S. Richardsen

Collection of british authors: Clarissa

The History of a Young Lady

S. Richardsen

Collection of british authors: Clarissa
The History of a Young Lady

ISBN/EAN: 9783742848512

Manufactured in Europe, USA, Canada, Australia, Japa

Cover: Foto ©Andreas Hilbeck / pixelio.de

Manufactured and distributed by brebook publishing software (www.brebook.com)

S. Richardsen

Collection of british authors: Clarissa

EACH VOLUME SOLD SEPARATELY.

COLLECTION OF BRITISH AUTHORS

TAUCHNITZ EDITION.

VOL. 596.

CLARISSA BY RICHARDSON

IN FOUR VOLUMES.

VOL. 2.

LEIPZIG: BERNHARD TAUCHNITZ.

PARIS: C. REINWALD, 15, RUE DES SAINTS PÈRES.

COLLECTION

OF

BRITISH AUTHORS.

VOL. 596.

CLARISSA BY S. RICHARDSON.

IN FOUR VOLUMES.

VOL. II.

CLARISSA;

OR,

THE HISTORY OF A YOUNG LADY:

COMPREHENDING

THE MOST IMPORTANT CONCERNS
OF PRIVATE LIFE; AND PARTICULARLY SHEWING
THE DISTRESSES THAT MAY ATTEND THE
MISCONDUCT BOTH OF PARENTS AND CHILDREN,
IN RELATION TO MARRIAGE.

BY

S. RICHARDSON.

COMPLETE IN FOUR VOLUMES.

VOL. II.

LEIPZIG

BERNHARD TAUCHNITZ

1862.

THE HISTORY OF CLARISSA HARLOWE.

LETTER I.
Mr. Lovelace to John Belford, Esq.
St. Alban's, Monday night.

I snatch a few moments while my beloved is retired [as I hope, to rest] to perform my promise. No pursuit — nor have I apprehensions of any; though I must make my charmer dread that there will be one.

And now, let me tell thee, that never was joy so complete as mine! — But let me enquire — is not the angel flown away?

* * *

O no! she is in the next apartment! — Securely mine! — Mine for ever!

O ecstasy! — My heart will burst my breast,
To leap into her bosom!

I knew that the whole stupid family were in a combination to do my business for me. I told thee that they were all working for me, like so many under-ground moles; and still more blind than the moles are said to be, unknowing that they did so. I myself the director of their principal motions; which falling in with the malice of their little hearts, they took to be all their own.

But did I say my joy was perfect? — O no! — It receives some abatement from my disgusted pride. For how can I endure to think that I owe more to her relations' persecutions than to her favour for me? — Or even, as far as I know, to her preference of me to another man?

But let me not indulge this thought. Were I to do so, it might cost my charmer dear. Let me rejoice that she has passed the Rubicon: that she cannot return: that, as I have ordered it, the flight will appear to the implacables to be altogether with her own consent: and that if I doubt her love, I can put her to trials as mortifying to her niceness as glorious to my pride. — For, let me tell thee, dearly as I love her, if I thought there was but the shadow of a doubt in her mind, whether she preferred me to any man living, I would shew her no mercy.

Tuesday day-dawn.

But, on the wings of love, I fly to my charmer, who perhaps by this time is rising to encourage the tardy dawn. I have not slept a wink of the hour and half I lay down to invite sleep. It seems to me, that I am not so much body as to require such vulgar renovation.

But why, as in the chariot, as in the inn, at alighting, all heart-bursting grief, my dearest creature? So persecuted as thou wert persecuted! — So much in danger of the most abhorred compulsion! — Yet grief so *unsuspectedly* sincere for an escape so critical! — Take care — take care — O beloved of my soul! for jealous is the heart in which love has erected a temple to thee.

Yet, it must be allowed, that such a sudden transition must affect her; must ice her over. When a little more used to her new situation; when her hurries are at an end; when she sees how religiously I shall observe all her INJUNCTIONS; she will undoubtedly have the gratitude to distinguish between the confinement she has escaped from and the liberty she has reason to rejoice in.

She comes! — She comes! — and the sun is just rising to attend her! — Adieu! — Be half as happy as I am (for all diffidences, like night-fogs before the sun, disperse at her approach) and, next to myself, thou wilt be the happiest man in the world.

LETTER II.
Miss Clarissa Harlowe to Miss Howe.

Wednesday, April 12.

I WILL pursue my melancholy story.

Being thus hurried to the chariot, it would have been to no purpose to have refused entering into it, had he not in my fright lifted me in, as he did: and it instantly drove away at full gallop, and stopped not till it brought us to St. Alban's; which was just as the day shut in.

I thought I should have fainted several times by the way. With uplifted hands and eyes, God protect me! said I often to myself — can it be I that am here! — My eyes running over, and my heart ready to burst with sighs as involuntary as my flight.

How different, how inexpressibly different, the gay wretch; visibly triumphing (as I could not but construe his almost rapturous joy) in the success of his arts! But overflowing with complimental flourishes, yet respectfully distant his address, all the way we *flew;* for that, rather than *galloping*, was the motion of the horses; which took, as I believe, a round-about way, to prevent being traced.

I have reason to think there were other horsemen at his devotion; three or four different persons, above the rank of servants, galloping by us now and then, on each side of the chariot: but he took no notice of them; and I had too much grief, mingled with indignation, notwithstanding all his blandishments, to ask any questions about them, or any thing else.

Think, my dear, what were my thoughts on alighting from the chariot; having no attendant of my own sex; no clothes but what

I had on, and those little suited to such a journey as I had *already* taken, and was *still* to take: neither cloak nor hat, nor any thing but a handkerchief about my neck and shoulders: fatigued to death: my mind still more fatigued than my body: and in such a foam the horses, that every one in the inn we put up at guessed [they could not do otherwise] that I was a young giddy creature, who had run away from her friends. This it was easy to see, by their whispering and gaping: more of the people of the house also coming in by turns than were necessary for the attendance.

The mistress of the house, whom he sent in to me, shewed me another apartment; and seeing me ready to faint, brought me hartshorn and water; and then, upon my desiring to be left alone for half an hour, retired: for I found my heart ready to burst, on revolving every thing in my thoughts: and the moment she was gone, fastening the door, I threw myself into an old great chair, and gave way to a violent flood of tears, which a little relieved me.

Mr. Lovelace, sooner than I wished, sent up the gentlewoman, who pressed me, in his name, to admit my brother, or to come down to him: for he had told her I was his sister; and that he had brought me against my will, and without warning, from a friend's house, where I had been all the winter, in order to prevent my marrying against the consent of my friends, to whom he was now conducting me; and that having given me no time for a travelling dress, I was greatly offended at him.

So, my dear, your frank, your open-hearted friend, was forced to countenance this tale; which indeed suited me the better, because I was unable for some time to talk, speak, or look up: and so my dejection, and grief, and silence, might very well pass before the gentlewoman and her niece, who attended me, as a fit of sullenness.

The room I was in being a bed-chamber, I chose to go down, at his repeated message, attended by the mistress of the house, to that in which he was. He approached me with great respect, yet not exceeding a brotherly politeness, where a brother *is* polite: and, calling me his dearest sister, asked after the state of my mind: and hoped I would forgive him; for never brother half so well loved a sister as he me.

A wretch! how naturally did he fall into the character, although I was so much out of mine!

Unthinking creatures have some comfort in the shortness of their views: in their unapprehensiveness: and that they penetrate not beyond the present moment: in short that they *are* unthinking! — But, for a person of my thoughtful disposition, who has been accustomed to look forward, as well to the *possible* as to the *probable*, what comfort can I have in my reflections?

But let me give you the particulars of our conversation a little before and after our supper-time, joining both in one.

When we were alone, he besought me (I cannot say but with all the tokens of a passionate and respectful tenderness) to be better reconciled to myself and to him; he repeated all the vows of honour and inviolable affection that he ever made me: he promised to be wholly governed by me in every future step. He asked me to give him leave to propose, whether I chose to set out next day to either of his aunts?

I was silent. I knew not what to say nor what to do.

Whether I chose to have private lodgings procured for me in either of those ladies' neighbourhood, as were once my thoughts?

I was still silent.

Whether I chose to go to either of Lord M.'s seats; that of Berks, or that in the county we were in?

In lodgings, I said, any where, where he was not to be.

He had *promised this*, he owned; and he would religiously keep to his word, as soon as he found all danger of pursuit over, and that I was settled to my mind. But, if the place were indifferent to me, London was the safest, and the most private: and his relations should all visit me there, the moment I thought fit to admit them. His cousin Charlotte, particularly, should attend me as my companion, if I would accept of her, as soon as she was able to go abroad. Meantime, would I go to Lady Betty Lawrence's (Lady Sarah was a melancholy woman) I should be the most welcome guest she ever received.

I told him I wished not to go (immediately, however, and in the frame I was in, and likely not to be out of) to any of his relations: that my reputation was concerned to have *him* absent from me: — that, if I were in some private lodging, the meaner the less to be suspected (as it would be known that I went away by his means, and he would be supposed to have provided me handsome accommodations) it would be most suitable both to my mind and to my situation: that this might be best, I should think, in the country for *me*; in town for *him*. And no matter how soon he was known to be there.

If he might deliver his opinion, he said, it was, that since I declined going to any of his relations, London was the only place in the world to be private in. Every new comer in a country town or village excited a curiosity: a person of my figure [and many compliments he made me] would excite more. Even messages and letters, where none used to be brought, would occasion inquiry. He had not provided a lodging any where, supposing I would choose to go either to London, where accommodations of that sort might be fixed upon in an hour's time, or to Lady Betty's; or to Lord M.'s Hertfordshire seat, where was the housekeeper, an excellent woman, Mrs. Greme, such another as my Norton.

To be sure, I said, if I were pursued, it would be in their first passion; and some one of his relation's houses would be the place they would expect to find me at—I knew not what to do.

My pleasure should determine him, he said, be it what it would. Only that I were safe was all he was solicitous about. He had lodgings in town; but he did not offer to propose them. He knew I would have more objections to go to them than I could have to go to Lord M.'s or to Lady Betty's.

No doubt of it, I replied, with such an indignation in my manner, as made him run over with professions, that he was far from proposing them, or wishing for my acceptance of them. And again he repeated, that my honour and safety were all he was solicitous about; assuring me, that my will should be a law to him in every particular.

I was too peevish, and too much afflicted, and indeed too much incensed against him, to take well any thing he said.

I thought, myself, I said, extremely unhappy. I knew not what to determine upon: my reputation now, no doubt, utterly ruined: destitute of clothes: unfit to be seen by any body: my very indigence, as I might call it, proclaiming my folly to every one who saw me; who would suppose that I had been taken at advantage, or had given an undue one; and had no power over either my will or my actions; that I could not but think I had been dealt artfully with; — that he had seemed to have taken, what he might suppose, the just measure of my weakness, founded on my youth and inexperience: that I could not forgive myself for meeting him: that my heart bled for the distresses of my father and mother on this occasion: that I would give the world, and all my hopes in it, to have been still in my father's house, whatever had been my usage: that, let him protest and vow what he would, I saw something low and selfish in his love, that he could study to put a young creature upon making such a sacrifice of her duty and conscience: when a person, actuated by a generous love, must seek to oblige the object of it in every thing essential to her honour and to her peace of mind.

He was very attentive to all I said, never offering to interrupt me once. His answer to every article, almost methodically, shewed his memory.

"What I had said, he told me, made him very grave, and he would answer accordingly.

"He was grieved at his heart to find that he had so little share in my favour or confidence.

"As to my *reputation* (he must be very sincere with me); that could not suffer half so much by the step I so greatly regretted to have taken as by the confinement, and equally foolish and unjust treatment, I had met with from my relations: that every mouth was full of blame of them, of my brother and sister particularly; and of wonder at my patience: that he must repeat what he had written to me, he believed, more than once, that my friends themselves expected, that I should take a proper opportunity to free myself from their persecutions; why else did they confine me? That my exalted character, as he called it, would still bear me out with those who knew *me:* who knew my *brother's* and *sister's* motives; and who knew the wretch they were for compelling me to have.

"With regard to *clothes;* who, as matters were circumstanced, could expect that I should be able to bring away any others than those I had on at the time? For *present* use or wear, all the ladies of his family would take a pride to supply me: for *future*, the product of the best looms, not only in England, but throughout the world, were at my command.

"If I wanted *money*, as no doubt I must, he should be proud to supply me: would to Heaven, he might presume to hope there were but one interest between us!"

And then he would fain have had me to accept of a bank note of an hundred pounds: which, unawares to me, he put into my hand: but which, you may be sure, I refused with warmth.

"He was inexpressibly grieved and surprised, he said, to hear me say he had acted *artfully* by me. He came provided, according to my *confirmed* appointment" [a wretch to upbraid me thus!] "to redeem me from my persecutors; and little expected a change of sentiment, and that he should have so much difficulty to prevail upon me as he had met with: that perhaps I might think his offer to go *into the garden with me,* and to face my assembled relations, was a piece of *art only:* but that if I did, I wronged him: since to this hour, seeing my excessive uneasiness, he wished, with all his soul, he had been permitted to accompany me in. It was always his maxim to brave a threatened danger. Threateners, where they have an opportunity to put in force their threat, were seldom to be feared. But had he been assured of a private stab, or of as many death's wounds as there were persons in my family (made desperate as he should have been by my return), he would have attended me into the house."

So, my dear, what I have to do, is to hold myself inexcusable for meeting such a determined and audacious spirit; that's all! I have hardly any question now, but that he would have contrived some wicked stratagem or other to have got me away, had I met him at a midnight hour, as once or twice I had thoughts to do; and that would have been more terrible still.

He concluded this part of his talk with saying, "That he doubted not, but that had he attended me in, he should have come off in every one's opinion so well, that he should have had general leave to renew his visits."

He went on — "He must be so

bold as to tell me, that he should have paid a visit of this kind (but indeed accompanied by several of his trusty friends) had I *not* met him; and that very afternoon too: for he could not tamely let the dreadful Wednesday come, without making some effort to change their determinations."

What, my dear, was to be done with such a man!

"That therefore for my sake, as well as for his own, he had reason to wish that a disease so desperate had been attempted to be overcome by as desperate a remedy. We all know, said he, that great ends are sometimes brought about by the very means by which they are endeavoured to be frustrated."

My present situation, I am sure, thought I, affords a sad evidence of this truth!

I was silent all this time. My blame was indeed turned inward. Sometimes too I was half frighted at his audaciousness: at others, had the less inclination to interrupt him, being excessively fatigued, and my spirits sunk to nothing, with the view even of the best prospects with such a man.

This gave him opportunity to proceed: and that he did; assuming a still more serious air.

"As to what further remained for him to say, in answer to what I had said, he hoped I would pardon him; but, upon his soul, he was concerned, infinitely concerned, he repeated (his colour and his voice rising) that it was *necessary* for him to observe, how much I chose rather to have run the risk of being Solmes's wife, than to have it in my power to reward a man who, I must forgive him, had been as much insulted on my account as *I* had been on *his* — who had watched my commands, and (pardon me, madam) every *changeable* motion of your pen, all hours, in all weathers, and with a cheerfulness and ardour that nothing but the most faithful and obsequious passion could inspire."

I now, my dear, began to revive into a little more warmth of attention. —

"And all, madam, for what?" — How I stared! for he stopt then a moment or two — "*Only*," went he on, "to prevail upon you to free yourself from ungenerous and base oppression" —

Sir, Sir! indignantly, said I —

Hear me but out, dearest madam! — My heart is full — I *must* speak what I have to say — to be told (for your words are yet in my ears and at my heart!) that you would give the world, *and all your hopes in it*, to have been still in your cruel and gloomy father's house" —

Not a word, sir, against my father! — I will not bear that —

"*Whatever had been your usage:* — and you have a credulity, madam, against all probability, if you believe you should have avoided being Solmes's wife: that I have put you upon *sacrificing your duty and conscience* — yet, dearest creature! see you not the contradiction that your warmth of temper has surprised you into, when the reluctance you shewed to the last to leave your persecutors has cleared your conscience from the least reproach of this sort?" —

O sir! sir! are you so critical then? Are you so light in your anger as to dwell upon words? —

Indeed, my dear, I have since thought, that his anger was not owing to that sudden *impetus* which cannot be easily bridled: but rather was a sort of *manageable* anger, let loose to intimidate me.

"Forgive me, madam — I have just done — have I not, in your own opinion, hazarded my life to redeem you from oppression? — Yet is not my reward, after all, precarious? — For, madam, have *you not conditioned with me* (and, hard as the condition is, *most sacredly will I observe it*) *that all my hope must be remote?* That you are determined to have it in your power *to favour or reject me totally,* as you please?" —

See, my dear! in every respect my condition changed for the worse! Is it in *my power* to take your advice, if I should think it ever so right to take it?*

* Clarissa has been censured as behaving to Mr. Lovelace, in their first conversation at St. Alban's, and afterwards, with too much reserve, and even with haughtiness. Surely those who have thought her to blame on this account have not paid a due attention to the story. How early, as above, and in what immediately follows, does he remind her of the terms of distance which she prescribed to him before she was in his power, *in hopes to leave a door open for a reconciliation with her friends*, which her heart was set upon? And how artfully does he (unrequired) promise to ob-

"And have you not furthermore declared, proceeded he, *that you will engage to renounce me for ever, if your friends insist upon that cruel renunciation as the terms of being reconciled to you?*

"But, nevertheless, madam, all the merit of having saved you from an odious compulsion shall be mine: I glory in it, though I were to lose you for ever — *As I see I am but too likely to do*, from your present displeasure: and especially, *if your friends insist upon the terms you are ready to comply with.*

"That you are *your own mistress*, through *my* means, is, I repeat, my boast. As such, I humbly implore your favour — and *that only upon the conditions I have yielded to hope for it.* — As I now do *thus humbly* [the proud wretch falling on one knee] your forgiveness, for so long detaining your ear, and for all the plain dealing that my undesigning heart would not be denied to utter by my lips."

O sir, pray rise! — Let the obliged kneel, if one of us must kneel! But, nevertheless, proceed not in this strain, I beseech you. You have had a great deal of trouble about me: but had you let me know *in time,* that you expected to be rewarded for it at the price of serve the conditions which she in her present circumstances and situation (in pursuance of Miss Howe's advice) would gladly have dispensed with? — To say nothing of the resentment which she was under a *necessity* to shew at the manner of his getting her away, in order to justify to him *the sincerity of her refusal to go off with him.* See in her subsequent letter to Miss Howe, No. v. her own sense upon this subject.

my duty, I should have spared you much of it.

Far be it from me, sir, to depreciate merit so *extraordinary*. But let me say, that had it not been for the forbidden correspondence I was teased by you into; and which I had not continued (every letter, for many letters, intended to be the last) but because I thought you a sufferer from my friends; I had not been either confined or ill-treated: nor would my brother's low-meant violence have had a foundation to work upon.

I am far from thinking my case would have been so very desperate as you imagine, had I staid. My father loved me in his heart: he would not see me before; and I wanted *only* to *see* him, and to be *heard*, and a *delay of his sentence* was the least thing I expected from the trial I was to stand.

You are boasting of your merits, sir: let merit *be* your boast, nothing else can attract me. If *personal* considerations had principal weight with me, either in Solmes's disfavour, or in your favour, I should despise *myself*: if you value yourself upon them, in preference to the *person* of the poor Solmes, I shall despise *you*.

You may glory in your fancied merits in getting me away; but the cause of *your* glory, I tell you plainly, is *my* shame.

Make to yourself a title to my regard, which I can better approve of, or else you will not have so much merit with *me* as you have with *yourself*.

But here, sir, like the first pair, (I, at least, driven out of my paradise) are we recriminating. No more shall you need to tell me of your *sufferings* and your *merits:*— your *all hours* and *all weathers:* for I will bear them in memory as long as I live; and if it be impossible for me to *reward* them, be ever ready to own the obligation. All that I desire of you now, is to leave it to myself to seek for some private abode: to take the chariot with you to London, or elsewhere: and, if I have any further occasion for your assistance and protection, I will signify it to you, and be still further obliged to you.

You are warm, my dearest life! — But indeed there is no occasion for it. Had I any views unworthy of my faithful love for you, I should not have been so honest in my declarations.

Then he began again to vow the sincerity of his intentions.

But I took him up short; I am willing to *believe* you, sir. It would be insupportable but to suppose there were a *necessity* for such solemn declarations. [At this he seemed to collect himself, as I may say, into a little more circumspection.] If I thought there *were*, I would not sit with you here, in a public inn, I assure you, although cheated hither, as far as I know, by methods (you must excuse me, sir) which, but to *suspect*, will hardly let me have patience either with you or with myself. But no more of this just now: let me, I beseech you, *good sir,* bowing, [I was very angry!] let me only know whether you intend to leave me, or whether I have only escaped from one confinement to another?

Cheated hither as far as you know, madam! Let you *know* (and with that air too, charming, though grievous to my heart!) *if you have only escaped from one confinement to another* — amazing! perfectly amazing! and can there be a necessity for me to answer this? You are absolutely your own mistress. — It were very strange if you were not. *The moment you are in a place of safety* I will leave you. To one condition only give me leave to beg your consent: it is this, that you will be pleased, now you are so entirely in your own power, to renew a promise *voluntarily* made before; *voluntarily*, or I would not *now* presume to request it; for although I would not be thought capable of growing upon concession, yet I cannot bear to think of losing the ground your goodness had given me room to hope I had gained; "That, make up how you please with your relations, you will never marry any other man, while I am living and single, unless I should be so wicked as to give new cause for high displeasure."

I hesitate not to confirm this promise, sir, upon your *own* condition. In what manner do you expect me to confirm it?

Only, madam, by your word.

Then I never will.

He had the assurance (*I was now in his power*) to salute me as a sealing of my promise, as he called it. His motion was so sudden, that I was not aware of it. It would have looked *affected* to be very angry; yet I could not be pleased, considering this as a leading *freedom* from a spirit so audacious and encroaching: and he might see that I was not.

He passed all that by with an air peculiar to himself— Enough, enough, dearest madam! And now let me beg of you but to conquer this dreadful uneasiness, which gives me to apprehend too much for my jealous love to bear; and it shall be my whole endeavour to deserve your favour, and to make you the happiest woman in the world, as I shall be the happiest of men.

I broke from him to write to you my preceding letter; but refused to send it by his servant, as I told you. The mistress of the house helped me to a messenger, who was to carry what you should give him to Lord M.'s seat in Hertfordshire, directed for Mrs. Greme, the housekeeper there. And early in the morning, for fear of pursuit, we were to set out that way; and there he proposed to change the chariot-and-six for a chaise-and-pair of his own, which he had at that seat, as it would be a less noticed conveyance.

I looked over my little stock of money; and found it to be no more than seven guineas and some silver: the rest of my stock was but fifty guineas, and that five more than I thought it was when my sister challenged me as to the sum I had by me*: and those I left in my escritoire, little intending to go away with him.

Indeed my case abounds with a shocking number of indelicate circumstances. Among the rest, I was forced to account to *him*, who knew I could have no clothes but what I had on, how I came to have linen with you (for he could not but know I sent for it); lest he should imagine I had an early design to go away with him, and made that a *part of the preparation*.

He most heartily wished, he said, for my mind's sake, that your mother would have afforded me her protection; and delivered himself upon this subject with equal *freedom* and concern.

There are, my dear Miss Howe, a multitude of punctilios and decorums, which a young creature must dispense with, who, in a situation like mine, makes a man the intimate attendant of her person. I could now, I think, give twenty reasons stronger than any I have heretofore mentioned, why women of the *least delicacy* should never think of incurring the danger and disgrace of taking the step I have been drawn in to take but with horror and aversion; and why they should look upon the man who should tempt them to it as the vilest and most selfish of seducers.

* * *

BEFORE five o'clock (Tuesday morning) the maid-servant came up to tell me my *brother* was ready, and that breakfast also waited for me in the parlour. I went down with a heart as heavy as my eyes, and received great acknowledgments and compliments from him on being so soon dressed, and ready (as he interpreted it) to continue our journey.

He had the thought which I had not (for what had I to do with thought who had it not when I stood most in need of it?) to purchase for me a cloak and hat, without saying any thing to me. He must reward himself, the artful encroacher said, before the landlady and her maids and niece, for his forethought; and would salute his pretty sullen sister!— He took his reward; and, as he said, a tear with it. While he assured me, still before them [a vile wretch!] that I had nothing to fear from meeting with parents who so dearly loved me.—

How could I be complaisant, my dear, to such a man as this?

When we had got into the chariot, and it began to move, he asked me whether I had any objection to go to Lord M.'s Hertfordshire seat? His lordship, he said, was at his Berkshire one.

I told him, I chose not to go, *as yet*, to any of his relations; for that would indicate a plain defiance to my own. My choice was to go to a private lodging, and for him to be at a distance from me; at least, till I heard how things were taken by my friends — for that, although I had but little hopes of a reconciliation as it *was!*

* See Vol. I. Letter xliii.

yet if they knew I was in his protection, or in that of any of his friends (which would be looked upon as the same thing) there would not be room for any hopes at all.

I should govern him as I pleased, he solemnly assured me, in every thing. But he still thought *London* was the best place for me; and if I were once safe there, and in a lodging to my liking, he would go to M. Hall. But as I approved not of London, he would urge it no further.

He proposed, and I consented, to put up at an inn in the neighbourhood of *the Lawn* (as he called Lord M.'s seat in this county) since I chose not to go thither. And here I got two hours to myself, which I told him I should pass in writing another letter to you (meaning my narrative, which, though greatly fatigued, I had begun at St. Alban's), and in one to my sister, to apprise the family (whether they were solicitous about it or not) that I was well; and to beg that my clothes, some particular books, and the fifty guineas I had left in my escritoire, might be sent me.

He asked, if I had considered whither to have them directed?

Indeed, not I, I told him: I was a stranger to —

So was he, he interrupted me; but it struck him by chance —

Wicked story-teller!

But, added he, I will tell you, madam, how it shall be managed — if you don't choose to go to London, it is, nevertheless, best that your relations should *think* you there; for then they will absolutely despair of finding you. If you write, be pleased to direct, To be left for you, at Mr. Osgood's, near Soho Square. Mr. Osgood is a man of reputation; and this will effectually amuse them.

Amuse them, my dear! — Amuse whom? — My father! — My uncles! — But it must be so! —— *All his expedients ready, you see!*

I had no objection to this: and I have written accordingly. But what answer I shall have, or whether any, that is what gives me no small anxiety.

This, however, is one consolation, that if I have an answer, and although my brother should be the writer, it cannot be more severe than the treatment I have of late received from him and my sister.

Mr. Lovelace staid out about an hour and a half; and then came in, impatiently sending up to me no less than four times to desire admittance. But I sent him word as often that I was busy; and at last, that I should be so till dinner was ready. He then hastened that, as I heard him now and then, with a hearty curse upon the cook and waiters.

This is another of his perfections. I ventured afterwards to check him for his free words, as we sat at dinner.

Having heard him swear at his servant when below, whom, nevertheless, he owns to be a good one;

It is a sad life, said I, these innkeepers live, Mr. Lovelace.

No; pretty well I believe — but why, madam, think you, that fellows who eat and drink at other men's cost, or they are sorry innkeepers, should be entitled to pity?

Because of the soldiers they are obliged to quarter! who are generally, I believe, wretched profligates. Bless me! said I, how I heard one of them swear and curse just now at a modest meek man, as I judge by his low voice and gentle answers! — Well do they make it a proverb — *Like a trooper!*

He bit his lip; arose; turned upon his heel; stept to the glass; and looking *confidently* abashed, if I may so say, Ay, madam, said he, these troopers are sad swearing fellows. I think their officers should chastise them for it.

I am sure they deserve chastisement, replied I: for swearing is a most *unmanly* vice, and cursing as *poor* and *low* a one; since it proclaims the profligate's want of power and his wickedness at the same time; for, could such a one *punish* as he *speaks*, he would be a fiend!

Charmingly observed, by my soul, madam! — The next trooper I hear swear and curse, I'll tell him what an *unmanly* and what a *poor* wretch he is.

Mrs. Greme came to pay her *duty* to me, as Mr. Lovelace called it; and was very urgent with me to go to her lord's house; letting me know what handsome things she had heard her lord, and his two nieces, and all the family, say of me; and what wishes for several months past they had put up for the honour she now hoped would soon be done them all.

This gave me some satisfaction, as it confirmed from the mouth of a very good sort of woman all that Mr. Lovelace had told me.

Upon inquiry about a private lodging, she recommended me to a sister-in-law of hers, eight miles from thence. — Where I now am. And what pleased me the better, was, that Mr. Lovelace (of whom I could see she was infinitely observant) obliged her, of his own motion, to accompany me in the chaise; himself riding on horseback, with his two servants, and one of Lord M.'s. And here we arrived about four o'clock.

But, as I told you in my former, the lodgings are inconvenient. Mr. Lovelace indeed found great fault with them: and told Mrs. Greme (who had said that they were not worthy of us) that they came not up even to her account of them. As the house was a mile from a town, it was not proper for him, he said, to be so far distant from me, lest any thing should happen; and yet the apartments were not separate and distinct enough for me to like them, he was sure.

This must be agreeable enough from him, you will believe.

Mrs. Greme and I had a good deal of talk in the chaise about him: she was very easy and free in her answers to all I asked and has, I find, a very serious turn.

I led her on to say to the following effect; some part of it not unlike what Lord M.'s dismissed bailiff had said before; by which I find that all the servants have a like opinion of him.

"That Mr. Lovelace was a generous man: that it was hard to say, whether the servants of her lord's family loved or feared him most: that her lord had a very great affection for him: that his two noble aunts were not less fond of him: that his cousins Montague were as good-natured young ladies *as ever lived:* that Lord M. and Lady Sarah, and Lady Betty, had proposed several ladies to him, before he made his addresses to me; and even since; despairing to move me and my friends in his favour. — But that he had no thoughts of marrying at all, she had heard him say, if it were not to me: that as well her lord as the two ladies his sisters were a good deal concerned at the ill-usage he received from my family: but admired my character, and wished to have him married to me (although I were not to have a shilling) in preference to any other person, from the opinion they had of the influence I should have over him. That, to be sure, Mr. Lovelace was a wild gentleman: but wildness was a distemper which would cure itself. That her lord delighted in his company, whenever he could get it: but that they often fell out; and his lordship was always forced to submit — indeed, was half afraid of him, she believed; for Mr. Lovelace would do as he pleased. She mingled a thousand pities often, that he acted not up to the talents lent him — yet would have it, that he had fine qualities to found a reformation upon: and, when the happy day came, would make amends for all: and of this all his friends were so assured, that they wished for nothing so earnestly, as for his marriage."

This, indifferent as it is, is better than my brother says of him.

The people of the house here are very honest-looking industrious folks: Mrs. Sorlings is the gentlewoman's name. The farm seems well stocked, and thriving. She is a widow; has two sons, men grown, who vie with each other which shall take most pains in promoting the common good; and they are both of them, I already see, more respectful to two modest young women their sisters, than my brother was to his sister.

I believe I must stay here longer than at first I thought I should.

I ought to have mentioned, that, before I set out for this place, I received your kind letter*. Every thing is kind from so dear a friend.

I own, that after I had told you of my absolute determination not to go away with him, you might well be surprised, at your first

* See Vol. I. Letter xc.

hearing that I was actually gone. The Lord bless me, my dear, I myself, at times, can hardly believe it is I, that have been led to take so strange a step.

I have not the better opinion of Mr. Lovelace for his extravagant volubility. He is too full of professions. He says too many fine things *of* me, and *to* me. True respect, true value, I think, lies not in words: words *cannot* express it: the silent awe, the humble, the doubting eye, and even the hesitating voice, better shew it by much, than, as our beloved Shakspeare says,

—— The rattling tongue
Of saucy and audacious eloquence.

The man indeed at times is all upon the *ecstatic;* one of his phrases. But, to my shame and confusion, I must say, that I know too well to what to attribute his transports. In one word, it is to his *triumph*, my dear. And, to impute it to *that* perhaps equally exposes my vanity, and condemns my folly.

We have been alarmed with notions of a pursuit, founded upon a letter from his intelligencer.

How do different circumstances either sanctify or condemn the same action! — What care ought we to take not to confound the distinctions of right and wrong, when *self* comes in the question! — I condemned in Mr. Lovelace the corrupting of a servant of my father's; and now I am glad to give a kind of *indirect* approbation of that fault, by inquiring of him what he hears, by that or any other way, of the manner in which my relations took my flight. A preconcerted, forward, and artful flight, it must undoubtedly appear to them. How grievous is that to think of! Yet *how*, as I *am situated*, can I put them right?

Most heavily, he says, they take it; but shew not so much grief as rage. And he can hardly have patience to hear of the virulence and menaces of my brother against himself. Then a merit is made to me of his forbearance.

What a satisfaction am I robbed of, my dearest friend, when I reflect upon my inconsiderateness! O that I had it still in my power to say I *suffered* wrong, rather than *did* wrong! That others were more wanting in their kindness to me, than I in duty (where duty is owing) to them.

Fie upon me! for *meeting the seducer!* — Let all end as happily as it now may, I have laid up for myself *remorse for my whole life.*

What still more concerns me is, that every time I see this man, I am still at a greater loss than before what to make of him. I watch every turn of his countenance: and I think I see very deep lines in it. He looks with more meaning, I verily think, than he used to look; yet not more serious; not less gay — I don't know how he looks — but with more confidence a great deal than formerly; and yet he never wanted that.

But here is the thing; I behold him with *fear* now, as conscious of the power my indiscretion has given him over me. And well may *he* look more elate, when he sees me deprived of all the self-supposed significance, which adorns and exalts a person who has been accustomed to respect; and who now, by a *conscious inferiority*, allows herself *to be overcome*, and in a state of *obligation*, as I may say, to a man who from an humble suitor to her for her favour, assumes the consequence and airs of a protector.

I shall send this, as my former, by a poor man, who travels every day with pedlary matters. He will leave it at Mrs. Knollys's, as you direct.

If you hear any thing of my father and mother, and of their health, and how my friends were affected by my unhappy step, pray be so good as to write me a few lines by the messenger, if his waiting for them can be known to you.

I am afraid to ask you, whether, upon reading that part of my narrative already in your hands, you think any sort of extenuation lies for

Your unhappy
CLARISSA HARLOWE.

LETTER III.

Mr. Lovelace to John Belford, Esq.

Tuesday, Wed. Apr. 11, 12.

You claim my promise, that I will be as particular as possible, in all that passes between me and my goddess. Indeed, I never had a more illustrious subject to exercise my pen upon. And, moreover, I have leisure; for by her good will, my access would be as difficult to her, as that of the humblest slave to an eastern monarch. Nothing, then, but inclination to write can be wanting: and since our friendship, and your obliging attendance upon me at the White Hart, will not excuse that, I will endeavour to keep my word.

I parted with thee and thy brethren with a full resolution, thou knowest, to rejoin ye, if she once again disappointed me, in order to go together (attended by our servants, for show-sake) to the gloomy father; and demand audience of the tyrant upon the freedoms taken with my character. In short, to have tried by fair means, if fair would do, to make him change his resolutions; and treat his charming *daughter* with less inhumanity, and *me* with more civility.

I told thee my reasons for not going in search of a letter of countermand. I was right; for if I had, I should have found such a one; and had I received it, she would not have met me. Did she think, that after I had been more than once disappointed, I would not keep her to her promise; that I would not hold her to it, when I had got her in so deeply?

The moment I heard the door unbolt, I was sure of her. That motion made my heart bound to my throat. But when that was followed with the presence of my charmer, flashing upon me all at once in a flood of brightness, sweetly dressed, though all unprepared for a journey, I trod air, and hardly thought myself a mortal.

Thou shalt judge of her dress, as at the moment I first beheld her she appeared to me, and as, upon a nearer observation, she really was. I am a critic, thou knowest, in women's dresses. Many a one have I taught to dress, and helped to undress. But there is such a native elegance in this lady, that she surpasses all that I could imagine surpassing. But then her person adorns what she wears, more than dress can adorn her; and that's her excellence.

Expect therefore a faint sketch of her admirable person with her dress.

Her wax-like flesh (for after all, flesh and blood I think she is) by its delicacy and firmness, answers for the soundness of her health. Thou hast often heard me launch out in praise of her complexion. I never in my life beheld a skin so *illustriously fair*. The lily and the driven snow it is nonsense to talk of: her lawn and her laces one might indeed compare to those: but what a whited wall would a woman appear to be, who had a complexion which would justify such unnatural comparisons? But this lady is all glowing, all charming flesh and blood: yet so clear, that every meandering vein is to be seen in all the lovely parts of her which custom permits to be visible.

Thou hast heard me also describe the wavy ringlets of her shining hair, needing neither art nor powder; of itself an ornament, defying all other ornaments: wantoning in and about a neck that is beautiful beyond description.

Her head-dress was a Brussels-lace cap, peculiarly adapted to the charming air and turn of her features. A sky-blue ribband illustrated that. But although the weather was somewhat sharp, she had not on either hat or cloak-hood; for besides that she loves to use herself hardily (by which means, and by a temperance truly exemplary, she is allowed to have given high health and vigour to an originally tender constitution) she seems to have intended to shew me, that she was determined not to stand to her appointment. O Jack! that such a sweet girl should be a rogue!

Her gown was a pale primrose-coloured paduasoy: the cuffs and robings curiously embroidered by the fingers of this ever-charming Arachne, in a running pattern of violets and their leaves; the light in the flowers silver; gold in the leaves. A pair of diamond snaps in her ears. A white handkerchief wrought by the same inimitable fingers concealed — O Belford!. what still more inimitable beauties did it not conceal! — And I saw, all the way we rode, the bounding heart (by its throbbing motions I saw it!) dancing beneath the charming umbrage.

Her ruffles were the same as her cap. Her apron a flowered lawn.

Clarissa. II.

Her coat white satin, quilted: blue satin her shoes, braided with the same colour, without lace; for what need has the prettiest foot in the world of ornament? neat buckles in them: and on her charming arms a pair of black velvet glove-like muffs of her own invention; for she makes and gives fashions as she pleases. — Her hands velvet of themselves, thus uncovered the freer to be grasped by those of her adorer.

I have told thee what were *my* transports, when the undrawn bolt presented to me my long-expected goddess. — *Her* emotions were more sweetly feminine, after the first moments; for then the fire of her starry eyes began to sink into a less dazzling languor. She trembled: nor knew she how to support the agitations of a heart she had never found so ungovernable. She was even fainting, when I clasped her in my supporting arms. What a precious moment that! How near, how sweetly near the throbbing partners!

By her dress, I saw, as I observed before, how unprepared she was for a journey; and not doubting her intention once more to disappoint me, I would have drawn her after me. Then began a contention the most vehement that ever I had with woman. It would pain thy friendly heart to be told the infinite trouble I had with her. I begged, I prayed, on my knees, yet in vain, I begged and prayed her to answer her own appointment: and had I not happily provided for such a struggle, knowing whom I had to deal with, I had certainly failed in my design; and as certainly would have accompanied her in, without thee and thy brethren: and who knows what might have been the consequence?

But my honest agent answering my signal, *though not quite so soon as I expected*, in the manner thou knowest I had prescribed, They are coming! they are coming! — Fly, fly, my beloved creature, cried I, drawing my sword with a flourish, as if I would have slain half an hundred of the supposed intruders: and, seizing her trembling hands, I drew her after me so swiftly, that *my* feet, winged by love, could hardly keep pace with *her* feet, agitated by fear. — And so I became her emperor.

I'll tell thee all, when I see thee: and thou shalt then judge of *my* difficulties, and of *her* perverseness. And thou wilt rejoice with me at my conquest over such a watchful and open-eyed charmer.

But seest thou not now (as I think I do) the wind-outstripping fair one flying *from* her love *to* her love? Is there not such a game? — Nay, flying from friends she was resolved not to abandon, to the man she was determined not to go off with? — *The sex! the sex, all over!* — Charming contradiction! — Hah, hah, hah, hah! — I must here — I must here, lay down my pen, to hold my sides: for I must have my laugh out now the fit is upon me.

* * *

I believe — I believe — Hah, hah, hah! I believe, Jack, my dogs conclude me mad: for here has one of them popt in, as if to see what ailed me; or whom I had with me. The whorson caught the laugh, as he went out. — Hah, hah, hah! — An *im-pudent* dog! — O Jack, knewest thou my conceit, and were but thy laugh joined to mine, I believe it would hold me for an hour longer.

But O, my best beloved fair one, repine not thou at the arts by which thou suspectest thy fruitless vigilance has been overwatched. — Take care, that thou provokest not new ones, that may be still more worthy of thee. If once thy emperor decrees thy fall, thou shalt greatly fall. Thou shalt have cause, if that come to pass, which may come to pass (for why wouldst thou put off marriage to so long a day, as till thou hast reason to be convinced of my reformation, dearest?) thou shalt have cause, never fear, to sit down more satisfied with thy stars, than with thyself. And come the worst to the worst, glorious terms will I give thee. Thy garrison, with general *Prudence* at the head, and governor *Watchfulness* bringing up the rear, shall be allowed to march out with all the honours due to so brave a resistance. And all thy sex, and all mine, that hear of my stratagems, and of thy conduct, shall acknowledge the fortress as nobly won as defended.

"Thou wilt not dare, methinks I hear thee say, to attempt to reduce such a goddess as this, to a standard unworthy of her excellencies. It is impossible, Lovelace, that thou shouldst intend to break through oaths and protestations so solemn."

That I *did not* intend it, is certain. That I *do* intend it, I cannot (my heart, my reverence for her will not let me) say. But knowest thou not my aversion to the state of shackles? — And is she not IN MY POWER?

"And wilt thou, Lovelace, abuse that power which" —

Which what, Belford? — Which I obtained not by her own consent, but *against* it.

"But which thou never hadst obtained, had she not esteemed thee above all men."

And which I had never taken so much pains to obtain, had I not loved her above all women. So far upon a par, Jack! and if thou pleadest honour, ought not honour to be mutual? If mutual, does it not imply mutual trust, mutual confidence? And what have I had of *that* from her to boast of? — Thou knowest the whole progress of our warfare: for a warfare it has truly been; and far, very far, from an amorous warfare too. Doubts, mistrusts, upbraidings, on her part; humiliations the most abject, on mine. Obliged to assume such airs of reformation, that every varlet of ye has been afraid I should reclaim in good earnest. And hast thou not thyself frequently observed to me, how awkwardly I returned to my usual gaiety, after I had been within a mile of her father's

2*

garden-wall, although I had not seen her?

Does she not deserve to pay for all this? — To make an honest fellow like an hypocrite; what a vile thing is that!

Then thou knowest what a *false* little rogue she has been. How little conscience she has made of disappointing me. Hast thou not been a witness of my ravings, on this score? Have I not, in the height of them, vowed revenge upon the faithless charmer? — And if I *must* be forsworn, whether I answer her expectations, or follow my own inclinations; and if the option be in my own power; can I hesitate a moment which to choose?

Then, I fancy by her circumspection, and her continual grief, that she *expects* some mischief from me. I don't care to disappoint any body I have a value for.

But O the noble, the exalted creature! Who can avoid hesitating when he thinks of an offence against her? Who can but pity—

Yet on the other hand, so loth at last to venture, though threatened to be forced into the nuptial fetters with a man whom to look upon as a rival, is to disgrace myself! — So sullen, now she has ventured! — What title has she to pity; and to a pity which her pride would make her disclaim?

But I resolve not *any way*. I will see how *her* will works; and how *my* will leads me on. I will give the combatants fair play, and yet every time I attend her, I find that she is less in *my* power; more in *hers*.

Yet, a foolish little rogue! to forbid me to think of marriage till I am a reformed man! Till the implacables of her family change their natures, and become placable.

It is true, when she was for making those conditions, she did not think, that without *any*, she should *be cheated out of herself*; for so the dear soul, as I may tell thee in its place, phrases it.

How it swells my pride, to have been able to outwit such a vigilant charmer! I am taller by half a yard in my imagination than I was. I look *down* upon every body now. Last night I was still more extravagant. I took off my hat, as I walked, to see if the lace were not scorched, supposing it had brushed down a star; and, before I put it on again, in mere wantonness and heart's ease, I was buffeting the moon.

In short, my whole soul is joy. When I go to bed I laugh myself asleep: and I awake either laughing or singing — yet nothing nearly in view, neither — for why? — *I am not yet reformed enough!*

I told thee at the time, if thou rememberest, how capable this restriction was of being turned upon the over-scrupulous dear creature, could I once get her out of her father's house; and were I disposed to punish her for her family's faults, and for the infinite trouble she herself had given me. Little thinks she, *that I have kept an account of both:* and that, when my heart is soft, and all her own, I can but turn to my *memoranda,* and harden myself at once.

O my charmer, look to it: abate of thy haughty airs! Value not thyself upon thy sincerity, if thou *art* indifferent to me! I will not bear it *now. Art thou not in my* POWER? — Nor, if thou lovest me, think, that the female affectation of denying thy love, will avail thee *now,* with a heart so proud and so jealous as mine? — Remember, moreover, that all thy family sins are upon thy head! —

But ah! Jack, when I see my angel, when I am admitted to the presence of this radiant beauty, what will become of all this vapouring?

But be my end what it may, I am obliged by thy penetration, fair one, to proceed by the sap. *Fair and softly. A wife at any time.* Marriage will be always in my power.

When put to the university, the same course of *initial studies* will qualify the yonker for the one line or for the other. The *genius* ought to point out the future lawyer, divine, or physician! — So the same cautious conduct, with such a vigilance, will do either for the *wife,* or for the *no-*wife. When I reform, I'll marry. 'Tis time enough for the *one,* the *lady* must say — for the *other,* say *I!*

But how I ramble! — This it is to be in such a situation, that I know not what to resolve upon.

I'll tell thee my *inclinings,* as I proceed. The *pro's* and the *con's* I'll tell thee: but being got too far from the track I set out in, I will close here. I may however write every day something, and send it as opportunity offers.

Regardless, nevertheless, I shall be in all I write, of connection, accuracy, or of any thing but of my own imperial will and pleasure.

LETTER IV.
Miss Howe to Miss Clarissa Harlowe.

Wednesday night, April 12.

I HAVE your narrative, my dear. You are the same noble creature you ever were. Above disguise, above art, above attempting to extenuate a failing.

The only family in the world, yours, surely, that could have driven such a daughter upon such extremities.

But you must not be so very much too good for *them,* [and for the *case.*

You lay the blame so properly and so unsparingly *upon your meeting him,* that nothing can be added to that subject by your worst enemies, were they to see what you have written.

I am not surprised, now I have read your narrative, that so bold and so contriving a man — I am forced to break off —

* * *

You stood it out much better and longer — here again comes my bustling, jealous mother!

* * *

DON'T be so angry at yourself. Did you not do for the best at the time? As to your first fault, *the answering his letters;* it was almost incumbent upon you to assume the guardianship of such a family, when the bravo of it had run riot as he did, and brought himself into danger.

Except your mother, who has no will of her own, have any of them common sense? —

Forgive me, my dear — here is that stupid uncle Antony of yours. A pragmatical, conceited, positive — He came yesterday, in a fearful pucker and puffed, and blowed, and stumped about our hall and parlour, while his message was carried up.

My mother was dressing. These widows are as starched as the old bachelors. She would not see him in a dishabille for the world — *What can she mean by it?*

His errand was to set her against you, and to shew their determined rage on your going away. The issue proved too evidently that this was the principal end of his visit.

The odd creature desired to speak with her alone. I am not used to such exceptions whenever any visits are made to my mother.

When she was *primmed out*, down she came to him. They locked themselves in. The two positive heads were put together — close together I suppose; for I listened, but could hear nothing distinctly, though they both seemed full of their subject.

I had a good mind, once or twice, to have made them open the door. Could I have been sure of keeping but tolerably my temper, I would have *demanded* admittance. But I was afraid, if I had obtained it, that I should have forgot it was my mother's house, and been for turning him out of it. To come to rave against and abuse my dearest, dearest, faultless friend! and the ravings to be encouraged, and perhaps joined in, in order to justify themselves; the one for contributing to drive that dear friend out of her father's house; the other for refusing her temporary asylum, till the reconciliation could have been effected, which her dutiful heart was set upon; and which it would have become the love which my mother had ever pretended for you, to have meditated for — could I have had patience!

The *issue*, as I said, shewed what the errand was — Its first appearance, after the old fusty fellow was marched off [*you must excuse me, my dear*] was in a kind of gloomy, Harlowe-like reservedness in my mother; which upon a few resenting flirts of mine, was followed by a rigorous prohibition of correspondence.

This put us, you may suppose, upon terms not most agreeable; I desired to know, if I were prohibited *dreaming* of you? — For, my dear, you have all my sleeping as well as waking hours.

I can easily allow for your correspondence with your wretch at first (and yet your motives were excellent) by the effect this prohibition has upon me; since, if possible, it has made me love you better than before; and I am more desirous than ever of corresponding with you.

But I have nevertheless a much more laudable motive — I should think myself the unworthiest of creatures, could I be brought to slight a dear friend, and such a meritorious one, in her distress. — I would die first — and so I told my mother. And I have desired her not to watch me in my retired hours; nor to insist upon my lying with her constantly, which she now does more earnestly than ever. 'Twere better, I told her, that the Harlowe Betty were borrowed to be set over me.

Mr. Hickman, who greatly honours you, has, unknown to me, interposed so warmly in your favour with my mother, that it makes for him no small merit with me.

I cannot, at present, write to every particular, unless I would be in *set* defiance. — Tease, tease, tease, for ever! The same thing, though answered fifty times over, in every hour to be repeated — Lord bless me! what a life must my poor father — but let me remember to whom I am writing.

If this ever-active, ever mischievous monkey of a man, this Lovelace, contrived as you suspect — but here comes my mother again — ay, stay a little longer, my mamma, if you please — I can but be suspected! I can but be chidden for making you wait; and chidden I am sure to be, whether I do or not, in the way you, my good mamma, are *Antony'd* into.

Bless me! how impatient she is! — How she thunders at the door! — This moment, madam! — How came I to double-lock myself in! — What have I done with the key! — Deuce take the key! — Dear madam! — You flutter one so!

* * *

You may believe, my dear, that I took care of my papers before I opened the door. We have had a charming dialogue — she flung from me in a passion —

So what's now to be done? — Sent for down in a very peremptory manner, I assure you. What an incoherent letter will you have, when I can get it to you! But now I know where to send it, Mr. Hickman shall find me a messenger. Yet, if he be detected, poor soul, he will be *Harlowed-off*, as well as his *meek mistress*.

Thursday, April 13.

I HAVE this moment your continuation letter. And am favoured, at present, with the absence of my Argus-ey'd mother. —

Dear creature! I can account for all your difficulties. A young lady of your delicacy! — and with such a man! — I must be brief —

The man's a fool, my dear, with all his pride, and with all his complaisance, *and affected regards to your injunctions.* Yet his ready inventions —

Sometimes I think you should go to Lady Betty's. I know not what to advise you to do. — I *should*, if you were not so intent upon reconciling yourself to your relations. Yet they are implacable.

You can have no hopes from them. Your uncle's errand to my mother may convince you of that; and if you have an answer to your letter to your sister, that will confirm you, I dare say.

You need not to have been afraid of asking me, whether upon reading your narrative, I thought any extenuation could lie for what you have done! I have, as above, before I had your question, told you my mind as to that. — And I repeat, that I think, your *provocations and inducements* considered, you are free from blame: at least the freest, that ever young creature was who took such a step.

But *you took it not* — you were *driven on one side*, and, possibly, *tricked on the other*. — If any woman on earth shall be circumstanced as you were, and shall hold out so long as you did, against her persecutors on one hand, and her seducer on the other, I will forgive her for all the rest of her conduct, be it what it will.

All your acquaintance, you may suppose, talk of nobody but you. Some indeed bring your admirable character for a plea against you: but nobody does, or *can*, acquit your father and uncles.

Every body seems apprized of your brother's and sister's motives. Your flight is, no doubt, the very thing they aimed to drive you to, by the various attacks they made upon you; unhoping (as they must do all the time) the success of their schemes in Solmes's behalf. They knew, that if once you were restored to favour, the suspended love of your father and uncles, like a river breaking down a temporary obstruction, would return with double force; and that then you would expose and triumph over all their arts. — And now, I hear they *enjoy* their successful malice.

Your father is all rage and violence. He ought, I am sure, to turn his rage inward. All your family accuse you of acting with *deep art;* and are put upon supposing that you are actually *every hour exulting over them*, with your man, in the success of it.

They all pretend now, that your trial of Wednesday was to be the last.

Advantage would indeed, my mother owns, have been taken of your yielding, if you had yielded. But had you not been to be prevailed upon, they would have given up their scheme, and taken your promise for renouncing Lovelace — believe them who will!

They own, however, that a minister was to be present — Mr. Solmes was to be at hand — and your father was previously to try his authority over you, in order to make you sign the settlements — all of it a romantic contrivance of your wild-headed foolish brother, I make no doubt. Is it likely that he and Bell would have given way to your restoration to favour, supposing it in their power to hinder it, on any other terms than those their hearts had been so long set upon?

How they took your flight, when

they found it out, may be better supposed than described.

Your aunt Hervey, it seems, was the first that went down to the ivy summer-house, in order to acquaint you that their search was over. Betty followed her; and they not finding you there, went on towards the cascade, according to a hint of yours.

Returning by the garden door, they met a servant [*they don't say it was that Joseph Leman; but it is very likely that it was he*] running, as he said, from pursuing Mr. Lovelace (a great hedge stake in his hand, and out of breath) to alarm the family.

If it were this fellow, and if he were employed in the double agency of cheating them and cheating you, what shall we think of the wretch you are with? — Run away from him my dear, if so — no matter to whom — or marry him, if you cannot.

Your aunt and all your family were accordingly alarmed by this fellow — *evidently when too late for pursuit*. They got together; and when a *posse*, ran to the place of interview; and some of them as far as to the tracks of the chariot-wheels, without stopping. And having heard the man's tale upon the spot, a general lamentation, a mutual upbraiding, and rage, and grief, were echoed from the different persons, according to their different tempers and conceptions. And they returned like fools as they went.

Your brother, at first, ordered horses and armed men to be got ready for a pursuit. Solmes and your uncle *Tony* were to be of the party. But your mother and your aunt Hervey dissuaded them from it, for fear of adding evil to evil; not doubting but Lovelace had taken measures to support himself in what he had done; and especially when the servant declared, that he saw you run with him as fast as you could set foot to the ground; and that there were several armed men on horseback at a small distance off.

* * *

My mother's absence was owing to a suspicion, that the Knollys's were to assist in our correspondence. She made them a visit upon it. *She does every thing at once.* And they have promised, that no more letters shall be left there, without her knowledge.

But Mr. Hickman has engaged one Filmer, a husbandman in the lane we call Finch-lane, near us, to receive them. Thither you will be pleased to direct yours, under cover, to Mr. John Soberton; and Mr. Hickman himself will call for them there; and there shall leave mine. It goes against me too to make him so useful to me. — He looks already so proud upon it! I shall have him [who knows?] give himself airs — he had best consider, that the favour he has been long aiming at, may put him into a very dangerous, a very ticklish situation. He that can oblige, may disoblige — happy for some people not to have it in their power to offend!

I will have patience, if I can for

a while, to see if these bustlings in my mother will subside — but, upon my word, I will not long bear this usage.

Sometimes I am ready to think, that my mother carries it thus on purpose to tire me out, and to make me the sooner marry. If I find it to be so, and that Hickman, in order to make a merit with me, is in the low plot, I will never bear him in my sight.

Plotting wretch, as I doubt your man is, I wish to Heaven that you were married, that you might brave them all, and not be forced to hide yourself, and be hurried from one inconvenient place to another. I charge you, omit not to lay hold on any handsome opportunity that may offer for that purpose.

Here again comes my mother —

* * *

We look mighty glum upon each other, I can tell you. She had not best *Harlowe* me at this rate — I won't bear it.

I have a vast deal to write. I know not what to write first. Yet my mind is full, and ready to run over.

I am got into a private corner of the garden, to be out of her way. — Lord help these mothers! — Do they think they can prevent a daughter's writing, or doing any thing she has a mind to do, by suspicion, watchfulness, and scolding? — They had better place a confidence in one by half — a generous mind scorns to abuse a generous confidence.

You have a nice, a very nice part to act with this wretch — who yet has, I think, but one plain path before him. I pity you — but you must make the best of the lot you have been forced to draw. Yet I see your difficulties. — But, if he do not offer to abuse your confidence, I would have you *seem* at least to place some in him.

If you think not of marrying soon, I approve of your resolution to fix somewhere out of his reach. And if he know not where to find you, so much the better. Yet I verily believe, they would force you back, could they but come at you, if they were not afraid of *him*.

I think, by all means, you should demand of both your trustees to be put in possession of your own estate. Meantime I have sixty guineas at your service. I beg you will command them. Before they are gone, I'll take care you shall be further supplied. I don't think you'll have a shilling or a shilling's worth of your own from your relations, unless you extort it from them.

As they believe you went away by your own consent, they are, it seems, equally surprised and glad that you have left your jewels and money behind you, and have contrived for clothes so ill. Very little likelihood this shows of their answering your request.

Indeed every one who knows not what I *now* know, must be at a loss to account for your *flight*, as they will call it. And how, my dear, can one report it with any tolerable advantage to you? — To say, you *did not intend it* when you met him, who will believe it? — to say, that a person of your known steadiness and punctilio was *over-persuaded* when you gave him the meeting, how will that sound? — To say, you were *tricked out of yourself*, and people were to give credit to it, how disreputable! — And while *unmarried*, and *yet with him*, the man a man of such a character, what would it not lead a censuring world to think?

I want to see how you put it in your letter for your clothes.

As you may depend upon all the little spiteful things they can offer, instead of sending what you write for, pray accept the sum I tender. What will seven guineas do? — And I will find a way to send you also any of my clothes and linen for present supply. I beg, my dear Clarissa, that you will not put your Anna Howe upon a foot with Lovelace, in refusing to accept of my offer. If you do not oblige me, I shall be apt to think that you rather incline to be obliged to *him*, than to favour *me*. And if I find this, I shall not know how to reconcile it with your delicacy in other respects.

Pray inform me of every thing that passes between you and him. My cares for you (however needless, from your own prudence) make me wish you to continue to be very minute. If any thing occur that you would tell me of if I were present, fail not to put it down in writing, although, from your natural diffidence, it should not appear to you altogether so worthy of your pen, or of my knowing. A stander-by may see more of the game than one that plays. Great consequences, like great folks, generally owe their greatness to small causes, and little incidents.

Upon the whole, I do not now think it is in your power to dismiss him when you please. I apprized you beforehand, that it would not. I repeat, therefore, that were I you, I would at least *seem* to place some confidence in him. So long as he is decent, you may. Very visibly observable, to such delicacy as yours, must be that behaviour in him, which will make him unworthy of *some* confidence.

Your relations, according to what old Antony says to *my mother*, and *she to me*, (by way of threatening, that you will not gain your supposed ends upon them by your flight) seem to expect that you will throw yourself into lady Betty's protection; and that she will offer to mediate for you: and they vow, that they will never hearken to any terms of accommodation that shall come from that quarter. They might speak out, and say, from *any* quarter; for I dare aver, that your brother and sister will not let them cool — at least, till their uncles have made such dispositions, and perhaps your father too, as they would have them make.

As this letter will apprize you of an alteration in the place to which you must direct your next, I send it by a friend of Mr. Hickman, who may be depended upon. He has business in the neighbourhood of Mrs. Sorlings; and he knows her. He will return to Mr. Hickman this night; and bring back any letter you shall have ready to send, or can get ready. It is moonlight. He'll not mind waiting for you. I choose not to send by any of Mr. Hickman's servants — at present, however. Every hour is now, or may be, important; and may make an alteration in your resolutions necessary.

I hear, at this instant, my mother calling about her, and putting every body into motion. She will soon, I suppose, make *me* and *my* employment the subjects of her inquiry.

Adieu, my dear. May Heaven preserve you, and restore you with honour as unsullied as your mind to

Your ever affectionate
ANNA HOWE.

LETTER V.
Miss Clarissa Harlowe to Miss Howe.

Thursday afternoon, April 13.

I AM infinitely concerned, my ever dear and ever kind friend, that I am the sad occasion of the displeasure between your mother and you. — How many persons have I made unhappy!

Had I not to console myself, that my error is not owing to wicked precipitation, I should be the most miserable of all creatures. As it is, I am enough punished in the *loss of my character*, more valuable to me than my life; and in the *cruel doubts and perplexities* which, conflicting with my hopes, and each getting the victory by turns, harrow up my soul between them.

I think, however, that you should obey your mother, and decline a correspondence with me; at least for the present. Take care how you fall into my error; for that *begun with carrying on a prohibited correspondence;* a correspondence which I thought it in my power to discontinue at pleasure. My talent is scribbling; and I the readier fell into this freedom, as I found delight in writing; having motives too, which I thought laudable; and, at one time, the permission of all my friends to write to him*.

Yet as to this correspondence, what hurt could arise from it, if your mother could be prevailed upon to permit it to be continued? — So much prudence and discretion as you have; and you, in writing to me, lying under no temptation of following so bad an example, as I have set — my letters too occasionally filled with self-accusation.

I thank you, my dear, most cordially I thank you, for your kind offers. You may be assured, that I will sooner be beholden to you, than to any body living. To Mr. Lovelace the last. Do not

* See Vol. I. p. 17, 18.

therefore think, that by declining your favours, I have an intention to lay myself under obligation to him.

I am willing to hope (notwithstanding what you write) that my friends will send me my little money, together with my clothes. They are too considerate, some of them, at least, to permit that I should be put to such *low* difficulties. Perhaps, they will not be in haste to oblige me. But, if not, I cannot yet want. I believe you think, I must not dispute with Mr. Lovelace the expenses of the road and lodgings, till I can get a fixed abode. But I hope soon to put an end even to those sort of obligations.

Small hopes indeed of a reconciliation from your account of my uncle's visit to your mother, in order to set her against an almost-friendless creature whom once he loved! *But is it not my duty to try for it?* Ought I to widen my error by obstinacy and resentment, because of *their* resentment; which must appear reasonable to them, as they suppose my flight premeditated; and as they are made to believe, that I am capable of triumphing *in it,* and *over them,* with the *man they hate?* When I have done all in my power to restore myself to their favour, I shall have the less to reproach myself with.

These considerations make me waver about following your advice, in relation to marriage; and the rather, as he is so full of complaisance with regard to my former conditions, which he calls my *injunctions*. Nor can I now, that my friends, as you inform me, have so strenuously declared *against accepting of the mediation of the ladies of Mr. Lovelace's family,* put myself into their protection, unless I am resolved to give up all hopes of a reconciliation with my own.

Yet if any happy introduction *could* be thought of to effect this desirable purpose, how shall terms be proposed to my father, while this man is with me, or near me? On the other hand, should they in his absence get me back by force (and this, you are of opinion, they would attempt to do, but in fear of him), how will their severest acts of compulsion be justified by my flight from them! — Meanwhile, to what censures, as you remind me, do I expose myself, while he and I are together, and unmarried! — Yet [can I with patience ask the question?] *is it in my power?* — O my dear Miss Howe! and am I so reduced, as that, to save the poor remains of my reputation in the world's eye, I must *watch the gracious motion* from the man's lips?

Were my cousin Morden in England, all might still perhaps be determined happily.

If no other mediation than his can be procured to set on foot the wished-for reconciliation, and if my situation with Mr. Lovelace alter not in the interim, I must endeavour to keep myself in a state of independence till he arrives, that I may be at liberty to govern myself by his advice and direction.

I will acquaint you, as you desire, with all that passes between Mr. Lovelace and me. Hitherto I have not discovered any thing in his behaviour that is *very* exceptionable. Yet I cannot say, that I think the respect he shews me, an easy, unrestrained, and natural respect, although I can hardly tell where the fault is.

But he has, doubtless, an arrogant and encroaching spirit. Nor is he so polite as his education, and other advantages, might have made one expect him to be. He seems, in short, to be one, who has always had too much of his own will to study to accommodate himself to that of others.

As to the placing of some confidence in him, I shall be as ready to take your advice in this particular, as in all others, and as he will be to deserve it. But *tricked away* as I was by him, not only *against my judgment, but my inclination*, can *he*, or any *body*, expect, that I should immediately treat him with complaisance, as if I acknowledged obligation to him for carrying me away? — If I did, must he not either think me a vile dissembler *before* he gained that point, or *afterwards?*

Indeed, indeed, my dear, I could tear my hair, on reconsidering what you write (as to the probability that the dreaded Wednesday was more dreaded than it needed to be) to think, that I should be thus tricked by this man; and that, in all likelihood, through his vile agent Joseph Leman. So premeditated and elaborate a wickedness as it must be! — Must I not, *with such a man*, be wanting *to myself*, if I were *not* jealous and vigilant? — Yet what a life to live for a spirit *so open*, and naturally *so unsuspicious*, as mine?

I am obliged to Mr. Hickman for the assistance he is so kindly ready to give to our correspondence. He is so *little likely* to make to himself an additional merit with the *daughter* upon it, that I shall be very sorry, if he risk any thing with the *mother* by it.

I am now in a state of obligation: so must rest satisfied with whatever I cannot help. Whom have I the power, once so precious to me, of obliging? — What I mean, my dear, is, that I ought, perhaps, to expect, that my influences over you are weakened by my indiscretion. Nevertheless, I will not, if I can help it, *desert myself*, nor give up the privilege you used to allow me, of telling you what I think of such parts of your conduct as I may not approve.

You must permit me therefore, severe as your mother is against an undesigning offender, to say that I think your liveliness to her inexcusable — to pass over, for this time, what nevertheless concerns me not a little, the free treatment you almost *indiscriminately* give to my relations.

If you will not, for your *duty's* sake, forbear your tauntings and impatience, let me beseech you, that you will for *mine*. — Since otherwise, your mother may apprehend, that my example, like a leaven, is working itself into the mind of her beloved daughter. And may not such an apprehension give her an irreconcileable displeasure against me?

I inclose the copy of my letter to my sister, which you are desirous to see. You will observe, that although I have not demanded my estate in form, and of my trustees, yet that I have hinted at leave to retire to it. How joyfully would I keep my word, if they would accept of the offer I renew! — It was not proper I believe you will think, on many accounts, to own that I was carried off against my inclination. I am, my dearest friend,

Your ever-obliged and affectionate
CL. HARLOWE.

LETTER VI.
To Miss Arabella Harlowe.

[*Inclosed to Miss Howe, in the preceding.*]
MY DEAR SISTER,   St. Alban's, April 11.

I HAVE, I confess, been guilty of an action which carries with it a rash and undutiful appearance. And I should have thought it an inexcusable one, had I been used with less severity than I have been of late; and had I not had too great reason to apprehend, that I was to be made a sacrifice to a man I could not bear to think of. But what is done, is done — perhaps I could wish it had not; and that I had trusted to the relenting of my dear and honoured parents. — Yet this from no other motives, but those of duty to them. — To whom I am ready to return (if I may not be permitted to retire to *the Grove*) on conditions which I before offered to comply with.

Nor shall I be in any sort of dependence upon the person by whose means I have taken this *truly reluctant step*, inconsistent with any reasonable engagement I shall enter into, if I am not further precipitated. Let me not have it to say, now at this important crisis! that I have a sister, but not a friend in that sister. My reputation, dearer to me than life, (whatever you may imagine from the step I have taken) is suffering. A little lenity will, even yet, in a great measure, restore it, and make that pass for a temporary misunderstanding only, which otherwise will be a stain as durable as life, upon a creature who has already been treated with great *unkindness*, to use no harsher a word.

For your own sake, therefore, for my brother's sake, by whom (I must say) I have been thus precipitated, and for all the family's sake, aggravate not my fault, if, on recollecting every thing, you think it one; nor by widening the unhappy difference, expose a sister for ever — Prays

Your affectionate
CL. HARLOWE.

I shall take it for a very great favour, to have my clothes directly sent me, together with fifty guineas, which you will find in my escritoire (of which I inclose the key); as also the divinity and miscellany classes of my little library; and, if it be thought fit, my jewels — Directed for *me*, to be left till called for, at Mr. Osgood's, near Soho-Square.

LETTER VII.

Mr. Lovelace to John Belford, Esq.

Mr. Lovelace in continuation of his last letter, (No. iii.) gives an account to his friend (pretty much to the same effect with the lady's) of all that passed between them at the Inns, in the journey, and till their fixing at Mrs. Sorlings'; to avoid repetition, those passages in his narrative are only extracted, which will serve to embellish hers; to open his views; or to display the humorous talent he was noted for.

At their alighting at the inn at St. Alban's on Monday night, thus he writes;

The people who came about us, as we alighted, seemed by their jaw-fallen faces, and goggling eyes, to wonder at beholding a charming young lady, majesty in her air and aspect, so composedly dressed, yet with features so discomposed, come off a journey which had made the cattle smoke, and the servants sweat. I read their curiosity in their faces, and my beloved's uneasiness in hers. She cast a conscious glance, as she alighted, upon her habit, which was *no habit;* and repulsively, as I may say, quitting my assisting hand, hurried into the house. * * *

Ovid was not a greater master of metamorphoses than thy friend. To the mistress of the house I instantly changed her into a sister, brought off by surprise from a near relation's (where she had wintered) to prevent her marrying a confounded rake [I love always to go as near the truth as I can] whom her father and mother, her elder sister, and all her loving uncles, aunts, and cousins abhorred. This accounted for my charmer's expected sullens; for her displeasure when she was to join me again, were it to hold; for her unsuitable dress upon the road; and, at the same time, gave her a proper and seasonable assurance of my honourable views.

Upon the debate between the lady and him, and particularly upon that part where she upbraids him with putting a young creature upon making a sacrifice of her duty and conscience, he writes:

All these, and still more mortifying things, she said.

I heard her in silence. But when it came to my turn, I pleaded, I argued, I answered her, as well as I could. — And when humility would not do, I raised my voice, and suffered my eye to sparkle with anger; hoping to take advantage of that sweet cowardice which is so amiable in the sex, and to which my victory over this proud beauty is principally owing.

She was not intimidated, however, and was going to rise upon me in her temper; and would have broken in upon my defence. But when a man talks to a woman upon such subjects, let her be ever so much in *all*, 'tis strange, if he cannot throw out a tub to the whale; — that is to say, if he cannot divert her from resenting one bold thing, by uttering two or three full as bold; but for which more favourable interpretations will lie.

To that part, where she tells him of the difficulty she made to correspond with him at first, thus he writes:

Very true, my precious! — And innumerable have been the difficulties thou hast made me struggle with. But one day thou mayest wish, that thou hadst spared this boast; as well as those other pretty haughtinesses. "That thou didst not reject Solmes for *my* sake: that *my* glory, if I valued myself upon carrying thee off, was *thy* shame: that I have more merit with *myself* than with thee, or any body else: [*What a coxcomb she makes me, Jack!*] That thou wishest thyself in thy father's house again, *whatever were to be the consequence.*" — If I forgive thee, charmer, for these hints, for these reflections, for these wishes, for these contempts, I am not the Lovelace I have been reputed to be; and that thy treatment of me shews that thou thinkest I am.

In short, her whole air throughout this debate, expressed a majestic kind of indignation, which implied a believed superiority of talents over the person to whom she spoke.

Thou hast heard me often expatiate upon the pitiful figure a man must make, whose wife *has*, or *believes* she has, more sense than himself. A thousand reasons could I give why I ought not to think of marrying Miss Clarissa Harlowe: at least till I can be sure, that she loves me with the preference I must expect from a wife.

I begin to stagger in my resolutions. Ever averse as I was to the hymeneal shackles, how easily will old prejudices recur! Heaven give me the heart to be honest to my Clarissa! — There's a prayer, Jack! If I should not be heard, what a sad thing would that be, for the most admirable of women! — Yet, as I do not often trouble Heaven with my prayers, who knows but this may be granted?

But there lie before me such charming difficulties, such scenery for intrigue, for stratagem, for enterprise. — What a horrible thing, that my talents point all that way! — When I know what is honourable and just; and would almost wish to be honest! — *Almost* I say; for such a varlet am I, that I cannot altogether wish it, for the soul of me! — Such a triumph over the whole sex, if I can subdue this lady! My maiden vow, as I may call it! — For did not the sex begin with me? — And does this lady spare me? Thinkest thou, Jack, that I should have spared my Rosebud, had I been set at defiance thus?—Her grandmother besought me, at first, *to spare her Rosebud;* and when a girl is put, or puts herself into a man's power, what can he wish for *further?* while I always considered opposition and resistance as a challenge to do my worst.*

Why, why, will the dear creature take such pains to appear all ice to me?—Why will she, by *her* pride awaken *mine?* — Hast thou not seen, in the above, how contemptuously she treats me?—What have I not suffered *for* her, and even *from* her?—Ought I to bear being told, that she will despise me, if I value myself above that odious Solmes?

Then she cuts me short in all my ardours. To *vow fidelity,* is by a cursed turn upon me, to shew that there is reason, in my own opinion, for doubt of it. The very same reflection upon me once before.** In my power, or out of my power, all one to this lady. — So, Belford, my poor vows are crammed down my throat, before they can well rise to my lips. And what can a lover say to his mistress, if she will neither let him lie nor swear?

One little piece of artifice I had recourse to. When she pushed so hard for me to leave her, I made a request to her, upon a condition she could not refuse; and pretended as much gratitude upon her granting it, as if it were a favour of the last consequence.

And what was this? but to promise what she had before promised, "Never to marry any other man, while I am living, and single, unless I should give her cause for high disgust against me." This, you know, was promising nothing, because she could be offended at any time, and was to be the sole judge of the offence. But it shewed her, how reasonable and just my expectations were; and that I was no encroacher.

She consented; and asked what security I expected? Her word only.

She gave me her word: but I besought her excuse for sealing it: and in the same moment (since to have waited for consent would have been asking for a denial) saluted her. And, believe me, or not, but, as I hope to live, it was the first time I had the courage to touch her charming lips with mine. And this I tell thee, Belford, that that single pressure (as modestly put too, as if I were as much a virgin as herself, that she might not be afraid of me another time) delighted me more than ever I was delighted by the *ultimatum* with any other woman. — So precious do awe, reverence, and apprehended prohibition, make a favour!

And now, Belford, I am only afraid, that I shall be *too* cunning; for she does not at present talk enough for me. I hardly know what to make of the dear creature yet.

---
* See Vol. I. p. 157.
** See Vol. I. p. 260.

I topt the brother's part on Monday night before the landlady at St. Alban's; asking my sister's pardon for carrying her off so unprepared for a journey; prated of the joy my father and mother, and all our friends, would have on receiving her; and this with so many circumstances, that I perceived, by a look she gave me, that went through my very veins, that I had gone too far. I apologized for it indeed when alone; but could not penetrate for the soul of me, whether I made the matter better or worse by it.

But I am of too frank a nature: my success, and the joy I have because of the jewel I am half in possession of, has not only unlocked my bosom, but left the door quite open.

This is a confounded sly sex. Would she but speak out, as I do — But I must learn reserves of her.

She must needs be unprovided of money: but has too much pride to accept of any from me. I would have had her go to town [*To town, if possible, must I get her to consent to go*] in order to provide herself with the richest of silks which that can afford. But neither is this to be assented to. And yet, as my intelligencer acquaints me, her implacable relations are resolved to distress her all they can.

These wretches have been most gloriously raving, ever since her flight; and still, thank Heaven, continue to rave; and will, I hope for a twelve-month to come. Now, at last, it is my day!

Bitterly do they regret, that they permitted her poultry visits, and garden walks, which gave her the opportunity to effect an escape which they suppose pre-concerted. For, as to her dining in the ivy-bower, they had a cunning design to answer upon her in that permission, as Betty told Joseph her lover.*

They lost, they say, an excellent pretence for confining her *more* closely on my threatening to rescue her, if they offered to carry her against her will to old Antony's moated house.** For this, as I told thee at the Hart, and as I once hinted to the dear creature herself,*** they had it in deliberation to do; apprehending, that I might attempt to carry her off, either with or without her consent, on some one of those connived-at excursions.

But here my honest Joseph, who gave me the information, was of admirable service to me. I had taught him to make the Harlowes believe, that I was as communicative to *my* servants, as their stupid James was to Joseph: § Joseph, as they supposed, by tampering with Will,§§ got all my secrets, and was acquainted with all my motions; and having also undertaken to watch all those of his

---
* Vol. I. p. 420.
** See Vol. I. Let. lxxix. and Let. lxxxii. Par. 1.
*** Ibid. Let. lxxix. Par. 4. See also Let. lxxxix. Par. 3.
§ Ibid. Let. xc. Par. 6. and 39.
§§ This will be further explained in Letter xvii. of this volume.

young lady*, the wise family were secure; and so was my beloved; and so was I.

I once had it in my head (and I hinted it to thee ** in a former) in case such a step should be necessary, to attempt to carry her off by surprise from the woodhouse; as it is remote from the dwelling-house. This had I attempted, I should certainly have effected by the help of the confraternity: and it would have been an action worthy of us all. — But Joseph's conscience, as he called it, stood in my way; for he thought it must have been known to be done by his connivance. I could, I dare say, have overcome this scruple, *as easily as I did many of his others*, had I not depended at one time upon her meeting me at a midnight or late hour [and, if she had, she never would have gone back]; at other times, upon the cunning family's doing my work for me, equally against their knowledge, or their wills.

For well I knew, that James and Arabella were determined never to leave off their foolish trials and provocations, till, by tiring her out, they had either made her Solmes's wife, or guilty of some such rashness as should throw her for ever out of the favour of both her uncles; though they had too much malice in their heads to intend service to me by their persecutions of her.

* See Vol. I. p. 137 160,
** Ibid. p. 161.

LETTER VIII.

Mr. Lovelace to John Belford, Esq.

In Continuation.

I OBLIGED the dear creature highly, I could perceive, by bringing Mrs. Greme to attend her, and to suffer that good woman's recommendation of lodgings to take place, on her refusal to go to *the Lawn.*

She must believe all my views to be honourable, when I had provided for her no particular lodgings, leaving it to her choice, whether she would go to M. Hall, to the Lawn, to London, or to either of the dowagers of my family.

She was visibly pleased with my motion of putting Mrs. Greme into the chaise with her, and riding on horseback myself.

Some people would have been apprehensive of what might pass between her and Mrs. Greme. But as all my relations either know or believe the justice of my intentions by her, I was in no pain on that account: and the less, as I have been always above hypocrisy, or wishing to be thought better than I am. And indeed, what occasion has a man to be an hypocrite, who has hitherto found his views upon the sex better answered, for his being known to be a rake? Why, even my beloved here denied not to correspond with me, though her friends had taught her to think me a libertine — Who then would be trying a *new* and *worse* character?

And then Mrs. Greme is a pious

matron, and would not have been biassed against the truth on any consideration. She used formerly, while there were any hopes of my reformation, to pray for me. She hardly continues the good custom, I doubt; for her worthy lord makes no scruple occasionally to rave against me to man, woman, and child, as they come in his way. He is very undutiful, as thou knowest. Surely, I may say so; since all duties are reciprocal. But for Mrs. Greme, *poor woman!* when my lord has the gout, and is at the Lawn, and the chaplain not to be found, she prays by him, or reads a chapter to him in the Bible, or some other good book.

Was it not therefore right, to introduce such a good sort of woman to the dear creature; and to leave them, without reserve, to their own talk! — And very busy in talk I saw they were, as they rode; and *felt* it too; for most charmingly glowed my cheeks.

I hope I shall be honest, I once more say: but as we frail mortals are not our own masters at all times, I must endeavour to keep the dear creature unapprehensive, until I can get her to *our acquaintance's in London*, or to some *other safe place there*. Should I, in the interim, give her the least room for suspicion; or offer to restrain her; she can make her appeals to strangers, and call the country in upon me; and, perhaps, throw herself upon her relations on their own terms. And were I now to lose her, how unworthy should I

be to be the prince and leader of such a confraternity as ours! How unable to look up among men! or to shew my face among women!

As things at present stand, she dare not own, that she went off against her own consent; and I have taken care to make all the *Implacables* believe, that she escaped *with it.*

She has received an answer from Miss Howe, to the letter written to her from St. Alban's.*

Whatever are the contents, I know not; but she was drowned in tears at the perusal of it. And I am the sufferer.

Miss Howe is a charming creature too; but confoundedly smart and spiritful. I am a good deal afraid of her. Her mother can hardly keep her in. I must continue to play off *old Antony*, by my *honest Joseph*, upon that mother, in order to manage that daughter, and oblige my beloved to an absolute dependence upon myself.**

Mrs. Howe is impatient of contradiction. So is Miss. A young lady who is sensible that she has all the maternal requisites herself, to be under maternal control; — fine ground for a man of intrigue to build upon! — A mother over-notable; a daughter over-sensible; and their Hickman, who is — over-neither: but merely a passive —

Only that I have an object still more desirable! —

* Vol. I. Letter xci. xlvii.
** See Vol. I. p. 137.

Yet how unhappy, that these two young ladies lived so near each other, and are so well acquainted! Else how charmingly might I have managed them both: But *one* man cannot have every woman worth having — pity though — when the man is such a VERY clever fellow!

LETTER IX.

Mr. Lovelace to John Belford, Esq.

In Continuation.

NEVER was there such a pair of scribbling lovers as we; yet perhaps whom it so much concerns to keep from each other what each writes. She *won't* have any thing else to do. I *would*, if she'd let me. I am not reformed enough for a husband. — *Patience is a virtue*, Lord M. says. *Slow and sure*, is another of his sentences. If I had not a great deal of that virtue, I should not have waited the Harlowes' own time of ripening into execution my plots upon themselves and upon their goddess daughter.

My beloved has been writing to her saucy friend, I believe, all that has befallen her, and what has passed between us hitherto. She will possibly have fine subjects for her pen, if she be as minute as I am.

I would not be so barbarous as to permit old Antony to set Mrs. Howe against her, did I not dread the consequences of the correspondence between the two young ladies. So lively the one, so vigilant, so prudent both, who would not wish to out wit such girls, and to be able to twirl them round his finger?

My charmer has written to her sister for her clothes, for some gold, and for some of her books. What books can tell her more than she knows? But I can. So she had better study *me*.

She *may* write. She must be obliged to me at last with all her pride. Miss Howe indeed will be ready enough to supply her; but I question, whether she can do it without her mother, who is as covetous as the grave. And my agent's agent, old Antony, has already given the mother a hint which will make her jealous of *pecuniaries*.

Besides, if Miss Howe has money by her, I can put her mother upon borrowing it of her: nor blame me, Jack, for contrivances that have their foundation in generosity. Thou knowest my spirit; and that I should be proud to lay an obligation upon my charmer to the amount of half, nay, to the whole, of my estate. Lord M. has more for me than I can ever wish for. My predominant passion is *girl*, not *gold;* nor value I *this*, but as it helps me to *that*, and gives me independence.

I was forced to put it into the sweet novice's head, as well for *my* sake as for *hers* (lest we should be traceable by *her* direction), whither to direct the sending of her clothes, if they incline to do her that small piece of justice.

If they do I shall begin to dread a reconciliation; and must be forced to muse for a contrivance or two, to prevent it; and *to avoid mischief.* For that (as I have told honest Joseph Leman) is a great point with me.

Thou wilt think me a sad fellow, I doubt. But are not all rakes sad fellows? — And art not thou, to thy little power, as bad as any? If thou dost all that's in thy head and in thy heart to do, thou art worse than I; for I do not, I assure thee.

I proposed, and she consented, that her clothes, or whatever else her relations should think fit to send her, should be directed to thy cousin Osgood's. Let a special messenger, at my charge, bring me any letter, or portable parcel, that shall come. If not portable, give me notice of it. But thou'lt have no trouble of this sort from her relations, I dare be sworn. And in this assurance, I will leave them, I think, to act upon their own heads. A man would have no more to answer for than needs must.

But one thing, while I think of it; *which is of great importance to be attended to* — you must hereafter write to me in character, as I shall do to you. It would be a confounded thing to be blown up by a train of my own laying. And who knows what opportunities a man in love may give against himself? In changing a coat or waistcoat, something might be forgotten. I once suffered that way. Then for the sex's curiosity, it is but remembering, in order to guard against it, that the name of their common mother was Eve.

Another thing remember; I have changed my name: changed it without an act of parliament. "Robert Huntingford" it is now. Continue *esquire.* It is a respectable addition, although every sorry fellow assumes it, almost to the banishment of the usual travelling one of *captain.* "To be left till called for, at the post-house at Hertford."

Upon naming thee, she asked thy character. I gave thee a better than thou deservest, in order to do credit to *myself.* Yet I told her, that thou wert an awkward fellow; and this to do credit to *thee,* that she may not, if ever she be to see thee, expect a cleverer man than she'll find. Yet thy *apparent* awkwardness befriends thee not a little: for wert thou a sightly mortal, people would discover nothing extraordinary in thee, when they conversed with thee: whereas, seeing a bear, they are surprised to find in thee any thing that is like a man. Felicitate thyself then upon thy defects; which are evidently thy principal perfections; and which occasion thee a distinction which otherwise thou wouldst never have.

The lodgings we are in at present are not convenient. I was so delicate as to find fault with them, as communicating with each other, because I knew *she* would; and told her, that were I sure she was safe from pursuit, I would leave her in them (since such was her earnest desire and expectation), and go to London.

She must be an infidel against all reason and appearances, if I do not banish even the *shadow* of mistrust from her heart.

Here are two young likely girls, daughters of the widow Sorlings; that's the name of our landlady.

I have only, at present, admired them in their dairy-works. How greedily do the sex swallow praise! — Did I not once in the streets of London, see a well-dressed handsome girl laugh, bridle, and visibly enjoy the praises of a sooty dog, a chimney-sweeper; who, with his empty sack cross his shoulder, after giving her the way, stopt, and held up his brush and shovel in admiration of her? — Egad, girl, thought I, I despise thee as Lovelace: but were I the chimney-sweeper, and could only contrive to get into thy presence, my life to thy virtue, I would have thee.

So pleased was I with the younger Sorlings, for the elegance of her works, that I kissed her, and she made me a courtesy for my condescension: and blushed, and seemed *sensible all over*: encouragingly, yet innocently, she adjusted her handkerchief, and looked towards the door, as much as to say, she would not tell, were I to kiss her again.

Her eldest sister popt upon her. The conscious girl blushed again, and looked so confounded, that I made an excuse for her, which gratified both. Mrs. Betty, said I, I have been so much pleased with the neatness of your dairy-works, that I could not help saluting your sister: you have *your* share of merit in them, I am sure — give me leave — Good souls! — I like them both — she courtesied too! — How I love a grateful temper! O that my Clarissa were but half so acknowledging!

I think I must get one of them to attend my charmer when she removes — the mother seems to be a notable woman. She had not best, however, be *too* notable: since, were she by suspicion to give a face of difficulty to the matter, it would prepare me for a trial with one or both the daughters.

Allow me a little rodomontade, Jack — but really and truly my heart is fixed. I can think of no creature breathing of the sex, but my Gloriana.

LETTER X.

Mr. Lovelace to John Belford, Esq.

In Continuation.

This is Wednesday; the day that I was to have lost my charmer for ever to the hideous Solmes! With what high satisfaction and heart's-ease can I now sit down, and triumph over my men in straw at Harlowe Place! Yet 'tis perhaps best for them, that she got off as she did. Who knows what consequences might have followed upon my attending her in; or (if she had not met me) upon my projected visit, followed by my myrmidons!

But had I even gone in with her unaccompanied, I think I had but little reason for apprehension:

for well thou knowest, that *the tame spirits* which value themselves upon reputation, and are held within the skirts of the law by political considerations only, may be compared to an infectious spider, which will run into his hole the moment one of his threads is touched by a finger that can crush him, leaving all his toils defenceless and to be brushed down at the will of the potent invader. While a silly fly, that has neither courage nor strength to resist, no sooner gives notice, by its buz and its struggles, of its being entangled, but out steps the self-circumscribed tyrant, winds round and round the poor insect, till he covers it with his bowel-spun toils; and when so fully secured, that it can neither move leg nor wing, suspends it, as if for a spectacle to be exulted over: then stalking to the door of his cell, turns about, glotes over it at a distance; and, sometimes advancing, sometimes retiring, preys at leisure upon its vitals.

But now I think of it, will not this comparison do as well for the *entangled girls*, as for the *tame spirits?* — Better o' my conscience! — 'Tis but comparing the spider to us brave fellows; and it *quadrates.*

Whatever our hearts are in, our heads will follow. Begin with *spiders,* with *flies,* with what we will, girl is the centre of gravity, and we all naturally tend to it.

Nevertheless, to recur: I cannot but observe, that these *tame spirits* stand a poor chance in a fairly offensive war with such of us mad fellows, as are above all law, and scorn to sculk behind the hypocritical screen of reputation.

Thou knowest, that I never scruple to throw myself amongst numbers of adversaries; the more the safer: one or two, no fear, will take the part of a single adventurer, if not *intentionally*, in *fact;* holding him in, while others hold in the principal antagonist, to the augmentation of their mutual prowess, till both are prevailed upon to compromise, or one to absent: so that upon the whole, the law-breakers have the advantage of the law-keepers, all the world over; at least for a time, and till they have run to the end of their race. Add to this, in the question between me and the Harlowes, that the whole family of them must know that they have injured me — must therefore be afraid of me. Did they not, at their own church, cluster together like bees, when they saw me enter it? nor knew they which should venture out first, when the service was over.

James, indeed, was not there. If he had, he would perhaps have endeavoured to *look* valiant. But there is a sort of valour in the *face,* which by its over bluster shews fear in the *heart:* just such a face would James Harlowe's have been, had I made them a visit.

When I have had such a face and such a heart as I have described to deal with, I have been all calm and serene, and left it to the friends of the blusterer (as I have done to the Harlowes) to do my work for me.

I am about mustering up in my memory, all that I have ever done, that has been thought praise-worthy, or but barely tolerable. I am afraid thou canst not help me to many remembrances of this sort; because I never was so bad as since I have known thee.

Have I not had it in my heart to do *some* good that thou canst remind me of? Study for me, Jack. I have recollected some instances which I think will *tell in*—but see if thou canst not help me to some which I may have forgot.

This I may venture to say, that the principal blot in my escutcheon is owing to these girls, these confounded girls. But for *them*, I could go to church with a good conscience: but when I do, there they are. Every where does Satan spread his snares for me: but, now I think of it, what if our governors should appoint churches for the *women* only, and others for the *men?* — Full as proper, I think, for the promoting of *true piety* in both [much better than the Synagogue-lattices] as separate boarding-schools for their *education*.

There are already male and female dedications of churches.

St. Swithin's, St. Stephen's, St. Thomas's, St. George's, and so forth, might be appropriated to the men; and Santa Catharina's, Santa Anna's, Santa Maria's, Santa Margaretta's, for the women.

Yet, were it so, and life to be the forfeiture of being found at the female churches, I believe that I, like a second Clodius, should change my dress, to come at my Portia or Pompeia, though one the daughter of a Cato, the other the wife of a Cæsar.

But how I *excurse!*— Yet thou usedst to say, thou likedst my excursions. If thou dost, thou'lt have enow of them: for I never had a subject I so much adored; and with which I shall probably be compelled to have so much patience before I strike the blow: if the blow I do strike.

But let me call myself back to my *recordation* subject — Thou needest not remind me of my *Rose-bud*. I have her in my head; and moreover have contrived to give my fair-one an hint of that affair, by the agency of honest Joseph Leman*; although I have not reaped the hoped-for credit of her acknowledgment.

That's the devil; and it was always my hard fate — every thing I do that is good, is but as I *ought!* — every thing of a contrary nature is brought into the most glaring light against me — is this fair? ought not a balance to be struck; and the credit carried to my account? — Yet I must own, too, that I half grudge Johnny this blooming maiden; for, in truth, I think a fine woman too

* See Vol. I. p. 293, 317.

rich a jewel to hang about a poor man's neck.

Surely, Jack, if I am guilty of a fault in my universal adorations of the sex, the *women* in general ought to love me better for it.

And so they do, I thank them heartily; except here and there a covetous little rogue comes cross me, who, under the pretence of loving virtue for its own sake, wants to have me all to herself.

I have rambled enough.

Adieu, for the present.

LETTER XI.
Miss Clarissa Harlowe to Miss Howe.

Thursday night, April 13.

I ALWAYS loved writing, and my unhappy situation gives me now enough of it; and you, I fear, too much. I have had another very warm debate with Mr. Lovelace. It brought on the subject which you advised me not to decline, when it handsomely offered. And I want to have either your acquittal or blame for having suffered it to go off without effect.

The impatient wretch sent up to me several times, while I was writing my last to you, to desire my company: yet his business nothing particular; only to hear *him* talk. The man seems pleased with his own volubility; and, whenever he has collected together abundance of smooth things, he wants me to find an ear for them! Yet he need not; for I don't often gratify him either with giving him the praise for his verboseness, or showing the pleasure in it, that he would be fond of.

When I had finished the letter, and given it to Mr. Hickman's friend, I was going up again, and had got up half a dozen stairs; when he besought me to stop, and hear what he had to say.

Nothing, as I said, to any new purpose had he to offer; but complainings; and those in a manner, and with an air, as I thought, that bordered upon insolence. He could not live, he told me, unless he had more of my company, and of my *indulgence* too, than I had yet given him.

Hereupon I stept down, and into the parlour, not a little out of humour with him; and the more, as he has very *quietly taken up his quarters here*, without talking of removing, as he had promised.

We began instantly our angry conference. He provoked me, and I repeated several of the plainest things I had said in our former conversations; and particularly told him, that I was every hour more and more dissatisfied with myself, and with him: that he was not a man, who, in my opinion, improved upon acquaintance: and that I should not be *easy till he had left me to myself.*

He might be surprised at my warmth, perhaps: but really the man looked so like a simpleton, hesitating, and having nothing to say for himself, or that should excuse the peremptoriness of his demand upon me (when he knew I had been writing a letter which a gentleman waited for), that I flung from him, declaring, that I would be mistress of my own time, and of my own actions, and not be called to account for either.

He was very uneasy till he could again be admitted into my company, and when I was obliged to see him, which was sooner than I liked, never did man put on a more humble and respectful demeanour.

He told me, that he had, upon this occasion, been entering into himself, and had found a great deal of reason to blame himself for an impatiency and inconsideration, which, although he meant nothing by it, must be very disagreeable to one of my delicacy. That having always aimed at a *manly sincerity* and *openness of heart*, he had not till now discovered, that both were very consistent with that *true* politeness, which he feared he had too much disregarded, while he sought to avoid the contrary extreme; knowing, that in me he had to deal with a lady, who despised an hypocrite, and who was above all flattery. But from this time forth, I should find such an alteration in his whole behaviour, as might be expected from a man who knew himself to be honoured with the presence and conversation of a person *who had the most delicate mind in the world* — that was his flourish.

I said, that he might perhaps expect congratulation upon the discovery he had just now made, to wit, that *true politeness* and *sincerity* were reconcilable: but that I, who had, by a perverse fate, been thrown into his company, had abundant reason to regret that he had no sooner found this out. — Since, I believed, very few men of *birth* and *education* were strangers to it.

He knew not, *neither*, that he had so badly behaved himself, as to deserve so very severe a rebuke.

Perhaps not, I replied: but he might, if so, make another discovery from what I had said; which might be to *my own* disadvantage: since, if he had so much reason to be satisfied with *himself*, he would see what an ungenerous person he spoke to, who, when he seemed to give himself airs of humility, which, perhaps, he thought beneath him to assume, had not the civility to make him a compliment upon them; but was ready to take him at his word.

He had long, with infinite pleasure, the pretended *flattery-hater* said, admired my *superior* talents, and a wisdom in so young a lady, perfectly surprising.

Let me, madam, said he, stand ever so low in your opinion, I shall believe all you say to be just; and that I have nothing to do, but to govern myself for the future by your example, and by the standard you shall be pleased to give me.

I know better, sir, replied I, than to value myself upon your volubility of speech. As you pretend to pay so preferable a regard to sincerity, you should confine yourself to the strict rules of truth, when you speak of me to myself: and then although you shall be so kind as to imagine you have *reason* to make me a compliment, you will have much more to pride yourself in those arts which have made so *extraordinary* a young creature so great a fool.

Really, my dear, the man deserves not politer treatment. — And then has he not made a fool, an egregious fool of me? — I am afraid he himself thinks he has.

I am surprised! I am amazed, madam, returned he, at so strange a turn upon me! — I am very unhappy, that nothing I can do or say will give you a good opinion of me! — Would to heaven that I knew what I *can* do to obtain the honour of your confidence!

I told him, *that I desired his absence*, of all things. I saw not, I said, that my friends thought it worth their while to give me disturbance: therefore if he would set out for London, or Berkshire, or whither he pleased, it would be most agreeable to me, and most reputable too.

He would do so, he *intended to do so*, the moment I was in a place to my liking — in a place convenient for me.

This, sir, will be so, when you are not here to break in upon me, and make the apartments inconvenient.

He did not think this place safe, he replied; and as I intended not to stay here, he had not been so solicitous, as otherwise he should have been, to enjoin privacy to his servants, nor to Mrs. Greme at her leaving me; and there were two or three gentlemen in the neighbourhood, he said, with whose servants his gossiping fellows had scraped acquaintance: so that he could not think of leaving me here unguarded and unattended. — But fix upon any place in England where I could be out of danger, and he would go to the furthermost part of the king's dominions, if by doing so he could make me easy.

I told him plainly that I should never be in humour with myself for *meeting him*; nor with him, for *seducing me away*: that my regrets increased, instead of diminished: that my reputation was wounded: that nothing I could do would now retrieve it: and that he must not wonder if I every hour grew more and more uneasy both with myself and him: that upon the whole, I was willing to take care of myself; and when *he* had left me I should best know what to resolve upon, and whither to go.

He wished he were at liberty, without giving me offence, or being thought to intend to *infringe the articles I had stipulated and insisted upon*, to make one humble proposal to me. But the *sacred regard* he was determined *to pay to all my injunctions* (reluctantly as I had on Monday last put it into his power to serve me) would not permit him to make it, unless I would promise to excuse him, if I did not approve of it.

I asked, in some confusion, what he would say?

He prefaced and paraded on; and then out came, with great diffidence and many apologies, and a bashfulness which sat very awkwardly upon him, a proposal of speedy solemnization: which, he said would put all right; and make my first three or four months (which otherwise must be passed in obscurity and apprehension) a round of visits and visitings to and from all his relations; to Miss Howe; to whom I pleased: and would pave the way to the reconciliation I had so much at heart.

Your advice had great weight with me just then, as well as *his reasons,* and the consideration of my *unhappy situation:* but what could I say? I wanted somebody to speak for me.

The man saw I was not angry at his motion. I only blushed; and that I am sure I did up to the ears; and looked silly and like a fool.

He wants not courage. Would he have had me catch at his first, at his *very* first word? — I was *silent* too — and do not the bold sex take silence for a mark of a favour? — Then, *so lately* in my father's house! Having also declared to him in my letters, before I had your advice, that I would not think of marriage till he had passed through a state of probation, as I may call it — how was it possible I could encourage, with *very* ready signs of approbation, such an early proposal? especially so soon after the free treatment he had provoked from me. If I were to die, I could not.

He looked at me with great confidence; as if (notwithstanding his contradictory bashfulness) he would look me through: while my eye but now-and-then could glance at him — he begged my pardon with great humility: he was *afraid* I would think he deserved no other answer but that of a *contemptuous silence.* True love was fearful of offending [take care, Mr. Lovelace, thought I, how yours is tried by that rule]. Indeed so *sacred a regard* [foolish man!] would he have *to all my declarations* made *before I honoured him —*

I would hear him no further; but withdrew in a confusion *too visible,* and left him to make his nonsensical flourishes to himself.

I will only add, that, if he really wishes for a speedy solemnization he never could have had a luckier time to press for my consent to it. But he let it go off; and indignation has taken place of it. And now it shall be a point with me, to get him at a distance from me.

I am, my dearest friend,
Your ever faithful and obliged
Cl. H.

LETTER XII.
Mr. Lovelace to John Belford, Esq.

Thursday, April 13.

Why, Jack, thou needest not make such a *wonderment,* as the girls say, if I should have taken large strides already towards reformation: for dost thou not see, that while I have been so assiduously, night and day, pursuing this single charmer, I have infinitely less to answer for, than otherwise I should have had? Let me see, how many days and nights? — Forty, I believe, after open trenches, spent in the sap only, and never a mine sprung yet!

By a moderate computation, a dozen kites might have fallen while I have been only trying to ensnare this single lark. Nor yet do I see when I shall be able to bring her to my lure: more innocent days yet, therefore! — But reformation for my stalking-horse, I hope, will be a sure, though a slow method to effect all my purposes.

Then, Jack, thou wilt have a merit too in engaging my pen, since thy time would be otherwise worse employed: and, after all, who knows but by creating new habits, at the expense of the old, a real reformation may be brought about? I have promised it; and I believe there is a pleasure to be found in being good, reversing that of Nat. Lee's madmen,

— Which none but good men know.

By all this, seest thou not, how greatly preferable it is, on twenty accounts, to pursue a difficult, rather than an easy chase? I have a desire to inculcate this pleasure upon thee, and to teach thee to fly at nobler game than daws, crows, and wigeons: I have a mind to shew thee from time to time, in the course of the correspondence thou hast so earnestly wished me to begin on this illustrious occasion that these exalted ladies may be abased, and to obviate one of the objections that thou madest to me when we were last together that the pleasure which attends these nobler aims remunerates not the pains they bring with them; since, like a paltry fellow as thou wert, thou assertedst that all women are alike.

Thou knowest nothing, Jack, of the delicacies of intrigue: nothing of the glory of outwitting the witty and the watchful: of the joys that fill the mind of the inventive or contriving genius, ruminating which to use of the different webs that offer to him for the entanglement of a haughty charmer, who in her day has given him unnumbered torments. — Thou, Jack, who, like a dog at his ease, contentest thyself to growl over a bone thrown out to thee, dost not know the joys of a chase, and in pursuing a winding game: these I will endeavour to rouse thee to, and thou wilt have reason doubly and trebly to thank me, as well because of the present delight, as with regard to thy prospects beyond the moon.

To this place I had written, purely to amuse myself, before I was admitted to my charmer. But now I have to tell thee, that I was quite right in my conjecture, that she would set up for herself, and dismiss me: for she has declared in so many words, that such was her resolution: and why? Because, to be plain with me, the more she saw of *me*, and of *my ways*, the less she liked of either.

This cut me to the heart! — I did not cry, indeed! — Had I been a *woman*, I should though, and that most plentifully: but I pulled out a white cambrick handkerchief: *that* I could command, but not my *tears*.

She finds fault with my protestations; with my professions; with my vows: I cannot curse a servant, the only privilege a master is known by, but I am supposed to be a trooper* — I must not say, by my soul; nor, as I hope to be saved. Why, Jack, how particular this is! Would she not have me think, I have a precious soul, as well as she? — If she thinks my salvation hopeless, what a *devil* [another exceptionable word!] does she propose to reform me for? — So I have not an ardent expression left me.

* * *

WHAT can be done with a woman who is above flattery, and despises all praise but that which flows from the approbation of her own heart?

Well, Jack, thou seest it is high time to change my measures. I must run into the *pious* a little faster than I had designed.

What a sad thing would it be, were I, after all, to lose her person, as well as her opinion! the only time that further acquaintance, and no blow struck nor suspicion given, ever lessened me in a lady's favour! — A cursed mortification! — 'Tis certain I can have no

* See p. 13.

pretence for holding her, if she will go. — No such thing as force to be used, or so much as hinted at! — Lord send us safe at London! — That's all I have for it now: and yet it must be the least part of my speech.

But why will this admirable creature urge her destiny? Why will she defy the power she is absolutely dependent upon? Why will she still wish to my face, that she had never left her father's house? Why will she deny me her company, till she makes me lose my patience, and lay myself open to her resentment? And why, when she is offended, does she carry her indignation to the utmost length that a scornful beauty, in the *very height* of her *power* and *pride*, can go?

Is it prudent, thinkest thou, in *her* circumstances, to tell me, *repeatedly* to tell me, "That she is every hour more and more dissatisfied with herself and me? That I am not one, who improve upon her in my conversation and address?" [Couldst *thou*, Jack, bear this from a captive?] "That she shall not be easy while she is with me? That she was thrown upon me by a perverse fate? That she knows better than to value herself upon my volubility? That if I think she deserves the compliments I make her, I may pride myself in those arts, by which I have made a fool of so extraordinary a person? That she shall never forgive herself for *meeting me*, nor me for *seducing* her away?" [*her very words*] "That her regrets increase instead of diminish? That she will take care of herself; and since her friends think it not worth while to pursue her, she will be left to her own care? That I shall make Mrs. Sorlings's house more agreeable by my absence?—And go to Berks, to town, or wherever I will" [to the devil, I suppose] "with all her heart?"

The impolitic charmer!—To a temper so vindictive as she thinks mine! To a free-liver, as she believes me to be, who has her in his power! I was *before*, as thou knowest, balancing; now this scale, now that the heaviest. I only waited to see how *her* will would work, how *mine* would lead me on. Thou seest what bias hers takes — and wilt thou doubt that mine will be determined by it? Were not her faults, before this, numerous enough? Why will she put me upon looking back?

I will sit down to argue with myself by-and-by, and thou shalt be acquainted with the result.

If thou didst but know, if thou hadst but beheld, what an abject slave she made me look like! I had given myself high airs, as *she* called them: but they were airs that shewed my love for her: that shewed I could not live out of her company. But she took me down with a vengeance! She made me look about me. So much advantage had she over me; such severe turns upon me; by my soul, Jack, I had hardly a word to say for myself. I am ashamed to tell thee what a poor creature she made me look like! But I could have told her something that would have humbled her pretty pride at the instant, had she been in a *proper* place, and *proper* company about her.

To such a place then — and where she cannot fly me — and *then* to see how my will works, and what can be done by the *amorous see-saw;* now humble, now proud; now expecting or demanding; now submitting, or acquiescing — till I have tired resistance.

But these hints are at present enough. I may further explain myself as I go along; and as I confirm or recede in my future motions. If she *will* revive past disobligations! If she *will* — but no more, no more, as I said, *at present,* of threatenings.

LETTER XIII.
Mr. Lovelace to John Belford, Esq.

In Continuation.

AND do I not see that I shall need nothing but patience, in order to have all power with me? For what shall we say, if all these complaints of a character wounded; these declarations of increasing regrets for meeting me; of resentments never to be got over for my *seducing* her away; these angry commands to leave her: — what shall we say, if all were to mean nothing but MATRIMONY? And what if my forbearing to enter upon that subject come out to be the true cause of her petulance and uneasiness!

I had once before played about the skirts of the irrevocable obligation; but thought myself obliged to speak in clouds, and to run away from the subject, as soon as she took my meaning, lest she should imagine it to be *ungenerously urged*, now she was in some sort in my power, as she had forbid me beforehand, to touch upon it, till I were in a state of visible reformation, and till a reconciliation with her friends was probable. But now, out-argued, out-talented, and pushed so vehemently *to leave* one whom I had no good pretence to *hold*, if she *would* go; and who could so easily, if I had given her cause to doubt, have thrown herself into other protection, or have returned to Harlowe Place and Solmes; I spoke out upon the subject, and offered reasons, although with infinite doubt and hesitation [*lest she should be offended at me,* Belford!] why she should assent to the legal tie, and make me the happiest of men. And O how the blushing cheek, the downcast eye, the silent yet trembling lip, and the heaving bosom, a sweet collection of heightened beauties, gave evidence, that the tender was not mortally offensive!

Charming creature! thought I [*but I charge thee, that thou let not any of thy sex know my exultation* *] is it so *soon* come to this? —

* Mr. Lovelace might have spared this caution on this occasion, since many of the sex [we mention it with regret] who on the first publication had read thus far, and even to the lady's first escape, have been readier to censure her for overniceness, as we have observed in a former note, page 8, than him for artifices and exultations not less cruel and ungrateful, than ungenerous and unmanly.

Am I *already* lord of the destiny of a Clarissa Harlowe? Am I *already* the reformed man thou resolvest I *should* be, before I had the *least* encouragement given me? Is it thus, that *the more thou knowest me, the less thou seest reason to approve of me?* — And can art and design enter into a breast so celestial? To banish me from thee, to insist so rigorously upon my absence, in order to bring me closer to thee, and make the blessing dear? — Well do *thy* arts justify *mine;* and encourage me to let loose my plotting genius upon thee.

But let me tell thee, charming maid, if thy wishes are at all to be answered, that thou hast yet to account to me for thy reluctance to go off with me, at a crisis when thy going off was necessary to avoid being forced into the nuptial fetters with a wretch, that were he not thy aversion, thou wert no more honest to thy own merit, than to me.

I am *accustomed* to be preferred, let me tell thee, by thy equals in rank too, though thy inferiors in merit; but who is not so? And shall I marry a woman, who has given me reason to doubt the preference she has for me?

No, my dearest love, I have too sacred a regard for thy *injunctions*, to let them be broken through, even by thyself. Nor will I take in thy full meaning by blushing silence only. Nor shalt thou give me room to doubt whether it be necessity or love, that inspires this condescending impulse.

Upon these principles, what had

I to do, but to construe her silence into contemptuous displeasure? And I begged her pardon for making a motion, which I had so much *reason* to fear would offend her: for the future *I would pay a sacred* regard to her *previous injunctions*, and prove to her by all my conduct the truth of that observation, that true love is always fearful of offending.

And what could the lady say to this? methinks thou askest.

Say! — Why she looked vexed, disconcerted, teased; was at a loss, as I thought, whether to be more angry with herself, or with me. She turned about, however, as if to hide a starting tear: and drew a sigh into two or three but just audible quavers, trying to suppress it, and withdrew — leaving me master of the field.

Tell me not of politeness: tell me not of generosity: tell me not of compassion — is she not a match for me? *More* than a match! Does she not out-do me at every fair weapon? Has she not made me doubt her love? Has she not taken officious pains to declare that she was not averse to Solmes for any respect she had to me? and her sorrow for putting herself out of *his* reach; that is to say, for meeting me?

Then what a triumph would it be to the *Harlowe pride*, were I now to marry this lady? A family beneath my own! No one in it worthy of an alliance with, but her! My own estate not contemptible! Living within the bounds of it, to avoid dependence upon *their* betters, and obliged to no man living! My expectations still so much *more* considerable! My person, my talents — not to be despised, surely — yet rejected by them with scorn. Obliged to carry on an underhand address to their daughter, when two of the most considerable families in the kingdom have made overtures, which I have declined, partly for her sake, and partly because I never will marry, if *she* be not the person. To be forced to *steal* her away; not only from *them*, but from *herself!* and must I be brought to implore forgiveness and reconciliation from the Harlowes? — Beg to be acknowledged as the *son* of a gloomy tyrant; whose only boast is his riches? As a *brother* to a wretch who has conceived immortal hatred to me; and to a sister who was beneath my attempts, or I would have had her *in my own way*, and that with a tenth part of the trouble and pains that her sister has cost me; and, finally, as a *nephew* to uncles, who valuing themselves upon their *acquired* fortunes, would insult me as creeping to them on that account? — Forbid it the blood of the Lovelaces, that your *last*, and, let me say, not the *meanest* of your stock, should thus creep, thus fawn, thus lick the dust for a WIFE! —

Proceed anon.

LETTER XIV.

Mr. Lovelace to John Belford, Esq.

In Continuation.

But is it not the divine CLARISSA [*Harlowe* let me not say; my soul spurns them all but her] whom I am thus by implication threatening? If virtue be the true nobility, how is she ennobled, and how would an alliance with her ennoble, were not contempt due to the family from which she sprung, and prefers to me!

But again, let me stop. — Is there not something wrong, *has* there not been something wrong, in this divine creature? And will not the reflections upon that wrong (what though it may be construed in *my favour?**) make me unhappy, when *novelty* has lost its charms, and when, mind and person, she is all my own? Libertines are nicer, if *at all* nice, than other men. They seldom meet with the stand of virtue in the women whom they attempt. And by the frailty of those they have triumphed over, they judge of all the rest. "*Importunity* and *opportunity* no woman is proof against, especially from the persevering lover, who knows how to suit temptations to inclinations;" this, thou knowest, is a prime article of the rake's creed.

And what? (methinks thou askest with surprise) dost thou question this most admirable of women? — The virtue of a CLARISSA dost thou question?

I do not, I dare not question it. My reverence for her will not let me *directly* question it. But let me, in my turn, ask thee — Is not, may not her virtue be founded rather in *pride* than in *principle?* Whose daughter is she? — And is she not a *daughter?* If impeccable, how came she by her impeccability? The pride of setting an example to her sex has run away with her hitherto, and may have made her till *now* invincible. But is not that pride abated? — What may not both *men* and *women* be brought to do, in a *mortified state?* What mind is superior to calamity? Pride is perhaps the principal bulwark of female virtue. Humble a woman, and may she not be *effectually* humbled?

Then who says, Miss Clarissa Harlowe is the paragon of virtue? — Is virtue itself?

All who know her, and have heard of her, it will be answered.

Common bruit! — Is virtue to be established by common bruit only? — Has her virtue ever been *proved?* — Who has dared to try her virtue?

I told thee, I would sit down to argue with myself; and I have drawn myself into argumentation before I was aware.

Let me enter into a strict discussion of this subject.

I know how ungenerous an appearance what I *have* said, and what I have *further* to say, on this topic, will have from *me:* but am I not bringing virtue to the touch-

---

* The particular attention of such of the fair sex, as are more apt to read for the sake of amusement, than instruction, is requested to this letter of Mr. Lovelace.

stone, with a view to exalt it, if it come out to be proof? — "Avaunt then, for one moment, all consideration that may arise from a weakness which some would miscal *gratitude;* and is often times the corrupter of a heart not ignoble!"

To the test then — and I will bring this charming creature to the *strictest* test, "that all the sex, who may be shewn any passages in my letters" [and I know thou cheerest the hearts of all thy acquaintance with such detached parts of mine, as tend not to dishonour characters, or reveal names: and this gives me an appetite to oblige thee by *interlardment*] *that all the sex*, "I say, may see what they *ought to be;* what is *expected* from them; and if they have to deal with a person of reflection and punctilio [of *pride*, if thou wilt], how careful they ought to be, by a regular and uniform conduct, not to give him cause to think lightly of them for favours granted, which may be interpreted into *natural weakness*. For is not a wife the keeper of a man's honour? And do not her faults bring more disgrace upon a husband, than even upon herself?"

It is not for nothing, Jack, that I have disliked the life of shackles.

To the test then, as I said, since now I have the question brought home to me, whether I am to have a wife? And whether she be to be a wife at the *first* or at the *second* hand?

I will proceed fairly. I will do the dear creature not only strict, but generous justice; for I will try her by her own judgment, as well as by our principles.

She blames herself for having corresponded with me, a man of free character; and one indeed whose *first* view it was to draw her into this correspondence; and who succeeded in it, by means unknown to herself.

"Now, what were her inducements to this correspondence?" If not what her niceness makes her *think* blameworthy, why does she blame herself?

Has she been *capable* of error? Of persisting in that error?

Whoever was the *tempter*, that is not the thing; nor what the *temptation*. The *fact*, the *error*, is now before us.

Did she persist in it against parental prohibition?

She owns she did.

Was a daughter ever known who had higher notions of the filial duty, of the parental authority?

Never.

"What must be those inducements, how strong, that were *too strong* for duty, in a daughter so *dutiful?* — What must *my* thoughts have been of these inducements, what *my* hopes built upon them *at the time*, taken in this light?"

Well, but it will be said, that her principal view was to prevent mischief between her brother and her other friends, and the man vilely insulted by them all.

But why should *she* be more concerned for the safety of others, than they were for their own? And had not the *rencounter* then happened? "Was a person of virtue to be prevailed upon to break through her *apparent*, her *acknowledged* duty, upon *any* consideration?" And, if not, was she to be so prevailed upon to prevent an *apprehended* evil only?

Thou, Lovelace, the tempter (thou wilt again break out and say) to be the accuser!

But I am *not* the accuser. I am the arguer only, and, in my heart, all the time acquit and worship the divine creature. "But let me, nevertheless, examine, whether the acquittal be owing to her *merit*, or to my *weakness* — weakness the true name for love!"

But shall we suppose another motive? — And that is LOVE; a motive which all the world will excuse her for. "But let me tell all the world that do, *not* because they *ought*, but because all the world is apt to be misled by it."

Let LOVE then be the motive: — love of *whom?*

A *Lovelace*, is the answer.

"Is there but *one* Lovelace in the world? May not *more* Lovelaces be attracted by so fine a figure? By such exalted qualities? It was her character that drew me to her: and it was her beauty and good sense that rivetted my chains: and now all together make me think her a subject worthy of my attempts; worthy of my ambition."

But has she had the candour, the openness, to *acknowledge* that love?

She has not.

"Well then, if love be at the bottom, is there not another fault lurking beneath the shadow of that love? — Has she not *affectation?* — Or is it *pride of heart?*"

And what results? — "Is then the divine Clarissa capable of *loving* a man whom she ought *not* to love? And is she capable of *affectation?* And is her virtue founded in *pride?* — And, if the answer to these questions be affirmative, must she not then be a *woman?*"

And can she keep this love at bay? Can she make *him*, who has been accustomed to triumph over other women, tremble? Can she so conduct herself, as to make him, at times, question whether she loves *him* or *any* man; "yet not have the requisite command over the passion itself in steps of the highest consequence to her honour, as *she* thinks" [*I am trying her, Jack, by her own thoughts*], "but suffer herself to be provoked to promise to abandon her father's house, and go off with him; knowing his character; and even conditioning not to marry till improbable and remote contingencies were to come to pass? What though the provocations were such as would justify any other woman; yet was a CLARISSA to be susceptible to provocations which she thinks *herself* highly censurable for being so much moved by?"

But let us see the dear creature resolved to revoke her promise; yet *meeting* her lover; a bold and intrepid man, who was more than once before disappointed by her;

and who comes, as she knows, prepared to expect the fruits of her appointment, and resolved to carry her off. And let us see him actually carrying her off; and having her at his mercy — "May there not be, I repeat, *other* Lovelaces; other *like* intrepid persevering enterprisers; although they may not go to work in the same way?"

"And has then a CLARISSA (herself her judge) failed? — In such *great* points failed? — And may she not *further* fail? — Fail in the *greatest* point, to which all the other points, in which she *has* failed, have but a natural tendency?"

Nor say thou, that virtue, in the eye of heaven, is as much a *manly* as a *womanly* grace. By virtue in this place I mean chastity, and to be superior to temptation; my Clarissa out of the question. Nor ask thou, shall the man be guilty, yet expect the woman to be guiltless, and even unsuspectable? Urge thou not these arguments, I say, since the wife, by a failure, may do much more injury to the husband, than the husband can do to the wife, and not only to her husband, but to all his family, by obtruding another man's children into his possessions, perhaps to the exclusion of (at least to a participation with) his own; he believing them all the time to be his. In the eye of heaven, therefore, the sin *cannot* be equal. Besides, I have read in some place *that the woman was made for the man*, not *the man for the woman*.

Virtue then is less to be dispensed with in the woman than in the man.

Thou, Lovelace, (methinks some better man than thyself will say) to expect such perfection in a woman!

Yes, I, may I answer. Was not the great Cæsar a great rake as to women? Was he not called, by his very soldiers, on one of his triumphant entries into Rome, *the bald-pated-lecher?* and warning given of him to the *wives* as well as to the daughters of his fellow-citizens? Yet did not Cæsar repudiate his wife for being only in company with Clodius, or rather because Clodius, though by surprise upon her, was found in hers? And what was the reason he gave for it? — It was this (though a rake himself, as I have said) and only this — *the wife of Cæsar must not be suspected!* —

Cæsar was not a prouder man than Lovelace.

Go to then, Jack; nor say, nor let any body say, in thy hearing, that Lovelace, a man valuing himself upon his ancestry, is singular in his expectations of a wife's purity, though not pure himself.

As to my CLARISSA, I own, that I hardly think there ever was such an angel of a woman. But has she not, as above, already taken steps, which she herself condemns? Steps, which the world and her own family did not think her *capable* of taking? And for which her own family will not forgive her?

Nor think it strange, that I refuse to hear any thing pleaded in behalf of a standard virtue from high *provocations.* "Are not provocations and temptations the tests of virtue? A standard virtue must not be allowed to be *provoked* to destroy or annihilate itself.

"May not then the success of him who could carry her *thus far,* be allowed to be an encouragement for him to try to carry her *further?*" 'Tis but to try. Who will be afraid of a trial for this divine creature? "Thou knowest, that I have more than once, twice, or thrice, put to the fiery trial young women of name and character; and never yet met with one who held out a month; nor indeed so long as could puzzle my invention. I have concluded against the whole sex upon it." And now, if I have not found a virtue that cannot be corrupted, I will swear that there is not one such in the whole sex. Is not then the whole sex concerned that this trial should be made? And who is it that knows this lady, that would not stake upon her head the honour of the whole? — Let her who would refuse it, come forth, and desire to stand in her place.

I must assure thee, that I have a prodigious high opinion of virtue; as I have of all those graces and excellencies which I have not been able to attain myself. Every freeliver would not *say* this, nor *think* thus — every argument he uses, condemnatory of his own actions, as some would think. But ingenuousness was ever a signal part of my character. Satan, whom thou mayest, if thou wilt, in this case, call my instigator, put the good man of old upon the severest trials. "To his behaviour under these trials that good man owed his honour and his future rewards." An innocent person, if doubted, must wish to be brought to a fair and candid trial.

Rinaldo indeed, in Ariosto, put the Mantuan knight's cup of trial from him, which was to be the proof of his wife's chastity*—this was his argument for forbearing the experiment: "Why should I seek a thing I should be loth to find? My wife is a woman. The sex is frail. I cannot believe better of her than I do. It will be to my own loss, if I find reason to think worse." But Rinaldo would not have refused the trial of the lady, before she *became* his wife, and when he might have found his account in detecting her.

For my part, I would not have put the cup from me, though married, had it been but in hope of finding reason to confirm my *good* opinion of my wife's honour: and that I might know whether I had a snake or a dove in my bosom.

To my point — "What must that virtue be, which will not stand a trial?—What that woman, who would wish to shun it?"

Well then, a trial seems necessary for the *further* establishment

* The story tells us, that whoever drank of this cup, if his wife were chaste, could drink without spilling; if otherwise, the contrary.

of the honour of so excellent a creature.

And who shall put her to this trial? who, but the man who has, as she thinks, already induced her in *lesser* points to swerve? — And this for her *own sake* in a double sense — not only, as he has been able to make *some* impression, but as she *regrets* the impression made; and so may be presumed to be guarded against his further attempts.

The situation she is at present in, it must be confessed, is a disadvantageous one to her: but, if she overcome, that will redound to her honour.

Shun not, therefore, my dear soul, further trials, nor hate me for making them. — "For what woman can be said to be virtuous till she has been tried?

"Nor is *one* effort, *one* trial to be sufficient. Why? because a woman's heart may be at one time *adamant*, at another, *wax*" — as I have often experienced; and so, no doubt, hast thou.

A fine time of it, methinks, thou sayest, would the women have, if they were all to be tried! —

But, Jack, I am not for that, neither. Though I am a rake, I am not a rake's friend; except thine and company's.

And be this one of the morals of my tedious discussion — "Let the little rogues who would not be *put to the question*, as I may call it, choose accordingly. Let them prefer to their favour good honest sober fellows, who have not been used to play dog's tricks: who will be willing to take them as they *offer*; and, who being tolerable themselves, are not suspicious of others."

But what, methinks thou askest, is to become of the lady if she fail?

What? — why will she not, "*if once subdued*, be *always subdued?*" Another of our libertine maxims. And what an immense pleasure to a marriage-hater, what rapture to thought, to be able to prevail upon such a woman as Miss Clarissa Harlowe to live with him without real change of name!

But if she resist — if nobly she stand her trial? —

Why then I will marry her; and bless my stars for such an angel of a wife.

But will she not hate thee? — will she not refuse? —

No, no, Jack! — Circumstanced and situated as we are, I am not afraid of that. And hate me! why should she hate the man who loves her upon proof?

And then for a little hint at *reprisal* — am I not justified in my resolutions of trying *her* virtue; who is resolved, as I may say, to try *mine?* who has declared, that she will not marry me, till she has hopes of my reformation?

And now, to put an end to this sober argumentation, wilt thou not thyself (whom I have supposed an advocate for the lady, because I know that Lord M. has put thee upon using the interest he thinks thou hast in me, to persuade me to enter the pale; *wilt thou not thyself*) allow me to try if I cannot awaken the *woman* in her? — to try if she, with all that glowing symmetry of parts, and that full bloom of vernal graces, by which she attracts every eye, be really inflexible as to the grand article?

Let me begin then, as opportunity presents — I will: and watch her every step to find one sliding one; her every moment to find the moment critical. And the rather, as she spares not me, but takes every advantage that offers to puzzle and plague me; nor expects nor thinks me to be a good man.

If she be a *woman*, and *love* me, I shall surely catch her once tripping: for love was ever a traitor to its harbourer: and love *within*, and I *without*, she will be more than woman, as the poet says, or I *less* than man, if I succeed not.

Now, Belford, all is out. The lady is mine; shall be *more* mine. Marriage, I see, is in my power, now *she* is so; else perhaps it had not. If I can have her *without* marriage, who can blame me for trying? if *not*, great will be her glory, and my future confidence. And well will she merit the sacrifice I shall make her of my liberty; and from all her sex honours next to divine, for giving a proof, "that there was once a woman whose virtue no trials, no stratagems, no temptations, even from the man she hated not, could overpower."

Now wilt thou see all my circulation: as in a glass wilt thou see it. — CABALA, however, is the word*; nor let the secret escape thee even in thy dreams.

Nobody doubts that she is to be my wife. Let her pass for such, when I give the word. "Meantime reformation shall be my stalking-horse; some one of the women in London, if I can get her thither, my bird. And so much for this time."

LETTER XV.
Miss Howe to Miss Clarissa Harlowe.

[*In Answer to Letters* v. xi.]

Do not be so much concerned, my dearest friend, at the bickerings between my mother and me. We love one another dearly notwithstanding. If my mother had not me to find fault with, she must find fault with somebody else. And as to me, I am a very saucy girl; and were there not this occasion, there would be some other to shew it.

You have heard me *say*, that this was always the case between us. You could not *otherwise* have known it. For when *you* were with us, you harmonized us both; and, indeed, I was always more afraid of you than of my mother. But then that awe is accompanied with love. Your reproofs, as I have always found, are so charmingly mild and instructive; so evidently calculated to improve, and not to provoke; that a generous temper must be amended by them. But here now, mind my good mamma,

* This word, whenever used by any of these gentlemen, was agreed to imply an inviolable secret.

when you are not with us — *You shall, I tell you, Nancy. I will have it so. Don't I know best, I won't be disobeyed.* How can a daughter of spirit bear such language; such looks too with the language; and not have a longing mind to disobey?

Don't advise me, my dear, to subscribe to my mother's prohibition of correspondence with you. She has no reason for it. Nor would she of her own judgment have prohibited it. That odd old ambling soul your uncle (whose visits are frequenter than ever), instigated by your malicious and selfish brother and sister, is the occasion. And they only have borrowed my mother's lips, at the distance they are from you, for a sort of speaking trumpet for them. The prohibition, once more I say, cannot come from her heart: but if it did, is so much danger to be apprehended from my continuing to write to one of my own sex, as if I wrote to one of the other? Don't let dejection and disappointment, and the course of oppression which you have run through, weaken your mind, my dearest creature; and make you see inconveniencies, where there cannot possibly be any. If *your* talent is *scribbling,* as you call it; so is *mine* — and I will scribble on, at all opportunities; and to you; let 'em say what they will. Nor let your letters be filled with the self-accusations you mention: there is no cause for them. I wish, that your Anna Howe, who continues in her mother's house, were but half so good as Miss Clarissa Harlowe, who has been driven out of her father's.

I will say nothing upon your letter to your sister till I see the effect it will have. You hope, you tell me, that you shall have your money and clothes sent you, notwithstanding my opinion to the contrary — I am sorry to have it to acquaint you, that I have just now heard, that they have sat in council upon your letter; and that your mother was the only person, who was for sending you your things; and was over-ruled. I charge you therefore to accept of my offer, as by my last: and give me particular directions for what you want, that I can supply you with besides.

Don't set your thoughts so much upon a reconciliation, as to prevent your laying hold of any handsome opportunity to give yourself a protector; such a one as the man will be, who, I imagine, husband-like, will let nobody insult you but himself.

What could he mean, by letting slip such a one as that you mention? I don't know how to blame you; for how could you go beyond silence and blushes, when the foolish fellow came with his observances of the restrictions which you laid him under when in another situation? But as I told you above, you really strike people into awe. And, upon my word, you did not spare him.

I repeat what I said in my last, that you have a very nice part to act; and I will add, that you have a mind that is much too delicate for your part. But when the lover is exalted, the lady must be humbled. He is naturally proud and saucy. I doubt you must engage his *pride*, which he calls his *honour:* and that you must throw off a little more of the veil. And I would have you restrain your wishes before him, that you had not met him, and the like. What signifies wishing, my dear? He will not bear it. You can hardly expect that he will.

Nevertheless, it vexes me to the very bottom of my pride, that any wretch of that sex should be able to triumph over such a woman.

I cannot, however, but say, that I am charmed with your spirit. So much sweetness, where sweetness is requisite; so much spirit, where spirit is called for — what a *true* magnanimity!

But I doubt, in your present circumstances, you must endeavour after a little more of the reserve, in cases where you are displeased with him, and palliate a little. That humility which he puts on when you rise upon him, is not natural to him.

Methinks I see the man hesitating, and looking like the fool you paint him, under your corrective superiority! — But he is not a fool. Don't put him upon mingling resentment with his love.

You are very serious, my dear, in the first of the two letters before me, in relation to Mr. Hickman and me; and in relation to my mother and me. But as to the latter, you must not be too grave. If we are not well together at one time, we are not ill together at another. And while I am able to make her smile in the midst of the most angry fit she ever fell into on the present occasion (though sometimes she would not if she could help it), it is a very good sign: a sign that displeasure can never go deep, or be lasting. And then a kind word, or kind look, to her favourite Hickman, sets the one into raptures, and the other in tolerable humour, at any time.

But your case pains me at heart; and with all my levity, *both* the good folks must sometimes partake of that pain; nor will it be over, as long as you are in a state of uncertainty; and especially as I was not able to prevail for that protection for you which would have prevented the unhappy step, the necessity for which we both, with so much reason, deplore.

I have only to add (and yet it is needless to tell you) that I am, and ever will be,
Your affectionate friend
and servant,
Anna Howe.

LETTER XVI.
Miss Clarissa Harlowe to Miss Howe.

You tell me, my dear, that my clothes and the little sum of money I left behind me, will not be sent me. — But I will still hope. It is yet early days. When their passions subside, they will better consider of the matter! and especially as I have my ever dear and excellent mother for my friend in this request. O the sweet indulgence! How has my heart bled, and how does it still bleed for her!

You advise me not to depend upon a reconciliation. I do not, I cannot depend upon it. But nevertheless it is the wish next my heart. And as to this man, what can I do? You see, *that marriage is not absolutely in my own power*, if I were *inclined* to prefer it to the trial which I think I ought to have principally in view to make for a reconciliation.

You say, he is proud and insolent — indeed he is. But can it be your opinion, that he intends to humble me down to the level of his mean pride?

And what mean you, my dear friend, when you say, that I must throw off a *little more of the veil?* — Indeed I never knew that I wore one. Let me assure you, that if I see any thing in Mr. Lovelace that looks like a design to humble me, his insolence shall never make me discover a weakness unworthy of a person distinguished by your friendship; that is to say, unworthy either of my *sex*, or of my *former self*.

But I hope, as I am out of all other protection, that he is not capable of mean or low resentments. If he has had any extraordinary trouble on my account, may he not thank himself for it? He may; and lay it, if he pleases, to his *character;* which, as I have told him, gave at least a *pretence* to my brother against him. And then, did I ever make him any promises? Did I ever profess a love for him? Did I ever wish for the continuance of his address? Had not my brother's violence precipitated matters, would not my indifference to him in all likelihood (as I designed it should) have tired out his proud spirit* and made him set out for London, where he used chiefly to reside? And if he *had*, would there not have been an end of all his pretensions and hopes? For no encouragement had I given him: nor did I then correspond with him. Nor, believe me, should I have begun to do so — the fatal rencounter not having then happened; which drew me in afterwards for others' sakes (fool that I was!) and not for my own. And can you think, or can *he*, that even this but temporarily-intended correspondence (which, by the way, my mother** connived at) would have ended thus, had I not been driven on one hand, and teased on the other to continue it, the occasion which had at first induced it, continuing? What pretence then has he, were I to be absolutely in his power, to avenge himself on me, for the faults of others; and through which I have suffered more than he? It cannot, cannot be, that I should have cause to apprehend him to be so ungenerous, so bad, a man?

You bid me not be concerned at the bickerings between your

* See Vol. I. p. 22.
** See Vol. II. p. 24.

mother and you. Can I avoid concern, when those bickerings are on my account? That they are raised (instigated shall I say?) by my uncle, and my other relations, surely must add to my concern.

But I must observe, perhaps too critically for the state my mind is in at present, that the very sentences you give from your mother, are so many *imperatives*, which you take amiss, are very severe reflections upon yourself. For instance — *you shall*, *I tell you, Nancy*, implies that you had disputed her will — and so of the rest.

And further let me observe, with respect to what you say, that there cannot be the same reason for a prohibition of correspondence with me, as there was of mine with Mr. Lovelace; that I thought as little of bad consequences from my correspondence with him at the time, as you can do from yours with me, now. But, if *obedience be a duty*, the *breach* of it is a *fault*, however circumstances may differ. Surely there is no merit in setting up our own judgment against the judgment of our parents. And if it be punishable so to do, I have been severely punished; and that is what I warned you of from my own dear experience.

Yet, God forgive me! I advise thus against myself with very great reluctance: and, to say truth, have not strength of mind, at present, to decline it myself. But, if the occasion go not off, I will take it into further consideration.

You give me very good advice in relation to this man; and I thank you for it. When you bid me be more upon the *reserve* with him in expressing my displeasure, perhaps I may try for it; but to *palliate*, as you call it, that, my dearest Miss Howe, cannot be done, by
  Your own
   CLARISSA HARLOWE.

LETTER XVII.
Miss Clarissa Harlowe to Miss Howe.

You may believe, my dear Miss Howe, that the circumstances of the noise and outcry within the garden door, on Monday last, gave me no small uneasiness, to think that I was in the hands of a man, who could, by such vile premeditation, lay a snare to trick me out of myself, as I have so frequently called it.

Whenever he came in my sight, the thought of this gave me an indignation that made his presence disgustful to me; and the more, as I fancied I beheld in his face a triumph which reproached my weakness on that account; although perhaps it was only the same vivacity and placidness that generally sit upon his features.

I was resolved to task him upon this subject, the first time I could have patience to enter upon it with him. For, besides that it piqued me excessively from the nature of the artifice, I expected shuffling and evasion, if he were guilty, that would have incensed me: and, if not confessedly guilty, such unsatisfactory declarations, as still would have kept my mind doubtful and uneasy; and would, upon every new offence that he might give me, sharpen my disgust to him.

I have had the opportunity I waited for; and will lay before you the result.

He was making his court to my good opinion in very polite terms, and with great seriousness lamenting that he had lost it; declaring, that he knew not how he had deserved to do so; attributing to me an indifference to him, that seemed, to his infinite concern, hourly to increase. And he besought me to let him know my whole mind, that he might have an opportunity either to confess his faults and amend them, or clear his conduct to my satisfaction, and thereby entitle himself to a greater share of my confidence.

I answered him with quickness — Then, Mr. Lovelace, I will tell you one thing with a frankness, that is, perhaps more suitable to *my* character than to *yours* [*he hoped not, he said*], which gives me a very bad opinion of you, as a designing artful man.

I am all attention, madam.

I never can think tolerably of you, while the noise and voice I heard at the garden door, which put me into the terror you took so much advantage of, remains unaccounted for. Tell me fairly, tell me candidly the whole of that circumstance, and of your dealings with that wicked Joseph Leman; and according to your explicitness in this particular, I shall form a judgment of your future professions.

I will, without reserve, my dearest life, said he, tell you the whole; and hope that my sincerity in the relation will atone for any thing you may think wrong in the fact.

"I knew nothing, *said he*, of this man, this Leman, and should have scorned a resort to so low a method as bribing the servant of any family to let me into the secrets of that family, if I had not detected him in attempting to corrupt a servant of mine, to inform him of all my motions, of all my supposed intrigues, and, in short of every action of my private life, as well as of my circumstances and engagements; and this for motives too obvious to be dwelt upon.

"My servant told me of his offers, and I ordered him, unknown to the fellow, to let me hear a conversation that was to pass between them.

"In the midst of it, and just as he had made an offer of money for a particular piece of intelligence, promising more when procured, I broke in upon them, and by bluster, calling for a knife to cut off his ears (one of which I took hold of), in order to make a present of it, as I said, to his employers, I obliged him to tell me who they were.

"Your brother, madam, and your uncle Antony, he named.

"It was not difficult when I had given him my pardon on naming them (after I had set before him the enormity of the task he had undertaken, and the honourableness of my intentions to your dear self) to prevail upon him, by a larger reward, to serve me; since at the same time, he might preserve the favour of your uncle and brother, as I desired to know nothing but what related to myself, and to you, in order to guard us both against the effects of an ill-will, which all his fellow-servants, as well as himself, as he acknowledged, thought undeserved.

"By this means, I own to you, madam, I frequently turned his principles about upon a pivot of my own, unknown to themselves: and the fellow, who is always calling himself a *plain man*, and boasting of his *conscience*, was the easier, as I condescended frequently to assure him of my honourable views; and as he knew that the use I made of his intelligence, in all likelihood, prevented fatal mischiefs.

"I was the more pleased with his services, as (let me acknowledge to you, madam) they procured to you, unknown to yourself, a safe and uninterrupted egress (which perhaps would not otherwise have been continued to you so long as it was) to the garden and wood-house! For he undertook to them, to watch all your motions; and the more cheerfully (for the fellow loves you) as it kept off the curiosity of others."*

So, my dear, it comes out, that I *myself* was obliged to this deep contriver. -I sat in silent astonishment; and thus he went on.

"As to the circumstance, for which you think so hardly of me, I do freely confess, that having a suspicion that you would revoke your intention of getting away, and in that case apprehending that we should not have the time together that was necessary for that purpose; I had ordered him to keep off every body he could keep off, and to be himself within view of the garden door; for I was determined, if possible, to induce you to adhere to your resolution." —

But pray, sir, interrupting him, how came you to apprehend that I should revoke my intention? I had indeed deposited a letter to that purpose; but you had it not: and how, as I had reserved to myself the privilege of a revocation, did you know, but I might have prevailed upon my friends, and so have revoked upon good grounds?

"I will be very ingenuous, madam — you had made me hope that if you changed your mind, you would give me a meeting to apprize me of the reasons for it. I went to the loose bricks, and I saw the letter there: and as I knew your friends were immoveably fixed in their schemes, I doubted not but the letter was to revoke or suspend your resolution; and pro-

* See Vol. I. p. 160, 161.

bably to serve instead of a meeting too. I therefore let it lie, that if you *did* revoke, you might be under the necessity of meeting me for the sake of the expectation you had given me: and as I came prepared, I was resolved, pardon me, madam, whatever were your intentions that you should not go back. Had I taken your letter, I must have been determined by the contents of it, for the present, at least: but not having received it, and you having reason to think I wanted not resolution in a situation so desperate, to make your friends a personal visit, I depended upon the interview you had bid me hope for."

Wicked wretch, said I; it is my grief, that I gave you opportunity to take so exact a measure of my weakness! — But *would* you have presumed to visit the family, had I not met you?

Indeed I would. I had some friends in readiness, who were to have accompanied me to them. And had your father refused to give me audience, I would have taken my friends with me to Solmes.

And what did you intend to do to Mr. Solmes?

Not the least hurt, had the man been passive.

But had he *not* been passive as you call it, what would you have done to Mr. Solmes?

He was loth, he said, to tell me — yet not the least hurt to his *person*.

I repeated my question.

If he *must* tell me, he only proposed to carry off the *poor fellow*, and to hide him for a month or two. And this he would have done, let what would have been the consequence.

Was ever such a wretch heard of! — I sighed from the bottom of my heart; but bid him proceed from the part I had interrupted him at.

"I ordered the fellow, as I told you, madam, said he, to keep within view of the garden door; and if he found any parly between us, and any body coming (before you could retreat undiscovered), whose coming might be attended with violent effects, he should cry out; and this not only in order to save himself from their suspicions of him, but to give me warning to make off, and, if possible, to induce you (I own it, madam) to go off with me, according to your own appointment. And I hope all circumstances considered, and the danger I was in of losing you for ever, that the acknowledgment of this contrivance, or if you had *not* met me, *that* upon Solmes, will not procure me your hatred: for, had they come as *I* expected as well as *you*, what a despicable wretch had I been, could I have left you to the insults of a brother and others of your family, whose mercy was cruelty when they had *not* the pretence with which this detected interview would have furnished them."

What a wretch! said I. — But if, sir, taking your own account of this strange matter to be fact, any body were coming, how happened

Clarissa. II. 5

it, that I saw only that man Leman (I *thought* it was he) out of the door, and at a distance, look after us?

Very lucky! said he, putting his hand first in one pocket, then in another — I hope I have not thrown it away — it is, perhaps, in the coat I had on yesterday — little did I think it would be necessary to be produced — but I love to come to a demonstration whenever I can — I *may* be giddy — *may* be heedless — I *am* indeed — but no man, as to *you*, madam, ever had a sincerer heart.

He then stepping to the parlour door, called his servant to bring him the coat he had on yesterday. The servant did. And from the pocket rumpled up as a paper he regarded not, pulled out a letter, written by that Joseph, dated Monday night; in which "he begs pardon for crying out so soon — says, that his fears of being discovered to act on both sides, had made him take the rushing of a little dog (that always follows him) through the phyllirea-hedge, for Betty's being at hand, or some of his masters: and that when he found his mistake, he opened the door by his own key (which the contriving wretch confessed he had furnished him with), and inconsiderately ran out in a hurry, to have apprized him that his crying out was owing to his fright only:" and he added, "that they were upon the hunt for me, by the time he returned.*"

I shook my head — Deep! deep! deep! said I, at the best! — O Mr. Lovelace! God forgive and reform you! — But you are, I see plainly, (upon the whole of your own account) a very artful, a very designing man.

Love, my dearest life, is ingenious. Night and day have I racked my stupid brain [*O sir, thought I, not stupid! 'twere well perhaps if it were*] to contrive methods to prevent the sacrifice designed to be made of you, and the mischief that must have ensued upon it: so little hold in your affections: such undeserved antipathy from your friends: so much danger of losing you for ever from *both* causes. I have not had for the whole fortnight before last Monday, half an hour's rest at a time. And I own to you, madam, that I should never have forgiven myself, had I omitted any contrivance or forethought that would have prevented your return without me.

Again I blamed myself for meeting him: and justly, for there were many chances to one, that I had *not* met him. And if I had not, all his fortnight's contrivances, as to me, would have come to nothing; and perhaps, I might nevertheless have escaped Solmes. Yet had he resolved to come to Harlowe Place with his friends, and been insulted, as he certainly would have been, what mischiefs might have followed!

But his resolution to run away with and to hide the poor Solmes he tells him, he would contrive for him a letter of this nature to copy.

---

* See his letter to Joseph Leman, Vol. I. No. xciv. towards the end, where

for a month or so, O my dear! what a wretch have I let run away with *me*, instead of *Solmes.*

I asked him, if he thought such enormities as these, such defiances of the laws of society, would have passed unpunished?

He had the assurance to say, with one of his usual gay airs, that he should by this means have disappointed his enemies, and saved me from a forced marriage. He had no pleasure in such desperate pushes. Solmes he would not have *personally* hurt. He must have fled his country, for a time at least: and, truly, if he had been obliged to do so (as all his hopes of my favour must have been at an end), he would have had a fellow-traveller of his own sex out of our family, whom I little thought of.

Was ever such a wretch! — To be sure he meant my brother!

And such, sir, said I, in high resentment, are the uses you make of your corrupt intelligencer —

My corrupt intelligencer, madam! interrupted he, he is to this hour your brother's as well as mine. By what I have ingenuously told you, you may see who began this corruption. Let me assure you, madam, that there are many free things which I have been guilty of as *reprisals*, in which I would not have been the *aggressor.*

All that I shall further say on this head, Mr. Lovelace, is this: that as this vile double-faced wretch has probably been the cause of great mischief on both sides, and *still* continues, as you own, his wicked practices, I think it would be but just, to have my friends apprized what a creature *he* is whom some of them encourage.

What you please, madam, as to that — my service, as well as your brother's is now almost over for him. The fellow has made a good hand of it. He does not intend to stay long in his place. He is now actually in treaty for an inn, which will do his business for life. I can tell you further, that he makes love to your sister's Betty: and that *by my advice.* They will be married when he is established. An innkeeper's wife is every man's mistress; and I have a scheme in my head to set some engines at work to make *her* repent her saucy behaviour to you to the last day of her life.

What a wicked schemer are you, sir! — Who shall avenge upon you the still greater evils which you have been guilty of? — I forgive Betty with all my heart. She was not my servant; and but too probably, in what she did, obeyed the commands of her to whom she owed duty, better than I obeyed those to whom I owed more.

No matter for that, the wretch said [*to be sure, my dear, he must design to make me afraid of him*]: the decree was gone out — Betty must smart — smart too by an act of her own choice. He loved, he said, to make bad people their own punishers. — Nay, madam, excuse me; but if the fellow, if this Joseph, in *your* opinion, deserves punishment, mine is a complicated

5*

scheme; a man and his wife, cannot well suffer separately, and it may come home to *him* too.

I had no patience with him. I told him so. I see, sir, said I, I see, what a man I am with. Your *rattle* warns me of the *snake*. — And away I flung: leaving him seemingly vexed, and in confusion.

LETTER XVIII.

Miss Clarissa Harlowe to Miss Howe.

My plain-dealing with Mr. Lovelace, on seeing him again, and the free dislike I expressed to his ways, his manners, and his contrivances, as well as to his speeches, have obliged him to recollect himself a little. He will have it, that the menaces which he threw out just now against my brother and Mr. Solmes, are only the effect of an unmeaning pleasantry: that he has too great a stake in his country to be guilty of *such* enterprises as should lay him under a necessity of quitting it for ever. Twenty things, particularly, he says, he has suffered Joseph Leman to tell of him that *were not*, and *could not* be true, in order to make himself formidable in some people's eyes, and this purely with a view to *prevent mischief*. He is unhappy, as far as he knows, in a quick invention; in hitting readily upon expedients; and many things are reported of him which he never said, and many which he never did, and others which he has only talked of (as just now), and which he has forgot as soon as the words have passed his lips.

This may be so, in part, my dear. No one man so young could be so wicked as he has been reported to be. But such a man at the head of such wretches as he is said to have at his beck, all men of fortune and fearlessness, and capable of such enterprises as I have unhappily found him capable of, what is not to be apprehended from him!

His carelessness about his character is one of his excuses: a very bad one. What hope can a woman have of a man who values not his reputation? — These gay wretches may, in mixed conversation, divert for an hour, or so: but the man of probity, the man of virtue, is the man that is to be the partner for life. What woman, who could help it, would submit it to the courtesy of a wretch, who avows a disregard to all moral sanctions, whether he will perform his part of the matrimonial obligation, and treat her with tolerable politeness?

With these notions, and with these reflections, to be thrown upon such a man myself? — Would to heaven — but what avail wishes now? — To whom can I fly, if I would fly from him?

LETTER XIX.

Mr. Lovelace to John Belford, Esq.

Friday, April 14.

Never did I hear of such a parcel of foolish toads as these Harlowes! — Why, Belford, the lady must fall, if every hair of her head were a guardian angel, unless they were to make a visible appearance for her, or, snatching her from me at unawares, would draw her after them into the starry regions.

All I had to apprehend, was, that a daughter, so reluctantly carried off, would offer terms to her father, and would be accepted upon a mutual *concedence; they* to give up *Solmes; she* to give up *me.* And so I was contriving to do all I could to guard against the latter. But they seem resolved to perfect the work they have begun.

What stupid creatures are there in the world! This foolish brother not to know, that he who would be bribed to undertake a base thing by one, would be *over*-bribed to *retort* the baseness; especially when he could be put into the way to serve himself by both! — Thou, Jack, wilt never know one half of my contrivances.

He here relates the conversation between him and the lady (upon the subject of the noise and exclamations his agent made at the garden door) to the same effect as in the lady's letter, No. XVII. *and proceeds exulting.*

What a capacity for glorious mischief has thy friend! — yet how near the truth all of it! The only deviation, my asserting that the fellow made the noises by *mistake,* and through *fright,* and not by *previous direction*: had she known the precise truth, her anger, to be so taken in, would never have let her forgive me.

Had I been a military hero, I should have made gunpowder useless: for I should have blown up all my adversaries by dint of stratagem, turning their own devices upon them.

But these fathers and mothers — Lord help 'em! — Were not the powers of nature stronger than those of discretion, and were not that busy *dea bona* to afford her genial aids, till tardy prudence qualified parents to *manage* their future offspring, how few people would have children!

James and Arabella may have *their* motives; but what can be said for a father acting as *this* father has acted? What for a mother? What for an aunt? What for uncles? — Who can have patience with such fellows and fellow-esses?

Soon will the fair-one hear how high their foolish resentments run against her: and then will she, it is to be hoped, have a little more confidence in me. Then will I be jealous that she loves me not with the preference my heart builds upon: then will I bring her to confessions of grateful love: and then will I kiss her when I please; and not stand trembling, as now, like a hungry hound, who sees a delicious morsel within his reach, yet dares not leap at it for his life.

But I was *originally* a bashful mortal. Indeed I am bashful still with regard to this lady — bashful, yet know the sex so well! — But that indeed is the *reason* that I know it so well: — for, Jack, I have had abundant cause, when I have looked into *myself,* by way of comparison with the *other* sex, to conclude that a bashful man has a good deal of the soul of a woman; and so, like Tiresias, can tell what they think, and what they drive at, as well as themselves.

The modest ones and I, particularly, are pretty much upon a par. The difference between us is only, what they *think*, I *act*. But the immodest ones outdo the worst of us by a bar's length, both in thinking and acting.

One argument let me plead in proof of my assertion; that even we rakes love modesty in a woman; while the modest women as they are accounted (that is to say, the *slyest*) love, and generally prefer, an impudent man. Whence can this be, but from a likeness in nature? And this made the poet say, that every woman is a rake in her heart. It concerns them, by their *actions*, to prove the contrary, if they can.

Thus have I read in some of the philosophers, *that no wickedness is comparable to the wickedness of a woman.*[*] Canst thou tell me, Jack, who says this? Was it Socrates? For he had the devil of a wife — or who? Or is it Solomon? — King Solomon — thou rememberest to have read of such a king, dost thou not? SOL-O-MON, I learned in my infant state [my mother was a good woman] to answer, when asked, *who was the wisest man?* — But my indulgent questioner never asked me, how he came by the inspired part of his wisdom.

Come, come, Jack, you and I are not so very bad, could we but stop where we are.

He then gives the particulars of what passed between him and the lady on his menaces relating to her brother and Mr. Solmes, and of his design to punish Betty Barnes and Joseph Leman.

LETTER XX.

Miss Clarissa Harlowe to Miss Howe.

Friday, April 14.

I WILL now give you the particulars of a conversation that has just passed between Mr. Lovelace and me; which I must call agreeable.

It began with his telling me, that he had just received intelligence that my friends were on a sudden come to a resolution to lay aside all thoughts of pursuing me, or of getting me back; and that therefore he attended me to know my pleasure; and what I would do, or have *him* do?

I told him, that I would have him leave me directly; and that, when it was known to every body that I was absolutely independent of him, it would pass, that I had left my father's house because of my brother's ill usage of me: which was a plea that I might make with justice, and to the excuse of my father as well as of myself.

He mildly replied, that if we

---

[*] Mr. Lovelace is as much out in his conjecture of Solomon as of Socrates. The passage is in Ecclesiasticus, chap. xxv.

could be certain, that my relations would *adhere* to this their new resolution, he could have no objection, since such was my pleasure: but, as he was well assured, that they had taken it only from apprehensions, that a more *active* one might involve my brother (who had breathed nothing but revenge) in some fatal misfortune, there was too much reason to believe, that they would resume their former purpose the moment they should think they *safely* might.

This, madam, said he, is a risk I cannot run. You would think it strange if I could. And yet, as soon as I knew they had so given out, I thought it proper to apprize you of it, and to take your commands upon it.

Let me hear, said I, willing to try if he had any particular view, what *you* think most advisable?

'Tis very easy to say that, if I durst— *If I might not offend you*— if it were not to *break conditions that shall be inviolable with me.*

Say then, sir, what you *would* say. I can approve or disapprove, as I think fit.

Had not the man a fine opportunity here to speak out? He had. And thus he used it.

To wave, madam, what I *would* say till I have more courage to speak out [*more courage, Mr. Lovelace more courage, my dear!*] — I will only propose what I think will be most agreeable to *you* — suppose, *if you choose not to go to Lady Betty's*, that you take a turn cross the country to Windsor?

Why to Windsor?

Because it is a pleasant place: because it lies in the way either to Berkshire, to Oxford, or to London: *Berkshire*, where Lord M. is at present: *Oxford*, in the neighbourhood of which lives Lady Betty: *London*, whither you may retire at your pleasure: or if you will *have* it so, whither I may go, you staying at Windsor: and yet be within an easy distance of you, if any thing should happen, or if your friends should change their new taken resolution.

This proposal, however, displeased me not. But, I said, my only objection was, the distance of Windsor from Miss Howe, of whom I should be glad to be always within two or three hours' reach by a messenger, if possible.

If I had thoughts of any other place than Windsor or nearer to Miss Howe, he wanted but my commands, and would seek for proper accommodations: but, fix as I pleased, further or nearer, he had servants, and they had nothing else to do but to obey me.

A grateful thing then he named to me — to send for my Hannah, as soon as I should be fixed [*]; unless I would choose one of the young gentlewomen *here* to attend me; both of whom, as I had acknowledged, were very obliging; and he knew I had generosity

---

[*] See his reasons for proposing Windsor, p. 78, 79 — and her Hannah, p. 81.

enough to make it worth their while.

This of Hannah, he might see, I took very well. I said I had thoughts of sending for her, as soon as I got to more convenient lodgings. As to these young gentlewomen, it were pity to break in upon that usefulness which the whole family were of to each other: each having her proper part, and performing it with an agreeable alacrity: insomuch that I liked them all so well, that I could even pass my days among them were he to leave me; by which means the lodgings would be more convenient to me than now they were.

He need not repeat his objections to this place, he said: but as to going to Windsor, or wherever else I thought fit, or as to his personal attendance, or leaving me, he would assure me (he very agreeably said) that I could propose nothing in which I thought my reputation, and even my *punctilio*, concerned, that he would not cheerfully come into. And since I was so much taken up with my pen, he would instantly order his horse to be got ready, and would set out.

Not to be off my caution, Have you any acquaintance at Windsor? said I. — Know you of any convenient lodgings there?

Except the Forest, replied he, where I have often hunted, I know the least of Windsor, of any place so noted and so pleasant. Indeed, I have not a single acquaintance there.

Upon the whole I told him, that I thought his proposal of Windsor not amiss; and that I would remove thither, if I could get a lodging only for myself and an upper chamber for Hannah: for that my stock of money was but small, as was easy to be conceived; and I should be very loth to be obliged to any body. I added, that the sooner I removed the better; for that then he could have no objection to go to London, or Berkshire, as he pleased. And I should let every body know my independence.

He again proposed himself, in very polite terms, as my banker. But I, as civilly, declined his offer.

This conversation was to be, all of it, in the main, agreeable. He asked whether I would choose to lodge in the town of Windsor or out of it?

As near the castle, I said, as possible, for the convenience of going constantly to the public worship; an opportunity I had been long deprived of.

He should be very glad, he told me, if he could procure me accommodations in any one of the canon's houses; which he imagined would be more agreeable to me than any other, on many accounts. And as he could depend upon my promise never to have any other man but himself, on the condition to which he had so cheerfully subscribed, he should be easy; since it was now his part, *in earnest*, to set about recommending himself to my favour, by the *only* way he knew it could be done. Adding, with a very serious air — I am but a young man, madam; but I have run a long course: let not your purity of mind incline you to despise me for the acknowledgment. It is high time to be weary of it, and to reform; since, like Solomon, I can say, there is nothing new under the sun: but that it is my belief, that a life of virtue can afford such pleasures, on reflection, as will be for ever blooming, for ever new!

I was agreeably surprised. I looked at him, I believe, as if I doubted my ears and my eyes. His aspect however became his words.

I expressed my satisfaction in terms so agreeable to him, that he said, he found a delight in this early dawning of a better day to him, and in *my* approbation, which he had never received from the success of the most favoured of his pursuits.

Surely, my dear, the man *must* be in earnest. He could not have *said* this; he could not have *thought* it, had he not. What followed made me still readier to believe him.

In the midst of my wild vagaries, said he, I have ever preserved a reverence for religion, and for religious men. I always called another cause, when any of my libertine companions, in pursuance of Lord Shaftesbury's test, (which is a part of the rake's creed, and what I may call the *whetstone of infidelity*) endeavoured to turn the sacred subject into ridicule. On this very account I have been called by good men of the clergy, who nevertheless would have it that I was a *practical* rake, *the decent rake:* and indeed I had too much pride in my shame, to disown the name of *rake*.

This, madam, I am the readier to confess, as it may give you hope, that the generous task of my reformation, which I flatter myself you will have the goodness to undertake, will not be so difficult a one as you may have imagined; for it has afforded me some pleasure in my retired hours, when a temporary remorse has struck me for any thing I have done amiss, that I should one day take delight in another course of life: for, unless we *can*, I dare say, no durable *good* is to be expected from the endeavour. Your example, madam, must do all, must confirm all*.

The divine grace, or favour, Mr. Lovelace, must do all, and confirm all. You know not how much you please me, that I can talk to you in this dialect.

And I then thought of his generosity to his pretty rustic; and of his kindness to his tenants.

Yet, madam, be pleased to remember one thing: reformation cannot be a *sudden* work. I have infinite vivacity: it is that which runs away with me. Judge, dearest madam, by what I am going to confess, that I have a prodigious

* That he proposes one day to reform, and that he has sometimes good motions, see Vol. I. p. 159.

way to journey on, before a good person will think me tolerable; since though I have read in some of our *perfectionists* enough to make a better man than myself either run into madness or despair about the grace you mention; yet I cannot enter into the meaning of the word, nor into the modus of its operation. Let me not then be checked, when I mention your example for my *visible* reliance; and instead of using such words, till I can better understand them, suppose all the rest included in the profession of that reliance.

I told him, that, although I was somewhat concerned at his expression, and surprised at so much *darkness*, as (for want of another word) I would call it, in a man of his talents and learning; yet I was pleased with his ingenuousness. I wished him to encourage this way of thinking. I told him, that his observation, that no *durable* good was to be expected from any new course where there was not a delight taken in it, was just: but that the delight would follow by use.

And twenty things of this sort I even preached to him; taking care, however, not to be tedious, nor to let my expanded heart give him a contracted or impatient brow. And, indeed, he took visible pleasure in what I said, and even hung upon the subject, when I, to try him, once or twice, seemed ready to drop it: and proceeded to give me a most agreeable instance, that he could at times think both deeply and seriously. — Thus it was.

He was once, he said, dangerously wounded in a duel, in the left arm, baring it, to shew me the scar: that this (notwithstanding a great effusion of blood, it being upon an artery) was followed by a violent fever, which at last fixed upon his spirits; and *that* so obstinately, that neither did he desire life nor his *friends* expect it: that for a month together, his heart, as he thought, was so totally changed that he despised his former courses, and particularly that rashness, which had brought him to the state he was in, and his antagonist (who, however, was the aggressor) into a much worse: that in this space he had thoughts which at times still gave him pleasure to reflect upon: and although these promising prospects changed, as he recovered health and spirits, yet he parted with them with so much reluctance, that he could not help shewing it in a copy of verses, *truly blank* ones he said; some of which he repeated (and advantaged by the grace which he gives to every thing he repeats): I thought them very tolerable ones; the sentiments, however, much graver than I expected from him.

He has promised me a copy of the lines: and then I shall judge better of their merit; and so shall you. The tendency of them was, "That, since sickness only gave him a proper train of thinking, and that his restored health brought with it a return of his evil habits, he was ready to renounce the gifts of nature for those of contemplation."

He further declared, that although these good motions went off (as he had owned) on his recovery, yet he had better hopes now, from the influence of my example, and from the reward before him, if he persevered: and that he was the more hopeful that he should, as his present resolution was made in a full tide of health and spirits; and when he had nothing to wish for but perseverance, to entitle himself to my favour.

I will not throw cold water, Mr. Lovelace, said I, on a rising flame: but look to it! for I shall endeavour to keep you up to this spirit. I shall measure your value of me by this test: and I would have you bear those charming lines of Mr. Rowe for ever in your mind: you, who have, by your own confession, so much to repent of; and indeed, as the scar, you shewed me, will, in one instance, remind you to your dying day.

The lines, my dear, are from that poet's Ulysses; you have heard me often admire them; and I repeated them to him:

Habitual evils change not on a sudden:
But many days must pass, and many
    sorrows;
Conscious remorse and anguish must be
    felt,
To curb desire, to break the stubborn
    will,
And work a second nature in the soul,
Ere virtue can resume the place she lost:
'Tis else DISSIMULATION —

He had often read these lines, he said; but never *tasted* them before. — By his *soul* (the unmortified creature swore), and as *he* hoped *to be saved*, he was *now* in earnest in his good resolutions. He had said, *before* I repeated those lines from Rowe, that habitual evils could not be changed on a *sudden*: but he hoped, he should not be thought a *dissembler*, if he were not enabled to *hold* his good purposes; since ingratitude and dissimulation were vices that of all others he abhorred.

May you ever abhor them, said I. They are the most odious of all vices.

I hope, my dear Miss Howe, I shall not have occasion in my future letters, to contradict these promising appearances. Should I have *nothing* on his side to combat with, I shall be very far from being happy, from the sense of my fault, and the indignation of all my relations. — So shall not fail of condign punishment for it, from my inward remorse on account of my forfeited character. But the least ray of hope could not dart in upon me, without my being willing to lay hold of the very first opportunity to communicate it to *you*, who take so generous a share in all my concerns.

Nevertheless, you may depend upon it, my dear, that these agreeable assurances, and hopes of his begun reformation, shall not make me forget my caution. Not that I think, at worst, any more than you, that he dare to harbour a thought injurious to my honour: but he is very various, and there is an *apparent*, and even an *acknowledged* unfixedness in his temper, which at times gives me uneasiness. I am resolved therefore to keep him at distance from my person and my thoughts as much as I can: for whether *all* men are or are not encroachers, I am sure Mr. Lovelace is one.

Hence it is that I have always cast about, and will continue to cast about, what ends he may have in view from *this* proposal, or from *that* report. In a word, though hopeful of the *best*, I will always be fearful of the *worst*, in every thing that admits of doubt. For it is better, in such a situation as mine, to apprehend without cause, than to subject myself to surprise for want of forethought.

Mr. Lovelace is gone to Windsor, having left two servants to attend me. He purposes to be back to-morrow.

I have written to my aunt Hervey, to supplicate her interest in my behalf, for my clothes, books, and money; signifying to her, "That, if I may be restored to the favour of my family, and allowed a negative only, as to any man who may be proposed to me, and be used like a daughter, a niece, and a sister, I will stand by my offer to live single, and submit, as I ought, to a negative from my father." Intimating, nevertheless, "That it were perhaps better, after the usage I have received from my brother and sister, that I may be allowed to be distant from them, as well for their sakes as for my own" (meaning, as I suppose it will be taken, at my dairy-house) — offering "to take my father's directions as to the manner I shall live in, the servants I shall have, and in every thing that shall shew the dutiful subordination to which I am willing to conform."

My aunt will know by my letter to my sister how to direct to me, if she be permitted to favour me with a line.

I am equally earnest *with her* in *this* letter, as I was with my *sister* in *that* I wrote to *her*, to obtain for me a speedy reconciliation, that I may not be further precipitated; intimating, "That, by a timely lenity, all may pass for a misunderstanding only, which, otherwise, will be thought equally disgraceful to them and to me; appealing to her for the necessity I was under to do what I did." —

Had I owned that I was overreached, and forced away against my intention, might they not, as a proof of the truth of my assertion, have insisted upon my immediate return to them? And, if I did *not* return, would they not have reason to suppose, that I had *now* altered my mind (if such were my mind), or had not the *power* to return? — Then were I to have gone back, must it not have been upon their own terms? *No conditioning with a father!* is a maxim with my father and with my uncles. If I would have gone, Mr. Lovelace would have opposed it. So I must have been under his control, or have run away *from* him, as it is supposed I did *to* him, from Harlowe Place. In what a giddy light would this have made me appear! — Had he constrained me, could I have appealed to my friends for *their* protection, without risking the very consequences, to prevent which (setting up myself presumptuously, as a middle person between flaming spirits) I have run into such terrible inconveniences.

But, after all, must it not give me great anguish of mind, to be forced to sanctify, as I may say, by my seeming *after*-approbation, a measure I was so artfully tricked into, and which I was so much resolved not to take?

How one evil brings on another is sorrowfully witnessed to by
 Your ever obliged and affectionate
  Cl. Harlowe.

LETTER XXI.

Mr. Lovelace to John Belford, Esq.

Friday, April 14.

Thou hast often reproached me, Jack, with my vanity, without distinguishing the humorous turn that accompanies it; and for which at the same time, that thou robbest me of the merit of it, thou admirest me highly. *Envy* gives thee the *indistinction: nature* inspires the *admiration:* unknown to thyself it inspires it. But thou art too clumsy and too shortsighted a mortal, to know how to account even for the impulses by which thou thyself art moved.

Well, but this acquits thee not of my charge of vanity, Lovelace, methinks thou sayest.

And true thou sayest: for I have indeed a confounded parcel of it. But, if men of parts may not be allowed to be vain, who should? And yet, upon second thoughts, men of parts have the least occasion of any to be vain; since the world (so few of *them* are there in it) are ready to find them out, and extol them. If a fool can be made sensible that there is a man who has more understanding than *himself*, he is ready enough to conclude, that such a man must be a very extraordinary creature.

And what, at this rate, is the general conclusion to be drawn from the premises? — Is it not, that *no* man ought to be vain? — But what if a man can't help it! — This, perhaps, may be *my* case. But there is nothing upon which I value myself so much as upon my *inventions.* And for the soul of me I cannot help letting it be seen that I do. Yet this vanity may be a means, perhaps, to overthrow me with this sagacious lady.

She is very apprehensive of me, I see. I have studied before her and Miss Howe, as often as I have been with them, to pass for a giddy, thoughtless creature. What a folly then to be so *expatiatingly* sincere in my answer to her home put, upon the noises within the garden? — But such success having attended that contrivance [success, Jack, has blown many a man up!] my cursed *vanity* got uppermost, and kept down my *caution*. The menace to have secreted Solmes, and that other, that I had thoughts to run away with her foolish brother, and of my project to revenge her upon the two servants, so much terrified the dear creature, that I was forced to sit down to muse after means to put myself right in her opinion.

Some favourable incidents, at the time, tumbled in from my agent in her family; at least such as I was determined to *make* favourable: and therefore I desired admittance; and this before she could resolve any thing against me; that is to say, while her admiration of my intrepidity kept resolution in suspense.

Accordingly, I prepared myself to be all gentleness, all obligingness, all serenity; and as I have now-and-then, and always *had*, more or less, good motions pop up in my mind, I encouraged and collected every thing of this sort that I had ever had from novicehood to maturity [*not long in recollecting, Jack*], in order to bring the dear creature into good humour with me:* and who knows, thought I, if I can hold it, and proceed, but I may be able to lay a foundation fit to build my grand scheme upon! — Love, thought I, is not *naturally* a doubter: FEAR is: I will try to banish the latter: nothing then but love will remain, CREDULITY is the god of love's *prime minister;* and they never are asunder.

* He had said, p. 58, that he would make reformation his stalking-horse, &c.

He then acquaints his friend with what passed between him and the lady, in relation to his advices from Harlowe Place, and to his proposals about lodgings, pretty much to the same purpose as in her preceding letter. When he comes to mention his proposal of the Windsor lodgings, thus he expresses himself:

Now, Belford, can it enter into thy leaden head what I meant by this proposal? — I know it cannot. And so I'll tell thee.

To leave her for a day or two, with a view to *serve her by my absence*, would, as I thought, look like confiding in her favour. I could not think of leaving her, thou knowest, while I had reason to believe her friends would pursue us; and I began to apprehend that she would suspect that I made a pretence of that intentional pursuit to keep about her and with her. But now that they had declared against it, and that they would *not* receive her if she went back (a declaration she had better hear first from me than from Miss Howe, or any other) what should hinder me from giving her this mark of my obedience; especially as I could leave Will, who is a clever fellow, and can do any thing but write and spell, and Lord M.'s Jonas (not as guards, to be sure, but as attendants only); the latter to be dispatched to me occasionally by the former, whom I could acquaint with my motions?

Then I wanted to inform myself, why I had not congratulatory letters from Lady Sarah and Lady Betty, and from my cousins Montague, to whom I had written, glorying in my beloved's escape; which letters, if properly worded, might be made necessary to shew her as matters proceed.

As to Windsor, I had no design to carry her particularly thither: but somewhere it was proper to name, as she condescended to ask my advice about it. London I durst not; but very cautiously: and so as to make it her own option: for I must tell thee, that there is such a perverseness in the sex, that when they ask your advice, they do it only to know your opinion, that they may oppose it: though, had not the thing in question been *your* choice, perhaps it had been *theirs*.

I could easily give reasons *against* Windsor, after I had pretended to be there; and this would have looked the better, as it was a place of my own nomination; and shewn her that I had no fixed scheme. Never was there in woman such a sagacious, such an all-alive apprehension, as in this. Yet it is a grievous thing to an honest man to be suspected.

Then, in my going or return, I can call upon Mrs. Greme. She and my beloved had a great deal of talk together. If I knew what it was about; and that *either*, upon their first acquaintance, was for benefitting herself by the *other;* I might contrive to serve them *both* without hurting *myself;* for these are the most prudent ways of doing friendships, and what are not followed by regrets, though the *served* should prove ungrateful. Then Mrs. Greme corresponds by pen and ink with her farmer-sister where we are: something may possibly arise *that* way, either of a convenient nature, *which I may pursue;* or of an inconvenient, *which I may avoid.*

Always be careful of back doors, is a maxim with me in all my exploits. Whoever knows me, knows that I am no proud man. I can talk as familiarly to servants as to principals, when I have a mind to make it worth their while to oblige me in any thing. Then servants are but as the common soldiers in an army. They do all the mischief; frequently without malice, and merely, *good souls!* for mischief-sake.

I am most apprehensive about Miss Howe. She has a confounded deal of wit, and wants only a subject, to shew as much roguery: and should I be outwitted with all my sententious, boasted conceit of my own *nostrum-mongership* — [*I love to plague thee, who art a pretender to accuracy*, and a surface-skimmer *in learning, with* out-of-the-way *words and phrases*] I should certainly hang, drown, or shoot myself.

Poor Hickman! I pity him for the prospect he has with such a virago! But the fellow's a fool, God wot! And now I think of it, it is absolutely necessary for complete happiness in the married state that one *should* be a fool [an argument I once held with this very Miss Howe]. But then the fool should know the other's superiority, otherwise the obstinate one will disappoint the wise one.

But my agent Joseph has helped to secure this quarter, as I have hinted to thee more than once.

LETTER XXII.

Mr. Lovelace to John Belford, Esq.

In Continuation.

But is it not a confounded thing that I cannot fasten an obligation upon this proud beauty? I have two motives in endeavouring to prevail upon her to accept of money and raiment from me: one; the real pleasure I should have in the accommodating of the haughty maid; and to think there was something near her and upon her, that I could call *mine;* the other in order to abate her severity, and humble her a little.

Nothing more effectually brings down a proud spirit, than a sense of lying under pecuniary obligations. This has always made me solicitous to avoid laying myself under any such: yet sometimes, formerly, have I been put to it, and cursed the tardy revolution of the quarterly periods. And yet I ever made shift to avoid anticipations: *I never would eat the calf in the cow's belly*, as Lord M.'s phrase is: for what is that, but to hold our lands upon *tenant-courtesy*, the vilest of all tenures? To be denied a fox-chase, for fear of breaking down a fence upon my own grounds? To be cla-moured at for repairs *studied* for rather than really *wanted?* To be prated to by a bumpkin with his hat on, and his arms folded, as if he defied your expectations of that sort; his foot firmly fixed as if upon his own ground, and you forced to take his arch leers and stupid gibes? he intimating by the whole of his conduct, that he had had it in his power to oblige you, and, if you behave civilly, may oblige you again? — I, who think I have a right to break every man's head I pass by, if I like not his looks, to bear this! — No more could I do it, than I could borrow of an insolent uncle, or inquisitive aunt, who would thence think themselves entitled to have an account of all my life and actions laid before them for their review and censure.

My charmer, I see, has a pride like my own: but she has no *distinction* in her pride: nor knows the pretty fool, that there is nothing nobler, nothing more delightful, than for lovers to be conferring and receiving obligations from each other. In this very farm-yard, to give thee a familiar instance, I have more than once seen this remark illustrated. A strutting rascal of a cock have I beheld chuck, chuck, chuck, chuck-ing his mistress to him, when he has found a single barley-corn, taking it up with his bill, and letting it drop five or six times, still repeating his chucking invitation: and when two or three of his feathered ladies strive who shall be the first for't [O *Jack*, a cock *is a Grand Signor of a bird!*] he directs the bill of the foremost to it; and when she has got the dirty pearl, he struts over her with an erected crest, and with an exulting chuck — a chuck-aw-aw-aw, circling round her with dropt wings, sweeping the dust in humble courtship: while the obliged she, half-shy, half-willing, by her cowring tail, prepared wings, yet seemingly affrighted eyes and contracted neck, lets one see that she knows the barley-corn was not all he called her for.

When she comes to that part of his narrative where he mentions the proposing of the lady's maid Hannah, or one of the young Sorlings's, to attend her, thus he writes:

Now, Belford, canst thou imagine what I meant by proposing Hannah, or one of the girls here, for her attendant? I'll give thee a month to guess.

Thou wilt not pretend to guess, thou say'st.

Well, then, I'll tell thee.

Believing she would certainly propose to have that favourite wench about her, as soon as she was a little settled, I had caused the girl to be inquired after, with an intent to make interest, somehow or other, that a month's warning should be insisted on by her master or mistress, or by some other means, which I had not determined upon, to prevent her coming to her. But fortune fights for me. The wench is luckily ill; a violent rheumatic disorder, which has obliged her to leave her place, confines her to her chamber. Poor Hannah! How I pity the girl! These things are very hard upon industrious servants! — I intend to make the poor wench a small present on the occasion — I know it will oblige my charmer.

And so, Jack, *pretending not to know any thing of the matter*, I pressed her to send for Hannah. She knew I had always a regard for this servant, because of her honest love to her lady: but now I have greater regard for her than ever. Calamity, though a poor servant's calamity, will rather increase than diminish good-will, with a truly generous master or mistress.

As to one of the young Sorlings's attendance, there was nothing at all in proposing that; for if either of them had been chosen by *her*, and permitted by the *mother*, [*two chances in that!*] it would have been only till I had fixed upon another. And, if afterwards they had been loth to part, I could easily have given my beloved a jealousy, which would have done the business; or to the girl, who would have quitted her *country dairy*, such a relish for a *London one*, as would have made it very convenient for her to fall in love with Will; or perhaps I could have done still better for her with Lord M.'s chaplain, who is very desirous of standing well with his lord's presumptive heir.

Clarissa. II. 6

A blessing on thy honest heart, Lovelace! thou'lt say; for thou art for providing for every body!

He gives an account of the serious part of their conversation, with no great variation from the lady's account of it: and when he comes to that part of it, where he bids her remember, that reformation cannot be a sudden thing, he asks his friend:

Is not this fair play? Is it not dealing ingenuously? Then the observation, I will be bold to say, is founded in *truth* and *nature*. But there was a little touch of *policy* in it besides; that the lady, if I should fly out again, should not think me too gross an hypocrite: for, as I plainly told her, I was afraid, that my fits of reformation were *but* fits and sallies; but I hoped her example would fix them into habits. But it is so discouraging a thing to have my monitor so very good! — I protest I know not how to look up at her! Now, as I am thinking, if I could pull her down a little nearer to my own level; that is to say, could prevail upon her to do something that would argue *imperfection*, something *to repent of;* we should jog on much more equally, and be better able to comprehend one another: and so the comfort would be mutual, and the remorse not all on one side.

He acknowledges that he was greatly affected and pleased with the lady's serious arguments at the time; but even then was apprehensive that his temper would not hold. Thus he writes:

This lady says serious things in so agreeable a manner (and then her voice is all harmony when she touches a subject she is pleased with), that I could have listened to her for half a day together. But yet I am afraid, if she *falls*, as they call it, she will lose a good deal of that *pathos*, of that noble self-confidence, which gives a good person, as I now see, a visible superiority over one *not* so good.

But, after all, Belford, I would fain know why people call such free livers as you and me *hypocrites*. — That's a word I hate; and should take it very ill to be called by it. For myself, I have as good motions, and, perhaps, have them as frequently as any body: all the business is, they don't hold; or, to speak more in character, *I don't take the care some do to conceal my lapses.*

LETTER XXIII.

Miss Howe to Miss Clarissa Harlowe.

Saturday, April 15.

Though pretty much pressed in time, and oppressed by my mother's watchfulness, I will write a few lines upon the new light that has broken in upon your gentleman; and send it by a particular hand.

I know not what to think of him upon it. He talks well; but judge him by Rowe's lines, he is certainly a *dissembler*, odious as the sin of hypocrisy, and, as he says, that other of ingratitude, are to him.

And pray, my dear, let me ask, could he have triumphed, as it is said he has done, over so many of our sex, had he not been egregiously guilty of *both* sins?

His ingenuousness is the thing that staggers me: yet is he cunning enough to know, that whoever accuses himself first, blunts the edge of an adversary's accusation.

He is certainly a man of sense: there is more hope of such a one than of a fool: and there must be a *beginning* to a reformation. These I will allow in his favour.

But this, that follows, I think, is the only way to judge of his specious confessions and self-accusations. — Does he confess any thing that you knew not before, or that you are not likely to find out from others? — If nothing else, what does he confess to his own disadvantage? You have heard of his duels: you have heard of his seductions. — All the world has. He *owns*, therefore, what it would be to no purpose to *conceal;* and his ingenuousness is a salvo —"Why, this, madam, is no more than Mr. Lovelace *himself* acknowledges."

Well, but what is now to be done! — You must make the best of your situation: and as you say, so say I, I hope that will not be bad; for I like all that he has proposed to you of Windsor, and his canon's house. His readiness to leave you, and go himself in quest of a lodging, likewise looks well. And I think there is nothing can be so properly done, as (whether you get to a canon's house or not) that the canon should join you together in wedlock as soon as possible.

I much approve, however, of all your cautions, of all your vigilance, and of every thing you have done, but of your *meeting* him. Yet, in my disapprobation of that, I judge by the *event* only; for who would have divined it would have concluded as it did? But he is the devil, by his own account: and had he run away with the wretched Solmes, and your more wretched brother, and been himself transported for life, he should have had my free consent for all three.

What use does he make of that Joseph Leman! — His ingenuousness, I must once more say, confounds me; but if, my dear, you can forgive your brother for the part he put that fellow upon acting, I don't know whether you ought to be angry at Lovelace. Yet I have wished fifty times, since Lovelace got you away, that you were rid of him, whether it were by a burning fever, by hanging, by drowning, or by a broken neck, provided it were before he laid you under a necessity to go into mourning for him.

I repeat my hitherto-rejected offer. May I send it safely by your old man? I have reasons for not sending it by Hickman's servant, unless I had a bank-note. Inquiring for such may cause dis-

6*

trust. My mother is so busy, so inquisitive — I don't love suspicious tempers.

And here she is continually in and out — I must break off.

* * *

Mr. Hickman begs his most respectful compliments to you, with offer of his services. I told him I would oblige him, because minds in trouble take kindly any body's civilities: but that he was not to imagine that he particularly obliged me by this, since I should think the man or woman either blind or stupid who admired not a person of your exalted merit for your own sake, and wished not to serve you without view to other reward than the honour of serving you.

To be sure, that was his principal motive, with great daintiness he said it: but with a kiss of his hand, and a bow to my feet, he hoped, that that fine lady's being my friend did not lessen the merit of the reverence he really had for her.

Believe me ever, what you, my dear, shall ever find me,

Your faithful and affectionate
ANNA HOWE.

LETTER XXIV.
Miss Clarissa Harlowe to Miss Howe.

Sat. afternoon.

I DETAIN your messenger while I write in answer to yours; the poor old man not being very well.

You dishearten me a good deal about Mr. Lovelace. I may be too willing from my sad circumstances to think the best of him. If his pretences to reformation are *but* pretences, what must be his intent? But can the heart of man be so very vile? Can he, *dare* he, mock the Almighty? But may I not, from one very sad reflection, think better of him; that I am thrown too much into his power, to make it *necessary* for him (except he were to intend the *very utmost* villany by me) to be such a shocking hypocrite? He must, at least, be in earnest at the *time* he gives the better hopes. Surely he must. You yourself must join with me in this hope, or you could not wish me to be so dreadfully yoked.

But, after all, I had rather, much rather, be independent of him, and of his family, although I have an high opinion of them; at least till I see what my own may be brought to. — Otherwise, I think it were best for me, at once, to cast myself into Lady Betty's protection. All would then be conducted with decency, and perhaps many mortifications would be spared me. But then I must be *his* at all adventures, and be thought to defy my own family. And shall I not first see the issue of *one* application? And yet I cannot make this till I am settled somewhere, and at a distance from him.

Mrs. Sorlings shewed me a letter this morning, which she had received from her sister Greme last night; in which Mrs. Greme (hoping I would forgive her forward zeal, if her sister thinks fit to shew her letter to me) "wishes, and that for all the noble family's sake, (and she hopes she may say for my own) that I will be pleased to yield to make his honour, as she calls him, happy." She grounds her *officiousness*, as she calls it, upon what he was so *condescending* [her word also] to say to her yesterday, in his way to Windsor, on her *presuming* to ask if she might soon give him joy? "That no man ever loved a woman as he loves me: that no woman ever so well deserved to be beloved: that in every conversation he admires me still more: that he loves me with such a purity, as he had never believed himself capable of, or that a mortal creature could have inspired him with; looking upon me as all *soul;* as an angel sent down to save *his;"* and a great deal more of this sort: "but that he apprehends my consent to make him happy is at a greater distance than he wishes, and complained of the too severe restrictions I had laid upon him before I honoured him with my *confidence:* which restrictions *must be as sacred to him as if they were parts of the marriage contract,"* &c.

What, my dear, shall I say to this? How shall I take it? Mrs. Greme is a good woman. Mrs. Sorlings is a good woman. And this letter agrees with the conversation between Mr. Lovelace and me, which I thought, and still think, so agreeable*. Yet what

* This letter, Mrs. Greme (with no bad design on her part) was put upon writing by Mr. Lovelace himself, as will be seen Letter xxxi.

means the man by *foregoing the opportunities* he has had to declare himself? — What mean his complaints *of my restrictions* to Mrs. Greme? He is not a bashful man.— But you say, I inspire people with an awe of me.— An awe, my dear! — As how?

I am quite petulant, fretful, and peevish, with myself, at times, to find, that I am bound so see the workings of this *subtle*, or this *giddy* spirit, which shall I call it?

How am I punished, as I frequently think, for my vanity, in hoping to be an *example* to young persons of my sex! Let me be but a *warning*, and I will now be contented. For, be my destiny what it may, I shall never be able to hold up my head again among my best friends and worthiest companions.

It is one of the cruellest circumstances that attends the faults of the inconsiderate, that she makes all who love her unhappy, and gives joy only to her own enemies, and to the enemies of her family.

What an useful lesson would this afford, were it properly inculcated at the time that the *tempted mind* was balancing upon a doubtful adventure?

You know not, my dear, the worth of a virtuous man; and, noble-minded as you are in most particulars, you partake of the common weakness of human nature, in being apt to slight what is in your own power.

You would not think of using Mr. Lovelace, were he your suitor, as you do the much worthier Mr.

Hickman — would you? — You know who says in my mother's case, "Much *will* bear, much *shall* bear, all the world through*." Mr. Hickman, I fancy, would be glad to know the lady's name who made such an observation. He would think it hardly possible but such a one should benefit by her own remark; and would be apt to wish his Miss Howe acquainted with her.

Gentleness of heart, surely, is not despicable in a man. Why, if it be, is the highest distinction a man can arrive at that of a *gentleman?* — A distinction which a prince may not deserve. For manners, more than birth, fortune, or title, are requisite in this character. Manners are indeed the essence of it. And shall it be generally said, and Miss Howe not be an exception to it (as once you wrote), that our sex are best dealt with by boisterous and unruly spirits**.

Forgive me, my dear, and love me as you used to do. For although my fortunes are changed, my heart is not: nor ever will, while it bids my pen tell you, that it must cease to beat, when it is not as much yours, as

Your
CLARISSA HARLOWE'S.

LETTER XXV.

Miss Clarissa Harlowe to Miss Howe.

Saturday evening.

MR. Lovelace has seen divers apartments at Windsor; but not one, he says, that he thought fit for me, and which, at the same time, answered my description.

He has been very solicitous to keep to the letter of my instructions; which looks well; and the better I like him, as, although he proposed that town, he came back dissuading me from it: for he said, that, in his journey from thence, he had thought Windsor, although of his own proposal, a wrong choice; because I coveted privacy, and that was a place generally visited and admired*.

I told him, that if Mrs. Sorlings thought me not an incumbrance, I would be willing to stay here a little longer; provided he would leave me, and go to Lord M.'s or to London, whichever he thought best.

He hoped, he said, that he might suppose me absolutely safe from the insults or attempts of my brother; and, therefore, if it would make me easier, he would obey, for a few days at least.

He again proposed to send for Hannah. I told him I designed to do so, through you — and shall I beg of you, my dear, to cause the honest creature to be sent to? Your faithful Robert, I think, knows where she is. Perhaps she will be permitted to quit her place directly, by allowing a month's wages, which I will repay her. He took notice of the serious humour he found me in, and of the redness of my eyes. I had just

* See Vol. I. p. 44.
** See Vol. I. p. 225.

* This inference of the lady in his favour is exactly what he had hoped for. See p. 79.

been answering your letter: and had he not approached me, on his coming off his journey, in a very respectful manner; had he not made an unexceptionable report of his inquiries, and been so ready to go from me, at the very first word; I was prepared (notwithstanding the good terms we parted upon when he set out for Windsor) to have given him a very unwelcome reception: for the contents of your last letter had so affected me, that the moment I saw him, I beheld with indignation the seducer, who had been the cause of all the evils I suffer, and have suffered.

He hinted to me, that he had received a letter from Lady Betty, and another (as I understood him) from one of the Miss Montagues. If they take notice of *me* in them, I wonder that he did not acquaint me with the contents. I am afraid, my dear, that his relations are among those who think I have taken a rash and inexcusable step. It is not to my *credit* to let *even them* know how I have been *frighted out of myself:* and yet perhaps they would hold me unworthy of their alliance, if they were to think my flight a voluntary one. O, my dear, how uneasy to us are our reflections upon every doubtful occurrence, when we know we have been prevailed upon to do a wrong thing!

Sunday morning.

Ah! this man, my dear! We have had warmer dialogues than ever yet we have had. At fair argument I find I need not fear him;[*] but he is such a wild, such an ungovernable creature, [*he* reformed!] that I am half-afraid of him.

He again, on my declaring myself uneasy at his stay with me here, proposed that I would put myself into Lady Betty's protection; assuring me that he thought he could not leave me at Mrs. Sorlings's with safety to myself. And upon my declining to do that for the reasons I gave you in my last[**], he urged me to make a demand of my estate.

He knew it, I told him, to be my resolution not to litigate with my father.

Nor would he put me upon it, he replied, but as the *last* thing. But if my spirit would not permit me to *be obliged*, as I called it, to any body; and yet if my relations would refuse me my own; he knew not how I could keep up that spirit, without being put to inconveniences, which would give him infinite concern — unless-unless-unless, he said hesitating, as if afraid to speak out — Unless I would take the only method I *could* take to obtain the possession of my own.

What is *that*, sir?

Sure the man saw by my looks, when he came with his creeping *unless's*, that I guessed what he meant.

Ah! madam, can you be at a loss to know what that method is? — They will not dispute with a

[*] See this confirmed by Mr. Lovelace p. 33.
[**] See p. 84.

man that right which they would contest with *you*.

Why said he with a *man* instead of with him? Yet he looked as if he wanted to be encouraged to say more.

So, sir, you would have me employ a lawyer, would you, notwithstanding what I have ever declared as to litigating with my father?

No, I would not, my dearest creature, snatching my hand, and pressing it with his lips — except you would make *me* the lawyer.

Had he said *me* at first, I should have been above the affectation of mentioning a lawyer.

I blushed. The man pursued not the subject so ardently, but that it was more easy as well as more natural to avoid it than to fall into it.

Would to heaven he might, without offending! — But I *so* over-awed him! — [*over-awed* him! — *your** notion my dear!] And so the over-awed, bashful man went off from the subject, repeating his proposal, that I would demand my own estate, or empower some man of the law to demand it, if I *would not* [he put in] empower a happier man to demand it. But it could not be amiss, he thought, to acquaint my two trustees, that I intended to assume it.

I should know better what to do, I told him, when he was at a distance from me, and *known* to be so. I suppose, sir, that if my father should propose my return, and engage never to mention Solmes to me, nor any other man,

* See p. 58, 59.

but by *my consent*, and I agree, upon that condition, to think no more of you, you will acquiesce. I was willing to try whether he had the regard to *all* my previous declarations which he pretended to have to *some* of them.

He was struck into confusion. What say you, Mr. Lovelace? You know all you mean is for my good. Surely I am my own mistress: surely I need not ask your leave to make what terms I please for myself, *so long as I break none with you?*

He hemmed twice or thrice. — Why, madam, why madam, I cannot say — then pausing — and rising from his seat, with petulance; I see plainly enough, said he, the reason why none of my proposals can be accepted: at *last* I am to be a sacrifice to your reconciliation with your implacable family.

It has always been your respectful way, Mr. Lovelace, to treat my family in this free manner. But pray, sir, when you call *others* implacable, see that you deserve not the same censure *yourself*.

He must needs say, there was no love lost between some of my family and him; but he had not deserved of *them* what they had of him.

Yourself being judge, I suppose, sir?

All the world, you yourself, madam, being judge.

Then, sir, let me tell you, had you been less upon your defiances, they would not have been irritated so much against you. But nobody ever heard, that avowed despite to the relations of a person was a proper courtship, either to that person or to her friends.

Well, madam, all that I know is, that their malice against me is such, that if you determine to sacrifice *me*, you may be reconciled when you please.

And all that I know, sir, is, that if I do give my father the power of a negative, and he will be contented with *that*, it will be but my *duty* to give it him; and if I preserve one to myself, I shall break through no obligation to *you*.

Your duty to your capricious *brother*, not to your *father*, you mean, madam.

If the dispute lay between my brother and me at *first*, surely, sir, a father may choose which party he will take.

He *may*, madam — but that exempts him not from blame for all that, if he take the wrong —

Different people will judge differently, Mr. Lovelace, of the right and the wrong. *You* judge as you please. Shall not others as *they* please? And who has a right to control a father's judgment in his own family, and in relation to his own child?

I know, madam, there is no arguing with you. But, nevertheless, I had hoped to have made myself some little merit with you, so as that I might not have been the *preliminary sacrifice* to a reconciliation.

Your hope, sir, had been better grounded, if you had had my consent to my abandoning of my father's house —

Always, madam, and for ever, to be reminded of the choice you would have made of that d—n'd Solmes — rather than —

Not so hasty! not so rash, Mr. Lovelace! I am convinced that there was no intention to marry me to that Solmes on Wednesday. So I am told they now give out, in order to justify themselves at your expense. Every body living, madam, is obliged to you for your kind thoughts but I.

Excuse me, *good* Mr. Lovelace [waving my hand and bowing], that I am willing to think the best of my father.

Charming creature! said he, with what a bewitching air is that said! — And with a vehemence in his manner would have snatched my hand. But I withdrew it, being much offended with him.

I think, madam, my sufferings for your sake might have entitled me to some favour.

My sufferings, sir, for your impetuous temper, set against *your* sufferings, for *my sake*, I humbly conceive, leave me very little your debtor.

Lord! madam [assuming a drolling air] what have you suffered! — Nothing but what you can easily forgive. You have been *only* made a prisoner in your father's house, by the way of doing credit to your judgment! — You have *only* had an innocent and faithful servant turned out of your service because you loved her — you have *only* had your sister's confident servant set over you, with leave to tease and affront you! —

Very well, sir!

You have *only* had an insolent brother take upon him to treat you like a slave, and as insolent a sister to undermine you in every body's favour, on pretence to keep you out of hands, which, if as vile as they vilely report, are not, however, half so vile and cruel as their own!

Go on, sir, if you please!

You have *only* been persecuted, in order to oblige you to have a sordid fellow, whom you have professed to hate, and whom every body despises! The licence has been *only* got! the parson has *only* been had in readiness! The day a near, a *very* near day, has been *only* fixed! And you were *only* to be searched for your correspondencies, and still closer confined, till the day came, in order to deprive you of all means of escaping the snare laid for you! — But all this you can forgive! You can wish you had stood all this; inevitable as the compulsion must have been! — And the man who, at the hazard of his life, has delivered you from all these mortifications, is the only person you *cannot* forgive!

Can't you go on, sir? You see I have patience to hear you. Can't you go on, sir?

I can, madam, with *my* sufferings: which I confess ought not to be mentioned, were I at last to be rewarded in the manner I hoped.

Your sufferings, then, if you please, sir?

— Affrontingly forbidden your father's house, after encouragement given, without any reasons they knew not before to justify the prohibition: forced upon a rencounter I wished to avoid: the first I ever, so provoked, wished to avoid. And that, because the wretch was your brother!

Wretch, sir! — And my brother! — This could be from no man breathing but from him before me!

Pardon me, madam! — But oh! how unworthy to be your brother! — The quarrel grafted upon an old one when at college; he universally known to be the aggressor; revived for views equally sordid, and injurious both to yourself and me — giving life to him who would have taken away mine!

Your *generosity* THIS, sir; not your sufferings: A little more of your *sufferings*, if you please; — I hope you do not repent that you did not murder my brother!

My private life hunted into! My morals decried! Some of the accusers not unfaulty!

That's an aspersion, sir!

Spies set upon my conduct! One hired to bribe my own servant's fidelity; perhaps to have poisoned me at last, if the honest fellow had not —

Facts, Mr. Lovelace! — Do you want facts in the display of your sufferings? — None of your *perhaps's* I beseech you!

Menaces every day, and defiances, put into every one's mouth against me! Forced to creep about in disguises — and to watch *all hours* —

And in *all weathers*, I suppose, sir — that, I remember, was once your grievance! *In all weathers*, sir*! and all these hardships arising from yourself, not imposed by me.

— Like a thief, or an eves-dropper, proceeded he: and yet neither by birth nor alliances unworthy of *their* relation, whatever I may be and am of their admirable daughter: of whom they, every one of them, are at least *as* unworthy! — These, madam, I call sufferings: *justly* call so; if at last I am to be sacrificed to an imperfect reconciliation — *imperfect*, I say: for, can you expect to live so much as *tolerably* under the same roof, after all that has passed with that brother and sister?

O sir, sir! what sufferings have yours been! And all for my sake, I warrant! — I can never reward you for them! — Never think of me more, I beseech you — how can you have patience with me? — Nothing has been owing to your own behaviour, I presume; nothing to your defiances for defiances: nothing to your resolution declared more than once, that you *would* be related to a family, which, nevertheless, you would not stoop to ask a relation of: nothing, in short, to courses which every body blamed you for, you not thinking it worth your

* See p. 7 and 9.

while to justify yourself. Had I not thought you used in an ungentlemanly manner, as I have heretofore told you, you had not had my notice by pen and ink*. That notice gave you a supposed security, and you generously defied my friends the more for it: and this brought upon me (perhaps not undeservedly) my father's displeasure; without which, my brother's private pique, and selfish views, would have wanted a foundation to build upon: so that for all that followed of my treatment and your redundant *only's*, I might thank you principally, as you may yourself, for all your *sufferings*, your *mighty* sufferings! — And if, voluble sir, you have founded any merit upon them, be so good as to revoke it: and look upon *me*, with my forfeited reputation, as the only sufferer — for what — pray hear me out, sir, [for he was going to speak] have you suffered in, but your pride? your reputation *could not* suffer: *that* it was beneath you to be solicitous about. And had you not been an unmanageable man, I should not have been driven to the extremity, I now every hour, as the hour passes, deplore — with this additional reflection upon myself, that I ought not to have *begun*, or having begun, not *continued* a correspondence with one who thought it not worth his while to clear his own character for *my sake*, or to submit to my father for his *own*, in a point wherein every father ought to have an option —

* See p. 9.

Darkness, light; light, darkness; by my soul; — just as you please to have it. O charmer of my heart! snatching my hand, and pressing it between both his, to his lips in a strange wild way, Take me, take me to yourself: mould me as you please: I am wax in your hands; give me your own impression; and seal me for ever yours. — We were born for each other! — You to make me happy, and save a soul — I am all error, all crime. I see what I ought to have done. But do you think, madam, I can willingly consent to be sacrificed to a partial reconciliation, in which I shall be so great, so irreparable a sufferer! — Any thing but *that* — include me in your terms: prescribe to me: promise for me as you please — put a halter about my neck, and lead me by it, upon condition of forgiveness on that disgraceful penance, and of a prostration as servile, to your father's presence (your brother absent); and I will beg his consent at his feet, and bear any thing but spurning from him, because he is your father. But to give you up upon cold conditions, d——n me [said the shocking wretch] if I either will or can!

These were his words, as near as I can remember them: for his behaviour was so strangely wild and fervent, that I was perfectly frighted. I thought he would have devoured my hand. I wished myself a thousand miles distant from him.

I told him, I by no means approved of his violent temper: he was too boisterous a man for my liking. I saw *now*, by the conversation that had passed, what was his boasted regard to my *injunctions;* and should take my measures accordingly, as he should *soon* find. And with a half-frighted earnestness, I desired him to withdraw and leave me to myself.

He obeyed: and that with extreme complaisance in his manner, but with his complexion greatly heightened, and a countenance as greatly dissatisfied.

But, on recollecting all that passed, I plainly see, that he means not, if he can help it, to leave to me the liberty of refusing him; which I had nevertheless preserved a *right* to do; but looks upon me as *his*, by a strange sort of obligation, for having run away with me *against my will*.

Yet you see he but touches upon the edges of matrimony neither. And that at a time generally, when he has either excited my passions or apprehensions; so that I cannot at once descend. But surely this cannot be his design. — And yet such seemed to be his behaviour to my sister*, when he provoked her to refuse him and so tamely submitted, as he did, to her refusal. — But he dare not. — What can one say of so various a man? — I am now again out of conceit with him. I wish I were fairly out of his power.

He has sent up three times to

* See Vol. I. p. 13.

beg admittance; in the two last with unusual earnestness. But I have sent him word, I will first finish what I am about.

What to do about going from this place I cannot tell. I could stay here with all my heart, as I have said to him: the gentlewoman and her daughters are desirous that I will: although not very convenient for them, I believe, neither: but I see he will not leave me while I do — so I *must* remove somewhere.

I have long been sick of myself: and now I am more and more so. But let me not lose your good opinion. If I do, that loss will complete the misfortunes of
Your
Cl. Harlowe.

LETTER XXVI.
Miss Clarissa Harlowe to Miss Howe.

Sunday night, April 16.

I may send to you, although you are forbid to write to me; may I not? — For that is not a *correspondence* (is it?) where letters are not answered.

I am strangely at a loss what to think of this man. He is a perfect Proteus. I can but write according to the shape he assumes at the time. Don't think *me* the changeable person, I beseech you, if in one letter I contradict what I wrote in another; nay, if I seem to contradict what I said in the same letter: for he is a perfect chameleon; or rather more variable than the chameleon; for that it is said cannot assume the *red* and the *white;* but this man *can*. And though *black* seems to be his natural colour, yet has he taken great pains to make me think him nothing but *white*.

But you shall judge of him as I proceed. Only, if I any where appear to you to be credulous, I beg you to set me right: for you are a stander-by, as you say in a former*. — Would to heaven I were not to play! For I think, after all, I am held to a desperate game.

Before I could finish my last to you, he sent up twice more to beg admittance. I returned for answer, that I would see him at my own time: I would neither be invaded nor prescribed to.

Considering how we parted, and my delaying his *audience*, as he sometimes calls it, I expected him to be in no very good humour, when I admitted of his visit; and by what I wrote, you will conclude that *I* was not. Yet mine soon changed when I saw his extreme humility at his entrance, and heard what he had to say.

I have a letter, madam, said he, from Lady Betty Lawrence, and another from my cousin Charlotte. But of these more by-and-by. I came now to make my humble acknowledgment to you, upon the arguments that passed between us so lately.

I was silent, wondering what he was driving at.

I am a most unhappy creature, proceeded he: unhappy from a strange impatiency of spirit, which

See p. 27.

I cannot conquer. It always brings upon me deserved humiliation. But it is more laudable to acknowledge than to persevere, when under the power of conviction.

I was still silent.

I have been considering what you proposed to me, madam, that I should acquiesce with such terms as you should think proper to comply with, in order to a reconciliation with your friends.

Well, sir.

And I find all just, all right, on your side; and all impatience, all inconsideration, on mine.

I stared, you may suppose. Whence this change, sir? and so soon?

I am so much convinced that you must be in the right in all you think fit to insist upon, that I shall for the future mistrust myself; and, if it be possible, whenever I differ with you, take an hour's time for recollection, before I give way to that vehemence, which an opposition, to which I have not been accustomed, too often gives me.

All this is mighty good, sir: but to what does it tend?

Why, madam, when I came to consider what you had proposed as to the terms of reconciliation with your friends; and when I recollected, that you had always *referred to yourself* to *approve or reject* me, according to my *merits* or *demerits*: I plainly saw, that it was rather a *condescension* in you, that you were pleased to ask my consent to those terms than that you were imposing a *new law*: and I now, madam, beg your pardon for my impatience: whatever terms you think proper to come into with your relations, which will enable you to honour me with the *conditional* effect of your promise to me, to these be pleased to consent: and if I lose you, insupportable as that thought is to me, yet, as it must be by my own fault, I ought to thank myself for it.

What think you, Miss Howe? — Do you believe he can have any view in this? — I cannot see any he could have; and I thought it best, as he put it in so right a manner, to appear not to doubt the sincerity of his confession, and to accept of it as sincere.

He then read to me part of lady Betty's letter; turning down the beginning, which was a little too severe upon him, he said, for my eye: and I believe, by the style, the remainder of it was in a *corrective* strain.

It was too plain, I told him, that he must have great faults, that none of his relations could write to him, but with a mingled censure for some bad action.

And it is as plain, my dearest creature, said he, that you, who know not of any such faults, but by surmise, are equally ready to condemn me. — Will not charity allow you to infer, that *their* charges are no better grounded? — And that my principal fault has been carelessness of my character, and too little solicitude to clear myself when aspersed? Which, I do assure you, is the case.

Lady Betty, in her letter, expresses herself in the most obliging manner in relation to me. "She wishes him so to behave, as to encourage me to make him soon happy. She desires her compliments to me; and expresses her impatience to see, as her niece, so *celebrated a lady* [those are her high words]. She shall take it for an honour, she says, to be put into a way to oblige me. She hopes I will not too long delay the ceremony; because that performed, will be to her, and to Lord M. and Lady Sarah, a sure pledge of her nephew's merits and good behaviour.

She says, "She was always sorry to hear of the hardships I had met with on his account: that he will be the most ungrateful of men, if he make not all up to me: and that she thinks it incumbent upon all their family, to supply to me the lost favour of my own: and, for her part, nothing of that kind, she bids him assure me, shall be wanting."

Her ladyship observes, "That the treatment he had received from my family, would have been more unaccountable than it was, with such natural and accidental advantages as he had, had it not been owing to his own careless manners. But she hopes that he will convince the Harlowe family, that they had thought worse of him than he had deserved; since now it was in his power to establish his character for ever. This she prays to God to enable him to do, as well for his own honour as for the honour of their *house*," was the magnificent word.

She concludes with "desiring to be informed of our nuptials the moment they are celebrated, that she may be with the earliest in felicitating me on the happy occasion."

But her ladyship gives me no direct invitation to attend her before the marriage, which I might have expected from what he had told me.

He then shewed me part of Miss Montague's more sprightly letter, "congratulating him upon the honour he had obtained, of the *confidence of so admirable a lady.*" These are her words. *Confidence*, my dear! Nobody, indeed, as you say, will believe otherwise, were they to be told the truth: and you see that Miss Montague (and all his family, I suppose) think the step I have taken an *extraordinary one.* "*She* also wishes for his speedy nuptials; and to see her new cousin at M. Hall: as do Lord M. she tells him and her sister, and in general all the well-wishers of their family.

"Whenever this happy day shall be passed, she proposes, she says, to attend me, and to make one in my train to M. Hall, if his lordship shall continue as ill of the gout as he is at present. But that should he get better, he will himself attend me, she is sure, and conduct me thither: and afterwards quit either of his three seats to us, till we shall be settled to our mind."

This young lady says nothing in excuse for not meeting me on the road, or St. Alban's, as he had made me expect she would: yet mentions *her having been indisposed*. Mr. Lovelace had also told me, that Lord M. *was ill of the gout;* which Miss Montague's letter confirms.

But why did not the man shew me these letters last night? Was he afraid of giving me too much pleasure?

LETTER XXVII.
Miss Clarissa Harlowe to Miss Howe.

You may believe, my dear, that these letters put me in good humour with him. He saw it in my countenance, and congratulated himself upon it. Yet I cannot but repeat my wonder, that I could not have the contents of them communicated to me last night*.

He then urged me to go directly to Lady Betty's, on the strength of her letter.

But how, said I, can I do that, were I even out of all hope of a reconciliation with my friends, (which yet, however unlikely to be effected, is my duty to *attempt*) as her ladyship has given me no particular invitation?

That, he was sure, was owing to her doubt that it would be accepted — else she had done it with the greatest pleasure in the world.

That doubt itself, I said, was enough to deter me: since her ladyship, who knew so well the boundaries of the fit and the unfit, by her not expecting I would accept of an invitation, had she given it, would have reason to think me very forward if I had accepted it; and much more forward to go without it. Then, said I, I thank *you*, sir, I have no clothes fit to go any whither, or to be seen by any body.

O, I was fit to appear in the drawing-room, were full dress and jewels to be excused; and should make the most amiable [he must mean *extraordinary*] figure there. He was astonished at the elegance of my dress. By what art he knew not, but I appeared to such advantage, as if I had a different suit every day. Besides, his cousins Montague would supply me with all I wanted for the present; and he would write to Miss Charlotte accordingly, if I would give him leave.

Do you think me the jay in the fable? said I. Would you have me visit the owners of the borrowed dresses in their own clothes? Surely, Mr. Lovelace, you think I have either a very low or a very confident mind.

Would I choose to go to London (for a few days only) in order to furnish myself with clothes?

Not at your expense, sir, said I, in an angry tone.

I could not have appeared in earnest to him, in my displeasure at his artful contrivances to get me away, if I were not occasionally to shew my real fretfulness upon the destitute condition to which he has reduced me. When people set out wrong together, it is very difficult to avoid recriminations.

* The reader will see how Miss Howe accounts for this in p. 112.

He wished he knew but my mind that should direct him in his proposals, and it would be his delight to observe it, whatever it were.

My mind is, that you, sir, should leave me — how often must I tell you so?

If I were any where but here, he would obey me, he said, if I insisted upon it. But if I would assert my right, that would be infinitely preferable, in his opinion, to any other measure *but one* (*which he durst only hint at*): for then admitting *his* visits, or refusing them, as I pleased, (granting a correspondence by letter only) it would appear to all the world, that what I had done was but in order to do myself justice.

How often, Mr. Lovelace, must I repeat, that I will not litigate with my father? Do you think that my unhappy circumstances will alter my notions of my own duty so far as I shall be enabled to perform it? How can I obtain possession without litigation, and but by my trustees? One of them will be against me; the other is abroad. Then the remedy proposed by this measure, were I *disposed* to fall in with it, will require time to bring it to effect; and what I want is *present* independence, and your *immediate* absence.

*Upon his soul, the wretch swore, he did not think it safe, for the reasons he had before given, to leave me here. He wished I would think of some place, to which I should like to go. But he must take the liberty to say, that he hoped his behaviour had not been so exceptionable, as to make me so *very* earnest for his absence in the interim: and the less, surely, as I was almost *eternally* shutting up myself from him, although he presumed to assure me, that he never went from me but with a corrected heart, and with strengthened resolutions of improving by my example.

Eternally shutting myself up from you! repeated I — I hope, sir, that you will not pretend to take it *amiss*, that I expect to be uninvaded in my retirements. I hope you don't think me so weak a creature (novice as you have found me in a very capital instance) as to be fond of occasions to hear your fine speeches, especially as no *differing circumstances* require your overfrequent visits; nor that I am to be addressed to as if I thought hourly professions *needful* to assure me of your honour.

He seemed a little disconcerted.

You know, Mr. Lovelace, proceeded I, why I am so earnest for your absence. It is, that I may appear to the world independent of you; and in hopes, by that means, to find it less difficult to set on foot a reconciliation with my friends. And now let me add (in order to make you easier as to the terms of that hoped-for reconciliation) that since I find I have the good fortune to stand so well with your relations, I will, from time to time, acquaint you, by letter, when you are absent, with every step I shall take, and with every overture that shall be made to me: but not with an intention to render myself accountable to you, neither, as to my acceptance or non-acceptance of those overtures. They know that I have a power given me by my grandfather's will, to bequeath the estate he left me, with other of his bounties, in a way that may affect them, though not absolutely from them; this *consideration*, I hope, will procure me *some* from them when their passion subsides, and when they know I am independent of you.

Charming reasoning! And let him tell me, that the assurance I had given him was *all he wished for.* It was *more* than he could ask. What a happiness to have a woman of honour and generosity to depend upon! Had he, on his first entrance into the world, met with such a one, he had never been other than a man of strict virtue. — But all, he hoped, was for the best; since, in that case, he had never perhaps had the happiness he had now in view, because his relations had been always urging him to marry; and that before he had the honour to know me. And now, as he had not been so bad as some people's malice reported him to be, he hoped he should have near as much merit in his repentance as if he had never erred. — A fine rakish notion and hope! And too much encouraged, I doubt, my dear, by the generality of our sex!

This brought on a more serious question or two. You'll see by it what a creature an unmortified libertine is.

I asked him if he knew what he had said alluded to a sentence in the best of books, *That there was more joy in heaven —*

He took the words out of my mouth,

Over one sinner that repenteth, than over ninety-and-nine just persons, which need no repentance*, were his words.

Yes, madam, I thought of it as soon as I said it, but not before. I have read the story of the prodigal son, I'll assure you: and one day, when I am settled as I hope to be, will write a dramatic piece on the subject. I have at times had it in my head; and you will be too ready, perhaps, to allow me to be qualified for it.'

You so lately, sir, stumbled at a word, with which you must be better acquainted, ere you can be thoroughly master of such a subject, that I am amazed you should know any thing of the Scripture, and be so ignorant of that**.

O, madam, I have read the Bible as a fine piece of ancient history — but as I hope to be saved, it has for some few years past made me so uneasy, when I have popped upon some passages in it, that I have been forced to run to music or company to divert myself.

Poor wretch! lifting up my hands and eyes.

* Luke xv. 7. The parable is concerning the ninety-nine sheep, not the prodigal son, as Mr. Lovelace erroneously imagines.
** See p. 74.

The denunciations come so slap-dash upon one, so unceremoniously, as I may say, without even the By-your-leave of a rude London chairman, that they overturn one, horse and man, as St. Paul was overturned. There's another Scripture allusion, madam! The light, in short, as his was, is too glaring to be borne.

O, sir, do you want to be complimented into repentance and salvation? But pray, Mr. Lovelace, do you mean any thing at all, when you swear so often as you do, *By your soul*, or bind an asseveration with the words, *As you hope to be saved?*

O my beloved creature, shifting his seat; let us call another cause.

Why, sir, don't *I* neither use *ceremony* enough with you?

Dearest madam, forbear for the present: I am but in my noviciate. Your foundation must be laid brick by brick: you'll hinder the progress of the good work you would promote, if you tumble in a whole waggon-load at once upon me.

Lord bless me, thought I, what a character is that of a libertine! What a creature am I, who have risked what I have risked with such a one!— What a task before me, if my hopes continue, of reforming such a wild Indian as this — Nay, worse than a wild Indian; for a man who errs with his eyes open, and against conviction, is a thousand times worse for what he knows, and much harder to be reclaimed, than if he had never known any thing.

I was equally shocked *at* him, and concerned *for* him; and having laid so few bricks (to speak to his allusion), and those so ill-cemented, I was as willing as the gay inconsiderate, to call another cause, as he termed it — another cause, too, more immediately pressing upon me, from my uncertain situation.

I said, I took it for granted, that he assented to the reasoning he seemed to approve, and would leave me. And then I asked him, what he really, and in his most deliberate mind, would advise me to, in my present situation? He must needs see, I said, that I was at a great loss what to resolve upon; entirely a stranger to London, having no adviser, no protector, at present: himself, he must give me leave to tell him, greatly deficient in *practice*, if not in the *knowledge*, of those decorums, which, I had supposed, were always to be found in a man of birth, fortune, and education.

He imagines himself, I find, to be a very polite man, and cannot bear to be thought otherwise. He put up his lip — I am sorry for it, madam — [a man of breeding, a man of politeness, give me leave to say [colouring], is much more of a black swan with *you*, than with any lady I ever met with.

Then that is your misfortune, Mr. Lovelace, as well as mine, at present. Every woman of discernment, I am confident, knowing what I know of you now, would say as I say [*I had a mind to mortify a pride, that I am sure deserves to*

7*

be mortified]; that your politeness is not regular, nor constant. It is not *habit*. It is too much seen by fits and starts, and sallies, and those not spontaneous. You must be *reminded* into them.

O Lord! O Lord! — Poor I! — was the light, yet the half-angry wretch's self-pitying expression!

I proceeded. — Upon my word, sir, you are not the accomplished man, which your talents and opportunities would have led one to expect you to be. You are indeed in your noviciate, as to every laudable attainment.

LETTER XXVIII.
Miss Clarissa Harlowe.
In Continuation.

As this subject was introduced by himself, and treated so lightly by him, I was going on to tell him more of my mind; but he interrupted me — Dear, dear madam, spare me. I am sorry that I have lived to this hour for nothing at all. But surely you could not have quitted a subject so much more agreeable, and so much more *suitable*, I will say, to our present situation, if you had not too cruel a pleasure in mortifying a man, who the less needed to be mortified, as he *before* looked up to you with a diffidence in his own merits too great to permit him to speak half his mind to you. Be pleased but to return to the subject we were upon; and at another time I will gladly embrace correction from the only lips in the world so qualified to give it.

You talk of reformation sometimes, Mr. Lovelace, and in so talking, acknowledge errors. But I see you can very ill bear the reproof, for which perhaps you are not solicitous to avoid *giving* occasion. Far be it from me to take delight in finding fault; I should be glad for both our sakes, since my situation is what it is, that I could do nothing but praise you. But failures which affect a mind that need not be very delicate to be affected by them, are too glaring to be passed over in silence by a person who wishes to be thought in earnest in her own duties.

I admire your delicacy, madam, again interrupted he. Although I suffer by it, yet would I not have it otherwise: indeed I would not, when I consider of it. It is an angelic delicacy, which sets you above all our sex, and even above your own. It is *natural* to *you*, madam; so you may not think it extraordinary: but there is nothing like it on earth, said the flatterer. — What company has he kept?

But let us return to the former subject — you were so good as to ask me, what I would advise you to do: I want but to make you easy; I want but to see you fixed to your liking: your faithful Hannah with you, your reconciliation with those to whom you wish to be reconciled, set on foot, and in a train. And now let me mention to you different expedients; in hopes that some one of them may be acceptable to you.

"I will go to Mrs. Howe, or to Miss Howe, or to whomsoever you would have me to go, and endeavour to prevail upon them to receive you.*

"Do you incline to go to Florence to your cousin Morden? I will furnish you with an opportunity of going thither, either by sea to Leghorn, or by land through France. Perhaps I may be able to procure one of the ladies of my family to attend you. Either Charlotte or Patty would rejoice in such an opportunity of seeing France and Italy. As for myself, I will only be your escort, in disguise, if you will have it so, even in your *livery*, that your punctilio may not receive offence by my attendance."

I told him, I would consider of all he had said: but that I hoped for a line or two from my aunt Hervey, if not from my sister, to both of whom I had written; which, if I were to be so favoured, might help to determine me. Meantime, if he would withdraw, I would particularly consider of this proposal of his, in relation to my cousin Morden. And if it held its weight with me, so far as to write for your opinion upon it, he should know my mind in an hour's time.

He withdrew with great respect: and in an hour's time re-

* The reader, perhaps, need not be reminded that he had taken care from the first (See Vol. I. p. 137.) to deprive her of any protection from Mrs. Howe. See in his next Letter, p. 109. a repeated account of the same artifices, and his exultations upon his inventions to impose upon two such watchful ladies as Clarissa and Miss Howe.

turned. And then I told him it was unnecessary to trouble you for your opinion about it. My cousin Morden was soon expected. If he were not, I could not admit him to accompany me to him upon any condition. It was highly improbable that I should obtain the favour of either of his cousins' company: and if that *could* be brought about, it would be the same thing in the world's eye, as if he went himself.

This led us into another conversation: which shall be the subject of my next.

LETTER XXIX.

Miss Clarissa Harlowe.

In Continuation.

Mr. Lovelace told me, that on the supposition that his proposal in relation to my cousin Morden might not be accepted, he had been studying to find out, if possible, some other expedient that might be agreeable, in order to convince me, that he preferred my satisfaction to his own.

He then offered to go himself, and procure my Hannah to come and attend me. As I had declined the service of either of the young Mrs. Sorlings's, he was extremely solicitous, he said, that I should have a servant, in whose integrity I might confide.

I told him, that you would be so kind, as to send to engage Hannah, if possible.

If any thing, he said, should prevent Hannah from coming, suppose he himself waited upon

Miss Howe, to desire her to lend me *her* servant till I was provided to my mind?

I said, your mother's high displeasure at the step I had taken (as *she* supposed, voluntarily) had deprived me of any open assistance of that sort from *you*.

He was amazed, so much as Mrs. Howe herself used to admire me, and so great an influence as Miss Howe was supposed, and deserved to have over her mother, that Mrs. Howe should take upon herself to be so much offended with me. He wished, that the man who took such pains to keep up and inflame the passions of my father and uncles, were not at the bottom of this mischief too.

I was afraid, I said, that my brother *was:* or else my uncle Antony, I dared to say, would not have taken such pains to set Mrs. Howe against me, as I understood he had done.

Since I had declined visiting Lady Sarah, and Lady Betty, he asked me, if I would admit of a visit from his cousin Montague, and accept of a servant of hers for the present?

That was not, I said, an unacceptable proposal: but I would first see, if my friends would send me my clothes, that I might not make such a giddy and runaway appearance to any of his relations.

If I pleased, he would take another journey to Windsor, to make a more particular inquiry amongst the canons, or in any worthy family.

Were not his objections as to the publicness of the place, I asked him, as strong now as before?

I remember, my dear, in one of your former letters, you mentioned London as the most private place to be in*: and I said, that since he made such pretences against leaving me here, as shewed he had no intention to do so: and since he engaged to go from me, and leave me to pursue my own measures, if I were elsewhere; and since his presence made these lodgings inconvenient to me; I should not be disinclined to go to London, did I know any body there.

As he had several times proposed London to me, I expected that he would eagerly have embraced that motion from me. But he took not ready hold of it: yet I thought his eye approved of it.

We are both great watchers of each other's eyes; and indeed seem to be more than half afraid of each other.

He then made a grateful proposal to me; "that I would send for my Norton to attend me.**"

He saw by my eyes, he said, that he had at last been happy in an expedient, which would answer the wishes of us both. Why, said he, did not I think of it before? — And, snatching my hand, Shall I write, madam? shall I send? shall I go and fetch the worthy woman myself?

* See Vol. I. 373.
** The reader is referred to Mr. Lovelace's next Letter, for his motives in making the several proposals of which the lady is willing to think so well.

After a little consideration, I told him, that this was *indeed* a grateful motion: but that I apprehended, it would put her to a difficulty, which she would not be able to get over; as it would make a woman of her known prudence appear to countenance a fugitive daughter, in opposition to her parents; and as her coming to me would deprive her of my mother's favour, without its being in my power to make it up to her.

O my beloved creature! said he, *generously enough*, let not this be an obstacle. I will do every thing for Mrs. Norton you wish to have done. — Let me go for her.

More coolly than perhaps his generosity deserved, I told him, it was impossible but I must soon hear from my friends. I should not, meantime, embroil any body with them. Not Mrs. Norton especially, from whose interest in, and mediation with, my mother, I might expect some good, were she to keep herself in a neutral state: that besides, the good woman had a mind above her fortune; and would sooner want than be beholden to any body improperly.

Improperly! said he. — Have not persons of merit a *right* to all the benefits conferred upon them? — Mrs. Norton is so good a woman, that I shall think she lays me under an obligation, if she will put it in my power to serve her; although she were *not* to augment it, by giving me the opportunity, at the same time, of contributing to your pleasure and satisfaction.

How could this man, with such powers of right thinking, be so far depraved by evil habits, as to disgrace his talents by wrong acting?

Is there not room, after all, thought I, at the time, to hope (as he so lately led me to hope) that the example it will behove me, for *both* our sakes, to endeavour to set him, may influence him to a change of manners, in which both may find our account?

Give me leave, sir, said I, to tell you, there is a strange mixture in your mind. You must have taken *pains* to suppress many good motions and reflections, as they arose, or levity must have been surprisingly predominant in it. — But as to the subject we were upon, there is no taking any resolutions till I hear from my friends.

Well, madam, I can only say, I would find out some expedient, if I could, that should be agreeable to you. But since I cannot, will you be so good as to tell me, what you would wish to have done? Nothing in the world but I will comply with, excepting leaving you here, at such a distance from the place I shall be in, if any thing should happen; and in a place where my gossiping rascals have made me in manner public, for want of proper cautions at first.

These vermin, added he, have a pride they can hardly rein-in, when they serve a man of family. They boast of their master's pedigree and descent, as if they were related to him. Nor is any thing they know of him or of his affairs, a secret to one another, were it a matter that would hang him.

If so, thought I, men of family should take care to give them subjects worth boasting of.

I am quite at a loss, said I, what to do, or whither to go. Would you, Mr. Lovelace, in earnest, advise me to think of going to London?

And I looked at him with steadfastness. But nothing could I gather from his looks.

At first, madam, said he, I was for proposing London, as I was then more apprehensive of pursuit. But as your relations seem cooler on that head, I am the more indifferent about the place you go to.—So as *you* are pleased, so as *you* are easy, I shall be happy.

This indifference of his to London, I cannot but say, made me incline the more to go thither. I asked him (to hear what he would say) if he could recommend me to any *particular place* in London?

No, he said: none that was fit for me, or that I should like. His friend Belford, indeed, had very handsome lodgings near Soho Square, at a relation's whose wife was a woman of virtue and honour. These, as Mr. Belford was generally in the country, he could borrow till I were better accomodated.

I was resolved to rfuse these at the first mention, as I should any other he had named. Nevertheless, I will see, thought I, if he has really thoughts of these for me. If I break off the talk here, and he resume this proposal with earnestness in the morning, I shall apprehend, that he is less indifferent than he seems to be, about my going to London; and that he has already a lodging in his eye for me. And then I will not go at all.

But after such generous motions from him, I really think it a little barbarous to act and behave as if I thought him capable of the blackest and most ungrateful baseness. But his character, his principles, are so faulty!—He is so light, so vain, so various, that there is no certainty that he will be next hour what he is this. Then, my dear, I have no guardian now; no father, no mother! only God and my vigilance to depend upon. And I have no reason to expect a miracle in my favour.

Well, sir, said I, [rising to leave him] something must be resolved upon: but I will postpone this subject till to-morrow morning.

He would fain have engaged me longer; but I said I would see him as early as he pleased in the morning. He might think of any convenient place in London, or near it, meantime.

And so I retired from him. As I do from my pen; hoping for better rest for the few hours that remain of this night, than I have had of a long time.

Cl. Harlowe.

LETTER XXX.

Miss Clarissa Harlowe.

In Continuation.

Monday morning, April 17.

Late as I went to bed, I have had very little rest. Sleep and I have quarrelled; and although I court it, it will not be friends. I hope its fellow-irreconcileables at Harlowe Place enjoy its balmy comforts. Else, that will be an aggravation of my fault. My brother and sister, I dare say, want it not.

Mr. Lovelace, who is an early riser as well as I, joined me in the garden about six; and, after the usual salutations, asked me to resume our last night's subject. It was upon lodgings at London, he said.

I think you mentioned one to me, sir — Did you not?

Yes, madam, [but watching the turn of my countenance] rather as what you would be welcome to, than perhaps approve of.

I believe so too. To go to town upon an *uncertainty*, I own, is not agreeable: but to be obliged to any persons of your acquaintance, when I want to be thought independent of you; and to a person especially, to whom my friends are to direct to me, if they vouchsafe to take notice of me at all; is an absurd thing to mention.

He did not mention it as what he imagined I would accept, but only to confirm to me what he had said, that he himself knew of none fit for me.

Has not your family, madam, some one tradesman they deal with, who has conveniencies of this kind? I would make it worth such a person's while to keep the secret of your being at his house. Traders are dealers in pins, said he: and will be more obliged by a penny customer, than by a pound present, because it is in their way: — yet will refuse neither, any more than a lawyer or a man of office his fee.

My father's tradesmen, I said, would, no doubt, be the first employed to find me out. So that *that* proposal was as wrong as the other. And who is it that a creature so lately in favour with all her friends can apply to, in such a situation as mine, but must be, (at least) equally the friends of her relations.

We had a good deal of discourse upon the same topic. But, at last, the result was this — He wrote a letter to one Mr. Doleman, a married man, of fortune and character, (I excepting to Mr. Belford) desiring him to provide decent apartments ready furnished [*I had told him what they should be*] for a single woman; consisting of a bedchamber; another for a maid-servant; with the use of a dining-room or parlour. This letter he gave me to peruse; and then sealed it up, and dispatched it away in my presence, by one of his own servants, who having business in town, is to bring back an answer.

I attend the issue of it; holding myself in readiness to set out for London, unless you, my dear, advise the contrary.

LETTER XXXI.

Mr. Lovelace to John Belford, Esq.

Sat. Sunday, Monday.

He gives, in several letters, the substance of what is contained in the last seven of the lady's.
He tells his friend, that calling at the Lawn, in his way to M. Hall (for he owns that he went not to Windsor), he found the letters from Lady Betty Lawrence, and his cousin Montague, which Mrs. Greme was about sending to him by a special messenger.
He gives the particulars from Mrs. Greme's report, of what passed between the lady and her, as in p. 13, 14, and makes such declarations to Mrs. Greme of his honour and affection to the lady, as put her upon writing the letter to her sister Sorlings, the contents of which are given in p. 84, 85.
He then accounts, as follows, for the serious humour he found her in on his return:

Upon such good terms when we parted, I was surprised to find so solemn a brow upon my return, and her charming eyes red with weeping. But when I had understood she had received letters from Miss Howe, it was natural to imagine that that little devil had put her out of humour with me.

It is easy for me to perceive, that my charmer is more sullen when she receives, and has perused, a letter from that vixen, than at other times. But as the sweet maid shews, even then, more of *passive grief* than of *active spirit*, I hope she is rather lamenting than plotting. And, indeed, for what now should she plot? when I am become a reformed man, and am hourly improving in my morals? — Nevertheless, I must contrive some way or other to get at their correspondence — only to see the turn of it; that's all.

But no attempt of this kind must be made yet. A detected invasion in an article so sacred would ruin me beyond retrieve. Nevertheless, it vexes me to the heart to think that she is hourly writing her whole mind on all that passes between her and me, I under the same roof with her, yet kept at such awful distance, that I dare not break into a correspondence, that may perhaps be a means to defeat all my devices.

Would it be *very* wicked, Jack, to knock her messenger o' the head, as he is carrying my beloved's letters, or returning with Miss Howe's? — to attempt to bribe him, and not succeed, would utterly ruin me. And the man seems to be one *used to poverty*, one who can sit down satisfied with it, and enjoy it; contented with hand-to-mouth conveniences, and not aiming to live better to-morrow, than he does to-day, and than he did yesterday. Such a one is above temptation, unless it could come clothed in the guise of *truth* and *trust*. What likelihood of corrupting a man who has no hope, no ambition?

Yet the rascal has but *half* life, and groans under that. Should I be answerable in his case for a whole life?—But hang the fellow! let him live. Were I a king, or a minister of state, an Antonio Perez*, it were another thing. And yet, on second thoughts, am I not a *rake*, as it is called? and who ever knew a rake stick at any thing? But thou knowest, Jack, that the greatest half of my wickedness is vapour, to shew my invention; and to prove that I could be mischievous if I would.

When he comes to that part, where the lady says (p. 89) in a sarcastic way waving her hand, and bowing, "Excuse me, good Mr. Lovelace, that I am willing to think the best of my father," *he gives a description of her air and manner, greatly to her advantage; and says,*

I could hardly forbear taking her into my arms upon it, in spite of an expected *tempest*. So much wit, so much beauty, such a lively manner, and such exceeding quickness and penetration! O Belford! she must be nobody's but mine. I can now account for, and justify Herod's command to destroy Mariamne, if he returned not alive from his interview with Cæsar:' for were I to know, that it were but probable, that any other man were to have this charming creature, even after my death, the very thought would be enough to provoke me to cut that man's throat, were he a prince.

I may be deemed by this lady a rapid, a boisterous lover — and *she* may like me the less for it: but all the ladies I have met with till now, loved to raise a tempest, and to enjoy it: nor did they ever raise it, but I enjoyed it too! — Lord send us once happily to London.

Mr. Lovelace gives the following account of his rude rapture, when he seized her hand, and put her, by his WILD *manner, as she expresses it,* (p. 92) *into such terror.*

Darkness and light, I swore, were convertible at her pleasure: she could make any subject plausible. I was all error: she all perfection. And I snatched her hand; and, more than kissed it; I was ready to devour it. There was, I believe, a kind of phrensy in my manner, which threw her into a panic, like that of Semele perhaps, when the Thunderer, in all his majesty, surrounded with ten thousand celestial burning-glasses, was about to scorch her into a cinder.

* * *

HAD not my heart misgiven me, and had I not, just in time, recollected that she was not so much in my power, but that she might abandon me at her pleasure, having more friends in that house than I had, I should at that moment have made offers, that would have decided all, one way or other — But, apprehending that I had shewn too much meaning in my passion, I gave it another turn. — But little did the charmer think

---

* Antonio Perez was first minister of Philip II. king of Spain, by whose command he caused Don Juan de Escovedo to be assassinated; which brought on his own ruin, through the perfidy of his viler master. *Gedde's Tracts.*

what an escape either she or I had (as the event might have proved) from the sudden gust of passion, which had like to have blown me into her arms. She was born, I told her, to make me happy, and to save a soul. * * * *

He gives the rest of his vehement speech pretty nearly in the same words as the lady gives them. And then proceeds:

I saw she was frighted: and she would have had reason, had the scene been London: and that place in London, which I have in view to carry her to. She confirmed me in my apprehension, that I had alarmed her too much: she told me, that she saw what my boasted regard to her injunctions was; and she would take proper measures upon it, as I should soon find: that she was shocked at my violent airs; and if I hoped any favour from her, I must that instant withdraw, and leave her to her recollection.

She pronounced this in such a manner, as shewed she was set upon it; and having stepped out of the *gentle*, the *polite* part I had so newly engaged to act, I thought ready obedience was the best atonement. And indeed I was sensible, from her anger and repulses, that I wanted time myself for recollection. And so I withdrew, with the same veneration as a petitioning subject would withdraw from the presence of his sovereign. But, oh! Belford, had she had but the least patience with me — had she but made me think, that she would forgive this initiatory ardour — surely she will not be always thus guarded. —

I had not been a moment by myself, but I was sensible, that I had half forfeited my newly-assumed character. It is exceedingly difficult, thou seest, for an honest man to act in disguises: as the poet says, *thrust Nature back with a pitchfork, it will return.* I recollected, that what she had insisted upon was really a part of that declared will, before she left her father's house, to which in another case (to humble her) I had pretended to have an inviolable regard. And when I remembered her words, of *taking her measures accordingly*, I was resolved to sacrifice a leg or an arm to make all up again, before she had time to determine upon any new measures.

How seasonably to this purpose have come in my aunt's and cousin's letters.

* * *

I have sent in again and again to implore her to admit me to her presence. But she will conclude a letter she is writing to Miss Howe, before she will see me. — I suppose to give an account of what has just passed.

* * *

Curse upon her perverse tyranny! How she makes me wait for an humble audience, though she has done writing some time! a prince begging for her upon his knees should not prevail upon me to spare her, if I can but get her to London — Oons! Jack, I believe I have bit my lip through for vexation! — but one day *hers* shall smart for it.

Mr. Lovelace beginning a new date, gives an account of his admittance, and of the conversation that followed: which differing only in style from that the lady gives in the next letter, is omitted. He collects the lady's expressions, which his pride cannot bear: such as, that he is a stranger to the decorums that she thought inseparable from a man of birth and education; and that he is not the accomplished man he imagines himself to be; and threatens to remember them against her.

He values himself upon his proposals and speeches, which he gives to his friend pretty much to the same purpose that the lady does in her four last letters.

After mentioning his proposal to her that she would borrow a servant from Miss Howe, till Hannah could come, he writes as follows:

Thou seest, Belford, that my charmer has no notion, that Miss Howe herself is but a puppet danced upon my wires at second or third hand. To outwit, and impel, as I please, two *such girls* as these, who think they know every thing; and, by taking advantage of the pride and ill-nature of the old ones of both families, to play *them* off likewise at the very time they think they are doing me spiteful displeasure; what charming revenge! — then the sweet creature, when I wished that her *brother* was not at the bottom of Mrs. Howe's resentment, to tell me, that she was afraid he *was*, or her uncle would not have appeared against her to that lady! — pretty dear! how innocent!

But don't think me the *cause* neither of her family's malice and resentment. It is all in their hearts. I work but with their materials. They, if left to their own wicked direction, would perhaps express their revenge by fire and faggot; that is to say, by the private dagger, or by Lord Chief Justice's warrants, by law, and so forth: I only point the lightning, and teach it where to dart, without the thunder. In other words, I only guide the effects: the cause is in their malignant hearts: and while I am doing a little mischief, I prevent a great deal.

Thus he exults on her mentioning London.

I wanted her to propose London herself. This made me again mention Windsor. If you would have a woman do one thing, you must always propose another, and that the very contrary: the sex! the very sex! as I hope to be saved! — Why, Jack, they lay a man under the necessity to deal doubly with them! And, when they find themselves outwitted, they cry out upon an honest fellow, who has been too hard for them at their own weapons.

I could hardly contain myself. My heart was at my throat. — Down, down, said I to myself, exuberant exultation! A sudden cough befriended me; I again turned to her, all as *indifferenced over* as a girl at the first long-expected question, who waits for two more. I heard out the rest of her speech; and when she had done, instead of saying any thing to her of London, I advised her *to send for her Mrs. Norton.*

As I *knew* she would be afraid of lying under obligation, I could have proposed to do so much for the good woman and her son, as would have made her resolve that I should do nothing: this, however, not merely to avoid expense. But there was no such thing as allowing of the presence of Mrs. Norton. I might as well have had her mother or her aunt Hervey with her. Hannah, had she been able to come, and had she actually come, I could have done well enough with. What do I keep fellows idling in the country for, but to fall in love, and even to marry those whom I would have them to marry? Nor, upon second thoughts, would the presence of her Norton, or of her aunt, or even of her mother, have saved the dear creature, had I decreed her fall.

How unequal is a modest woman to the adventure, when she throws herself into the power of a rake! Punctilio will, at any time, stand for reason with such an one. She cannot break through a well-tested modesty. None but the impudent little rogues, who can name the parson and the church before you think of either, and undress and go to bed before you the next hour, should think of running away with a man.

* * *

I AM in the right train now. Every hour, I doubt not, will give me an increasing interest in the affections of this proud beauty. I have just carried *unpoliteness* far enough to *make her afraid of me;* and to shew her, that I am *no whiner.* Every instance of politeness, now, will give me double credit with her. My next point will be to make her acknowledge a *lambent* flame, a preference of me to all other men at least: and then my happy hour is not far off. An *acknowledged* reciprocality in love sanctifies every little freedom: and little freedoms beget greater. And if she call me *ungenerous,* I can call her *cruel.* The sex love to be called cruel. Many a time have I complained of cruelty, even in the act of yielding, because I knew it gratified the fair-one's pride.

Mentioning that he had only hinted at Mr. Belford's lodgings, as an instance to confirm what he had told her, that he knew of none in London fit for her, he says,

I had a mind to alarm her with something furthest from my purpose; for (as much as she disliked my motion,) I intended nothing by it: Mrs. Osgood is too pious a woman, and would have been more *her* friend than *mine.*

I had a view, moreover, to give her an high opinion of her own sagacity. I love, when I dig a pit, to have my prey tumble in with

Monday, April 17.

I HAVE just now received a fresh piece of intelligence from my agent, honest Joseph Leman. Thou knowest the history of poor Miss Betterton of Nottingham. James Harlowe is plotting to revive the resentments of her family against me. The Harlowes took great pains, some time ago, to endeavour to get to the bottom of that story. But now the foolish devils are resolved to do something in it, if they can. My head is working to make this booby squire a plotter, and a clever fellow, in order to turn his plots to my advantage, supposing his sister shall aim to keep me *at arm's length when in town, and to send me from her.* But I will, in proper time, let thee see Joseph's letter, and what I shall answer to it*. To know in time a designed mischief, is, with me, to disappoint it, and to turn it upon the contriver's head.

Joseph is plaguy squeamish again; but I know he only intends by his qualms to swell his merits with me. O Belford! Belford! what a vile corruptible rogue, whether in poor or in rich, is human nature!

* See Letters xliii, xliv. of this volume.

LETTER XXXII.

Miss Howe to Miss Clarissa Harlowe.

[In Answer to Letters xxiv—xxx. inclusive.]

Tuesday, April 18.

You have a most implacable family. Another visit from your uncle Antony has not only confirmed my mother an enemy to our correspondence, but has almost put her upon treading in their steps. —

But to other subjects:

You plead generously to Mr. Hickman. Perhaps, with regard to him, I may have done, as I have often done in singing — begun a note or key too high; and yet, rather than begin again, proceed, though I strain my voice, or spoil my tune. But this is evident, the man is the more observant for it; and you have taught me, that the spirit which is the humbler for ill usage, will be insolent upon better. So good and grave Mr. Hickman, keep your distance a little longer, I beseech you. You have erected an altar to me; and I hope you will not refuse to bow to it.

But you ask me, if I would treat Mr. Lovelace, were he to be in Mr. Hickman's place, as I do Mr. Hickman? Why, really, my dear, I believe I should not. — I have been very sagely considering this point of behaviour (in general) on both sides in courtship; and I will very candidly tell you the result. I have concluded that politeness, even to excess, is necessary, on the men's part, to bring us to listen to their first addresses, in order to induce us to bow our necks to a yoke so unequal. But, upon my conscience, I very much doubt whether a little intermingled insolence is not requisite from them, to keep up that interest, when once it has got footing. Men must not let us see, that we can make fools of them. And I think that *smooth* love, that is to say, a passion without rubs; in other words, a passion without passion; is like a sleepy stream that is hardly seen to give motion to a straw. So that, sometimes to make us fear, and even, for a short space, to *hate* the wretch, is productive of the *contrary* extreme.

If this be so, Lovelace, than whom no man was ever more polite and obsequious at the *beginning*, has hit the very point. For his turbulence *since*, his readiness to offend, and his equal readiness to humble himself (as he is known to be a man of sense, and of courage too,) must keep a woman's passion alive; and at last tire her into a non-resistance that shall make her as passive as a tyrant-husband would wish her to be.

I verily think that the different behaviour of our two heroes to their heroines makes out this doctrine to demonstration. I am so much accustomed, for my own part, to Hickman's whining, creeping, submissive courtship, that I now expect nothing but whine and cringe from him: and am so little moved with his nonsense, that I am frequently forced to go to my harpsichord, to keep me awake, and to silence his humdrum.

Whereas Lovelace keeps up the ball with a witness, and all his address and conversation is one continual game at racket.

Your frequent quarrels and reconciliations verify this observation: and I really believe, that, could Hickman have kept my attention alive after the Lovelace manner, only that he had preserved his morals, I should have married the man by this time. But then he must have *set out* accordingly. For now he can never, never recover himself, that's certain; but must be a dangler to the end of the courtship-chapter; and, what is still worse for him, a passive to the end of his life.

Poor Hickman! perhaps you'll say.

I have been called your echo — poor Hickman! said I.

You wonder, my dear, that Mr. Lovelace shewed you not over-night the letters of Lady Betty and his cousin. I don't like his keeping such a material and *relative* circumstance, as I may call it, one moment from you. By his communicating the contents of them to you next day, when you were angry with him, it looks as if he withheld them for *occasional pacifiers;* and if so, must he not have had a forethought that he might give you *cause* for anger? Of all the circumstances that have happened since you have been with him, I think I like this the least: this alone, my dear, small as it might look to an *indifferent* eye, in *mine* warrants all your caution. Yet I think, that Mrs.

Greme's letter to her sister Sorlings; his repeated motions for Hannah's attendance; and for that of one of the widow Sorlings's daughters; and, above all, for that of Mrs. Norton, are agreeable counterbalances. Were it not for these circumstances, I should have said a great deal more of the other. Yet what a foolish fellow to let you know over-night that he *had* such letters! — I can't tell what to make of him.

I am pleased with the contents of these ladies' letters; and the more, as I have caused the family to be again sounded, and find that they are all as desirous as ever of your alliance.

They really are (every one of them) your very great admirers: and, as for Lord M. he is so much pleased with you, and with the confidence, as he calls it, which you have reposed in his nephew, that he vows he will disinherit him, if he reward it not as he ought. You must take care, that you lose not both families.

I hear Mrs. Norton is enjoined, as she values the favour of the *other* family, not to correspond either with you or with me — Poor creatures! — But they are your — yet they are not your *relations*, neither, I believe. Had you had any other nurse, I should have concluded you had been changed. I suffer by their low malice — excuse me therefore.

You really hold this man to his good behaviour with more spirit than I thought you mistress of; especially when I judged of you by that meekness which you always contended for, as the proper distinction of the female character; and by the love, which (think as you please) you certainly have for him. You may rather be proud of, than angry at the imputation; since you are the only woman I ever knew, read, or heard of, whose love was so much governed by her prudence. But when once the indifference of the husband takes place of the ardour of the lover, it will be *your* turn: and, if I am not mistaken, this man, who is the only self-admirer I ever knew who was not a coxcomb, will rather, in his day, expect homage than pay it.

Your handsome husbands, my dear, make a wife's heart ache very often: and though you are as fine a person of a woman, at the least, as he is of a man, he will take too much delight in *himself* to think himself more indebted to your favour, than you are to his distinction and preference of you. But no man, take your finer mind, with your very fine person, can deserve you. So you must be contented, should your merit be under-rated; since that *must* be so, marry whom you will. Perhaps you will think I indulge these sort of reflections against your Narcissus's of men, to keep my mother's choice for me of Hickman in countenance with myself—I don't know but there is something in it; at least, enough to have given birth to the reflection.

I think there can be no objection to your going to London.

There, as in the centre, you will be in the way of hearing from every body, and sending to any body. And then you will put all his sincerity to the test, *as to his promised absence*, and such like.

But indeed, my dear, I think you have nothing for it but marriage. You may try (that you may say you *have* tried) what your relations can be brought to: but the moment they refuse your proposals, submit to the yoke, and make the best of it. He will be a savage indeed, if he makes you speak out. Yet, it is my opinion, that you *must* bend a little, for he cannot bear to be thought slightly of.

This was one of his speeches once: I believe designed for me. — "A woman who means one day to favour her lover with her hand, should shew the world for her *own* sake, that she distinguishes him from the common herd."

Shall I give you another fine sentence of his, and in the true libertine style, as he spoke it, throwing out his challenging hand? — "D—n him, if he would marry the first princess on earth, if he but thought she balanced a minute in her choice of *him*, or of an *emperor*."

All the world, in short, expect you to have this man. They think, that you left your father's house for this very purpose. The longer the ceremony is delayed, the worse appearance it will have in the world's eye: and it will not be the fault of some of your relations, if a slur be not thrown upon your reputation, while you continue unmarried. Your uncle Antony, in particular, speaks rough and vile things, grounded upon the morals of his *brother Orson*. But hitherto your admirable character has antidoted the poison; the detractor is despised, and every one's indignation raised against him.

I have written through many interruptions: and you will see the first sheet creased and rumpled, occasioned by putting it into my bosom on my mother's sudden coming upon me. We have had one very pretty debate, I will assure you; but it is not worth while to trouble you with the particulars. — But upon my word — no matter though. —

Your Hannah cannot attend you. The poor girl left her place about a fortnight ago, on account of a rheumatic disorder, which has confined her to her room ever since. She burst into tears, when Kitty carried to her your desire of having her with you; and called herself doubly unhappy, that she could not wait upon a mistress whom she so dearly loved.

Had my mother answered my wishes, I should have been sorry Mr. Lovelace had been the *first* proposer of my Kitty for your attendant, till Hannah should come. To be altogether among strangers, and a stranger to attend you every time you remove, is a very disagreeable thing. But your considerateness and bounty will make you faithful ones wherever you go.

You must take your own way: but, if you suffer any inconvenience, either as to clothes or money, that it is in my power to remedy, I will never forgive you. My mother (if *that* be your objection) need not know any thing of the matter.

We have all our defects: we have often regretted the particular fault, which, though in venerable characters, we must have been blind not to see.

I remember what you once said to me; and the caution was good: Let us, my Nancy, were your words; let us, who have not the same failings as those we censure, guard against *other* and *greater* in ourselves. Nevertheless, I must needs tell you, that my mother has vexed me a little very lately, by some instances of her jealous narrowness. I will mention one of them, though I did not intend it. She wanted to borrow thirty guineas of me: *only* while she got a note changed. I said I could lend her but eight or ten. Eight or ten would not do: she thought I was much richer. I could have told her, I was much cunninger than to let her know my stock; which on a review, I find ninety-five guineas; and all of them most heartily at your service.

I believe your uncle Tony put her upon this wise project; for she was *out of cash* in an hour after he left her. If he did, you will judge that they intend to distress you. If it will provoke *you* to demand your own in a legal way, I wish they would; since their putting you upon that course will justify the necessity of your leaving them. And as it is not for your credit to own, that you were tricked away contrary to your intention, this would afford a reason for your going off that I should make very good use of. You'll see, that I approve of Lovelace's advice upon this subject. I am not willing to allow the weight to your answer to him on that head, which perhaps *ought* to be allowed it.*

You must be the less surprised at the inventions of this man, because of his uncommon talents. Whatever he had turned his head to, he would have excelled in: or been (or done things) extraordinary. He is said to be revengeful, a very bad quality! I believe indeed, he is a devil in every thing but his foot — This, therefore, is my repeated advice — provoke him not too much against yourself; but unchain him; and let him loose upon your sister's vile Betty, and your brother's Joseph Leman. This is resenting *low:* but I know to whom I write, or else I would go a good deal *higher*, I'll assure you.

Your next, I suppose, will be from London. Pray direct it, and your future letters, till further notice, to Mr. Hickman, at his own house. He is entirely devoted to you. Don't take so heavily my mother's partiality and prejudices. I hope I am past a baby.

Heaven preserve you, and make you as happy as I think you deserve to be, prays

Your ever affectionate
ANNA HOWE.

* See p. 96.

LETTER XXXIII.

Miss Clarissa Harlowe to Miss Howe.

Wedn. morn. April 19.

I am glad, my dear friend, that you approve of my removal to London.

The disagreement between your mother and you gives me inexpressible affliction. I hope I think you both more unhappy than you are. But I beseech you let me know the particulars of the debate you call *a very pretty* one. I am well acquainted with your dialect. When I am informed of the whole, let your mother have been ever so severe upon me, I shall be easier a great deal. — Faulty people should rather deplore the occasion they have given for anger than resent it.

If I am to be obliged to any body in England for money, it shall be to you. Your mother need not know of your kindness to me, you say — but she *must* know it, if it be done, and if she challenge my beloved friend upon it; for would you either falsify or prevaricate? — I wish your mother could be made easy on this head. — Forgive me, my dear. — But I know — yet once she had a better opinion of me. — O my inconsiderate rashness! — Excuse me once more, I pray you. — Pride, when it is *native*, will shew itself sometimes in the midst of mortifications — but my spirit is down already.

* * *

I am unhappy that I cannot have my worthy Hannah. I am as sorry for the poor creature's illness as for my own disappointment by it. Come, my dear Miss Howe, since you press me to be beholden to you; and would think me proud if I absolutely refused your favour; pray be so good as to send her two guineas in my name.

If I have nothing for it, as you say, but matrimony, it yields a little comfort, that his relations do not despise the *fugitive*, as persons of their rank and quality-pride might be supposed to do, for having *been* a fugitive.

But O my cruel, thrice cruel uncle! to suppose — but my heart checks my pen, and will not let it proceed, on an intimation so extremely shocking as that which he supposes! — Yet if thus they have been persuaded, no wonder if they are irreconcileable.

This is all my hard-hearted brother's doings! — his surmisings! — God forgive him — prays his injured sister!

LETTER XXXIV.

Miss Clarissa Harlowe to Miss Howe.

Thursday, April 20.

Mr. Lovelace's servant is already returned with an answer from his friend Mr. Doleman, who has taken pains in his inquiries, and is very particular. Mr. Lovelace brought me the letter as soon as he had read it: and as he now knows that I acquaint you with every thing that offers, I desired him to let me send it to you for your perusal. Be pleased to return it by the first opportunity.

You will see by it, that his friends in town have a notion that we are actually married.

TO ROBERT LOVELACE, ESQ.

DEAR SIR, Tuesday night, April 18.

I AM extremely rejoiced to hear, that we shall so soon have you in town, after so long an absence. You will be the more welcome still, if what report says, be true; which is, that you are *actually married* to the fair lady upon whom we have heard you make such encomiums. Mrs. Doleman, and my sister, both wish you joy if you are; and joy upon your near prospect if you are not.

I have been in town for this week past, to get help, if I could, from my paralytic complaints; and am in a course for them. Which, nevertheless, did not prevent me from making the desired inquiries. This is the result.

You may have a first floor, well furnished, at a mercer's in Bedford Street, Covent Garden, with conveniencies for servants: and these either by the quarter or month. The terms according to the conveniences required.

Mrs. Doleman has seen lodgings in Norfolk Street and others in Cecil Street; but though the prospects to the Thames and Surry hills look inviting from both these streets, yet I suppose they are too near the city.

The owner of those in Norfolk Street would have half the house go together. It would be too much for your description therefore: and I suppose, that when you think fit to *declare your marriage*, you will hardly be in lodgings.

Those in Cecil Street, are neat and convenient. The owner is a widow of good character; but she insists that you take them for a twelvemonth certain.

You may have good accommodations in Dover Street, at a widow's, the relict of an officer in the guards, who dying soon after he had purchased his commission (to which he had a good title by service, and which cost him most part of what he had) she *was obliged to let lodgings.*

This may possibly be an objection. But she is very careful, she says, that she takes no lodgers, but of *figure* and *reputation*. She rents two good houses, distant from each other, only joined by a *large handsome passage*. The *inner-house* is the genteelest, and very elegantly furnished; but you may have the use of a very handsome parlour in the *outer-house*, if you choose to look into the street.

A little garden belongs to the inner-house, in which the old gentlewoman has displayed a true female fancy! having crammed it with vases, flower-pots, and figures, without number.

As these lodgings seemed to me the most likely to please you, I was more particular in my inquiries about them. The apartments she has to let are in the inner-house: they are a dining-room, two neat parlours, a withdrawing-room, two or three handsome bedchambers; one with a pretty light closet in it which looks into the little garden, all furnished in taste.

A *dignified clergyman*, his *wife*, and *maiden-daughter*, were the last who lived in them. They have but lately quitted them, on his being presented to a considerable church preferment in Ireland. The gentlewoman says that he took the lodgings but for *three months* certain; but liked them and *her usage* so well, that he continued in them *two years;* and left them with regret, though on so good an account. She bragged, that this was the way of all the lodgers she ever had, who staid with her *four times as long as they at first intended.*

I had some knowledge of the Colonel, who was always looked upon as a man of honour. His relict I never saw before. I think she has a *masculine air*, and is a *little forbidding at first*: but when I saw her behaviour to two agreeable *maiden gentlewomen*, her husband's nieces, whom, for *that* reason, she calls *doubly* hers, and heard their praises of *her*, I could impute her very bulk to good-humour; since we seldom see your sour peevish people plump. She lives *reputably*, and is, as I find, *aforehand* in the world.

If these, or any other of the lodgings I have mentioned, be not altogether to your lady's mind, she may continue in them *the less while*, and *choose others for herself.*

The widow consents that you shall take them for a *month only*, and *what* of them you please. The terms, she says, she will not fall out upon, when she knows what your lady expects, and what *her* servants are to do, or *yours* will undertake; for she observed that servants are generally worse to deal with than their masters or mistresses.

The lady may board or not, as she pleases.

As we *suppose you married*, but that you have reason, from family differences, to keep it private for the present, I thought it not amiss to hint as much to the widow (but as *uncertainty*, however); and asked her, if she could, in that case, accommodate you and your servants, as well as the lady and hers? She said, she could; and wished, by all means, it were to be so; since the circumstance of a person's *being single*, if not as well recommended as this lady, was *one of her usual exceptions.*

If none of these lodgings please, you need not doubt very handsome ones in or near Hanover Square, Soho Square, Golden Square, or in some of the new streets about Grosvenor Square. And Mrs. Doleman, her sister, and myself, most cordially join to offer to your good lady the best accommodations we can make for her at Uxbridge (and also for you, if you are the happy man we wish you to be) till she fits herself more to her mind.

Let me add, that the lodgings at the mercer's, those in Cecil Street, those at the widow's in Dover Street, any of them, may be entered upon at a day's warning. I am, my dear sir,

Your sincere and affectionate friend and servant,
Tno. DOLEMAN.

You will easily guess, my dear, when you have read the letter, *which* lodgings I made choice of. But first, to try him, (as in so material a point I thought I could not be too circumspect) I seemed to prefer those in Norfolk Street, for the very reason the writer gives why he thought I would *not;* that is to say, for its neighbourhood to a city so well governed as London is said to be. Nor should I have disliked a lodging in the heart of it, having heard but indifferent accounts of the liberties sometimes taken at the other end of the town. — Then seeming to incline to the lodgings in Cecil Street — then to the mercer's. But he made no visible preference: and when I asked his opinion of the widow gentlewoman's, he said, he thought those the most to my taste and convenience: but as he hoped that I would think lodgings necessary but for a very little while, he knew not which to give his vote for.

I then fixed upon the widow's; and he has written accordingly to Mr. Doleman, making my compliments to his lady and sister, for their kind offer.

I am to have the dining-room, the bed-chamber with the light closet, (of which, if I stay any time at the widow's, I shall make great use) and a servant's room; and we propose to set out on Saturday morning. As for a maid-servant, poor Hannah's illness is a great disappointment to me: but, as he observes, I can make the widow satisfaction for one of hers, till I can get a servant to my mind. And you know, I want not much attendance.

* * *

MR. Lovelace has just now, of his own accord, given me five guineas for poor Hannah. I send them inclosed. Be so good as to cause them to be conveyed to her; and to let her know from whom they came.

He has obliged me much by this little mark of his considerateness. Indeed I have had the better opinion of him ever since he proposed her return to me.

* * *

I HAVE just now *another* instance of his considerateness. He came to me, and said, that, on second thoughts, he could not bear that I should go up to town without some attendant, were it but for the look of the thing, to the London widow and her nieces, who, according to his friend's account, *lived so genteelly; and especially as I required him to leave me soon after I arrived there*, and so would be left alone among strangers. He therefore thought, that I might engage Mrs. Sorlings to lend me one of her two maids, or let one of her daughters go up with me, and stay till I were provided. And if the latter, the young gentlewoman, no doubt, would be glad of so good an opportunity to see the curiosities of the town, and would be a proper attendant on the same occasions.

I told him, as I had done before, that the two young gentlewomen were so equally useful in their way, and servants in a busy farm were so little to be spared, that I should be loth to take them off their laudable employments. Nor should I think much of diversions for one while; and so the less want an attendant out of doors.

And now, my dear, lest any thing should happen, in so variable a situation as mine, to over-cloud my prospects, (which at present are more promising than ever yet they have been since I quitted Harlowe Place,) I will snatch the opportunity to subscribe myself

Your not unhoping, and ever-obliged friend and servant,
CL. HARLOWE.

LETTER XXXV.
Mr. Lovelace to John Belford, Esq.

Thursday, April 20.

He begins with communicating to him the letter he wrote to Mr. Doleman, to procure suitable lodgings in town, and which he sent away by the lady's approbation: and then gives him a copy of the answer to it (See p. 116.): upon which he thus expresses himself:

Thou knowest the widow; thou knowest her nieces; thou knowest the lodgings; and didst thou ever read a letter more artfully couched, than this of Tom Doleman? Every possible objection anticipated! Every accident provided against! Every tittle of it plot proof!

Who could forbear smiling, to see my charmer, like a farcical dean and chapter, choose what was before chosen for her; and sagaciously (as *they* go in form to prayers, that Heaven would direct their choice) pondering upon the different proposals, as if she would make me believe, she had a mind for *some other?* The dear sly rogue looking upon me, too, with a view to discover some emotion in me. Emotions I had; but I can tell her, that they lay deeper than her eye could reach, though it had been a sunbeam.

No confidence in me, fair one! None at all, 'tis plain. Thou wilt not, if I were inclined to change my views, encourage me by a generous reliance on my honour! — And shall it be said, that I, a master of arts in love, shall be over-matched by so unpractised a novice?

But to see the charmer so far satisfied with my contrivance, as to borrow my friend's letter, in order to satisfy Miss Howe likewise! —

Silly little rogues! to walk out into by-paths on the strength of their own judgment! — When nothing but *experience* can enable them to disappoint us, and teach them grandmother wisdom! When they *have* it indeed, then may they sit down, like so many Cassandras, and preach caution to others; who will as little mind *them*, as they did *their* instructresses, whenever a fine handsome confident young fellow, such a one as thou knowest who, comes across them.

But, Belford, didst thou not mind that sly rogue Doleman's naming *Dover Street* for the widow's place of abode? — What dost think could be meant by that? — 'Tis impossible thou shouldst guess. So, not to puzzle thee about it, suppose the *widow Sinclair's in Dover Street* should be inquired after by some officious person, in order to come at characters [Miss Howe is as *sly* as the devil, and as busy to the full]; and neither such a name, nor such a house, can be found in that street, nor a house to answer the description; then will not the keenest hunter in England be at a fault?

But how wilt thou do, methinks thou askest, to hinder the lady from resenting the fallacy, and mistrusting thee the more on that account, when she finds it out to be in another street?

Pho! never mind that: either I shall have a way for it; or we shall thoroughly understand one another by that time; or, if we don't, she'll know enough of me, not to wonder at *such* a peccadillo.

But how wilt thou hinder the lady from apprizing her friend of the real name?

She must first know it herself, monkey, must she not?

Well, but how wilt thou do to hinder her from knowing the street, and her friend from directing letters thither; which will be the same thing as if the name were known?

Let me alone for that too.

If thou further objectest, that Tom Doleman is too great a dunce to write such a letter in answer to mine; — Canst thou not imagine, that, in order to save honest Tom all this trouble, I who know the town so well, could send him a copy of what he should write, and leave him nothing to do but transcribe?

What now sayest thou to *me*, Belford?

And suppose I had designed this task of inquiry for thee; and suppose the lady excepted against thee for no other reason in the world, but because of my value for thee? What sayest thou to the *lady*, Jack?

This it is to have leisure upon my hands! — What a matchless plotter thy friend! — Stand by, and let me swell! — I am already as big as an elephant; and ten times wiser! — Mightier too by far! Have I not reason to snuff the moon with my proboscis? — Lord help thee for a poor, for a very poor creature! — Wonder not, that I despise thee heartily; since the man who is disposed immoderately to exalt himself, cannot do it but by despising every body else in proportion.

I shall make good use of the *Dolemanic* hint of *being married*. But I will not tell thee all at once. Nor, indeed, have I thoroughly digested that part of my plot. When a general must regulate his motions by those of a watchful adversary, how can he say beforehand what he will, or what he will not do?

Widow SINCLAIR, didst thou not say, Lovelace?

Ay, Sinclair, Jack! — Remember the name! Sinclair, I repeat. She *has* no other. And her features being broad, and full-blown, I will suppose her to be of Highland extraction; as her husband the colonel [mind that too] was a Scot, as brave as honest.

I never forget the *minutiæ* in my contrivances. In all matters that admit of doubt, the *minutiæ* closely attended to, and provided for, are of more service than a thousand oaths, vows, and protestations made to supply the neglect of them, especially when jealousy has made its way in the working mind.

Thou wouldst wonder if thou knewest one half of my *providences*. To give thee but one — I have already been so good as to send up a list of books to be procured for the lady's closet, mostly at *second hand*. And thou knowest, that the women there are all well read. But I will not anticipate — besides, it looks as if I were afraid of leaving any thing to my old friend Chance: which has many a time been an excellent second to me; and ought not to be affronted or despised; especially by one who has the art of making unpromising incidents turn out in his favour.

LETTER XXXVI.
Miss Howe to Miss Clarissa Harlowe.

Wednesday, April 19.

I have a piece of intelligence to give you, which concerns you much to know. Your brother having been assured that you are not married, has taken a resolution to find you out, waylay you, and carry you off. A friend of his, a captain of a ship, undertakes to get you on ship-board; and to sail away with you, either to Hull or Leith, in the way to one of your brother's houses.

They are very wicked; for in spite of your virtue they conclude you to be *ruined*. But if they can be assured when they have you, that you are not, they will secure you till they can bring you out Mrs. Solmes. Meantime, in order to give Mr. Lovelace full employment, they talk of a prosecution which will be set up against him, for some crime they have got a notion of, which they think, if it do not cost him his life, will make him fly his country.

This is very early news. Miss Bell told it in confidence, and with mighty triumph over Lovelace, to Miss Lloyd: who is at present her favourite; though as much your admirer as ever. Miss Lloyd, being very apprehensive of the mischief which might follow such an attempt, told it to me, with leave to apprize you privately of it — and yet neither she nor I would be sorry perhaps, if Lovelace were to be fairly hanged — that is to say, if *you*, my dear, had no objection to it. But we cannot bear that such an admirable creature should be made the tennis-ball of two violent spirits — much less, that you should be seized, and exposed to the brutal treatment of wretches who have no bowels.

If you can engage Mr. Lovelace to keep his temper upon it, I think you should acquaint him with it, but not to mention Miss Lloyd. Perhaps his wicked agent may come at the intelligence, and reveal it to him. But I leave it to your own discretion to do as you think fit in it. All my concern is, that this daring and foolish project, if carried on, will be a means of throwing you more into his power than ever. But as it will convince you, that there can be no hope of a reconciliation, I wish you were actually married, let the cause for the prosecution hinted at be what it will, short of murder or a rape.

Your Hannah was very thankful for your kind present. She heaped a thousand blessings upon you for it. She has Mr. Lovelace's too by this time.

I am pleased with Mr. Hickman, I can tell you: — for he has sent her two guineas by the person who carries Mr. Lovelace's five, as from an unknown hand: nor am I, or you, to know it. But he does a great many things of this sort; and is as silent as the night in his charities; for nobody knows of them, till the gratitude of the benefited will not let them be concealed. He is now and then my almoner, and I believe always adds to my little benefactions.

But his time is not come to be praised to his face for these things; nor does he seem to want that encouragement.

The man has certainly a good mind. Nor can we expect in one man every good quality. But he is really a silly fellow, my dear, to trouble his head about me, when he sees how much I despise his whole sex; and must of course make a common man look like a fool, were he not to make *himself* look like one, by wishing to pitch his tent so oddly. Our likings and dislikings, as I have often thought, are seldom governed by prudence, or with a view to happiness. The eye, my dear, the wicked eye — has such a strict alliance with the heart — and both have such enmity to the judgment! — What an unequal union, the mind and body! All the senses, like the family at Harlowe Place, in a confederacy against that which would animate, and give honour to the whole, were it allowed its proper precedence.

Permit me, I beseech you, before you go to London, to send you forty-eight guineas. I mention that sum to oblige you, because, by accepting back the two to Hannah, I will hold you indebted to me fifty. — Surely *this* will induce you! You know that I cannot want the money. I told you, that I have near double that sum; and that the half of it is more than my mother knows I am mistress of. You are afraid, that my mother will question me on this subject; and then you think I must own the truth — but little as I love equivocation, and little as you would allow of it in your Anna Howe, it is hard, if I cannot (were I to be put to it ever so closely) find something to say, that would bring me off, and not impeach my veracity. With so little money as you have, what can you do at such a place as London? — You don't know what occasion you may have for messengers, intelligence, and such-like. If you don't oblige me, I shall not think your spirit so much down as you say it is, and as, in this one particular, I think it ought to be.

As to the state of things between my mother and me, you know enough of her temper, not to need to be told, that she never espouses or resents with indifference. Yet will she not remember, that I am *her* daughter. No, truly, I am all my *papa's girl*.

She was very sensible, surely, of the violence of my poor father's temper, that she can so long remember *that*, when acts of tenderness and affection seem quite forgotten. Some daughters would be tempted to think, that control sat very heavy upon a mother who can endeavour to exert the power she has over a child, and regret, for years after death, that she had not the same over a husband.

If this manner of expression becomes not me, of my mother, the fault will be somewhat extenuated by the love I always bore to my father, and by the reverence I shall ever pay to his memory: for he was a fond father, and perhaps would have been as tender a husband, had not my mother and he been too much of a temper to agree.

The misfortune was, in short, that, when *one* was out of humour, the *other* would be so too: yet neither of their tempers *comparatively* bad. Notwithstanding all which, I did not imagine, girl as I was in my father's lifetime, that my mother's part of the yoke sat so heavy upon her neck as she gives me room to think it did whenever she is pleased to disclaim *her* part of me.

Both parents, as I have often thought, should be very careful, if they would secure to themselves the undivided love of their children, that, of all things, they should avoid such *durable* contentions with each other, as should distress their children in choosing their party, when they would be glad to reverence *both* as they ought.

But here is the thing: there is not a better manager of her affairs in the sex, than my mother; and I believe a *notable* wife is more impatient of control, than an *indolent* one. An indolent one, perhaps, thinks she has something to *compound* for; while women of the other character, I suppose, know too well their own significance to think highly of that of any body else. All must be their own way. In one word, because they are *useful*, they will be *more* than useful.

I do assure you, my dear, were I a man, and a man who loved my quiet, I would not have one of these managing wives on any consideration. I would make it a matter of serious inquiry beforehand, whether my mistress's qualifications, if I heard she was notable, were *masculine* or *feminine* ones. If indeed I were an indolent supine mortal, who might be in danger of becoming the property of my steward, I would then perhaps choose to marry for the qualifications of a steward.

But, setting my mother out of the question, because she *is* my mother, have I not seen how Lady Hartley pranks up herself above all her sex, because she knows how to manage affairs that do not *belong* to her sex to manage? — Affairs that do no credit to her as a woman to understand; *practically* I mean; for the *theory* of them may not be amiss to be known.

Indeed, my dear, I do not think a *man-woman* a pretty character at all: and, as I said, were I a man, I would sooner choose a dove, though it were fit for nothing, but as the play says, to go tame about house, and breed, than a wife that is setting at work (my insignificant self *present* perhaps) every busy hour my never-resting servants, those of the stud not excepted; and who, with a besom in her hand, as I may say, would be continually filling me with apprehensions, that she wanted to sweep me out of my own house as useless lumber.

Were indeed the mistress of a family (like the wonderful young lady I so *much* and so *justly* admire) to know how to confine herself within her own respectable rounds of the needle, the pen, the housekeeper's bills, the dairy for her amusement; to see the poor fed from superfluities that would otherwise be wasted; and exert herself in all the really useful branches of domestic management; then would she move in her proper sphere; then would she render herself *amiably* useful, and *respectably* necessary; then would she become the *mistress*-wheel of the family [whatever you think of your Anna Howe, I would not have her be the *master*-wheel]; and every body would love her; as every body did you, before your insolent brother came back, flushed with his unmerited acquirements, and turned all things topsy-turvy.

If you *will* be informed of the particulars of our contention, after you have known in general, that *your* unhappy affair was the subject; why then, I think I must tell you.

Yet how shall I? — I feel my cheek glow with mingled shame and indignation — know then, my dear, — that I have been — as I may say — that I have been *beaten* — indeed 'tis true. My mother thought fit to slap my hands to get from me a sheet of a letter she caught me writing to you; which I tore, because she should not read it, and burnt it before her face.

I know this will trouble you: so spare yourself the pains to tell me it does.

Mr. Hickman came in presently after. I would not see him. I am either too much a woman to be beat, or too much a child to have an humble servant. — So I told my mother. What can one oppose but sullens, when it would be unpardonable so much as to *think* of lifting up a finger?

In the Harlowe-style, she *will* be obeyed, she says: and even Mr. Hickman shall be forbid the house, if he contributes to the carrying on of a correspondence which she will not suffer to be continued.

Poor man! He stands a whimsical chance between us. But he knows he is *sure* of my mother; but not of me. 'Tis easy then for him to choose his party, were it not his inclination to serve you, as it surely *is*. And this makes him a merit with me, which otherwise he would not have had; notwithstanding the good qualities which I have just now acknowledged in his favour. For, my dear, let my faults in other respects be what they may, I will pretend to say, that I have in my own mind those qualities which I praised him for. And if we are to come together, I could for that reason better dispense with them in him. — So if a husband, who has a bountiful-tempered wife, is not a niggard, nor seeks to restrain her, but has an opinion of all she does, that is enough for him: as, on the contrary, if a bountiful-tempered husband has a frugal wife, it is best for both. For one to give, and the other to give, except they have prudence, and are at so good an understanding with each other, as to compare notes, they may perhaps put it out of their power to be *just*.

Good frugal doctrine, my dear! But this way of putting it, is middling the matter between what I have learnt of my mother's *over*-prudent and your *enlarged* notions. — But from doctrine to fact —

I shut myself up all that day; and what little I did eat, eat alone. But at night she sent up Kitty, with a command, upon my obedience, to attend her at supper.

I went down: but most gloriously in the sullens. YES, and NO, were great words with me, to every thing she asked, for a good while.

That behaviour, she told me, should not do for her.

Beating should not with me, I said.

My bold resistance, she told me, had provoked her to slap my hand: and she was sorry to have been so provoked. But again insisted, that I would either give up my correspondence absolutely, or let her see all that passed in it.

I must not do either, I told her. It was unsuitable both to my inclination and to my honour, at the instigation of base minds, to give up a friend in distress.

She rung all the maternal changes upon the words duty, obedience, filial obligation, and so forth.

I told her, that a duty too rigorously and unreasonably exacted had been your ruin, if you *were* ruined.

If I were of age to be married, I hope she would think me capable of *making*, or at least of *keeping*, my own friendships, such a one especially as this, with a *woman* too, and one whose friendship she herself, till this distressful point of time, had thought the most useful and edifying that I had ever contracted.

The greater the merit, the worse the action: the finer the talents, the more dangerous the example.

There were other duties, I said, besides the filial one; and I hoped I need not give up a suffering friend, especially at the instigation of those by whom she suffered. I told her that it was very hard to annex such a condition as that to my duty; when I was persuaded, that both duties might be performed, without derogating from either: that an unreasonable command (she must excuse me; I must say it, though I were slapped again) was a degree of tyranny: and I could not have eccepted, that at these years I should be allowed no will, no choice of my own! where a woman only was concerned, and the devilish sex not in the question.

What turned most in favour of her argument was, that I desired to be excused from letting her read all that passes between us. She insisted much upon this: and since, she said, you were in the hands of the most intriguing man in the world; and a man, who had made a jest of her favourite Hickman, as she has been told; she knows not what consequences, unthought-of by you or me, may flow from such a correspondence.

So you see, my dear, that I fare the worse on Mr. Hickman's account! My mother *might* see all that passes between us, did I not know, that it would cramp your spirit, and restrain the freedom of your pen, as it would also the freedom of mine: and were she not moreover so firmly attached to the contrary side, that inferences, consequences, strained deductions, censures, and constructions the most partial, would for ever be hauled in to tease me, and would perpetually subject us to the necessity of debating and canvassing.

Besides, I don't choose that she should know how much this artful wretch has outwitted, as I may call it, a person so much his superior in all the nobler qualities of the human mind.

The generosity of your heart, and the greatness of your soul, full well I know; but do not offer to dissuade me from this correspondence.

Mr. Hickman, immediately on the contention above, offered his service; and I accepted of it, as you will see by my last. He thinks, though he has all honour for my mother, that she is unkind to us both. He was pleased to tell me (with an air, as I thought) that he not only *approved* of our correspondence, but admired the steadiness of my friendship; and having no opinion of your *man*, but a great one of *me*, thinks that my advice or intelligence from time to time may be of use to you; and on this presumption said, that it would be a thousand pities that you should suffer for want of either.

Mr. Hickman pleased me in the main of his speech; and it is well the general tenor of it was agreeable; otherwise I can tell him, I should have reckoned with him for his word *approve;* for it is a style I have not yet permitted him to talk to me in. And you see, my dear, what these men are — no sooner do they find that you have favoured them with the power of doing you an agreeable service, but they take upon them to *approve*, forsooth, of your actions! By which is implied a right to *disapprove*, if they think fit.

I have told my mother how much you wish to be reconciled to your relations, and how independent you are upon Lovelace.

Mark the end of the latter assertion, she says. And as to reconciliation, she knows that nothing will do (and will have it, that nothing *ought* to do) but your returning back, without presuming to condition with them. And this if you do, she says, will best shew your independence on Lovelace.

You see, my dear, what your duty is, in my mother's opinion.

I suppose your next directed to Mr. Hickman, at his own house, will be from London.

Heaven preserve you in honour and safety, is my prayer.

What you do for change of clothes, I cannot imagine.

It is amazing to me what your relations can mean by distressing you as they seem resolved to do.

I see they will throw you into his arms, whether you will or not.

I send this by Robert, for dispatch sake; and can only repeat the hitherto rejected offer of my best services. Adieu, my dearest friend. Believe me ever,

Your affectionate and faithful
ANNA HOWE.

LETTER XXXVII.

Miss Clarissa Harlowe to Miss Howe.

Thursday, April 20.

I SHOULD think myself utterly unworthy of your friendship did my own concerns, heavy as they are, so engross me, that I could not find leisure for a few lines to declare to my beloved friend my sincere disapprobation of her conduct, in an instance where she is so *generously* faulty, that the consciousness of that very generosity may hide from her the fault, which I, more than any other, have reason to deplore, as being the unhappy occasion of it.

You know, you say, that your account of the contentions between your mother and you will trouble me; and so you bid me spare myself the pains to tell you that they do.

You did not use, my dear, to forbid me thus *beforehand*. You were wont to say, you loved me the better for my expostulations with you on that acknowledged warmth and quickness of your temper which your own good sense taught you to be apprehensive of. What though I have so miserably fallen, and am unhappy? If ever

I had any judgment worth regarding, it is now as much worth as ever, because I can give it as freely against myself as against any body else. And shall I not, when there seems to be an infection in my fault, and that it leads you likewise to resolve to carry on a correspondence against prohibition, expostulate with you upon it; when whatever consequences flow from your disobedience, they but widen my error, which is as the evil root, from which such sad branches spring?

The mind that can glory in being capable of so noble, so firm, so unshaken a friendship as that of my dear Miss Howe; a friendship which no casualty or distress can lessen, but which increases with the misfortunes of its friend — such a mind must be above taking amiss the well-meant admonitions of that distinguished friend. I will not therefore apologize for my freedom on this subject: and the less need I, when that freedom is the result of an affection, in the very instance, so *absolutely* disinterested, that it tends to deprive myself of the only comfort left me.

Your acknowledged sullens; your tearing from your mother's hands the letter she thought she had a right to see; and burning it, as you own, before her face; your refusal to see the man, who is so willing to obey you for the sake of your unhappy friend, and this purely to vex your mother; can you think, my dear, upon this brief recapitulation of hardly one half of the faulty particulars you give, that these faults are excusable in one who so well knows her duty?

Your mother had a good opinion of me once: is not that a reason why she should be more regarded now, when I have, *as she believes*, so deservedly forfeited it? A prejudice in favour is as hard to be totally overcome, as a prejudice in disfavour. In what a strong light, then, must that error appear to her, that should so totally turn her heart against me, herself not a principal in the case?

There are other duties, you say, besides the filial duty: but that, my dear, must be a duty prior to all other duties; a duty anterior, as I may say, to your very birth: and what duty ought not to give way to that, when they come in competition?

You are persuaded, that the duty to your friend, and the filial duty, may be performed without derogating from either. Your *mother* thinks otherwise. What is the conclusion to be drawn from these premises?

When your mother sees how much *I* suffer in my reputation from the step I have taken, from whom she and all the world expected better things, how much reason has she to be watchful over you! One evil draws on another after it; and how knows she, or any body, where it may stop?

Does not the person who will vindicate, or seek to extenuate, a faulty step in another, [in this light must your mother look upon the matter in question between her and you] give an indication either of a culpable will, or a weak judgment; and may not she apprehend, that the censorious will think, that such a one might probably have equally failed under the same *inducements* and *provocations*, to *use your own words*, as applied to me in a former letter?

Can there be a stronger instance in human life, than mine has so early furnished within a few months past (not to mention the uncommon provocations to it, which I have met with), of the necessity of the continuance of a watchful parent's care over a daughter; let that daughter have obtained ever so great a reputation for her prudence?

Is not the space from sixteen to twenty-one, that which requires this care, more than at any time of a young woman's life? For in that period, do we not generally attract the eyes of the other sex, and become the subject of their addresses, and not seldom of their attempts? And is not that the period in which our conduct or misconduct gives us a reputation or disreputation, that almost inseparably accompanies us throughout our whole future lives?

Are we not likewise then most in danger from *ourselves*, because of the distinction with which we are apt to behold particulars of that sex?

And when our dangers multiply, both from *within* and *without*, do not our parents know, that their vigilance ought to be doubled?

And shall that necessary increase of care sit uneasy upon us, because we are grown up to stature and womanhood?

Will you tell me, if so, what is the precise stature and age, at which a good child shall conclude herself absolved from the duty she owes to a parent?—And at which a parent, after the example of the dams of the brute creation, is to lay aside all care and tenderness for her offspring?

Is it so hard for you, my dear, to be treated like a child? And can you not think it as hard for a good parent to imagine herself under the unhappy *necessity* of so treating her woman-grown daughter?

Do you think, if your mother had been *you*, and you your *mother*, and *your* daughter had struggled with you, as you did with her, that you would not have been as apt as your mother was to have slapped your daughter's hands, to have made her quit her hold, and give up the prohibited letter?

Your mother told you with great truth, that you *provoked* her to this harshness; and it was great condescension in her (and not taken notice of by you as it deserved) to say that she was *sorry for it*.

At *every* age on this side matrimony (for then we come under another sort of protection, though that is far from abrogating the filial duty) it will be found, that the wings of our parents are our most necessary and most effectual safeguard from the vultures, the hawks, the kites, and other villainous birds of prey, that hover over us with a view to seize and destroy us the first time we are caught wandering out of the eye or care of our watchful and natural guardians and protectors.

Hard as you may suppose it, to be denied the *continuance* of a correspondence once so much approved, even by the venerable denier; yet, if your mother think my fault to be of such a nature, as that a correspondence with me will cast a shade upon my reputation; all my own friends having given me up — that hardship is to be submitted to. And must it not make her the more strenuous to support her own opinion when she sees the first fruits of this tenaciousness on your side, is to be *gloriously in the sullens,* as you call it; and in a disobedient opposition?

I know that you have an humorous meaning in that expression, and that this turn, in most cases, gives a delightful poignancy both to your conversation and correspondence; but indeed, my dear, *this* case will not bear humour.

Will you give me leave to add to this tedious expostulation, that I by no means approve of some of the things you write, in relation to the manner in which your father and mother lived — at times lived — only *at times,* I dare say; though perhaps too often.

Your mother is answerable to *any body,* rather than to her *child,* for whatever was wrong in her conduct, if any thing *was* wrong, towards Mr. Howe: a gentleman, of whose memory I will only say, that it *ought* to be revered by you — but yet, should you not examine yourself, whether your displeasure at your mother had no part in your revived reverence for your father, at the time you wrote?

No one is perfect: and although your mother may not be so right to remember disagreeablenesses against the departed, yet should you not want to be reminded on *whose* account, and on *what* occasion she remembered them. You cannot judge, nor ought you to *attempt* to judge, of what might have passed between both, to embitter and keep awake disagreeable remembrances in the survivor.

LETTER XXXVIII.
Miss Clarissa Harlowe.

In Continuation.

But this subject must not be pursued. Another might, with more pleasure, (though not with more approbation) upon one of your lively excursions. It is upon the high airs you give yourself upon the word *approve.*

How comes it about, I wonder, that a young lady so noted for a predominating generosity, should not be uniformly generous? That your generosity should fail in an instance, where policy, prudence, gratitude, would not permit it to fail? Mr. Hickman (as you confess) has indeed a worthy mind. If I had not long ago known that, he would never have found an advocate in me for my Anna Howe's favour to him. Often and often have I been concerned, when I was your happy guest, to see him, after a conversation in which he had well supported his part in your absence, sink at once into silence the moment you came into company.

I have told you of this before: and I believe I hinted to you once, that the superciliousness you put on *only* to him, was capable of a construction, which at the time would have very little gratified your pride to have had made; since it would have been as much in *his* favour as in *your* disfavour.

Mr. Hickman, my dear, is a *modest* man. I never see a modest man, but I am sure (if he has not wanted opportunities) that he has a treasure in his mind, which requires nothing but the *key of encouragement* to unlock it, to make him shine — while a confident man, who, to *be* confident, must think as meanly of his company as highly of himself, enters with magisterial airs upon any subject; and, depending upon his assurance to bring himself off when found out, talks of more than he is master of.

But a *modest* man! — O, my dear, shall not a modest woman distinguish and wish to consort with a modest man? — A man, *before* whom, and *to* whom, she may open her lips secure of his good opinion of all she says, and of his just and polite regard for her judgment? and who must therefore inspire her with an agreeable self-confidence.

What a lot have I drawn! — We are all indeed apt to turn teachers — but, surely, I am better enabled to talk, to write, upon these subjects, than ever I was. But I will banish *myself*, if possible, from an address which, when I began to write, I was determined to confine wholly to your own particular.

My dearest, dearest friend, how ready are you to tell us what *others* should do, and even what a *mother* should have done! But indeed you once, I remember, advanced, that, as different attainments required different talents to master them, so in the writing way, a person might not be a bad critic upon the works of others, although he might himself be unable to write with excellence. But will you permit me to account for all this readiness of finding fault, by placing it to human nature, which being sensible of the defects of human nature (that is to say, of its *own* defects) loves to be *correcting?* But in exercising that talent, chooses rather to turn its eye *outward* than *inward?* In other words, to employ itself rather in the *out-door* search than in the *in-door* examination.

And here give me leave to add (and yet it is with tender reluctance) that although you say very pretty things of notable wives; and although I join with you in opinion, that husbands may have as many inconveniencies to encounter *with* as conveniencies to boast *of*, from women of that character; yet Lady Hartley perhaps would have had milder treatment from your pen, had it not been dipped in gall with a mother in your eye.

As to the money you so generously and repeatedly offer, don't be angry with me, if I again say, that I am very desirous that you should be able to aver, without the least qualifying or reserve, that nothing of that sort has passed between us. I know your mother's strong way of putting the *question she is intent upon* having answered. But yet I promise that I will be obliged to nobody but you when I have occasion.

LETTER XXXIX.
Miss Clarissa Harlowe.
In Continuation.

AND now, my dear, a few words as to the prohibition laid upon you; a subject that I have frequently touched upon, but cursorily, because I was afraid to trust myself with it, knowing that my judgment, if I did, would condemn my practice.

You command me not to attempt to dissuade you from this correspondence; and you tell me how kindly Mr. Hickman approves of it: and how obliging he is to me, to permit it to be carried on under cover to him — but this does not quite satisfy me.

I am a very bad casuist; and the pleasure I take in writing to you, who are the only one to whom I can disburden my mind, may make me, as I have hinted, very partial to my own wishes: — else, if it were not an artful evasion beneath an open and frank heart to wish to be complied with, I would be glad methinks to be permitted still to write to you; and only to have such *occasional returns* by Mr. Hickman's pen, as well as cover, as might set me right when I am wrong; confirm me when right; and guide me where I doubt. This would enable me to proceed in the difficult path before me with more assuredness. For whatever I suffer from the censures of others, if I can preserve your good opinion, I shall not be altogether unhappy, let what will befal me.

And indeed, my dear, I know not how to *forbear* writing. I have now no other employment or diversion. And I must write on, although I were not to send it to any body. You have often heard me own the advantages I have found from writing down every thing of moment that befals me; and of all I *think*, and of all I *do*, that may be of future use to me; for, besides that this helps to form one to a style, and opens and expands the ductile mind, every one will find, that many a good thought evaporates in thinking; many a good resolution goes off, driven out of memory perhaps by some other not so good: But when I set down what I *will* do, or what I *have* done, on this or that occasion: the resolution or action is before me, either to be adhered to, withdrawn, or amended; and I have entered into compact with myself, as I may say; having given it under my own hand to *improve*, rather than to go *backward*, as I live longer.

I would willingly, therefore, write to *you*, if I *might*; the rather as it would be the more inspiring to have some end in view in what I write; some friend to please; besides merely seeking to gratify my passion for scribbling.

But why, if your mother will permit our correspondence on communicating to her all that passes in it, and if she would condescend to one only condition, may it not be complied with?

Would she not, do you think, my dear, be prevailed upon to have the communication made to her, *in confidence?*

If there were any prospect of a reconciliation with my friends, I should not have so much regard for my *pride*, as to be afraid of *any body's* knowing how much I have been *outwitted*, as you call it. I would, in *that* case (when I had left Mr. Lovelace) acquaint your mother and all my own friends with the whole of my story. It would behove me so to do, for my own reputation, and for their satisfaction.

But if I have no such prospect, what will the communication of my reluctance to go away with Mr. Lovelace, and of his arts to frighten me away, avail me? Your mother has hinted, that my friends would insist upon my returning to them (as a proof of the truth of my plea) to be disposed of, without condition, at their pleasure. If I scrupled this, my brother would rather triumph over me than keep my secret. Mr. Lovelace, whose pride already so ill brooks my regrets for meeting him, (when he thinks, if I had not, I must have been Mr. Solmes's wife) would perhaps treat me with indignity: and thus, deprived of all refuge and protection, I should become the scoff of men of intrigue; and be thought, with too great an appearance of reason, a disgrace to my sex — while that avowed love, *however indiscreetly shewn*, which is followed by marriage, will find more excuses made for it *than generally it ought to find.*

But, if your mother will receive the communication in confidence, pray shew her all that I have written or shall write. If my past conduct in that case shall not be found to deserve *heavy* blame, I shall then perhaps have the benefit of *her* advice, as well as *yours*. And if after a re-establishment in her favour, I shall wilfully deserve blame for the time to come, I will be content to be denied yours as well as hers for ever.

As to cramping my spirit, as you call it, (were I to sit down to write what I know your mother must see) that, my dear, is already cramped. And do not think so unhandsomely of your mother, as to fear that she would make *partial* constructions against me. Neither you nor I can doubt, but that, had she been left unprepossessedly to herself, she would have shewn favour to me. And so, I dare say, would my uncle Antony. Nay, my dear, I can extend my charity still further: for I am sometimes of opinion, that were my brother and sister *absolutely certain*, that they had so far ruined me in-the opinion of both my uncles, as that they need not be apprehensive of my clashing with their interests; they would not oppose a pardon, although they might not wish a reconciliation; especially if I would make a few sacrifices to them: which, I assure you, I should be inclined to make were I wholly free and independent on this man. You know I never valued myself upon worldly acquisitions, but as they enlarged my power to do things I loved to do. And if I were denied the power, I must, as I now do, curb my inclination.

Do not, however, think me guilty of an affectation in what I have said of my brother and sister. Severe enough I am sure it is, in the most favourable sense. And an indifferent person will be of opinion, that *they* are much better warranted than ever, for the sake of the family-honour, to seek to ruin me in the favour of all my friends.

But to the former topic — try, my dear, if your mother will, upon the condition above given, permit our correspondence, on seeing all we write, but if she will not, what a selfishness would there be in my love to you, were I to wish you to forego your duty for my sake!

And now, one word as to the freedom I have treated you with in this tedious expostulatory address. I presume — upon your forgiveness of it, because few friendships are founded on such a basis as ours; which is, "freely to *give* reproof, and thankfully to *receive* it, as occasions arise; that so either may have opportunity to clear up mistakes, to acknowledge and amend errors, as well in behaviour as in words and deeds; and to rectify and confirm each other in the judgment each shall form upon persons, things, and circumstances." And all this upon the following consideration: "That it is much more eligible, as well as honourable, to be corrected with the gentleness that may be expected from an undoubted friend, than by continuing either blind or wilful, to expose ourselves to the censures of an envious, and perhaps malignant world."

But it is as needless, I dare say, to remind you of this, as it is to *repeat* my request, so often repeated, that you will not, in your turn, spare the follies and the faults of

Your ever affectionate
CL. HARLOWE.

Subjoined to the above.

I said, that I would avoid writing any thing of my own particular affairs in the above address, if I could.

I will write one letter more, to inform you how I stand with this man. But, my dear, you must permit that one, and your answer to it, (for I want your advice upon the contents of mine) and the copy of one I have written to my aunt, to be the last that shall pass between us, while the prohibition continues.

I fear, I very much fear, that my unhappy situation will draw me in to be guilty of evasion, of little affectations, and of curvings from the plain, simple truth, which I was wont to delight in, and prefer to every other consideration. But allow me to say, and this for your sake, and in order to lessen your mother's fears of any ill consequences that she might apprehend from our correspondence, that if I am at any time guilty of a failure in these respects, I will not *go on in it*, but endeavour to recover my lost ground, that I may not bring error into habit.

I have deferred going to town, at Mrs. Sorlings's earnest request; but have fixed my removal to Monday, as I shall acquaint you in my next.

I have already made a progress in that next; but having an unexpected opportunity, will send this by itself.

LETTER XL.

Miss Howe to Miss Clarissa Harlowe.

Friday morning, April 21.

My mother will not comply with your condition, my dear. I hinted it to her as from myself. But the *Harlowes* (excuse me) have got her entirely in with them. It is a scheme of mine, she told me, formed to draw her into your party against your parents. Which, for her own sake, she is very careful about.

Don't be so much concerned about my mother and me, once more, I beg of you. We shall do well enough together — now a falling out, now a falling in. It used to be so, when you were not in the question.

Yet do I give you my sincerest thanks for every line of your reprehensive letters; which I intend to read as often as I find my temper rises.

I will freely own, however, that I winced a little at first reading them. But I see, that on every reperusal, I shall love and honour you still more, if possible, than before.

Yet I think I have one advantage over you, and which I will hold through this letter, and through all my future letters; that is, that I will treat you as freely as you treat me; and yet will never think an *apology necessary to you for my freedom*.

But that you so think with respect to me is the effect of your gentleness of temper, with a little sketch of implied reflection on the warmth of mine. Gentleness in a woman you hold to be no fault: nor do I a little due or provoked warmth — but what is this but praising on both sides what neither of us can help; nor perhaps *wish* to help? You can no more go out of your road than I can go out of mine. It would be a pain to either to do so: what then is it in either's approving of her own natural bias, but making a virtue of necessity?

But one observation I will add, that were *your* character and *my* character to be truly drawn, mine would be allowed to be the most natural. Shades and lights are equally necessary in a fine picture. Yours would be surrounded with such a flood of brightness, with such a glory, that it would indeed dazzle; but leave one heartless to imitate it.

O may you not suffer from a base world for your gentleness; while my temper, by its warmth, keeping all imposition at distance, though less amiable in general, affords me not reason, as I have mentioned heretofore, to wish to make an exchange with you!

I should indeed be inexcusable to open my lips by way of contradiction to my mother, had I such a fine spirit as yours to deal with. Truth is truth, my dear! Why should narrowness run away with the praises due to a noble expansion of heart? If every body would speak out, as I do, (that is to say give praise where only praise is due; dispraise where due likewise) *shame*, if not *principle*, would mend the world — nay, shame would *introduce* principle in a generation or two. Very true, my dear. Do you apply. I dare not. — For I *fear* you almost as much as I *love* you.

I will give you an instance, nevertheless, which will a-new demonstrate, that none but very generous and noble-minded people, ought to be implicitly obeyed. You know what I said above, that *truth* is *truth*.

Inconveniencies will sometimes arise from having to do with persons of modesty and scrupulousness. Mr. Hickman, you say, is a *modest* man. He put your corrective packet into my hand with a very fine bow, and a self-satisfied air [*we'll consider what you say of this honest man by-and-by, my dear*]: his strut was not gone off, when in came my mother as I was reading it.

When some folks find their anger has made them considerable, they will be always angry, or seeking occasion for anger.

Why, now, Mr. Hickman — why, now, Nancy, — [as I was huddling the packet into my pocket at her entrance] you have a letter brought you this instant. — While the *modest* man, with his pausing brayings, Mad-a—maddam, looked as if he knew not whether he had best to run, and leave me and my mother to fight it out, or to stand his ground and see fair play.

It would have been poor to tell a lie for it. She flung away. I went out at the opposite door to read the contents; leaving Mr. Hickman to exercise his *white teeth* upon his thumb nails.

When I had read your letters, I went to find out my mother. I told her the generous contents, and that you desired that the prohibition might be adhered to. I proposed your condition, as from myself; and was rejected, as above.

She supposed she was finely painted between two "young creatures, who had more wit than prudence:" and instead of being prevailed upon by the generosity of your sentiments, made use of your opinion only 'to confirm her own, and renewed her prohibitions, charging me to return no other answer but that she *did* renew them adding, that they should stand till your relations were reconciled to you; hinting as if she had *engaged for as much:* and expected my compliance.

I thought of your reprehensions and was *meek*, though not pleased. And let me tell you, my dear, that as long as I can satisfy my own mind, that good is intended, and that it is hardly possible that evil should ensue from our correspondence — as long as I know, that this prohibition proceeds originally from the same spiteful minds which have been the occasion of all these mischiefs — as long as I know, that it is not your fault if your relations are not reconciled to you; and that upon conditions which no reasonable people would refuse — you must give me leave, with all deference to your judgment, and to your excellent lessons (*which would reach almost every case of this kind but the present*) to insist upon your writing to me, and that minutely, as if this prohibition had not been laid.

It is not from humour, from perverseness, that I insist upon this. I cannot express how much my heart is in your concerns. And you must, in short, allow me to think, that if I can do you service by writing, I shall be better justified in *continuing* to write than my mother is in her prohibition.

But yet, to satisfy you all I can, I will as seldom return answers while the interdict lasts, as may be consistent with my notions of friendship, and with the service I owe you and can do you.

As to your expedient of writing by Hickman [and now, my dear, your *modest man* comes in and as you love modesty in that sex, I will do my endeavour, by holding him at a proper distance, to keep him in your favour] I know what you mean by it, my sweet friend. It is to make that man significant with me. As to the correspondence, THAT *shall* go on, I do assure you, be as scrupulous as you please — so that *that* will not suffer if I do *not* close with your proposal as to him.

I must tell you, that I think it will be honour enough for him to have his name made use of so frequently betwixt us. This, of itself, is placing a confidence in him, that will make him walk bolt upright, and display his *white* hand, and his *fine diamond ring;* and most mightily lay down his services *and* his pride to oblige, *and* his diligence, *and* his fidelity, *and* his contrivances to keep our secret *and* his excuses, and his evasions to my mother, when challenged by her; with fifty *ands* beside: and will it not moreover give him pretence and excuse oftener than ever to pad-nag it hither to good Mrs. Howe's fair daughter?

But to admit him into my company tête-à-tête, and into my closet, as often as I would wish to write to you; I only to dictate to his pen — my mother all the time supposing that I was going to be heartily in love with him — to make him master of my *heart*, as I may say, when I write to you — indeed, my dear, I *won't*. Nor, were I married to the best HE in England, would I honour him with the communication of my correspondencies.

No, my dear, it is sufficient, surely, for him to parade it in the character of our letter-conveyer, and to be honoured in a cover, and never fear but, modest as you think him, he will make enough of that.

You are always blaming me for want of generosity to this man, and for abuse of power. But I profess, my dear, I cannot tell how to help it. Do, dear now, let me spread my plumes a little, and now-and-then make myself feared. This is my time you know, since it would be no more to *my* credit than to *his* to give myself those airs when I am married. He has a joy when I am pleased with him, that he would not know but for the pain my displeasure gives him.

Men, no more than *women*, know how to make a moderate use of power. Is not that seen every day, from the prince to the peasant? If I do not make Hickman quake now-and-then, he will endeavour to make me fear. All the animals in the creation are more or less in a state of hostility with each other. The wolf that runs away from a lion, will devour a lamb the next moment. I remember, that I was once so enraged at a game chicken, that was continually pecking at another (a poor humble one, as I thought him) that I had the offender caught, and without more ado, in a *pet of humanity*, wrung his neck off. What followed this execution? Why that other grew insolent as soon as *his* insulter was gone, and was continually pecking at one or two under *him*. Peck and be hanged, said I, — I might as well have preserved the first; for I see it is the *nature of the beast*.

Excuse my flippancies. I wish I were with you. I would make you smile in the midst of your gravest airs, as I used to do. O that you had accepted of my offer to attend you! But *nothing that I offer* will you accept. — Take care! — You will make me very angry with you: and when I am, you know I value nobody: for, dearly as I love you, I must be, and cannot always help it, Your saucy
ANNA HOWE.

LETTER XLI.

Miss Clarissa Harlowe to Miss Howe.

Friday, April 21.

MR. LOVELACE communicated to me this morning early, from his intelligencer, the news of my brother's scheme. I like him the better for making very light of it; and for his treating it with contempt. And indeed, had I not had the hint of it from you, I should have suspected it to be some contrivance of his, in order to hasten me to town, where he has long wished to be himself.

He read me the passage in that Leman's letter, which is pretty much to the effect of what you wrote to me from Miss Lloyd; with this addition, that one Singleton, a master of a Scots vessel, is the man who is to be the principal in this act of violence.

I have seen him. He has been twice entertained at Harlowe Place, as my brother's friend. He has the air of a very bold and fearless man; and I fancy it must be his project; as my brother, I suppose, talks to every body of the rash step I have taken; for he did not spare me before he had this seeming reason to censure me.

This Singleton lives at Leith; so, perhaps I am to be carried to my brother's house not far from that port.

Putting these passages together, I am not a little apprehensive, that the design, lightly as Mr. Lovelace, from his fearless temper, treats it, may be attempted to be carried into execution; and of the consequences that may attend it, if it be.

I asked Mr. Lovelace, seeing him so frank and cool, what he would advise me to do.

Shall I ask *you*, madam, what are your own thoughts? — Why I return the question, said he, is because you have been so very earnest, that I should leave you as soon as you are in London, that I know not what to propose without offending you.

My opinion is, said I, that I should studiously conceal myself from the knowledge of every body but Miss Howe; and that you should leave me; since they will certainly conclude, that where *one* is the *other* is not far off: and it is easier to trace *you* than *me*.

You would not surely wish, said he, to fall into your brother's hands by such a violent measure as this? I propose not to throw myself officiously in their way; but should they have reason to think I avoided them, would not that whet their diligence to find you, and their courage to attempt to carry you off; and subject me to insults that no man of spirit can bear?

Lord bless me! said I, to what has this one fatal step that I have been betrayed into —

Dearest madam, let me beseech you to forbear this harsh language, when you see, by this new scheme, how determined they were upon carrying their old ones, had you not been *betrayed*, as you call it. Have I offered to defy the laws of society, as this brother of yours must do, if any thing be intended by this project? I hope you will be pleased to observe, that there are as violent and as wicked enterprisers as myself — but this is so very wild a project, that I think there can be no room for apprehensions from it. I know your brother well. When at college, he had always a romantic turn: but never had a head for any thing but to puzzle and confound himself. A half-invention, and a whole conceit; but not master of talents to do himself good, or others harm, but as those others gave him the power by their own folly.

This is very volubly run off, sir! — But violent spirits are but too much alike; at least in their methods of resenting. You will not presume to make yourself a less innocent man surely, who had determined to brave my whole family in person, if my folly had not saved you the rashness, and *them* the insult —

Dear madam! — Still must it be *folly, rashness!* — It is as impossible for you to think tolerably of any body *out* of your own family, as it is for any one *in it* to *deserve* your love! Forgive me, dearest creature! if I did not love you as never man loved a woman, I might appear more indifferent to preferences so undeservedly made. But let me ask you, madam, what have you borne from *me?* What cause have I given you to treat me with so much severity, and so little confidence: and what have you not borne from *them?* Malice and ill-will, indeed, sitting in judgment upon my character, may not give sentence in my favour: but what *of your own knowledge* have you against me?

Spirited questions, were they not, my dear? — And they were asked with as spirited an air. I was startled. But I was resolved not to desert myself.

Is this a *time*, Mr. Lovelace, is this a *proper* occasion taken, to give yourself these high airs to me, a young creature destitute of protection? It is a surprising question you ask me. Had I aught against you *of my own knowledge* — I can tell you, sir — and away I would have flung.

He snatched my hand, and besought me not to leave him in displeasure. He pleaded his passion for me, and my severity to him, and partiality for those from whom I had suffered so much; and whose intended violence, he said, was now the subject of our deliberation.

I was forced to hear him.

You condescended, dearest creature, said he, to ask my advice. It is very easy, give me leave to say, to advise you what to do. I hope I may, on this *new* occasion, speak without offence, *notwithstanding your former injunctions* — you see that there can be no hope of reconciliation with your relations. Can you, madam, consent to honour with your hand a wretch whom you have never yet obliged with one *voluntary* favour!

What a *recriminating*, what a *reproachful way*, my dear, was this of putting a question of this nature!

I expected not from him, at the time, and just as I was very angry with him, either the question or the manner. I am ashamed to recollect the confusion I was thrown into; all your advice in my head at the moment: yet his words so prohibitory. He confidently seemed to enjoy my confusion; [indeed, my dear, *he knows not what respectful love is!*] and gazed upon me as if he would have looked me through.

He was still more declarative afterwards, indeed, as I shall mention by-and-by: but it was half extorted from him.

My heart struggled violently between resentment and shame, to be thus teased by one who seemed to have all his passions at command, at a time when I had very little over *mine!* till at last I burst into tears, and was going from him in high disgust: when, throwing his arms about me, with an air, however, the most tenderly respectful, he gave a *stupid* turn to the subject.

It was far from his heart, he said, to take so much *advantage* of the *streight* which the discovery of my brother's foolish project had brought me into, as to renew, *without my permission*, a proposal which I had hitherto discountenanced, and which for *that* reason —

And then he came with his *half-sentences*, apologizing for what he had not so much as *half-proposed*.

Surely he had not the insolence to intend to tease me, to see if I could be brought to speak what became me not to speak — but, whether he had or not, it *did* tease me; insomuch that my very heart was fretted, and I broke out at last into fresh tears, and a declaration that I was very unhappy. And just then recollecting how like a tame fool I stood with his arms about me, I flung from him with indignation. But he seized my hand as I was going out of the room, and upon his knees besought my stay for one moment: and then, in words the most clear and explicit, tendered himself to my acceptance, as the most effectual means to disappoint my brother's scheme, and set all right.

But what could I say to this? — Extorted from him, as it seemed to me, rather as the effect of his compassion than his love? What *could* I say? I paused, I looked silly — I am sure I looked *very* silly. He suffered me to pause, and look silly; *waiting for* me *to say something:* and at last (ashamed of my confusion, and aiming to make an *excuse for it*) I told him that I desired he would avoid such measures as might add to the uneasiness which, it must be visible to him, I had, when he reflected upon the irreconcileableness of my friends, and upon what might follow from this unaccountable project of my brother.

He promised to be governed by me in every thing. And again the wretch, instead of pressing his former question, asked me, *if I forgave him for the humble suit he had made to me?* What had I to do, but to try for a palliation of my confusion, since it served me not?

I told him I had hopes it would not be long before Mr. Morden arrived; and doubted not, that that gentleman would be the readier to engage in my favour, when he found, that I made no other use of *his* (Mr. Lovelace's) assistance than to free myself from the addresses of a man so disagreeable to me as Mr. Solmes: I must therefore wish, that every thing might remain as it was, till I could hear from my cousin.

This, although teased by him as I was, was not, you see, my dear, a *denial*. But he must throw himself into a heat, rather than try to persuade; which any other man, in his situation, I should think, would have done: and this warmth obliged me to adhere to my seeming negative.

This was what he said, with a vehemence that must harden any woman's mind, who had a spirit above being frighted into passiveness.

Good God! and will you, madam, still resolve to shew me, that I am to hope for no share in your favour, while any the remotest prospect remains, that you will be received by my bitterest enemies, at the price of my utter rejection?

This was what I returned, with warmth, and with a salving art *too* — You have seen, Mr. Lovelace, how much my brother's violence can affect me: but you will be mistaken if you let loose yours upon me, with a thought of terrifying me into measures the contrary of which you have acquiesced with.

He only besought me to suffer his *future actions* to speak for him; and if I saw him worthy of any favour, that I would not let him be the *only* person within my knowledge who was not entitled to my consideration.

You refer to a *future time*, Mr. Lovelace; so do I, for the *future proof* of a merit you seem to think for the *past time* wanting: and *justly* you think so. And I was again going from him.

One word more he begged me to hear — he was determined studiously to avoid all mischief, and every step that might lead to mischief, let my brother's proceedings, short of a violence upon my person, be what they would: but if any attempt that should extend to that were to be made, would I have him to be a quiet spectator of my being seized, or carried back, or on board, by this Singleton; or, in case of extremity, was he not permitted to stand up in my defence?

Stand up in my defence! Mr. Lovelace! — I should be very miserable were there to be a call for that. But do you think I might not be *safe* and *private* in London? By your friend's description of the widow's house, I should think I might be safe there.

The widow's house, he replied, as described by his friend, being *a back house within a front one*, and *looking to a garden rather than to a street*, had the *appearance* of privacy: but if, when there, it was not approved, it would be easy to find another more to my liking — though, as to his part, the method he would advise should be, to write to my uncle Harlowe as one of my trustees, and wait the issue of it here at Mrs. Sorlings's, fearlessly directing it to be answered *hither*. To be afraid of little spirits was but to encourage insults, he said. The substance of the letter should be, "To demand as a right what they would refuse if requested as a courtesy: to acknowledge that I had put myself [too well, he said, did their treatment justify me] into the protection of the *ladies* of his family [by whose orders, and Lord M.'s, he himself would appear to act]: but that upon my own terms; which were such, that I was under no obligation to those ladies for the favour; it being no more than they would have granted to any one of my sex, equally distressed." If I approved not of this method, happy should he think himself, he said, if I would honour him with the opportunity of making such a claim in his own name — but this was a point [with his *buts* again in the same breath!] that *he durst but just touch upon.* He hoped, however, that I would think their violence a sufficient inducement for me to take such a wished-for resolution.

Inwardly vexed, I told him, that he himself had proposed to leave me when I was in town: that I expected he would: and that, when I was known to be absolutely independent, I should consider what to write and what to do: but that, while he was with me, I neither would nor could.

He would be very sincere with me, he said: this project of my brother's had changed the face of things. He must, before he left me, see whether I should or should not approve of the London widow and her family, if I chose to go thither. They might be people whom my brother might buy. But if he saw they were persons of integrity, he then might go for a day or two, or so. But he must needs say, he could not leave me longer at a time.

Do you propose, sir, said I, to take up your lodgings in the house where I shall lodge?

He did not, he said, as he knew the use I intended to make of his absence, and my punctilio — and yet the house where he had lodgings was new-fronting, and not in condition to receive him: but he could go to his friend Belford's, in Soho; or perhaps he might reach to the same gentleman's house at Edgware, over night, and return on the mornings, till he had reason to think this wild project of my brother's laid aside. But to no greater distance till then should he care to venture.

The result of all was, to set out on Monday next for town. I hope it will be in a happy hour.

CL. HARLOWE.

LETTER XLII.

Mr. Lovelace to John Belford, Esq.

Friday, April 21.

As it was not probable that the lady could give so particular an account of her own confusion, in the affecting scene she mentions on Mr. Lovelace's offering himself to her acceptance; the following extracts are made from his letter of the above date.

AND now, Belford, what wilt thou say, if, like the fly buzzing about the bright taper, I had like to have singed the silken wings of my liberty? Never was man in greater danger of being caught in his own snares: all my views anticipated; all my schemes untried: the admirable creature not brought to town; nor one effort made to know if she be really angel or woman.

I offered myself to her acceptance, with a suddenness, 'tis true, that gave her no time to wrap herself in reserves; and in terms *less tender* than *fervent*, tending to upbraid her for her past indifference, and to remind her of her injunctions: for it was the fear of her brother, not her love of me, that had inclined her to dispense with those injunctions.

I never beheld so sweet a confusion. What a glory to the pencil, could it do justice to it, and to the mingled impatience which visibly informed every feature of the most meaning and most beautiful face in the world! She hemmed twice or thrice: her look, now so charmingly silly, then so sweetly significant; till at last the lovely teaser, teased by my hesitating expectation of her answer, out of all power of articulate speech, burst into tears, and was turning from me with precipitation, when, presuming to fold her in my happy arms — O think not, best beloved of my heart, said I, think not, that this motion, which you may believe to be so contrary to your *former injunctions*, proceeds from a design to avail myself of the cruelty of your relations: if I have disobliged you by it, (and you know with what *respectful tenderness* I have presumed to hint it) it shall be my utmost care for the future — there I stopped —

Then she spoke; but with vexation — I am — I am — *very* unhappy — tears trickling down her crimson cheeks; and her sweet face, as my arms still encircled the finest waist in the world, sinking upon my shoulder: the dear creature so absent, that she knew not the honour she permitted me.

But why, but why unhappy, my dearest life? said I: — all the gratitude that ever overflowed the heart of the most obliged of men —

Justice to myself there stopped my mouth: for what *gratitude* did I owe her for obligations so involuntary?

Then recovering herself, and her usual reserves, and struggling to free herself from my clasping arms, How now, sir! said she, with a cheek more indignantly glowing, and eyes of fiercer lustre.

I gave way to her angry struggle; but absolutely overcome by so charming a display of innocent confusion, I caught hold of her hand as she was flying from me; and kneeling at her feet, O my angel, said I, (quite destitute of reserve, and hardly knowing the tenor of my own speech; and had a parson been there, I had certainly been a gone man), receive the vows of your faithful Lovelace. Make him yours, and only yours, for ever. This will answer every end. Who will dare to form plots

Clarissa. II.   10

and stratagems against my wife? that you are not so, is the ground of all their foolish attempts, and of their insolent hopes in Solmes's favour. — O be mine! — I beseech you (thus on my knee I *beseech* you) to be mine. We shall then have all the world with us. And every body will applaud an event that every body expects.

Was the devil in me! I no more intended all this ecstatic nonsense, than I thought the same moment of flying in the air! all power is with this charming creature. It is I, not she, at this rate, that must fail in the arduous trial.

Didst thou ever before hear of a man uttering solemn things by an involuntary impulse, in defiance of premeditation, and of all his own proud schemes? But this sweet creature is able to make a man forego every purpose of his heart, that is not favourable to her. And I verily think I should be inclined to spare her all further trial [and yet what trial has she had?] were it not for the contention that her vigilance has set on foot, *which* shall overcome the *other*. Thou knowest my generosity to my uncontending Rosebud — and sometimes do I qualify my ardent aspirations after even this very fine creature, by this reflection: — that the most charming woman on earth, were she an empress, can excel the meanest, in the customary visibles only — such is the equality of the dispensation, to the prince and the peasant, in this prime gift WOMAN.

Well, but what was the result of this involuntary impulse on my part? — wouldst thou not think I was taken at my offer? — an offer so solemnly made, and on one knee too?

No such thing! — the pretty trifler let me off as easily as I could have wished.

Her brother's project; and to find that there were no hopes of a reconciliation for her; and the apprehension she had of the mischiefs that might ensue — these, not *my offer*, nor *love of me*, were the causes to which she ascribed all her sweet confusion — an *ascription* that is high treason against my sovereign pride — to make marriage with *me*, but a second-place refuge; and as good as to tell me, that her confusion was owing to her concern that there were no hopes that my enemies would accept of her intended offer to renounce a man who had ventured his life for her, and was still ready to run the same risk in her behalf!

I re-urged her to make me happy — but I was to be postponed to her cousin Morden's arrival. On him are now placed all her hopes. I raved; but to no purpose.

Another letter was to be sent, or had been sent, to her aunt Hervey; to which she hoped an answer.

Yet sometimes I think, that fainter and fainter would have been her procrastinations, had I been a man of courage — *but so fearful was I of offending!*

A confounded thing! the man to be so bashful; the woman to

want so much courting! — how shall two such come together; no kind mediatress in the way?

But I must be contented. 'Tis seldom, however, that a love *so ardent* as mine meets with a spirit *so resigned* in the *same person*. But true love, I am now convinced, only wishes: nor has it any active will but that of the adored object.

But, O the charming creature, again of herself to mention London! had Singleton's plot been of *my own contriving*, a more happy expedient could not have been thought of to induce her to resume her purpose of going thither; nor can I divine what could be her reason for postponing it.

I inclose the letter from Joseph Leman, which I mentioned to thee in mine of Monday last,* with my answer to it. I cannot resist the vanity that urges me to the communication. Otherwise, it were better, perhaps, that I suffer thee to imagine, that this lady's stars fight against her, and dispense the opportunities in my favour, which are only the consequences of my own superlative invention.

LETTER XLIII.
To Robert Lovelace, Esq. his honner.
Sat. April 15.

MAY IT PLEASE YOUR HONNER,

This is to let your honner kno', as how I have been emploied in a bisness I would have been excused from, if so be I could. For it is to gitt evidense from a young man, who has of late com'd out to be my cuzzen by my grandmother's side; and but lately come to live in these partes, about a very vile thing, as younge master calls it, relating to 'your honner. God forbid I should call it so without your leafe. It is not for so plane a man as I be, to tacks my betters. It is consarning one Miss Batirton, of Notingam; a very pritty crature, belike.

Your honner got her away, it seems, by a false letter to her, macking believe as howe her shecuzzen, that she derely loved, was coming to see her; and was tacken ill upon the rode: and so Miss Batirton set out in a shase, and one sarvant, to fet her cuzzen from the inne where she laid sick, as she thote: and the sarvant was tricked, and braute back the shase; but Miss Batirton was not harde off for a month, or so. And when it came to passe, that her frends founde her out, and would have prossekutid your honner, your honner was gone abroad; and so she was broute to bed, as one may say, before your honner's return: and she got colde in her lyin-inn, and lanquitched, and soon died: and the child is living; but your honner never troubles your honner's hedd about it in the least. And this and some such other matters of verry bad reporte, Squier Solmes was to tell my young lady of, if so be she would have harde him speke, before we lost her sweet company, as I may say, from heere.*

I hope your honner will excuse me. But I was forsed to tell all I

See p. 111.

* See Vol. I. p. 271.

harde, because they had my cuzzen in to them, and he would have said he had tolde me: so could not be melely mouthed, for fear to be blone up, and plese your honner.

Your honner helped me to many ugly stories to tell against your honner to my younge master, and younge mistress; butt did not tell me about this.

I most humbelly besecche your honner to be good and kinde and fethful to my dearest younge lady, now you have her; or I shall brake my harte for having done some dedes that have helped to bring things to this passe. Pray youre dere good honner, be just! prayey do! — as God shall love ye! prayey do! — I cannot write no more for this pressent, for verry fear and grief —

But now I am cumm'd to my writing agen, will youre honner be pleased to tell me, if as how there be any danger to your honner's life from this bisness; for my cuzzen is actlie hier'd to go down to Miss Batirton's frendes to see if they will stir in it: for you must kno' your honner', as how he lived in the Batirton family at the time, and could be a good evidense, and all that.

I hope it was not so verry bad, as Titus says it was; for hee ses as how there was a rape in the case betwixt you *at furste*, and plese your honner; and my Cuzzen Titus is a very honist younge man as ever brocke bred. This is his carackter; and this made me willinger to owne him for my relation, when we came to talck.

If there should be danger of your honner's life, I hope your honner will not be hanged like as one of us common men: only have your hedd cut off, or so: and yet it is pity such a hedd should be lossed: but if as how it shoulde be prossekutid to that furr, which God forbid, be plesed natheless to thinck of youre fethful Joseph Leman, before your hedd be condemned; for after condemnation, as I have been told, all will be the king's, or the shreeve's.

I thote as how it was best to acquent your honner of this; and for you to let me kno' if I could do any thing to sarve your honner, and prevent mischief with my Cuzzen Titus, on his coming back from Nottingham, before he mackes his reporte.

I have gin him a hint already: for what, as I sed to him, Cuzzen Titus, signifies stirring up the coles, and macking of strife, to make rich gentilfolkes live at variance, and to be cutting of throtes, and such-like?

Verry trewe, sed little Titus. And this, and plese your honner, gis me hopes of him, if so be your honner gis me direction; sen', as God kno'es, I have a poor, a verry poor invenshon; only a willing mind to prevent mischief, that is the chief of my aim, and always was, I bless my God! — els I could have made much mischief in my time; as indeed any sarvant may. Your honner natheless praises my invenshon every now-and-then:

alas! and plese your honner, what invenshon should such a plane man as I have? — but when your honner sets me agoing by *your* fine invenshon, I can do well enuff. And I am sure I have a hearty good will to deserve your honner's faver, if I mought.

Two days, as I may say, off and on, have I been writing this long letter. And yet I have not sed all I would say. For, be it knone unto your honner, as how I do not like that Capten Singleton, which I told you of *in my two last letters*. He is always laying his hedd and my young master's hedd together; and I suspect much if so be some mischef is not going on between them: and still the more, as because my eldest younge lady semes to be joined to them sometimes.

Last week my younge master sed before my fase, *My harte's blood boiles over, Captain Singelton, for revenge upon this* — and he called your honner by a name it is not for such a won as me to say what. Capten Singelton whispred my younge master, being I was by. So younge master sed, *You may say any thing before Joseph; for, althoff he looks so seelie, he has as good a harte, and as good a hedd, as any sarvante in the worlde nede to have.* My conscience touched me just then. But why shoulde it? when all I do is to prevente mischeff; and seing your honner has so much patience, which younge master has not; so am not affeard of telling your honner any-thing whatsomever.

Any furthermore, I have suche a desire to desarve your honner's bounty to me, as mackes me let nothing pass I can tell you of, to prevent harm: and too-besides your honner's goodness about the Blew Bore; which I have so good an accounte of! — I am sure I shall be bounden to bless your honner the longest day I have to live.

And then the Blew Bore is not all neither; sen', and plese your honner, the pretty sowe (God forgive me for gesting in so serus a matter) runs in my hedd likewise. I believe I shall love her, mayhap more than your honner would have me; for she begins to be be kind and good-humered, and listens, and plese your honner, licke as *if she was among beans*, when I talke about the Blew Bore, and all that.

Prayey, your honner, forgive the gesting of a poor plane man. We common fokes have our joys, and plese your honner, lick as our betters have; and if we be sometimes snubbed, we can find our underlings to snub them agen; and if not, we can get a wife mayhap, and snub her: so are masters some how or others oursells.

But how I try your honner's patience! — Sarvants will shew their joyful hartes, tho'ff but in partinens, when encouredg'd.

Be plesed from the prems's to let me kno' if as how I can be put upon any sarvice to sarve your honner, and to sarve my deerest younge lady; which God grant! for I begin to be affearde for her, hearing what pepel talck — to be sure your honner will not do her no *harme*, as a man may say. But I kno' your honner must be good to so wonderous a younge lady. How can you help it? — But heere my conscience smites me, that *but for some of my stories, which your honner taule me, my old master and my old lady, and the two old squires, would not have been abell to be half so hard-harted as they be, for all what my younge master and younge mistress sayes.*

And here is the sad thing; they cannot come to clere up matters with my deerest younge lady, because, as *your honner has ordered it*, they have these stories as if bribed by me out of your honner's sarvant; which must not be known for fere you should kill'n and me too, and blacken the briber! — Ah! your honner! I doute as that I am a very vild fellow (Lord bless my soul, I pray God) and did not intend it.

But if my deerest younge lady should come to harm, and plese your honner, the horsepond at the Blew Bore — but the Lord preserve us from all bad mischeff, and all bad cudes, I pray the Lord! — For tho'ff your honner is kind to me in worldly pelff, yet *what shall a man get to loos his soul*, as holy Skrittuer says, and plese your honner?

But natheless I am in hope of reppentence hereafter, being but a younge man, if I do wrong thro' ignorens: your honner being a grate man, and a grate wit; and I a poor crature, not worthy notice; and your honner able to answer for all. But howsomever I am
Your honner's fethful sarvant
in all dewtie,
JOSEPH LEMAN.
April 15 and 16.

LETTER XLIV.

Mr. Lovelace to Joseph Leman.

HONEST JOSEPH, Monday, April 17.

You have a worse opinion of your invention than you ought to have. I must praise it again. Of a plain man's head, I have not known many better than yours. How often have your forecast and discretion answered my wishes in cases which I could not foresee, not knowing how my general directions would succeed, or what might happen in the execution of them? you are too doubtful of your own abilities, honest Joseph; that's your fault. But it being a fault that is owing to natural *modesty*, you ought rather to be *pitied* for it than *blamed*.

The affair of Miss Betterton was a youthful frolic. I love dearly to exercise my invention. I do assure you, Joseph, 'that I have ever had more pleasure in my contrivances, than in the end of them. I am no sensual man; but a man of spirit — one woman is like another — *you understand me, Joseph* — in coursing, all the sport is made by the winding hare. A barn-door chick is better eating. *Now you take me, Joseph.*

Miss Betterton was but a tradesman's daughter. The family indeed were grown rich; and aimed at a new line of gentry; and were unreasonable enough to expect a man of my family would marry her. I was honest. I gave the young lady no hope of that; for she put it to me. She resented: kept up, and was kept up. A little innocent contrivance was necessary to get her out — but no rape in the case, I assure you, Joseph — she loved me: I loved her. Indeed, when I got her to the inn, I asked her no questions. It is cruel to ask a modest woman for her consent. It is creating difficulties to both. Had not her friends been officious, I had been constant and faithful to her to this day, as far as I know — for then I had not known my angel.

I went not abroad upon *her* account. She loved me too well, to have appeared against me. She refused to sign a paper they had drawn up for her, to found a prosecution upon: and the brutal creatures would not permit the midwife's assistance, till her life was in danger; and, I believe, to this her death was owing.

I went into mourning for her, though abroad at the time. A distinction I have ever paid to those worthy creatures who died in childbed by me.

I was ever nice in my loves. These were the rules I laid down to myself on my entrance into active life: to set the mother above want, if her friends were cruel, and if I could not get her a husband worthy of her: to shun common women: a piece of justice I owed to innocent ladies, as well as to myself: to marry off a former mistress, if possible, before I took to a new one: to maintain a lady handsomely in her lying-in: to provide for the little one, if it lived, according to the degree of its mother: to go into mourning for the mother if she died. And the promise of this was a great comfort to the pretty dears as they grew near their times.

All my errors, all my expenses, have been with and upon women. So I could acquit my conscience (acting thus honourably by them) as well as my discretion as to point of fortune.

All men love women: and find me a man of more honour in these points if you can, Joseph.

No wonder the sex love me as they do!

But *now* I am strictly virtuous. I am reformed. So I have been for a long, long time: resolving to marry, as soon as I can prevail upon the most admirable of women to have me. I think of nobody else. It is impossible I should. I have spared very pretty girls for her sake. Very true, Joseph! so set your honest heart at rest — you see the pains I take to satisfy your qualms.

But, as to Miss Betterton — no rape in the case, I repeat. Rapes are unnatural things: and more rare than are imagined, Joseph. I should be loth to be put to such a streight. I never was. Miss Betterton was taken from me against her own will. In that case, her friends, not I, committed the rape.

I have contrived to see the boy twice, unknown to the aunt, who takes care of him; loves him; and would not now part with him, on any consideration.

The boy is a fine boy, I thank God. No father need be ashamed of him. He will be well provided for. If not, I would take care of him. He will have his mother's fortune. They curse the father, ungrateful wretches! but bless the boy — upon the whole, there is nothing vile in this matter on my side; a great deal on the Bettertons.

Wherefore, Joseph, be not thou in pain, either for *my* head, or for *thy* own neck; nor for the Blue Boar; nor for thy pretty sow.

I love your jesting. Jesting better becomes a poor man, than qualms. — I love to have you jest. All we say, all we do, all we wish for, is a jest. He that makes life itself not so, is a sad fellow, and has the worst of it.

I doubt not, Joseph, but you have had your joys, as you say, as well as your betters. May you have more and more, honest Joseph! — He that grudges a poor man joy, ought to have none himself. Jest on therefore: jesting, I repeat, better becomes thee than qualms.

I had no need to tell you of Miss Betterton: did I not furnish you with stories enough without hers against myself, to augment your credit with your cunning masters? besides, I was loth to mention Miss Betterton, her friends being all living, and in credit. I loved her too: for she was taken from me, by her cruel friends, while our joys were young.

But enough of dear Miss Betterton. *Dear*, I say; for death *endears*. — Rest to her worthy soul! — there, Joseph, off went a deep sigh to the memory of Miss Betterton!

As to the journey of little Titus [I now recollect the fellow by his name] let that take its course; a lady dying in childbed eighteen months ago; no process begun in her lifetime; refusing herself to give evidence against me while she lived — pretty circumstances to found an indictment for a rape upon!

As to your young lady, the ever admirable Miss Clarissa Harlowe, I always courted her for a wife. Others rather expected marriage from the vanity of their own hearts, than from my promises. For I was always careful of what I promised. You know, Joseph, that I have gone beyond my promises to *you*. I do to every body: and why? because it is the best way of shewing, that I have no grudging, or narrow spirit. A promise is an obligation. *A just man will keep his promise. A generous man will go beyond it.* This is my rule.

If you doubt my honour to your young lady, it is more than she does. She would not stay with me an hour if she did. Mine is the steadiest heart in the world. Hast thou not reason to think it so? —

why this squeamishness then, honest Joseph?

But it is because thou *art* honest: so I forgive thee. Whoever loves my divine Clarissa, loves me.

Let James Harlowe call me what names he will. For his sister's sake I will bear them. Do not be concerned for me. Her favour will make me rich amends. His own vilely malicious heart will make his blood *boil over* at any time: and when it does, thinkest thou that I will let it touch my conscience? — and if not *mine*, why should it touch *thine?* Ah! Joseph, Joseph! what a foolish teaser is thy conscience! — such a conscience, as gives a plain man trouble, when he intends to do for the best, is weakness, not conscience.

But say what thou wilt, write all thou knowest or hearest of, to me: I'll have patience with every body. Why should I not, when it is as much the desire of my heart, as it is of thine, to prevent mischief?

So now, Joseph, having taken all this pains to satisfy thy conscience, and answer all thy doubts, and to banish all thy fears; let me come to a *new point*.

Your endeavours and mine, which were designed, *by round-about ways*, to reconcile all, even against the wills of the most obstinate, have not, we see, answered the end we hoped they would answer; but, on the contrary, have widened the unhappy differences between our families. But this has not been either your fault or mine: it is owing to the black pitch-like blood of your venomous-hearted young master, *boiling over*, as he owns, that our honest wishes have hitherto been frustrated.

Yet we must proceed in the same course; we shall tire them out in time, and they will propose terms; and when they do, they shall find how reasonable mine shall be, little as they deserve from me.

Persevere therefore, Joseph; honest Joseph, persevere; and, unlikely as you may imagine the means, our desires will be at last obtained.

We have nothing for it now, but to go through with our work in the way we have begun. For since (as I told you in my last) my beloved mistrusts you, she will blow you up, if she be *not* mine; if she *be*, I can and will protect you; and as, if there will be any fault, in her opinion, it will be rather mine than yours, she *must* forgive you, and keep her husband's secrets, for the sake of his reputation: else she will be guilty of a great failure in her duty. So, now you have set your hand to the plough, Joseph, there is no looking back.

And what is the consequence of all this? one labour more, and that will be all that will fall to your lot; at least, of consequence.

My beloved is resolved not to

think of marriage till she has tried to move her friends to a reconciliation with her. You know they are determined not to be reconciled. She has it in her head, I doubt not, to make me submit to the people I hate; and if I did, they would rather insult me, than receive my condescension as they ought. She even owns, that she will renounce me, if they insist upon it, provided they will give up Solmes! So, to all appearance, I am still as far as ever from the happiness of calling her mine: indeed I am more likely than ever to lose her (if I cannot contrive some way to avail myself of the present critical situation); and then, Joseph, all I have been studying, and all you have been doing, will signify nothing.

At the place were we are, we cannot long be private. The lodgings are inconvenient for us, while both together, and while she refuses to marry. She wants to get me at a distance from her. There are extraordinary convenient lodgings in my eye in London, where we could be private, and all mischief avoided. When *there* (if I *get* her thither), she will insist, that I shall leave her. Miss Howe is for ever putting her upon contrivances. That, you know, is the reason I have been obliged, by your means, to play the family off at Harlowe Place upon Mrs. Howe, and Mrs. Howe upon her daughter — Ah, Joseph! — little need for your fears for my angel: *I* only am in danger — but were I the free liver I am reported to be, all this could I get over with a wet finger, as the saying is.

But, by the help of one of your hints, I have thought of an expedient which will do every thing; and raise your reputation, though already so high, higher still. This Singleton, I hear, is a fellow who loves enterprising: the view he has to get James Harlowe to be his principal owner in a larger vessel which he wants to be put into the command of, may be the subject of their present close conversation. But since he is taught to have so good an opinion of you, Joseph, cannot you (still pretending an abhorrence of me, and of my contrivances), propose to Singleton to propose to James Harlowe (who so much thirsts for revenge upon me), to assist him with his whole ship's crew, upon occasion, to carry off his sister to Leith, where both have houses, or elsewhere?

You may tell them, that if this can be effected, it will make me raving mad; and bring your young lady into all their measures.

You can inform them, *as from my servant*, of the distance she keeps me at, in hopes of procuring her father's forgiveness, by cruelly giving me up, if insisted upon.

You can tell them, that as the only secret my servant has kept from you, is the place we are in, you make no doubt, that a two-guinea bribe will bring that out, and also an information when I shall be at a distance from her, that the enterprise may be conducted with safety.

You may tell them (still as from my servant) that we are about removing from inconvenient lodgings to others more convenient (which is true); and that I must be often absent from her.

If they listen to your proposal, you will promote your interest with Betty, by telling it to her as a secret. Betty will tell Arabella of it. Arabella will be overjoyed at any thing that will help forward her revenge upon me; and will reveal it (if her brother do not), to her uncle Antony. He probably will whisper it to Mrs. Howe. She can keep nothing from her daughter, though they are always jangling. Her daughter will acquaint my beloved with it. And if it will not, or if it will, come to my ears from some of those, you can write it to me, as in confidence, by way of preventing mischief; which is the study of us both.

I can then shew it to my beloved. Then will she be for placing a greater confidence in me. That will convince me of her love, which now I am sometimes ready to doubt. She will be for hastening to the safer lodgings. I shall have a pretence to stay about her person as a guard. She will be convinced, that there is no expectation to be had of a reconciliation. You can give James Harlowe and Singleton continual false scents, as I shall direct you; so that no mischief can possibly happen.

And what will be the happy, happy, thrice happy consequence? — The lady will be mine in an honourable way. We shall all be friends in good time. The two guineas will be an agreeable addition *to the many gratuities I have helped you to, by the like contrivances, from this stingy family.* Your reputation, both for head and heart, as I hinted before, will be heightened. The Blue Boar will also be yours. Nor shall you have the least difficulty about raising money to buy the stock, if it be worth your while to have it.

Betty will likewise then be yours. You have both saved money, it seems. The whole Harlowe family, whom you have so faithfully served, ['tis serving them surely, to prevent the mischief which their violent son would have brought upon them] will throw you in somewhat towards housekeeping. I will still add to your store. So nothing but happiness before you.

Crow, Joseph, crow! A dunghill of thy own in view: servants to snub at thy pleasure: a wife to quarrel with, or to love, as thy humour leads thee. *Landlord* and *landlady* at every word: to be paid, instead of paying, for thy eating and drinking. But not thus happy only in thyself; happy in promoting peace and reconciliation between two good families, in the long run; without hurting any christian soul. O Joseph, honest Joseph! what envy wilt thou raise! — And who would be squeamish with such prospects before him?

This one labour, I repeat, crowns the work. If you can get but such a design entertained by them, whether they prosecute it or not, it will be equally to the purpose of

Your loving friend,
R. LOVELACE.

LETTER XLV.

Miss Clarissa Harlowe to Mrs. Hervey.

[Inclosed in her last to Miss HOWE.]

HONOURED MADAM, Thursday, April 20.

HAVING not had the favour of an answer to a letter I took the liberty to write to you on the 14th, I am in some hopes that it may have miscarried; for I had much rather it should, than to have the mortification to think that my aunt Hervey deemed me unworthy of the honour of her notice.

In this hope, having kept a copy of it, and not being able to express myself in terms better suited to the unhappy circumstances of things, I transcribe and inclose what I then wrote*. And I humbly beseech you to favour the contents of it with your interest.

Hitherto it is in my power to perform what I undertake for in this letter; and it would be very grievous to me to be precipitated upon measures, which may render the desirable reconciliation more difficult.

* The contents of the Letter referred to are given, p. 76.

If, madam, I were permitted to write to you with the hopes of being answered, I could clear my intention with regard to the step I have taken, although I could not perhaps acquit myself to some of my severest judges, of an imprudence previous to it. You, I am sure, would pity me, if you knew all I could say, and how miserable I am in the forfeiture of the good opinion of all my friends.

I flatter myself, that *their* favour is yet retrievable. But, whatever be the determination at Harlowe Place, do not *you*, my dearest aunt, deny me the favour of a few lines, to inform me if there can be any hope of a reconciliation upon terms less shocking than those heretofore endeavoured to be imposed upon me; or if (which God forbid!) I am to be for ever reprobated.

At least, my dear aunt, procure for me the justice of my wearing apparel, and the little money and other things which I wrote to my sister for, and mention in the inclosed to you; that I may not be destitute of common conveniencies, or be under a necessity to owe an obligation for such, where (at present, however) I would least of all owe it.

Allow me to say, that had I designed what happened, I might (as to the money and jewels at least) have saved myself some of the mortifications which I have suffered, and which I still further apprehend, if my request be not complied with.

If you are permitted to encourage an eclaircissement of what I hint, I will open my whole heart to you, and inform you of every thing.

If it be any pleasure to have me mortified, be pleased to let it be known, that I am extremely mortified: and yet it is *entirely* from my own reflections that I am so; having nothing to find fault with in the behaviour of the person from whom every evil was apprehended.

The bearer, having business your way, will bring me your answer on Saturday morning, if you favour me according to my hopes. I knew not that I should have this opportunity till I had written the above.

I am, my dearest aunt,
Your ever dutiful
CL. HARLOWE.

Be pleased to direct for me, if I am to be favoured with a few lines, to be left at Mr. Osgood's, near Soho Square; and nobody shall ever know of your goodness to me, if you desire it to be kept a secret.

LETTER XLVI.

[Miss Howe to Miss Clarissa Harlowe.

Saturday, April 22.

I CANNOT for my life account for your wretch's teasing ways. But he certainly doubts your love of him. In this *he* is a *modest* man, as well as *somebody* else; and tacitly confesses, that he does not deserve it.

Your Israelitish hankerings after the Egyptian onions (testified still more in your letter to your aunt); your often-repeated regrets for meeting him; for being betrayed away by him — these he cannot bear.

I have been looking back on the whole of his conduct, and comparing it with his general character; and find that he is more *consistently*, more *uniformly*, mean, revengeful, and proud, than either of us once imagined.

From his cradle, as I may say, as an *only child*, and a *boy*, humorsome, spoiled, mischievous; the governor of his governors.

A libertine in his riper years, hardly regardful of appearances; and despising the sex in general, for the faults of particulars of it, who made themselves too cheap to him?

What has been his behaviour in your family, a CLARISSA in view, (from the time your foolish brother was obliged to take a life from him) but defiance for defiances? — Getting you into his power by terror, by artifice. What politeness can be expected from such a man?

Well, but what in such a situation is to be done? Why, you must despise him: you must hate him — if you can — and run away from him — but whither? Whither indeed, now that your brother is laying foolish plots to put you in a still worse condition, as it may happen?

But if you cannot despise and hate him; if you care not to break with him; you must part with some punctilios: and if the so doing bring not on the solemnity, you must put yourself into the protection of the ladies of his family.

Their respect for you is of itself a security for his honour to you, if there could be any room for doubt. And at least, you should remind him of his offer to bring one of the Miss Montague's to attend you at your new lodgings in town, and accompany you till all is happily over.

This, you'll say, will be as good as *declaring* yourself to be his. *And so let it.* You ought not now to think of any thing else but to be *his.* Does not your brother's project convince your more and more of this?

Give over then, my dearest friend, any thoughts of this hopeless reconciliation, *which has kept you balancing thus long.* You own, in the letter before me, that he made very explicit offers, though you give me not the very words. And he gave his reasons, I perceive, with his wishes, that you should accept them: which very few of the sorry fellows do; whose plea is generally but a compliment to our self-love— *that we must love them,* however presumptuous and unworthy, *because they love us.*

Were I in *your place,* and had *your* charming delicacies, I should, perhaps, do as you do. No doubt but I should expect that the man should urge me with respectful warmth; that he should supplicate with constancy, and that all his words and actions should tend to the one principal point — nevertheless, if I suspected art or delay, founded upon his doubts of my love, I would either condescend to clear up his doubts, or renounce him for ever.

And in this last case, I, your Anna Howe, would exert myself, and either find you a private refuge, or resolve to share fortunes with you.

What a wretch, to be so easily answered by your reference to the arrival of your cousin Morden! But I am afraid that you were too scrupulous: — for did he not resent that reference?

Could we have *his* account of the matter, I fancy, my dear, I should think you over, nice, overdelicate.* Had you laid hold of his *acknowledged* explicitness, he would have been as much in *your* power, as now you seem to be in *his* — you wanted not to be told, that the person who had been tricked into such a step as you had taken, must of necessity submit to many mortifications.

But were it to *me,* a girl of spirit as I am thought to be, I do assure you, I would, in a quarter of an hour, (all the time I would allow to punctilio in such a case as yours) know what he drives at: since either he must mean *well* or *ill;* if *ill,* the sooner you know it, the better; if *well,* whose modesty

* The reader who has seen his account, which Miss Howe could not have seen, when she wrote thus, will observe that it was not possible for a person of Clarissa's true delicacy of mind to act otherwise than she did, to a man so cruelly and so insolently artful.

is it he distresses, but that of his own wife?

And methinks you should endeavour to avoid all exasperating recriminations, as to what you have heard of his failure in morals; especially while you are so happy, as not to have occasion to speak of them by experience.

I grant that it gives a worthy mind some satisfaction in having borne its testimony against the immoralities of a bad one. But that correction which is unseasonably given, is more likely either to harden or make an hypocrite, than to reclaim.

I am pleased, however, as well as you with his making light of your brother's *wise* project. — Poor creature! and must master Jemmy Harlowe, with his half-wit, pretend to plot and contrive mischief, yet rail at Lovelace for the same things? — A witty villain deserves hanging at once (and without ceremony, if you please:) but a half-witted one deserves broken bones first, and hanging afterwards. I think Lovelace has given his character in few words.*

Be angry at me, if you please; but as sure as you are alive, now that this poor creature, whom some call your brother, finds he has succeeded in making you fly your father's house, and that he has nothing to fear but your getting into your *own*, and into an independence of him, he thinks himself equal to any thing, and so has a mind to fight Lovelace with his own weapons.

* See p. 140.

Don't you remember his pragmatical triumph, as told you by your aunt, and prided in by that saucy Betty Barnes, from his own foolish mouth?*

I expect nothing from your letter to your aunt. I hope Lovelace will never know the contents of it. In every one of yours, I see that he as warmly resents as he dares, the little confidence you have in him. I should resent it too, were I he; and knew I deserved better.

Don't be scrupulous about clothes, if you think of putting yourself into the protection of the ladies of his family. They know how matters stand between you and your relations, and love you never the worse for the silly people's cruelty.

I know you won't demand possession of your estate. But give *him* a right to demand it for you; and that will be still better.

Adieu, my dear! May Heaven guide and direct you in all your steps, is the daily prayer of

Your ever affectionate
and faithful
ANNA HOWE.

LETTER XLVII.

Mr. Belford to Robert Lovelace, Esq.

Friday, April 21.

THOU, Lovelace, hast been long the *entertainer;* I the *entertained.* Nor have I been solicitous to animadvert, as thou wentest along, upon thy inventions, and their tendency. For I believed, that with all thy airs, the unequalled

* See Vol. I. p. 417, 418, 420.

perfections and fine qualities of this lady would always be her protection and security. But now that I find thou hast so far succeeded as to induce her to come to town, and to choose her lodgings in a house, the people of which will too probably damp and suppress any honourable motions which may arise in thy mind in her favour, I cannot help writing: and that professedly in her behalf.

My inducements to this are not owing to virtue: but if they *were* what hope could I have of affecting thee, by pleas arising from it? Nor would such a man as thou art be deterred, were I to remind thee of the vengeance which thou mayest one day expect, if thou insultest a woman of her character, family, and fortune.

Neither are gratitude and honour motives to be mentioned in a woman's favour, to men such as we are, who consider all those of the sex as fair prize, over whom we can obtain a power. For *our honour*, and *honour*, in the *general acceptation* of the word, are two things.

What then is my motive? — What, but the true friendship that I bear thee, Lovelace; which makes me plead *thy own sake*, and *thy family's sake*, in the justice thou owest to this incomparable creature; who, however, so well deserves to have *her sake* to be mentioned as the principal consideration.

Last time I was at M. Hall, thy noble uncle so earnestly pressed me to use my interest to persuade thee to enter the pale, and gave me so many family reasons for it, that I could not help engaging myself heartily on his side of the question; and the rather as I knew, that thy own intentions with regard to this fine woman were then worthy of *her*. And of this I assured his lordship; who was half afraid of thee, because of the ill usage thou receivedst from her family. But now, that the case is altered, let me press the matter home to thee, from *other* considerations.

By what I have heard of this lady's perfections from every mouth, as well as from thine, and from every letter thou hast written, where wilt thou find such another woman? And why shouldst thou tempt her virtue? — Why shouldst thou wish to try where there is no reason to doubt?

Were I in thy case, and designed to marry, and if I preferred a woman as I know thou dost this, to all the women in the world, I should dread to make further trial, knowing what *we* know of the sex, for *fear* of succeeding; and especially if I doubted not, that if there were a woman in the world virtuous at heart, it is she.

And let me tell thee, Lovelace, that in this lady's situation, the trial is not a fair trial. Considering the depth of thy plots and contrivances: considering the opportunities which I see thou must have with her, in spite of her own heart; all her relations' follies acting in concert, though unknown to themselves, with thy wicked scheming head: considering how destitute of protection she is: considering the house she is to be in, where she will be surrounded with thy implements; *specious*, *well-bred*, and *genteel* creatures, not easily to be detected when they are disposed to preserve appearances, especially by a young, unexperienced lady wholly unacquainted with the town: considering all these things, I say, what glory, what cause of triumph, wilt thou have, if she should be overcome? — Thou, too, a man born for intrigue, full of invention, intrepid, remorseless, able patiently to watch for thy opportunity, not hurried, as most men, by gusts of violent passion, which often nip a project in the bud, and make the snail that was just putting out his horns to meet the inviter, withdraw into its shell — a man who has no regard to his word or oath to the sex; the lady scrupulously strict to *her* word, incapable of art or design; apt therefore to believe well of others — it would be a miracle if she stood such an attempter, such attempt, and such snares, as I see will be laid for her. And after all, I see not when men are so frail *without* importunity, that so much should be expected from women, daughters of the same fathers and mothers, and made up of the same brittle compounds, (education all the difference) nor where the triumph is in subduing them.

May there not be other Lovelaces, thou askest, who, attracted by her beauty, may endeavour to prevail with her*?

No; there cannot, I answer, be such another man, person, mind, fortune, and thy character, as above given, taken in. If thou imaginest there could, such is thy pride, that thou wouldst think the worse of thyself.

But let me touch upon thy predominant passion, *revenge;* for *love* is but second to that, as I have often told thee, though it has set thee into raving at me: what poor pretences for revenge are the difficulties thou hadst in getting her off; allowing that she had run a risk of being Solmes's wife, had she staid? If these are other than pretences, why thankest thou not those who, by their persecutions of her, answered thy hopes, and threw her into thy power? — Besides, are not the pretences thou makest for further trial, most ingratefully, as well as *contradictorily*, founded upon the supposition of error in her, occasioned by her *favour* to thee?

And let me, for the utter confusion of thy poor pleas of this nature, ask thee — would she, in thy opinion, had she *willingly gone off with thee*, have been entitled to *better* quarter? — For a mistress indeed she might: but wouldst thou for a *wife* have had cause to like her half so well, as now?

Has she not demonstrated, that even the highest provocations were not sufficient to warp her from her duty to her parents, though a na-

* See p. 54, 55.

tive, and, as I may say, an originally *involuntary* duty, because *native?* And is not this a charming earnest that she will sacredly observe a still higher duty into which she proposes to enter, when she does enter, by *plighted* vows, and entirely as a *volunteer?*

That she loves thee, wicked as thou art, and cruel as a panther, there is no reason to doubt. Yet, what a command has she over herself, that such a penetrating self-flatterer as thyself, art sometimes ready to doubt it! Though persecuted on the one hand, as she was, by her own family, and attracted, on the other, by the splendour of thine; every one of whom courts her to rank herself among them?

Thou wilt perhaps think, that I have departed from my proposition, and pleaded the *lady's sake* more than *thine* in the above—but no such thing. All that I have written, is more in *thy* behalf than in *hers;* since she may make *thee* happy; but it is next to impossible, I should think, if she preserve her delicacy, that thou canst make *her* so. What is the love of a rakish heart? There cannot be *peculiarity* in it. But I need not give my further reasons. Thou wilt have ingenuousness enough, I dare say, were there occasion for it, to subscribe to my opinion.

I plead not for the state from any great liking to it myself. Nor have I, at present, thoughts of entering into it. But, as thou art the last of thy name; as thy family is of note and figure in thy country; and as thou thyself thinkest that thou shalt one day marry: is it possible, let me ask thee, that thou canst have such another opportunity as thou now hast, if thou lettest this slip? A woman, in her family and fortune, not unworthy of thine own, (though thou art so apt, from pride of ancestry, and pride of heart, to speak slightly of the families thou dislikest; so celebrated for beauty; and so noted at the same time for prudence, for *soul*, (I will say, instead of *sense*) and for virtue.

If thou art not so narrow-minded an elf, as to prefer thine own *single* satisfaction to *posterity*, thou who shouldst wish to beget children for duration, wilt not postpone till the rake's usual time; that is to say, till diseases, or years, or both, lay hold of thee; since in that case thou wouldst intitle thyself to the curses of thy legitimate progeny for giving them a being altogether miserable: a being which they will be obliged to hold upon a worse tenure than that *tenant-courtesy*, which thou callest the *worst**; to wit, upon the *doctor's courtesy;* thy descendants also propagating (if they shall live, and be able to propagate) a wretched race, that shall entail the curse, or the *reason* for it, upon remote generations.

Wicked as the sober world accounts you and me, we have not yet, it is to be hoped, got over all compunction. Although we find religion against us, we have not yet presumed to make a religion to suit our practices. We despise

* See p. 80.

those who do. And we know better than to be even *doubters.* In short, we believe a future state of rewards and punishments. But as we have so much youth and health in hand, we hope to have time for repentance. That is to say, in plain English, [nor think thou me too grave, Lovelace; *thou* art grave sometimes, though not often] we hope to live to sense, as long as sense can relish, and purpose to reform when we can sin no longer.

And shall this admirable woman suffer for her generous endeavours to set on foot thy reformation; and for insisting upon proofs of the sincerity of thy professions before she will be thine?

Upon the whole matter, let me wish thee to consider well what thou art about, before thou goest a step further in the path which thou hast chalked out for thyself to tread, and art just going to enter upon. Hitherto all is so far right, that if the lady mistrusts thy honour, she has no *proofs.* Be honest to her, then, in *her* sense of the word. None of thy companions, thou knowest, will offer to laugh at what *thou* dost. And if they *should,* (on thy entering into a state which has been so much ridiculed by thee, and by all of us) thou hast one advantage — it is this; that thou canst not be ashamed.

Deferring to the post-day to close my letter, I find one left at my cousin Osgood's, with direction to be forwarded to the lady. It was brought within these two hours by a particular hand, and has a Harlowe seal upon it. As it may therefore be of importance, I dispatch it with my own, by my servant, post haste*.

I suppose you will soon be in town. Without the lady, I hope. Farewell.

Be honest, and be happy.

J. BELFORD.

Sat. April 22.

LETTER XLVIII.

Mrs. Hervey to Miss Clarissa Harlowe.

[*In Answer to Letter* xlv.]

DEAR NIECE,

It would be hard not to write a few lines, so much pressed to write, to one I ever loved. Your former letter I received; yet was not at liberty to answer it. I break my word to answer you now.

Strange informations are every day received about you. The wretch you are with, we are told, is every hour triumphing and defying — must not these informations aggravate? You know the uncontrollableness of the man. He loves his own humour better than he loves you — though so fine a creature as you are! I warned you over and over: no young lady was ever more warned! — Miss Clarissa Harlowe to do such a thing!

You might have given your friends the meeting. If you had *held* your aversion, it would have been complied with. As soon as I was entrusted myself with their *intention* to give up the point, I gave you a hint — a dark one, per-

* This Letter was from Miss Arabella Harlowe. See Let. ll.

haps* — but who would have thought — O Miss: — such an artful flight! — Such *cunning* preparation!

But you want to clear up things —*what* can you clear up? Are you not gone off? — With a Lovelace too? *What*, my dear, would you clear up?

You did not *design* to go, you say. Why did you meet him then, chariot-and-six, horsemen, all prepared by him? O, my dear, how art produces art! — Will it be believed? — If it *would*, what power will he thought to have had over you! — He — who? — *Lovelace!* — the vilest of libertines! — Over whom? — A *Clarissa!* — Was your love for such a man above your reason? Above your resolution? What credit would a belief of this, *if* believed, bring you? — How mend the matter? — Oh! that you had stood the next meeting!

I'll tell you all that was intended if you had.

It was, indeed, imagined, that you would not have been able to resist your father's entreaties and commands. He was resolved to be all condescension, if anew you had not provoked him. *I love my Clary Harlowe*, said he, but an hour before the killing tidings were brought him; *I love her as my life: I will kneel to her, if nothing else will do, to prevail upon her to oblige me.*

Your father and mother (the reverse of what should have been!) would have humbled themselves to *you*: and if you could have denied

* See Vol. I. p. 418, 419.

them, and refused to sign the settlements previous to the meeting, they would have yielded, although with regret.

But it was presumed, so naturally sweet your temper, so self-denying, as they thought you, that you could *not* have withstood them, notwithstanding all your dislike of the *one* man, without a greater degree of headstrong passion for the *other*, than you had given any of us reason to expect from you.

If you *had*, the meeting on Wednesday would have been a lighter trial to you. You would have been presented to all your assembled friends, with a short speech only "that this was the young creature, till very lately faultless, condescending, and obliging; now having cause to glory in a triumph over the wills of father, mother, uncles, the most indulgent; over family interests, family views; and preferring her own will to every body's; and this for a transitory preference to *person* only; there being no comparison between the men as to their *morals*."

Thus complied with and perhaps blessed, by your father and mother, and the consequences of your disobedience deprecated in the solemnest manner by your inimitable mother, your *generosity* would have been appealed to, since your duty would have been found too weak an inducement, and you would have been bid to withdraw for one half-hour's consideration: then would the settlements have been again tendered for your signing, by the person least disobliging to you; by your good Norton perhaps; she perhaps seconded by your father again: and if again refused, you would again have been led in, to declare such your refusal. Some restrictions, which you yourself had proposed, would have been insisted upon. You would have been permitted to go home with me, or with your uncle Antony (with *which* of us was not agreed upon, because they hoped you might be persuaded) there to stay till the arrival of your cousin Morden; or till your father could have borne to see you; or till assured, that the views of Lovelace were at an end.

This the intention, your father so set upon your compliance, so much in hopes that you would have yielded, that you would have been prevailed upon by methods so condescending and so gentle; no wonder that *he*, in particular, was like a distracted man, when he heard of your flight — of your flight so *premeditated;*—with your ivy summer-house dinings, your arts to blind me, and all of us!—naughty, naughty young creature!

I, for my part, would not believe it, when told of it. Your uncle Hervey would not believe it. We rather expected, we rather feared, a still more desperate adventure. There could be but one more desperate; and I was readier to have the cascade first resorted to, than the garden back-door. — Your mother fainted away, while her heart was torn between the two apprehensions. — Your father, poor man! your father was beside himself for near an hour — what imprecations! — what dreadful imprecations! — To this day he can hardly bear your name: yet can think of nobody else. Your merits, my dear, but aggravate your fault. — Something of fresh aggravation every hour — how can any favour be expected?

I am sorry for it; but am afraid nothing you ask will be complied with.

Why mention you, my dear, the saving you from mortifications, who have gone off with a man? What a poor pride is it to stand upon any thing else?

I dare not open my lips in your favour. Nobody dare. Your letter must stand by itself. This has caused me to send it to Harlowe Place. Expect therefore great severity. May you be enabled to support the lot you have drawn! O, my dear! how unhappy have you made every body! Can *you* expect to be happy? Your father wishes you had never been born. Your poor mother — but why should I afflict you? There is now no help! — You must be changed, indeed, if you are not very unhappy yourself in the reflections your thoughtful mind must suggest to you.

You must now make the best of your lot. Yet *not* married it seems!

It is in your power, you say, to perform whatever you shall undertake to do. You may deceive yourself: you hope that your reputation and the favour of your friends may be retrieved. Never, never, both, I doubt; if either. Every offended person (and that is all who loved you, and are related to you) must *join* to restore you: when can these be of *one* mind in a case so notoriously wrong?

It would be very grievous, you say, to be precipitated upon measures, that may make the desirable reconciliation more difficult. Is it *now*, my dear, a time for you to be afraid of being *precipitated?* At *present*, if *ever*, there can be no thought of reconciliation. The *upshot* of your precipitation must first be seen. There may be murder yet as far as we know. Will the man you are with part willingly with you? If *not*, what may be the consequence? If he *will* — Lord bless me! what shall we think of his reasons for it? — I will fly this thought. — I know your purity — but, my dear, are you not out of all protection? — Are you not unmarried? — Have you not (making your daily prayers useless) thrown yourself into temptation? And is not the man the most wicked of plotters?

You have hitherto, you say (and I think, my dear, with an air unbecoming your declared penitence) *no fault to find with the behaviour of a man from whom every evil was apprehended:* like Cæsar to the Roman augur, who had bid him *beware of the ides of March: The ides of March*, said Cæsar, seeing the augur among the crowd, as he marched in state to the senate-house, from which he never was to return alive, *the ides of March are come. But they are not past,* the augur replied. Make the application, my dear: may you be able to make this reflection upon his good behaviour to the last of your knowledge of him! May he behave himself better to you, than he ever did to any body else over whom he had power! Amen!

No answer, I beseech you. I hope your messenger will not tell any body that I have written to you. And I dare say you will not shew this letter to Mr. Lovelace — for I have written with the less reserve, depending upon your prudence.

You have my prayers.

My Dolly knows not that I write. Nobody does*: not even Mr. Hervey.

Dolly would have several times written: but having defended your fault with heat, and with a partiality that alarmed us [such a fall as yours, my dear, must be alarming to all parents] she has been forbidden, on pain of losing our favour for ever: and this at your family's request, as well as by her father's commands. You have the poor girl's hourly prayers, I will, however, tell you, though she knows not that I do, as well as those of

Your truly afflicted aunt,

Friday, April 21. D. Hervey.

* Notwithstanding what Mrs. Hervey here says, it will be hereafter seen that this severe letter of hers was written in private concert with the implacable Arabella.

LETTER XLIX.
Miss Clarissa Harlowe to Miss Howe.

With the preceding.

Sat. morn. April 22.

I HAVE just now received the enclosed from my aunt Hervey. Be pleased, my dear, to keep her secret of having written to the unhappy wretch her niece.

I may go to London, I see, or where I will. No matter what becomes of me.

I was the willinger to suspend my journey thither, till I heard from Harlowe Place. I thought if I could be encouraged to hope for a reconciliation, I would let this man see, that he should not have me in his power, but upon my own terms, if at all.

But I find I must be *his*, whether I will or not; and perhaps through still greater mortifications than those great ones which I have already met with — and must I be so absolutely thrown upon a man, with whom I am not at all satisfied?

My letter is sent, you see, to Harlowe Place. My heart aches for the reception it may meet with there.

One comfort only arises to me from its being sent; that my aunt will clear *herself* by the communication, from the supposition of having corresponded with the poor creature whom they have all determined to reprobate. It is no small part of my misfortune that I have weakened the confidence one dear friend has in another, and made one look cool upon another.

My poor cousin Dolly, you see, has reason for regret on this account, as well as my aunt. Miss Howe, my dear Miss Howe, is but too sensible of the effects of my fault, having had more words with her mother on my account, than ever she had on any other. Yet the man who has drawn me into all this evil, I must be thrown upon! — Much did I consider, much did I apprehend, *before* my fault, supposing I *were* to be guilty of it: but I saw it not in all its shocking lights.

And now, to know that my father, an hour before he received the tidings of my supposed flight, owned that he loved me as his life; that he would have been all condescension; that he would — Oh! my dear, how tender, how mortifyingly tender now in him! My aunt need not have been afraid, that it should be known that she has sent me such a letter as this! — A father to kneel to his child! — There would not indeed have been any bearing of that! — What I should have done in such a case, I know not. Death would have been much more welcome to me than such a sight, on such an occasion, in behalf of a man so very, very disgustful to me! — But I had deserved annihilation, had I suffered my father to kneel in vain.

Yet, had but the sacrifice of *inclination* and *personal preference* been *all*, less than KNEELING should have done. My *duty* should have been the conqueror of my *inclination*. But an aversion — an aversion so *very* sincere! — The triumph of a cruel and ambitious brother, ever so uncontroulable, joined with the insults of an envious sister, bringing wills to *theirs*, which otherwise would have been favourable to *me:* the marriage duties, so absolutely indispensable, so solemnly to be engaged for: the marriage intimacies [permit me to say to you, my friend, what the purest, although with apprehension, must think of] so *very* intimate: myself one, who never looked upon any duty, much less a voluntary vowed one, with indifference; could it have been honest in me to have given my hand to an odious hand, and to have consented to such a more than reluctant, such an *immiscible* union, if I may so call it? — For life too! — Did not I *think* more and deeper than most young creatures think; did I not *weigh*, did I not *reflect;* I might perhaps have been less obstinate — *delicacy*, (may I presume to call it?) *thinking, weighing, reflection*, are not blessings (I have not found them such) in the degree I have them. I wish I had been able, in some very nice cases, to have known what *indifference* was; yet not to have my *ignorance* imputable to me as a fault. Oh! my dear! the finer sensibilities, if I may suppose mine to be such, make not happy.

What a method had my friends intended to take with me? This, I dare say, was a method chalked out by my brother. *He*, I suppose, was to have presented me to all my assembled friends, as the daughter capable of preferring her own will to the wills of them all. It would have been a sore trial, no doubt. Would to Heaven, however, I had stood it— let the issue have been what it would, would to Heaven I had stood it!

There may be murder, my aunt says. This looks as if she knew of Singleton's rash plot. Such an *upshot*, as she calls it, of this unhappy affair, Heaven avert!

She flies a thought, that I can *less* dwell upon — a *cruel* thought — but she has a poor opinion of the purity she compliments me with, if she thinks that I am not, by God's grace, above temptation, from this sex. Although I never saw a man, whose *person* I could like, before this man; yet his faulty character allowed me but little merit from the indifference I pretended to on his account. But now, I see him *in nearer lights*, I like him less than ever. Unpolite, cruel, insolent! — Unwise! A trifler with his own happiness; the destroyer of mine! — His last treatment — *my fate too visibly in his power* — *master of his own wishes* [shame to say it] *if he knew what to wish for*. — Indeed I never liked him so little as now. Upon my word, I think I could hate him (if I do not already hate him) sooner than any man I ever thought tolerably of — a good reason why: because I have been more disappointed in my expectations of him; although they never were so high, *as to have made him my choice in preference to the single life, had that been permitted me.* Still, if the giving him up for ever will make my path to reconciliation easy, and if they will signify as much to me, they shall see that I never will be *his:* for I have the vanity to think my soul his soul's superior.

You will say I rave: forbidden to write to my aunt, and taught to despair of reconciliation, you, my dear, must be troubled with my passionate resentments. What a wretch was I to give him a meeting, since by that I put it out of my power to meet my assembled friends! — All would now, if I had met them, 'have been over; and who can tell when my present distresses will? — Rid of both men, I had been now perhaps at my aunt Hervey's or at my uncle Antony's; wishing for my cousin Morden's arrival; who might have accommodated all.

I *intended*, indeed, to have stood it; and, if I had, how know I by whose name I might now have been called? For how should I have resisted a condescending, a *kneeling* father, had he been able to have kept his temper with me?

Yet my aunt says, he would have relented, if *I* had not. Perhaps he would have been moved by my humility, before he could have shewn such *undue* condescension. . Such temper as he would have received me with might have been improved upon in my favour. And that he had designed *ultimately* to relent, how it clears my friends (at least to themselves) and condemns me! O why were my aunt's hints [I remember them now] so very dark? — Yet I intended to have returned after the interview; and then perhaps she would have explained herself. — O this artful, this designing Lovelace! — Yet I must repeat, that most ought I to blame myself for meeting him.

But far, far be banished from me fruitless recrimination! Far banished, *because* fruitless! Let me wrap myself about in the mantle of my own integrity, and take comfort in my unfaulty intention! Since it is now too late to look back, let me collect all my fortitude, and endeavour to stand those shafts of angry Providence, which it will not permit me to shun! That, whatever the trials may be, which I am destined to undergo, I may not behave unworthily in them; and may come out amended by them.

Join with me in this prayer, my beloved friend; for your own honour's sake, as well as for love's sake, join with me in it: lest a deviation on my side, should, with the censorious, cast a shade upon a friendship which has no levity in it; and the basis of which is improvement, as well in the greater as lesser duties.

CL. HARLOWE.

LETTER L.

Miss Clarissa Harlowe to Miss Howe.

Sunday afternoon, April 23.

O MY best, my *only* friend! now indeed is my heart broken! it has received a blow it never will recover. Think not of corresponding with a wretch who now seems absolutely devoted. How can it be otherwise, if a parent's curses have the weight I always attributed to them, and have heard so many instances in confirmation of that weight!—Yes, my dear Miss Howe, superadded to all my afflictions, I have the consequences of a father's curse to struggle with! How shall I support this reflection!—my past and my present situation so much authorizing my apprehensions!

I have, at last, a letter from my unrelenting sister. Would to Heaven I had not provoked it by my second letter to my aunt Hervey! It lay ready for me, it seems. The thunder slept till I awakened it. I inclose the letter itself. Transcribe it I cannot. There is no bearing the thoughts of it: for [shocking reflection!] the curse extends to the life beyond this.

I am in the depth of vapourish despondency. I can only repeat, shun, fly, correspond not with a wretch so devoted as

CL. HARLOWE.

LETTER LI.

To Miss Clarissa Harlowe.

To be left at Mr. Osgood's, near Soho Square.

Friday, April 21.

It was *expected* you would send again to me, or to my aunt Hervey. The enclosed has lain ready for you therefore by direction. You will have no answer from any body, write to *whom* you will, and as *often* as you will, and *what* you will.

It was designed to bring you back by proper authority, or to send you whither the disgraces you have brought upon us all should be in the likeliest way, after a while, to be forgotten. But I believe that design is over: so you may *range* securely—nobody will think it worth while to give themselves any trouble about you. Yet my mother has obtained leave to send you your clothes of all sorts: but your clothes only. This is a favour you'll see by the within letter not *designed* you: and *now* not granted for your sake, but because my poor mother cannot bear in her sight any thing you used to wear. Read the enclosed, and tremble.

ARABELLA HARLOWE.

TO THE MOST UNGRATEFUL AND UNDUTIFUL OF DAUGHTERS.

Harlowe Place, April 15.

SISTER THAT WAS!

For I know not what name you are *permitted*, or *choose* to go by.

You have filled us all with distraction. My father, in the first agitations of his mind, on discovering your wicked, your shameful elopement, imprecated on his knees a fearful curse upon you. Tremble at the recital of it!—No less, than "that you may meet your punishment both *here* and *hereafter*, by means of the very wretch, in whom you have chosen to place your wicked confidence."

Your clothes will not be sent you. You seem, by leaving them behind you, to have been secure of them, whenever you demanded them, but perhaps you could think of nothing but meeting your fellow: nothing but how to get off with your forward self! — For every thing seems to have been forgotten but what was to contribute to your wicked flight — yet you judged right, perhaps, that you would have been detected, had you endeavoured to get away your clothes. — Cunning creature! not to make one step that we could guess at you by! Cunning to effect your own ruin, and the disgrace of all the family!

But does the wretch put you upon writing for your things, for fear you should be too expensive to him? — That's it, I suppose.

Was there ever a giddier creature! — Yet this is the celebrated, the blazing Clarissa — Clarissa *what? Harlowe*, no doubt! — And Harlowe it will be, to the disgrace of us all!

Your drawings and your pieces are all taken down; as is also your own whole-length picture, in the Vandyke taste, from your late parlour: they are taken down, and thrown into your closet, which will be nailed up, as if it were not a part of the house; there to perish together: for who can bear to see them? Yet, how did they use to be shewn to every body; the former, for the magnifying of your dainty finger works; the latter, for the imputed dignity (dignity now in the dust!) of your boasted figure; and this by those fond parents from whom you have run away with so *much*, yet with so *little* contrivance!

My brother vows revenge upon your libertine — for the *family's sake*, he vows it — not for *yours!* — For he will treat you, he declares, like a common creature, if ever he sees you: and doubts not that this will be your fate.

My uncle Harlowe renounces you for ever.

So does my uncle Antony.

So does my aunt Hervey.

So do *I*, base unworthy creature! the disgrace of a good family, and the property of an infamous rake, as questionless you will soon find yourself, if you are not already.

Your books, since they have not taught you what belongs to your family, to your sex, and to your education, will not be sent you. Your money neither. Nor yet the jewels so undeservedly made yours. For it is wished you may be seen a beggar along London streets.

If all this is heavy, lay your hand to your heart, and ask yourself why you have deserved it?

Every man whom your pride taught you to reject with scorn (Mr. Solmes excepted, who, however, has reason to rejoice that he missed you) triumphs in your shameful elopement; and now knows how to account for his being refused.

Your worthy Norton is ashamed of you, and mingles her tears with your mother's; both reproaching themselves for their shares in you, and in so fruitless an education.

Every body, in short, is ashamed of you: but none more than
ARABELLA HARLOWE.

LETTER LII.

Miss Howe to Miss Clarissa Harlowe.

Tuesday, April 25.

BE comforted; be not dejected; do not despond, my dearest and best beloved friend. God Almighty is just and gracious, and gives not his assent to rash and inhuman curses. Can you think that Heaven will seal to the black passions of its depraved creatures? If it did, malice, envy, and revenge would triumph; and the best of the human race, blasted by the malignity of the worst, would be miserable in both worlds.

This outrageousness shews only what manner of spirit they are of, and how much their sordid views exceed their parental love. 'Tis all owing to rage and disappointment—disappointment in designs proper to be frustrated.

If you consider this malediction as it ought to be considered, a person of your piety must and will rather pity and pray for your *rash father* than terrify *yourself* on the occasion. None but God can curse. Parents, or others, whoever they be, can only pray to him to curse: and such prayers can have no weight with a just and all-perfect Being, the motives to which are unreasonable, and the end proposed by them cruel.

Has not God commanded us *to bless, and curse not?* Pray for your father then, I repeat, that he incur not the malediction he has announced on you; since he has broken, as you see, a command truly divine; while you, by obeying that other precept, which enjoins us *to pray for them that persecute and curse us*, will turn the curse into a blessing.

My mother blames them for this wicked letter of your sister; and she pities you; and of her own accord, wished me to write to comfort you, for this once: for she says it is pity your heart, which was so noble (and when the sense of your fault, and the weight of a parent's curse, are so strong upon you) should be quite broken.

Lord bless me, how your aunt writes!—Can there be two rights and two wrongs in palpable cases! — But, my dear, she *must* be wrong: so they all have been, justify themselves now as they will. They can only justify themselves *to* themselves from selfish principles, resolving to *acquit*, not fairly to *try* themselves. Did your unkind aunt, in all the tedious progress of your contentions with them, give you the least hope of their relenting?— Her dark hints now I recollect, as well as you. But why was any thing good or hopeful to be darkly hinted?— How easy was it for *her*, who pretended always to love you; for *her*, who can give such flowing licence to her pen for your hurt; to have given you one word, one line (in confidence) of their pretended change of measures!

But do not mind their after-pretences, my dear—all of them

serve but for tacit confessions of their vile usage of you. I will keep your aunt's secret, never fear. I would not, on any consideration, that my mother should see her letter.

You will now see, that you have nothing left, but to overcome all scrupulousness, and marry as soon as you have an opportunity. Determine so to do, my dear.

I will give you a motive for it, regarding myself. For this I have resolved, and this I have vowed [O friend, the best beloved of my heart, be not angry with me for it]! "That so long as your happiness is in suspense, I will never think of marrying." In justice to the man I shall have, I have vowed this: for, my dear, must I not be miserable if you are so? And what an unworthy wife must I be to any man who cannot have interest enough in my heart to make his obligingness a balance for an affliction he has not caused?

I would shew Lovelace your sister's abominable letter, were it to me. I inclose it. It shall not have a place in this house. This will enter him of course into the subject which you now ought to have most in view. Let him see what you suffer for him. He cannot prove base to such an excellence. I should never enjoy my head or my senses should this man prove a villain to you! — With a merit so exalted, you may have punishment more than enough for your involuntary fault in that husband.

I would not have you be too sure that their project to seize you is over. The words intimating that it *is* over, in the letter of that abominable Arabella, seem calculated to give you security. — She only says, she *believes* that design is over. — And I do not yet find from Miss Lloyd that it is disavowed. So it will be best, when you are in London, to be private, and, for fear of the worst, to let every direction be to a *third place;* for I would not, for the world, have you fall into the hands of such flaming and malevolent spirits by surprise.

I will myself be content to direct to you at *some third place;* and I shall then be able to aver to my mother, or to any other, if occasion be, *that I know not where you are.*

Besides, this measure will make you less apprehensive of the consequences of their violence, should they resolve to attempt to carry you off in spite of Lovelace.

I would have you direct to Mr. Hickman, even your answer to this. I have a reason for it. Besides, my mother, notwithstanding this particular indulgence, is very positive. They have prevailed upon her, I know, to give her word to this purpose — spiteful poor wretches! How I hate in particular your foolish uncle Antony.

I would not have your thoughts dwell on the contents of your sister's shocking letter; but pursue other subjects — the subjects before you. And let me know your progress with Lovelace, and what he says to this diabolical curse. So far you may enter into this hateful subject. I expect that this will aptly introduce the grand topic between you, without needing a mediator.

Come, my dear, when things are at worst they will mend. Good often comes when evil is expected. — But if you despond, there can be no hopes of cure. Don't let them break your heart; for that it is plain to me is now what some people have in view to do.

How poor to withhold from you your books, your jewels, and your money! As money is all you can at present want, since they will vouchsafe to send your clothes, I send fifty guineas by the bearer, inclosed in single papers in my *Norris's Miscellanies*. I charge you, as you love me, return them not.

I have more at your service. So if you like not your lodgings or his behaviour when you get to town, leave both them and him directly.

I would advise you to write to Mr. Morden without delay. If he intends for England, it may hasten him. And you will do very well till he can come. But surely Lovelace will be infatuated, if he secure not his happiness by *your consent*, before that of Mr. Morden's is made needful on his arrival.

Once more, my dear, let me beg of you to be comforted. Manage with your usual prudence the stake before you, and all will still be happy. Suppose yourself to be *me*, and me to be *you* [you *may* — for your distress is mine]; and then you will add full day to these but glimmering lights which are held out to you by

Your ever affectionate and faithful
ANNA HOWE.

I hurry this away by Robert. I will enquire into the truth of your aunt's pretences about the change of measures which she says they intended in case you had not gone away.

LETTER LIII.

Miss Clarissa Harlowe to Miss Howe.

Wednesday morning, April 26.

YOUR letter, my beloved Miss Howe, gives me great comfort. How sweetly do I experience the truth of the wise man's observation, *That a faithful friend is the medicine of life!*

Your messenger finds me just setting out for London: the chaise at the door. Already I have taken leave of the good widow, who has obliged me with the company of her eldest daughter, at Mr. Lovelace's request, while he rides by us. The young gentlewoman is to return in two or three days with the chaise, in its way to my Lord M.'s Hertfordshire seat.

I received my sister's dreadful letter on Sunday, when Mr. Lovelace was out. He saw, on his return, my *extreme anguish and dejection;* and he was told *how much worse I had been:* for I had fainted away more than once.

I think the contents of it have touched my head as well as my heart.

He would fain have seen it. But I would not permit that, because of the threatenings he would have found in it against himself. As it *was*, the effect it had upon me, made him break out into execrations and menaces. I was so ill, that he himself advised me to delay going to town on Monday, as I proposed to do.

He is extremely regardful and tender of me. All that you supposed *would* follow this violent letter, from him, *has* followed it. He has offered himself to my acceptance in so unreserved a manner, that I am concerned I have written so freely and so diffidently of him. Pray, my dearest friend, keep to yourself every thing that may appear disreputable of him from me.

I must acquaint you, that his kind behaviour, and my low-spiritedness, co-operating with your former advice, and my unhappy situation, made me the very Sunday evening *receive unreservedly his declarations:* and now indeed I am more in his power than ever.

He presses me every hour [indeed as *needlessly* as *unkindly*] for fresh tokens of my esteem *for* him, and confidence in him. And, as I have been brought to *some verbal concessions*, if he should prove unworthy, I am sure I shall have great reason to blame this violent letter: for I have no resolution at all. Abandoned thus of all my natural friends, of whose returning favour I have now no hopes, and only you to pity me, and *you* restrained, as I may say, I have been forced to turn my desolate heart to such protection as I could find.

All my comfort is, that your advice repeatedly given to the same purpose, in your kind letter before me, warrants me. I now set out the more cheerfully to London on that account: for before a heavy weight hung upon my heart! and although I thought it best and safest to go, yet my spirits sunk, I know not why, at every motion I made towards a preparation for it.

I hope no mischief will happen on the road. — I hope these violent spirits will not meet.

Every one is waiting for me. — Pardon me, my best, my kindest friend, that I return your Norris. In these more promising prospects, I cannot have occasion for your favour. Besides, I have some hope, that with my clothes they will send me the money I wrote for, although it is denied me in the letter. If they do not, and if I should have occasion, I can but signify my wants to so ready a friend. And I have promised to be obliged only to you. But I had rather methinks you should have it *still to say*, if challenged, that nothing of this nature has been either requested or done. I say this, with a view entirely to my future hopes of recovering your mother's favour, which, next to that of my own father and mother, I am most solicitous to recover.

I must acquaint you with one thing more, notwithstanding my

hurry; and that is, that Mr. Lovelace offered either to attend me to Lord M.'s, or to send for his chaplain yesterday. He pressed me to consent to this proposal most earnestly; and even seemed desirous rather to have the ceremony pass here than in London: for when there, I had told him, it was time enough to consider of so weighty and important a matter. Now, upon the receipt of your kind, your consolatory letter, methinks I could almost wish it had been *in my power* to comply with his earnest solicitations. But this dreadful letter *has unhinged my whole frame.* Then some *little punctilio* surely is necessary. No preparation made. No articles drawn. No licence ready. Grief so extreme: no pleasure in prospect, nor so much as in wish — O, my dear, who could think of entering into so solemn an engagement? Who, *so* unprepared, could seem to be *so* ready?

If I could flatter myself that my indifference to all the joys of this life proceeded from *proper* motives, and not rather from the disappointments and mortifications my pride has met with, how much rather, I think, should I choose to be wedded to my shroud, than to any man on earth!

Indeed I have at present no pleasure but in *your* friendship. Continue that to me, I beseech you. If my heart rises hereafter to a capacity of more, it must be built on that foundation.

My spirits sink again, on setting out. Excuse this depth of vapourish dejection, which forbids me even *hope*, the cordial that keeps life from stagnating, and which never was denied me till within these eight-and-forty hours.

But 'tis time to relieve you.

Adieu, my best beloved and kindest friend! Pray for your
CLARISSA.

LETTER LIV.

Miss Howe to Miss Clarissa Harlowe.

Thursday, April 27.

I AM sorry you sent back my Norris. But you must be allowed to do as you please. So must I, in my turn. We must neither of us perhaps expect absolutely of the other what is the rightest to be done: and yet few folks, so young as we are, *better* know *what that rightest is.* I cannot separate myself from you, although I give a double instance of my vanity in joining myself with you in this particular assertion.

I am most heartily rejoiced that your prospects are so much mended; and that, as I hoped, good has been produced out of evil. What must the man have been, what must have been his views, had he not taken such a turn, upon a letter so vile, and upon a treatment so unnatural; himself principally the occasion of it.

You *know best* your *motives* for suspending: but I wish you *could* have taken him at offers so earnest.* Why should you not have

* Mr. Lovelace, in his next letter, tells his friend how extremely ill the lady

permitted him to send for Lord M.'s chaplain? If punctilio only was in the way, and want of a licence, and of proper preparations, and such like, my service to you, my dear; and there is ceremony tantamount to your ceremony.

Do not, do not, my dear friend, *again* be so very melancholy a decliner, as to prefer a shroud, when the matter you wish for is in your power; and when, as you have justly said heretofore, persons *cannot die when they will.*

But it is a strange perverseness in human nature, that we slight that when near us, which at a distance we wish for.

You have now but one point to pursue; that is marriage: let that be solemnized. Leave the rest to Providence; and, to use your own words in a former letter, follow as that leads. You will have a handsome man; a genteel man; he would be a *wise* man, if he were not vain of his endowments, and wild and intriguing: but while the eyes of many of our sex, taken by so specious a form and so brilliant a spirit, encourage that vanity, you must be contented to stay till grey hairs and prudence enter upon the stage together. You would not have every thing in the same man.

I believe Mr. Hickman treads no crooked paths; but he hobbles most ungracefully in a straight one. Yet Mr. Hickman, though he *pleases* not my eye, nor *diverts* my ear, will not, as I believe, *disgust* the one nor *shock* the other. Your man, as I have lately said, will always keep up attention; you will always be alive with him, though perhaps more from fears than hopes: while Mr. Hickman will neither say any thing to keep one awake, nor yet by shocking adventures make one's slumbers uneasy.

I believe I now know which of the two men so prudent a person as *you* would, at first, have chosen; nor doubt I, that you can guess which *I* would have made choice of, if I might. But proud as we are, the proudest of us all can *only* refuse, and many of us accept the but half-worthy, for fear a still worse should offer.

If the men had chosen their mistresses for spirits like their own, although Mr. Lovelace, at the long run, might have been *too many for me*, I don't doubt but I should have given heart-ake for heart-ake, for one half-year at least: while you, with my dull-swift, would have glided on *as* serenely, *as* calmly, *as* accountably, as the succeeding seasons; and varying no otherwise than they, to bring on new beauties and conveniencies to all about you.

* * *

I was going on in this style — but my mother broke in upon me, with a prohibitory aspect. "She

was; recovering from fits to fall into stronger fits, and nobody expecting her life. She has not, he says, acquainted Miss Howe how *very* ill she was. In p. 180, she tells Miss Howe, that her motives for suspending were not *merely ceremonious ones.*

gave me leave for one letter only."
— She had just parted with your odious uncle; and they have been in close conference again.

She has vexed me. I must lay this by till I hear from you again; not knowing whither to send it.

Direct me to a *third place*, as I desired in my former.

I told my mother, (on her challenging me) that I was writing indeed, and to you: but it was only to amuse myself: for I protested *that I knew not where to send to you.*

I hope that your next may inform me of your nuptials, although the next to that were to acquaint me that he was the ungratefullest monster on earth, as he must be if not the kindest husband in it.

My mother has vexed me. But so, on revising, I wrote before — but she has *unhinged me*, as you call it: pretended to catechise Hickman, I assure you, for contributing to our supposed correspondence. Catechised him *severely* too, upon my word! — I believe I have a sneaking kindness for the sneaking fellow; for I cannot endure that any body should treat him like a fool but myself.

I believe, between you and me, the good lady forgot herself. I heard her loud. She possibly imagined that my father was come to life again. Yet the meekness of the man might have soon convinced her, I should have thought; for my father, it seems, would talk as loud as she, I suppose, (though within a few yards of each other) as if both were out of their way, and were hallooing at half a mile's distance to get in again.

I know you'll blame me for this sauciness — but I told you I was vexed: and if I had not a spirit, my parentage on both sides might be doubted.

You must not chide me too severely, however, because I have learned of you not to defend myself in an error: and I own I am wrong: and that's enough: you won't be so generous in this case as you are in every other if you don't think it is.

Adieu, my dear! I must, I will love you; and love you for ever! So subscribes your

ANNA HOWE.

LETTER LV.

From Miss Howe.

Inclosed in the above.

Thursday, April 27.

I HAVE been making inquiry, as I told you I would, whether your relations had really (before you left them) resolved upon that change of measures which your aunt mentions in her letter! and by laying together several pieces of intelligence, some drawn from my mother, through your uncle Antony's communications; some from Miss Lloyd, by your sister's; and some by a third way, that I shall not tell you of; I have reason to think the following a true state of the case.

"That there was no intention of a change of measures, till within two or three days of your going away. On the contrary, your brother and sister, though they had no hope of prevailing with you in Solmes's favour, were resolved never to give over their persecutions till they had pushed you upon taking some step, which, by help of *their good offices*, should be deemed inexcusable by the half-witted souls they had to play upon.

"But that at last your mother (tired with, and perhaps, ashamed of the passive part she had acted) thought fit to declare to Miss Bell, that she was determined to try to put an end to the family feuds; and to get your uncle Harlowe to second her endeavours.

"This alarmed your brother and sister; and then a change of measures was resolved upon. Solmes's offers were however too advantageous to be given up; and your father's condescension was now to be their sole dependence, and (as *they* give it out) the trying of what that would do with you, their last effort."

And, indeed, my dear, this must have succeeded, I verily think, with such a daughter as they had to deal with, could that father, who never, I dare say, kneeled in his life, but to his God, have so far condescended as your aunt writes he would.

But then, my dear, what would this have done? — Perhaps you would have given Lovelace the *meeting*, in hopes to pacify him, and prevent mischief; supposing that they had given you time, and not hurried you directly into the state. But if you had *not* met him, you see, that he was resolved to visit them, and well attended too: and what must have been the consequence?

So that, upon the whole, we know not but matters may be best as they *are*, however disagreeable that *best* is.

I hope your considerate and thoughtful mind will make a good use of this hint. Who would not with patience sustain even a great evil, if she could persuade herself, that it was kindly dispensed, in order to prevent a *still* greater? — Especially, if she could sit down, as you can, and acquit her own heart!

Permit me one further observation — do we not see, from the above state of the matter, what might have been done before, *by the worthy person* of your family, had she exerted the *mother*, in behalf of a child so meritorious, yet so much oppressed?

Adieu, my dear. I will be ever yours,

ANNA HOWE.

Clarissa, in her answer to the first of the two last letters, chides her friend for giving so little weight to her advice, in relation to her behaviour to her mother. It may be proper to insert here the following extracts from that answer; though a little before the time.

You assume, my dear, *says she*, your usual, and ever-agreeable style, in what you write of the two gentlemen, and how unaptly you think they have chosen; Mr. Hickman in addressing you; Mr. Lovelace me. But I am inclinable to believe, that with a view to happiness, however two mild tempers might agree, two high ones would make sad work of it, both at one time violent and unyielding. You two might indeed have racqueted the ball betwixt you, as you say. But Mr. Hickman, by his gentle manners, seems formed for you, if you go not too far with him. If you do, it would be a tameness in him to bear it, which would make a man more contemptible than Mr. Hickman can ever deserve to be made. Nor is it a disgrace for even a brave man, who knows what a woman is to vow to him *afterwards*, to be very obsequious *beforehand*.

Do you think it is to the credit of Mr. Lovelace's character, that he can be offensive and violent? — Does he not, as all such spirits must, subject himself to the necessity of making submissions for his excesses, far more mortifying to a proud heart than those condescensions which the high-spirited are so apt to impute as a weakness of mind in such a man as Mr. Hickman?

Let me tell you, my dear, that Mr. Hickman is such a one, as would rather bear an affront *from* a lady, than offer one *to* her. He had rather, I dare say, that she should have occasion to ask *his* pardon, than he *hers*. But, my dear, *you have outlived your first passion;* and had the second man been an angel, he would not have been more than indifferent to you.

My motives for suspending, *proceeds she*, were not *merely ceremonious ones*. I was really very ill. I could not hold up my head. The contents of my sister's letters had pierced my heart. Indeed, my dear, I was *very* ill. And was I, moreover, to be as ready to accept his offer, as if I were afraid *he never would repeal it?*

I see with great regret that your mamma is still immoveably bent against our correspondence. What shall I do about it? — It goes against me to continue it, or to wish you to favour me with returns. — Yet I have so managed my matters, that I have no friend but you to advise with. It is enough to make one indeed wish to be married to this man, though a man of errors; as he has worthy relations of my own sex; and I should have some friends, I hope; — and having *some*, I might have more — for as money is said to increase money, so does the countenance of persons of character increase friends; while the destitute *must* be destitute. — It goes against my heart to beg of you to discontinue corresponding with me; and yet it is against my conscience to carry it on against parental prohibition. But I dare not use all the arguments against it that I could use — and why? — For fear I should convince you; and you should reject me as the rest of my friends have done. I leave therefore the determination of this point upon you. — I am not, I find, to be trusted with it. But be *mine* all the fault, and all the punishment, if it be punishable! — And certainly it must, when it can be the cause of those over lively sentences wherewith you conclude the letter I have before me, and which I must no further animadvert upon, because you forbid me to do so.

To the second letter, among other things, she says,

So, my dear, you seem to think, that there was a *fate* in my error. The cordial, the considerate friend, is seen in the observation you make on this occasion. Yet since things have happened as they have, would to Heaven I could hear, that all the world acquitted my father, or at least, my mother! whose character, before these family feuds broke out, was the subject of every one's admiration. Don't let any body say from you, so that it may come to *her* ear, that she might, by a timely exertion of her fine talents, have saved her unhappy child. You will observe, my dear, that *in her own good time*, when she saw that there was not likely to be an end to my brother's persecutions, she resolved to exert herself. But the pragmatical daughter, *by the fatal meeting*, precipitated all, and frustrated her indulgent designs. O, my love, I am now convinced, by dear experience, that while children are so happy as to have parents or guardians, whom they *may* consult, they should not presume, (no, not with the best and purest intentions) to follow their own conceits, in material cases.

A ray of hope of future reconciliation darts in upon my mind, from the intention you tell me my mother had to exert herself in my favour, had I not gone away. And my hope is the stronger, as this communication points out to me, that my *uncle Harlowe's interest* is likely, in my mother's opinion, to be of weight, if it could be engaged. It will behove me, perhaps, to apply to that dear uncle, if a proper occasion offer.

LETTER LVI.

Mr. Lovelace to John Belford, Esq.

Monday, April 24.

FATE is weaving a whimsical web for thy friend; and I see not but I shall be inevitably manacled.

Here have I been at work, dig, dig, dig, like a cunning miner, at one time, and spreading my snares like an artful fowler, at another, and exulting in my contrivances to get this inimitable creature absolutely into my power. Every thing made for me. Her brother and uncles were but my pioneers: her father stormed as I directed him to storm. Mrs. Howe was acted by the springs I set at work: her daughter was moving for me, and yet imagined herself plump against me, and the dear creature herself had already run her stubborn neck into my gin, and knew not that she was caught, for I had not drawn my springes close about her; and just as all this was completed, wouldst thou believe, that I should be my own enemy, and her friend? — that I should be so totally diverted from all my favourite purposes, as to propose to marry her before I went to town, in order to put it out of my own power to resume them?

When thou knowest this, wilt thou not think that my black angel plays me booty, and has taken it into his head to urge me on to the indissoluble tie, that he might be more sure of me (from the complex transgressions to which he will certainly stimulate me, when wedded) than perhaps he thought he could be from the simple sins, in which I have so long allowed myself, that they seem to have the plea of habit?

Thou wilt be still the more surprised, when I tell thee, that there seems to be a coalition going forward between the black angels and the white ones; for here has hers induced her in one hour, and by one retrograde accident, to *acknowledge* what the charming creature never before acknowledged, a preferable favour for me. She even avows an intention to be mine: — mine, without reformation-conditions. — She permits me to talk of love to her: of the irrevocable ceremony: yet, another extraordinary! postpones that ceremony; chooses to set out for London; and even to go to the widow's in town.

Well, but how comes all this about? methinks thou askest. — Thou, Lovelace, dealest in wonders; yet aimest not at the *marvellous* — how did all this come about?

I will tell thee — I was *in danger of losing my charmer for ever*. — She was soaring upward to her native skies. She was got above earth, by means, too, of the *earth-born:* and something extraordinary was to be done to keep her with us sublunaries. And what so effectually as the soothing voice of love, and the attracting offer of matrimony from a man not hated, can fix the attention of the maiden heart, aching with uncertainty; and before impatient of the questionable question?

This in short, was the case — while she was refusing all manner of obligation to me, keeping me at haughty distance, in hopes that her cousin Morden's arrival would soon fix her in a full and absolute independence of me: disgusted likewise at her adorer, for holding himself the reins of his own passions, instead of giving them up to her controul — she writes a letter urging an answer to a letter before sent, for her apparel, her jewels, and some gold, which she had left behind her; all which was to save her pride from obligation, and to promote the independence her heart was set upon. And what followed but a shocking answer, made still more shocking by the communication of a father's curse upon a daughter deserving only blessings! — A curse upon the curser's heart, and a double one upon the transmitter's, the spiteful, the envious Arabella!

Absent when it came; on my

return I found her recovering from fits, again to fall into stronger fits; and nobody expecting her life; half a dozen messengers dispatched to find me out. Nor wonder at her being so affected; she, whose filial piety gave her dreadful faith in a father's curses; and the curse of this gloomy tyrant extending (to use her own words, when she could speak) *to both worlds* — O that it had turned, in the moment of its utterance, to a mortal quinsy, and sticking in his gullet, had choked the old execrator, as a warning to all such unnatural fathers!

What a miscreant had I been, not to have endeavoured to bring her back, by all the endearments, by all the vows, by all the offers that I could make her!

I *did* bring her back. More than a father to her: for I have given her a life her unnatural father had well nigh taken away: shall I not cherish the fruits of my own benefaction? I was earnest in my vows to marry; and my ardour to urge the present time was a *real* ardour. But extreme dejection with a mingled delicacy, that in her dying moments I doubt not she will preserve, have caused her to refuse me the *time*, though not the solemnity; for she has told me, that now she must be wholly in my protection [*being destitute of every other!*] — More indebted, still, thy friend, as thou seest, to her cruel relations, than to herself for her favour!

She has written to Miss Howe an account of their barbarity; but has not acquainted her how very ill she was.

Low, very low, she remains; yet, dreading her stupid brother's enterprise, she wants to be in London; where, but for *this* accident, and (wouldst thou have believed it?) for *my persuasions*, seeing her so very ill, she would have been this night; and we shall actually set out on Wednesday morning, if she be not worse.

And now for a few words with thee on thy heavy preachment of Saturday last.

Thou art apprehensive that the lady is now truly in danger; and it is a miracle, thou tellest me, if she withstand such an attempter; "Knowing what we know of the sex, thou sayest, thou shouldst dread, wert thou me, to make further trial, lest thou shouldst succeed. And, in another place, tellest me, that thou pleadest not for the state for any favour thou hast for it."

What an advocate art thou for matrimony!

Thou wert ever an unhappy fellow at argument. Does the trite stuff with which the rest of thy letter abounds, in *favour* of wedlock, strike with the force that this which I have transcribed does *against* it?

Thou takest great pains to convince me, and that from the distresses the lady is reduced to (chiefly by her friends' persecutions and implacableness, I hope thou wilt own, and not from me, as yet) that the proposed trial will not be a fair trial. But let me ask thee, is not calamity the test of virtue? and wouldst thou not have me value this charming creature upon *proof* of her merits?—Do I not intend to reward her by marriage, if she stand that *proof*?

But why repeat I what I have said before? Turn back, thou egregious arguer, turn back to my long letter of the 13th*; and thou wilt there find every syllable of what thou hast written, either answered or invalidated.

But I am not angry with thee, Jack. I love opposition. As gold is tried by fire, and virtue by temptation, so is sterling wit by opposition. Have I not, before thou settest out as an advocate for my fair one, often brought thee in, as making objeictons to my proceedings, for no other reason than to exalt myself by proving thee a man of straw? As Homer raises up many of his champions, and gives them terrible names, only to have them knocked on the head by his heroes.

However, take to thee this one piece of advice—evermore be sure of being in the right, when thou presumest to sit down to correct thy master.

And another, if thou wilt—never offer to invalidate the force which a virtuous education ought to have on the sex, by endeavouring to find excuses for *their* frailty from the frailty of ours. For, are we not devils to each other? They tempt us: we tempt them. Because we *men* cannot resist temptation,

* See Letter xlv. p. 52—58.

is that a reason that *women* ought not, when the whole of their education is caution and warning against our attempts? Do not their grandmothers give them one easy rule — men are to ask — women are to deny.

Well, but to return to my principal subject; let me observe, that be my future resolutions what they will as to this lady, the contents of the violent letter she has received, have set me at least a month forward with her. I can now, as I hinted, talk of love and marriage, without control or restriction; her injunctions no more my terror.

In this sweetly familiar way shall we set out together for London. Mrs. Sorlings's eldest daughter, at my motion, is to attend her in the chaise; while I ride by way of escort: for she is extremely apprehensive of the Singleton plot; and has engaged me to be all patience, if any thing should happen on the road. But nothing I am sure *will* happen: for, by a letter received just now from Joseph, I understand, that James Harlowe has already laid aside his stupid project: and this by the earnest desire of all those of his friends to whom he had communicated it; who were afraid of the consequences that might attend it. But it is not over with *me*, however; although I am not determined at present as to the uses I may make of it.

My beloved tells me, she shall have her clothes sent her: she hopes also her jewels, and some gold, which she left behind her. But Joseph says, clothes *only* will be sent. I will not, however, tell her that: on the contrary, I say, there is no doubt but they will send *all* she wrote for. The greater her disappointment *from them*, the greater must be her dependence on me.

But after all, I hope I shall be enabled to be honest to a merit so transcendent. The devil take thee though for thy opinion given so mal-à-propos, that she *may be* overcome.

If thou designest to be honest, methinks thou sayest, why should not Singleton's plot be over with *thee*, as it is with her *brother?*

Because (if I *must* answer thee) where people are so modestly doubtful of what they are able to do, it is good to leave a loop-hole. And let me add, that when a man's heart is set upon a point, and any thing occurs to beat him off, he will find it very difficult, when the suspending reason ceases, to forbear resuming it.

LETTER LVII.
Mr. Lovelace to John Belford, Esq.

Tuesday, April 25.

ALL hands at work in preparation for London. What makes my heart beat so strong? why rises it to my throat, in such half-choking flutters, when I think of what this removal may do for me? I am hitherto resolved to be honest: and that increases my wonder at these involuntary commotions. 'Tis a plotting villain of a heart: it ever was; and ever will be, I doubt. Such a joy when any roguery is going forward! — I so little its master! — A head likewise so well turned to answer the triangular varlet's impulses! — No matter. I will have one struggle with thee, old friend; and if I cannot overcome thee now, I never will again attempt to conquer thee.

The dear creature continues extremely low and dejected. Tender blossom! how unfit to contend with the rude and ruffling winds of passion, and haughty and insolent controul! — Never till now from under the wing (it is not enough to say of indulging, but) of *admiring* parents; the mother's bosom only fit to receive this charming flower!

This was the reflection, that, with mingled compassion, and augmented love, arose to my mind, when I beheld the charmer reposing her lovely face upon the bosom of the widow Sorlings, from a recovered fit, as I entered soon after she had received her execrable sister's letter. How lovely in her tears! — and as I entered, her lifted-up face significantly bespeaking my protection, as I thought. And can I be a villain to such an angel! — I hope not — but why, Belford, why, once more, puttest thou me in mind, that she *may be* overcome? and why is her own reliance on my honour so late and so reluctantly shewn?

But, after all, so low, so dejected continues she to be, that I am terribly afraid I shall have a vapourish wife, if I *do* marry. I should then be doubly undone. Not that I shall be *much at home with her, perhaps, after the first fortnight, or so.* But when a man has been ranging, like the painful bee, from flower to flower, perhaps for a month together, and the thoughts of home and a wife begin to have their charms with him, to be received by a Niobe, who, like a wounded vine, weeps her vitals away, while she but involuntarily curls about him; how shall I be able to bear that?

May heaven restore my charmer to health and spirits, I hourly pray — that a man may see whether she can love any body but her father and mother! In *their* power, I am confident, it will be, at any time, to make her husband joyless, and that, as I hate them so heartily, is a shocking thing to reflect upon. — Something *more* than woman, an *angel* in some things; but a *baby* in others: so father-sick! so family-fond! — what a poor chance stands a husband with such a wife, unless, forsooth, they vouchsafe to be reconciled to her, and *continue* reconciled!

It is infinitely better for her and for me, that we should not marry. What a delightful manner of life [O that I could persuade her to it!] would the life of honour be with such a woman! The fears, the inquietudes, the uneasy days, the restless nights; all arising from doubts of having disobliged me! Every absence dreaded to be an absence for ever! And then, how amply rewarded, and rewarding, by the rapture-causing return. Such a passion as this keeps love in a continual fervour; makes it all alive. The happy pair, instead of sitting dozing and nodding at each other in opposite chimney-corners in a winter evening, and over a wintry love, always new to each other, and having always something to say.

Thou knowest, in my verses to my Stella, my mind on this occasion. I will lay those verses in her way, as if undesignedly, when we are together at the widow's; that is to say, if we do not soon go to church by consent. She will thence see what my notions are of wedlock. If she receives them with any sort of temper, that will be a foundation; and let *me* alone to build upon it.

Many a girl has been *carried*, who never would have been *attempted*, had she shewed a proper resentment, when her ears or her eyes were first invaded. I have tried a young creature by a bad book, a light quotation, or an indecent picture; and if she has borne that, or only blushed, and not been angry and more especially if she has leered and smiled; that girl have I, and old Satan, put down for our own. O how I could warn these little rogues if I would! Perhaps envy, more than virtue, will put me upon setting up beacons for them, when I grow old and joyless.

Tuesday afternoon.

If you are in London when I get thither, you will see me soon. My charmer is a little better than she was. Her eyes shew it, and her harmonious voice, hardly audible the last time I saw her, now begins to cheer my heart once more. But yet she has no love, no sensibility! — There is no addressing her with those *meaning*, yet *innocent* freedoms (innocent, *at first setting out*, they may be called) which soften others of her sex. The more strange this, as she now acknowledges preferable favour for me; and is highly susceptible of grief. Grief mollifies and enervates. The grievèd mind looks round it, silently implores consolation, and loves the soother. Grief is ever an inmate with joy. Though they won't shew themselves at the same window at *one* time; yet they have the whole house in common between them.

LETTER LVIII.
Mr. Lovelace to John Belford, Esq.

Wedn. April 26.

At last my lucky star has directed us into the desired port, and we are safely landed. Well says Rowe:

The wise and active conquer difficulties
By daring to attempt them. Sloth and folly
Shiver and shrink at sight of toil and hazard,
And *make* th' impossibility they *fear*.

But in the midst of my exultation, something, I know not what to call it, checks my joys, and glooms over my brighter prospects. If it be not conscience, it is wondrously like what I thought so, many, many years ago.

Surely, Lovelace, methinks thou sayest, thy good motions are not gone off already! surely thou will not now at last be a villain to this lady!

I can't tell what to say to it. Why would not the dear creature accept of me, when I so sincerely offered myself to her acceptance. Things already appear with a very different face *now I have got her here*. Already have our mother and her daughters been about me: "Charming lady! what a complexion! what eyes! what majesty in her person! — O Mr. Lovelace, you are a happy man! — *You owe us such a lady!*" — Then they remind me of my revenge, and of my hatred to her whole family.

Sally was so struck with her, at first sight, that she broke out to me in these lines of Dryden:

— Fairer to be seen
Than the fair lily on the flow'ry green!
More fresh than May herself in blossoms new!

I sent to thy lodgings within half an hour after our arrival, to receive thy congratulations upon it: but thou wert at Edgeware, it seems.

My beloved, who is charmingly amended, is retired to her constant employment, writing. I must content myself with the same amusement, till she shall be pleased to admit me to her presence: for already have I given to every one her cue.

And, among the rest, who dost thou think is to be her maid servant? — Deb. Butler.

Ah, Lovelace!

And ah, Belford! it can't be otherwise. But what dost think Deb's name is to be? — Why, Dorcas, Dorcas Wykes. And won't it be admirable, if either through fear, fright, or good liking, we can get my beloved to accept of Dorcas Wykes for a bedfellow?

In so many ways will it be now in my power to have the dear creature, that I shall not know which of them to choose!

But here comes the widow, with Dorcas Wykes in her hand; and I am to introduce them both to my fair one.

* * *

So — the honest girl is accepted — of good parentage: but, through a neglected education, plaguy illiterate — she can neither write, nor read writing. A kinswoman of Mrs. Sinclair — could not therefore well be refused, the widow in person recommending her; and the wench only taken till her Hannah can come. What an advantage has an imposing or forward nature over a courteous one! So here may something arise to lead into correspondences, and so forth. To be sure, a person need not be *so wary, so cautious of what she writes, or what she leaves upon her table or toilette, when her attendant cannot read.*

It would be a miracle, as thou sayest, if this lady can save herself — and having gone so far, how can I recede? — Then my revenge upon the Harlowes! to have run away with a daughter of theirs, to make her a Lovelace — to make her one of a family so superior to her own, what a triumph, as I have heretofore observed* to *them!* — But to run away with her, and to bring her to my lure in the *other* light, what a mortification of their pride! what a gratification of my own!

Then these women are continually at me. These women, who, before my whole soul and faculties were absorbed in the love of this single charmer, used always to oblige me with the flower and first fruits of their garden! Indeed, indeed, my goddess should not have chosen this London widow's — but I dare say, if I *had,* she would *not.* People who will be dealing in contradiction, ought to pay for it. And to be punished by the consequences of our own choice, what a moral lies there! — What a deal of good may I not be the occasion of from a little evil!

Dorcas is a neat creature, both in person and dress; her countenance not vulgar. And I am in hopes, as I hinted above, that her lady will accept of her for her bedfellow, in a strange house, for a week or so. But I saw she had a dislike to her at her very first appearance: yet I thought the girl behaved very modestly — over-did it a little perhaps — her lady shrunk back, and looked shy upon her. The doctrine of sympathies and antipathies is a surprising doctrine. — But Dorcas will be excessively obliging, and win her

* See p. 51.

lady's favour soon. I doubt not. I am secure in one of the wench's qualities however — she is not to be corrupted. A great point that — Since a lady and her maid, when heartily of one party, will be too hard for half a score devils.

The dear creature was no less shy when the widow first accosted her at her alighting. Yet I thought that honest Doleman's letter had prepared her for her masculine appearance.

And now I mention that letter, why dost thou not wish me joy, Jack?

Joy of what?

Why, joy of my nuptials. — Know then, that *said* is *done* with me, when I have a mind to have it so; and that we are actually man and wife: only that consummation has not passed — bound down to the contrary of that, by a solemn vow, till a reconciliation with her family take place. The women here are told so. They know it before my beloved knows it; and that, thou wilt say, is odd.

But how shall I do to make my fair-one keep her temper on the intimation? *Why, is she not here?* — at Mrs. Sinclair's? But if she will hear reason, I doubt not to convince her, that she ought to acquiesce.

She will insist, I suppose, upon my leaving her, and that I shall not take up my lodgings under the same roof. But circumstances are changed since I first made her that promise. I have taken all the vacant apartments; and must carry this point also.

I hope in a while to get her with me to the public entertainments. She knows nothing of the town, and has seen less of its diversions than ever woman of her taste, her fortune, her endowments did see. She has indeed a natural politeness, which transcends all acquirement. The most capable of any one I ever knew, of judging what an *hundred* things are by seeing *one* of a like nature. Indeed she took so much pleasure in her own chosen amusements, till persecuted out of them, that she had neither leisure nor inclination for the town diversions.

These diversions will amuse. And the deuce is in it, if a little susceptibility will not put forth, now she receives my address; especially if I can manage it so, as to be allowed to live under *one* roof with her. What though the sensibility be at first faint and reluctant, like the appearance of an early spring-flower in frosty weather, which seems afraid of being nipt by an easterly blast: that will be enough for me.

I hinted to thee in a former[*], that I had provided books for the lady's in-door amusement. Sally and Polly are readers. My beloved's light closet was their library. And several pieces of devotion have been put in, bought on purpose, at *second-hand*.

I was always for forming a judgment of the reading part of the sex by their books. The observations I have made on this occasion have been of great use to

[*] See p. 122.

me, as well in England as out of it. This sagacious lady may possibly be as curious in this point as her Lovelace.

So much for the present. Thou seest that I have a great deal of business before me. Yet I will write again soon.

Mr. Lovelace sends another letter with this; in which he takes notice of young Miss Sorlings's setting out with them, and leaving them at Barnet: but, as its contents are nearly the same with those in the lady's next letter, it is omitted.

LETTER LIX.

Miss Clarissa Harlowe to Miss Howe.

Wednesday afternoon, April 26.

At length, my dearest Miss Howe, I am in London, and in my new lodgings. They are neatly furnished, and the situation, for the town, is pleasant.

But, I think you must not ask me, how I like the old gentlewoman. Yet she seems courteous and obliging. Her kinswomen just appeared to welcome me at my alighting. They seem to be genteel young women. But more of their aunt and of them, as I shall see more.

Miss Sorlings has an uncle at Barnet, whom she found so very ill, that her uneasiness on that account (having large expectations from him) made me comply with her desire to stay with him. Yet I wished, as her uncle did not expect her, that she would see me settled in London; and Mr. Lovelace was still more earnest that she would, offering to send her back again in a day or two, and urging, that her uncle's malady threatened not a sudden change. But leaving the matter to *her choice,* (after she knew what *would have been mine,* she made me not the expected compliment. Mr. Lovelace, however, made her a handsome present at parting.

His genteel spirit on all occasions makes me often wish him more consistent.

As soon as I arrived, I took possession of my apartment. I shall make good use of the light closet in it, if I stay here any time.

One of his attendants returns in the morning to the Lawn; and I made writing to you by him, an excuse for my retiring.

And now give me leave to chide you, my dearest friend, for your rash, and I hope revocable resolution, not to make Mr. Hickman the happiest man in the world, while my happiness is in suspense. Suppose I were to be unhappy, what, my dear, would this resolution of yours avail me? Marriage is the highest state of friendship: if happy, it lessens our cares by dividing them, at the same time that it doubles our pleasures by a mutual participation. Why, my dear, if you love me, will you not rather give *another* friend to one who has *not two* that she is sure of? — Had you married on your mother's last birth-day, as she would have had you, I should not, I dare say, have wanted a refuge, that would have saved me many mortifications and much disgrace.

* * *

Here I was broke in upon by Mr. Lovelace; introducing the widow leading in a kinswoman of hers to attend me, if I approved of her, till my Hannah should come, or till I had provided myself with some other servant. The widow gave her many good qualities; but said, that she had one great defect; which was, that she could not write, nor read writing; that part of her education having been neglected when she was young: but for discretion, fidelity, obligingness, she was not to be outdone by any body. She commended her likewise for her skill at the needle.

As for her *defect*, I can easily forgive that. She is very likely and genteel; too genteel indeed, I think, for a servant. But, what I like least of all in her, she has a strange sly eye. I never saw such an eye — half-confident, I think. But indeed Mrs. Sinclair herself (for that is the widow's name,) has an odd winking eye; and her respectfulness seems too much studied, methinks, for the London ease and freedom. But people can't help their looks, you know; and after all, she is extremely civil and obliging. And as for the young woman, (Dorcas is her name) she will not be long with me.

I accepted her: how could I do otherwise, (if I had had a mind to make objections, which in my present situation I had not) her aunt present, and the young woman also present; and Mr. Lovelace officious in his introducing them to oblige me? But, upon their leaving me, I told *him* (who seemed inclinable to begin a conversation with me) that I desired that this apartment might be considered as my retirement: that when I saw him it might be in the dining-room (which is up a few stairs; for this back house, being once two, the rooms do not all of them very conveniently communicate with each other;) and that I might be as little broken in upon as possible, when I am here. He withdrew very respectfully to the door; but there stopt, and asked for my company *then* in the dining-room. If he were about setting out for other lodgings, I would go with him now, I told him; but, if he did not just then go, I would first finish my letter to Miss Howe.

I see he has no mind to leave me, if he can help it. My brother's scheme may give him a pretence to try to engage me to dispense with his promise. But if I *now do*, I must acquit him of it entirely. My approbation of his tender behaviour in the midst of my grief has given him a right, as he seems to think, of addressing me with all the freedom of an approved lover. I see by this man, that when once a woman embarks with this sex, there is no receding. One concession is but the prelude to another with them. He has been ever since Sunday last continually complaining of the distance I keep him at; and thinks himself entitled now, to call in question my value for him; strengthening his doubts by my former declared readiness to give him up to a reconciliation with my friends — and yet has himself fallen off from that *obsequious tenderness,* if I may couple the words, which drew from me the concessions he builds upon.

While we were talking at the door, my new servant came up, with an invitation to us both to tea. I said *he* might accept of it, if he pleased; but I must pursue my writing: and not choosing either tea or supper, I desired him to make my excuses below, as to both; and inform them of !my choice to be retired as much as possible: yet to promise for me my attendance on the widow and her nieces at breakfast in the morning.

He objected particularity in the eye of strangers, as to avoiding supper.

You know, said I, and you can tell them, that I seldom eat suppers. My spirits are low. You must never urge me against a declared choice. Pray, Mr. Lovelace, inform them of all my particularities. If they are obliging, they will allow for them. I come not hither to make new acquaintance.

I have turned over the books I found in my closet; and am not a little pleased with them; and think the better of the people of the house for their sakes.

Stanhope's gospels; Sharpe's, Tillotson's and South's sermons; Nelson's Feasts and Fasts; a sacramental piece of the Bishop of Man, and another of Dr. Gauden, Bishop of Exeter; and Innett's Devotions; are among the devout books: and among those of a lighter turn, the following not ill-chosen ones: a Telemachus in French, another in English; Steele's, Rowe's, and Shakspeare's Plays; that genteel comedy of Mr. Cibber, the Careless Husband, and others of the same author; Dryden's Miscellanies; the Tatlers, Spectators, and Guardians, Pope's and Swift's and Addison's Works.

In the blank leaves of the Nelson and Bishop Gauden, is Mrs. Sinclair's name; and in those of most of the others, either Sarah Martin or Mary Horton, the names of the two nieces.

* * *

I am exceedingly out of humour with Mr. Lovelace: and have great reason to be so. As you will allow, when you have read the conversation I am going to give you an account of; for he would not let me rest till I gave him my company in the dining room.

He began with letting me know, that he had been out to inquire after the character of the widow, which was the more necessary, he said, as he supposed that I would *expect his frequent absence.*

I *did,* I said; and that he would not think of taking up his lodging in the same house with me. But what, said I, is the result of your inquiry?

Why, indeed, the widow's character was, in the main, what he liked well enough. But as it was Miss Howe's opinion, as I had told him, that my brother had not given over his scheme; as the widow lived by letting lodgings; and had others to let in the same part of the house, which might be taken by an enemy; he knew no better way than for him to take them all, as it could not be for a long time *unless I would think of removing to others.*

So far was well enough: but as it was easy for me to see, that he spoke the slighter of the widow, in order to have a pretence to lodge here himself, I asked him his intention in that respect. And he frankly owned, that if I chose to stay here, he could not, as matters stood, think of leaving me for six hours together; and he had prepared the widow to expect, that we should be here but for a few days; — only till we could fix ourselves in a house suitable to our condition; and this, that I might be under the less embarrassment, if I pleased to remove.

Fix *our*-selves in a house, and *we* and *our*, Mr. Lovelace — pray in what light?

He interrupted me — Why, my dearest life, if you will hear me with patience — yet I am half afraid, that I have been too forward, as I have not consulted you upon it — but as my friends in town, according to what Mr. Doleman has written in the letter you have seen, conclude us to be married —

Surely, sir, you have not presumed —

Hear me out, dearest creature — you have received with favour my addresses — you have made me hope for the honour of your consenting hand: yet, by declining my most fervent tender of myself to you, at Mrs. Sorlings's, have given me apprehensions of delay: I would not for the world be thought so ungenerous a wretch, now you have honoured me with your confidence, *as to wish to precipitate you:* yet your brother's schemes are not given up. Singleton, I am afraid, is actually in town! his vessel lies at Rotherhithe — your brother is absent from Harlowe Place; indeed not with Singleton yet, as I can hear. If you are *known* to be mine, or if you are but *thought* to be so, there will probably be an end of your brother's contrivances. The widow's character may be as worthy *as it is said to be.* But the worthier she is, the more danger, if your brother's agent should find us out; since she may be persuaded, that she ought in conscience to take a parent's part, against a child who stands in opposition to them. But if she believes us married, her good character will stand us in stead, and she will be of our party. — Then I have taken care to give her a reason why two apartments are requisite for us at the hour of retirement.

I perfectly raved at him. I would have flung from him in resentment; but he would not let me:

and what could I do? Whither go, the evening advanced? I am astonished at you! said I. — If you are a man of honour, what need of all this strange obliquity? You delight in crooked ways — let me know, since I *must* stay in your company, (for he held my hand) let me know all you have said to the people below. — Indeed, indeed, Mr. Lovelace, you are a very unaccountable man.

My dearest creature, need I to have mentioned any thing of this? and could I not have taken up my lodgings in this house unknown to you, if I had not intended to make you the judge of all my proceedings? But *this* is what I have told the widow before her kinswomen and before your new servant. — "That indeed we were privately married at Hertford; but that you had preliminarily bound me under a solemn vow, which I am most religiously resolved to keep, to be contented with separate apartments, and even not to lodge under the same roof, till a certain reconciliation shall take place, which is of high consequence to both." And further, that I might convince you of the purity of my intentions, and that my whole view in this was to prevent mischief, I have acquainted them, "that I have solemnly promised to behave to you before every body, as if we were only betrothed, and not married; not even offering to take any of those innocent freedoms which are not refused in the most punctilious loves."

And then he solemnly vowed to me the strictest observance of the same respectful behaviour to me.

I said, that I was not by any means satisfied with the tale he had told, nor with the necessity he wanted to lay me under, of appearing what I was not: that every step he took was a wry one, a needless wry one: and since he thought it necessary to tell the people below any thing about me, I insisted that he should unsay all he had said, and tell them the truth.

What he had told them, he said, was with so many circumstances, that he could sooner die than contradict it. And still he insisted upon the propriety of appearing to be married, for the reasons he had given before — and, dearest creature, said he, why this high displeasure with me upon so well-intended an expedient? You know that I cannot wish to shun your brother, or his Singleton, but upon your account. The first step I would take, if left to myself, would be to find them out. *I have always acted in this manner, when any body has presumed to give out threatenings against me.*

'Tis true I should have consulted you first, and had your leave. But since you dislike what I have said, let me implore you, dearest madam, to give the only proper sanction to it, by naming an early day. Would to heaven that were to be to-morrow! — For God's sake let it be to-morrow! But if not, [was it his business, my dear, before I spoke (yet he seemed to be afraid of me) to say *if not?*

let me beseech you, madam, if my behaviour shall not be to your dislike, that you will not to-morrow, at breakfast-time, discredit what I have told them. The moment I give you cause to think, that I take any advantage of your concession, that moment revoke it, and expose me as I shall deserve. — And once more, let me remind you, that I have no view either to serve or save myself by this expedient. It is only to prevent a probable mischief, for your own mind's sake; and for the sake of those who deserve not the least consideration from me.

What could I say? What could I do? — I verily think, that had he urged me again, in a *proper manner*, I should have consented (little satisfied as I am with him) to give him a meeting to-morrow morning at a more solemn place than in the parlour below.

But this I resolve, that he shall not have my consent to stay a night under this roof. He has now given me a stronger reason for this determination than I had before.

* * *

Alas! my dear, how vain a thing to say, what we will or what we will not do, when we have put ourselves into the power of this sex! — He went down to the people below, on my desiring to be left to myself; and staid till their supper was just ready; and then, desiring a moment's *audience*, as he called it, he besought my leave to stay that one night, promising to set out either for Lord M.'s or for Edgeware to his friend Belford's, in the morning, after breakfast. But if I were against it, he said he would not stay supper, and would attend me about eight next day — yet he added, that my denial would have a very particular appearance to the people below, from what he had told them; and the more, as he had actually agreed for all the vacant apartments (indeed only for a month) for the reason he before hinted at: but I need not stay here two days, if, upon conversing with the widow and her nieces in the morning, I should have any dislike to them.

I thought, notwithstanding my resolution abovementioned, that it would seem too punctilious to deny him, under the circumstances he had mentioned: — having, besides, no reason to think he would obey me; for he looked as if he were determined to debate the matter with me. And now as I see no likelihood of a reconciliation with my friends, and as I have actually received his addresses, I thought I would not quarrel with him, if I could help it, especially as he asked to stay but for one night, and could have done so without my knowing it; and you being of opinion, that the proud wretch, distrusting his own merits with me, or at least my regard for him, will probably bring me to some concessions in his favour — for all these reasons, I thought proper to yield *this* point: yet I was so vexed with him on the *other*, that it was impossible for me to comply with that grace which a concession should be made with, or not made at all.

This was what I said — What you *will* do, you *must* do, I think. You are very ready to promise; very ready to depart from your promise. You say, however, that you will set out to-morrow for the country. You know how ill I have been. I am not well enough now to debate with you upon your encroaching ways. I am utterly dissatisfied with the tale you have told below. Nor will I promise to appear to the people of the house to-morrow what I am not.

He withdrew in the most respectful manner, beseeching me only to favour him with such a meeting in the morning, as might not make the widow and her nieces think he had given me reason to be offended with him.

I retired to my own apartment, and Dorcas came to me soon after to take my commands. I told her, that I required very little attendance, and always dressed and undressed myself.

She seemed concerned, as if she thought I had repulsed her; and said, it should be her whole study to oblige me.

I told her, that I was not difficult to be pleased: and should let her know from time to time what assistance I should expect from her. But for that night I had no occasion for her further attendance.

She is not only genteel, but is well-bred, and well-spoken.—She must have had what is generally thought to be the polite part of education: but it is strange, that fathers and mothers should make so light, as they generally do, of that preferable part, in girls, which would improve their minds, and give a grace to all the rest.

As soon as she was gone, I inspected the doors, the windows, the wainscot, the dark closet as well as the light one; and finding very good fastening to the door, and to all the windows, I had again recourse to my pen.

* * *

Mrs. Sinclair is just now gone from me. Dorcas, she told me, had acquainted her, that I had dismissed her for the night. She came to ask me how I liked my apartment, and to wish me good rest. She expressed her concern, that they could not have my company at supper. Mr. Lovelace, she said, had informed them of my love of retirement. She assured me, that I should not be broken in upon. She highly extolled *him*, and gave *me* a share in the praise, as to person. But was sorry, she said, that she was likely to lose us so soon as Mr. Lovelace talked of.

I answered her with suitable civility; and she withdrew with great tokens of respect. With greater, I think, than should be from distance of years, as she was the wife of a gentleman; and as the appearance of every thing about her, as well house as dress, carries the marks of such good circumstances, as require not abasement.

If, my dear, you *will* write

against prohibition, be pleased to direct, *To Miss Lætitia Beaumont; to be left till called for, at Mr. Wilson's, in Pall Mall.*

Mr. Lovelace proposed this direction to me, not *knowing* of your desire that our letters should pass by a third hand. As his motive for it was, that my brother might not trace out where we are, I am glad, as well from this instance as from others, that he seems to think he has done mischief enough already.

Do you know how my poor Hannah does?

Mr. Lovelace is so full of his contrivances and expedients, that I think it may not be amiss to desire you to look carefully to the seals of my letters, as I shall to those of yours. If I find him base in this particular, I shall think him capable of any evil; and will fly him as my worst enemy.

LETTER LX.
Miss Howe to Miss Clarissa Harlowe.
With her two last Letters, No. liv. lv. inclosed.

Thursday night, April 27.

I HAVE yours; just brought me. Mr. Hickman has helped me to a lucky expedient, which, with the assistance of the post, will enable me to correspond with you every day. An honest higgler, [Simon Collins his name] by whom I shall send this, and the two inclosed, (now I have your directions whither) goes to town constantly on Mondays, Wednesdays, and Fridays; and can bring back to me from Mr. Wilson's what you shall have caused to be left for me.

I congratulate you on your arrival in town, so much amended in spirits. I must be brief. I hope you'll have no cause to repent returning my Norris; it is forthcoming on demand.

I am sorry your Hannah can't be with you. She is very ill still; but not dangerously.

I long for your account of the women you are with. If they are not right people, you will find them out in one breakfasting.

I know not what to write upon his reporting to them that you are actually married. His reasons for it are plausible. But he delights in odd expedients and inventions.

Whether you like the people or not, do not, by your noble sincerity and plain dealing, make yourself enemies. You are in the *world* now, you know.

I am glad you had thoughts of taking him at his offer, if he had re-urged it. I wonder he did not. But if he do not soon, and in such a way as you *can* accept of it, don't think of staying with him.

Depend upon it, my dear, he will not leave you either night or day, if he can help it, now he has got footing.

I should have abhorred him for his report of your marriage, had he not made it with such circumstances as leave it still in your power to keep him at distance. If once he offer at the *least* familiarity — but this is needless to say to you. He can have, I think, no other design but what he professes; because he must needs think, that his report of being married to you must increase your vigilance.

You may depend upon my looking narrowly into the sealings of your letters. If, as you say, he be base in that point, he will be so in every thing: but to a person of your merit, of your fortune, of your virtue, he cannot be base. The man is no fool. It is his interest, as well with regard to his expectations from his own friends, as from you, to be honest. Would to heaven, however, that you were *really* married! This is now the predominant wish of

Your
ANNA HOWE.

LETTER LXI.
Miss Clarissa Harlowe to Miss Howe.
Thursday morning, eight o'clock.

I AM more and more displeased with Mr. Lovelace, on reflection, for his boldness in hoping to make me, though but *passively*, as I may say, testify to his great untruth. And I shall like him still less for it, if his view in it does not come out to be *the hope of accelerating my resolution in his favour*, by the difficulty it will lay me under as to my behaviour to him. He has sent me his compliments by Dorcas, with a request that I will permit him to attend me in the dining-room, — perhaps, that he may guess from thence, whether I will meet him in good humour, or not: but I have answered, that as I shall see him at breakfast-time I desired to be excused.

Ten o'clock.

I TRIED to adjust my countenance, before I went down, to an easier air than I had a heart, and was received with the highest tokens of respect by the widow and her two nieces: agreeable young women enough in their persons; but they seemed to put on an air of reserve; while Mr. Lovelace was easy and free to all, as if he were of long acquaintance with them: gracefully enough, I cannot but say; an advantage which travelled gentlemen have over other people.

The widow, in the conversation we had after breakfast, gave us an account of the military merits of the Colonel her husband, and, upon this occasion, put her handkerchief to her eyes twice or thrice. I hope for the sake of her sincerity, she wetted it, because she would be *thought* to have done so; but I saw not that she did. She wished that I might never know the loss of a husband so dear to me, as her beloved Colonel was to her: and she again put her handkerchief to her eyes.

It must, no doubt, be a most affecting thing to be separated from a good husband, and to be left in difficult circumstances besides, and that not by *his* fault, and exposed to the insults of the base and ungrateful, as she represented her case to be at his death. This moved me a good deal in her favour.

You know, my dear, that I have an open and free heart; and naturally have as open and free a countenance; at least my complimenters have told me so. At once, where I like, I mingle minds without reserve, encouraging reciprocal freedoms, and am forward to dissipate diffidences. But with these two nieces of the widow I never can be intimate — I don't know why.

Only that circumstances, and what passed in conversation, encouraged not the notion, or I should have been apt to think, that the young ladies and Mr. Lovelace were of longer acquaintance than of yesterday. For he, by stealth, as it were, cast glances sometimes at them, which they returned; and, on my ocular notice, their eyes fell, as I may say, under my eye, as if they could not stand its examination.

The widow directed all her talk to me, as to Mrs. Lovelace; and I with a very ill grace bore it. And once she expressed more forwardly than I thanked her for, her wonder that any vow, any consideration, however weighty, could have force enough with so charming a couple, as she called him and me, to make us keep separate beds.

Their eyes, upon this hint, had the advantage of mine. Yet was I not conscious of guilt. How know I then, upon recollection, that my censures upon theirs are not too rash? There are, no doubt, many truly modest persons (putting myself out of the question) who, by blushes at an injurious charge, have been suspected, by those who cannot distinguish between the confusion which guilt will be attended with, and the noble consciousness that overspreads the face of a fine spirit, to be thought but capable of an imputed evil.

The great Roman, as we read, who took his surname from one part in three (the fourth not then discovered) of the world he had triumphed over, being charged with a mean crime to his soldiery, chose rather to suffer exile (the punishment due to it, had he been found guilty) than to have it said, that Scipio was questioned in public, on so scandalous a charge. And think you, my dear, that Scipio did not blush with indignation, when the charge was first communicated to him?

Mr. Lovelace, when the widow expressed her forward wonder, looked sly and leering, as if to observe how I took it: and said, they might take notice that his regard for my will and pleasure (calling me his dear creature) had greater force upon him than the oath by which he had bound himself.

Rebuking both him and the widow, I said, it was strange to me to hear an oath or vow so lightly treated, as to have it thought but of second consideration, whatever were the first.

The observation was just, Miss Martin said; for that nothing could excuse the breaking of a solemn vow, be the occasion of making it what it would.

I asked after the nearest church; for I have been too long a stranger to the sacred worship. They named St. James's, St. Anne's, and another in Bloomsbury; and the two nieces said they oftenest went to St. James's church, because of the good company, as well as for the excellent preaching.

Mr. Lovelace said, the Royal Chapel was the place he oftenest went to, when in town. Poor man! little did I expect to hear he went to any place of devotion.

I asked, if the presence of the visible king of, comparatively, but a small territory, did not take off, too generally, the requisite attention to the service of the invisible King and Maker of a thousand worlds?

He believed this might be so with such as came from curiosity, when the royal family were present. But otherwise, he had seen as many contrite faces at the Royal Chapel, as any where else: and why not? Since the people about court have as deep scores to wipe off, as any people whatsoever.

He spoke this with so much levity, that I could not help saying, that nobody questioned but he knew how to choose his company.

Your servant, my dear, bowing, were his words; and, turning to them, You will observe upon numberless occasions, ladies, as we are further acquainted, that my beloved never spares me upon these topics. But I admire her as much in her reproofs, as I am fond of her approbation.

Miss Horton said, there was a time for every thing. She could not but say, that she thought innocent mirth was mighty becoming in young people.

Very true, joined in Miss Martin. And Shakspeare says well, *That youth is the spring of life, the bloom of gaudy years;* [with a theatrical air she spoke it:] and for her part, she could not but admire in Mr. Lovelace that charming vivacity which so well suited his time of life.

Mr. Lovelace bowed. The man is fond of praise. More fond of it, I doubt, than of deserving it. Yet this sort of praise he *does* deserve. He has, you know, an easy free manner, and no bad voice: and this praise so expanded his gay heart, that he sung the following lines from Congreve, as he told us they were:

Youth does a thousand pleasures bring,
 Which from decrepit age will fly;
Sweets, that wanton in the bosom of the
 spring,
In winter's cold embraces die.

And this for a compliment, as he said, to the two nieces. Nor was it thrown away upon them. They encored it; and his compliance fixed them in my memory.

We had some talk about meals, and the widow very civilly offered to conform to any rules I would set her. I told her how easily I was pleased, and how much I chose to dine by myself, and that from a plate sent me from any single dish. But I will not trouble you, my dear, with such particulars.

They thought me very singular; and with reason: but as I liked them not so *very* well as to forego my own choice in compliment to them, I was the less concerned for what they thought. — And still the less, as Mr. Lovelace had put me very much out of humour with him.

They, however, cautioned me against melancholy. I said, I should be a very unhappy creature if I could not bear my own company.

Mr. Lovelace said, that he must let the ladies into my story, and then they would know how to allow for my ways. But, *my dear, as you love me*, said the confident wretch, give as little way to melancholy as possible. Nothing but the sweetness of your temper, and your high notions of a duty that never can be deserved where you place it, can make you so uneasy as you are. — Be not angry, *my dear love*, for saying so (seeing me frown, I suppose): and snatched my hand and kissed it. — I left him with them, and retired to my closet and my pen.

Just as I have written thus far, I am interrupted by a message from him, that he is setting out on a journey, and desires to take my commands. — So here I will leave off, to give him a meeting in the dining-room.

* * *

I was not displeased to see him in his riding-dress.

He seemed desirous to know how I liked the gentlewomen below. I told him, that although I did not think them *very* exceptionable, yet as I wanted not, in my present situation, new acquaintance, I should not be fond of cultivating theirs.

He urged me still further on this head.

I could not say, I told him, that I greatly liked either of the young gentlewomen, any more than their aunt: and that were my situation ever so happy they had much too gay a turn for me.

He did not wonder, he said, to hear me say so. He knew not any of the sex who had been accustomed to shew themselves at the town diversions and amusements, that would appear tolerable to me. *Silence* and *blushes*, madam, are now no graces with our fine ladies in town. Hardened by frequent public appearances, they would be as much ashamed to be found guilty of these weaknesses as men.

Do you defend these two gentlewomen, sir, by reflections upon half the sex? But you must second me, Mr. Lovelace, (and yet I am not fond of being thought particular) in my desire of breakfasting and supping (when I *do* sup) by myself.

If I would have it so, to be sure it should be so. The people of the house were not of consequence enough to be apologized to, in any point where my pleasure was concerned. And if I should dislike them still more on further knowledge of them, he hoped I would think of *some other lodgings*.

He expressed a good deal of regret at leaving me, declaring, that it was absolutely in obedience to my commands; but that he could not have consented to go, while my brother's schemes were on foot, if I had not done him the credit of my countenance in the report he had made that we were married; which, he said, had bound all the family to his interest, so that he could leave me with the greater security and satisfaction.

He hoped, that on his *return* I would name his happy day; and the rather, as I might be convinced, by my brother's projects, that no reconciliation was to be expected.

I told him, that perhaps I might write one letter to my uncle Harlowe. He once loved me. I should be easier when I had made one direct application. I might possibly propose such terms, in relation to my grandfather's estate, as might procure me their attention; and I hoped he would be long enough absent to give me time to write to him, and receive an answer from him.

That, he must beg my pardon, he could not promise. He would inform himself of Singleton's and my brother's motions; and if on his return he found no reason for apprehension, he would go directly to Berks, and endeavour to bring up with him his cousin Charlotte, who, he hoped, would induce me to give him an earlier day than at present I *seemed to think of*. — I *seemed to think of*, my dear, very acquiescent, as I should imagine!

I told him, that I should take that young lady's company for a great favour.

I was the more pleased with this motion, as it came from himself, and with no ill grace.

He earnestly pressed me to accept of a bank note: but I declined it. And then he offered me his servant William for my attendant in his absence; who, he said, might be dispatched to him if any thing extraordinary fell out. I consented to that.

He took his leave of me in the most respectful manner, only kissing my hand. He left the bank note, unobserved by me, upon the table. You may be sure I shall give it him back at his return.

I am in a much better humour with him than I was.

Where doubts of any person are removed, a mind not ungenerous is willing, by way of amends for having conceived those doubts, to construe every thing that happens, *capable* of a good construction, in that person's favour. Particularly, I cannot but be pleased to observe, that although he speaks of the ladies of his family with the freedom of relationship, yet it is always with tenderness. And from a man's kindness to his relations of the sex, a woman has some reason to expect his good behaviour to herself, when married, if she be willing to deserve it from him.

And thus, my dear, am I brought to sit down satisfied with this man, where I find room to infer that he is not by nature a savage. But how could a creature, who gave a man an opportunity to run away with her, expect to be treated by that man with a very high degree of politeness?

But why, now, when fairer prospects seem to open, why these melancholy reflections? will my beloved friend ask of her Clarissa.

Why? Can you ask why, my dearest Miss Howe, of a creature, who, in the world's eye, has enrolled her name among the giddy and the inconsiderate; who labours under a parent's curse, and the cruel uncertainties which must arise from reflecting, that, equally against duty and principle, she has thrown herself into the power of a man, and that man an immoral one?—Must not the sense she has of her inconsideration darken her most hopeful prospects? Must it not even rise strongest upon a thoughtful mind when her hopes are the fairest? Even her pleasures, were the man to prove better than she expects, coming to her with an abatement, like that which persons who are in possession of ill-gotten wealth must then most poignantly experience, (if they have reflecting and unscared minds) when, all their wishes answered, (if the wishes of such persons can ever be wholly answered) they sit down in hopes to *enjoy* what they have unjustly obtained, and find their own reflections their greatest torment.

May you, my dear friend, be always happy in your reflections, prays

Your ever affectionate
CL. HARLOWE.

Mr. Lovelace, in his next letter, triumphs on his having carried his two great points of making the lady yield to pass for his wife to the people of the house, and to his taking up his lodging in it, though but for one night. He is now, he says, in a fair way, and doubts not but that he shall soon prevail, if not by persuasion, by surprise. Yet he pretends to have some little remorse, and censures himself as acting the part of the grand tempter. But having succeeded thus far, he cannot, he says, forbear trying, according to the resolution he had before made, whether he cannot go further. He gives the particulars of their debates on the above-mentioned subjects, to the same effect as in the lady's last letters.

And now, Belford, will I give thee an account of our first breakfast conversation.

All sweetly serene and easy was the lovely brow and charming aspect of my goddess, on her descending among us; commanding reverence from every eye; a courtesy from every knee; and silence, awful silence, from every quivering lip: while she, armed with conscious worthiness and superiority, looked and behaved as an empress would look and behave among her vassals; yet with a freedom from pride and haughtiness, as if born to dignity, and to a behaviour habitually gracious.

It will by this time be seen, that his whole merit with regard to this lady lies in doing justice to her excellencies both of mind and person, though to his own condemnation. Thus he begins his succeeding letter:

He takes notice of the jealousy, pride, and vanity of Sally Martin and Polly Horton, on his respectful behaviour to the lady: *creatures who, brought up too high for their fortunes, and to a taste of pleasure, and the public diversions, had fallen an easy prey to his seducing arts* (as will be seen in the *conclusion* of this work): *and who, as he observes,* "had not yet got over that distinction in their love which makes a woman prefer one man to another."

How difficult is it, *says he,* to make a woman subscribe to a preference against herself, though ever so visible; especially where love is concerned! This violent, this partial little devil, Sally, has the insolence to compare herself with my angel — yet owns her to be an angel. I charge you, Mr. Lovelace, said she, shew none of your extravagant acts of kindness before me to this sullen, this gloomy beauty — I cannot bear it. Then was I reminded of her first sacrifice.

What a rout do these women make about nothing at all! Were it not for what the *learned bishop,* in his letter from Italy, calls the entanglements of amour, and *I* the delicacies of intrigue, what is there, Belford, in all they can do for us?

How do these creatures endeavour to stimulate me! A fallen woman is a worse devil than even a profligate man. The former is incapable of remorse: that am not I — nor ever shall they prevail upon me, though aided by all the powers of darkness, to treat this admirable creature with indignity. — So far, I mean, as indiguity can be separated from the trials which will prove her to be either woman or angel.

Yet with them I am a craven. I might have had her before now, if I would. If I would treat her as flesh and blood, I should find her such. They thought I knew, if any man living did, that if a man made a goddess of a woman, she would assume the goddess; that if power were given her, she would exert that power to the giver, if to nobody else: and D—r's wife is thrown into my dish, who, thou knowest, kept her ceremonious husband at haughty distance, and whined in private to her insulting footman. O how I cursed the blaspheming wretches! They will make me, as I tell them, hate their house, and remove from it. And by my soul, Jack, I am ready at times to think that I should not have brought her hither, were it but on Sally's account. And yet, without knowing either Sally's heart, or Polly's, the dear creature resolves against having any conversation with them but such as she cannot avoid. I am not sorry for this, thou mayest think; since jealousy in woman is not to be concealed from woman. And Sally has no command of herself.

What dost think!—Here this little devil Sally, not being able, as she told me, to support life under my displeasure, was going into a fit: but when I saw her *preparing* for it, I went out of the room; and so she thought it would not be worth her while to shew away.

In this manner he mentions what his meaning was in making the lady the compliment of his absence:

As to leaving her; if I go but for *one* night, I have fulfilled my promise: and if she think not, I can mutter and grumble, and yield again, and make a merit of it; and then, unable to live out of her presence, soon return. Nor are women ever angry at bottom for being disobeyed through excess of love. They like an uncontrollable passion. They like to have every favour ravished from them; and to be eaten and drank quite up by a voracious lover. Don't I know the sex?—Not so, indeed, as yet, my Clarissa: but, however, with *her* my frequent egresses will make me look new to her, and create little busy scenes between us. At the least, I may surely, without exception, salute her at parting and at return; and will not those occasional freedoms (which civility will warrant) by degrees familiarize my charmer to them?

But here, Jack, what shall I do with my uncle and aunts, and all my loving cousins? For I understand that they are more in haste to have me married than I am myself.

LETTER LXII.

Miss Clarissa Harlowe to Miss Howe.

Friday, April 28.

Mr. Lovelace is returned already. My brother's projects were his pretence. I could not but look upon this short absence as an evasion of his promise; especially as he had taken such precautions with the people below; and as he knew that I proposed to keep close within doors. I cannot bear to be dealt meanly with; and angrily insisted that he should directly set out for Berkshire, in order to engage his cousin, as he had promised.

O my dearest life, said he, why will you banish me from your presence? I cannot leave you for so long a time as you seem to expect I should. I have been hovering about town ever since I left you. Edgware was the furthest place I went to; and there I was not able to stay two hours, for fear, at this crisis, any thing should happen. Who can account for the workings of an apprehensive mind, when all that is dear and valuable to it is at stake? You may spare yourself the trouble of writing to any of your friends, till the solemnity has passed that shall entitle me to give weight to your application. When they know we are married, your brother's plots will be at an end; and your father and mother, and uncles, must be reconciled to you. Why then should you hesitate a moment to confirm my happiness? Why, once more, would you banish me from you? Why will you not give the man, who has brought you into difficulties, and who so honourably wishes to extricate you from them, the happiness of doing so?

He was silent. My voice failed to second the inclination I had to say something not wholly discouraging to a point so warmly pressed.

I'll tell you, my angel, resumed he, what I propose to do, if you approve of it. I will instantly go out to view some of the handsome new squares or fine streets round them, and make a report to you of any suitable house I find to be let. I will take such a one as you shall choose, and set up an equipage befitting our condition. You shall direct the whole. And on some early day, either before or after we fix, [it must be at your own choice] be pleased to make me the happiest of men. And then will every thing be in a desirable train. You shall receive in your own house (if it can be so soon furnished as I wish) the compliments of all my relations. Charlotte shall visit you in the interim: and if it take up time, you shall choose whom you will honour with your company, first, second, or third in the summer months; and on your return you shall find all that was wanting in your new habitation supplied; and pleasures in a constant round shall attend us. O my angel, take me to you, instead of banishing me from you, and make me yours for ever.

You see, my dear, that there was no *day* pressed for, I was not uneasy about that; and the sooner recovered myself as there was not. But, however, I gave him no reason to upbraid me for refusing his offer of going in search of a house.

He is accordingly gone out for this purpose. But I find that he intends to take up his lodging here to-night; and if to-night, no doubt on other nights, while he is in town. As the doors and windows of my apartment have good fastenings; as he has not, in all this time, given me cause for apprehension; as he has the pretence of my brother's schemes to plead; as the people below are very courteous and obliging; Miss Horton especially, who seems to have taken a great liking to me, and to be of a gentler temper and manners than Miss Martin; and as we are now in a tolerable way—I imagine it would look particular to them all, and bring me into a debate with a man, who (let him be set upon what he will) has always a great deal to say for himself, if I were to insist upon his promise: on all these accounts, I think, I will take no notice of his lodging here, if he don't — let me know, my dear, your thoughts of every thing.

You may believe I gave him

back his bank note the moment I saw him.

Friday evening.

Mr. Lovelace has seen two or three houses; but none to his mind. But he has heard of one which looks promising, he says, and which he is to inquire about in the morning.

Saturday morning.

He has made his inquiries, and actually seen the house he was told of last night. The owner of it is a young widow lady; who is inconsolable for the death of her husband; *Fretchville* her name. It is furnished quite in taste, every thing being new within these six months. He believes, if I like not the furniture, the use of it may be agreed for, with the house, for a time certain: but, if I like it, he will endeavour to take the one and purchase the other directly.

The lady sees nobody; nor are the best apartments above-stairs to be viewed till she is either absent or gone into the country; which she talks of doing in a fortnight or three weeks at furthest; and to live there retired.

What Mr. Lovelace saw of the house (which were the saloon and two parlours) was perfectly elegant; and he was assured all is of a piece. The offices are also very convenient; coach-house and stables adjoining.

He shall be very impatient, he says, till I see the whole; nor will he, if he finds he can have it, look further till I have seen it, except any thing else offer to my liking. The price he values not.

He now does nothing but talk of the *ceremony;* but not indeed of the *day*. I don't want him to urge that — but I wonder he does not.

He has just now received a letter from Lady Betty Lawrence, by a particular hand; the contents principally relating to an affair she has in chancery. But in the postscript she is pleased to say very respectful things of me.

They are all impatient, she says, for the happy day being over; which they flatter themselves will *ensure his reformation.*

He hoped, he told me, that I would *soon* enable him to answer *their* wishes and *his own.*

But, my dear, although the opportunity was so inviting, he urged not for the *day*. Which is the *more extraordinary*, as he was so pressing for marriage before we came to town.

He was very earnest with me to give him, and four of his friends, my company on Monday evening, at a little collation. Miss Martin and Miss Horton, cannot, he says, be there, being engaged in a party of their own with two daughters of Colonel Solcombe, and two nieces of Sir Antony Holmes, upon an annual occasion. But Mrs. Sinclair will be present, and she gave him hope of the company of a young lady of very great fortune and merit, (Miss *Partington*) an heiress, to whom Colonel Sinclair, it seems, in his lifetime was guardian, and who therefore calls Mrs. Sinclair mamma.

I desired to be excused. He had laid me, I said, under a most disagreeable necessity of appearing as a married person, and I would see as few people as possible who were to think me so.

He would not urge it, he said, if I were *much* averse: but they were his select friends: men of birth and fortune; who longed to see me. It was true, he added, that they, as well as his friend Doleman, believed we were married; but they thought him under the restrictions that he had mentioned to the people below. I might be assured, he told me, that his politeness before them should be carried into the highest degree of reverence.

When he is set upon any thing, there is no knowing, as I have said heretofore, what one *can* do*. But I will not, if I can help it, be made a show of; especially to men of whose characters and principles I have no good opinion. I am, my dearest friend,

Your ever affectionate
CL. HARLOWE.

Mr. Lovelace in his next letter gives an account of his quick return: of his reasons to the lady for it: of her displeasure upon it: and of her urging his absence from the safety she was in from the situation of the house, except she were to be traced out by his visits.

I was confoundedly puzzled, *says he*, on this occasion, and on her insisting upon the execution of a too-ready offer which I made her to go down to Berks, to bring

* See p. 195. See also Vol. I. p. 296.

up my cousin Charlotte to visit and attend her. I made miserable excuses: and, fearing that they would be mortally resented, as her passion began to rise upon my saying Charlotte was delicate, which she took strangely wrong, I was obliged to screen myself behind the most solemn and explicit declarations.

He then repeats those declarations, to the same effect with the account she gives of them.

I began, *says he*, with an intention to keep my life of honour in view, in the declarations I made her; but, as it has been said of a certain orator in the House of Commons, who more than once, in a long speech, convinced himself as he went along, and concluded against the side he set out intending to favour, so I in earnest pressed without reserve for matrimony in the progress of my harangue, which state I little thought of urging upon her with so much strength and explicitness.

He then values himself upon the delay that his proposal of taking and furnishing a house must occasion.
He wavers in his resolutions whether to act honourably or not by a merit so exalted.
He values himself upon his own delicacy, in expressing his indignation against her friends, for supposing what he pretends his heart rises against them for presuming to suppose.

But have I not reason, *says he*,

to be angry with her, for not praising me for this my delicacy, when she is so ready to call me to account for the least failure in punctilio? — However, I believe I can excuse her too, upon this generous consideration [for *generous* I am sure it is, because it is against myself]; that her mind being the essence of delicacy, the least want of it shocks her; while the meeting with what is so very extraordinary to *me*, is too familiar to her to obtain her notice *as* an extraordinary.

He glories in the story of the house, and of the young widow possessor of it, Mrs. Fretchville he calls her; and leaves it doubtful to Mr. Belford, whether it be a real or a fictitious story.

He mentions his different proposals in relation to the ceremony which he so earnestly pressed for; and owns his artful intention in avoiding to name the day.

And now, *says* he, I hope soon to have an opportunity to begin my operations; since all is *halcyon* and security.

It is impossible to describe the dear creature's sweet and silent confusion when I touched upon the matrimonial topics.

She *may* doubt. She *may* fear. The wise in all important cases will doubt, and will fear, till they are sure. But her apparent willingness to think well of a spirit so inventive, and so machinating, is a happy prognostic for me. O these reasoning ladies! — How I love these reasoning ladies! — 'Tis all over with them when once love has crept into their hearts: for then will they employ all their reasoning powers to *excuse* rather than to *blame* the conduct of the *doubted* lover, let appearances against him be ever so strong.

Mowbray, Belton, and Tourville, long to see my angel, and will be here. She has *refused* me; but *must be present* notwithstanding. So generous a spirit as mine is cannot enjoy its happiness without communication. If I raise not your envy and admiration both at once, but half-joy will be the joy of having such a charming fly entangled in my web. She therefore must comply. And thou must come. And then will I shew thee the pride and glory of the Harlowe family, my implacable enemies; and thou shalt join with me in my triumph over them all.

I know not what may still be the perverse beauty's fate; I want thee therefore to see and admire her, while she is serene and full of hopes: before her apprehensions are realized, if realized they are to be; and if evil apprehensions of me she really has: before her beamy eyes have lost their lustre: while yet her charming face is surrounded with all its virgin glories; and before the plough of disappointment has thrown up furrows of distress upon every lovely feature.

If I can procure you this honour, you will be ready to laugh out, as I have often much ado to forbear, at the puritanical behaviour of the mother before this lady. Not an oath, not a curse, nor the least free word, escapes her lips. She minces in her gait. She prims up her horse mouth. Her voice, which, when she pleases, is the voice of thunder, is sunk into an humble whine. Her stiff hams, that have not been bent to a civility for ten years past, are now limbered into courtesies three deep at every word. Her fat arms are crossed before her; and she can hardly be prevailed upon to sit in the presence of my goddess.

I am drawing up instructions for ye all to observe on Monday night.

Saturday night.

Most confoundedly alarmed! — Lord, sir, what do you think? cried Dorcas—my lady is resolved to go to church to-morrow! I was at quadrille with the women below — To church! said I; and down I laid my cards. *To church!* repeated they, each looking upon the other. We had done playing for *that* night.

Who could have dreamt of such a whim as this?—Without notice! without questions! Her clothes not come; No leave asked!—Impossible she should think of being *my wife!* Besides, she don't consider, if she go to church I must go too!—Yet not to ask for my company!—Her brother and Singleton ready to snap her up, as far as she knows!—Known by her clothes—her person, her features, so distinguished!—Not such another woman in England! To church of all places!—Is the devil in the girl? said I, as soon as I could speak.

Well, but to leave this subject till to-morrow morning, I will now give you the instructions I have drawn up for yours and your companion's behaviour on Monday night.

Instructions to be observed by John Belford, Richard Mowbray, Thomas Belton, and James Tourville, Esquires of the Body to General Robert Lovelace, on their admission to the presence of his goddess.

Ye must be sure to let it sink deep into your heavy heads, that there is no such lady in the world as Miss Clarissa Harlowe; and that she is neither more nor less than Mrs. Lovelace, though at present, to my shame be it spoken, a virgin.

Be mindful also, that your old mother's name, after that of *her* mother when a maid, is Sinclair: that her husband was a lieutenant-colonel, and all that *you*, Belford, know from honest Doleman's letter of her,* that let your brethren know.

Mowbray and Tourville, the two greatest blunderers of the four, I allow to be acquainted with the widow and nieces, from the knowledge they had of the colonel. They will not forbear familiarities of speech to the mother, as of longer acquaintance than a day. So I have suited their parts to their capacities. They may praise the widow and the colonel for people of great honour — but not too grossly; nor to labour the

* See p. 117, & seq.

point so as to render themselves suspected.

The mother will lead ye into her own and the colonel's praises; and Tourville and Mowbray may be both her vouchers — I and you, and Belton, must be only hearsay confirmers.

As poverty is generally suspectible, the widow must be got handsomely aforehand! and no doubt but she is. The elegance of her house and furniture, and her readiness to discharge all demands upon her, which she does with ostentation enough, and which makes her neighbours, I suppose, like her the better, demonstrate this. She will propose to do handsome things by her two nieces. Sally is near marriage — with an eminent woollen-draper in the Strand, if ye have a mind to it; for there are five or six of them there.

The nieces may be inquired after, since they will be absent, as persons respected by Mowbray and Tourville, for their late worthy uncle's sake.

Watch ye diligently every turn of my countenance: every motion of my eye; for in my eye and in my countenance will ye find a sovereign regulator. I need not bid you respect me mightily: your allegiance obliges you to that: and who that sees me, respects me not?

Priscilla Partington (for her looks so innocent, and discretion so deep, yet seemingly so softly) may be greatly relied upon. She will accompany the mother, gorgeously dressed, with all her Jew's extravagance flaming out upon her; and first, *induce*, then *countenance* the lady. She has her cue, and I hope will make her acquaintance coveted by my charmer.

Miss Partington's history is this: the daughter of Colonel Sinclair's brother-in-law: that brother-in-law may have been a Turkey merchant, or any merchant, who died confoundedly rich: the colonel one of her guardians [*collateral credit in that to the old one*]; whence she always calls Mrs. Sinclair *mamma*; though not succeeding to the trust.

She is just come to pass a day or two, and then to return to her surviving guardian's at Barnet.

Miss Partington has suitors a little hundred (her grandmother, an alderman's dowager, having left her a great additional fortune); and is not trusted out of her guardian's house, without an old gouvernante, noted for discretion, except to her mamma Sinclair; with whom now-and-then she is permitted to be for a week together.

Pris. will mamma-up Mrs. Sinclair, and will undertake to court her guardian to let her pass a delightful week with her — Sir Edward Holden, he may as well be, if your shallow pates will not be clogged with too many circumstantials. Lady Holden, perhaps, will come with her; for she always delighted in her mamma Sinclair's company; and talks of her, and

14*

her good management, twenty times a day.

Be it principally thy part, Jack, who art a parading fellow, and aimest at wisdom, to keep thy brother-varlets from blundering; for, as thou must have observed from what I have written, we have the most watchful and most penetrating lady in the world to deal with: a lady worth deceiving! but whose eyes will pierce to the bottom of your shallow souls the moment she hears you open. Do thou therefore place thyself between Mowbray and Tourville: their toes to be played upon and commanded by thine, if they go wrong: thy elbows to be the ministers of approbation.

As to your general behaviour; no hypocrisy! — I hate it: so does my charmer. If I had studied for it, I believe I *could* have been an hypocrite: but my general character is so well known, that I should have been suspected at once, had I aimed at making myself too white. But what necessity can there be for hypocrisy, unless the generality of the sex were to *refuse* us for our immoralities? the best of them love to have the credit of reforming us. Let the sweet souls try for it: if they fail, their intent was good. That will be a consolation to them. And as to *us*, our work will be the easier; our sins the fewer: since they will draw themselves in with a very little of our help; and we shall save a parcel of cursed falsehoods, and appear to be what we *are* both to angels and men. — Meantime their very grandmothers will acquit us, and reproach them with their *self-do*, *self-have;* and as having *erred against knowledge*, and ventured against *manifest appearances.* What folly therefore for men of our character to be hypocrites!

Be sure to instruct the rest, and do thou thyself remember not to talk obscenely. You know I never permitted any of you to talk obscenely. Time enough for that, when you grow old, and can ONLY talk. Besides, ye must consider Prisc.'s *affected* character, my goddess's *real* one. Far from obscenity therefore, do not so much as touch upon the double-entendre. What! as I have often said, cannot you touch a lady's heart, without wounding her ear?

It is *necessary*, that ye should appear worse men than myself. You cannot help appearing so, you'll say. Well then, there will be the less restraint upon you — the less restraint, the less affectation. — And if Belton begins his favourable subject in behalf of *keeping*, it may make me take upon myself to oppose him: but fear not; I shall not give the argument all my force.

She must have some curiosity, I think, to see what sort of men my companions are: she will not expect any of you to be saints. Are you not men born to considerable fortunes, although ye are not all of you men of parts? who is it in this mortal life, that *wealth does not mislead?* And as it gives people the *power of being mis-*

chievous, does it not require great virtue to forbear the use of that power? Is not the devil said to be the God of this world? Are we not children of this world? Well then! let me tell thee my opinion — it is this: That were it not for the *poor* and the *middling*, the world would probably, long ago, have been destroyed by fire from heaven. Ingrateful wretches the rest, thou wilt be apt to say, to make such sorry returns, as they generally do make, to the *poor* and the *middling*.

This dear lady is prodigiously learned in *theories*. But as to *practics*, as to *experimentals*, must be, as you know from her tender years, a mere novice. Till she knew me, I dare say, she did not believe, whatever she had read, that there were such fellows in the world, as she will see in you four. I shall have much pleasure in observing how she'll stare at her company, when she finds me the politest man of the five.

And so much for instructions general and particular for your behaviour on Monday night.

And let me add, that you must attend to every minute circumstance, whether you think there be reason in it, or not. Deep, like golden ore, frequently lies my meaning, and richly worth digging for. The hint, of *least* moment, as *you* may imagine it, is often pregnant with events of the *greatest*. Be implicit. Am I not your general? did I ever lead you on that I brought you not off with safety and success, sometimes to your own stupid astonishment?

And now, methinks, thou art curious to know, what can be my view in risking the displeasure of my fair-one, and alarming her fears, after four or five halcyon days have gone over our heads? I'll satisfy thee.

The visitors of the two nieces will crowd the house. Beds will be scarce. Miss Partington, a sweet modest genteel girl, will be prodigiously taken with my charmer; will want to begin a friendship with her. A share in her bed, for one night only, will be requested. Who knows, but on that very Monday night I may be so unhappy as to give *mortal offence* to my beloved? *the shiest birds may be caught napping.* Should she *attempt to fly me* upon it, cannot I *detain her?* should she *actually fly*, cannot I *bring her back* by authority civil or uncivil, if I have evidence upon evidence that she acknowledged, though but tacitly, her marriage? — and *should I, or should I not* succeed, and she *forgive me*, or if she but descend to *expostulate*, or if she *bear me in her sight;* then will she be all my own. All delicacy is my charmer. I long to see how such a delicacy, on *any* of these occasions, will behave, and in my situation it behoves me to provide against every accident.

I must take care, knowing what an eel I have to deal with, that the little wriggling rogue does not slip through my fingers. How silly should I look staring after her, when she had shot from me into the muddy river, her family, from which with so much difficulty I have taken her.

Well then; here are — let me see — how many persons are there who, after Monday night, will be able to swear, that she has gone by my name, answered to my name, had no other view in leaving her friends, but to go by my name? her own relations neither able nor willing to deny it. — First, here are *my* servants; her servant Dorcas; Mrs. Sinclair; Mrs. Sinclair's two nieces; and Miss Partington.

But for fear these evidences should be suspected, here comes the jet of the business — "No less than four worthy gentlemen of fortune and family, who were all in company such a night particularly, at a collation to which they were invited by Robert Lovelace, of Sandoun-hall, in the county of Lancaster, Esquire, in company with Magdalen Sinclair, widow, and Priscilla Partington, spinster, and the lady complainant, when the said Robert Lovelace addressed himself to the said lady, on a multitude of occasions as *his* wife; as they and others did, as Mrs. Lovelace: every one complimenting and congratulating her upon her nuptials; and that she received such their compliments and congratulations with no other visible displeasure or repugnance, than such as a young bride, full of blushes and pretty confusion, might be supposed to express upon such contemplative revolvings as those compliments would naturally inspire." Nor do thou rave at me, Jack, nor *rebel:* — Dost think I brought the dear creature hither for nothing? And here's a faint sketch of my plot. — Stand by, varlets — tanta-ra-ra-ra! — Veil your bonnets, and confess your master!

LETTER LXIII.

Mr. Lovelace to John Belford, Esq.

Sunday.

HAVE been at church, Jack — behaved admirably well too! My charmer is pleased with me now: for I was exceedingly attentive to the discourse, and very ready in the auditor's part of the service. — Eyes did not much wander. How could they, when the loveliest object, infinitely the loveliest in the whole church, was in my view.

Dear creature! how fervent, how amiable, in her devotions! I have got her to own *that she prayed for me.* I hope a prayer from so excellent a mind will not be made in vain.

There is, after all, something beautifully solemn in devotion. The sabbath is a charming institution to *keep* the heart right, when it *is* right. One day in seven, how reasonable! — I think I'll go to church once a day often. I fancy it will go a great way towards making me a reformed man. To see multitudes of well-appearing people all joining in one reverend act: an exercise how worthy of a rational being! Yet it adds a sting or two to my former stings, when I think of my projects with regard to this charming creature. In my conscience, I believe if I were to go constantly to church, I could not pursue them.

I had a scheme come into my head while there: but I will renounce it, because it obtruded itself upon me in so good a place. Excellent creature! How many *ruins* has she prevented by attaching me to herself; by engrossing my whole attention!

But let me tell thee what passed between us in my first visit of this morning; and then I will acquaint thee more largely with my good behaviour at church.

I could not be admitted till after eight. I found her ready prepared to go out. I pretended to be ignorant of her intention, having charged Dorcas not to own that she had told me of it.

Going abroad, madam? — with an air of indifference.

Yes, sir; I intend to go to church.

I hope, madam, I shall have the honour to attend you.

No! she designed to take a chair, and go to the next church.

This startled me: a chair to carry her to the next church from Mrs. Sinclair's, her right name not Sinclair, and to bring her back hither in the face of people who might not think well of the house! — there was no permitting that. Yet I was to appear indifferent. But said, I should take it for a favor, if she would permit me to attend her in a coach, as there was time for it, to St. Paul's.

She made objections to the gaiety of my dress; and told me, that if she went to St. Paul's, she could go in a coach without *me*.

I objected Singleton and her brother, and offered to dress in the plainest suit I had.

I beg the favour of attending you, dear madam, said I. I have not been at church a great while: we shall sit in different stalls: and the next time I go, I hope it will be to give myself a title to the greatest blessing I can receive.

She made some further objections: but at last permitted me the honour of attending her.

I got myself placed in her eye, that the time might not seem tedious to me; for we were there early. And I gained her good opinion, as I mentioned above, by my behaviour.

The subject of the discourse was particular enough: it was about a prophet's story or parable of an ewe lamb taken by a rich man from a poor one, who dearly loved it, and whose only comfort it was: designed to strike remorse into David, on his adultery with Uriah's wife Bathsheba, and his murder of the husband. These women, Jack, have been the occasion of all manner of mischief from the beginning! Now, when David, full of indignation, swore [King David would swear, Jack: but how shouldst thou know who King David was? The story is in the bible] that the rich man should surely die; Nathan, which was the prophet's name, and a good ingenious fellow, cried out, (which were the words of the text) *Thou art the man!* — By my soul I thought the parson looked directly at me: and at that moment I cast my eye full on my ewelamb. But I must tell thee too, that I thought a good deal of my Rosebud. — A better man than King David in *that* point, however, thought I!

When we came home we talked upon the subject; and I shewed my charmer my attention to the discourse, by letting her know where the doctor made the most of his subject, and where it might have been touched to greater advantage: for it is really a very affecting story, and has as pretty a contrivance in it as ever I read. And this I did in such a grave way, that she seemed more and more pleased with me; and I have no doubt that I shall get her to favour me to-morrow night with her company at my collation.

Sunday evening.

We all dined together in Mrs. Sinclair's parlour. All *excessively* right! The two nieces have topped their parts; Mrs. Sinclair hers. Never so easy as now! — "She really thought a little oddly of these people at first, she said: Mrs. Sinclair seemed very forbidding! Her nieces were persons with whom she could not wish to be acquainted. But really we should not be too hasty in our censures. Some people improve upon us. The widow seems *tolerable*." She went no further than *tolerable*. "Miss Martin and Miss Horton are young people of good sense, and have read a great deal. What Miss Martin particularly said of marriage, and of her humble servant, was very solid. She believes with such notions she cannot make a bad wife." — I have said Sally's humble servant is a woollen-draper of great reputation; and she is soon to be married.

I have been letting her into thy character, and into the characters of my other three esquires, in hopes to excite her curiosity to see you to-morrow night. I have told her some of the *worst*, as well as *best* parts of your characters, in order to exalt myself, and to obviate any sudden surprises, as well as to teach her, what sort of men she may expect to see, if she will oblige me with her company.

By her after-observations upon each of you, I shall judge what I may or may not do to *obtain* or *keep* her good opinion; what she will *like*, or what *not;* and so pursue the one, or avoid the other, as I see proper. — So, while she is penetrating into your shallow heads, I shall enter *her* heart, and know what to bid *my own* to hope for.

The house is to be taken in three weeks; all will be over in three weeks, or bad will be my luck! — Who knows but in three days? — Have I not carried that great point of making her pass for my wife to the people below? And that other great one, of fixing myself here night and day? — What woman ever escaped me, who lodged under one roof with me?— The house too, THE house; the people, people after my own heart: her servants, Will, and Dorcas, both *my* servants — *three days* did I say! Pho! pho! pho! — *Three hours!*

* * *

I HAVE carried my third point; but so extremely to the dislike of my charmer that I have been threatened, for suffering Miss Partington to be introduced to her without her leave. Which laid her under a necessity to deny or comply with the urgent request of so fine a young lady; who had engaged to honour me at my collation, on condition that my beloved would be present at it.

To be obliged to appear before my friends as what she was not! She was for insisting, that I should acquaint the women here with the truth of the matter, and not go on propagating stories for her countenance; making her a sharer in my guilt.

But what points will not perseverance carry? especially when it is covered over with the face of yielding *now*, and, Parthian like, returning to the charge *anon*. Do not the sex carry all their points with their men by the same methods? Have I conversed with them so freely as I have done, and learnt nothing of them? Didst thou ever know that a woman's denial of any favour, whether the least or the greatest, that my heart was set upon, stood her in any stead? The more perverse she, the more steady I; that is my rule.

But the point thus so much against her will carried, I doubt thou wilt see in her more of a sullen than of an obliging charmer. For when Miss Partington was withdrawn, "What was Miss Partington to her? In her situation she wanted no new acquaintance. And what were my four friends to her in her present circumstances? She would assure me, if ever again —" and there she stopped with a twirl of her hand.

When we meet, I will, in her presence, tipping thee a wink, shew thee the motion, for it was a very pretty one. Quite new. Yet have I seen an hundred pretty passionate twirls too, in my time, from other fair ones. How universally engaging it is to put a woman of sense, to whom a man is not married, in a passion, let the reception given to every ranting scene in our plays testify. Take care, my charmer, now thou art come to delight me with thy angry twirls, that thou temptest me not to provoke a *variety of them* from one, whose every motion, whose every air carries in it so much sense and soul.

But, angry or pleased, this charming creature must be all loveliness. Her features are all harmony, and made for one another. No other feature could be substituted in the place of any one of hers, but must abate of her perfection: and think you that I do not long to have your opinion of my fair prize?

If you love to see features that glow, though the heart is frozen, and never yet was thawed; if you love fine sense, and adages flowing through teeth of ivory, and lips of coral; an eye that penetrates all things; a voice that is harmony itself; an air of grandeur, mingled with a sweetness that cannot be described; a politeness that, if ever equalled, was never excelled —you'll see all these excellencies, and ten times more, in this my GLORIANA.

Mark her majestic fabrick!—She's a temple
Sacred by birth, and built by hands divine;
Her soul the deity that lodges there:
Nor is the pile unworthy of the god.

Or, to describe her in a softer style with Rowe,

The bloom of op'ning flowers, unsully'd beauty,
Softness, and sweetest innocence she wears,
And looks like nature in the world's first spring.

Adieu, varlets four!—At six on Monday evening I expect ye all.

LETTER LXIV.

Miss Clarissa Harlowe to Miss Howe.

Sunday, April 30.

Mr. Lovelace in his last letters having taken notice of the most material passages contained in this letter, the following extracts from it are only inserted.
She gives pretty near the same account that he does of what passed between them on her resolution to go to church; and of his proposal of St. Paul's, and desire of attending her. She praises his good behaviour there; as also the discourse, and the preacher: is pleased with its seasonableness: gives particulars of the conversation between them afterwards, and commends the good observations he made upon the sermon.

I AM willing, says she, to have hopes of him: but am so unable to know how to depend upon his seriousness for an hour together, that all my favourable accounts of him in this respect must be taken with allowance.

Being very much pressed, I could not tell how to refuse dining with the widow and her nieces this day. I am better pleased with them, than I ever thought I should be. I cannot help blaming myself for my readiness to give severe censures, where reputation is concerned. People's ways, humours, constitutions, educations, and opportunities allowed for, my dear, many persons, as far as I know, may appear blameless, whom others of different humours and educations are too apt to blame; and who, from the same fault, may be as ready to blame *them*. I will therefore make it a rule to myself for the future, never to judge peremptorily on first appearances. But yet I must observe that these are not people I should choose to be intimate with, or whose ways I can like: although, for the stations they are in, they may go through the world with tolerable credit.

Mr. Lovelace's behaviour has

been such, as makes me call this, so far as it is passed, an agreeable day. Yet, when easiest as to him, my situation with my friends takes place in my thoughts, and causes me many a tear.

I am the more pleased with the people of the house, because of the persons of rank they are acquainted with, and who visit them.

Sunday evening.

I AM still well pleased with Mr. Lovelace's behaviour. We have had a good deal of serious discourse together. The man has really just and good notions. He confesses how much he is pleased with this day, and hopes for many such. Nevertheless, he ingenuously warned me, that his unlucky vivacity might return: but he doubted not, that he should be fixed at last by my example and conversation.

He has given me an entertaining account of the four gentlemen he is to meet to-morrow-night: *entertaining*, I mean, for his humorous description of their persons, manners, &c. but such a description as is far from being to their praise: yet he seemed rather to design to divert my melancholy by it, than to degrade them. I think at bottom, my dear, that he must be a good-natured man; but that he was spoiled young for want of check or control.

I cannot but call this, my circumstances considered, an happy day to the end of it. Indeed, my dear, I think I could prefer him to all the men I ever knew, were he but to be always what he has been this day. You see how ready I am to own all you have charged me with, when I find myself out. It is a difficult thing, I believe, sometimes, for a young creature that is able to deliberate with herself, to know when she loves, or when she hates: but I am resolved, as much as possible, to be determined both in my hatred and love by *actions*, as they make the man worthy or unworthy.

She dates again on Monday, and declares herself highly displeased at Miss Partington's being introduced to her: and still more for being obliged to promise to be present at Mr. Lovelace's collation. She foresees, she says, a murdered evening.

LETTER LXV.

Miss Clarissa Harlowe to Miss Howe.

Monday night, May 1.

I HAVE just escaped from the very disagreeable company I was obliged, so much against my will, to be in. As a very particular relation of this evening's conversation would be painful to me, you must content yourself with what you shall be able to collect from the outlines, as I may call them, of the characters of the persons; assisted by the little histories Mr. Lovelace gave me of each yesterday.

The names of the gentlemen are Belton, Mowbray, Tourville, and Belford. These four, with Mrs. Sinclair, Miss Partington, the great heiress mentioned in my last, Mr. Lovelace, and myself, made up the company.

I gave you before, the favourable side of Miss Partington's character, such as it was given me by Mrs. Sinclair, and her nieces. I will now add a few words from my own observation upon her behaviour in *this* company.

In *better* company perhaps she would have appeared to less disadvantage: but, notwithstanding her *innocent looks*, which Mr. Lovelace also highly praised, he is the last person whose judgment I would take upon real modesty. For I observed, that, upon some talk from the gentlemen, not free enough to be openly censured, yet too indecent in its implication to come from well-bred persons, in the company of virtuous people, this young lady was very ready to apprehend; and yet, by smiles and simperings, to encourage, rather than discourage, the culpable freedoms of persons, who, in what they went out of their way to say, must either be guilty of absurdity, meaning *nothing;* or meaning *something* of rudeness.*

But indeed I have seen women, of whom I had a better opinion, than I can say I have of Mrs. Sinclair, who have allowed *gentlemen*, and *themselves* too, in greater liberties of this sort, than I have thought consistent with that purity of manners which ought to be the distinguishing characteris-

* Mr. Belford in Letter cxxvi. reminds Mr. Lovelace of some particular topics which passed in their conversation, extremely to the lady's honour.

tic of our sex: for what are *words*, but the *body* and *dress* of *thought?* And is not the mind of a person strongly indicated by its outward dress?

But to the *gentlemen;* as they must be called in right of their ancestors, it seems; for no other do they appear to have:

Mr. BELTON has had an university education, and was designed for the gown; but that not suiting with the gaiety of his temper, and an uncle dying, who devised to him a good estate, he quitted the college, came up to town, and commenced fine gentleman. He is said to be a man of sense. — Mr. Belton dresses gaily, but not quite foppishly: drinks hard; keeps all hours, and glories in doing so; games, and has been hurt by that pernicious diversion: he is about thirty years of age: his face is of a fiery red, somewhat bloated and pimply: and his irregularities threaten a brief duration to the sensual dream he is in: for he has a short consumptive cough, which seems to denote bad lungs; yet makes himself and his friends merry by his stupid and inconsiderate jests upon very threatening symptoms which ought to make him more serious.

Mr. MOWBRAY has been a great traveller; speaks as many languages as Mr. Lovelace himself, but not so fluently: is of a good family; seems to be about thirty-three or thirty-four: tall and comely in his person: bold and daring in his look: is a large-boned strong man: has a great scar in his forehead, with a dent, as if his scull had been beaten in there; and a seamed scar in his right cheek. — He dresses likewise very gaily: has his servants always about him, whom he is continually calling upon, and sending on the most trifling messages; half a dozen instances of which we had in the little time I was among them; while they seem to watch the turn of his fierce eye, to be ready to run, before they have half his message, and serve him with fear and trembling. Yet to his equals the man seems tolerable: he talks not amiss upon public entertainments and diversions: especially upon those abroad: yet has a romancing air: and avers things strongly, which seem quite improbable. Indeed, he *doubts* nothing, but what he ought to *believe:* for he jests upon sacred things; and professes to hate the clergy of all religions. He has high notions of *honour*, a word hardly ever out of his mouth; but seems to have no great regard to *morals*.

Mr. Tourville occasionally told his age; just turned of thirty-one. He is also of an ancient family; but in his person and manners, more of what I call the coxcomb, than any of his companions. He dresses richly; would be thought elegant in the choice and fashion of what he wears: yet, after all, appears rather tawdry than fine. One sees by the care he takes of his outside, and the notice he bespeaks from *every one* by his *own* notice of himself, that the inside takes up the least of his attention. He dances finely, Mr. Lovelace says: is a master of music; and singing is one of his principal excellencies. They prevailed upon him to sing; and he obliged them both in Italian and French; and, to do him justice, his songs in both were decent. They were all highly delighted with his performance; but his greatest admirers were, Mrs. Sinclair, Miss Partington, and *himself.* To me he appeared to have a great deal of affectation.

Mr. Tourville's conversation and address are insufferably full of those really gross affronts upon the understanding of our sex, which the moderns call *compliments*, and are intended to pass for so many instances of good breeding, though the most hyperbolical, unnatural stuff that can be conceived, and which can only serve to shew the insincerity of the *complimenter*, and the ridiculous light in which the *complimented* appears in his eyes, if he supposes a woman capable of relishing the romantic absurdities of his speeches.

He affects to introduce into his common talk Italian and French words; and often answers an English question in French, which language he greatly prefers, to the barbarously hissing English. But then he never fails to translate into this his *odious* native tongue the words and the sentences he speaks in the other two — lest, perhaps, it should be questioned whether he understands what he says.

He loves to tell stories: always calls them *merry*, *facetious*, *good*, or *excellent*, before he begins, in order to bespeak the attention of the hearers; but never gives himself concern in the *progress* or *conclusion* of them, to make good what he promises in his *preface*. Indeed he seldom brings any of them to a conclusion; for if his company have patience to hear him out, he breaks in upon himself by so many parenthetical intrusions, as one may call them, and has so many incidents springing in upon him, that he frequently drops his own thread, and sometimes sits down satisfied half way; or, if at other times he would resume it, he applies to his company to help him in again, with a *devil fetch him* if he remembers what he was driving at — but enough, and too much of Mr. Tourville.

Mr. Belford is the fourth gentleman, and one of whom Mr. Lovelace seems more fond than any of the rest; for he is a man of tried bravery, it seems; and this pair of friends came acquainted upon occasion of a quarrel (possibly about a woman) which brought on a challenge, and a meeting at Kensington Gravel-pits; which ended without unhappy consequences, by the mediation of three gentlemen strangers, just as each had made a pass at the other.

Mr. Belford, it seems, is about seven or eight-and-twenty. He is the youngest of the five, except Mr. Lovelace: and they are perhaps the wickedest; for they seem to lead the other three as they please. Mr. Belford, as the others, dresses gaily; but has not those advantages of person, nor from his dress, which Mr. Lovelace is too proud of. He has, however, the appearance and air of a gentleman. He is well read in classical authors, and in the best English poets and writers: and, by his means, the conversation took now-and-then a more agreeable turn: and I, who endeavoured to put the best face I could upon my situation, as I passed for Mrs. Lovelace with them, made shift to join in it, at such times, and received abundance of compliments from all the company, on the observations I made.*

Mr. Belford seems good-natured and obliging; and, although very complaisant, not so fulsomely so as Mr. Tourville; and has a polite and easy manner of expressing his sentiments on all occasions. He seems to delight in a logical way of argumentation, as also does Mr. Belton. These two attacked each other in this way; and both looked at us women, as if to observe whether we did not admire their learning, or, when they had said a smart thing, their wit. But Mr. Belford had visibly the advantage of the other, having quicker parts, and by taking the worst side of the argument, seemed to *think* he had. Upon the whole of his behaviour and conversation, he put me in mind of that character in Milton:

* See Letter cxxvi. above referred to.

— His tongue
Dropt manna, and could make the worse
   appear
The better reason, to perplex and dash
Maturest counsels; for his thoughts were
   low;
To vice industrious: but to nobler deeds
Tim'rous and slothful: — yet he pleased
   the ear.

How little soever matters in general may be to our liking, we are apt, when hope is strong enough to permit it, to endeavour to make the best we can of the lot we have drawn; and I could not but observe often, how much Mr. Lovelace excelled all his four friends in every thing they seemed desirous to excel in. But, as to wit and vivacity, he had no equal there. All the others gave up to him, when his lips began to open. The haughty Mowbray would call upon the prating Tourville for silence, and would elbow the supercilious Belton into attention, when Lovelace was going to speak. And when he had spoken, the words, Charming fellow! with a free word of admiration or envy, fell from every mouth.

He has indeed so many advantages in his person and manner, that what would be inexcusable in another, would, if one watched not over one's self, and did not endeavour to distinguish what is the essence of right and wrong, look becoming in him.

Mr. Belford, to my no small vexation and confusion, with the forwardness of a favoured and intrusted friend, singled me out, on Mr. Lovelace's being sent for down, to make me congratulatory compliments on my supposed nuptials; which he did with a caution, not to insist too long on the rigorous vow I had imposed upon a man so universally admired —

"See him among twenty men," said he, "all of distinction, and nobody is regarded but Mr. Lovelace."

It must, indeed, be confessed, that there is in his whole deportment a natural dignity, which renders all insolent or imperative demeanour as unnecessary as inexcusable. Then that deceiving sweetness which appears in his smiles, in his accent, in his whole aspect and address, when he thinks it worth his while to oblige or endeavour to attract, how does this shew, that he was *born* innocent, as I may say; that he was not *naturally* the cruel, the boisterous, the impetuous creature; which the wicked company he may have fallen into have made him! For he has, besides, an open, and, I think, an honest countenance. Don't *you* think so, my dear? On all these specious appearances, have I founded my hopes of seeing him a reformed man.

But it is amazing to me, I own, that with so much of the gentleman, such a general knowledge of books and men, such a skill in the learned as well as modern languages, he can take so much delight as he does in the company of such persons as I have described, and in subjects of frothy impertinence, unworthy of his talents, and his natural and acquired advantages. I can think but of one reason for it, and that must argue a very low mind, his VANITY; which makes him desirous of being considered as the head of the people he consorts with. A man to love praise, yet to be content to draw it from such contaminated springs!

One compliment passed from Mr. Belford to Mr. Lovelace, which hastened my quitting the shocking company.—"You are a happy man, Mr. Lovelace," said he, upon some fine speeches made him by Mrs. Sinclair, and assented to by Miss Partington: "you have so much courage and so much wit, that neither man nor woman can stand before you."

Mr. Belford looked at me when he spoke: yes, my dear, he smilingly looked at me: and he looked upon his complimented friend: and all their *assenting*, and therefore *affronting* eyes, both men's and women's, were turned upon your Clarissa: at least, my self-reproaching heart made me think so; for that would hardly permit my eye to look up.

Oh! my dear, were but a woman, who gives reason to the world to think her to be in love with a man, [and this must believed to be my case: or to what can my *supposed* voluntary going off with Mr. Lovelace be imputed?] to reflect one moment on the exaltation she gives *him*, and the disgrace she brings upon *herself*; the low pity, the silent contempt, the insolent sneers and whispers, to which she makes herself obnoxious from a censuring world of both sexes; how would she despise herself! and how much more eligible would she think death itself than such a discovered debasement.

What I have thus in general touched upon, will account to you, why I could not more particularly relate what passed in this evening's conversation: which, as may be gathered from what I have written, abounded with *approbatory* accusations, and *supposed* witty retorts.

LETTER LXVI.

Miss Clarissa Harlowe to Miss Howe.

Monday midnight.

I AM very much vexed and disturbed at an odd incident. Mrs. Sinclair has just now left me; I believe in displeasure, on my declining to comply with a request she made me: which was, to admit Miss Partington to a share in my bed; her house being crowded by her niece's guests, and by their attendants, as well as by those of Miss Partington.

There might be nothing in it; and my denial carried a stiff and ill-natured appearance. But instantly upon her making the request, it came into my thought, "that I was in a manner a stranger to every body in the house; not so much as a servant I could call my own, or of whom I had any great opinion: that there were four men of free manners in the house, *avowed* supporters of Mr. Lovelace in matters of offence; himself a man of enterprise; all, as far as I knew, (and as I had reason to think by their noisy mirth after I left them) drinking deeply: that Miss Partington herself is not so bashful a person as she was represented to me to be: that *officious pains* were taken to give me a good opinion of her: and that Mrs. Sinclair made a greater parade in prefacing the request, than such a request needed. To deny, thought I, can only carry an appearance of singularity to people who *already* think me singular. To consent, may possibly, if not probably, be attended with inconveniencies. The consequences of the alternative so very disproportionate, I thought it more prudent to incur the censure, than to risk the inconvenience."

I told her, that I was writing a long letter: that I should choose to write till I were sleepy: and that a companion would be a restraint upon me, and I upon her.

She was loth, she said, that so delicate a young creature, and so great a fortune as Miss Partington, should be put to lie with Dorcas in a press-bed. She should be very sorry if she had asked an improper thing. She had never been so put to it before. And Miss would stay up with *her* till I had done writing.

Alarmed at this urgency, and it being easier to persist in a denial *given* than to give it at *first*, I said, Miss Partington should be welcome to my whole bed, and I would retire into the dining-room, and there, locking myself in, write all the night.

The poor thing, she said, was afraid to lie alone. To be sure Miss Partington would not put me to such an inconvenience.

She then withdrew: but returned; begged my pardon for returning: but the poor child, she said, was in tears. Miss Partington had never seen a young lady she so much admired, and so much wished to imitate, as me. The dear girl hoped that nothing had passed in her behaviour, to give me dislike to her. — Should she bring her to me?

I was very busy, I said. The letter I was writing was upon a very important subject. I hoped to see the young lady in the morning: when I would apologize to her for my particularity. And then Mrs. Sinclair hesitating and moving towards the door (though she turned round to me again), I desired her (*lighting her*) to take care how she went down.

Pray, madam, said she, on the stairs-head, don't give yourself all this trouble. God knows my heart, I meant no affront: but, since you seem to take my freedom amiss, I beg you will not acquaint Mr. Lovelace with it; for he perhaps will think me bold and impertinent.

Now, my dear, is not this a particular incident: either as I have made it, or as it was designed? I don't love to do an uncivil thing; and if nothing were meant by the request, my refusal deserves to be called uncivil. Then I have shewn a suspicion of vile usage by it, which surely dare not be meant. If *just* I ought to apprehend every thing, and fly the house and the

man as I would an infection. If
not just, and if I cannot contrive
to clear myself of having entertained suspicions, by assigning
some other plausible reason for
my denial, the very *staying here*
will have an appearance not at all
reputable to myself.

I am now out of humour with
him, with myself, with all the
world, but you. His companions
are shocking creatures. Why,
again I repeat, should he have
been desirous to bring me into
such company? Once more, I like
him not. Indeed I do not like
him!

LETTER LXVII.

'Miss Clarissa Harlowe to Miss Howe.
Tuesday, May 2.

WITH infinite regret I am
obliged to tell you, that I can
write no longer to you, or receive
letters from you. Your mother
has sent me a letter inclosed in a
cover to Mr. Lovelace, directed for
him at Lord M.'s, (and which was
brought him just now) reproaching me on this subject in very
angry terms, and forbidding me,
"as I would not be thought to intend to make her and you unhappy, to write to you without her
leave."

This, therefore, is the last you
must receive from me till happier
days: and as my prospects are
not very bad, I presume we shall
soon have leave to write again;
and even to see each other; since
an alliance with a family so honourable as Mr. Lovelace's is, will
not be a disgrace.

She is pleased to write, "that
if I would wish to *inflame* you, I
should let you know her written
prohibition: but if otherwise, find
some way of my own accord (without bringing *her* into the question)
to decline a correspondence, which
I must know she has for some time
past forbidden." But all I can
say is, to beg of you *not* to be inflamed; — to beg of you not to let
her *know*, or even by your behaviour to her on this occasion, *guess*,
that I have acquainted you with
my reason for declining to write to
you. For how else, after the
scruples I have heretofore made
on this very subject, yet proceeding to correspond, can I honestly
satisfy you about my motives for
this sudden stop? So, my dear, I
choose, you see, rather to rely
upon your discretion, than to
feign reasons with which you
would not be satisfied, but, with
your usual active penetration, sift
to the bottom, and at last find me
to be a mean and low qualifier;
and that with an implication injurious to you, that I supposed
you had not prudence enough to
be trusted with the naked truth.

I repeat that my prospects are
not bad. "The house, I presume,
will soon be taken. The people
here are very respectful, notwithstanding my nicety about Miss
Partington. Miss Martin, who is
near marriage with an eminent
tradesman in the Strand, just now
in a very respectful manner, asked
my opinion of some patterns of
rich silks for the occasion. The
widow has a less forbidding ap-

pearance than at first. Mr. Lovelace, on my declared dislike of his four friends, has assured me, that neither they nor any body else shall be introduced to me without my leave.

These circumstances I mention (as you will suppose) that your kind heart may be at ease about me; that you may be induced by them to acquiesce with your mother's commands, (*cheerfully* acquiesce) and that for *my sake*, lest I should be thought an *inflamer;* who am, with very contrary intentions, my dearest and best-beloved friend,

Your ever obliged and affectionate,
CL. HARLOWE.

LETTER LXVIII.
Miss Howe to Miss Clarissa Harlowe.
Wedn., May 3.

I AM astonished that my mother should take such a step — purely to exercise an unreasonable act of authority; and to oblige the most remorseless hearts in the world. If I find that I can be of use to you either by advice or information, do you think I will not give it? — Were it to any person, much *less* dear to me than you are, do you think, in such a case, I would forbear giving it?

Mr. Hickman, who pretends to a little casuistry, in such nice matters, is of opinion, that I ought not to decline a correspondence thus circumstanced. And it is well he is; for my mother having set me up, I must have somebody to quarrel with.

This I will come into if it will make you easy — I will forbear to write to *you* for a few days, if nothing extraordinary happen, and till the rigour of her prohibition is abated. But be assured, that I will not dispense with your writing to *me*. My heart, my conscience, my honour will not permit it.

But how will I help myself? — How! — easily enough. For I do assure you, that I want but very little further provocation to fly privately to London. And if I do, I will not leave you till I see you either honourably married, or absolutely quit of the wretch: and in this last case, I will take you down with me, in defiance of the whole world; or, if you refuse to go with me, stay with you, and accompany you as your shadow whithersoever you go.

Don't be frighted at this declaration. There is but one consideration, and but one hope, that withhold me, watched as I am, in all my retirements; obliged to read to her without a voice; to work in her presence without fingers; and to lie with her every night against my will. The *consideration* is, lest you should apprehend that a step of this nature would look like a doubling of your fault, in the eyes of such as think your going away a fault. The *hope* is, that things will still end happily, and that some people will have reason to take shame to themselves for the sorry part they have acted. Nevertheless I am often balancing — but your resolving to give up the correspondence at this crisis, will turn the scale. *Write*, therefore, or *take the consequence.*

A few words upon the subject of your last letters — I know not whether your brother's wise project be given up or not. A dead silence reigns in your family. Your brother was absent three days: then at home one; and is now absent: but whether with Singleton or not, I cannot find out.

By your account of your wretch's companions, I see not but they are a set of *infernals*, and he the *Beelzebub*. What could he mean, as you say, by his earnestness to bring you into such company, and to give you such an opportunity to make him and them reflecting glasses to one another? The man's a *fool*, to be sure, my dear — a *silly fellow*, at least — the wretches must put on the *best* before you, no doubt, — lords of the creation! — Noble fellows these! — Yet who knows how many poor despicable souls of our sex the worst of them has had to whine after him!

You have brought an inconvenience upon yourself, as you observe, by your refusal of Miss Partington for your bed-fellow. Pity you had not admitted her! Watchful as *you* are, what *could* have happened? If violence were intended, he would not stay for the *night.* You might have sat up after her, or not gone to bed. Mrs. Sinclair pressed it too far. You were over-scrupulous.

If any thing happen to delay your nuptials, I would advise you to remove: but if you marry, perhaps you may think it no great matter to stay where you are, till you take possession of your own estate. The knot once tied, and with so resolute a man, it is my opinion, your relations will soon resign what they cannot legally hold: and, were even a litigation to follow, you will not be *able*, nor ought you to be *willing*, to help it: for your estate will then be his right; and it will be unjust to wish it to be withheld from him.

One thing I would advise you to think of: and that is, of proper settlements: it will be to the credit of your prudence and of his justice (and the more as matters stand) that something of this should be done before you marry. Bad as he is, nobody accounts him a sordid man. And I wonder he has hitherto been silent on that subject.

I am not displeased with his proposal about the widow lady's house. I think it will do very well. But if it must be three weeks before you can be certain about it, surely you need not put off his day for that space: and he may bespeak his equipages. Surprising to me as well as to you, that he could be so acquiescent.

I repeat — continue to write to me. I insist upon it; and as minutely as possible: or, take the consequence. I send this by a particular hand. I am, and ever will be,

Your most affectionate
ANNA HOWE.

LETTER LXIX.

Miss Clarissa Harlowe to Miss Howe.

Thursday, May 4.

I FOREGO every other engagement, I suspend every wish, I banish every other fear, to take up my pen, to beg of you, that you will not think of being *guilty* of such an act of love as I can never thank you for; but must for ever regret. If I *must* continue to write to you, I must. I know full well your impatience of control, when you have the least imagination that your generosity or friendship is likely to be wounded by it.

My dearest, dearest creature, would you incur a maternal, as I have a paternal, malediction? Would not the world think there was an infection in my fault, if it were to be followed by Miss Howe? There are some points so flagrantly wrong, that they will not bear to be argued upon. This is one of them. I need *not* give reasons against such a rashness. Heaven forbid that it should be known that you had it but once in your *thought*, be your motives ever so noble and generous, to follow so bad an example; the rather, as that you would, in such a case, want the extenuations that might be pleaded in my favour; and particularly that one of being *surprised* into the unhappy step.

The restraint your mother lays you under would not have appeared heavy to you but on my account. Would you have once thought it a hardship to be admitted a part of her bed? — How did I use to be delighted with such a favour from *my* mother! How did I love to work in her presence! — So did you in the presence of yours once. And to read to her in winter evenings I know was one of your joys. — Do not give me cause to reproach *myself* on the reason that may be assigned for the change in *you*.

Learn, my dear, I beseech you learn, to subdue your own passions. Be the motives what they will, excess is excess. Those passions in our sex, which we take no pains to subdue, may have one and the same source with those infinitely blacker passions, which we used so often to condemn in the violent and headstrong of the other sex, and which may be only heightened in them by *custom*, and their *free education*. Let us both, my dear, ponder well this thought; look into ourselves, and fear.

If I write, as I find I must, I insist upon *your* forbearing to write. Your silence to *this* shall be the sign to me, that you will not think of the rashness you threaten me with; and that you will obey your mother as to *your own* part of the correspondence, however: especially, as you can inform and advise me in every weighty case by Mr. Hickman's pen.

My trembling writing will shew you, my dear, impetuous creature,

what a trembling heart you have given to
Your ever obliged,
Or, if you take so rash a step,
Your for ever disobliged,
CLARISSA HARLOWE.

My clothes were brought to me just now. But you have so much discomposed me, that I have no heart to look into the trunks. Why, why, my dear, will you fright me with your flaming love! Discomposure gives distress to a weak heart, whether it arise from friendship or enmity.

A servant of Mr. Lovelace carries this to Mr. Hickman for dispatch sake. Let that worthy man's pen relieve my heart from this new uneasiness.

LETTER LXX.

Mr. Hickman to Miss Clarissa Harlowe.

[*Sent to Wilson's by a particular hand.*]

MADAM, Friday, May 5.

I HAVE the honour of dear Miss Howe's commands, to acquaint you, without knowing the occasion, that she is excessively concerned for the concern she has given you in her last letter: and that, if you will but write to her, under cover as before, she will have no thoughts of what you are so very apprehensive about. — Yet she bid me write, "That if she has but the *least* imagination that she can *serve* you, and *save* you," those are her words, "all the censures of the world will be but of second consideration with her." I have great temptations on this occasion to express my own resentments upon your present state; but not being fully apprized of what that is — only conjecturing from the disturbance upon the mind of the dearest lady in the world to me, and the most sincere of friends to you, that *that* is not altogether so happy as were to be wished; and being, moreover, forbid to enter into the cruel subject, I can only offer, *as I do*, my best and faithfullest services! and wish you a happy deliverance from all your troubles. For I am,

Most excellent young lady,
Your faithful and most obedient servant,
CH. HICKMAN.

LETTER LXXI.

Mr. Lovelace to John Belford, Esq.

Tuesday, May 2.

MERCURY, as the fabulist tells us, having the curiosity to know the estimation he stood in among mortals, descended in disguise, and in a statuary's shop cheapened a Jupiter, then a Juno, then one then another, of the *Dii majores;* and at last asked, what price that same statue of *Mercury* bore? O sir, says the artist, buy one of the others, and I'll throw you in that for nothing.

How sheepish must the god of thieves look upon this rebuff to his vanity!

So thou! a thousand pounds wouldst thou give for the good opinion of this single lady — to be only thought tolerable, and not quite unworthy of her conversation, would make thee happy. And at parting last night, or rather this morning, thou madest me promise a few lines to Edgware, to let thee know what she thinks of thee, and of thy brethren.

Thy thousand pounds, Jack, is all thy own: for most heartily does she dislike ye all — thee as much as any of the rest.

I am sorry for it too, as to thy part; for two reasons — *one*, that I think the motive for thy curiosity was fear or consciousness: whereas that of the arch thief was vanity, intolerable vanity: and he was therefore justly sent away with a blush upon his cheeks to heaven, and could not brag — the *other*, that I am afraid, if she dislikes *thee*, she dislikes *me:* for are we not birds of a feather?

I must never talk of reformation, she told me, having such companions, and taking such delight, as I seemed to take, in their frothy conversation.

I, no more than you, Jack, imagined she could possibly like ye: but then, as *my* friends, I thought a person of her education would have been more sparing of her censures.

I don't know how it is, Belford; but women think themselves entitled to take any freedoms with us, while we are unpolite, forsooth, and I can't tell what, if we don't tell a pack of cursed lies, and make black white, in *their* favour — teaching us to be hypocrites, yet stigmatising us at other times, for deceivers.

I defended ye all as well as I could: but you know there was no attempting aught but a palliative defence, to one of her principles.

I will summarily give thee a few of my pleas.

"To the *pure*, every little deviation seemed offensive: yet I saw not, that there was any thing amiss the whole evening, either in the words or behaviour of any of my friends. Some people could talk but upon *one* or *two* subjects: she upon *every one:* no wonder, therefore, *they* talked to what they understood best; and to mere objects of sense. Had she honoured us with more of *her* conversation, she would have been less disgusted with *ours;* for she saw how every one was prepared to admire her, whenever she opened her lips. You in particular, had said, when she retired, that virtue itself spoke when she spoke: but that you had such an awe upon you, after she had favoured us with an observation or two on a subject started, that you should ever be afraid in her company, to be found *most* exceptionable, when you intended to be *least* so."

Plainly, she said, she neither liked my companions, nor the house she was in.

I liked not the house any more than she: though the people were very obliging, and she had owned they were less exceptionable to herself, than at first: and were we not about another of our own?

She did not like Miss Partington — let her fortune be what it would, and she had heard a great deal said of her fortune; she should not choose an intimacy with her. She thought it was a hardship to be put upon such a difficulty as she was put upon the preceding night, when there were lodgers in the front-house, whom they had reason to be freer with, than, upon so short an acquaintance, with her.

I pretended to be an utter stranger as to this particular; and, when she explained herself upon it, condemned Mrs. Sinclair's request, and called it a confident one.

She *artfully* made lighter of her denial of the girl for a bedfellow, than she *thought* of it, I could see that; for it was plain, she supposed there was room for me to think she had been either *over nice*, or *over cautious*.

I offered to resent Mrs. Sinclair's freedom.

No; there was no great matter in it. It was best to let it pass. It might be thought more particular in her to deny such a request, than in Mrs. Sinclair to make it, or in Miss Partington to expect it to be complied with. But as the people below had a large acquaintance, she did not know how often she might have her retirements invaded, if she gave way. And indeed, there were levities in the behaviour of that young lady, which she could not so far pass over as to wish an intimacy with her.

I said, I liked Miss Partington as little as *she* could. Miss Partington was a silly young creature; who seemed too likely to justify the watchfulness of her guardians over her. — But, nevertheless, as to her general conversation and behaviour last night, I must own, that I thought the girl (for *girl* she was, as to discretion) not exceptionable; only carrying herself like a free good-natured creature who believed herself secure in the honour of her company.

It was very well said of me, she replied: but, if that young lady were so well satisfied with her company, she must needs say, that I was very kind to suppose her such an *innocent*—for her own part, she had seen nothing of the London world: but thought, she must tell me plainly, that she never was in such company in her life; nor ever again wished to be in such.

There, Belford! — *Worse off than Mercury! — Art thou not?*

I was nettled. Hard would be the lot of *more* discreet women, as far as I knew, than Miss Partington, were they to be judged by so rigid a virtue as hers.

Not so, she said: but if I really saw nothing exceptionable to a virtuous mind, in that young person's behaviour, my ignorance of *better* behaviour was, she must needs tell me, as pitiable as *hers*: and it were to be wished, that minds *so* paired, for their own sakes, should never be separated.

See, Jack, *what I get by my charity!*

I thanked her heartily. But said, that I must take the liberty to observe that good folks were generally so uncharitable, that, devil take me, if I would choose to be good, were the consequence to be, that I must think hardly of the whole world besides.

She congratulated me upon my charity; but told me, that to *enlarge her own*, she hoped it would not be expected of her to approve of the *low company* I had brought her into last night.

No exception for thee, Belford! Safe is thy thousand pounds.

I saw not, I said, begging her pardon, that she liked *any body*. [*Plain dealing for plain dealing, Jack! — Why then did she abuse my friends?*] — However, let me but know whom and what she did or did not like: and, if possible, I would like and dislike the very same persons and things.

She bid me then in a pet, *dislike myself*.

Cursed severe! — *Does she think she must not pay for it one day or one night?* — And if one, many; that's my comfort.

I was in such a train of being happy, I said, before my earnestness to procure her to favour my friends with her company, that I wished the devil had had, as well my friends as Miss Partington — and yet I must say, that I saw not how good people could answer half their end, which is to reform the wicked by precept as well as example, were they to accompany *only* with the good.

I had like to have been blasted by two or three flashes of lightning from her indignant eyes; and she turned scornfully from me, and retired to her own apartment.

Once more Jack, *safe, as thou seest, is thy thousand pounds.*

She says I am not a polite man; but is she, in the instance before us, more polite for a woman?

And now dost thou not think, that I owe my charmer some revenge for her cruelty in obliging such a fine young creature, and so vast a fortune, as Miss Partington, to crowd into a press-bed with Dorcas, the maid-servant of the proud refuser? — Miss Partington too (with tears) declaring by Mrs. Sinclair, that would Mrs. Lovelace do her the honour of a visit at Barnet, the best bed and best room in her guardian's house, should be at her service. Thinkest thou that I could not guess at her dishonourable fears of me? — That she apprehended that the supposed *husband* would endeavour to take possession of *his own?* — And that Miss Partington would be willing to contribute to such a piece of justice?

Thus, then, thou both remindest, and defiest me, charmer! — And since thou reliest more on thy own precaution than upon my honour, be it unto thee, fair one, as thou apprehendest!

And now, Jack, let me know, what thy opinion, and the opinions of thy brother varlets, are of my Gloriana.

I have just now heard, that Hannah hopes to be soon well enough to attend her young lady, when in London. It seems the girl has had no physician. I must send her one, out of pure love and respect to her mistress. Who knows but medicine may *weaken* nature, and *strengthen* the disease? — As her malady is not a *fever*, very likely it may do so. — But perhaps the wench's hopes are too forward. *Blustering weather in this month yet.* — And that is bad for rheumatic complaints.

LETTER LXXII.
Mr. Lovelace to John Belford, Esq.
Tuesday, May 2.

JUST as I had sealed up the inclosed, comes a letter to my beloved, in a cover to me, directed to Lord M.'s. From whom, thinkest thou? — From Mrs. Howe! —

And what the contents?

How should I know unless the dear creature had communicated them to me? But a very cruel letter I believe it is, *by the effect it had upon her*. The tears ran down her cheeks as she read it; and her colour changed several times. No end of her persecutions, I think!

"What a cruelty in my fate!" said the sweet lamenter. — "Now the *only* comfort of my life must be given up!"

Miss Howe's correspondence, no doubt.

But *should* she be so much grieved at this? This correspondence was prohibited before, and that, to the *daughter*, in the strongest terms: but yet carried on by *both;* although a *brace of impeccables,* an't please ye. Could they expect that a mother would not vindicate her authority? — and finding her prohibition ineffectual with her perverse *daughter*, was it not reasonable to suppose she would try what effect it would have upon her *daughter's friend?* — And now, I believe, the end will be effectually answered; for my beloved, I dare say, will make a point of conscience of it.

I hate cruelty, especially in *women:* and should have been more concerned for this instance of it in Mrs. Howe, had I not had a stronger instance of the same in my beloved to Miss Partington; for how did she know, since she was so much afraid for *herself*, whom Dorcas might let in to that innocent and *less watchful* young lady? But nevertheless I must needs own, that I am not very sorry for this prohibition, let it *originally* come from the *Harlowes* or *from whom it will;* because I make no doubt, that it is owing to Miss Howe, in a great measure, that my beloved is so much upon her guard, and thinks so hardly of me. And who can tell, *as characters here are so tender*, and *some disguises so flimsy,* what consequences might follow this undutiful correspondence? I say, therefore, I am not sorry for it. Now will she not have any body to compare notes with: any body to alarm her: and I may be saved the guilt and disobligation of inspecting into a correspondence that has long made me uneasy.

How every thing works for me! — Why will this charming creature make *such contrivances* necessary, as will increase my trouble, and my guilt too, as some will account it? But why, rather, I should ask, will she fight against her stars?

LETTER LXXIII.

Mr. Belford to Robert Lovelace, Esq

Edgeware, Tuesday night, May 2.

WITHOUT staying for the promised letter from you to inform us what the lady says of *us*, I write to tell you, that we are all of one opinion with regard to *her*; which is, that there is not of her age, a finer woman in the world, as to her understanding. As for her person, she is at the age of bloom, and an admirable creature; a perfect beauty; but this *poorer* praise, a man, who has been honoured with her conversation, can hardly descend to give; and yet she was brought amongst us contrary to her will.

Permit me, dear Lovelace, to be a means of saving this excellent creature from the dangers she hourly runs from the most plotting heart in the world. In a former, I pleaded your own family, Lord M.'s wishes particularly; and then I had not seen her: but now I join her sake, *honour's* sake, motives of justice, generosity, gratitude, and humanity, which are all concerned in the preservation of so fine a woman. Thou knowest not the anguish I should have had (whence arising, I cannot devise) had I not known before I set out this morning, that the incomparable creature had disappointed thee in thy cursed view of getting to admit the specious Partington for a bedfellow.

I have done nothing but talk of this lady ever since I saw her. There is something *so awful*, and yet *so sweet*, in her aspect, that were I to have the Virtues and the Graces all drawn in one piece, they should be taken, every one of them, from different airs and attitudes in her. She was born to adorn the age she was given to, and would be an ornament to the first dignity. What a piercing, yet gentle eye; every glance, I thought, mingled with love and fear of you! What a sweet smile darting through the cloud that overspread her fair face, demonstrating that she had more apprehensions and grief at her heart than she cared to express!

You may think what I am going to write too flighty; but, by my faith, I have conceived such a profound reverence for her sense and judgment, that far from thinking the man excusable who should treat her basely, I am ready to regret that such an angel of a woman should even marry. She is in my eye all mind: and were she to meet with a man all mind likewise, why should the charming qualities she is mistress of, be endangered? Why should such an angel be plunged so low as into the vulgar offices of domestic life? Were she mine, I should hardly wish to see her a mother, unless there were a kind of moral certainty, that minds like hers could be propagated. For why, in short, should not the work of bodies be left to *mere* bodies? I know, that you yourself have an opinion of her little less exalted. Belton, Mowbray, Tourville, are all of my mind; are full of her praises; and swear it would be a million of pities to ruin a woman, in whose fall none but devils can rejoice.

What must that merit and excellence be, which can extort this from *us*, free livers like yourself, and all of us your partial friends, who have joined with you in your just resentments against the rest of her family, and offered our assistance to execute your vengeance on them? But we cannot think it reasonable, that you should punish an innocent creature, who loves you so well, and who is in your protection, and has suffered so much for you, for the faults of her relations.

And here let me put a serious question or two. Thinkest thou, truly admirable as this lady is, that the *end* thou proposest to thyself, if obtained, is answerable to the *means*, to the trouble thou givest thyself, and to the perfidies, tricks, stratagems, and contrivances thou hast already been guilty of, and still meditatest? In every real excellence she surpasses all her sex. But in the article thou seekest to subdue her for, a mere sensualist, a Partington, a Horton, a Martin, would make a sensualist a thousand times happier than she either will or can.

Sweet are the joys that come with willingness.

And wouldst thou make *her* unhappy for a whole life, and *thyself* not happy for a single moment?

Hitherto, it is not too late; and that perhaps is as much as can be said, if thou meanest to preserve her esteem and good opinion, as well as person; for I think it is impossible she can get out of thy hands now she is in this cursed house. O that damned hypocritical *Sinclair*, as thou callest her! How was it possible she should behave so speciously as she did all the time the lady staid with us! — Be honest and marry; and be thankful that she will condescend to have thee. If thou dost not, thou wilt be the worst of men; and wilt be condemned in this world and the next: as I am sure thou oughtest, and shouldest too, wert thou to be judged by one, who never before was so much touched in a woman's favour, and whom thou knowest to be

Thy partial friend,
J. BELFORD.

Our companions consented, that I should withdraw to write to the above effect. They can make nothing of the characters we write in; so I read this to them. They approve of it; and of their own motion each man would set his name to it. I would not delay sending it, for fear of some detestable scheme taking place.

THOMAS BELTON,
RICHARD MOWBRAY,
JAMES TOURVILLE.

Just now are brought me both yours. I vary not my opinion, nor forbear my earnest prayers to you in her behalf, notwithstanding her dislike of me.

LETTER LXXIV.

Mr. Lovelace to John Belford, Esq.

Wednesday, May 3.

WHEN I have already taken pains to acquaint thee in full with regard to my views, designs, and resolutions with regard to this admirable woman, it is very extraordinary, that thou shouldest vapour as thou dost in her behalf, when I have made no trial, no attempt; and yet givest it as thy opinion in a former letter, that advantage *may be* taken of the situation she is in; and that she *may be* overcome.

Most of thy reflections, particularly that which respects the difference as to the joys to be given by the virtuous and the libertine of her sex, are fitter to come in as after reflections, than as *antecedencies.*

I own with thee, and with the poet, *that sweet are the joys that come with willingness* — but is it to be expected, that a *woman of education*, and a *lover of forms*, will yield before she is attacked? And have I so much as summoned this to surrender? I doubt not but I shall meet with difficulty. I must therefore make my first effort by surprise. There may possibly be some *cruelty* necessary: but there may be *consent in struggle:* there may be *yielding in resistance.* But the first conflict over, whether the following may not be weaker and weaker, till *willingness* ensue, is the point to be tried. I will illustrate what I have said by the simile of a bird new caught. We begin, when boys, with birds; and when grown up, go on to women; and both perhaps, in turn, experience our sportive cruelty.

Hast thou not observed the charming gradations by which the ensnared volatile has been brought to bear with its new condition? How, at first, refusing all sustenance, it beats and bruises itself against its wires, till it makes its gay plumage fly about, and overspread its well secured cage. Now it gets out its head; sticking only at its beautiful shoulders: then, with difficulty, drawing back its head, it gasps for breath, and erectly perched, with meditating eyes, first surveys, and then attempts, its wired canopy. As it gets breath, with renewed rage, it beats and bruises again its pretty head and sides, bites the wires, and pecks at the fingers of its delighted tamer. Till at last, finding its efforts ineffectual, quite tired and breathless, it lays itself down, and pants at the bottom of the cage, seeming to bemoan its cruel fate and forfeited liberty. And after a few days, its struggles to escape still diminishing as it finds it to no purpose to attempt it, its new habitation becomes familiar; and it hops about from perch to perch, resumes its wonted cheerfulness, and every day sings a song to amuse itself, and reward its keeper.

Now, let me tell thee, that I have known a bird actually starve itself, and die with grief, at its being caught and caged. But never did I meet with a woman, who was so silly. — Yet have I heard the dear souls most vehemently threaten their own lives on such an occasion. But it is saying nothing in a woman's favour, if we do not allow her to have *more sense than a bird.* And yet we must all own, that it is more difficult to catch a *bird* than a *lady.*

To pursue the comparison — if the disappointment of the captivated lady be very great, she will threaten, indeed, as I said: she will even refuse her sustenance for some time, especially if you intreat her much, and she thinks she gives you concern by her refusal. But then the stomach of the dear sullen one will soon return. 'Tis pretty to see how she comes to by degrees: pressed by appetite, she will first steal, perhaps, a weeping morsel by herself; then be brought to piddle and sigh, and sigh and piddle, before you: now and then, if her viands be unsavoury, swallowing with them a relishing tear or two: then she comes to eat and drink, to oblige you: then resolves to live for your sake: her exclamations will, in the next place, be turned into blandishments; her vehement upbraidings into gentle murmuring — How *dare* you, traitor! — into, How *could* you, dearest! She will draw you to her, instead of pushing you from her: no longer, with unsheathed claws, will she resist you; but, like a pretty, playful, wanton kitten, with gentle paws, and concealed talons, tap your cheek, and with intermingled smiles, and tears, and caresses, implore your consideration for her, and your *constancy:* all the favour she then has to ask of you! — And this is the time, were it given to man to confine himself to one object, to be happier every day than another.

Now, Belford, were I to go no further than I have gone with my beloved Miss Harlowe, how shall I know the difference between *her* and *another* bird? To let her fly now what a pretty jest would that be! — How do I know, except I try, whether she may not be brought to sing me a fine song, and to be as well contented as I have brought other birds to be, and very shy ones too?

But now let us reflect a little upon the confounded partiality of us human creatures. I can give two or three familiar, and if they were *not familiar,* they would be *shocking,* instances of the cruelty both of men and women, with respect to other creatures, perhaps as worthy as (at least more innocent than) themselves. By my soul, Jack, there is more of the savage in human nature than we are commonly aware of. Nor is it, after all, so much amiss, that we sometimes avenge the more innocent animals upon our own species.

To particulars:

How usual a thing is it for women as well as men without the least remorse, to ensnare, to cage, and torment, and even with burning knitting-needles to put out the eyes of the poor feathered songster [thou seest I have not yet done with birds]; which however, in proportion to its bulk, has more life than themselves (for a bird is all soul); and of consequence has as much feeling as the human creature! When, at the same time, if an honest fellow, by the gentlest persuasion, and the softest arts, has the good luck to prevail upon a mewed up lady, to countenance her own escape, and she consents to break cage, and be set a-flying into the all-cheering air of liberty, mercy on us! what an outcry is generally raised against him!

Just like what you and I once saw raised in a paltry village near Chelmsford, after a poor hungry fox, who watching his opportunity, had seized by the neck, and shouldered, a sleek-feathered goose: at what time we beheld the whole vicinage of boys and girls, old men, and old women, all the furrows and wrinkles of the latter filled up with malice for the time; the old men armed with prongs, pitchforks, clubs, and catsticks; the old women with mops, brooms, fire-shovels, tongs, and pokers; and the younger fry with dirt, stones, and brick-bats, gathering as they ran like a snowball, in pursuit of the wind-outstripping prowler; all the mongrel curs of the *circumjacencies*, yelp, yelp, yelp, at their heels, completing the horrid chorus.

Rememberest thou not this scene? Surely thou must. My imagination, inflamed by a tender sympathy for the danger of the adventurous marauder, represents it to my eye, as if it were but yesterday. And dost thou not recollect how generously glad we were, as if our own case, that honest Reynard, by the help of a lucky stile, over which both old and young tumbled upon one another, and a winding course, escaped their brutal fury, and flying catsticks; and how, in fancy, we followed him to his undiscovered retreat; and imagined we beheld the intrepid thief enjoying his dear-earned purchase with a delight proportioned to his past danger?

I once made a charming little savage severely repent the delight she took in seeing her tabby favourite make cruel sport with a pretty sleek bead-eyed mouse, before she devoured it. Egad, my love, said I to myself, as I sat meditating the scene, I am determined to lie in wait for a fit opportunity to try how *thou* wilt like to be tost over *my* head, and be caught again: how *thou* wilt like to be patted from me and pulled to me. Yet will I rather give life than take it away, as this barbarous quadruped has at last done by her prey. And after all was over between my girl and me,

I reminded her of the incident to which my resolution was owing.

Nor had I at another time any mercy upon the daughter of an old epicure, who had taught the girl, without the least remorse, to roast lobsters alive; to cause a poor pig to be whipt to death; to scrape carp the contrary way of the scales, making them leap in the stew-pan, and dressing them in their own blood for sauce. And this for luxury-sake, and to provoke an appetite; which I had without stimulation, in my way, and that I can tell thee a very ravenous one.

Many more instances of the like nature could I give, were I to leave nothing to thyself, to shew that the best take the same liberties, and perhaps worse, with some sort of creatures, that we take with others; all *creatures* still! and creatures too, as I have observed above, replete with strong life, and sensible feeling! If therefore people pretend to mercy, let mercy go through all their actions. I have read somewhere, *that a merciful man is merciful to his beast.*

So much at present for those parts of thy letter in which thou urgest to me motives of compassion for the lady.

But I guess at thy principal motive in this thy earnestness in behalf of this charming creature. I know that thou correspondest with Lord M. who is impatient, and has long been desirous, to see me shackled. And thou wantest to make a merit with the uncle, with a view to one of his nieces. But knowest thou not, that *my consent* will be wanting to complete thy wishes? — And what a commendation will it be of thee to such a girl as Charlotte, when I shall acquaint her with the affront thou puttest upon the whole sex, by asking, *Whether I think my reward, when I have subdued the most charming woman in the world, will be equal to my trouble?* — Which, thinkest thou, will a woman of spirit soonest forgive; the undervaluing varlet who *can put such a question;* or him, who *prefers the pursuit and conquest of a fine woman to all the joys of life?* Have I not known even *a virtuous woman,* as she would be thought, vow everlasting antipathy to a man who gave out, that she was *too old for him to attempt?* And did not Essex's personal reflection on Queen Elizabeth, that she was *old and crooked,* contribute more to his ruin than his treason?

But another word or two, as to thy objection relating to my trouble and reward.

Does not the keen foxhunter endanger his neck and his bones in pursuit of a vermin, which, when killed, is neither fit food for men nor dogs?

Do not the hunters of the nobler game value the venison less than the sport?

Why then should I be reflected upon, and the sex affronted, for my patience and perseverance in the most noble of all chases; and for not being a poacher in love, as thy question may be *made to imply?*

Learn of thy master, for the future, to treat more respectfully a sex that yields us our principal diversions and delights.

Proceed anon.

LETTER LXXV.
Mr. Lovelace in Continuation.

WELL sayest thou, that mine is the *most plotting heart in the world*. Thou dost me honour; and I thank thee heartily. Thou art no bad judge. How like Boileau's parson, I strut behind my double chin! Am I not obliged to deserve thy compliment? And wouldst thou have me repent of a murder before I have committed it?

"The Virtues and Graces are this lady's handmaids. She was certainly born to adorn the age she was given to." — Well said, Jack — "And would be an ornament to the first dignity." But what praise is that, unless the first dignity were adorned with the first merit? — Dignity! gewgaw! —*First dignity!* thou idiot! — Art thou, who knowest *me*, so taken with ermine and tinsel? — I, who have won the gold, am only fit to wear it. For the future therefore correct thy style, and proclaim her the ornament of the happiest man, and (respecting herself and sex) the greatest conqueror in the world.

Then, that she *loves me*, as thou imaginest, by no means appears clear to me. Her conditional offers to renounce me; the little confidence she places in me; entitle me to ask, What merit can she have with a man, who won her in spite of herself; and who fairly, in set and obstinate battle, took her prisoner?

As to what thou inferrest from her *eye* when with us, thou knowest nothing of her *heart* from that, if thou imaginest there was one glance of love shot from it. Well did I note her eye, and plainly did I see that it was all but just civil disgust to me and to the company I had brought her into. Her early retiring that night, against all entreaty, might have convinced thee, that there was very little of the gentle in her heart for me. And her eye never knew what it was to contradict her heart.

She is, thou sayest, *all mind*. So say I. But why shouldst thou imagine, that such a mind as hers, meeting with such a one as mine; and, to dwell upon the word, *meeting* with an inclination in hers; should not propagate minds like her own?

Were I to take thy stupid advice, and marry; what a figure should I make in rakish annals! The lady in my power; yet not having *intended* to put herself in my power; declaring against love, and a rebel to it: so much open-eyed caution: no confidence in my honour; her family expecting the worst *hath* passed; herself seeming to expect, that the worst will be attempted: [Priscilla Partington for that!] What! wouldst thou not have me act in character?

But why callest thou the lady

innocent? And why sayest thou *she loves me?*

By *innocent*, with regard to me, and not taken as a general character, I must insist upon it, she is *not* innocent. Can *she* be innocent, who, by wishing to shackle me in the prime and glory of my youth, with such a capacity as I have for noble mischief,* would make my perdition more certain, were I to break, as I doubt I should, the most solemn vow I could make? I say no man ought to take even a common oath, who thinks he cannot keep it. This is conscience! This is honour! — And when I think I can keep the marriage vow, then will it be time to marry.

No doubt of it, as thou sayest, the devils would rejoice in the fall of such a woman. But this is my confidence, that I shall have it in my power to marry when I will. And if I do her this *justice*, shall I not have a claim to her *gratitude?* And will she not think herself the obliged, rather than the obliger? Then let me tell thee, Belford, it is impossible so far to hurt the *morals of this lady*, as thou and thy brother varlets have hurt others of the sex, who are now casting about the town firebrands and double death. Take ye that thistle to mumble upon.

* * *

A SHORT interruption. I now resume.

That the morals of this lady cannot fail, is a consideration that will lessen the guilt on both sides. And if, when subdued, she knows but how to middle the matter between virtue and love, then will she be a wife for me: for already I am convinced, that there is not a woman in the world that is love-proof and plot-proof, if she be not the person.

And now imagine (the charmer overcome) thou seest me sitting supinely cross-kneed, reclining on my sofa, the god of love dancing in my eyes, and rejoicing in every mantling feature; the sweet rogue, late such a proud rogue, wholly in my power, moving up slowly to me, at my beck, with heaving sighs, half-pronounced upbraidings from murmuring lips, her finger in her eye, and quickening her pace at my *Come hither, dearest!*

One hand stuck in my side, the other extended to encourage her bashful approach — *Kiss me, love!* — *Sweet*, as Jack Belford says, *are the joys that come with willingness.*

She tenders her purple mouth [her coral lips will be purple then, Jack!] Sigh not so deeply, my beloved! — happier hours await thy humble love, than did thy proud resistance.

Once more bend to my ardent lips the swanny glossiness of a neck late so stately. —

There's my precious!

Again!

Obliging loveliness!

O my ever-blooming glory! I have tried thee enough. To-morrow's sun —

---

* See Letter xix. Paragr. 4.

Then I rise, and fold to my almost talking heart the throbbing-bosomed charmer.

And now shall thy humbled pride confess its obligation to me!

To-morrow's sun — and then I disengage myself from the bashful passive, and stalk about the room — To-morrow's sun shall gild the altar at which my vows shall be paid thee!

Then, Jack, the rapture! then the darted sunbeams from her gladdened eye, drinking up at one sip, the precious distillation from the pearl-dropt cheek! Then hands ardently folded, eyes seeming to pronounce, God bless my Lovelace! to supply the joy-locked tongue: her transports too strong, and expressions too weak, to give utterance to her grateful meanings! — All — all the studies — all the studies of her future life vowed and devoted (when she can speak) to acknowledge and return the perpetual obligation!

If I could bring my charmer to this, would it not be the eligible of eligibles? — Is it not worth trying for? — As I said, I can marry her when I will. She *can* be nobody's but mine, neither for shame, nor by choice, nor yet by address: for who, that knows my character, believes that the worst she dreads, is *now* to be dreaded?

I have the highest opinion that man can have (thou knowest I have) of the merit and perfections of this admirable woman; of her virtue and honour too, although thou, in a former, art of opinion, that she *may be overcome*.* Am I not therefore obliged to go further, in order to contradict thee, and, as I have often urged, to be *sure*, that she is what I really think her to be, and, if I am ever to marry her, hope to find her.

Then this lady is mistress of our passions: no one ever had to so much perfection the art of moving. This all her family know, and have equally feared and revered her for it. This I know too; and doubt not more and more to experience. How charmingly must this divine creature warble forth (if a proper occasion be given) her melodious elegiacs! — Infinite beauties are there in a weeping eye. I first taught the two nymphs below to distinguish the several airs of the *lamentable* in a new subject, and how admirably some, more than others, become their distresses.

But to return to thy objections — thou wilt perhaps tell me, in the names of thy brethren, as well as in thy own name, that among all the objects of your respective attempts, there was not one of the rank and merit of my charming Miss Harlowe.

But let me ask, has it not been a constant maxim with us, that the greater the *merit* on the woman's side, the nobler the victory on the man's? And as to *rank*, sense of honour, sense of shame, pride of family, may make rifled rank get up, and shake itself to rights: and if any thing come of it, such a one may suffer only in her pride, by

* See Letter xlvii. Paragr. 9.

16*

being obliged to take up with a second-rate match instead of a first; and, as it may fall out, be the *happier*, as well as the more *useful*, for the misadventure; since (taken off of her public gaddings, and *domesticated* by her disgrace) she will have reason to think herself obliged to the man who has saved her from *further reproach;* while *her* fortune and alliance will lay an obligation upon him; and her past fall, if she have prudence and consciousness, will be his present and future security.

But a *poor* girl [such a one as my *Rosebud* for instance] having no recalls from education; being driven out of every family that pretends to reputation; persecuted most perhaps by such as have only kept their secret better; and having no refuge to fly to — the common, the stews, the street, is the fate of such a poor wretch; penury, want, and disease, her sure attendants; and an untimely end perhaps closes the miserable scene.

And will you not now all join to say, that it is more manly to attack a lion than a sheep? — Thou knowest, that I always illustrated my eagleship by aiming at the noblest quarries: and by disdaining to make a stoop at wrens, phyl-tits,* and wagtails.

* *Phyl-tits*, q. d. *Phyllis-tits*, in opposition to *Tom-tits*. It needs not now be observed, that Mr. Lovelace, in the wanton gaiety of his heart, often takes liberties of coining words and phrases in his letters to this his familiar friend. See his ludicrous reason for it in Letter xxi. Parag. *antepenult.*

The worst respecting myself, in the case before me, is that my triumph, when completed, will be so glorious a one, that I shall never be able to keep up to it. All my future attempts must be poor to this. I shall be as unhappy, after a while, from my reflections upon this conquest, as Don John of Austria was, in his, on the renowned victory of Lepanto, when he found that none of his future achievements could keep pace with his early glory.

I am sensible that my pleas and my reasoning may be easily answered, and perhaps justly censured; but by whom censured? Not by any of the confraternity, whose constant course of life, even long before I became your general, to this hour, has justified what ye now in a fit of squeamishness, and through envy, condemn. Having, therefore, vindicated myself and my intentions to you, that is all I am at present concerned for.

Be convinced then, that *I* (according to *our* principles) am right, *thou* wrong; or, at least, be silent. But I *command thee to be convinced.* And in thy next be sure to tell me that thou art.

LETTER LXXVI.

Mr. Belford to Robert Lovelace, Esq.

Edgeware, Thursday, May 4.

I know that thou art so abandoned a man, that to give thee the best reasons in the world against what thou hast once resolved upon, will be but acting the madman whom once we saw trying to buffet down a hurricane with his hat. I hope, however, that the lady's merit will still avail her with thee. But, if thou persistest; if thou wilt avenge thyself on this sweet lamb, which thou hast singled out from a flock thou hatest, for the faults of the dogs who kept it: if thou art not to be moved by beauty, by learning, by prudence, by innocence, all shining out in one charming object; but she must fall, fall by the man whom she has chosen for her protector; I would not for a thousand worlds have thy crime to answer for.

Upon my faith, Lovelace, the subject sticks with me, notwithstanding I find I have not the honour of the lady's good opinion. And the more, when I reflect upon her father's brutal curse, and the villainous hard-heartedness of all her family. But, nevertheless, I should be desirous to know (*if thou wilt proceed*) by what gradations, arts, and contrivances thou effectest thy ingrateful purpose. And, O Lovelace, I conjure thee, if thou art a *man*, let not the specious devils thou hast brought her amongst be suffered to triumph over her; nor make her the victim of *unmanly artifices*. If she yield to *fair seduction*, if I may so express myself; if thou canst raise a weakness in her by love, or by arts not inhuman; I shall the less pity her; and shall then conclude, that there is not a woman in the world who can resist a bold and resolute lover.

A messenger is just now arrived from my uncle. The mortification, it seems, is got to his knee; and the surgeons declare that he cannot live many days. He therefore sends for me directly, with these shocking words, *That I will come and close his eyes.* My servant or his must of necessity be in town every day on his case, or on other affairs; and one of them shall regularly attend you for any letter or commands. It will be charity to write to me as often as you can. For although I am likely to be a considerable gainer by the poor man's death, yet I cannot say that I at all love these scenes of death and the doctor so near me. The *doctor* and *death* I should have said; for that is the natural order, and, generally speaking, the one is but the harbinger to the other.

If, therefore, you decline to oblige me, I shall think you are displeased with my freedom. But let me tell you, at the same time, that no man has a right to be displeased at freedoms taken with him for faults he is not ashamed to be guilty of.

J. BELFORD.

LETTER LXXVII.
Miss Clarissa Harlowe to Miss Howe.

I THANK you and Mr. Hickman for his letter, sent me with such kind expedition; and proceed to obey my dear menacing tyranness.

She then gives the particulars of what passed between herself and Mr. Lovelace on Tuesday morning, in relation to his four friends, and to Miss Partington, pretty much to the same effect as in Mr. Lovelace's letter, No. I. And then proceeds:

He is constantly accusing me of over-scrupulousness. He says, "I am always out of humour with him: that I could not have behaved more reservedly to Mr. Solmes: and that it is contrary to all his hopes and notions, that he should not, in so long a time, find himself able to inspire the person whom he hoped so soon to have the honour to call his, with the least distinguishing tenderness for him beforehand."

Silly and partial encroacher! not to know *to what to attribute the reserve I am forced to treat him with!* But his *pride* has eaten up his *prudence*. It is indeed a dirty low pride, that has swallowed up the *true* pride, which should have set him above the vanity that has overrun him.

Yet he pretends that he has no pride but in obliging me: and is always talking of his reverence and humility, and such sort of stuff: but of this I am sure, that he has, as I observed the first time I saw him*, too much regard to his own person, greatly to value that of his wife, marry whom he will; and I must be blind, if I did not see that he is exceedingly vain of his external advantages, and of that address, which, if it has *any* merit in it to an outward eye, is perhaps owing more to his confidence than to any thing else.

Have you not beheld the man, when I was your happy guest, as

* See Vol. I. p. 15.

he walked to his chariot, looking about him, as if to observe what eyes his specious person and air had attracted?

But indeed we have seen homely coxcombs as proud as if they had persons to be proud of; at the same time that it was apparent, that the pains they took about themselves but the more exposed their defects.

The man who is fond of being thought *more* or *better* than *he is*, as I have often observed, but provokes a scrutiny into his pretensions; and that generally produces contempt. For pride, as I believe I have heretofore said, is an infallible sign of weakness; of *something wrong in the head or heart, or in both*. He that exalts himself insults his neighbour; who is provoked to question in him even that merit, which, were he modest, would perhaps be allowed to be his due.

You will say that I am very grave: and so I am. Mr. Lovelace is extremely sunk in my opinion since Monday night: nor see I before me any thing that can afford me a pleasing hope. For what, with a mind *so unequal as his*, can be my *best* hope?

I think I mentioned to you in my former, that my clothes were brought me. You fluttered me so, that I am not sure I did. But I know I designed to mention that they were. They were brought me on Thursday; but neither my few guineas with them, nor any of my books, except a *Drexelius on Eternity*, the good old *Practice of*

Piety, and a *Francis Spira*. My brother's wit, I suppose. He thinks he does well to point out death and despair to me. I wish for the one, and every now-and-then am on the brink of the other.

You will the less wonder at my being so very solemn, when, added to the above, and to my uncertain situation, I tell you, that they have sent me with these books a letter from my cousin Morden. It has set my heart against Mr. Lovelace. Against myself too. I send it inclosed. If you please, my dear, you may read it here.

COL. MORDEN TO MISS CLARISSA HARLOWE.

Florence, April 13.

I AM extremely concerned to hear of a difference betwixt the rest of a family so near and dear to me, and *you*, still dearer to me than any of the rest.

My cousin James has acquainted me with the offers you have had, and with your refusals. I wonder not at either. Such charming promises at so early an age as when I left England; and those promises, as I have often heard, so greatly exceeded, as well in your person as mind; how much must you be admired! How few must there be worthy of you!

Your parents, the most indulgent in the world, to a child the most deserving, have given way it seems to your refusal of several gentlemen. They have contented themselves at last to name one with *earnestness* to you because of the address of another whom they cannot approve.

They had not reason, it seems, from your behaviour, to think you greatly averse: so they proceeded; perhaps too hastily for a delicacy like yours. But when all was fixed on their parts, and most extraordinary terms concluded in your favour; terms which abundantly shew the gentleman's just value for you; you flew off with a warmth and vehemence little suited to that sweetness which gave grace to all your actions.

I know very little of either of the gentlemen: but of Mr. Lovelace I know more than of Mr. Solmes. I wish I could say more to his advantage than I can. As to every qualification but *one*, your brother owns there is no comparison. But that *one* outweighs all the rest together. It cannot be thought that Miss Clarissa Harlowe will dispense with MORALS in a husband.

What, my dearest cousin, shall I plead first to you on this occasion? Your duty, your interest, your temporal, and your eternal welfare, do and may all depend upon this single point, *the morality of a husband*. A woman who has a wicked husband may find it difficult to *be* good, and out of her power to *do* good; and is therefore in a worse situation than the man can be in, who has a bad wife. You preserve all your religious regards, I understand. I wonder not that you do. I should have wondered had you not. But what can you promise yourself, as to perseverance in them, with an immoral husband?

If your parents and you differ in sentiment on this important occasion, let me ask you, my dear cousin, who ought to give way? I own to you, that I should have thought there could not any where have been a more suitable match for you than with Mr. Lovelace, had he been a moral man. I should have very little to say against a man, of whose actions I am not to set up myself as a judge, did he not address my cousin. But, on this occasion, let me tell you, my dear Clarissa, that Mr. Lovelace cannot possibly deserve you. He *may* reform, you'll say: but he may *not*. Habit is not soon or easily shaken off. Libertines, who are libertines in defiance of talents, of superior lights, of conviction, hardly ever reform but by miracle, or by incapacity. Well do I know my own sex. Well am I able to judge of the probability of the reformation of a licentious young man, who has not been fastened upon by sickness, by affliction, by calamity; who has a prosperous run of fortune before him: his spirits high: his will uncontrolable: the company he keeps, perhaps such as himself, confirming him in all courses, assisting him in all his enterprises.

As to the other gentleman, suppose, my dear cousin, you do not like him at *present*, it is far from being unlikely that you will *hereafter:* perhaps the more for not liking him *now*. He can hardly sink *lower* in your opinion: he may *rise*. Very seldom is it that *high* expectations are so much as *tolerably* answered. How indeed can they, when a fine and extensive imagination carries its expectation infinitely beyond reality, in the highest of our sublunary enjoyments? A woman adorned with such an imagination sees no defect in a favoured object (the less, if she be not conscious of any wilful fault in herself) till it is too late to rectify the mistakes occasioned by her generous credulity. But suppose a person of your talents were to marry a man of inferior talents; who, in this case, can be so happy in *herself* as Miss Clarissa Harlowe? What delight do you take in doing good! How happily do you devote the several portions of the day to your own improvement, and to the advantage of all that move within your sphere! — and *then*, such is your taste, such are your acquirements in the politer studies, and in the politer amusements; such your excellence in all the different parts of economy fit for a young lady's inspection and practice, that your friends would wish you to be taken off as little as possible by regards that may be called merely *personal.*

But as to what may be the consequence respecting yourself, respecting a young lady of your talents, from the preference you are suspected to give to a libertine, I would have you, my dear cousin, consider what that may be. A mind so pure, to mingle with a mind impure! And will not such a man as this engross all your solicitudes? Will he not perpetually fill you with anxieties for him and for yourself? — The divine and civil powers defied, and their sanctions broken through by him, on every not merely *accidental* but *meditated* occasion. To be agreeable to him, and to hope to preserve an interest in his affections, you must probably be obliged to abandon all your own laudable pursuits. You must enter into his pleasures and distastes. You must give up your own virtuous companions for his profligate ones — perhaps be forsaken by yours, because of the scandal he daily gives. Can you hope, cousin, with such a man as this to be *long* so good as you *now* are? If not, consider which of your present laudable delights you would choose to give up? Which of his culpable ones to follow him in? How could you brook to go backward, instead of forward, in those duties which you now so exemplarily perform? And how do you know, if you once give way, where you shall be suffered, where you shall be *able* to stop?

Your brother acknowledges that Mr. Solmes is not near so agreeable in person as Mr. Lovelace. But what is *person* with such a lady as I have the honour to be now writing to? He owns likewise that he has not the address of Mr. Lovelace: but what is a *mere* personal advantage is a plausible *address*, without *morals?* A woman had better take a husband whose manners she were to fashion, than to find them ready fashioned to her hand, at the price of his morality; a price that is often paid for travelling accomplishments. O, my dear cousin, were you but with us here at Florence, or at Rome, or at Paris (where also I resided for many months) to see the gentlemen whose supposed *rough* English manners at setting out are to be polished, and what their improvements are in their return through the same places, you would infinitely prefer the man in his *first* stage, to the same man in his *last*. You find the difference on their return — a fondness for foreign fashions, an attachment to foreign vices, a supercilious contempt of his own country and countrymen (himself more despicable than the *most* despicable of those he despises); these, with an unblushing effrontery, are too generally the attainments that concur to finish the travelled gentleman!

Mr. Lovelace, I know, deserves to have an exception made in his favour; for he is really a man of parts and learning; he was esteemed so both here and at Rome; and a fine person, and a generous turn of mind, gave him great advantages. But you need not be told, that a libertine man of sense does infinitely more mischief than a libertine of weak parts is able to do. And this I will tell you further, that it was Mr. Lovelace's own fault that he was not still more respected than he was among the *literati* here. There were, in short, some liberties in which he indulged himself, that endangered his person and his liberty; and made the best and most worthy of those who honoured him with their notice give him up; and his stay both at Florence and at Rome shorter than he designed.

This is all I choose to say of Mr. Lovelace. I had much rather have had reason to give him a quite contrary character. But as to rakes or libertines in general, I, who know them well, must be allowed, because of the mischiefs they have *always* in their *hearts*, and *too often* in their *power*, to do your sex, to add still a few more words upon this topic.

A libertine, my dear cousin, a *plotting*, an *intriguing* libertine, must be generally *remorseless — unjust* he must always be. The noble rule of doing to others what he would have done to himself is the first rule he breaks; and every day he breaks it; the oftener the greater his triumph. He has great contempt for your sex. He believes no woman chaste, because he is a profligate. Every woman who *favours him*, *confirms him* in his wicked incredulity. He is always plotting to extend the mischiefs he delights in. If a woman loves such a man, how can she bear the thought of dividing her interest in his affections with half the town, and that perhaps the dregs of it? Then so sensual! — How will a young lady of your delicacy bear with so sensual a man? A man who makes a jest of his vows; and who perhaps will break your spirit by the most unmanly insults. To be a libertine, at *setting out*, all compunction, all humanity, must be overcome. To *continue* to be a libertine, is to continue to be every thing vile and inhuman. Prayers, tears, and the most abject submission, are but fuel to his pride: wagering perhaps with lewd companions, and not, improbably, with lewder women, upon instances which he boasts of to them of your patient sufferings, and broken spirit, and bringing them home to witness to both.

I write what I know *has* been.

I mention not fortunes squandered, estates mortgaged or sold, and posterity robbed — nor yet a multitude of other evils, too shocking, to be mentioned to a person of your delicacy.

All these, my dear cousin, to be shunned, all the evils I have named to be avoided; the power of doing all the good you have been accustomed to do, preserved, nay, increased by the separate provision that will be made for you: your charming diversions and exemplary employments, all maintained; and every good habit perpetuated: and all by *one* sacrifice, the fading pleasure of the eye! Who would not, (since every thing is not to be met with in one man; who would not) to preserve so many essentials, give up so light, so unpermanent a pleasure?

Weigh all these things, which I might insist upon to more advantage, did I think it needful to one of your prudence — weigh them well, my beloved cousin;

and if it be not the will of your parents that you should continue single, resolve to oblige them; and let it not be said that the powers of fancy shall (as in many others of your sex) be too hard for your duty and your prudence. The less agreeable the man, the more obliging the compliance. Remember, that he is a sober man — a man who has a reputation to lose, and whose reputation, therefore, is a security for his good behaviour to you.

You have an opportunity offered you to give the highest instance that can be given of filial duty. Embrace it. It is worthy of you. It is expected *from* you; however, for your inclination-sake, we may be sorry that you are called upon to give it. Let it be said that you have been able to lay an obligation upon your parents (a proud word, my cousin!) which you could not do, were it not laid *against* your inclination! — Upon parents who have laid a thousand upon you: who are set upon this point: who will not give it up: who have given up many points to you, even of this very nature: and in their turn, for the sake of their own authority, as well as judgment, expect to be obliged.

I hope I shall soon, in person congratulate you upon this your meritorious compliance. To settle and give up my trusteeship is one of the principal motives of my leaving these parts. I shall be glad to settle it to every one's satisfaction; to yours particularly.

If on my arrival I find a happy union, as formerly, reign in a family so dear to me, it will be an unspeakable pleasure to me; and I shall perhaps so dispose my affairs, as to be near you for ever.

I have written a very long letter, and will add no more, than that I am, with the greatest respect, my dearest cousin,

Your most affectionate and faithful servant,
Wm. Morden.

I will suppose, my dear Miss Howe, that you have read my cousin's letter. It is now in vain to wish it had come sooner. But if it *had*, I might perhaps have been so rash as to give Mr. Lovelace the *fatal meeting*, as I little thought of going away with him.

But I should hardly have given him the *expectation* of so doing, *previous* to the meeting, which made him come prepared; and the revocation of which he so artfully made ineffectual.

Persecuted as I was, and little expecting so much condescension, as my aunt, to my great mortification, has told me, (and you confirm) I should have met with, it is, however, hard to say what I should or should not have done as to *meeting him*, had it come in time: but this effect I verily believe it would have had — to have made me insist with all my might on going over, out of all their ways, to the kind writer of the instructive letter, and on making a father (a protector, as well as a friend) of a kinsman, who is one of my trustees. This, circumstanced as I was, would have been a natural, at least an unexceptionable protection. — But I *was to be* unhappy! And how it cuts me to the heart, to think that I can already subscribe to my cousin's character of a libertine, so well drawn in the letter which I suppose you now to have read!

That a man of a character which ever was my abhorrence should fall to my lot! — But, depending on my own strength; having no reason to apprehend danger from headstrong and disgraceful impulses; I too little perhaps cast up my eyes to the supreme Director: in whom, mistrusting myself, I ought to have placed my whole confidence — and the more, when I saw myself so perseveringly addressed by a man of this character.

Inexperience and presumption, with the help of a brother and sister who have low ends to answer in my disgrace, have been my *ruin!* — A hard word, my dear! But I repeat it upon deliberation: since, let the best happen which *now* can happen, my reputation is destroyed; a rake is my portion; and what that portion is, my cousin Morden's letter has acquainted you.

Pray keep it by you till called for. I saw it not myself (having not the heart to inspect my trunks) till this morning. I would not for the world this man should see it; because it might occasion mischief between the most violent spirit, and the most settled brave one in the world, as my cousin's is said to be.

This letter was inclosed (opened) in a blank cover. Scorn and detest me as they will, I wonder that one line was not sent with it — were it but to have more particularly pointed the design of it, in the same generous spirit that sent me the Spira.

The sealing of the cover was with black wax. I hope there is no new occasion in the family to give reason for black wax. But if there were, it would to be sure have been mentioned, and laid at my door — perhaps too justly!

I had begun a letter to my cousin; but laid it by, because of the uncertainty of my situation, and expecting every day for several days past to be at a greater certainty. You bid me write to him some time ago, you know. Then it was I began it: for I have great pleasure in obeying you in all I may. So I ought to have; for you are the only friend left me. And, moreover, you generally honour me with your own observance of the advice I take the liberty to offer you: for I pretend to say, I give better advice than I have taken. And so I had need. For, I know not how it comes about, but I am, in my own opinion, a poor lost creature: and yet cannot charge myself with one criminal or faulty inclination. Do you know, my dear, how this can be?

Yet I can tell you *how*, I believe — one devious step at setting out! That must be it: — which, pursued, has led me so far out of my path, that I am in a wilderness of doubt and error: and never, never, shall find my way out of it: for, although but one pace away at first, it has led me hundreds and hundreds of miles out of my path: and the poor estray has not one kind friend, nor has met with one directing passenger, to help her to recover it.

But I, presumptuous creature must rely so much upon my own knowledge of the right path! — little apprehending that an *ignis fatuus* with its false fires (and yet I had heard enough of such) would arise to mislead me! and now, in the midst of fens and quagmires, it plays around me, and around me, throwing me back again, whenever I think myself in the right track. But there is one common point, in which all shall meet, err widely as they may. In that I shall be laid quietly down at last: and then will all my calamities be at an end.

But how I stray again; stray from my intention; I would only have said, that I had begun a letter to my cousin Morden some time ago: but that now I can never end it. You will believe I cannot: for how shall I tell him that all his compliments are misbestowed? That all his advice is thrown away? All his warnings vain? And that even my highest expectation is to be the wife of that free liver, whom he so pathetically warns me to shun?

Let me, however, have your prayers joined with my own (my fate depending, as it seems, upon the *lips of such a man*) "that, whatever shall be my destiny, that dreadful part of my father's malediction, that I may be punished by the man in whom he supposes I put my confidence, may not take place; that this, for *Mr. Lovelace's* own sake, and for the sake of *human nature*, may not be! Or, if it be necessary, in support of the parental authority, that I should be punished by *him*, that it may not be by his *premeditated* or *wilful* baseness; but that I may be able to acquit his *intention*, if not his *action!*" Otherwise, my fault will appear to be doubled in the eye of the event-judging world. And yet, methinks, I would be glad that the unkindness of my father and uncles, whose hearts have already been too much wounded by my error, may be justified in every article, excepting in this heavy curse: and that my father will be pleased to withdraw that before it be generally known: at least that most dreadful part of it which regards futurity!

I must lay down my pen. I must brood over these reflections. Once more, before I inclose my cousin's letter, I will peruse it. And then I shall have it by heart.

LETTER LXXVIII.

Miss Clarissa Harlowe to Miss Howe.

Sunday night, May 7.

When you reflect upon my unhappy situation, which is attended with so many indelicate and even shocking circumstances, some of which my pride will not let me think of with patience; all aggravated by the contents of my cousin's affecting letter; you will not wonder that the vapourishness which has laid hold of my heart should rise to my pen. And yet it would be more kind, more friendly in me, to conceal from *you*, who take such a generous interest in my concerns, that worst part of my griefs, which communication and complaint cannot relieve.

But to whom can I unbosom myself but to you? When the man who ought to be my protector, as he has brought upon me all my distresses, adds to my apprehensions; when I have not even a servant on whose fidelity I can rely, or to whom I can break my griefs as they arise; and when his bountiful temper and gay heart attach every one to him: and I am but a *cypher*, to give *him* significance, and *myself* pain?— These griefs, therefore, do what I can, will sometimes burst into tears; and these, mingling with my ink, will blot my paper. And I know you will not grudge me the temporary relief.

But I shall go on in the strain I left off with in my last, when I intended rather to apologise for my melancholy. But let what I have above written, once for all, be my apology. My misfortunes have given you a call to discharge the noblest offices of the friendship we have vowed to each other, in advice and consolation; and it would be an injury to it, and to you, to suppose it needed even that call.

She then tells Miss Howe, that now her clothes are come, Mr. Lovelace is continually teasing her to go abroad with him in a coach attended by whom she pleases of her own sex, either for the air, or to the public diversions.

She gives the particulars of a conversation that has passed between them on that subject, and his several proposals. But takes notice that he says not the least word of the solemnity which he so much pressed for before they came to town; and which, as she observes, was necessary to give propriety to his proposals.

Now, my dear, *says she*, I cannot bear the life I live. I would be glad at my heart to be out of his reach. If I were, he should soon *find the difference*. If I must be humbled, it had better be by those to whom I owe duty, than by him. My aunt writes in her letter*, that she dare not propose any thing in my favour. You tell me, that, upon enquiry you find** that, had I not been unhappily seduced away, a change of measures was actually resolved upon; and that my mother, particularly, was determined to exert herself for the restoration of the family peace; and, in order to succeed the better, had thoughts of trying to engage my uncle Harlowe in her party.

Let me build on these foundations. I can but try, my dear.

* See Letter xlviii.   ** Letter lv.

It is my duty to try all *probable* methods to restore the poor outcast to favour. And who knows but that once indulgent uncle, who has very great weight in the family, may be induced to interpose in my behalf? I will give up all right and title to my grandfather's devises and bequests, with all my heart and soul, to whom they please, in order to make my proposal palatable to my brother. And that my surrender may be effectual, I will engage never to marry.

What think you, my dear, of this expedient? Surely, they cannot resolve to renounce me for ever. If they look with impartial eyes upon what has happened, they will have something to blame *themselves* for, as well as *me*.

I presume, that you will be of opinion that this expedient is worth trying. But here is my difficulty: if I should write, my hard-hearted brother has so strongly confederated them all against me, that my letter would be handed about from one to another, till he had hardened every one to refuse my request; whereas, could my uncle be engaged to espouse my cause, as from *himself*, I should have some hope; as I presume to think he would soon have my mother and my aunt of his party.

What, therefore, I am thinking of, is this — "Suppose Mr. Hickman, whose good character has gained him every body's respect, should put himself in my uncle Harlowe's way? And (as if from your knowledge of the state of things between Mr. Lovelace and me) assure him not only of the above particular, but that I am under no obligations that shall hinder me from taking his directions?"

I submit the whole to your discretion, whether to pursue it at all, or in what manner. But if he *be* pursued, and if my uncle refuses to interest himself in my favour upon Mr. Hickman's application as from you (for so, for obvious reasons, it must be put) I can then have no hope; and my next step, in the mind I am in, shall be to throw myself into the protection of the ladies of his family.

It were an impiety to adopt the following lines, because it would be throwing upon the decrees of Providence a fault too much my own. But often do I revolve them, for the sake of the general similitude which they bear to my unhappy, yet undesigned error.

To you, great gods! I make my last
    appeal:
Or clear my virtues, or my crimes reveal.
If wand'ring in the maze of life I run,
And backward tread the steps I sought
    to shun,
Impute my error to your own decree:
My feet are guilty: but my heart is free.

The lady dates again on Monday, to let Miss Howe know, that Mr. Lovelace, on observing her uneasiness, had introduced to her Mr. Mennell, Mrs. Fretchville's kinsman who managed all her affairs. She calls him a young officer of sense and politeness, who gave her an account of the house and furniture, to the same *effect that Mr. Lovelace had done before;* as also of the melancholy way Mrs. Fretchville is in.*

She tells Miss Howe how extremely urgent Mr. Lovelace was with the gentleman, to get Mrs. Lovelace (as he now always calls her before company) a sight of the house: and that Mr. Mennell undertook that very afternoon to shew her all of it, except the apartment Mrs. Fretchville should be in when she went. But that she chose not to take another step till she knew how she approved of her scheme to have her uncle sounded, and with what success, if tried, it would be attended.

Mr. Lovelace, in his humourous way, gives his friend an account of the lady's peevishness and dejection, on receiving a letter with her clothes. He regrets that he has lost her confidence; which he attributes to his bringing her into the company of his four companions. Yet he thinks he must excuse them, and censure her for over-niceness; for that he never saw men behave better, at least not them.

Mentioning his introducing Mr. Mennell to her.

Now, Jack, says he, was it not very kind of Mr. Mennell [Captain Mennell I sometimes called him; for among the military men there is no such officer, thou knowest, as a *lieutenant* or an *ensign* — was it not very kind in him] to come along with me so readily as he did, to satisfy my beloved about the vapourish lady and the house?

But who is Capt. Mennell? methinks thou askest: I never heard of such a man as Captain Mennell.

Very likely. But knowest thou not young Newcomb, honest Doleman's nephew?

O-ho! It is he?

It is. And I have changed his name by virtue of my own single authority. Knowest thou not that I am a great name-father? Preferment I bestow, both military and civil. I give estates, and take them away at my pleasure. Quality too I create. And by a still more valuable prerogative, I *degrade*, by virtue of my own imperial will, without any other act of forfeiture than for my own convenience. What a poor thing is a monarch to me!

But Mennell, now he has seen this angel of a woman, has qualms! that's the devil! — I shall have enough to do to keep him right. But it is the less wonder that *he* should stagger, when a few hours conversation with the same lady could make four much more hardened varlets find *hearts* — only, that I am confident that I shall at last reward her virtue, if her virtue overcome me, or I should find it impossible to persevere — for at times I have confounded qualms myself. But say not a word of them to the confraternity: nor laugh at me for them thyself.

* See Letter xlii.

In another letter, dated Monday night, he writes as follows:

This perverse lady keeps me at such a distance, that I am sure something is going on between her and Miss Howe, notwithstanding the prohibition from Mrs. Howe, to both: and as I have thought it some degree of merit in myself to punish others for their transgressions, I am of opinion that both these girls are punishable for their breach of parental injunctions. And as to their letter-carrier, I have been inquiring into his way of living; and finding him to be a common poacher, a deer-stealer, and warren-robber, who, under pretence of higgling, deals with a set of customers who constantly take all he brings, whether fish, fowl, or venison, I hold myself justified (since Wilson's conveyance must at present be sacred) to have him stripped and robbed, and what money he has about him given to the poor; since, if I take not money as well as letters, I shall be suspected.

To serve one's self, and punish a villain at the same time, is serving public and private. The law was not made for such a man as me. And I *must* come at correspondencies so disobediently carried on.

But, on second thoughts, if I could find out that the dear creature carried any of her letters in her pockets, I can get her to a play or to a concert, and she may have the misfortune to lose her pockets.

But how shall I find this out; since her Dorcas knows no more of her dressing and undressing than her Lovelace? For she is dressed for the day before she appears even to her servant. Vilely suspicious! Upon my soul, Jack, a suspicious temper is a punishable temper. If a woman suspects a rogue in an honest man, is it not enough to make the honest man who knows it a rogue? But, as to her pockets, I think my mind hankers after them, as the less mischievous attempt. But they cannot hold all the letters that I should wish to see. And yet a woman's pockets are half as deep as she is high. Tied round the sweet *Levities*, I presume, as ballast-bags, lest the wind, as they move with full sail, from whale-ribbed canvas, should blow away the gipsies.

He then, in apprehension that something is meditating between the two ladies, or that something may be set on foot to get Miss Harlowe out of his hands, relates several of his contrivances, and boasts of his instructions given in writing to Dorcas, and to his servant Will Summers; and says, that he has provided against every possible accident, even to bring her back if she should escape, or in case she should go abroad, and then refuse to return; and hopes so to manage, as that, should he make an attempt, whether he succeeded in it or not, he may have a pretence to detain her.

He then proceeds as follows:

I have ordered Dorcas to cultivate by all means her lady's favour; to lament her incapacity as to writing and reading; to shew letters to her lady, as from pretended country relations; to beg her advice how to answer them, and to get them answered; and to be always aiming at scrawling with a pen, lest inky fingers should give suspicion. I have moreover given the wench an ivory-leaved pocket-book, with a silver pencil, that she may make memoranda on occasion.

And, let me tell thee, that the lady has already (at Mrs. Sinclair's motion) removed her clothes out of the trunks they came in, into an ample mahogany repository, where they will lie at full length; and which has drawers in it for linen. A repository that used to hold the richest suits which some of the nymphs put on, when they are to be dressed out to captivate or to ape quality. For many a countess, thou knowest, has our mother equipped; nay, two or three duchesses, who live upon *quality-terms* with their lords. But this to such as will come up to her price, and can make an appearance like quality themselves on the occasion: for the reputation of persons of birth must not lie at the mercy of every *under-degreed* sinner.

A master-key, which will open every lock in this chest, is put into Dorcas's hands; and she is to take care, when she searches for papers, before she removes any thing, to observe how it lies, that she may replace all to a hair. Sally and Polly can occasionally help to transcribe. Slow and sure with such an Argus-eyed charmer must be all my movements.

It is impossible that one so young and so inexperienced as she is, can have all the caution from herself; the behaviour of the women so unexceptionable; no revellings, no company ever admitted into this inner-house; all genteel, quiet, and easy in it; the nymphs well-bred and well-read; her first disgusts to the old one got over. — It must be Miss Howe, therefore, [who once was in danger of being taken in by one of our class, by honest Sir George Colmar, as thou hast heard] that makes my progress difficult.

Thou seest, Belford, by the above *precautionaries*, that I forget nothing. As the song says, it is not to be imagined

On what slight strings
Depend those things
On which men build their glory!

So far, so good. I shall never rest till I have discovered, in the first place, where the dear creature puts her letters; and in the next till I have got her to a play, to a concert, or to take an airing with me out of town for a day or two.

* * *

I gave thee just now some of *my* contrivances. Dorcas, who is ever attentive to all her lady's motions, has given me some instances of her *mistress's* precautions. She wafers her letters, it seems, in two places; pricks the wafers; and then seals upon them. No doubt but the same care is taken with regard to those brought to her, for she always examines the seals of the latter before she opens them.

I must, I must come at them. This difficulty augments my curiosity. Strange, so much as she writes, and at all hours, that not one sleepy or forgetful moment has offered in our favour!

A fair contention, thou seest; nor plead thou in her favour her *youth*, her *beauty*, her *family*, her *fortune*. CREDULITY, she has none; and with regard to her TENDER YEARS, am I not a *young fellow* myself? As to BEAUTY; pr'ythee, Jack, do thou, to spare my modesty, make a comparison between my Clarissa, for a *woman*, and thy Lovelace for a *man*. For her FAMILY, that was not known to its country a century ago: and I hate them all but her. Have I not cause? — For her FORTUNE; fortune, thou knowest, was ever a *stimulus* with me; and this for reasons not ignoble. Do not girls of fortune adorn themselves on purpose to engage our attention? Seek they not to draw us into their snares? Depend they not, generally, on their *fortunes*, in the views they have upon us, more than on their *merits?* Shall we deprive them of the benefit of their *principal* dependence? — Can I, in particular, marry *every girl*, who wishes to obtain my notice? If, therefore, in support of the libertine principles for which none of the sweet rogues hate us, a woman of fortune is brought to yield homage to her emperor, and any consequences attend the *subjugation*, is not such a one shielded by her fortune, as well from insult and contempt, as from indigence — all, then, that admits of debate between my beloved and me, is only this — which of the two has more *wit*, more *circumspection* — and that remains to be tried.

A sad life, however, this life of doubt and suspense, for the poor lady to live, as well as for me; that is to say, if she be not *naturally* jealous. — If she be, her uneasiness is constitutional, and she cannot help it; nor will it, in that case, hurt her. For a suspicious temper will *make* occasions for doubt, if none were to offer to its hand. My fair-one, therefore, if naturally suspicious, is obliged to me for saving her the trouble of *studying* for these occasions — but, after all, the plainest paths in our journeys through life are the safest and best, I believe, although it is not given me to choose them. I am not, however, singular in the pursuit of the more intricate paths; since there are thousands, and ten thousands, who had rather fish in troubled waters than in smooth.

LETTER LXXIX.
Mr. Lovelace to John Belford, Esq.

Tuesday, May 9.

I AM a very unhappy man. This lady is said to be one of the sweetest tempered creatures in the world: and so I thought her. But to *me* she is one of the most perverse. I never was supposed to be an ill-natured mortal neither. How can it be? I imagined for a long while that we were born to make each other happy: but quite the contrary; we really seem to be sent to plague each other.

I will write a comedy, I think: I have a title ready; and that's half the work. *The Quarrelsome Lovers.* 'Twill do. There's something new and striking in it. Yet, more or less, all lovers quarrel. Old Terence has taken notice of that; and observes upon it, that lovers *falling out* occasions lovers *falling in*; and a better understanding of course. 'Tis natural that it should be so. But with *us*, we fall out so often, without falling in once; and a second quarrel so generally happens before a first is made up; that it is hard to guess what event our loves will be attended with. But perseverance is my glory, and patience my handmaid, when I have in view an object worthy of my attempts. What is there in an easy conquest? Hudibras questions well,

What mad lover ever dy'd
To gain a soft and easy bride?
Or, for a lady tender-hearted,
In purling streams or hemp departed?

But I will lead to the occasion of this preamble.

I had been out. On my return, meeting Dorcas on the stairs — Your lady in her chamber, Dorcas? In the dining-room, sir: and if ever you hope for an opportunity to come at a letter, it must be now. For at her feet I saw one lie, which, as may be seen by its open folds, she has been reading, with a little parcel of others she is now busied with — all pulled out of her pocket, as I believe: so, sir, you'll know where to find them another time.

I was ready to leap for joy, and instantly resolved to bring forward an expedient which I had held in petto; and entering into the dining-room with an air of transport, I boldly clasped my arms about her, as she sat; she huddling up her papers in her handkerchief all the time; the dropped paper unseen. O my dearest life, a lucky expedient have Mr. Mennell and I hit upon just now. In order to hasten Mrs. Fretchville to quit the house, I have agreed, if you approve of it, to entertain her cook, her housemaid, and two men-servants, (about whom she was very solicitous) till you are provided to your mind. And that no accommodations may be wanted, I have consented to take the household linen at an appraisement.

I am to pay down five hundred pounds, and the remainder as soon as the bills can be looked up, and the amount of them adjusted. Thus will you have a charming house entirely ready to receive you. Some of the ladies of my family will soon be with you: they will not permit you long to suspend my happy day. And that nothing may be wanting to gratify your utmost punctilio, I will till then consent to stay here at Mrs. Sinclair's, while you reside at your new house; and leave the rest to your own generosity. O my beloved creature, will not this be agreeable to you? I am sure it will — it must — and clasping her closer to me, I gave her a more fervent kiss than ever I had dared to give her before. I permitted not my ardour to overcome my discretion however; for I took care to set my foot upon the letter, and scraped it further from her, as it were behind her chair.

She was in a passion at the liberty I took. Bowing low, I begged her pardon; and stooping still lower, in the same moment, took up the letter, and whipt it into my bosom.

Pox on me for a puppy, a fool, a blockhead, a clumsy varlet, a mere Jack Belford! — I thought myself a much cleverer fellow than I am! — Why could I not have been followed in by Dorcas; who might have taken it up while I addressed her lady?

For here, the letter being unfolded, I could not put it in my bosom, without alarming her ears, as my sudden motion did her eyes. — Up she flew in a moment: Traitor! Judas! her eyes flashing lightning, and a perturbation in her eager countenance so charming! — What have you taken up? — And then, what for both my ears I durst not have done to her, she made no scruple to seize the stolen letter, though in my bosom.

What was to be done on so palpable a detection? — I clasped her hand, which had hold of the ravished paper, between mine: O my beloved creature! said I, can you think I have not some curiosity? Is it possible you can be thus for ever employed; and I, loving narrative letter-writing above every other species of writing, and admiring your talent that way, should not (thus upon the dawn of my happiness, as I presume to hope) burn with a desire to be admitted into so sweet a correspondence?

Let go my hand! — stamping with her pretty foot: How dare you, sir! — At this rate, I see — too plainly I see — and more she could not say: but, gasping, was ready to faint with passion and affright; the devil a bit of her accustomed gentleness to be seen in her charming face, or to be heard in her musical voice.

Having gone thus far, loth, very loth was I to lose my prize — once more I got hold of the rumpled-up letter! — *Impudent man!* were her words: stamping again. *For God's sake*, then it was. I let go my prize, lest she should faint away; but had the pleasure first to find my hand within both hers, she trying to open my reluctant fingers. How near was my heart at that moment to my hand, throbbing to my fingers' ends, to be thus familiarly, although angrily, treated by the charmer of my soul!

When she had got it in her possession, she flew to the door. I threw myself in her way, shut it, and, in the humblest manner, besought her to forgive me. And yet do you think the Harlowe-hearted charmer (notwithstanding the agreeable annunciation I came in with) would forgive me? — No truly; but pushing me rudely from the door, as if I had been nothing, [yet do I love to try, so innocently to try, her strength too!] she gaining that force through passion which I had lost through fear, out she shot to her own apartment [thank my stars she could fly no further!]; and as soon as she entered it, in a passion still, she double-locked and double-bolted herself in. This my comfort, on reflection, that upon a greater offence it cannot be worse.

I retreated to my own apartment, with my heart full: and my man Will not being near me, gave myself a plaguy knock on the forehead with my double fist.

And now is my charmer shut up from me: refusing to see me; refusing her meals. She resolves *not to see me*, that's more: — Never again, if she can help it; and *in the mind she is in* — I hope she has said.

The dear creatures, whenever they quarrel with their humble servants, should always remember this saving clause, that they may not be forsworn.

But thinkest thou that I will not make it the subject of one of my first plots to inform myself of the reason why all this commotion was necessary on so slight an occasion as this would have been, were not the letters that pass between these ladies of a treasonable nature.

Wednesday Morning.

No admission to breakfast, any more than to supper. I wish this lady is not a simpleton, after all. I have sent up in Capt. Mennell's name.

A message from Capt. Mennell, madam.

It won't do. She is of baby age. She cannot be — a Solomon, I was going to say, in every thing. Solomon, Jack, was the wisest man. But didst ever hear who was the wisest woman? I want a comparison for this lady. Cunning women and witches we read of without number. But I fancy *wisdom* never entered into the character of a woman. It is not a requisite of the sex. Women, indeed, make better sovereigns than men: but why is that? — Because the women-sovereigns are governed by men, the men-sovereigns by women. — Charming, by my soul! For hence we guess at the rudder by which both are steered.

But to put wisdom out of the question, and to take *cunning* in; that is to say, to consider woman *as* a woman: what shall we do, if this lady has something extraordinary in her head? Repeated charges has she given to Wilson, by a particular messenger, to send any letter directed for her the moment it comes.

I must keep a good look-out. She is not now afraid of her brother's plot. I shan't be at all surprised, if Singleton calls upon Miss Howe as the only person who *knows*, or is *likely to know*, where Miss Harlowe is; pretending to have affairs of importance, and of particular service to her, if he can but be admitted to her speech — of compromise, who knows, from her brother?

Then will Miss Howe warn her to keep close. Then will my protection be again necessary. This will do, I believe. Any thing from Miss Howe must.

Joseph Leman is a vile fellow with her, and my implement. Joseph, *honest* Joseph, as I call him, may hang himself. I have played him off enough, and have very little further use for him. No need to wear one plot to the stumps, when I can find new ones every hour.

Nor blame me for the use I make of my talents. Who that has such will let 'em be idle?

Well then, I will find a Singleton; that's all I have to do.

Instantly find one! — Will!

Sir —

This moment call me hither thy cousin Paul Wheatley, just come from sea, whom thou wert recommending to my service, if I were to marry, and keep a pleasure-boat.

Presto — Will's gone — Paul will be here presently. Presently will he be gone to Mrs. Howe's. If Paul be Singleton's mate, coming from his captain, it will do as well as if it were Singleton himself.

Sally, a little devil, often reproaches me with the slowness of my proceedings. But in a play does not the principal entertainment lie in the *first four acts?* Is not all in a manner over when you come to the *fifth?* And what a vulture of a man must he be, who souses upon his prey, and in the same moment trusses and devours?

But to own the truth. I have overplotted myself. To make my work secure, as I thought, I have frighted the dear creature with the sight of my four Hottentots, and I shall be a longtime, I doubt, before I can recover my lost ground. And then this cursed family at Harlowe Place have made her out of humour with *me*, with *herself*, and with *all the world*, but Miss Howe, who, no doubt, is continually adding difficulties to my other difficulties.

I am very unwilling to have recourse to measures which these demons below are continually urging me to take; because I am sure that at last I shall be brought to make her legally mine.

One complete trial over, and I think I will do her noble justice!

* * *

Well, Paul's gone — gone already — has all his lessons. A notable fellow! — Lord W.'s necessary-man was Paul before he went to sea. A more sensible rogue Paul than Joseph! Not such a pretender to piety neither as the other. At what a price have I bought that Joseph! I believe I must punish the rascal at last: but must let him marry first: then (though that may be punishment enough) I shall punish two at once in the man and his wife. And how richly does Betty deserve punishment for her behaviour to my goddess?

But now I hear the rusty hinges of my beloved's door give me creaking invitation. My heart creaks and throbs with respondent trepidations: whimsical enough though! For what relation has a lover's heart to a rusty pair of hinges? But they are the hinges that open and shut the door of my beloved's bedchamber. Relation enough in that.

I hear not the door shut again. I shall receive her commands, I hope, anon. What signifies her keeping me thus at a distance? She must be mine, let me do or offer what I will. Courage whenever I assume, all is over: for, should she think of escaping from hence, whither can she fly to avoid me! Her parents will not receive her. Her uncles will not entertain her. Her beloved Norton is in their direction, and cannot. Miss Howe dare not. She has not one friend in town but me—is entirely a stranger to the town. And what then is the matter with me, that I should be thus unaccountably over-awed and tyrannized over by a dear creature who wants only to know how impossible it is that she should escape me, in order to be as humble to me as she is to her persecuting relations!

Should I even make the grand attempt, and fail, and should she hate me for it, her hatred can be but temporary. She has already incurred the censure of the world. She must therefore choose to be mine, for the sake of soldering up her reputation in the eye of that impudent world. For, who that knows me, and knows that she has been in my power, though but for twenty-four hours, will think her spotless as to fact, let her inclination be what it will? And then *human nature* is such a well-known rogue, that every man and woman judges by what each knows of him or herself, that *inclination* is no more to be trusted, where an opportunity is given, than *I* am; especially where a woman young and blooming loves a man well enough to go off with him; for such will be the world's construction in the present case.

She calls her maid Dorcas. No doubt, that I may hear her harmonious voice, and to give me an opportunity to pour out my soul at her feet; to renew all my vows; and to receive her pardon for the past offence: and then, with what pleasure shall I begin upon a new score, and afterwards wipe out that; and begin another, and another, till the *last* offence passes, and there can be *no other?* And once, after that, to be forgiven, will be to be forgiven for ever.

* * *

The door is again shut. Dorcas tells me, that her lady denies to admit me to dine with her; a favour I had ordered the wench to beseech her to grant me, the next time she saw her — not uncivilly, however, denies — coming to by degrees! Nothing but the last offence, the honest wench tells me, in the language of her principals below, will do with her. The last offence is meditating. Yet this vile recreant heart of mine plays me booty.

But here I conclude; though the tyranness leaves me nothing to do but to read, write, and fret.

Subscription is formal between us. Besides I am so totally hers, that I cannot say how much I am thine or any other person's.

LETTER LXXX.
Miss Clarissa Harlowe to Miss Howe.

Tuesday May 9.

IF, my dear, you approve of the application to my uncle Harlowe, I wish it may be made as soon as possible. We are quite out again. I have shut myself up from him. The offence indeed not *very* great — and yet it is too. He had like to have got a letter. One of yours. But never will I write again, or reperuse my papers, in an apartment where he thinks himself entitled to come. He did not read a line of it. Indeed he did not. So don't be uneasy. And depend upon future caution.

Thus it was. The sun being upon my closet, and Mr. Lovelace abroad —

She then gives Miss Howe an account of his coming by surprise upon her: of his fluttering speech: of his bold address: of her struggle with him for the letter, &c.

And now, my dear, *proceeds she,* I am more and more convinced, that I am too much in his power to make it prudent to stay with him. And if my friends *will* but give me hope, I will resolve to abandon him for ever.

O my dear! he is a fierce, a foolish, an insolent creature! — And in truth, I hardly expect that we *can* accommodate. How much unhappier am I already with him than my mother ever was with my father after marriage! Since (and that without any reason, any pretence in the world for it) he is for breaking my spirit *before* I am his, and while I am, or ought to be, [O my folly, that I am not!] in my own power.

Till I can know whether my friends will give me hope or not, I must do what I never studied to do before in my case; that is, try to keep this difference open: and yet it will make me look *little in my own eyes;* because I shall mean by it more than I can own. But this is one of the consequences of a step I shall ever deplore! The natural fruits of all engagements, where the minds are unpaired — *dis-paired*, in my case, may I say.

Let this evermore be my caution to individuals of my sex — guard your eye: — 'twill ever be in a combination against your judgment. If there are two parts to be taken, it will for ever, traitor as it is, take the wrong one.

If you ask me, my dear, how this caution befits me? let me tell you a secret, which I have but very lately found out upon self-examination, although you seem to have made the discovery long ago; that had not my foolish eye been too much attached, I had not taken the pains to attempt, so officiously as I did, the prevention of mischief between him and some of my family, which first induced the correspondence between us, and was the occasion of bringing the apprehended mischief with double weight upon myself. My vanity and conceit, as far as I know, might have part in the inconsiderate measure: for does it not look as if I thought myself more capable of obviating difficulties than any body else of my family?

But you must not, my dear, suppose my heart to be still a confederate with my eye. That deluded eye now clearly sees its fault, and the misled heart despises it for it. Hence the application I am making to my uncle: hence it is, that I can say, (I think truly) that I would atone for my fault at any rate, even by the sacrifice of a limb or two, if that would do.

Adieu, my dearest friend! — May your heart never know the hundredth part of the pain mine at present feels! prays
    Your
        Clarissa Harlowe.

LETTER LXXXI.
Miss Howe to Miss Clarissa Harlowe.
Wednesday, May 10.

I *will* write! No *man* shall write for me.* No *woman* shall hinder

* Clarissa proposes Mr. Hickman to write for Miss Howe. See Letter lxix. Parag. 5, et ult.

me from writing. Surely I am of age to distinguish between reason and caprice. I am not writing to a man, am I? — If I were carrying on a correspondence with a fellow of whom my mother disapproved, and whom it might be improper for me to encourage, my own honour and my duty would engage my obedience. But as the case is so widely different, not a word more on this subject, I beseech you!

I much approve of your resolution to leave this wretch, if you can make up with your uncle.

I hate the man — most heartily do I hate him, for his teasing ways. The very reading of your account of them teases me almost as much as they can you. May you have encouragement to fly the foolish wretch!

I have other reasons to wish you may: for I have just made an acquaintance with one who knows a vast deal of his private history. The man is really a villain, my dear! an execrable one! if all be true that I have heard! and yet I am promised other particulars. I do assure you, my dear friend, that, had he a dozen lives, he might have forfeited them all, and been dead *twenty crimes* ago.

If ever you condescend to talk familiarly with him again, ask him after Miss Betterton, and what became of her. And if he shuffle and prevaricate as to her, question him about Miss Lockyer. — O, my dear, the man's a villain! I will have your uncle sounded, as you desire, and that immediately. But yet I am afraid of the success, and this for several reasons. 'Tis hard to say what the sacrifice of your estate would do with some people: and yet I must not, when it comes to the test, permit you to make it.

As your Hannah continues ill, I would advise you to try to attach Dorcas to your interest. Have you not been impoliticly shy of her?

I wish you could come at some of his letters. Surely a man of his negligent character cannot be always guarded. If *he be*, and if you cannot engage *your* servant, I shall suspect them both. Let him be called upon at a short warning when he is writing, or when he has papers lying about, and so surprise him into negligence.

Such inquiries, I know, are of the same nature with those we make at an inn in travelling, when we look into every corner and closet for fear of a villain; yet should be frighted out of our wits were we to find one. But 'tis better to detect such a one when awake and up, than to be attacked by him when in bed and asleep.

I am glad you have your clothes. But no money! No books but a *Spira*, a *Drexelius*, and a *Practice of Piety!* Those who sent the latter ought to have kept it for themselves — but I must hurry myself from this subject.

You have exceedingly alarmed me by what you hint of his attempt to get one of my letters. I am assured by my new informant, that he is the head of a gang of wretches, (those he brought you among, no doubt, were some of them) who join together to betray innocent creatures, and to support one another afterwards by violence; and were he to come at the knowledge of the freedoms I take with him, I should be afraid to stir out without a guard.

I am sorry to tell you, that I have reason to think that your brother has not laid aside his foolish plot. A sun-burnt, sailor-looking fellow was with me just now, pretending great service to you from Captain Singleton, could he be admitted to your speech. I pleaded ignorance as to the place of your abode. The fellow was too well instructed for me to get any thing out of him.

I wept for two hours incessantly on reading yours, which inclosed that from your cousin Morden.* My dearest creature, do not desert yourself. Let your Anna Howe obey the call of that friendship which has united us as one soul, and endeavour to give you consolation.

I wonder not at the melancholy reflections you so often cast upon yourself in your letters, for the step you have been forced upon on one hand, and tricked into on the other. A strange fatality! *As if it were designed to shew the vanity of all human prudence.* I wish, my dear, as you hint, that both you and I have not *too much* prided ourselves in a perhaps too conscious superiority over others.

* See Letter lxxvii.

But I will stop — how apt are weak minds to look out for judgments in any extraordinary event! 'Tis so far right, that it is better, and safer, and juster, to arraign ourselves, or our dearest friends, than Providence; which must always have wise ends to answer in its dispensations.

But do not talk, as in one of your former, of being a warning only.*—You will be as excellent an example as ever you hoped to be, as well as a warning: and that will make your story, to all that shall come to know it, of double efficacy: for were it that such a merit as yours could not ensure to herself noble and generous usage from a libertine heart, who will expect any tolerable behaviour from men of his character?

If you think yourself inexcusable for taking a step that put you into the way of delusion, *without any intention to go off with him*, what must those giddy creatures think of themselves, who, without half your provocations and inducements, and without any regard to decorum, leap walls, drop from windows, and steal away from their parents' house, to the seducer's bed, in the same day?

Again, if you are so ready to accuse yourself for dispensing with the prohibitions of the most unreasonable parents, which yet were but half-prohibitions at first, what ought those to do who wilfully shut their ears to the advice of the most reasonable; and that

* See Letter xxiv.

perhaps, where apparent ruin, or *undoubted inconvenience*, is the consequence of the *predetermined* rashness?

And, lastly, to all who will know your story, you will be an excellent *example* of watchfulness, and of that caution and reserve by which a prudent person, who has been supposed to be a little misled, endeavours to mend her error; and, never once losing sight of her duty, does all in her power to recover the path she has been rather driven out of than chosen to swerve from.

Come, come, my dearest friend, consider but these things; and steadily, without desponding, pursue your earnest purposes to amend what you think has been amiss; and it may not be a misfortune in the end that you have erred; especially as so little of your will was in your error.

And indeed I must say that I use the words *misled*, and *error*, and such like, only in compliment to your own too ready self-accusations, and to the opinion of one to whom I owe duty: for I think in my conscience that every part of your conduct is defensible; and that those only are blameable who have no other way to clear themselves but by condemning you.

I expect, however, that such melancholy reflections as drop from your pen but too often, will mingle with all your future pleasures, were you to marry Lovelace, and were he to make the best of husbands.

You were immensely happy, above the happiness of a mortal creature, before you knew him: every body almost worshipped you: envy itself, which has of late reared up its venomous head against you, was awed, by your superior worthiness, into silence and admiration. You were the soul of every company where you visited. Your elders have I seen declining to offer their opinions upon a subject till you had delivered yours; often, to save themselves the mortification of retracting *theirs*, when they heard yours. Yet, in all this, your sweetness of manners, your humility and affability, caused the subscription every one made to your sentiments, and to your superiority, to be equally unfeigned and unhesitating; for they saw that their applause, and the preference they gave you to themselves, subjected not themselves to insults, nor exalted you into any visible triumph over them: for you had always something to say on every point you carried that raised the yielding heart, and left every one pleased and satisfied with themselves, though they carried not off the palm.

Your works were shewed or referred to wherever fine works were talked of. Nobody had any but an inferior and second-hand praise for diligence, for economy, for reading, for writing, for memory, for facility in learning every thing laudable, and even for the more envied graces of person and dress, and an all-surpassing elegance in both, where you were known, and those subjects talked of.

The poor blessed you every step you trod: the rich thought you their honour, and took a pride that they were not obliged to descend from their own class for an example that did credit to it.

Though all men wished for you, and sought you, young as you were; yet, had not those who were brought to address you been encouraged out of sordid and spiteful views, not one of them would have dared to lift up his eyes to you.

Thus happy in all about you, thus making happy all within your circle, could you think that nothing would happen to you, to convince you *that you were not to be exempted from the common lot?* — To convince you *that you were not absolutely perfect;* and that *you must not expect to pass through life without trial, temptation, and misfortune?*

Indeed, it must be owned that no trial, no temptation, worthy of your virtue, and of your prudence, could well have attacked you sooner, because of your tender years, nor more effectually, than those heavy ones under which you struggle, since it must be allowed, that your equanimity and foresight made you superior to common accidents; for are not most of the troubles that fall to the lot of common mortals brought upon themselves either by their *too large desires,* or *too little deserts?* — Cases both, from which you stood exempt. — It was therefore to be some *man*, or some *worse spirit in the shape of one*, that, formed on purpose, was to be sent to invade you; while as many other such spirits as there are persons in your family were permitted to take possession, severally, in one dark hour, of the heart of every one of it, there to sit perching, perhaps, and directing every motion to the motions of the seducer without, in order to irritate, to provoke, to push you forward *to meet him*.

Upon the whole, there seems, as I have often said, to have been a kind of fate in your error, if it *were* an error and this perhaps admitted *for the sake of a better example to be collected from your* SUFFERINGS! *than could have been given, had you never erred:* for, my dear, the time of ADVERSITY *is your* SHINING-TIME. I see it evidently, that adversity must call forth graces and beauties which could not have been brought to light in a run of that prosperous fortune which attended you from your cradle till now; admirably as you *became*, and, as we all thought, greatly as you *deserved* that prosperity.

All the matter is, the trial must be grievous to you. It is to *me:* it is to all who love you, and looked upon you as one set aloft to be admired and imitated, and not as a mark, as you have lately found, for envy to shoot its shafts at.

Let what I have written above have its due weight with you, my dear; and then, as warm imaginations are not without a mixture of enthusiasm, your Anna Howe, who, on re-perusal of it, imagines it to be in a style superior to her usual style, will be ready to flatter herself that she has been in a manner inspired with the hints that have comforted and raised the dejected heart of her suffering friend; who, from such hard trials, in a bloom so tender, may find at times her spirits sunk too low to enable her to pervade the surrounding darkness, which conceals from her the hopeful dawning of the better day which awaits her.

I will add no more at present, than that I am

Your ever faithful and affectionate

ANNA HOWE.

LETTER LXXXII.

Miss Clarissa Harlowe to Miss Howe.

Friday, May 12.

I MUST be silent, my exalted friend, under praises that oppress my heart with a consciousness of not deserving them; at the same time that the generous designs of those praises raises and comforts it: for it is a charming thing to stand high in the opinion of those we love; and to find that there are souls that can carry their friendships beyond accidents, beyond body, and ties of blood. Whatever, my dearest creature, is *my* shining-time, the time of a *friend's* adversity is *yours*. And it would be almost a fault in me to regret those afflictions, which give you an opportunity so gloriously to exert those qualities, which not only ennoble our sex, but dignify human nature.

But let me proceed to subjects less agreeable.

I am sorry you have reason to think Singleton's projects are not at an end. But who knows what the sailor had to propose? — yet, had any good been intended me, this method would hardly have been fallen upon.

Depend upon it, my dear, your letters shall be safe.

I have made a handle of Mr. Lovelace's bold attempt and freedom, as I told you I would, to keep him ever since at a distance, that I may have an opportunity to see the success of the application to my uncle, and to be at liberty to embrace any favourable overtures that may arise from it. Yet he has been very importunate, and twice brought Mr. Mennell from Mrs. Fretchville to talk about the house. — *If I should be obliged to make up with him again, I shall think I am always doing myself a spite.*

As to what you mention of his newly-detected crimes; and your advice to attach Dorcas to my interest; and to come at some of his letters; these things will require more or less of my attention, as I may hope favour or not from my uncle Harlowe.

I am sorry that my poor Hannah continues ill. Pray, my dear, inform yourself, and let me know, whether she wants any thing that befits her case.

I will not close this letter till to-morrow is over; for I am resolved to go to church; and this as well for the sake of my duty, as to see if I am at liberty to go out when I please without being attended or accompanied.

Sunday, May 14.

I have not been able to avoid a short debate with Mr. Lovelace. I had ordered a coach to the door. When I had notice that it was come, I went out of my chamber to go to it; but met him dressed on the stairs-head, with a book in his hand, but without his hat and sword. He asked with an air very solemn, yet respectful, if I were going abroad. I told him I was. He desired leave to attend me, if I were going to church. I refused him. And then he complained heavily of my treatment of him; and declared that he would not live such another week as the past, for the world.

I owned to him very frankly, that I had made an application to my friends: and that I was resolved to keep myself to myself till I knew the issue of it.

He coloured, and seemed surprised. But checking himself in something he was going to say, he pleaded my danger from Singleton, and again desired to attend me.

And then he told me, that Mrs. Fretchville had desired to continue a fortnight longer in the house. She found, said he, that I was unable to determine about entering upon it; and now who knows *when* such a vapourish creature will come to a resolution? This, madam, has been an unhappy week; for had I not stood upon such bad terms with you, *you might have been now mistress of that house;* and probably had my cousin Montague, if not Lady Betty, actually with you.

And so, sir, taking all you say for granted, your cousin Montague cannot come to Mrs. Sinclair's? What, pray, is her objection, to Mrs. Sinclair's? Is this house fit for me to live in a month or two, and not fit for any of your relations for a few days? — And Mrs. Fretchville has *taken more time too!* — Then pushing by him, I hurried down stairs.

He called to Dorcas to bring him his sword and hat; and following me down into the passage, placed himself between me and the door; and again desired leave to attend me.

Mrs. Sinclair came out at that instant, and asked me, if I did not choose a dish of chocolate?

I wish, Mrs. Sinclair, said I, you would take this man in with you to your chocolate. I don't know whether I am at liberty to stir out without his leave or not.

Then turning to him, I asked, if he kept me there his prisoner?

Dorcas just then bringing him his sword and hat, he opened the street door, and taking my reluctant hand, led me, in a very obsequious manner, to the coach. People passing by, stopped, stared, and whispered — but he is so graceful in his person and dress, that he generally takes every eye.

I was uneasy to be so gazed at; and he stepped in after me, and the coachman drove to St. Paul's.

He was very full of assiduities all the way; while I was as reserved as possible: and when I returned, dined, as I had done the greatest part of the week, by myself.

He told me, upon my resolving to do so, that although he would continue his passive observance till I knew the issue of my application; yet I must expect that *then* I should not rest one moment till I had fixed his happy day: for that his very soul was fretted with my slights, resentments, and delays.

A wretch! when I can say, to my infinite regret, on a *double* account, that all he complains of is owing to himself!

O that I may have good tidings from my uncle!

Adieu! my dearest friend — this shall lie ready for an exchange (as I hope for one to-morrow from you) that will decide, as I may say, the destiny of
Your
Cl. Harlowe.

LETTER LXXXIII.

Miss Howe to Mrs. Judith Norton.

Thursday, May 11.

GOOD MRS. NORTON,

Cannot you, without naming me as an adviser, who am hated

by the family, contrive a way to let Mrs. Harlowe know, that in an accidental conversation with me, you had been assured that my beloved friend pines after a reconciliation with her relations? That she has hitherto, in hopes of it, refused to enter into any obligation that shall be in the least an hinderance to it: that she would fain avoid giving Mr. Lovelace a right to make her family uneasy in relation to her grandfather's estate: that all she wishes for still is to be indulged in her choice of a single life, and, on that condition, would make her father's pleasure her's with regard to that estate: that Mr. Lovelace is continually pressing her to marry him; and all his friends likewise: but that I am sure she has so little liking to the man, because of his faulty morals, and of the antipathy of her relations to him, that if she had any hope given her of a reconciliation, she would forego all thoughts of him, and put herself into her father's protection. But that their resolution must be speedy; for otherwise she would find herself obliged to give way to his pressing entreaties: and it might then be out of her power to prevent disagreeable litigations.

I do assure you, Mrs. Norton, upon my honour, that our dearest friend knows nothing of this procedure of mine: and therefore it is proper to acquaint you, in confidence, with my grounds for it. — These are they:

She had desired me to let Mr. Hickman drop hints to the above effect to her uncle Harlowe: but indirectly, as from *himself*, lest, if the application should not be attended with success, and Mr. Lovelace (who already takes it ill that he has so little of her favour) come to know it, she may be deprived of *every* protection, and be perhaps subjected to great inconveniences from so haughty a spirit.

Having this authority from her, and being very solicitous about the success of the application, I thought that if the weight of so good a wife, mother, and sister, as Mrs. Harlowe is known to be, were thrown into the same scale with that of Mr. John Harlowe (supposing he *could* be engaged) it could hardly fail of making a due impression.

Mr. Hickman will see Mr. John Harlowe to-morrow: by that time you may see Mrs. Harlowe. If Mr. Hickman finds the old gentleman favourable, he will tell him, that you will have seen Mrs. Harlowe upon the same account; and will advise him to join in consultation with her how best to proceed to melt the most obdurate hearts in the world.

This is the fair state of the matter, and my true motive for writing to you. I leave all, therefore, to your discretion; and most heartily wish success to it; being of opinion that Mr. Lovelace cannot possibly deserve our admirable friend: nor indeed know I the man who does.

Pray acquaint me by a line of the result of your interposition. If it prove not such as may be reasonably hoped for, our dear friend shall know nothing of this step from me; and pray let her not from you. For in that case, it would only give deeper grief to a heart already too much afflicted. I am, dear and worthy Mrs. Norton,

Your true friend,
ANNA HOWE.

LETTER LXXXIV.
Mrs. Norton to Miss Howe.

DEAR MADAM, Saturday, May 13.

My heart is almost broken, to be obliged to let you know, that such is the situation of things in the family of my ever-dear Miss Harlowe, that there can be at present no success expected from any application in her favour. Her poor mother is to be pitied. I have a most affecting letter from her; but must not communicate it to you; and she forbids me to let it be known that she writes upon the subject; although she is compelled, as it were, to do it, for the ease of her own heart. I mention it therefore in confidence.

I hope in God that my beloved young lady has preserved her honour inviolate. I hope there is not a man breathing who could attempt a sacrilege so detestable. I have no apprehension of a failure in a virtue so established. God for ever keep so pure a heart out of the reach of surprises and violence! Ease, dear madam, I beseech you, my over-anxious heart, by one line, by the bearer, although but by *one* line, to acquaint me (as surely you can) that her honour is unsullied. — If it be not, adieu to all the comforts this life can give: since none will it be able to afford

To the poor
JUDITH NORTON.

LETTER LXXXV.
Miss Howe to Mrs. Judith Norton.

Saturday evening, May 13.

DEAR GOOD WOMAN,

YOUR beloved's honour is inviolate! — *must* be inviolate! and *will* be so, in spite of men and devils. Could I have had hope of a reconciliation, all my view was, that she should not have had this man. — All that can be said now, is, she must run the risk of a bad husband: she, of whom no man living is worthy!

You pity her mother — so do not *I!* I pity no mother that puts it out of her power to shew maternal love, and humanity, in order to patch up for herself a precarious and sorry quiet, which every blast of wind shall disturb.

I hate tyrants in every form and shape: but paternal and maternal tyrants are the worst of all: for they can have no bowels.

I repeat, that I pity *none* of them. Our beloved friend *only* deserves pity. She had never been in the hands of this man, but for them. She is quite blameless. You don't know all her story. Were I to tell you that she had no intention to go off with this man, it would avail her nothing. It would only serve to condemn, with those

who drove her to extremities, *him* who now must be her refuge. I am
Your sincere friend and servant,
ANNA HOWE.

LETTER LXXXVI.
Mrs. Harlowe to Mrs. Norton.

[*Not communicated till the Letters came to be collected.*]

Saturday, May 13.

I RETURN an answer in writing, as I promised, to your communication. But take no notice either to my Bella's Betty (who I understand sometimes visits you) or to the poor wretch herself, nor to any body, that I do write. I charge you don't. My heart is full: writing may give some vent to my griefs, and perhaps I may write what lies most upon my heart, without confining myself strictly to the present subject.

You know how dear this ingrateful creature ever was to us all. You know how sincerely we joined with every one of those who ever had seen her, or conversed with her; to praise and admire her; and exceeded in our praise even the bounds of that modesty, which, because she was our own, should have restrained us; being of opinion, that to have been silent in the praise of so apparent a merit must rather have argued blindness or affection in us, than that we should incur the censure of vain partiality to our own.

When therefore any body congratulated us on such a daughter, we received their congratulations without any diminution. If it was said, You are happy in this child! we owned, that no parents ever were happier in a child. If more particularly, they praised her dutiful behaviour to us, we said, She knew not how to offend. If it was said, Miss Clarissa Harlowe has a wit and penetration beyond her years; we, instead of disallowing it, would add — And a judgment no less extraordinary than her wit. If her prudence was praised, and a *forethought*, which every one saw supplied what only *years* and *experience* gave to others; Nobody need to scruple taking lessons from Clarissa Harlowe, was our proud answer.

Forgive me, O forgive me, my dear Norton — but I know you will; for yours when good, was this child, and your glory as well as mine.

But have you not heard strangers, as she passed to and from church, stop to praise the angel of a creature, as they called her; when it was enough for those who knew who she was, to cry, *Why, it is Miss Clarissa Harlowe!* — as if every body were obliged to know, or to have heard of Clarissa Harlowe, and of her excellencies. While, *accustomed to praise*, it was too *familiar to her*, to cause her to alter either her look or her pace.

For my own part, I could not stifle a pleasure that had perhaps a faulty vanity for its foundation, whenever I was spoken of, or addressed to, as the mother of so sweet a child: Mr. Harlowe and I,

18*

all the time, loving each other the better for the share each had in such a daughter.

Still, still indulge the fond, the overflowing heart of a mother! I could dwell for ever upon the remembrance of what she *was*, would but that remembrance banish from my mind what she *is!*

In *her* bosom, young as she was, could I repose all my griefs — sure of receiving from *her* prudent advice as well as comfort; and both insinuated in so humble, in so dutiful a manner, that it was impossible to take those exceptions which the distance of years and character between a mother and a daughter would have made one apprehensive of from any other daughter. She was our glory when abroad, our delight when at home. Every body was even covetous of her company; and we grudged her to our brothers Harlowe and to our sister and brother Hervey. No other contention among us, than, but who should be next favoured by her. No chiding ever knew she from us, but the chiding of lovers, when she was for shutting herself up too long together from us, in pursuit of those charming amusements and useful employments, for which, however, the whole family was the better.

Our other children had reason (good children as they always were) to think themselves neglected. But they likewise were so sensible of their sister's superiority, and of the honour she reflected upon the whole family, that they confessed themselves eclipsed, without envying the eclipser. Indeed, there was not any body so equal with her, in their own opinions, as to envy what all aspired but to emulate. The dear creature, you know, my Norton, gave an eminence to us all!

Then her acquirements. Her skill in music, her fine needle-works, her elegance in dress; for which she was so much admired, that the neighbouring ladies used to say, that they need not fetch fashions from London; since whatever Miss Clarissa Harlowe wore was the best fashion, because her choice of *natural* beauties set those of *art* far behind them. Her genteel ease, and fine turn of person; her deep reading, and these, joined to her open manners, and her cheerful modesty — O my good Norton, what a sweet child was *once* my Clary Harlowe!

This, and more, *you* knew her to be; for many of her excellencies, were owing to yourself; and with the milk you gave her, you gave her what no other nurse in the world could give her.

And do you think, my worthy woman, do you think, that the wilful lapse of such a child is to be forgiven? Can she herself think that she deserves not the severest punishment for the abuse of such talents as were entrusted to her?

Her fault was a fault of premeditation, of cunning, of contrivance. She has deceived every body's expectations. Her whole sex, as well as the family she sprung from disgraced by it.

Would any body ever have believed that such a young creature as this, who had by her advice saved even her over-lively friend from marrying a fop, and a libertine, would herself have gone off with one of the vilest and most notorious of libertines? A man whose character she knew; and knew it to be worse than the character of him from whom she saved her friend; a man against whom she was warned: one who had her brother's life in his hands; and who constantly set our whole family at defiance.

Think for me, my good Norton; think what my unhappiness must be both as a wife and a mother. What restless days, what sleepless nights; yet my own rankling anguish endeavoured to be smoothed over, to soften the anguish of fiercer spirits, and to keep them from blazing out to further mischief! O this naughty, naughty girl, who *knew* so well what she did; and who could look so far into consequences, that we thought she would have died, rather than have done as she has done!

Her known character for prudence leaves her absolutely without excuse. How then can I offer to plead for her, if, through motherly indulgence, I would forgive her myself? — And have we not, moreover, suffered all the disgrace that *can* befal us? Has not she?

If *now* she has so little liking to his morals, had she not reason before to have *as* little? Or has she suffered by them in her own person? — O my good woman, I doubt — I doubt — will not the character of this man make one doubt an angel, if once in his power? The world will think the worst. I am told it does. So likewise her father fears; her brother hears; and what can *I* do?

Our *antipathy* to him she knew before, as well as his character. These therefore cannot be *new* *motives* without a *new reason.* — O my dear Mrs. Norton, how shall *I*, how can *you*, support ourselves under the apprehensions to which these thoughts lead?

He continually pressing her, you say, *to marry him: his friends likewise.* She has reason, no doubt she has reason, for this application to us; and her crime is glossed over, to bring her to us with new disgrace: whither, whither, does one guilty step lead the misguided heart! — and now, truly, to save a stubborn spirit, we are only to be *sounded*, that the application may be occasionally retracted or denied!

Upon the whole: were I inclined to plead for her, it is *now* the most improper of all times. *Now* that my brother Harlowe has discouraged (as he last night came hither on purpose to tell us) Mr. Hickman's insinuated application; and been applauded for it. *Now*, that my brother Antony is intending to carry his great fortune, through her fault, into another family: she expecting, no doubt, herself to be put into possession of her grandfather's estate, in consequence of a reconciliation, and as a reward for her fault: and insisting still upon the same terms which she offered before, and which were rejected—not through my fault, I am sure, rejected!

From all these things you will return such an answer as the case requires. It might cost me the peace of my whole life, at this time, to move for her. God forgive her! if I do, nobody else will. And let it, for your own sake, as well as mine, be a secret that you and I have entered upon this subject. And I desire you not to touch upon it again but by particular permission: for, O my dear good woman, it sets my heart a bleeding in as many streams as there are veins in it!

Yet think me not impenetrable by a proper contrition and remorse — but what a torment is it to have a will without a power!

Adieu! adieu! God give us both comfort; and to the *once* dear — the *ever*-dear creature, (for can a mother forget her child?) repentance, deep repentance, and as little suffering as may befit his blessed will, and her grievous fault, prays

Your real friend
CHARLOTTE HARLOWE.

LETTER LXXXVII.
Miss Howe to Miss Clarissa Harlowe.
Sunday, May 14.

How it is now, my dear, between you and Mr. Lovelace, I cannot tell. But wicked as the man is, I am afraid he must be your lord and master.

I called him by several very hard names in my last. I had but just heard of some of his vileness, when I sat down to write; so my indignation was raised. But on inquiry, and recollection, I find that the facts laid to his charge were all of them committed some time ago — not since he has had *strong* hopes of your favour. This is saying something for him. His generous behaviour to the innkeeper's daughter is a more recent instance to his credit; to say nothing of the universal good character he has as a kind landlord. And then I approve much of the motion he made to put you in possession of Mrs. Fretchville's house, while he continues at the other widow's till you agree that one house should hold you. I wish this were done. Be sure you embrace this offer, (if you do not soon meet at the altar) and get one of his cousins with you.

Were you once married, I should think you cannot be very unhappy, though you may not be so happy with him as you deserve to be. The stake he has in his country, and his reversions; the care he takes of his affairs; his freedom from obligation; nay, his pride with your merit, must be a tolerable security for you, I should think. Though particulars of his wickedness, as they come to my knowledge, hurt and incense me; yet, after all, when I give myself time to reflect, all that I have heard of him to his disadvantage was comprehended in the general character given of him long ago, by Lord M.'s and his own dismissed bailiff*, and which was confirmed to me by Mrs. Fortescue, as I heretofore told you**, and to you by Mrs. Greme***.

You can have nothing, therefore, I think, to be deeply concerned about, but his future good, and the bad example he may hereafter set to his own family. These indeed are very just concerns: but were you to *leave* him now, either *with* or *without* his consent, his fortune and alliances so considerable, his person and address so engaging, (every one excusing you now on those accounts, and because of your relations' follies) it would have a very ill appearance for your reputation. I cannot therefore, on the most deliberate consideration, advise you to think of that, while you have no reason to doubt his honour. May eternal vengeance pursue the villain, if he give room for an apprehension of this nature!

Yet his teasing ways are intolerable; his acquiescence with your slight delays, and his resignedness to the distance you now keep him at, (for a fault so much slighter, as he must think, than the punishment) are unaccountable: he doubts your love of *him*, that is very probable; but you have reason to be surprised at *his* want of ardour; a blessing so great within his *reach*, as I may say.

By the time you have read to this place, you will have no doubt of what has been the issue of the conference between the *two gentlemen.* I am equally shocked, and enraged against them all. Against them *all*, I say; for I have tried your good Norton's weight with your mother (though at first I did not intend to tell you so) to the same purpose as the gentleman sounded your uncle. Never were there such determined brutes in the world! Why should I mince the matter? Yet would I fain methinks make an exception for your mother.

Your uncle will have it that you are ruined. "He can believe every thing bad of a creature, he says, who could run away with a man; with such a one especially as Lovelace. They *expected* applications from you, when some heavy distress had fallen upon you. But they are all resolved not to stir an inch in your favour; no, not to save your life!"

My dearest soul, resolve to assert your right. Claim your own, and go and live upon it, as you ought. Then, if you marry not, how will the wretches creep to you for your reversionary dispositions!

You were accused (as in your aunt's letter) "of premeditation and contrivance in your escape." Instead of pitying *you*, the mediating person was called upon "to pity *them;* who once, your uncle said, doated upon you; who took no joy but in your presence; who devoured your words as you spoke them; who trod over again your footsteps, as you walked before them." — And I know not what of this sort.

* Vol. I. p. 21.   ** Ibid. p. 49-53.
*** See Vol. II. p. 13. 14.

Upon the whole, it is now evident to me, and so it must be to you, when you read this letter, that you must be his. And the sooner you are so, the better. Shall we suppose that marriage is not in your power? — I cannot have patience to suppose that.

I am concerned, methinks, to know how you will do to condescend (now you see you must be his) after you have kept him at such a distance; and for the revenge his pride may put him upon taking for it. But let me tell you, that if my going up, and sharing fortunes with you, will prevent such a noble creature from stooping too low; much more, were it likely to prevent your ruin; I would not hesitate a moment about it. What is the whole world to me, weighed against such a friend as you are? Think you, that any of the enjoyments of this life could be enjoyments to me, were you involved in calamities, from which I could either alleviate or relieve you, by giving up those enjoyments? And what in saying this, and acting up to it, do I offer you, but the fruits of a friendship your worth has created?

Excuse my warmth of *expression*. The warmth of my *heart* wants none. I am enraged at your relations; for, bad as what I have mentioned is, I have not told you all; nor now, perhaps, ever will. I am angry at my own mother's narrowness of mind, and at her indiscriminate adherence to old notions. And I am exasperated against your foolish, your low *vanity'd* Lovelace. But let us stoop to take the wretch as he is, and make the best of him, since you are destined to stoop, to keep grovelers and worldlings in countenance. He has not been guilty of direct indecency to you. Nor *dare* he — not so much of a devil as that comes to neither. Had he such villainous intentions, so much in his power as you are, they would have shewn themselves before now to such a penetrating and vigilant eye, and to such a pure heart as yours. Let us save the wretch then, if we can, though we soil our fingers in lifting him up out of his dirt.

There is yet, to a person of your fortune and independence, a good deal to do, if you enter upon those terms which ought to be entered upon. I don't find that he has once talked of settlements; nor yet of the licence. A foolish wretch! — But as your evil destiny has thrown you out of all other protection and mediation, you must be father, mother, uncle to yourself; and enter upon the requisite points for yourself. It is hard upon you; but indeed you must. Your situation requires it. *What room for delicacy now?* — or would you have *me* write to him? Yet that would be the same thing as if you were to write yourself. Yet write you should, I think, if you cannot speak. But speaking is certainly best: for words leave no traces; they pass as breath; and mingle with latitude. But the pen is a witness on record.

I know the gentleness of your

spirit; I know the laudable pride of your heart; and the just notion you have of the dignity of our sex, in these delicate points. But once more, all this is nothing now: your honour is concerned that the dignity I speak of should not be stood upon.

"Mr. Lovelace," would I say; yet hate the foolish fellow for his low, his stupid pride, in wishing to triumph over the dignity of his own wife; — "I am by your means deprived of every friend I have in the world. In what light am I to look upon *you?* I have well considered every thing. You have made some people, much against my liking, think me a *wife:* others know I am *not* married; nor do I desire any body should believe I am: do you think your being here in the same house with me can be to my reputation? you talk to me of Mrs. Fretchville's house." This will bring him to renew his last discourse on that subject, if he does not revive it of himself. "If Mrs. Fretchville knows not her own mind, what is her house to me? You talked of bringing up your cousin Montague to bear me company: if my brother's schemes be your pretence for not going yourself to *fetch her,* you can *write* to her. I insist upon bringing these two points to an issue: off or on ought to be indifferent to *me,* if so to *them.*"

Such a declaration must bring all forward. There are twenty ways, my dear, that you would find out for another in your circumstances. He will disdain, from his native insolence, to have it thought he has *any body* to consult. Well then, will he not be obliged to declare himself; and if he *does,* no delays on your side, I beseech you. Give him the day. Let it be a short one. It would be derogating from your own merit, and *honour* too, let me tell you, even although he should not be so explicit as he ought to be, to seem but to doubt his meaning; and to wait for that explanation for which I should for ever despise him, if he makes it necessary. Twice already have you, my dear, if not oftener, *modesty'd away* such opportunities as you ought not to have slipped. As to settlements, if they come not in naturally, e'en leave them to his own justice, and to the justice of his family. And there's an end of the matter.

This is *my* advice: mend it as circumstances offer, and follow *your own.* But indeed, my dear, this, or something like it, would I do. And let him tell me afterwards, if he dared or would, that he humbled down to his shoe-buckles the person it would have been his glory to exalt.

Support yourself meantime with reflections worthy of yourself. Though tricked into this man's power, you are not meanly subjugated to it. All his reverence you command, or rather, as I may say, inspire; since it was never known that he had any reverence for aught that was good, till you was with him: and he professes now-and-then to be so awed and charmed by your example, as that the force of it shall reclaim him.

I believe you will have a difficult task to keep him to it; but the more will be your honour, if you effect his reformation: and it is my belief, that if you *can* reclaim this great, this specious deceiver, who has, morally speaking, such a number of years before him, you will save from ruin a multitude of innocents; for those seem to me to have been the prey for which he has spread his wicked snares. And who knows but, for this very purpose, principally, a person may have been permitted to swerve, whose heart or will never was in her error, and who has so much remorse upon her for having, as she thinks, erred at all? Adieu, my dearest friend.

ANNA HOWE.

Inclosed in the above.

I must trouble you with my concerns, though your own are so heavy upon you. A piece of news I have to tell you. Your uncle Antony is disposed to marry. With *whom*, think you? With my mother. True indeed. Your family know it. All is laid with redoubled malice at your door. And there the *old soul* himself lays it.

Take no notice of this intelligence, not so much as in your letters to me, for fear of accidents.

I think it can't do. But were I to provoke my mother, that might afford a pretence. Else, I should have been with you before now, I fancy.

The first likelihood that appears to me of encouragement, I dismiss Hickman, that's certain. If my mother disoblige *me* in so important an article, I shan't think of obliging *her* in such another. It is impossible, surely, that the desire of *popping me off* to that honest man can be with such a view.

I repeat that it cannot come to any thing. But these *widows* — then such a love in us all, both old and young, of being courted and admired! — And so irresistible to their *elderships* to be flattered, that all power is not over with them; but that they may still class and prank it with their daughters. — It vexed me heartily, to have her tell me of this proposal with self-complaisant simperings; and yet she affected to speak of it, as if she had no intention to encourage it.

These antiquated bachelors (old before they believe *themselves* to be so) imagine that when they have once persuaded themselves to think of the state, they have nothing more to do than to make their minds known to the woman.

Your uncle's overgrown fortune is indeed a bait; a tempting one. A saucy daughter to be got rid of! The memory of the father of that daughter not precious enough to weigh much! — But let him advance if he dare — let her encourage — but I hope she won't.

Excuse me, my dear. I am nettled. They have *fearfully rumpled my gorget.* You'll think me faulty. So I won't put my name to this separate paper. Other hands may resemble mine. You did not see me write it.

LETTER LXXXVIII.

Miss Clarissa Harlowe to Miss Howe.

Monday afternoon, May 15.

Now indeed it is evident, my best, my only friend, that I have but one choice to make. And now do I find that I have carried my resentment against this man too far; since now I am to appear as if under an obligation to his patience with me for a conduct, which perhaps he will think (if not humoursome and childish) plainly demonstrative of my little esteem of him; of but a *secondary* esteem at least, where before, his pride rather than his merit, had made him expect a *first*. O my dear! to be cast upon a man that is not a *generous* man; that is indeed a *cruel* man! A man that is capable of creating a distress to a young creature, who by her evil destiny is thrown into his power; and then of *enjoying* it as I may say! [I verily think I may say so, of this savage!] — What a fate is mine!

You give me, my dear, good advice, as to the peremptory manner in which I ought to treat him; but do you consider to *whom* it is that you give it? — And then should I take it, and should he be capable of delay, I unprotected, desolate, nobody to fly to, in what a wretched light must I stand in his eyes; and, what is still worse, in my own! O my dear, see you not, *as I do*, that the *occasion* for this my indelicate, my shocking situation should never have been given by *me*, of all creatures; since I am unequal, utterly unequal, to the circumstances to which my inconsideration has reduced me! — What, *I* to challenge a man for a husband! — *I* to exert myself to quicken the delayer in his resolutions? And having, as you think, lost an opportunity, to begin to try to recal it, as *from myself*, and *for myself*! To *threaten* him, as I may say, into the marriage state! — O my dear! if this be right to be done, how difficult is it, where modesty and self (or where pride if you please) is concerned, to do that right? Or, to express myself in your words, to be father, mother, uncle, to myself! — Especially where one thinks a triumph over one is intended.

You say, you have tried Mrs. Norton's weight with my mother — bad as the returns are which my application by Mr. Hickman has met with, you tell me, "That you have not acquainted me with all the bad, nor, now perhaps, ever will." But why so, my dear? What *is* the bad, what *can* be the bad, which now you will never tell me of? — What worse than renounce me! and for ever! "My uncle, you say, believes me ruined: he declares that he can believe every thing bad of a creature who could run away with a man: and they have all made a resolution, not to stir an inch in my favour; no, not to save my life." — Have you worse than this, my dear, behind? — Surely, my father has not renewed his dreadful malediction! — Surely, if so, my mother has not joined in it! Have my uncles given it their sanction, and made it a family act? And themselves thereby more really faulty, than even THEY suppose me to be, though I the cause of that greater fault in them? — What, my dear, is the worst, that you will leave for ever unrevealed?

O Lovelace! why comest thou not just now, while these black prospects are before me? For, now, couldst thou look into my heart, wouldst thou see a distress worthy of thy barbarous triumph!

* * *

I was forced to quit my pen. And you say you have tried Mrs. Norton's weight with my mother?

What *is* done cannot be remedied: but I wish you had not taken a step of this importance to me without first consulting me. Forgive me, my dear, but I must tell you that that high-souled and noble friendship which you have ever avowed with so obliging and so uncommon a warmth, although it has been always the subject of my grateful admiration, has been often the ground of my apprehension, because of its unbridled fervour.

Well, but now to look forward, you are of opinion that I must be his: and that I cannot leave him with reputation to myself, whether with or without his consent. I must, if so, make the best of the bad matter.

He went out in the morning, intending not to return to dinner, unless (as he sent me word) I would admit him to dine with me.

I excused myself. The man, whose anger is now to be of such high importance to me, was, it seems, displeased.

As he (as well as I) expected that I should receive a letter from you this day by Collins, I suppose he will not be long before he returns; and then, possibly, he is to be mighty stately, mighty *mannish*, mighty *coy*, if you please! And then must I be very humble, very submissive, and try to insinuate myself into his good graces: with downcast eye, if not by speech, beg his forgiveness for the distance I have so perversely kept him at? — Yes, I warrant: — But I shall see how this behaviour will sit upon me! — You have always rallied me upon my meekness, I think: well then, I will try if I can be still meeker, shall I! — O my dear! —

But let me sit with my hands before me, all patience, all resignation; for I think I hear him coming up. Or shall I roundly accost him, in the words, in the form, which you, my dear, have prescribed?

He is come in. He has sent to me, all impatience, as Dorcas says, by his aspect. — But I cannot, cannot see him!

Monday night.

THE contents of your letter, and my own heavy reflections, rendered me incapable of seeing this expecting man. The first word he asked Dorcas, was, if I had received a letter since he had been out? She told me this; and her answer, that I had; and was fasting, and had been in tears ever since.

He sent to desire an interview with me.

I answered by her, that I was not very well. In the morning if better, I would see him as soon as he pleased.

Very humble! was it not, my dear? Yet he was *too royal* to take it for humility; for Dorcas told me, he rubbed one side of his face impatiently; and said a rash word, and was out of humour; stalking about the room.

Half an hour after, he sent again; desiring very earnestly, that I would admit him to supper with me. He would enter upon no subjects of conversation but what I should lead to.

So I should have been at *liberty*, you see, to *court him!*

I again desired to be excused.

Indeed, my dear, my eyes were swelled: I was very low-spirited; and could not think of entering all at once, after the distance I had kept him at for several days, into the freedom of conversation which the utter rejection I have met with from my relations, as well as your advice, has made necessary.

He sent up to tell me, that as he heard I was fasting, if I would promise to eat some chicken which Mrs. Sinclair had ordered for supper, he would acquiesce — *very kind in his anger! Is he not?*

I promised that I would. Can I be more *preparatively* condescending — how happy, I'll warrant, if I may meet him in a *kind* and *forgiving* humour!

I hate myself! But I won't be insulted. Indeed I won't for all this.

LETTER LXXXIX.
Miss Clarissa Harlowe to Miss Howe.
Tuesday, May 16.

I THINK, once more, we seem to be in a kind of train but through a storm. I will give you the particulars.

I heard him in the dining-room at five in the morning. I had rested very ill, and was up too. But opened not my door till six: when Dorcas brought me his request for my company.

He approached me, and taking my hand, as I entered the dining-room, I went not to bed, madam, till two, said he: yet slept not a wink. For God's sake, torment me not, as you have done for a week past.

He paused. I was silent.

At first, proceeded he, I thought your resentment of a curiosity, in which I had been disappointed, could not be deep; and that it would go off of itself: but when I found it was to be kept up till you knew the success of some new overtures which you had made, and which, complied with, might have deprived me of you for ever; how, madam, could I support myself under the thoughts of having, with such an union of interests, made so little impression upon your mind in my favour?

He paused again. I was silent. He went on.

I acknowledge that I have a *proud heart*, madam. I cannot but hope for some instances of previous and preferable favour, from the lady I am ambitious to call mine; and that her choice of me should not appear, not *flagrantly* appear, directed by the perverseness of her selfish persecutors, who are my irreconcileable enemies.

More to the same purpose, he said. You know, my dear, the room he had given me to recriminate upon him in twenty instances. I did not spare him.

Every one of these instances, said I, (after I had enumerated them) convinces me of your *pride* indeed, sir, but not of your *merit*. I confess, that I have as much *pride* as you can have, although I hope it is of another kind than that you so *readily avow*. But if, sir, you have the least mixture in yours of that pride which may be expected, and thought laudable in a man of your birth, alliances, and fortune, you should rather wish, I will presume to say, to promote what you call my pride, than either to suppress it, or to regret that I have it. It is *this* my acknowledged pride, proceeded I, that induces me to tell you, sir, that I think it beneath me to disown what have been my motives for declining, for some days past, any conversation with you, or visit from Mr. Mennell, that might lead to points out of my power to determine upon, until I heard from my uncle Harlowe; whom, I confess, I have caused to be sounded, whether I might be favoured with his interest to obtain for me a reconciliation with my friends, upon terms which I had caused to be proposed.

I know not, said he, and suppose must not presume to ask, what those terms were. But I can but too well guess at them; and that I was to have been the preliminary sacrifice. But you must allow me, madam, to say, that as much as I admire the nobleness of your sentiments in general, and in particular that *laudable* pride which you have spoken of, I wish that I could compliment you with such an *uniformity* in it, as had set you as much above all submission to minds implacable and unreasonable (I hope I may, without offence, say, that your brother's and sister's are such) as it has above all favour and condescension to me.

Duty and *nature*, sir, call upon me to make the submissions you speak of: there is a father, there is a mother, there are uncles in the one case, to justify and demand those submissions. What, pray, sir, can be pleaded for the *condescension*, as you call it? Will you say, your merits, either with regard to *them*, or to *myself*, may?

This, madam, to be said, after the persecutions of those relations! After what you have suffered! After what you have made me hope! Let me, my dearest creature, ask you (we have been talking of *pride*) what sort of pride must *his* be, which can dispense with inclination and preference in the lady whom he adores? — What must be that love —

Love, sir! who talks of *love?* — Was not *merit* the thing we were talking of? — Have *I* ever professed, have *I* ever required of *you* professions of a passion of that nature! — But there is no end of these debatings; each *so* faultless, each *so* full of self —

I do not think myself *faultless*, madam: — but —

But what, sir! — Would you evermore argue with me, as if you were a child? — Seeking palliations, and making promises? — Promises of what, sir? Of being in future the man it is a shame a gentleman is not? — Of being the man —

Good God! interrupted he, with eyes lifted up, if *thou* wert to be thus severe —

Well, well, sir, [impatiently] I need only to observe, that all this vast difference in sentiment shews how unpaired our minds are — so let us —

Let us *what*, madam! — My soul is rising into tumults! And he looked so wildly, that I was a good deal terrified — Let us *what*, madam! —

I was, however, resolved not to desert myself — Why, sir, let us resolve to quit every regard for each other. — Nay, flame not out — I am a poor weak-minded creature in some things: but where what I *should be*, or not deserve to live, if I *am not*, is in the question, I have a great and invincible spirit, or my own conceit betrays me — let us resolve to quit every regard for each other that is more than civil. *This* you may depend upon; I will never marry any other man. I have seen enough of your sex; at least of *you*. — A single life shall ever be *my* choice: while I will leave you at liberty to pursue *your own*.

Indifference, *worse* than indifference! said he, in a passion —

Interrupting him — Indifference let it be — you have not (in my opinion at least) deserved that it should be other: if you have in *your own*, you have cause (at least your *pride* has) to hate me for misjudging you.

Dearest, dearest creature! snatching my hand with fierceness, let me beseech you to be *uniformly* noble! *Civil regards*, madam! — *Civil regards!* — Can you so expect to narrow and confine such a passion as mine!

Such a passion as yours, Mr. Lovelace, *deserves* to be narrowed and confined. It is either the passion *you* do not think it, or *I* do not. I question whether your mind is capable of being *so* narrowed and *so* widened, as is necessary to make it be what I wish it to be. Lift up your hands and your eyes, sir, in silent wonder, if you please; but what does that wonder express, what does it convince me of, but that we are not born for one another?

By my soul, said he, and grasped my hand with an eagerness that hurt it, we *were* born for one another: you *must* be mine — you *shall* be mine [and put his other arm round me] although my damnation were to be the purchase! I was still more terrified — Let me leave you, Mr. Lovelace, said I; or do you be gone from me. Is the passion you boast of to be thus shockingly demonstrated?

You must not go, madam! — You must not leave me in anger — I will return — I will return — when you can be less violent — less shocking.

And he let me go.

The man quite frighted me; insomuch, that when I got into my chamber, I found a sudden flow of tears a great relief to me.

In half an hour, he sent a little billet, expressing his concern for the vehemence of his behaviour, and entreating to see me.

I went. Because I could not help myself, I went.

He was full of his excuses — O my dear, what would you, even *you*, do with such a man as this; and in my situation?

It was very possible for him now, he said, to account for the workings of a beginning phrensy. For his part, he was near distraction. All last week to suffer as he had suffered; and now to talk of *civil regards* only, when he had hoped, from the nobleness of my mind —

Hope what you will, interrupted I, I must insist upon it, that our minds are by no means suited to each other. You have brought me into difficulties. I am deserted by every friend but Miss Howe. My true sentiments I will not conceal — it is against my will that I must submit to owe protection from a brother's projects, which Miss Howe thinks are not given over, to you, who have brought me into these straits: *not* with my own concurrence brought me into them; remember that —

I do remember that, madam! — So often reminded, how can I forget it?

Yet I *will* owe to you this protection, if it be necesary, in the earnest hope that you will *shun*, rather than *seek* mischief, if any further inquiry after me be made. But what hinders you from leaving me? — Cannot I send to you? The widow Fretchville, it is plain, knows not her own mind: the people here indeed are more civil to me every day than other: but I had rather have lodgings more agreeable to my circumstances. I best know what will suit them; and am resolved not to be obliged to any body. If you leave me, I will privately retire to some one of the neighbouring villages, and there wait my cousin Morden's arrival with patience.

I presume, madam, replied he, from what you have said, that your application to Harlowe Place has proved unsuccessful: I therefore hope that you will now give me leave to mention the terms in the nature of settlements, which I have long intended to propose to you; and which having till now delayed to do, through accidents not proceeding from myself, I had thoughts of urging to you *the moment you entered upon your new house;* and upon your finding yourself as independent in appearance as you are in *fact*. Permit me, madam, to propose these matters to you — not with an expectation of your *immediate answer;* but for your *consideration.*

Were not hesitation, a self-felt glow, a downcast eye, encouragement more than enough? And yet you will observe (as I now do on recollection) that he was in no great hurry to solicit for a *day;* since he had no thoughts of proposing settlements till I had got into my new house; and now, in his great complaisance to me, he desired leave to propose his terms, not with an expectation of my *immediate answer;* but for my *consideration* only — yet, my dear, your advice was too much in my head at this time. I hesitated.

He urged on upon my silence: he would call God to witness to the justice, nay to the *generosity* of his intentions to me, if I would be so good as to hear what he had to propose to me, as to settlements.

Could not the man have fallen into the subject without this *parade?* Many a point, you know, *is* refused, and *ought to be* refused, if leave be asked to introduce it; and when *once* refused, the refusal must in honour be adhered to — whereas, had it been *slid* in upon one, as I may say, it might have merited further consideration. If such a man as Mr. Lovelace knows not this, who should?

But he seemed to think it enough that he had asked my leave to propose his settlements. He took no advantage of my silence, as I presume men *as modest* as Mr. Lovelace would have done, in a like case: yet, gazing in my face very confidently, and seeming to expect my answer, I thought myself obliged to give the subject a more diffuse turn, in order to save myself the mortification of appearing too ready in my compliance, after such a distance as had been between us; and yet (in pursuance of your advice) I was willing to avoid the necessity of giving him such a repulse as might again throw us out of the course — a cruel alternative to be reduced to!

You talk of *generosity*, Mr. Lovelace, said I; and you talk of *justice;* perhaps, without having considered the force of the words, in the sense you use them on this occasion. — Let me tell you what *generosity* is, in my sense of the word — TRUE GENEROSITY is not confined to pecuniary instances: it is *more* than politeness: it is *more* than good faith: it is *more* than honour: it is *more* than *justice:* since all these are but duties, and what a worthy mind cannot dispense with. But TRUE GENEROSITY is greatness of soul. It incites us to do more by a fellow-creature than can be strictly required of us. It obliges us to hasten to the relief of an object that wants relief; anticipating even such a one's hope or expectation. Generosity, sir, will not surely permit a worthy mind to doubt of its honourable and beneficent intentions: much less will it allow itself to shock, to offend any one; and, least of all, a person thrown by adversity, mishap, or accident, into its protection.

What an opportunity had he to clear his intentions, had he been so disposed, from the *latter part* of this home observation! — But he ran away with the *first*, and kept to that.

Admirably defined! — he said — but who at this rate, madam, can be said to be *generous* to *you?* — Your *generosity* I implore; while *justice*, as it must be my sole merit, shall be my aim. Never was there a woman of such nice and delicate sentiments!

It is a reflection upon yourself, sir, and upon the company you have kept, if you think these notions either nice or delicate. Thousands of my sex are more nice than I; for they would have avoided the devious path I have been surprised into: the consequences of which surprise have laid me under the sad necessity of telling a man *who has not delicacy enough to enter into those parts of the female character which are its glory and distinction*, what true generosity is.

His divine monitress, he called me. He would endeavour to form his manners (as he had often promised) by my example. But he hoped I would now permit him to mention briefly the *justice* he proposed to do me, in the terms of the settlements; a subject so proper, *before now*, to have been entered upon; and which would have been entered upon long ago, had not my *frequent displeasure* [*I am ever in fault, my dear!*] taken from him the *opportunity* he had often wished for: but now, having ventured to lay hold of *this*, nothing should divert him from improving it.

I have no spirits, just now, sir, to attend to such weighty points. What you have a mind to propose, write to me: and I shall know what answer to return. Only one thing let me remind you of, that if you touch upon any subject, in which my father has a concern, I shall judge by your treatment of the father what value you have for the daughter.

He *looked* as if he would choose rather to speak than write: but had he *said* so, I had a severe return to have made upon him; as possibly he might see by *my* looks.

* * *

In this way are we now: a sort of calm, as I said, succeeding a storm. What may happen next, whether a storm or a calm, with such a spirit as I have to deal with, who can tell?

But, be that as it will, I think, my dear, I am not *meanly* off: and that is a great point with me; and which I know you will be glad to hear: if it were only, that I can see this man without losing any of that dignity [what other word can I use, speaking of *myself*, that betokens *decency*, and not *arrogance?*] which is so necessary to enable me to look *up*, or rather with the *mind's* eye, I may say, to look *down* upon a man of this man's cast

Although circumstances have so offered, that I could not take your advice as to the *manner* of dealing with him; yet you gave me so much courage by it, as has enabled me to conduct things to this issue; as well as determined me against leaving him: which *before*, I was thinking to do, at all adventures. Whether, when it came to the point, I *should* have done so, or not, I cannot say, because it would have depended upon his behaviour at the time.

But let his behaviour be what it will, I am afraid, (with you) that should any thing offer at last to oblige me to leave him, I shall not mend my situation in the world's eye; but the contrary. And yet I will not be treated by him with indignity while I have any power to help myself.

You, my dear, have accused me of having *modestyed away*, as you phrase it, several opportunities of being — being what, my dear? — Why, the wife of a libertine: and what a libertine and his wife are, my cousin Morden's letter tells us. — Let me here, once for all, endeavour to account for the motives of my behaviour to this man, and for the principles I have proceeded upon, as they appear to me upon a close self-examination.

Be pleased then to allow me to think, that my motives on this occasion arise not *altogether* from maidenly niceness; nor yet from the apprehension of what my present tormentor, and future husband, may think of a precipitate compliance, on such a disagreeable behaviour as his: but they arise principally from what offers to my own heart; respecting, as I may say, its own rectitude, its own judgment of the *fit* and the *unfit;* as I would, without study, answer *for* myself *to* myself, in the *first* place; to *him*, and to the *world*, in the *second* only. Principles that *are* in my mind; that I found there; implanted, no doubt, by the first gracious Planter: which therefore *impel* me, as I may say, to act up to them, that thereby I may, to the best of my judgment, be enabled to comport myself worthily in both states, (the single and the married) let others act as they will by *me*.

I hope, my dear, I do not deceive myself, and, instead of setting about rectifying what is amiss in my heart, endeavour to find excuses for habits and peculiarities which I am unwilling to cast off or overcome. The heart is very deceitful: do you, my dear friend, lay mine open, [*but surely it is always open before you!*] and spare me not, if you think it culpable.

This observation, once for all, as I said, I thought proper to make, to convince you, that, to the best of my judgment, my errors, in matters as well of lesser moment as of greater, shall rather be the fault of my judgment than of my will.

I am, my dearest friend,
   your ever obliged
      Clarissa Harlowe.

LETTER XC.

Miss Clarissa Harlowe to Miss Howe.

Tuesday night, May 16.

Mr. Lovelace has sent me, by Dorcas, his proposals, as follow:

"To spare a delicacy so extreme, and to obey you, I write: and the rather, that you may communicate this paper to Miss Howe, who may consult any of her friends you shall think proper to have intrusted on this occasion. I say, *intrusted;* because, as you know, I have given it out to several persons, that we are actually married.

"In the first place, madam, I offer to settle upon you, by way of jointure, your whole estate: and moreover to vest in trustees such a part of mine in Lancashire, as shall produce a clear four hundred pounds a-year, to be paid to your sole and separate use quarterly.

"My own estate is a clear, not nominal, 2000*l.* per annum. Lord M. proposes to give me possession either of that which he has in Lancashire [to which, by the way, I think I have a better title than he has himself] or that we call *the Lawn*, in Hertfordshire, upon my nuptials with a lady whom he so greatly admires; and to make that I shall choose a clear 1000*l.* per annum.

"My too great contempt of censure has subjected me to much slander. It may not, therefore, be improper to assure you, on the word of a gentleman, that no part of my estate was ever mortgaged: and that although I lived very expensively abroad, and made large drafts, yet that Midsummer-day next will discharge all that I owe in the world. My notions are not all bad ones. I have been thought, in pecuniary cases, *generous.* It would have deserved *another* name, had I not first been *just.*

"If, as your own estate is at present in your father's hands, you rather choose that I should make a jointure out of mine, tantamount to yours, be it what it will, it shall be done. I will engage Lord M. to write to *you* what he proposes to do on the happy occasion: not as your desire or expectation, but to demonstrate that no advantage is intended to be taken of the situation you are in with your own family.

"To shew the beloved daughter the consideration I have for her, I will consent that she shall prescribe the terms of agreement in relation to the large sums which must be in her father's hands, arising from her grandfather's estate. I have no doubt but he will be put upon making large demands upon you. All those it shall be in your power to comply with, for the sake of your own peace. And the remainder shall be paid into your hands, and be entirely at your disposal, as a fund to support those charitable donations which I have heard you so famed for *out* of your family; and for which you have been so greatly reflected upon *in* it.

"As to clothes, jewels, and the like, against the time you shall choose to make your appearance, it will be my pride, that you shall not be beholden for such of these as shall be answerable to the rank of both to those who have had the stupid folly to renounce a daughter they deserved not. You must excuse me, madam: you would mistrust my sincerity in the rest, could I speak of these people with less asperity, though so nearly related to you.

"These, madam, are my proposals. They are such as I always designed to make, whenever you would permit me to enter into the delightful subject. But you have been so determined to try every method for reconciling yourself to your relations, even by giving me absolutely up for ever, that you have seemed to think it but justice to keep me at a distance, till the event of that your *predominant* hope could be seen. It is *now* seen! — And although I *have been*, and perhaps still *am*, ready to regret the want of that preference I wished for from you as Miss Clarissa Harlowe; yet I am sure, as the husband of Mrs. Lovelace, I shall be more ready to adore than to blame you for the pangs you have given to a heart, the generosity, or rather *justice*, of which my implacable enemies have taught you to doubt: and this still the readier, as I am persuaded that those pangs never would have been given by a mind so noble, had not the doubt been entertained, perhaps with too great an appearance of reason; and as I hope I shall have it to reflect, that the moment the doubt shall be overcome the indifference will cease.

"I will only add, that if I have omitted any thing that would have given you further satisfaction; or if the above terms be short of what you would wish; you will be pleased to supply them as you think fit. And when I know your pleasure, I will instantly order articles to be drawn up conformably, that nothing in my power may be wanting to make you happy.

"You will now, dearest madam, judge how far all the rest depends upon yourself."

You see, my dear, what he offers. You see it is all my fault that he has not made these offers before. I am a strange creature! — To be to blame in *every thing*, and to *every body;* yet neither intend the ill at the time, nor know it to *be* the ill till too late, or so nearly too late, that I must give up all the delicacy he talks of, to compound for my fault!

I shall now judge how far the rest depends upon myself! So coldly concludes he such warm, and, in the main, unobjectionable proposals: would you not, as you read, have supposed that the paper would conclude with the most earnest demand of a day? — I own, I had that expectation so strong, resulting *naturally*, as I may say, from the premises, that without *studying* for dissatisfaction, I could not help being dissatisfied when I came to the conclusion.

But you say there is no help. I must perhaps make *further* sacrifices. All delicacy it seems is to be at an end with me! — But if so, this man knows not what every *wise* man knows, that prudence, and virtue, and delicacy of mind in a *wife*, do the husband more *real* honour in the eye of the world than the same qualities (were *she* destitute of them) in *himself*, do him: as the *want* of them in her does him more *dishonour:* for are not the wife's errors the husband's reproach? How *justly* his reproach is another thing.

I will consider this paper; and write to it, if I am able: for it seems now, *all the rest depends upon myself*.

LETTER XCI.

Wednesday morning, May 17.

Mr. Lovelace would fain have engaged me last night. But as I was not prepared to enter upon the subject of his proposals, (intending to consider them maturely) and was not highly pleased with his conclusion, I desired to be excused seeing him till morning; and the rather, as there is hardly any getting from him in tolerable time over-night.

Accordingly, about seven o'clock we met in the dining-room.

I find he was full of expectation that I should meet him with a very favourable, who knows but with a *thankful* aspect? And I immediately found by his fallen countenance, that he was under no small disappointment that I did not.

My dearest love, are you well? Why look you so solemn upon me? Will your indifference never be over? If I have proposed terms in any respect *short* of your expectation —

I told him, that he had very considerately mentioned my shewing his proposals to Miss Howe; and as I should have a speedy opportunity to send them to her by Collins, I desired to suspend any talk upon that subject till I had her opinion upon them.

Good God! — If there were but the least loophole! the least room for delay! — But he was writing a letter to Lord M. to give him an account of his situation with me, and could not finish it so satisfactorily, either to my lord or to himself, as if I would condescend to say whether the terms he had proposed were acceptable or not.

Thus far, I told him, I could say, that my principal point was peace and reconciliation with my relations. As to other matters, the genteelness of his own spirit would put him upon doing more for me than I should ask, or expect. Wherefore, if all he had to write about was to know what Lord M. would do on my account, he might spare himself the trouble; for that my utmost wishes, as to myself, were much more easily gratified than he perhaps imagined.

He asked me then, if I would so far permit him to touch upon the happy day, as to request the presence of Lord M. on the occasion, and to be my father? *Father* had a sweet and venerable sound with it, I said I should be glad to have a father who would own me! Was not this plain speaking, think you, my dear? Yet it rather, I must own, appears so to me on reflection, than was *designed* freely at the time. For I then, with a sigh from the bottom of my heart, thought of my *own father;* bitterly regretting, that I am an outcast from him and from my mother.

Mr. Lovelace, I thought, seemed a little affected at the *manner* of my speaking, and perhaps at the sad reflection.

I am but a very young creature, Mr. Lovelace, said I, (and wiped my eyes as I turned away my face) although you have *kindly,* and *in love to me*, introduced so much sorrow to me already: so you must not wonder that the word *father* strikes so sensibly upon the heart of a child ever dutiful till she knew you, and whose tender years still require the paternal wing.

He turned towards the window (rejoice with me, my dear, since I seem to be devoted to him, that the man is not absolutely impenetrable!): his emotion was visible; yet he endeavoured to suppress it. Approaching me again; again he was obliged to turn from me; angelic something, he said: but then, obtaining a heart more *suitable* to his wish, he once more approached me. — For his own part, he said, as Lord M. was so subject to the gout, he was afraid that the compliment he had just proposed to make him might, if made, occasion a *longer suspension* than he could bear to think of: and if it did, it would vex him to the heart that he had made it.

I could not say a single word to this, you know, my dear. But you will guess at my thoughts of what he said — So much passionate love, *lip deep!* So prudent, and so dutifully patient *at heart* to a relation he had till now so undutifully despised! — Why, why, am I thrown upon such a man, thought I!

He hesitated, as if contending with himself; and after taking a turn or two about the room, he was at a great loss what to determine upon, he said, because he had not the honour of knowing when he was to be made the happiest of men — would to God it might that very instant be resolved upon!

He stopped a moment or two, staring, in his usual confident way, in my downcast face [did I not, O my beloved friend, think you, want a father or a mother just then?] But if he could not, so *soon* as he wished, procure my consent to a day; in *that* case, he thought the compliment might *as well be* made to Lord M. as *not* — [*see my dear!*] Since the settlements might be drawn and engrossed in the intervenient time, which would pacify his impatience, *as no time would be lost.*

You will suppose how *I* was

affected by this speech, by repeating the substance of what *he* said upon it; as follows.

—But, by his soul, he knew not, so much was I upon the reserve, and so much latent meaning did my eye import, whether, when he most hoped to please me, he was not furthest from doing so. Would I vouchsafe to say, whether I approved of his compliment to Lord M. or not?

To leave it to *me* to choose whether the speedy day he ought to have urged for with earnestness should be accelerated or suspended!—Miss Howe, thought I, at that moment, says I must *not* run away from this man!

To be sure, Mr. Lovelace, if this matter be *ever to be*, it must be agreeable to me to have the full approbation of *one* side, since I cannot have that of the *other*.

If this matter be ever to be! Good God! what words are these at this time of day! And full *approbation* of *one* side? Why that word *approbation?* when the greatest pride of all my family is, that of having the honour of so dear a creature for their relation. Would to heaven, my dearest life, added he, that, without complimenting *any* body, to-morrow might be the happiest day of my life!—What say you, my angel? With a trembling impatience, that *seemed* not affected—What say you for *to-morrow?*

It was likely, my dear, I could say much to it, or name another day, had I been disposed to the latter, with such an *hinted delay from him*.

I was silent.

Next day, madam, if not to-morrow?

Had he given me *time* to answer, it could not have been in the affirmative, you must think—but *in the same breath*, he went on—or the *day after that?*—And taking both my hands in his, he stared me into a half-confusion—would *you* have had patience with him, my dear?

No, no, said I, as calmly as possible, you cannot think that I should imagine there can be reason for such a hurry. It will be most agreeable, to be sure, for my lord to be present.

I am all obedience and resignation, returned the wretch, with a self-pluming air, as if he had acquiesced to a proposal *made by me*, and had complimented me with a great piece of *self-denial*.

Is it not plain, my dear, that he designs to vex and tease me? Proud, yet mean, and foolish man, if so!—But you say all punctilio is at an end with me. Why, why, will he take pains to make a heart wrap itself up in reserve, that wishes only, and that for his sake, as well as my own, to observe due decorum?

Modesty, I think, required of me, that it should pass as he had put it: did it not?—I think it did. Would to heaven—but what signifies wishing?

But when he would have *rewarded himself*, as he had heretofore called it, for this self-supposed concession, with a kiss, I repulsed him with a just and very sincere disdain.

He seemed both vexed and surprised, as one who had made the most agreeable proposals and concessions, and thought them ungratefully returned. He plainly said, that he thought our situation would intitle him to such an innocent freedom: and he was both amazed and grieved to be thus scornfully repulsed.

No reply could be made by me on such a subject. I abruptly broke from him. I recollect, as I passed by one of the pier-glasses, that I saw in it his clenched hand offered in wrath to his forehead: the words *indifference, by his soul, next to hatred*, I heard him speak; and something of *ice* he mentioned: I heard not what.

Whether he intends to write to my lord, or to Miss Montague, I cannot tell. But *as all delicacy ought to be over with me now*, perhaps I am to blame to expect it from a man who may not know what it is. If he does *not*, and yet thinks himself very polite, and intends not to be otherwise, I am rather to be pitied, than he to be censured.

And after all, since I *must* take him as I find him, I *must*: that is to say, as a man so vain and so accustomed to be admired, that, not being conscious of internal defect, he has taken no pains to polish more than his outside: and as his proposals are higher than my expectations; and as, in his own opinion, he has a great deal to bear from *me*, I *will* (no new offence preventing) sit down to answer them; — and, if possible, in terms as unobjectionable to him, as his are to me.

But, after all, see you not, my dear, more and more, the mismatch that there is in our minds?

However, I am willing to compound for my fault, by giving up (if that may be all my punishment) the expectation of what is deemed happiness in this life, with such a husband as I fear he will make. In short, I will content myself to be a *suffering person* through the state to the end of my life. — A long one it cannot be! —

This may qualify him (as it may prove) from stings of conscience from misbehaviour to a *first* wife, to be a more tolerable one to a *second*, though not perhaps a better deserving one: while my story, to all who shall know it, will afford these instructions: *That the eye is a traitor, and ought ever to be mistrusted; that form is deceitful:* in other words; *that a fine person is seldom paired by a fine mind:* and *that sound principles, and a good heart, are the only bases on which the hopes of* a happy future, *either with respect to this world, or the other, can be built.*

And so much at present for Mr. Lovelace's proposals; of which I desire your opinion.*

* We cannot forbear observing in this place, that the lady has been particularly censured, even by some of her own sex, as *over nice* in her part of the above conversations: but surely this must be owing to want of attention to the cir-

Four letters are written by Mr. Lovelace from the date of his last, giving the state of affairs between him and the lady, pretty much the same as in hers in the same period, allowing for the humour in his, and for his resentments expressed with vehemence

cumstances she was in, and to her character, as well as the *character of the man she had to deal with*: for although she could not be supposed to know so much of his designs as the reader does by means of his letters to Belford; yet she was but too well convinced of his faulty morals, and of the necessity there was, from the whole of his behaviour to her, to keep such an encroacher, as she frequently calls him, at a distance. In Letter XXIX. the reader will see that upon some favourable appearance she blames herself for her readiness to suspect him. But his character, his principles, said she, *are so faulty; he is so light, so vain, so various! — Then, my dear, I have no guardian now, no father, no mother! Nothing but God and my own vigilance to depend upon!* In page 30 of this volume, *Must I not with such a man*, says she, *be wanting to myself, were I not jealous and vigilant?*
By this time the reader will see that she had still *greater* reason for her jealousy and vigilance. And Lovelace will tell the sex, as he does Letter CXXIV. of this volume, *That the woman who resents not initiatory freedoms must be lost. Love is an encroacher,* says he: *love never goes backward. Nothing but the highest act of love can satisfy an* indulged love.
But the reader perhaps is too apt to form a judgment of Clarissa's conduct in critical cases by *Lovelace's complaints of her coldness*; not considering his views upon her; and that she is proposed as an *example*; and therefore in her trials and distresses must not be allowed to dispense with those rules which perhaps some others of her sex, in her delicate situation, would not have thought themselves so strictly bound to observe; although, if she had *not* observed them, a *Lovelace* would have carried all his points.

on her resolution to leave him, *if her friends could be brought to be reconciled to her. — A few extracts from them will be only given.*

What, *says he*, might have become of me, and of my projects, had not her father, and the rest of the implacables, stood my friends?

After violent threatenings of revenge, he says,

'Tis plain she would have given me up for ever. Nor should I have been able to prevent her abandoning of me, unless I had *torn up the tree by the roots to come at the fruit;* which I hope *still to bring down by a gentle shake or two*, if I can but have patience to stay the ripening season.

Thus triumphing in his unpolite cruelty, he says,

After her haughty treatment of me, I am resolved she *shall* speak out. There are a thousand beauties to be discovered in the face, in the accent, in the *bush-beating* hesitations of a woman who is earnest about a subject which she wants to introduce, yet knows not how. Silly fellows, calling themselves generous ones, would value themselves for sparing a lady's confusion: but they are silly fellows indeed, and rob themselves of prodigious pleasure by their forwardness; and at the same time deprive her of displaying a world of charms, which only can be manifested on these occasions.

I'll tell thee beforehand how it will be with my charmer in this case — she will be about it, and about it, several times: but I will not understand her: at last, after half a dozen hem — ings, she will be obliged to speak out — *I think, Mr. Lovelace — I think, sir — I think you were saying some days ago* — still I will be all silence — her eyes fixed upon my shoe-buckles, as I sit over against her — ladies, when put to it thus, always admire a man's shoe-buckles, or perhaps some particular beauties in the carpet. *I think you said, that Mrs. Fretchville* — then a crystal tear trickles down each crimson cheek, vexed to have her virgin pride so little assisted. But, come, my meaning dear, cry I to myself, remember, what I have suffered *for* thee, and what I have suffered *by* thee! Thy tearful pausings shall not be helped out by me. Speak out, love! — O the sweet confusion! Can I rob myself of so many conflicting beauties by the precipitate charmer-pitying folly, by which a *politer* man [thou knowest, lovely, that I am no *polite* man!] betrayed by his own tenderness, and *unused* to female tears, would have been overcome? I will feign an irresolution of mind on the occasion, that she may not quite abhor me — that her reflections on the scene in my absence may bring to her remembrance some beauties in my part of it: an irresolution that will be owing to awe, to reverence, to profound veneration; and that will have more eloquence in it than words can have. Speak out then, love, and spare not.

Hard-heartedness, as it is called, is an *essential* of the *libertine's character*. Familiarized to the distresses he occasions, he is seldom betrayed by tenderness into a complaisant weakness unworthy of himself.

Mentioning the settlements, he says,

I am in earnest as to the terms. If I marry her [and I have no doubt that I shall, after my pride, my ambition, my *revenge*, if thou wilt, is gratified] I will do her noble justice. The more I do for such a prudent, such an excellent economist, the more shall I do for myself. — But, by my soul, Belford, her haughtiness shall be brought down to own both love and obligation to me. Nor will this sketch of settlements bring us forwarder than I would have it. Modesty of sex will stand my friend at any time. At the very altar, our hands joined, I will engage to make this proud beauty leave the parson and me, and all my friends who should be present, though twenty in number, to look like fools upon one another, while she took wing, and flew out of the church-door, or window, (if they were open, and the door shut) and this only by a single word.

He mentions his rash expression, that she should be his, although his damnation should be the purchase.

At that instant, *says he*, I was

upon the point of making a violent attempt, but was checked in the very moment, and but just in time to save myself, by the awe I was struck with on again casting my eye upon her terrified but lovely face, and seeing, as I thought, her spotless heart in every line of it.

O virtue, virtue! *proceeds he,* what is there in thee, that can thus against his will affect the heart of a Lovelace! — Whence these involuntary tremors, and fear of giving mortal offence? — What art thou, that acting in the breast of a feeble woman, canst strike so much awe into a spirit so intrepid! Which never before, no, not in my first attempt, young as I then was, and frightened at my own boldness, (till I found myself *forgiven*) had such effect upon me!

He paints in lively colours that part of the scene between him and the lady, where she says, the word *father* has a sweet and venerable sound with it.

I was exceedingly affected, *says he,* upon the occasion. But was ashamed to be surprised into such a fit of uumanly weakness — so *ashamed,* that I was resolved to subdue it at the instant, and to guard against the like for the future. Yet, at that moment, I more than half regretted, that I could not permit her to enjoy a triumph which she so well deserved to glory in — her youth, her beauty, her artless innocence, and her manner, equally beyond comparison or description. But her *indifference,* Belford! — That she could resolve to sacrifice me to the malice of my enemies; and carry on the design in so clandestine a manner — yet love her, as I do, to phrensy! — Revere her, as I do, to adoration! — These were the recollections with which I fortified my recreant heart against her! — Yet, after all, if she persevere, she must conquer! — Coward, as she has made me, that never was a coward before!

He concludes his fourth letter in a vehement rage, upon her refusing him, when he offered to salute her; having supposed, as he owns, that she would have been all condescension on his proposals to her.

This, *says he,* I will for ever remember against her, in order to steel my heart, that I may *cut through a rock of ice* to hers; and repay her for the disdain, the scorn, which glowed in her countenance, and was apparent in her air, at her abrupt departure from me, after such obliging behaviour on my side, and after I had so earnestly pressed her for an early day. The women below say, she hates me; she despises me! — And 'tis true: she does; she must — and why cannot I take their advice? I will not long, my fair one, be despised by *thee,* and laughed at by *them!*

Let me acquaint thee, Jack, *adds he by way of postscript,* that this effort of hers to leave me, if she could have been received; her sending for a coach on Sunday;

no doubt, resolving not to return, if she had gone out without me, (for did she not declare that she had thoughts to retire to some of the villages about town, where she could be safe and private?) have, altogether, so much alarmed me, that I have been adding to the written instructions for my fellow and the people below how to act in case she should elope in my absence: particularly letting Will know what he shall report to strangers, in case she shall throw herself upon any such, with a resolution to abandon me. To these instructions I shall further add, as circumstances offer.

LETTER XCII.
Miss Howe to Miss Clarissa Harlowe.

Thursday, May 18.

I HAVE neither time nor patience, my dear friend, to answer every material article in your last letters just now received. Mr. Lovelace's proposals are all I like of him. And yet (as you do) I think that he concludes them not with that warmth and earnestness which we might naturally have expected from him. Never in my life did I hear or read of so patient a man, with such a blessing in his reach. But wretches of his cast, between you and me, my dear, have not, I fancy, the ardours that honest men have. Who knows, as your Bell once spitefully said, but he may have half a dozen creatures to quit his hands of before he engages for life? — Yet I believe you must not expect him to be honest on this side of his grand climacteric.

He to suggest delay from a compliment to be made to Lord M. and to give time for settlements! *He*, a part of whose character it is, not to know what complaisance to his relations is — I have no patience with him! You did indeed want an interposing friend on the affecting occasion which you mention in yours of yesterday morning. But, upon my word, were I to have been that moment in your situation, and been so treated, I would have torn his eyes out, and left it to his own heart, when I had done, to furnish the reason for it.

Would to heaven to-morrow, without complimenting any body, might be his happy day! — Villain! After he had himself suggested the compliment! — And I think he accuses you of delaying! — Fellow, that he is — How my heart is wrung! —

But, as matters now stand betwixt you, I am very unseasonable in expressing my resentments against him. — Yet I don't know whether I am or not, neither; since it is the most cruel of fates, for a woman to be forced to have a man whom her heart despises. You must, at *least*, despise him; at times, however. His clenched fist offered to his forehead on your leaving him in just displeasure — I wish it had been a pole-ax, and in the hand of his worst enemy.

I will endeavour to think of some method, of some scheme to

get you from him, and to fix you safely somewhere till your cousin Morden arrives — a scheme to lie by you, and to be pursued as occasion may be given. You are sure that you can go abroad when you please? and that our correspondence is safe? I cannot, however (for the reasons heretofore mentioned respecting your own reputation) wish you to leave him while he gives you not cause to suspect his honour. But your heart I know would be the easier, if you were sure of some asylum in case of necessity.

Yet once more, I say I can have no notion that he can or dare to mean you dishonour. But then the man is a fool, my dear — that's all.

However, since you are thrown upon a fool, marry the fool, at the first opportunity; and though I doubt that this man will be the most ungovernable of fools, as all witty and vain fools are, take him as a punishment, since you cannot as a reward: in short, as one given to convince you that there is nothing but imperfection in this life.

And what is the result of all I have written, but this? Either marry, my dear, or get from them all, and from him too.

You intend the latter, you'll say, as soon as you have opportunity. That, as above hinted, I hope quickly to furnish you with: and then comes on a trial between *you* and *yourself*.

These are the very fellows that we women do not *naturally* hate. We don't always know what is and what is not, in our power to do. When some principal point we have long had in view becomes so critical, that we must of necessity choose or refuse, then perhaps we look about us; are affrighted at the wild and uncertain prospect before us; and after a few struggles and heart-aches, reject the untried new; draw in our horns, and resolve to *snail*-on, as we did before, in a tract we are acquainted with.

I shall be impatient till I have your next. I am, my dearest friend,

Your ever affectionate and faithful

ANNA HOWE.

LETTER XCIII.

Mr. Belford to Robert Lovelace, Esq.

Wednesday, May 17.

I CANNOT conceal from you any thing that relates to yourself so so much as the inclosed does. You will see what the noble writer apprehends from you, and wishes of you, with regard to Miss Harlowe, and how much at heart all your relations have it that you do honourably by her. They compliment me with an influence over you, which I wish with all my soul you would let me have in this article.

Let me once more entreat thee, Lovelace, to reflect, before it be too late (before the mortal offence be given), upon the graces and merits of this lady. Let thy frequent remorses at last end in one effectual remorse. Let not pride and wantonness of heart ruin thy fairer prospects. By my faith, Lovelace, there is nothing but vanity, conceit, and nonsense, in our wild schemes. As we grow older, we shall be wiser, and looking back upon our foolish notions of the present hour (our youth dissipated) shall certainly despise ourselves, when we think of the honourable engagements we might have made: thou, more especially, if thou lettest such a matchless creature slide through thy fingers. A creature pure from her cradle. In all her actions and sentiments uniformly noble. Strict in the performance of all her even *unrewarded* duties to the most *unreasonable of fathers*, what a *wife*, will she make the man who shall have the honour to call her his!

What apprehensions wouldst thou have had reason for, had she been prevailed upon by giddy or frail motives, for which one man, by importunity, might prevail as well as another?

We all know what an inventive genius thou art master of: we are all sensible, that thou hast *a head to contrive, and a heart to execute.* Have I not called thine *the plotting'st heart in the universe?* I called it so upon knowledge. What wouldst thou *more?* Why should it be the most *villainous*, as well as the most *able?* — Marry the lady; and *when* married let her know what a number of contrivances thou hadst in readiness to play off. Beg of her not to hate thee for the communication; and assure her that thou gavest them up from remorse, and in justice to her extraordinary merit; and let her have the opportunity of congratulating herself for subduing a heart so capable of what thou callest *glorious mischief.* This will give her room for triumph: and even *thee* no less: she, for *hers* over *thee;* thou, for *thine* over *thyself.*

Reflect likewise upon her sufferings for thee. Actually at the time thou art forming schemes to ruin her (at least in *her* sense of the word) is she not labouring under a father's curse laid upon her by thy means, and for thy sake? And wouldst thou give operation and completion to that curse, which otherwise cannot have effect?

And what, Lovelace, all the time is thy pride? — Thou that vainly imaginest that the whole family of the Harlowes, and that of the Howes too, are but thy machines, unknown to themselves, to bring about thy purposes, and thy revenge, what art thou more, or better, than the instrument even of her implacable brother, and envious sister, to perpetuate the disgrace of the most excellent of sisters, to which they are moved by vilely low and sordid motives? — Canst thou bear, Lovelace, to be thought the machine of thy inveterate enemy James Harlowe? — Nay, art not thou the cully of that still viler Joseph Leman, who serves himself as much by thy money, as he does thee by the double part he acts by thy direction? — And further still, art not thou the devil's agent, who only can, and who certainly will, suitably reward thee, if thou proceedest, and if thou effectest thy wicked purpose?

Could any man but thee put together upon paper the following questions with so much unconcern as thou seemest to have written them? — Give them a reperusal, O heart of adamant! "Whither can she fly to avoid me? Her parents will not receive her: her uncles will not entertain her: her beloved Norton is in their direction, and cannot: Miss Howe dare not. She has not one friend in town but ME: is entirely a stranger to the town."* — What must that heart be that can triumph in a distress so deep, into which she has been plunged by thy elaborate arts and contrivances? And what a sweet, yet sad reflection was that, which had like to have had its due effect upon thee, arising from thy naming Lord M. for her nuptial father? Her tender years inclining her to *wish* a father, and to *hope* a friend. — O, my dear Lovelace, canst thou resolve to be, instead of the father thou hast robbed her of, a devil?

Thou knowest that I have no interest, that I can have no view, in wishing thee to do justice to this admirable creature. For thy own sake, once more I conjure thee, for thy family's sake, and for the sake of our common humanity, let me beseech thee to be just to Miss Clarissa Harlowe.

No matter whether these expostulations are in character from me, or not. I *have* been and *am* bad enough. If thou takest my advice, which is (as the enclosed will shew) the advice of all thy family, thou wilt perhaps have it to reproach me, (and but perhaps neither) that thou art not a worse man than myself. But if thou dost not, and if thou ruinest such a virtue, all the complicated wickedness of ten devils, let loose among the innocent with full power over them, will not do so much vile and base mischief as thou wilt be guilty of.

It is said, that the prince on his throne is not safe, if a mind so desperate can be found, as values not its *own* life. So may it be said, that the most immaculate virtue is not safe, if a man can be met with, who has no regard to his own honour, and makes a jest of the most solemn vows and protestations.

Thou mayest by trick, chicane, and false colours, thou, who art worse than a piccaroon in love, overcome a poor lady, so entangled as thou hast entangled her; so unprotected as thou hast made her: but consider, how much more generous and just to her, and noble to thyself, it is to overcome *thyself*.

Once more, it is no matter whether my past or future actions countenance my preachment, as perhaps thou'lt call what I have written: but this I promise thee, that whenever I meet with a

* See p. 264.

woman of but one half of Miss Harlowe's perfections, who will favour me with her acceptance, I will take the advice I give, and marry. Nor will I attempt to try her honour at the hazard of my own. In other words, I will not degrade an excellent creature in *her own eyes*, by trials, when I have no cause for suspicion. And let me add, with respect to thy *eagleship's* manifestations of which thou boastest, in thy attempts upon the innocent and uncorrupted, rather than upon those whom thou humorously comparest to wrens, wagtails, and phyl-tits, as thou callest them,* that I hope I have it not once to reproach myself that I ruined the morals of any one creature, who otherwise would have been uncorrupted. Guilt enough in contributing to the *continued* guilt of other poor wretches, if I am one of those who take care she shall never *rise again*, when she has *once fallen*.

Whatever the capital devil, under whose banner thou hast listed, will let thee do, with regard to this incomparable woman, I hope thou wilt act with honour in relation to the inclosed, between Lord M. and me; since his lordship, as thou wilt see, desires that thou mayest not know he wrote on the subject; for reasons, I think, very far from being creditable to thyself: and that thou wilt take as meant the honest zeal for thy service of ·

Thy real friend,
J. BELFORD.

* See p. 244.

LETTER XCIV.

Lord M. to John Belford, Esq.

[*Inclosed in the preceding.*]

SIR, M. Hall, Monday, May 15.

IF any man in the world has power over my nephew, it is you. I therefore write this to beg you to interfere in the affair depending between him and the most accomplished of women, as every one says; and *what every one says must be true*.

I don't know that he has any bad designs upon her; but I know his temper too well not to be apprehensive upon such long delays: and the ladies here have been for some time in fear for her: Lady Sarah in particular, who (as you must know) is a wise woman, says that these delays, in the present case, must be from him, rather than from the lady.

He had always indeed a strong antipathy to marriage, and may think of playing his dog's tricks by her, as he has by so many others. If there's any danger of this, 'tis best to prevent it in time; for *when a thing is done, advice comes too late*.

He has always had the folly and impertinence to make a jest of me for using proverbs; but as they are the wisdom of whole nations and ages collected into a small compass, I am not to be shamed out of sentences that often contain more wisdom in them than the tedious harangues of most of our parsons and moralists. Let him laugh at them, if he pleases: you and I know better things, Mr.

Belford — *though you have kept company with a wolf, you have not learnt to howl of him.*

But, nevertheless, you must not let him know that I have written to you on this subject. I am ashamed to say it; but he has ever treated me as if I were a man of very common understanding; and would, perhaps, think never the better of the best advice in the world, for coming from me. *Those*, Mr. Belford, *who most love are least set by.* — *But who would expect velvet to be made out of a sow's ear!*

I am sure he has no reason, however, to slight me as he does. He may and will be the better for me, if he outlives me; though he once told me to my face, that I might do as I would with my estate; for that he, for his part, *loved his liberty as much as he despised money.* And at another time, twitting me with phrases, *that the man was above controul who wanted not either to borrow or flatter.* He thought, I suppose, that *I could not cover him with my wings without pecking at him with my bill*; though I never used to be pecking at him without very great occasion: and God knows he might have my very heart; if he would but endeavour to oblige me, by studying his own good; for that is all I desire of him. Indeed, it was his poor mother that first spoiled him: and I have been but too indulgent to him since. A fine grateful disposition, you'll say, to *return evil for good!* But that was always his way. It is a good saying, and which was verified by him with a witness — *Children, when little, make their parents fools; when great, mad.* Had his parents lived to see what I have seen of him, they would have been mad indeed.

This match, however, as the lady has such an extraordinary share of wisdom and goodness, might set all to rights; and if you can forward it, I would enable him to make whatever settlements he could wish; and should not be unwilling to put him in possession of another pretty estate besides. I am no covetous man, he knows. And, indeed, what is a covetous man to be likened to so fitly, as *to a dog in a wheel which roasts meat for others?* And what do I live for (as I have often said) but to see him and my two nieces well married and settled? May Heaven *settle him down to a better mind*, and turn his heart to more of goodness and consideration!

If the delays are on his side, I tremble for the lady; and if on hers, (as he tells my niece Charlotte) I could wish she were apprized that *delays are dangerous.* Excellent as she is, she ought not to depend on her merits with such a changeable fellow, and such a professed marriage-hater as he has been. *Desert and reward*, I can assure her, *seldom keep company together.*

But let him remember, that *vengeance, though it comes with leaden feet, strikes with iron hands.* If he behaves ill in this case, he may find it so. What a pity it is that a man of his talents and learning should be so vile a rake! Alas! alas! *Une poignée de bonne vie vaut mieux que plein muy de clergé;* a handful of good life is better than a whole bushel of learning.

You may throw in, too, as a friend, that should he provoke me, it may not be too late for me to marry. My old friend Wycherly did so, when he was older than I am, on purpose to plague his nephew: and in spite of this gout, I might have a child or two still. I have not been without some thoughts that way, when he has angered me more than ordinary: but these thoughts have gone off again hitherto, upon my considering that *the children of very young and very old men* (though I am not so very old neither) *last not long;* and that *old men, when they marry young women,* are said to *make much of death:* yet who knows but that matrimony might be good against the gouty humours I am troubled with?

No man is every thing — you, Mr. Belford, are a learned man. I am a peer. And do you (as you best know how) inculcate upon him the force of these wise sayings which follow, as well as those which went before; but yet so discreetly, as that he may not know that you *borrow your darts from my quiver.* These be they — *Happy is the man who knows his follies in his youth. He that lives well, lives long. Again, he that lives ill one year will sorrow for it seven.* And again, as the Spaniards have it — *who lives well sees afar off!* Far off indeed; for he sees into eternity, as a man may say. Then that other fine saying, *he who perishes in needless dangers, is the devil's martyr.* Another proverb I picked up at Madrid, when I accompanied Lord Lexington in his embassy to Spain, which might teach our nephew more mercy and compassion than is in his nature I doubt to shew; which is this, *that he who pities another remembers himself.* And this that is going to follow, I am sure he has proved the truth of a hundred times, *that he who does what he will, seldom does what he ought.* Nor is that unworthy of his notice, *young men's frolics old men feel.* My devilish gout, God help me — but I will not say what I was going to say.

I remember, that you, yourself, complimenting me for my taste in pithy and wise sentences, said a thing that gave me a high opinion of you; and it was this: *Men of talents,* said you, *are sooner to be convinced by short sentences than by long preachments, because the short sentences drive themselves into the heart, and stay here, while long discourses, though ever so good, tire the attention; and one good thing drives out another, and so on, till all is forgotten.*

May your good counsel, Mr. Belford, founded upon these hints which I have given, pierce his heart, and incite him to do what will be so happy for himself, and so necessary for the honour of that admirable lady whom I long to see his wife; and if I may, I will not think of one for myself.

20*

Should he abuse the confidence she has placed in him, I myself shall pray that vengeance may fall upon his head — *Raro* — I quite forget all my Latin: but I think it is, *Raro antecedentem scelestum deseruit pede pœna claudo*: Where vice goes before, vengeance (sooner or later) will follow. But why do I translate these things for you?

I shall make no apologies for this trouble. I know how well you love him and me: and there is nothing in which you could serve us both more importantly, than in forwarding this match to the utmost of your power. When it is done, how shall I rejoice to see you at M. Hall! Meantime I shall long to hear that you are likely to be successful with him, and am,

Dear sir,
Your most faithful friend and servant,
M.

Mr. Lovelace having not returned an answer to Mr. Belford's expostulatory Letter so soon as Mr. Belford expected, he wrote to him, expressing his apprehension that he had disobliged him by his honest freedom. Among other things, he says —

I pass my time here at Watford, attending my dying uncle, very heavily. I cannot, therefore, by any means dispense with thy correspondence. And why shouldst thou punish me, for having more conscience and more remorse than thyself? Thou who never thoughtest either conscience or remorse an honour to thee. And I have, besides, a melancholy story to tell thee, in relation to Belton and his Thomasine; and which may afford a lesson to all the keeping class.

I have a letter from each of our three companions in the time. They have all the wickedness that thou hast, but not the wit. Some new rogueries do two of them boast of, which, I think, if completed, deserve the gallows.

I am far from hating intrigue upon principle. But to have awkward fellows plot, and commit their plots to paper, destitute of the seasonings, of the *acumen*, which is thy talent, how extremely shocking must their letters be! — But do thou, Lovelace, whether thou art, or art not, determined upon thy measures with regard to the fine lady in thy power, enliven my heavy heart by thy communications; and thou wilt oblige

Thy melancholy friend,
J. BELFORD.

LETTER XCV.

Mr. Lovelace to John Belford, Esq.

Friday, night, May 19.

WHEN I have opened my views to thee so amply as I have done in my former letters, and have told thee, that my principal design is but to bring virtue to a trial, that, *if* virtue, it need not be afraid of; and that the reward of it will be marriage (that is to say, if, after I have carried my point, I cannot prevail upon her to live with me the life of honour*; for that thou

* See p. 57.

knowest is the wish of my heart); I am amazed at the repetition of thy wambling nonsense.

I am of opinion with thee, that some time hence, when I am *grown wiser*, I shall conclude that *there is nothing but vanity, conceit, and nonsense in my present wild schemes.* But what is this saying, but that I must be *first* wiser?

I do not intend *to let this matchless creature slide through my fingers.*

Art thou able to say half the things in her praise, that I have said, and am continually saying or writing?

Her gloomy father cursed the sweet creature, because she put it out of his wicked power to compel her to have the man she hated. Thou knowest how little merit she has with me on this score — and shall I not *try* the virtue I intend, upon full proof, to *reward*, because her father is a tyrant? — Why art thou thus eternally reflecting upon so excellent a woman, as if thou wert assured she would *fail in the trial?* — Nay, thou declarest, every time thou writest on the subject, that she *will*, that she must yield, *entangled as she is:* and yet makest her virtue the pretence of thy solicitude for her.

An *instrument of the vile James Harlowe*, dost thou call me? — O Jack! how could I curse thee! *I* an *instrument* of that brother! of that sister! But mark the end — and thou shalt see what will become of that brother and of that sister!

Play not against me my own acknowledged sensibilities, I desire thee. Sensibilities, which at the same time that they contradict thy charge of an *adamantine heart* in thy friend, thou hadst known nothing of, had I not communicated them to thee.

If I ruin such a virtue, sayest thou! — Eternal monotonist! — Again, *The most immaculate virtue may be ruined by men who have no regard to their honour, and who make a jest of the most solemn oaths*, &c. What must be the virtue that will be ruined *without oaths?* Is not the world full of these deceptions? And are not *lovers' oaths* a jest of hundreds of years standing? And are not cautions against the perfidy of our sex a necessary part of the female education?

I do intend to endeavour to overcome *myself;* but I must first try if I cannot overcome *this lady.* Have I not said, that the honour of the sex is concerned that I should *try?*

Whenever thou meetest with a woman of but half her perfections, thou wilt marry — Do, Jack.

Can a girl be *degraded by trials*, who is not *overcome?*

I am glad that thou takest crime to thyself for not endeavouring to convert the poor wretches whom *others* have ruined. I will not recriminate upon thee, Belford, as I might, when thou flatterest thyself, that thou never ruinedst the morals of any young creature, who otherwise would not have been corrupted — the palliating consolation of an Hottentot heart, determined rather to gluttonize on the garbage of other foul feeders than to reform. — But, tell me, Jack, wouldst thou have spared such a girl as my Rosebud, had I not, by my example, engaged thy generosity? Nor was my Rosebud the only girl I spared: when my power was acknowledged, who more merciful than thy friend?

It is *resistance* that inflames desire,
Sharpens the darts of love, and blows its fire.
Love is disarmed that meets with too much ease;
He languishes, and does not care to please.

The women know this as well as the men. They love to be addressed with spirit;

And therefore 'tis their golden fruit they guard
With so much care, to make possession hard.

Whence, for a by-reflection, the ardent, the complaisant gallant is so often preferred to the cold, the unadoring husband. And yet the sex do not consider, that variety and novelty give the ardour and the obsequiousness: and that, were the rake as much used to them as the husband is, he would be [and is to *his own wife*, if married] as indifferent to their favours as their husbands are; and the husband in his turn would, to another woman, be the rake. Let the women, upon the whole, take this lesson from a Lovelace — "Always to endeavour to make themselves as new to a husband, and to appear as elegant and as obliging to him as they are desirous to appear to a *lover*, and actually were to *him* as *such;* and then the *rake*, which all women love, will last longer in the *husband* than it generally does."

But to return: — If I have not sufficiently cleared my conduct to thee in the above; I refer thee once more to mine of the 13th of last month*. And pr'ythee, Jack, lay me not under a necessity to repeat the same things so often. I hope thou readest what I write *more than once*.

I am not displeased that thou art so apprehensive of my resentment, that I cannot miss a day without making thee uneasy. Thy conscience, 'tis plain, tells thee, that thou hast deserved my displeasure: and if it has convinced thee of *that*, it will make thee afraid of repeating thy fault. See that this be the consequence. Else now that thou hast told me how I can punish thee, it is very likely that I do punish thee by my silence, although I have as much pleasure in writing on this charming subject as thou canst have in reading what I write.

When a boy, if a dog ran away from me through fear, I generally looked about for a stone or a stick; and, if neither offered to my hand, I skimmed my hat after him, to make him afraid for something. What signifies power, if we do not exert it?

Let my lord know that thou *hast* scribbled to me. But give him not the contents of thy epistle. Though a parcel of crude stuff,

* See p. 49, & seq.

he would think there was something in it. Poor arguments will do, when brought in favour of what we like. But the stupid peer little thinks that this lady is a rebel to love. On the contrary, not only he, but all the world, believe her to be a volunteer in the service. So I shall incur blame, and she will be pitied, if any thing happen amiss.

Since my lord's heart is so set upon this match, I have written already, to let him know, "That my unhappy character has given my beloved an ungenerous diffidence of me. That she is so mother-sick and father-fond, that she had rather return to Harlowe Place than marry. That she is even apprehensive, that the step she has taken of going off with me will make the ladies of a family of such rank and honour as ours think slightly of her. That therefore I desire his lordship (though this hint, I tell him, must be very delicately touched) to write me such a letter as I can shew her (let him treat me in it ever so freely, I shall not take it amiss, I tell him, because I know his lordship takes pleasure in writing to me in a corrective style). That he may make what offers he pleases on the marriage. That I desire his presence at the ceremony; that I may take from his hand the greatest blessing that mortal man can give me."

I have not absolutely told the lady that I would write to his lordship to this effect; yet have given her reason to think I will. So that without the last necessity I shall not produce the answer I expect from him: for I am very loth, I own, to make use of any of my family's names for the furthering of my designs. And yet I must make all secure before I pull off the mask. *Was not this my motive for bringing her hither?*

Thus thou seest, that the old peer's letter came very seasonably. I thank thee for it. But as to his sentences, they cannot possibly do me good. I was early suffocated with his *wisdom of nations*. When a boy, I never asked any thing of him but out flew a *proverb;* and if the tendency of that was to deny me, I never could obtain the least favour. This gave me so great an aversion to the very word, that when a child, I made it a condition with my tutor, who was an honest parson, that I would not read my Bible at all, if he would not excuse me one of the wisest books in it: to which, however, I had no other objection, than that it was called *the Proverbs.* And as for Solomon, he was then a hated character with me, not because of his polygamy, but because I had conceived him to be such another musty old fellow as my uncle.

Well, but let us leave old saws to old men. — What signifies thy tedious whining over thy departing relation? Is it not generally agreed that he cannot recover? Will it not be kind in thee to put him out of his misery? I hear that he is pestered still with visits from doctors, and apothecaries, and surgeons; that they cannot cut so deep as the mortification has gone; and that in every visit, in every scarification, inevitable death is pronounced upon him. Why then do they keep tormenting him? Is it not to take away more of his living fleece than of his dead flesh? — When a man is given over, the fee should surely be refused. Are they not now robbing his heirs? — What hast thou to do, if the will be as thou'dst have it? — He sent for thee [did he not?] to close his eyes. He is but an *uncle*, is he?

Let me see, if I mistake not, it is in the Bible, or some other good book; can it be in Herodotus? — O, I believe it is in Josephus; a half-sacred and half-profane author. He tells us of a king of Syria, put out of his pain by his prime minister, or one who deserved to be so for his contrivance. The story says, if I am right, that he spread a wet cloth over his face, which killing him, he reigned in his place. A notable fellow! Perhaps this wet cloth, in the original, is what we now call *laudanum*; a potion that overspreads the faculties, as the wet cloth did the face of the royal patient; and the translator knew not how to render it.

But how like a forlorn varlet thou subscribest, *Thy melancholy friend*, J. BELFORD! Melancholy! for what? To stand by, and see fair play between an old man and death? I thought thou hadst been more of a man, thou that art not afraid of an acute death, a sword's point, to be so plaguily hipped at the consequences of a chronical one! — What though the scarificators work upon him day by day? It is only upon a *caput mortuum*: and pr'ythee *go to*, to use the *stylum veterum*, and learn of the *royal butchers;* who for sport (an hundred times worse men than thy Lovelace) widow ten thousand at a brush, and make twice as many fatherless — learn of *them*, I say, how to support a *single* death.

But art thou sure, Jack, it is a mortification? — My uncle once gave promises of such a root-and-branch distemper; but alas! it turned to a smart gout-fit; and *I* had the mortification instead of *him*. - - I have heard that bark in proper doses will arrest a mortification in its progress, and at last cure it. Let thy uncle's surgeon know, that it is worth more than his ears, if he prescribe one grain of the bark.

I wish *my* uncle had given *me* the opportunity of setting thee a better example: thou should'st have seen what a brave fellow I had been. And had I had occasion to write, my conclusion would have been this: "I hope the old Trojan's happy. In that hope I am so: and

"Thy rejoicing friend,
"R. LOVELACE."

Dwell not always, Jack, upon one subject. Let me have poor Belton's story. The sooner the better. If I can be of service to him, tell him, he may command me either in purse or person. Yet the former with a freer will than the latter: for how can I leave my goddess? But I'll issue my commands to my other vassals to attend thy summons.

If ye want *head*, let *me* know. If not, my quota on this occasion is *money*.

LETTER XCVI.
Mr. Belford to Robert Lovelace, Esq.

Saturday, May 20.

NOT one word will I reply to such an abandoned wretch as thou hast shewn thyself to be in thine of last night. I will leave the lady to the protection of that power who only can work miracles; and to her own merits. Still I have hopes that these will have her.

I will proceed, as thou desirest, to poor Belton's case; and the rather, as it has thrown me into such a train of thinking upon our past lives, our present courses, and our future views, as may be of service to both, if I can give due weight to the reflections that arise from it.

The poor man made me a visit on *Thursday*, in this my melancholy attendance. He began with complaints of his ill health and spirits, his hectic cough, and his increased malady of spitting blood; and then led to his story.

A confounded one it is; and which highly aggravates his other maladies: for it has come out, that his Thomasine (who, truly, would be new christened, you know, that her name might be nearer in sound to the christian name of the man whom she pretended to doat upon) has for many years carried on an intrigue with a fellow who had been hostler to her father (an innkeeper at Dorking); of whom, at the expense of poor Belton, she has made a gentleman; and managed it so, that having the art to make herself his cashier, she has been unable to account for large sums, which he thought forthcoming at demand, and had trusted to her custody, in order to pay off a mortgage upon his paternal estate in Kent, which his heart had run upon leaving clear, but which cannot now be done, and will soon be foreclosed. And yet she has so long passed for his wife, that he knows not what to resolve upon about her; nor about the two boys he was so fond of, supposing them to be his; whereas now he begins to doubt his share in them.

So KEEPING don't do, Lovelace. 'Tis *not* the eligible life. "A man may *keep a woman*," said the poor fellow to me, "but *not his estate!* — Two interests! — Then my tottering fabric!" pointing to his emaciated carcase.

We do well to value ourselves upon our *liberty*, or, to speak more properly, upon the liberties we take! We had need to run down matrimony as we do, and to make that state the subject of our frothy jests; when we frequently render

woman is in no danger of incurring (*legally*, at least) that guilt; and you yourself have broken through and overthrown in her all the fences and boundaries of moral honesty, and the modesty and reserves of her sex: and what tie shall hold her against inclination or interest? And what shall deter an attempter?

While a husband has this security from *legal* sanctions, that if his wife be detected in a criminal conversation with a man of fortune, (the *most* likely by bribes to seduce her) he may recover very great damages, and procure a divorce besides: which, to say nothing of the ignominy, is a consideration that must have some force upon *both* parties. And a wife must be vicious indeed, and a reflection upon a man's own choice, who, for the sake of change, and where there are no qualities to seduce, nor affluence to corrupt, will run so many hazards to injure her husband in the tenderest of all points.

But there are difficulties in procuring a divorce [and so there ought] — and none, says the rake, in parting with a mistress whenever you suspect her; or whenever you are weary of her, and have a mind to change her for another.

But must not the man be a brute indeed, who can cast off a woman whom he has seduced, [if he take her from the town, that's another thing] without some flagrant reason; something that will better justify him to *himself*, as well as to *her*, and to the *world*, than mere *power* and *novelty?*

But I don't see, if we judge by the *fact*, and by the *practice* of all we have been acquainted with of the *keeping-class*, that we know how to part with them when we have them.

That we know we *can* if we *will*, is all we have for it: and this leads us to bear many things from a *mistress* which we would not from a *wife*. But, if we are good-natured and humane: if the woman has *art* [and what woman *wants* it who has fallen by *art?* and to whose precarious situation *art* is so necessary?]: if you have given her the credit of being called by your name: if you have a settled place of abode, and have received and paid visits in her company, as your wife: if she has brought you children — you will allow that these are strong obligations upon you, in the world's eye, as well as to your own heart, against tearing yourself from such close connections. She will stick to you as your skin: and it will be next to flaying yourself to cast her off.

Even if there be *cause* for it, by infidelity, she will have managed ill if she have not her defenders. Nor did I ever know a cause or a person so *bad*, as to want advocates, either from ill-will to the one or pity to the other: and you will then be thought a hard-hearted miscreant: and even were she to go off without credit to *herself*, she will leave *you* as little, especially with all those whose good opinion a man would wish to cultivate.

Well, then, shall this poor privilege, that we may part with a woman, if we *will*, be deemed a balance for the other inconveniences? Shall it be thought by *us*, who are men of family and fortune, an equivalent for giving up *equality of degree;* and taking for the partner of our bed, and very probably more than the partner in our estates, (to the breach of all family-rule and order) a low-born, a low-educated creature, who has not brought any thing into the common stock; and can possibly make no returns for the solid benefits she receives, but those libidinous ones, which a man cannot boast of, but to *his* disgrace, nor think of, but to the shame of *both?*

Moreover, as the man advances in years, the fury of his libertinism will go off. He will have different aims and pursuits, which will diminish his appetite to ranging, and make such a regular life as the matrimonial and family life palatable to him, and every day more palatable.

If he has children, and has reason to think them *his*, and if his lewd courses have left him *any* estate, he will have cause to regret the *restraint* his boasted *liberty* has laid him under, and the valuable *privilege* it has deprived him of; when he finds, that it must descend to some relation, for whom, whether near or distant, he cares not one farthing; and who, perhaps, (if a man of virtue) has held him in the utmost contempt for his dissolute life.

And were we to suppose his estate in his power to bequeath as he pleases, why should a man resolve for the gratifying of his foolish humour only, to bastardize his race? Why should he wish to expose his children to the scorn and insults of the rest of the world? Why should he, whether they are sons or daughters, lay them under the necessity of complying with proposals of marriage, either *inferior as to fortune, unequal as to age?* Why should he deprive the children he loves, who themselves may be guilty of no fault, of the respect they would wish to have, and to deserve, and of the opportunity of associating themselves with *proper*, that is to say, with *reputable* company? And why should he make them think themselves under obligation to every person of character who will vouchsafe to visit them? What little reason, in a word, would such children have to bless their father's obstinate defiance of the laws and customs of his country; and for giving them a mother, of whom they could not think with honour; to whose *crime* it was that they owed their very beings, and whose example it was their duty to shun?

If the education and morals of these children are left to chance, as too generally they are, (for the man who has humanity and a feeling heart, and who is capable of fondness for his offspring, I take it for granted, will marry) the case is still worse; his crime is perpetuated, as I may say, by his children: and the sea, the army, perhaps the highway, for the boys; the common for the girls; too often point out the way to a worse catastrophe.

What, therefore, upon the whole, do we get by treading in these crooked paths, but danger, disgrace, and a too late repentance?

And, after all, do we not frequently become the cullies of our own libertinism; sliding into the very state with those half-worn-out doxies, which perhaps we might have entered into with their ladies; at least with their superiors both in degree and fortune? And all the time lived handsomely like ourselves; not sneaking into holes and corners; and, when we crept abroad with our women, looking about us, and at every one that passed us, as if we were confessedly accountable to the censures of all honest people.

My cousin Tony Jenyns thou knewest. He had not the actively mischievous spirit that thou, Belton, Mowbray, Tourville, and *myself*, have: but he imbibed the same notions we do, and carried them into practice.

How did he prate against wedlock! How did he strut about as a *wit* and a *smart!* And what a *wit* and a *smart* did all the boys and girls of our family (myself among the rest, then an urchin) think him for the airs he gave himself? — Marry! No, not for the world; what man of sense would bear the insolences, the petulances, the expensiveness of a wife! He could not for the heart of him think it tolerable, that a woman of *equal* rank and fortune, and, as it might happen, *superior* talents to his own, should look upon herself to have a right to share the benefit of that fortune which she brought him.

So, after he had fluttered about the town for two or three years, in all which time he had a better opinion of himself than any body else had, what does he do, but enter upon an affair with his fencing-master's daughter?

He succeeds; takes private lodgings for her at Hackney; visits her by stealth; both of them tender of reputations that were *extremely* tender, but which neither had quite given up; for rakes of either sex are always the last to condemn or cry down themselves: visited by nobody, nor visiting; the life of a thief, or of a man beset by creditors, afraid to look out of his own house, or to be seen abroad with her. And thus he went on for twelve years, and, though he had a good estate, hardly making both ends meet; for though no glare, there was no economy; and besides, he had every year a child, and very fond of his children was he. But none of them lived above three years: and being now, on the death of the dozenth, grown as dully sober as if he had been a real husband, his good Mrs. Thomas (for he had not permitted her to take his own name) prevailed upon him to think-the loss of her children a judgment upon the parents for their wicked way of life [a time will come, Lovelace, if we live to advanced years, in which reflection will take hold of the enfeebled mind]; and then it was not difficult for his woman to induce him, by way of compounding with heaven, to marry her. When this was done, he had leisure to sit down and contemplate; and to recollect the many offers of persons of family and fortune which he had declined in the prime of life: his expenses *equal* at least; his reputation not only *less* but *lost:* his enjoyment *stolen:* his partnership *unequal*, and such as he had always been ashamed of. But the women said, that after twelve or thirteen years' cohabitation, Tony did an honest thing by her. And that was all my poor cousin got by making his old mistress his new wife — not a drum, not a trumpet, not a fife, not a tabret, nor the expectation of a new joy, to animate him on?

What Belton will do with his Thomasine I know not; nor care I to advise him: for I see the poor fellow does not like that any body should curse her but himself. This he does very heartily. And so low is he reduced, that he blubbers over the reflection upon his past fondness for her cubs, and upon his present doubts of their being his: "What a d—n'd thing is it, Belford, if Tom and Hal should be the hostler dog's puppies, and not mine!"

Very true! and I think the strong health of the chubby-faced muscular whelps confirms the too great probability. But I say not so to him.

You, he says, are such a gay lively mortal, that this sad tale would make no impression upon you: especially now, that your whole heart is engaged as it is. *Mowbray* would be too violent upon it: he has not, he says, a feeling heart. *Tourville* has no discretion: and, a pretty jest! although he and his Thomasine lived without reputation in the world, (people guessing that they were not married, notwithstanding she went by his name) yet "he would not *too much* discredit the *cursed ingrate* neither!"

Could a man act a weaker part had he been really married; and were he sure he was going to separate from the mother of his own children?

I leave this as a lesson upon thy heart, without making any application: only with this remark, "That after we libertines have indulged our licentious appetites, reflecting (in the conceit of our vain hearts) both with our lips and by our lives, upon our ancestors and the good old ways, we find out, when we come to years of discretion, if we live till then, (what all who knew us found out before, that is to say; we find out) our own despicable folly: that those good old ways would have been the best for *us*, as well as for the rest of the world; and that in every step we have deviated from them, we have only

LETTER XCVII.
Mr. Lovelace to John Belford, Esq.
Saturday, May 20.

I AM pleased with the sober reflection with which thou concludest thy last: and I thank thee for it. Poor Belton: — I did not think his Thomasine would have proved so very a devil. But this must ever-lastingly be the risk of a keeper, who takes up with a low-bred girl. This I never did. Nor had I occasion to do it. Such a one as *I*, Jack, needed only, till now, to shake the stateliest tree, and the mellowed fruit dropt into my mouth: — always of Montaigne's taste, thou knowest — thought it a glory to subdue a girl of family. More truly delightful to me the seduction-progress than the crowning act: for that's a vapour, a bubble! And most cordially do I thank thee for thy indirect hint, that I am right in my present pursuit.

From such a woman as Miss Harlowe a man is secured from all the inconveniences thou expatiatest upon.

Once more, therefore, do I thank thee, Belford, for thy approbation: — a man need not, as thou sayest, sneak into *holes* and *corners*, and shun the day, in the company of such *a woman as this*. How friendly in thee thus to abet the favourite purpose of my heart! — Nor can it be a disgrace to me, to permit *such a lady* to be called by my name! — Nor shall I be at all concerned about the *world's* censure, if I live to the *years of discretion* which thou mentionest, should I be taken in, and prevailed upon to tread with her the good old path of my ancestors.

A blessing on thy heart, thou honest fellow! I *thought* thou wert in jest, and but acquitting thyself of an engagement to Lord M. when thou wert pleading for matrimony in behalf of this lady! — It could not be principle, I knew, in thee: it could not be compassion — a little *envy* indeed I suspected! — But now I see thee once more thyself: and once more, say I, a blessing on thy heart, thou true friend and very honest fellow!

Now will I proceed with courage in all my schemes, and oblige thee with the continued narrative of my progressions towards bringing them to effect! — But I could not forbear to interrupt my story to shew my gratitude.

LETTER XCVIII.
Mr. Lovelace to John Belford, Esq.

AND now will I favour thee with a brief account of our present situation.

From the highest to the lowest we are all extremely happy. — *Dorcas* stands well in her lady's graces. *Polly* has asked her advice in relation to a courtship-affair of her own. No oracle ever gave better. *Sally* has had a quarrel with her woollen-draper: and made my charmer lady-chancellor in it. She blamed Sally for behaving tyrannically to a man who loves her. Dear creature! to stand against a glass, and to shut her eyes because she will not see her face in it!—Mrs. *Sinclair* has paid *her* court to so unerring a judge, by requesting her advice with regard to both nieces.

This is the way we have been in for several days with the people below. Yet *sola* generally at her meals, and seldom at other times in their company. They now, used to her ways, [*perseverance must conquer*] never press her; so when they meet all is civility on both sides. Even married people, I believe, Jack, prevent abundance of quarrels, by seeing one another *but seldom*.

But how stands it between thyself and the lady, methinks thou askest, since her abrupt departure from thee, and undutiful repulse of Wednesday morning?

Why, pretty well in the main. Nay, *very* well. For why? The dear saucy-face knows not how to help herself. Can fly to no other protection. And has, besides, overheard a conversation [who would have thought she had been so near?] which passed between Mrs. Sinclair, Miss Martin, and myself, that very Wednesday afternoon, which has set her heart at ease with respect to several doubtful points.

Such as, particularly, "Mrs. Fretchville's unhappy state of mind—most humanely pitied by Miss Martin, who knows her very well—the husband she has lost, and herself (as Sally says) lovers from their cradles. Pity from one begets pity from another, be the occasion for it either strong or weak; and so many circumstances were given to poor Mrs. Fretchville's distress, that it was impossible but my beloved must *extremely* pity *her* whom the less tender-hearted Miss Martin *greatly* pitied.

"My Lord M.'s gout his only hindrance from visiting my spouse. Lady Betty and Miss Montague soon expected in town.

"My earnest desire is signified to have my spouse receive those ladies in her own house, if Mrs. Fretchville would but know her own mind; and I pathetically lamented the delay occasioned by her not knowing it.

"My intention to stay at Mrs. Sinclair's, *as I said I had told them before*, while my spouse resides in her own house, (when Mrs. Fretchville could be brought to quit it) in order to gratify her utmost punctilio.

"My passion for my beloved (which, as I told them in a high and fervent accent, was the truest that man could have for woman) I boasted of. It was, in short, I said, of the *true Platonic kind;* or I had no notion of what Platonic love was."

So it is, Jack; and must end as Platonic love generally does end.

"Sally and Mrs. Sinclair next praised, *but not grossly*, my beloved. Sally particularly admired her purity; called it exemplary; yet (to avoid suspicion) expressed her thoughts that she was *rather over-nice*, if she might presume to say so *before me*. But, nevertheless, she applauded me for the strict observation I made of my vow.

"I more freely blamed her reserves to me; called her cruel; inveighed against her relations; doubted her love. Every favour I asked of her denied me. Yet my behaviour to her as pure and delicate when alone as when before them — hinted at something that had passed between us that very day, that shewed her indifference to me in so strong a light, that I could not bear it. But that I would ask her for her company to the play of *Venice Preserved*, given out for Saturday night as a benefit play; the prime actors to be in it; and this to see if I were to be denied every favour. — Yet, for my own part, I *loved not tragedies;* though she did for the sake of the instruction, the warning, and the example generally given in them.

"I had too much *feeling*, I said. There was enough in the world to make our hearts sad, without carrying grief into our diversions, and making the distresses of others our own."

True enough, Belford; and I believe, generally speaking, that all the men of our cast are of my mind — they love not any tragedies but those in which they themselves act the parts of tyrants and executioners; and, afraid to trust themselves with serious and solemn reflections, run to comedies, in order to laugh away compunction on the distresses they have occasioned, and to find examples of men as immoral as themselves. For very few of our comic performances, as thou knowest, give us good ones. — I answer, however, for myself — yet thou, I think, on recollection, lovest to deal in the *lamentable*.

Sally answered for Polly, who was absent; Mrs. Sinclair for herself, and for all her acquaintance, even for Miss Partington, in preferring the comic to the tragic scenes. — And I believe they are right; for the devil's in it, if a confided-in rake does not give a girl enough of tragedy in his comedy.

"I asked Sally to oblige my fair one with her company. She was engaged [that was right, thou'lt suppose]. I asked Mrs. Sinclair's leave for Polly. To be sure, she answered, Polly would think it an honour to attend Mrs. Lovelace: but the poor thing was tender-hearted; and as the tragedy was deep, would weep herself blind.

"Sally, meantime, objected Singleton, that *I* might answer the objection, and save my beloved the trouble of making it, or debating the point with me; and on this occasion I regretted that her brother's projects were not laid aside; since, if they had been given up, I would have gone in person to bring up the ladies of my family to attend my spouse.

"I then from a letter just before received from one in her father's family, warned them of a person who had undertaken to find us out, and whom I thus in writing (having called for pen and ink) described that they might arm all the family against him" — "A sun-burnt, pock-fretten sailor, ill-looking, big-boned; his stature about six feet; an heavy eye, an over-hanging brow, a deck-treading stride in his walk; a couteau generally by his side; lips parched from his gums, as if by staring at the sun in hot climates; a brown coat; a coloured handkerchief about his neck; an oaken plant in his hand near as long as himself, and proportionably thick."

"No questions asked by this fellow must be answered. They should call *me* to him. But not let my beloved know a little of this, so long as it could be helped. And I added, that if her brother or Singleton came, and if they behaved civilly, I would, for *her sake*, be civil to *them*: and in this case, she had nothing to do, but to own her marriage, and there could be no pretence for violence on either side. But most fervently I swore, that if she were *conveyed away*, either by *persuasion* or *force*, I would directly, *on missing her but one day*, go to demand her at Harlowe Place, whether she were there or not; and if I recovered not a sister I would have a brother; and should find out a captain of a ship as well as he."

And now, Jack, dost thou think she'll attempt to get from me, do what I will?

"Mrs. Sinclair began to be afraid of mischief in her house — I was apprehensive that she would overdo the matter, and be out of character, I therefore winked at her. She primmed; nodded, to shew she took me; twanged out a heigh-ho through her nose, lapped one horse lip over the other, and was silent."

Here's preparation, Belford! — dost think I will throw it all away for any thing thou canst say, or Lord M. write? — *no indeed* — as my charmer says, when she bridles.

* * *

AND what must necessarily be the consequence of all this with regard to my beloved's behaviour to me? canst thou doubt, that it was all complaisance next time she admitted me into her presence?

Thursday we were very happy. All the morning *extremely* happy. I kissed her charming hand. — I need not describe to thee her hand and arm. When thou sawest her, I took notice that thy eyes dwelt upon them whenever thou couldst spare them from that beauty spot of wonders, her face — *fifty* times kissed her hand, I believe — once her cheek, intending her lip, but so rapturously, that she could not help seeming angry.

Had she not thus kept me at arms-length; had she not denied me those innocent liberties which our sex, from step to step, aspire to; could I but have gained access to her in her hours of heedlessness and dishabille [for full dress creates dignity, augments consciousness, and compels distance]; we had been familiarised to each other long ago. But keep her up ever so late; meet her ever so early; by breakfast-time, she is dressed for the day; and at her *earliest hour,* as nice as others dressed. All her forms thus kept up, wonder not that I have made so little progress in the proposed trial. — But how must all this distance stimulate!

Thursday morning, as I said, we were extremely happy — about *noon,* she numbered the hours she had been with me; all of them to me but as one minute; and desired to be left to herself. I was loth to comply: but observing the sunshine begin to shut in, I yielded.

I dined out. Returning, I talked of the house, and of Mrs. Fretchville — had seen Mennel — had pressed him to get the widow to quit. She pitied Mrs. Fretchville [another good effect of the overheard conversation] — had written to Lord M.; expected an answer soon from him. I was admitted to sup with her. I urged for her approbation or correction of my written terms. She again promised an answer as soon as she heard from Miss Howe.

Then I pressed for her company to the play on Saturday night. She made objections, as I had foreseen: her brother's projects, warmth of the weather, &c. But in such a manner, as if half afraid to disoblige me [another happy effect of the overheard conversation.] I soon got over these therefore; and she consented to favour me.

Friday passed as the day before.

Here were two happy days to both. Why cannot I make every day equally happy? it looks *as if it were in my power to do so.* Strange, I should thus delight in teasing a woman, I so dearly love! I must, I doubt, have something in my temper like Miss Howe, who loves to plague the man who puts himself in her power. — But I could not do thus by such an angel as this, did I not believe, that after her probation time shall be expired, and if she be not to be brought to *cohabitation* (my darling view) I shall reward her as she wishes.

Saturday is half-over. We are equally happy — Preparing for the play. Polly has offered her company, and is accepted. I have directed her where to weep: and this not only to shew her humanity, [a weeping eye indicates a gentle heart] but to have a pretence to hide her face with her fan or handkerchief. — Yet Polly is far from being every man's girl; and we shall sit in the gallery green box.

The woes of others, so well represented as those of Belvidera particularly will be, must, I hope, unlock and open my charmer's heart. Whenever I have been able to prevail upon a girl to permit me to attend her to a play, I have thought myself sure of her. The female heart (all gentleness and harmony by nature) expands, and forgets its forms, when its attention is carried out of itself at an agreeable or affecting entertainment — music, and perhaps a collation afterwards, co-operating. Indeed, I have no hope of such an effect here; but I have more than one end to answer by getting her to a play. To name but one—Dorcas has a *master-key*, as I have told thee. — But it were worth while to carry her to the play of *Venice Preserved*, were it but to shew her, that there have been, and may be, much deeper distresses than she can possibly know.

Thus exceedingly happy are we at present. I hope we shall not find any of Nat. Lee's left-handed gods at work, to dash our bowl of joy with wormwood.

R. LOVELACE.

LETTER XCIX.
Miss Clarissa Harlowe to Miss Howe.

Friday, May 19.

I WOULD not, if I could help it, be so continually brooding over the dark and gloomy face of my condition [all nature, you know, my dear, and every thing in it, has a bright and a gloomy side], as to be thought unable to enjoy a more hopeful prospect. And this, not only for my own sake, but for yours, who take such a generous concern in all that befals me.

Let me tell you then, my dear, that I have known four-and-twenty hours together not unhappy ones, my situation considered.

She then gives the particulars of the conversation which she had overheard between Mr. Lovelace, Mrs. Sinclair, and Miss Martin; but accounts more minutely than he had done for the opportunity she had of overhearing it, unknown to them.

She gives the reasons she has to be pleased with what she heard from each; but is shocked at the measure he is resolved to take, if he misses her but for one day. Yet is pleased that he proposes to avoid aggressive violence, if her brother and he meet in town.

Even Dorcas, says she, appears less exceptionable to me than before, and I cannot but pity her for her neglected education, as it is matter of so much regret to *herself:* else, there would not be much in it; as the low and illiterate are the most useful people in the commonwealth (since such constitute the labouring part of the public); and as a lettered education but too generally sets people above those servile offices by which the business of the world is carried on. Nor have I any doubt but there are, take the world through, twenty happy people among the unlettered, to one among those who have had a school education.

This, however, concludes not against learning or letters; since one would wish to lift to some little distinction, and more genteel usefulness, those who have capacity, and whose parentage one respects, or whose services one would wish to reward.

Were my mind quite at ease, I could enlarge, perhaps not unusefully, upon this subject; for I have considered it with as much attention as my years, and little experience and observation, will permit.

But the extreme illiterateness and indocility of this maid are surprising, considering that she wants not inquisitiveness, appears willing to learn, and, in other respects, has quick parts. This confirms to me what I have heard remarked, that there is a *docible season*, a learning-time, as I may say, for every person, in which the mind may be led step by step, from the lower to the higher, (year by year) to improvement. How industriously ought these seasons, as they offer, to be taken hold of by tutors, parents, and other friends, to whom the cultivation of the genius of children and youth is committed; since, once elapsed, and no foundation laid, they hardly ever return! — And yet it must be 'confessed, that there are some geniuses, which, like some fruits, ripen not till late. And industry and perseverance will do prodigious things — but for a learner to have those first rudiments to master at twenty years of age, suppose, which others are taught, and they themselves might have attained, at ten, what an up-hill labour?

These kind of observations you have always wished me to intersperse, as they arise to my thoughts. But it is a sign that my prospects are a little mended, or I should not, among so many more interesting ones, that my mind has been of late filled with, have had heart's ease enough to make them.

Let me give you my *reflections* on my more hopeful prospects.

I am now, in the first place, better able to account for the delays about the house than I was before — poor Mrs. Fretchville — though I know her not, I pity her! — Next, it looks well, that he had apprised the women (before this conversation with them) of his intention to stay in this house, after I was removed to the other. By the tone of his voice he seemed concerned for the appearance this new delay would have with me.

So handsomely did Miss Martin express herself of me, that I am sorry, methinks, that I judged so hardly of her, when I first came hither — free people may go a great way, but not all the way; and as such are generally unguarded, precipitate, and thoughtless, the same quickness, changeableness, and *suddenness* of spirit, as I may call it, may intervene (if the heart be not corrupted) to recover them to thought and duty.

His reason for declining to go in person to bring up the ladies of his family, while my brother and Singleton continue their machinations, carries no bad face with it; and one may the rather allow for *their* expectations, that so proud a spirit as his should attend them for this purpose, as he speaks of them sometimes as persons of punctilio.

Other reasons I will mention for my being easier in my mind than I was before I overheard this conversation.

Such, as, the advice he has received in relation to Singleton's mate; which agrees but too well with what you, my dear, wrote to me in your's of May the 10th.*

His not intending to acquaint *me* with it.

His cautions to the servants about the sailor, if he should come, and make inquiries about us.

His resolution to avoid violence, were he to fall in either with my brother, or this Singleton; and the easy method he has chalked out, in this case, to prevent mischief; since I need only *not to deny* my being his. But yet I should be exceedingly unhappy in my own opinion to be driven into such a tacit acknowledgment to any new persons, till I am so, although I have been led (so much against my liking) to give countenance to the belief of the persons below that we are married.

I think myself obliged, from what passed between Mr. Lovelace and me on Wednesday, and from what I overheard him say, to consent to go with him to the play; and the rather, as he had the discretion to propose one of the nieces to accompany me.

I cannot but acknowledge that I am pleased to find that he has actually written to Lord M.

I have promised to give Mr. Lovelace an answer to his proposals as soon as I have heard from you, my dear, on the subject.

I hope that in my next letter I shall have reason to confirm these favourable appearances. Favourable I must think them in the wreck I have suffered.

I hope, that in the trial which you hint may happen between *me* and *myself* (as you* express it) if he should so behave, as to oblige me to leave him, I shall be able to act in such a manner, as to bring no discredit upon myself in your eye: and that is all now that I have to wish for. But if I value him so much as you are pleased to suppose I do, the trial which you imagine will be so difficult to me, will not, I conceive, be upon getting from him, when the means to effect my escape are lent me; but how I shall behave when got from him: and if, like the Israelites of old, I shall be so weak as to wish to return to my Egyptian bondage.

I think it will not be amiss, notwithstanding the present favourable appearances, that you should perfect the scheme (whatever it be) which you tell me** you have thought of, in order to procure for me an asylum, in case of necessity. Mr. Lovelace is certainly a deep and dangerous man; and it is therefore but prudence to be watchful, and to be provided against the worst. Lord bless me, my dear, how am I reduced! — Could I ever have thought to be in such a situation, as to be obliged to stay with a man, of whose honour by me I could have but the *shadow* of a doubt! — but I will look forward, and hope the best.

* See p. 267.

* See p. 302.
** See p. 301, 302.

I am certain that your letters are safe. Be perfectly easy therefore on that head.

Mr. Lovelace will never be out of my company by his good will, otherwise I have no doubt that I am mistress of my goings-out and comings-in; and did I think it needful, and were I not afraid of my brother and Captain Singleton, I would oftener put it to trial.

LETTER C.
Miss Howe to Miss Clarissa Harlowe.
Saturday, May 20.

I DID not know, my dear, that you deferred giving an answer to Mr. Lovelace's proposals till you had my opinion of them. A particular hand, occasionally going to town, will leave this at Wilson's, that no delay may be made on that account.

I never had any doubt of the man's justice and generosity in matters of settlement: and all his relations are as noble in their spirits as in their descent: but *now*, it may not be amiss for you to wait, to see what returns my lord makes to his letter of invitation.

The scheme I think of is this:

There is a person, whom I believe you have seen with me; her name Townsend, who is a great dealer in Indian silks, Brussels and French laces, cambrics, linen, and other valuable goods: which she has a way of coming at, duty-free; and has a great vend for them (and for other curiosities which she imports) in the private families of the gentry round us.

She has her days of being in town, and then is at a chamber she rents at an inn in Southwark, where she keeps patterns of all her silks, and much of her portable goods, for the conveniency of her London customers. But her place of residence, and where she has her principal warehouse, is at Deptford, for the opportunity of getting her goods on shore.

She was first brought to me by my mother, to whom she was recommended on the supposal of my speedy marriage, "that I might have an opportunity to be as fine as a princess," was my mother's expression, "at a moderate expense."

Now, my dear, I must own, that I do not love to encourage these contraband traders. What is it, but bidding defiance to the laws of our country, when we do; and hurting fair traders; and at the same time robbing our prince of his legal due, to the diminution of those duties which possibly must be made good by new levies upon the public.

But, however, Mrs. Townsend and I, though I have not yet had dealings with her, are upon a very good foot of understanding. She is a sensible woman; she has been abroad, and often goes abroad in the way of her business, and gives very entertaining accounts of all she has seen. And having applied to me, to recommend her to you, (as it is her view to be known to young ladies who are likely to change their condition) I am sure I can engage her to give you protection at her house at Deptford; which, she says, is a populous village; and one of the last, I should think, in which you would be sought for. She is not much there, you will believe, by the course of her dealings, but, no doubt, must have somebody on the spot, in whom she can confide; and there, perhaps, you might be safe, till your cousin comes. And I should not think it amiss that you write to him immediately. I cannot suggest to you *what* you should write. That must be left to your own discretion. For you will be afraid, no doubt, of the consequence of a variance between the two men.

But, notwithstanding all this, and were I sure of getting you safely out of his hands, I will nevertheless forgive you, were you to make all up with him, and marry to-morrow. Yet I will proceed with my projected scheme in relation to Mrs. Townsend; though I hope there will be no occasion to prosecute it, since your prospects seem to be changed, and since you have had *twenty-four not unhappy hours together*. How my indignation rises for this poor consolation in the courtship [*courtship* must I call it?] of such a woman! let me tell you, my dear, that were you once your own absolute and independent mistress, I should be tempted, notwithstanding all I have written, to wish you the wife of any man in the world, rather than the wife either of Lovelace or of Solmes.

Mrs. Townsend, as I have recollected, has two brothers, each a master of a vessel; and who knows, as she and they have concerns together, but that, in case of need, you may have a whole ship's crew at your devotion? If Lovelace give you cause to leave him, take no thought for the people at Harlowe Place. Let *them* take care of one another. It is a care they are *used* to. The law will help to secure *them*. The wretch is no assassin, no night-murderer. He is an *open*, because a *fearless* enemy; and should he attempt any thing that would make him obnoxious to the laws of society, you might have a fair riddance of him, either by flight or the gallows; no matter which.

Had you not been so minute in your account of the circumstances that attended the opportunity you had of overhearing the dialogue between Mr. Lovelace and two of the women, I should have thought the conference contrived on purpose for your ear.

I shewed Mr. Lovelace's proposals to Mr. Hickman, who had chambers once in Lincoln's-Inn, being designed for the law had his elder brother lived. He looked so wise, so proud, and so important, upon the occasion; and wanted to take so much consideration about them — would take them home, if I pleased — and weigh them well — and so forth — and the like — and all that — that I had no patience with him, and snatched them back with anger.

O dear! — to be so angry, an't please me, for his zeal! —

Yes, zeal without knowledge, I said — like most other zeals — if there were no objections that struck him at once, there were none.

So *hasty*, dearest madam! —

And so *slow*, un-dearest sir, I could have said — but SURELY, said I, with a look which implied, *Would you rebel, sir!*

He begged my pardon — *saw* no objection, indeed! — but might he be allowed once more —

No matter — no matter — I would have shewn them to my mother, I said, who though of no inn of court, knew more of these things than half the lounging lubbers of them; and that at first sight — only that she would have been angry at the confession of our continued correspondence.

But my dear, let the articles be drawn up, and engrossed; and solemnize upon them; and there's no more to be said.

Let me add, that the sailor-fellow has been tampering with my Kitty, and offered a bribe, to find where to direct to you. Next time he comes, I will have him laid hold of; and if I can get nothing out of him, will have him drawn through one of our deepest fish-ponds. His attempt to corrupt a servant of mine will justify my orders.

I send this letter away directly. But will follow it by another; which shall have for its subject only my mother, myself, and your uncle Antony. And as your prospects are more promising than they have been, I will endeavour to make you smile upon the occasion. For you will be pleased to know, that my mother has had a formal tender from that grey goose, which may make her skill in settlements useful to herself, were she to encourage it.

May your prospects be still more and more happy, prays

Your own
ANNA HOWE.

LETTER CI.

Miss Howe to Miss Clarissa Harlowe.

Sat. Sunday, May 20, 21.

Now, my dear, for the promised subject. *You must not ask me* how I came by the *originals* [such they really are] that I am going to present you with: for my mother would not read to me those parts of your uncle's letter which bore hard upon myself, and which leave him without any title to mercy from me: nor would she let me hear but what she pleased of hers in answer; for she has condescended to answer him — with a denial, however; but such a denial as no one but an *old bachelor* would take from a widow.

Any body, except myself, who could have been acquainted with such a fal-lal courtship as this must have been had it proceeded, would have been glad it had gone on: and I dare say, but for the saucy daughter, it had. My good mamma, in that case, would have been ten years the younger for it, perhaps: and could I but have approved of it, I should have been considered by her as if ten years older than I am: since, very likely, it would have been: "We widows, my dear, know not how to keep men at a distance — so as to give them pain, in order to try their love. — You must advise me, child: you must teach me to be cruel — yet not *too* cruel neither — so as to make a man heartless, who has no time, God wot, to throw away." Then would my behaviour to Mr. Hickman have been better liked; and my mother would have bridled like her daughter.

O my dear, how might we have been diverted by the practisings for the recovery of the *long-for-gottens!* could I have been sure that it would have been in my power to have put them asunder, in the Irish style, *before they had come together*. But there's no trusting to a widow whose goods and chattels are in her own hands, addressed by an old bachelor who has *fine things*, and offers to leave her *ten thousand pounds better* than he found her, and sole mistress, besides, of all her *notables!* for these, as you will see by-and-by, are his proposals.

The old Triton's address carries the writer's marks upon the very superscription — *To the equally amiable, and worthily admired* [there's for you!] *Mrs.* ANNABELLA HOWE, *widow*, the last word added, I suppose, as *esquire* to a man, as a word of honour: or for fear the *Bella* to *Anna*, should not enough distinguish the person meant from the spinster [vain hussy you'll call me, I know]: and then follows: — *These humbly present.* — Put down as a memorandum, I presume, to make a leg, and behave handsomely, at presenting it; he intending, very probably, to deliver it himself.

And now stand by — to see

Enter OLD NEPTUNE.

His head adorned with seaweed, and a crown of cockle shells; as we see him decked out in Mrs. Robinson's ridiculous grotto.

MADAM, Monday, May 15.

I DID make a sort of resolution ten years ago never to marry. I saw in other families, where they lived *best*, you will be pleased to mark that, *queernesses* I could not away with. Then liked well enough to live single for the sake of my brother's family; and for one child in it more than the rest. But that girl has turned us all off the hinges: and why I should deny myself any comforts for them, as will not thank me for so doing, I don't know.

So much for my motives as from self and family: but the dear Mrs. Howe makes me go further.

I have a very great fortune, I bless God for it, all of my own getting, or most of it; you will be pleased to mark that; for I was the youngest brother of three. You have also, God be thanked, a great estate, which you have improved by your own frugality and wise management. Frugality, let me stop to say, is one of the greatest virtues in this mortal life, because it enables us to do justice to *all*, and puts it in our power to benefit *some* by it, as we see they *deserve*.

You have but one child; and I am a bachelor, and have never a one — all bachelors cannot say so: wherefore your daughter may be the better for me, if she will keep up with my humour; which was never thought bad: especially to my equals. Servants, indeed, I don't matter being angry with, when I please: they are paid for bearing it, and too often deserve it; as we have frequently taken notice of to one another. And, moreover, if we keep not servants at a distance, they will be familiar. I always made it a rule to find fault, whether reasonably or not, that so I might have *no reason* to find fault. Young women and servants in general (as worthy Mr. Solmes observes) are better governed by fear than love. But this my humour as to servants will not affect either you or miss, you know.

I will make very advantageous settlements; such as any common friend shall judge to be so. But must have all in my own power, while I live: because, you know, madam, it is as creditable to the wife, as to the husband, that it should be so.

I aim not at fine words. We are not children; though it may be hoped we shall have some; for I am a very healthy sound man, I bless God for it: and never brought home from my voyages and travels *a worser* constitution than I took out with me. I was none of those, I will assure you. But this I will undertake, that, if you are the survivor, you shall be at the *least* ten thousand pounds the better for me. What in the contrary case, I shall be the better for you, I leave to you, as you shall think my kindness to you shall deserve.

But one thing, madam, I shall be glad of, that Miss Howe might not live with us then [she need not know I write thus] — but go home to Mr. Hickman, as she is upon the point of marriage, I hear: and if she behaves dutifully, as she should do, to us both, she shall be the better; for so I said before.

You shall manage all things, both mine and your own; for I know but little of land-matters. All my opposition to you shall be out of love, when I think you take too much upon you for your health.

It will be very pretty for you, I should think, to have a man of experience, in a long winter's evening, to sit down by you, and tell you stories of foreign parts, and the customs of the nations he has consorted with. And I have fine curiosities of the Indian growth, such as ladies love, and some that even my niece Clary, when she was good, never saw. These, one by one as you are kind to me, (which I make no question of, because I shall be kind to you) shall all be yours. — Prettier entertainment by much, than sitting with a *too smartish* daughter, sometimes out of humour, and thwarting, and vexing, as daughters will (when women grown especially, as I have heard you often observe); and thinking their parents old, without paying them the reverence due to years; when, as in your case, I make no sort of doubt, they are young enough to wipe their noses. You understand me, madam.

As for me myself, it will be very happy, and I am delighted with the thinking of it, to have, after a pleasant ride, or so, a lady of like experience with myself to come home to, and but one interest betwixt us: to reckon up our comings-in together; and what this day and this week has produced — O how this will increase love! — most mightily will it increase it! — and I believe I should never love you enough, or be able to shew you all my love.

I hope, madam, there need not be such maiden niceties and hangings-off, as I may call them, between us, (for hanging-off sake) as that you will deny me a line or two to this proposal, written down, although you would not answer me so readily when I spoke to you; your daughter being, I suppose, hard by; for you looked round you, as if not willing to be overheard. So I resolved to write: that my writing may stand as upon record for my upright meaning; being none of your Lovelaces; you will mark that, madam; but a downright, true, honest, faithful Englishman. So hope you will not disdain to write a line or two to this my proposal: and I shall look upon it as a great honour, I will assure you, and be proud thereof. What can I say more? — For you are your own mistress, as I am my own master: and you shall *always* be your own mistress, be pleased to mark that; for so a lady of your prudence and experience ought to be.

This is a long letter. But the subject requires it; because I would not write *twice* where once would do. So would explain my sense and meaning at one time.

I have had writing in my head *two whole months, very near;* but hardly knew how (being unpractised in these matters) to begin to write. And now, good lady, be favourable to

Your most humble lover,
and obedient servant,
ANT. HARLOWE.

Here's a letter of courtship, my dear! — And let me subjoin to it, that if now, or hereafter, I should treat this hideous lover, who is so free with me to my mother with asperity, and you should be disgusted at it; I shall think you don't give me that preference in your love which you have in mine.

And now, which shall I first give you; the answer of my good mamma, or the dialogue that passed between the widow-mother, and the pert daughter, upon her letting the latter know that she had a love-letter?

I *think* you shall have the *dialogue*. But let me premise one thing; that if you *think* me too free, you must not let it run in your head that I am writing of *your* uncle, or of *my* mother; but of a couple of old lovers, no matter whom. Reverence is too apt to be forgotten by children where the *reverends* forget *first* what belongs to their own characters. A *grave* remark, and therefore at *your* service, my dear.

Well then, suppose my mamma (after twice coming into my closet to me, and as often going out, with very meaning features, and lips ready to burst open but still closed, as if by compulsion, a speech going off in a slight cough, that never went near the lungs) grown more resolute the third time of entrance, and sitting down by me, thus begin.

Mother. I have a very serious matter to talk with you upon, Nancy, when you are disposed to attend to matters *within* ourselves, and not let matters *without* ourselves wholly engross you.

A good *selv—ish* speech! — But I thought that friendship, gratitude, and humanity, were matters that ought to be deemed of the most *intimate* concern to us. But not to dwell upon words.

Daughter. I am *now* disposed to attend to every thing my mamma is *disposed* to say to me.

M. Why then, child — why then, my dear — (and the good lady's face looked *so* plump, *so* smooth, and *so* shining!) — I see you are all attention, Nancy! — But don't be surprised! — Don't be uneasy! — But I have — I have — where is it? — [and yet it lay next her heart, never another near it — so no difficulty to have found it] — I have a *letter*, my dear! — [and out from her bosom it came, but she still held it in her hand] I have a *letter*, child. — It is — it is — it is from — from a *gentleman:* I assure you! — [lifting up her head and smiling.]

There is no delight to a daughter, thought I, in such surprises as seem to be *collecting*. I will deprive my mother of the satisfaction of making a *gradual* discovery.

D. From Mr. Antony Harlowe, I suppose, madam?

M. [Lips drawn closer: eye raised] Why, my dear! — I cannot but own — but how, I wonder, could you think of Mr. Antony Harlowe?

D. How, madam, could I think of any body *else?*

M. How could you think of any body *else!* — [angrily and drawing back her face.] But do you know the subject, Nancy?

D. You have told it, madam, by your manner of breaking it to me. But, indeed, I questioned not that he had *two* motives in his visits here — both equally agreeable to me; for all that family love me dearly.

M. No love lost, if so, between you and them. But this [*rising*] is what I get — so like your papa!

— I never could open my heart to him!

D. Dear madam, excuse me. Be so good as to open your heart to *me.* — I don't love the Harlowes — But pray excuse me.

M. You have put me quite out with your forward temper! [angrily sitting down again.]

D. I will be all patience and attention. May I be allowed to read his letter?

M. I wanted to *advise* with you upon it. — But you are such a strange creature! — You are always for answering one before one speaks!

D. You'll be so good as to forgive me, madam. — But I thought every body (he among the rest) knew that you had always declared against a second marriage.

M. And so I have. But then it *was in the mind I was in.* Things may offer —

I stared.

M. Nay, don't be surprised! — I don't intend — I don't intend —

D. Not, perhaps, in *the mind you are in,* madam.

M. Pert creature! [rising again] — We shall quarrel, I see! — There's no —

D. Once more, dear madam, I beg your excuse. I will attend in silence. — Pray, madam, sit down again — pray do [she sat down] — May I see the letter?

M. No; there are some things in it you won't — like. Your temper is known, I find, to be unhappy. But nothing *bad* against you; intimations, on the contrary, that you shall be the better for him, if you oblige him.

Not a living soul but the Harlowes, I said, thought me ill-tempered: and I was contented that *they* should, who could do as they had done by the most universally acknowledged sweetness in the world.

Here we broke out a little; but, at last, she read me some of the passages in the letter. But not the *most mightily* ridiculous; yet I could hardly keep my countenance neither, especially when she came to that passage which mentions his *sound health;* and at which she stopped; she best knew why — but soon resuming —

M. Well now, Nancy, tell me what *you* think of it.

D. Nay, pray, madam, tell me what *you* think of it.

M. I expect to be answered by an answer: not by a question! — You don't *use* to be so shy to speak your mind.

D. Not when my mamma commands me to do so.

M. Then speak it now.

D. Without hearing the whole of the letter?

M. Speak to what you *have* heard.

D. Why then, madam — you won't be my mamma Howe, if you give way to it.

M. I am surprised at your assurance, Nancy!

D. I mean, madam, you will then be my mamma Harlowe.

M. O dear heart! — But I am not a fool.

And her colour went and came.

D. Dear madam [but, indeed I don't love a Harlowe — that's what I meant] I *am* your child, and *must* be your child, do what you will.

M. A very pert one, I am sure, as ever mother bore! And you *must* be my child do what I *will!* — as much as to say, you would not if you could help it, if I —

D. How could I have such a thought! — It would be *forward*, indeed, if I had — when I don't know what your *mind* is as to the proposal: — when the proposal is so very advantageous a one too.

M. [Looking a little less discomposed] Why, indeed, ten thousand pounds —

D. And to be sure of outliving him, madam!

This staggered her a little.

M. Sure! — Nobody can be sure — but it is very likely that —

D. Not at all, madam. You were going to read something (but stopped) about his constitution: his sobriety is well known — why, madam, these gentlemen who have used the sea, and been in different climates, and come home to relax from cares in a temperate one, and are sober — are the likeliest to live long of any men in the world. Don't you see that his very skin is a fortification of buff?

M. Strange creature!

D. God forbid, that any body I love and honour, should *marry a man* in hopes to *bury him* — but suppose, madam, at your time of life —

M. My time of life? — Dear heart — what is my time of life, pray?

D. Not old, madam; and that you are not, may be your danger!

As I hope to live (my dear) my mother smiled, and looked not displeased with me.

M. Why, indeed, child — why, indeed, I must needs say — and then I should choose to do nothing (froward as you are sometimes) to hurt *you*.

D. Why, as to that, madam, I can't expect that you should deprive yourself of any satisfaction —

M. Satisfaction, my dear! — I don't say it would be a *satisfaction* — but could I do any thing that would benefit *you*, it would perhaps be an inducement to hold one conference upon the subject.

D. My fortune already will be more considerable than my match, if I am to have Mr. Hickman.

M. Why so? — Mr. Hickman has fortune enough to entitle him to yours.

D. If *you* think so, that's enough.

M. Not but I should think the worse of myself, if I desired any body's death: but I think, as you say, Mr. Antony Harlowe is a healthy man, and bids fair for a long life.

Bless me, thought I, how shall I do to know whether this be an objection or a recommendation?

D. Will you forgive me, madam?

M. What would the girl say? [Looking as if she was half afraid to hear what.]

D. Only, that if you marry a man of *his* time of life, you stand two chances instead of one, to be a nurse at *your* time of life.

M. Saucebox!

D. Dear madam! — what I mean is only that these healthy old men sometimes fall into lingering disorders all at once. And I humbly conceive, that the infirmities of age are too uneasily borne with, where the remembrance of the pleasanter season comes not in to relieve the healthier of the two.

M. A strange girl! — Yet his healthy constitution an objection just now — but I always told you, that you know either too much to be argued with, or too little for me to have patience with you.

D. I can't but say, I should be glad of your commands, madam, how to behave myself to Mr. Antony Harlowe next time he comes.

M. How to behave yourself! — Why, if you retire with contempt of him, when he next comes, it will be but as you have been used to do of late.

D. Then he *is* to come again, madam?

M. And suppose he be?

D. I can't help it, if it be your pleasure, madam. He desires a line in answer to his fine letter. If he come, it will be in pursuance of that line, I presume?

M. None of your arch and pert leers, girl! — you know I won't bear them. I had a mind to hear what you would say to this matter. I have not written, but I shall presently.

D. It is mighty good of you, madam, (I hope the man will think so) to answer his first application by letter. — Pity *he should write twice, if once will do.*

M. That fetch won't let you into my intention, as to what I shall write. It is too saucily put.

D. Perhaps I can guess at your intention, madam, were it to become me so to do.

M. Perhaps I would not make a *Mr. Hickman* of any man; using him the worse for respecting me.

D. Nor, perhaps, would I, madam, if I *liked* his respects.

M. I understand you. But, perhaps, it is in *your* power to make me hearken, or not, to Mr. Harlowe.

D. Young men, who have probably a good deal of time before them, need not be in haste for a wife. Mr. Hickman, poor man! must stay his time, or take his remedy.

M. He bears more from you than a man ought.

D. Then, I doubt, he gives a reason for the treatment he meets with.

M. Provoking creature!

D. I have but one request to make to you, madam.

M. A *dutiful* one, I suppose. What is it, pray?

D. That if *you* marry, *I* may be permitted to live single.

M. Perverse creature, I'm sure!

D. How can I expect, madam, that you should refuse such terms? *Ten thousand pounds!* — at the *least* ten thousand pounds! — A very handsome proposal! — So many *fine things* too, to give you *one by one!* — Dearest madam, forgive me! — I hope it is not yet so far gone, that rallying *this man* will be thought want of duty to *you.*

M. Your rallying of *him*, and your reverence to *me*, it is plain, have *one* source.

D. I hope not, madam. But ten thousand pounds —

M. Is no unhandsome proposal.

D. Indeed I think so. I hope, madam, you will not be behindhand with him in generosity.

M. He won't be ten thousand pounds the better for me, if he survive me.

D. No, madam; he can't expect that, as you have a daughter, and as he is a *bachelor, and has not a child!* — Poor old soul!

M. Old soul, Nancy! — And thus to call him for being a bachelor, and not having a child? — Does this become you?

D. Not *old soul* for that, madam — but half the sum; five thousand pounds; you can't engage for less, madam.

M. That sum has *your* approbation then? [looking as if she'd be even with me.]

D. As he leaves it to your generosity, madam, to reward his kindness to you, it *can't* be less. — Do, dear madam, permit me, without incurring your displeasure, to call him *poor old soul* again.

M. Never was such a whimsical creature! — [turning away to hide her involuntary smile, for I believe I looked very archly! at least I intended to do so] — I hate that wicked sly look. You give yourself very free airs — don't you?

D. I snatched her hand, and kissed it — My dear mamma, be not angry with your girl! — You have told me, that you were very lively formerly.

M. Formerly! Good lack! — But were I to encourage his proposals, you may be sure, that for Mr. Hickman's sake, as well as yours, I should make a wise agreement.

D. You have both lived to years of prudence, madam.

M. Yes, I suppose I am an *old soul* too.

D. He also is for making a *wise agreement*, or hinting at once, at least.

M. Well, the short and the long I suppose is this: I have not your consent to marry.

D. Indeed, madam, you have not my *wishes* to marry.

M. Let me tell you, that if prudence consist in wishing well to *one's-self*, I see not but the *young flirts* are as prudent as the *old souls*.

D. Dear madam, would you blame me, if to wish you *not* to marry Mr. Antony Harlowe, is to wish well to *myself?*

M. You are mighty witty. I wish you were as dutiful.

D. I am more dutiful, I hope, than witty; or I should be a fool, as well as a saucebox.

M. Let *me* judge of both — parents are only to live for their children, let them deserve it or not. That's *their* dutiful notion!

D. Heaven forbid that I should

wish, if there be two interests between my mother and me, that my mother postpone her own for mine! or give up any thing that would add to the real comforts of her life, to oblige me! — Tell me, my dear mamma, if you think the closing with this proposal *will?*

M. I say, that ten thousand pounds is such an acquisition to one's family, that the *offer* of it deserves a civil return.

D. Not the *offer*, madam: the *chance* only! — If indeed you have a view to an increase of family, the money may provide.

M. You can't keep within tolerable bounds! — That saucy fleer I cannot away with —

D. Dearest, dearest madam, forgive me; but *old soul* ran in my head again! — Nay, indeed and upon my word, I will not be robbed of that charming smile! And again I kissed her hand.

M. Away, bold creature! Nothing can be so provoking as to be made to smile when one would choose, and *ought*, to be angry.

D. But, dear madam, if it be to *be*, I presume you won't think of it before *next winter*.

M. What now would the pert one be at?

D. Because he only proposes to entertain you with pretty stories of foreign nations in a winter's evening. Dearest, dearest madam, let me have the reading of his letter through. I will forgive him all he says about *me*.

M. It may be a very difficult thing, perhaps, for a man of the best sense to write a love-letter that may not be cavilled at.

D. That's because lovers in their letters hit not the medium. They either write too much nonsense, or too little. But do you call this *odd* soul's letter [no more will I call him *old* soul, if I can help it] a love-letter?

M. Well, well, I see you are averse to this matter. I am not to be your *mother; you* will live single, if *I* marry. I had a mind to see if generosity governed you in your views. I shall pursue my own inclinations; and if *they* should happen to be suitable to yours, pray let me, for the future, be better rewarded by you, than hitherto I have been.

And away she flung, without staying for a reply. — Vexed, I dare say, that I did not better approve of the proposal — were it only that the merit of denying might have been all her own, and to lay the stronger obligation upon her saucy daughter.

She wrote such a *widow-like* refusal when she went from me, as might not exclude hope in any other wooer; whatever it may do in Mr. Tony Harlowe.

It will be my part, to take care to beat her off the visit she half promises to make him, (as you will see in her answer) upon condition that he withdraw his suit. For who knows what effect the old bachelor's exotics [*far-fetched and dear-bought*, you know, is a proverb] might otherwise have upon a woman's mind, wanting nothing but unnecessaries, gewgaws, and fineries, and offered such as are not easily to be met with, or purchased?

Well, but now I give you leave to read here, in this place, the copy of my mother's answer to your uncle's letter. Not one comment will I make upon it. I know my duty better. And here, therefore, taking the liberty to hope that I may, in your present less disagreeable, though not wholly agreeable situation, provoke a smile from you, I conclude myself,

Your ever affectionate and faithful
ANNA HOWE.

MRS. ANNABELLA HOWE TO ANTONY HARLOWE, ESQ.

MR. ANTONY HARLOWE,

SIR,   Friday, May 19.

It is not usual, I believe, for our sex to answer by pen and ink the first letter on these occasions. The *first* letter! How odd is that! as if I expected another; which I do not. But then I think, as I do not judge proper to encourage your proposal, there is no reason why I should not answer in civility where so great a civility is intended. Indeed, I was always of opinion that a person was entitled to that, and not to ill-usage, because he had a respect for me. And so I have often and often told my daughter.

A woman, I think, makes but a poor figure in a man's eye afterwards, and does no reputation to her sex neither, when she behaves like a tyrant to him beforehand.

To be sure, sir, if I were to change my condition, I know not a gentleman whose proposal could be more agreeable. Your nephew and your nieces have enough without you: my daughter is a fine fortune without me, and I should take care to double it, living or dying, were I to do such a thing: so nobody need to be the worse for it. But Nancy would not think so.

All the comfort I know of in children, is that when young they do with us what they will, and all is pretty in them, to their very faults; and when they are grown up, they think their parents must live for them only, and deny themselves every thing for their sakes. I know Nancy could not bear a father-in-law. She would fly at the very thought of my being in earnest to give her one. Not that I stand in fear of my daughter neither. It is not fit I should. But she has her poor papa's spirit. A very violent one that was. And one would not choose, you know, sir, to enter into an affair, that one knows one must renounce a daughter for, or she a mother. — Except indeed one's heart were *much* in it; which, I bless God, mine is not.

I have now been a widow these ten years; nobody to control me: and I am said not to bear control: so, sir, you and I are best as we are, I believe; nay, I am sure of it; for we want not what either has: having both more than we know what to do with. And I

22*

know I could not be in the least accountable for any of my ways.

My daughter, indeed, though she is a fine girl, as girls go, [she has too much sense indeed for one of her sex; and knows she has it] is more a check to me than one would wish a daughter to be: for who would choose to be always snapping at each other? But she will soon be married; and then not living together, we shall only come together when we are pleased, and stay away when we are not; and so, like other lovers, never see any thing but the best sides of each other.

I own, for all this, that I love her dearly; and she me, I dare say: so would not wish to provoke her to do otherwise. Besides, the girl is so much regarded every where, that having lived so much of my prime a widow, I would not lay myself open to her censures, or even to her indifference, you know.

Your generous proposal requires all this explicitness. I thank you for your good opinion of me. When I know you acquiesce with this my civil refusal, [and indeed, sir, I am as much in earnest in it, as if I had spoken plainer] I don't know but Nancy and I may, with your permission, come to see your fine things; for I am a great admirer of rarities that come from abroad.

So, sir, let us only converse occasionally as we meet, as we used to do, without any other view to each other than good wishes: which I hope may not be lessened for this declining. And then I shall always think myself

Your obliged servant,
ANNABELLA HOWE.

P. S. I sent word by Mrs. Lorimer, that I would write an answer: but would take time for consideration. So hope, sir, you won't think it a slight I did not write sooner.

LETTER CII.

Mr. Lovelace to John Belford, Esq.

Sunday, May 21.

I AM too much disturbed in my mind to think of any thing but revenge; or I did intend to give thee an account of Miss Harlowe's observations on the play. *Miss Harlowe's* I say. Thou knowest that I hate the name of *Harlowe;* and I am exceedingly out of humour with her, and with her saucy friend.

What's the matter *now?* thou'lt ask.

Matter enough; for while we were at the play, Dorcas, who had her orders, and a key to her lady's chamber, as well as a master-key to her drawers and mahogany chest, closet-key and all, found means to come at some of Miss Howe's last written letters. The vigilant wench was directed to them by seeing her lady take a letter out of her stays, and put it to the others, before she went out with me — afraid, as the women upbraidingly tell me, that I should find it *there.*

Dorcas no sooner found them, than she assembled three ready writers of the *non-apparents;* and

Sally and *she*, and *they*, employed themselves with the utmost diligence in making extracts, according to former directions, from these cursed letters, for my use. *Cursed*, I may well call them — such abuses! such virulence! — O this little fury Miss Howe! — Well might her saucy friend (who has been equally free with me, or the occasion could not have been given) be so violent as she lately was, at my endeavouring to come at one of these letters.

I was sure that this fair one, at so early an age, with a constitution so firm, health so blooming, eyes so sparkling, expectations therefore so lively, and hope so predominating, could not be absolutely, and from her own vigilance, so guarded, and so apprehensive, as I have found her to be.

Sparkling eyes, Jack, when the poetical tribe have said all they can for them, are an infallible sign of a rogue, or room for a rogue, in the heart.

Thou mayest go on with thy preachments, and Lord M. with his wisdom of nations, I am now more assured of her than ever. And now my revenge is up, and joined with my love, all resistance must fall before it. And most solemnly do I swear that Miss Howe shall *come in for her snack*.

And here, just now, is another letter brought from the same little virulent devil. I hope to procure transcripts from that too, very speedily, if it be put to the rest; for the saucy fair one is resolved to go to church this morning; not so much from a spirit of devotion, I have reason to think, as to try whether she can go out without check, control, or my attendance.

* * *

I have been denied breakfasting with her. Indeed she was a little displeased with me last night: because, on our return from the play, I obliged her to pass the rest of the night with the women and me, in their parlour, and to stay till near one. She told me, at *parting*, that she expected to have the whole next day to herself. I had not read the extracts then, so was all affectionate respect, awe, and distance; for I had resolved to begin a new course, and if possible, to banish all jealousy and suspicion from her heart; and yet I had no reason to be much troubled at her past suspicions; since, if a woman will continue with a man whom she suspects, when she can get from him, or *thinks* she can, I am sure it is a very hopeful sign.

* * *

She is gone. Slipped down before I was aware. She had ordered a chair, on purpose to exclude my personal attendance. But I had taken proper precautions. Will attended her by consent; Peter, the house servant, was within Will's call.

I had, by Dorcas, represented her danger from Singleton, in order to dissuade her from going at all, unless she allowed me to attend her; but I was answered, with her usual saucy smartness, that if there were no cause of fear of being met with at the play-house, when there were but two play-houses, surely there was less at church, when there were so *many* churches. The chairmen were ordered to carry her to St. James's church.

But she would not be so careless of obliging me, if she knew what I have already come at, and how the women urge me on; for they are continually complaining of *the restraint they lie under* in their behaviour; in their attendance; neglecting *all their concerns in the front house; and keeping this elegant back one entirely free from company*, that she may have no suspicion of them. They doubt not my generosity, they say; but *why* for my own sake, in Lord M.'s style, *should I make so long a harvest of so little corn?*

Women, ye reason well. I think I will begin my operations the moment she comes in.

* * *

I have come at the letter brought her from Miss Howe to-day. Plot, conjuration, sorcery, witchcraft, all going forward! I shall not be able to see this *Miss Harlowe* with patience. As the nymphs below ask, so do I, why is *night* necessary? and Sally and Polly upbraidingly remind me of my first attempts upon themselves. Yet *force* answers not my end — and yet it may, if there be truth in that part of the libertine's creed, *that once subdued is always subdued!* And what woman answers *affirmatively* to the question?

* * *

She is returned; but refuses to admit me: and insists upon having the day to herself. Dorcas tells me that she believes her denial is from motives of piety — oons, Jack, is there impiety in seeing me!—Would it not be the highest act of piety to reclaim me? and is this to be done by her refusing to see me, when she is in a devouter frame than usual? — But I hate her, hate her heartily! She is old, ugly, and deformed. — But O the blasphemy! Yet she is an Harlowe; and I do and *can* hate her for that.

But since I must not see her, [she will be mistress of her *own will*, and of her *time* truly!] let me fill up *my* time by telling thee what I have come at.

The first letter the women met with is dated April 27*. Where can she have put the *preceding* ones! — It mentions Mr. Hickman as a busy fellow between them. Hickman had best take care of himself. She says in it, *I hope you have no cause to repent returning my Norris — it is forthcoming on demand.* Now what the devil can this mean! — Her Norris forthcoming on demand! — The devil take me, if I am *out-Norris'd!* — If such innocents can allow themselves to plot (to *Norris*) well may I.

She is sorry, that *her Hannah can't be with her* — And what if she could? — What could Hannah do for her in *such a house as this?*

The women in the house are to be found out in one breakfasting. The women are enraged at both the correspondents for this; and more

* See Letter lx.

than ever make a point of my subduing her. I had a good mind to give Miss Howe to them in full property. Say but the word, Jack, and it shall be done.

She is glad that Miss Harlowe had thoughts, of taking me at my word. She wondered I did not offer again. Advises her, if I don't soon, not to stay with me. Cautions her *to keep me at a distance; not to permit the least familiarity* — See Jack! see Belford! — Exactly as I thought! — Her vigilance all owing to a cool friend; who can sit down quietly, and give that advice, which in her own case she could not take. What an encouragement to me to proceed in my devices, when I have reason to think that my beloved's reserves are owing more to Miss Howe's cautions, than to her own inclinations! But *it is my interest to be honest,* Miss Howe tells her — INTEREST, fools! — I thought these girls knew that my *interest* was ever subservient to my *pleasure.*

What would I give to come at the copies of the letters to which those of Miss Howe are answers!

The next letter is dated May 3*. In this the little termagant expresses her astonishment, that her mother should write to Miss Harlowe, to forbid her to correspond with her daughter. Mr. Hickman, she says, is of opinion, *that she ought not to obey her mother.* How the creeping fellow trims between both! I am afraid that I must punish him, as well as this virago;

* See Letter lxviii.

and I have a scheme rumbling in my head, that wants but half an hour's musing to bring into form that will do my business upon both. I cannot bear that the parental authority should be thus despised, thus trampled under foot — but observe the vixen, *'Tis well he is of her opinion: for her mother having set her up she must have somebody to quarrel with.* — Could a Lovelace have allowed himself a greater licence? This girl's a devilish rake in her heart. Had she been a man, and one of us, she'd have outdone us all in enterprise and spirit.

She wants but very little further provocation, she says, *to fly privately to London. And if she does, she will not leave her till she sees her either honourably married, or quit of the wretch.* Here, Jack, the transcriber Sally has added a prayer — "For the Lord's sake, dear Mr. Lovelace, get this fury to London;" — her fate, I can tell thee, Jack, if we had her among us, should not be so long deciding as her friend's. What a gantlope would she run, when I had done with her, among a dozen of her own pitiless sex, whom my charmer shall never see! — But more of this anon.

I find by this letter, that my saucy captive had been drawing the characters of every varlet of ye. Nor am I spared in it more than you. *The man's a fool to be sure, my dear.* Let me perish if they either of them find me one; *A silly fellow, at least.* Cursed contemptible! — *I see not but they are a set of in-*

fernals — there's for thee, Belford — *and he the Belzebub* — there's for thee, Lovelace! — And yet she would have her friend marry a Belzebub. — And what have any of us done (within the knowledge of Miss Harlowe) that she should give such an account of us, as should excuse so much abuse from Miss Howe! — But the occasion that shall warrant this abuse is to come!

She blames her for *not admitting Miss Partington to her bed — watchful as you are, what could have happened? — If violence were intended, he would not stay for the night.* I am ashamed to have this hinted to me by this virago. Sally writes upon this hint — "See, sir, what is expected from you. An hundred and an hundred times we have told you of this" — And so they have. But to be sure, the advice from *them* was not of half the efficacy as it will be from *Miss Howe* — *You might have sat up after her, or not gone to bed*, proceeds she.

But can there be such apprehensions between them, yet the one advise her to stay, and the other resolve to wait my imperial motion for marriage? I am glad I know that.

She approves of my proposal of Mrs. Fretchville's house. She puts her upon expecting settlements; upon naming a day: and concludes with insisting upon her writing, notwithstanding her mother's prohibitions: or bids her *take the consequence.* Undutiful wretches! How I long to vindicate against them both the insulted parental character!

Thou wilt say to thyself by this time, And can this proud and insolent girl be the same Miss Howe, who sighed for honest Sir George Colmar; and who, but for this her beloved friend, would have followed him in all his broken fortunes, when he was obliged to quit the kingdom?

Yes, she is the *very* same. And I always found in others, as well as in myself, that a first passion, thoroughly subdued, made the conqueror of it a rover; the conqueress a tyrant.

Well, but now comes mincing, in a letter from one who has the *honour of dear Miss Howe's commands** to acquaint Miss Harlowe, that Miss Howe is *excessively concerned for the concern she has given her.*

I have great temptations, on this occasion, says the prim Gothamite, *to express my own resentments upon your present state.*

My own resentments! — And why did he not fall into this *temptation!* — Why, truly, because he knew not what that state was which gave him so *tempting* a subject — *only by a conjecture*, and so forth.

He then dances in his style, as he does in his gait! To be sure, to be sure, he must have made the grand tour, and come home by the way of Tipperary.

And being moreover forbid, says the prancer, *to enter into the cruel subject* — this prohibition was a mercy to thee, friend Hickman!

* See Letter lxx.

— But why *cruel subject*, if thou knowest not what it is, but conjecturest only from the disturbance it gives to a girl, that is her mother's disturbance, will be thy disturbance, and the disturbance in turn of every body with whom she is intimately acquainted, unless I have the humbling of her?

In another letter,* the little fury professes, *that she will write, and that no man shall write for her*, as if some medium of that kind had been proposed. She approves of her fair friend's intention *to leave me, if she can be received by her relations*. I am *a wretch, a foolish wretch.* She hates me for my teasing ways. She has just made an acquaintance with one who knows a vast deal of my private history. A curse upon her, and upon her historiographer! — *The man is really a villain, an execrable one.* Devil take her! Had I a dozen lives, I might have forfeited them all twenty crimes ago. An odd way of reckoning, Jack!

. Miss Betterton, Miss Lockyer are named — *the man* (she irreverently repeats) she again calls *a villain.* Let me perish, I repeat, if I am called a villain for nothing!
— She *will have her uncle* (as Miss Harlowe requests) *sounded about receiving her.* *Dorcas is to be attached to her interest: my letters are to be come at by surprise or trick.*

What thinkest thou of this, Jack?

Miss Howe is alarmed at my attempt to come at a letter of hers. Were I to come at the knowledge

* See Letter lxxxi.

of her freedoms with my character, she says, *she should be afraid to stir, out without a guard.* I would advise the vixen to get her guard ready.

I am at the head of a gang of wretches [thee, Jack, and thy brother varlets, she owns she means] *who join together to betray innocent creatures, and to support one another in their villainies* — What sayest thou to this, Belford!

She wonders not at her melancholy reflections for meeting me, for being forced upon me, and tricked by me. I hope, Jack, thou'lt have done preaching after this!

But she comforts her, *that she will be both a warning and example to all her sex.* I hope the sex will thank me for this.

The nymphs had not time, they say, to transcribe all that was worthy of my resentment in this letter: so I must find an opportunity to come at it myself. Noble rant, they say, it contains — but I am a *seducer*, and a hundred vile fellows, in it. — *And the devil*, it seems, *took possession of my heart, and of the hearts of all her friends, in the same dark hour, in order to provoke her to meet me.* Again, *there is a fate in her error*, she says — *Why then should she grieve?* — *Adversity is her shining time*, and I can't tell what — yet never to thank the man to whom she owes the *shine!*

In the next letter*, wicked as I am, *she fears I must be her lord and master.*

I hope so.

* See Letter lxxxvii.

She retracts what she said against me in her last. — My behaviour to my Rosebud; Miss Harlowe to take possession of Mrs. Fretchville's house; I to stay at Mrs. Sinclair's; the stake I have in my country; my reversions; my economy; my person; my address [something like in all this!]; are brought in my favour, to induce her now *not* to leave me. How do I love to puzzle these *long-sighted* girls!

Yet *my teasing ways*, it seems, are intolerable. — Are women only to tease, I trow? — The sex may thank themselves for teaching me to out-tease them. So the headstrong Charles XII. of Sweden taught the Czar Peter to beat him, by continuing a war with the Muscovites against the ancient maxims of his kingdom.

May eternal vengeance PURSUE *the villain* [thank heaven she does not say *overtake*] *if he give room to doubt his honour!* — — Women can't swear, Jack — — sweet souls! they can only curse.

I am said *to doubt her love* — — Have I not reason? And she, *to doubt my ardour* — — Ardour, Jack! — Why, 'tis very right — women, as Miss Howe says, and as every rake knows, love ardours.

She apprises her of the *ill success of the application made to her uncle* — by Hickman, no doubt — I must have this fellow's ears in my pocket, very quickly, I believe.

She says, *she is equally shocked and enraged against all her family: Mrs. Norton's weight has been tried upon Mrs. Harlowe; as well as Mr.* *Hickman's upon the uncle: but never were there*, says the vixen, *such determined brutes in the world. Her uncle concludes her ruined already.* Is not that a call upon me, as well as a reproach? — *They all expected applications from her when in distress — but were resolved not to stir an inch to save her life.* She was accused *of premeditation and contrivance.* Miss Howe *is concerned*, she tells her, *for the revenge my pride may put me upon taking for the distance she has kept me at —* and well she may. — It is now evident to her, that she must be mine (for her *cousin* Morden, it seems, is set against her too) — an act of necessity, of convenience! — Thy friend, Jack, to be already made a woman's convenience? Is this to be borne by a Lovelace?

I shall make great use of this letter. From Miss Howe's hints of what passed between her uncle Harlowe and Hickman, [*it must* be Hickman] I can give room for my *invention* to play; for she tells her, that *she will not reveal all.* I must endeavour to come at this letter myself. I must have the very words: extracts will not do. This letter, when I have it, must be my compass to steer by.

The fire of friendship then blazes and crackles. I never before imagined that so fervent a friendship could subsist between two sister-beauties, both toasts. But even *here* it may be inflamed by opposition, and by that contradiction which gives vigour to female spirits of a warm and romantic turn.

She raves about *coming up, if by so doing she could prevent so noble a creature from stooping too low, or save her from ruin.* — One reed to support another! I think I will contrive to bring her up.

How comes it to pass that I cannot help being pleased with this virago's spirit, though I suffer by it? Had I her but here, I'd engage in a week's time to teach her submission without reserve. What pleasure should I have in breaking such a spirit! I should wish for her but one month, in all, I think. She would be too tame and spiritless for me after that. How sweetly pretty to see the two lovely friends, when humbled and tame, both sitting in the darkest corner of a room, arm in arm, weeping and sobbing for each other! — And I their emperor, their then *acknowledged* emperor, reclining at my ease in the same room, uncertain to which I should first, Grand Signor like, throw out my handkerchief!

Again mind the girl: *she is enraged at the Harlowes: she is angry at her own mother; she is exasperated against her foolish and low-vanity'd Lovelace.* Foolish, a little toad! [God forgive me for calling a virtuous girl, a toad!] *Let us stoop to lift the wretch out of his dirt, though we soil our fingers in doing it! He has not been guilty of direct indecency to you.* — It seems *extraordinary* to Miss Howe that I have not. *Nor dare he* — she should be sure of that. If women have such things in their heads, why should not I in my heart? — *Not so much of a devil as that comes to neither.*

Such villainous intentions would have shewn themselves before now if I had them. — Lord help them! —

She then puts her friend upon urging for *settlements, licence,* and so forth. — *No room for delicacy now,* she says; and tells her what she shall say, *to bring all forward from me.* Is it not as clear to thee, Jack, as it is to me, that I should have carried my point long ago, but for this vixen? *She reproaches her for having* MODESTY'D *away* as she calls it, *more than one opportunity that she ought not to have slipt.* — Thus thou seest, that the noblest of the sex mean nothing in the world by their shyness and distance, but to pound the poor fellow they dislike not, when he comes into their purlieus.

Though *trick'd into this man's power,* she tells her, *she is not meanly subjugated to it.* There are hopes of my reformation, it seems, *from my reverence for her; since before her I never had any reverence for what was good!* I am *a great, a specious deceiver.* I thank her for this, however. A good moral use, she says, may be made of *my having prevailed upon her to swerve.* I am glad that any good may flow from my actions.

Annexed to this letter is a paper, the most saucy that ever was written of a mother, by a daughter. There are in it such free reflections upon widows and bachelors, that I cannot but wonder how Miss Howe came by her learning. Sir George Colmar, I can tell thee, was a greater fool than thy friend, if she had it all for nothing.

The contents of this paper acquaint Miss Harlowe, that her uncle Antony has been making proposals of marriage to her mother.

The old fellow's heart ought to be a tough one, if he succeed; or she who broke that of a much worthier man, the late Mr. Howe, will soon get rid of him.

But be this as it may, the stupid family is made more irreconcileable than ever to their goddess-daughter for old Antony's thoughts of marrying: so I am more secure of her than ever. And yet I believe at last, that my tender heart will be moved in her favour. For I did not *wish* that she should have *nothing* but persecution and distress. — But why loves she the *brutes*, as Miss Howe justly calls them, so much; *me* so little?

I have still more unpardonable transcripts from other letters.

LETTER CIII.
Mr. Lovelace to John Belford, Esq.

The next letter is of such a nature, that I dare say, these proud rogues would not have had it fall into my hands for the world*.

I see by it to what her displeasure with me, in relation to my proposals, was owing. They were not summed up, it seems, with the warmth, with the *ardour* which she had expected.

This whole letter was transcribed by Dorcas, to whose lot it

* See Letter xcii.

fell. Thou shalt have copies of them all at full length shortly.

Men of our cast, this little devil says, *she fancies cannot have the ardours that honest men have.* Miss Howe has very pretty fancies, Jack. Charming girl! Would to heaven I knew whether my fair-one answers her as freely as she writes! 'Twould vex a man's heart, that this virago should have come honestly by her *fancies*.

Who knows but I may have half a dozen creatures to get off my hands, before I engage for life? — Yet, lest this should mean me a compliment, as if I would reform, she adds her belief, *that she must not expect me to be honest on this side my grand climacteric.* She has an high opinion of her sex, to think they can charm so long a man so well acquainted with their *identicalness*.

He to suggest delays, she says, *from a compliment to be made to Lord M.!* Yes, *I*, my dear — because a man has not been accustomed to be dutiful, must he never be dutiful? — In so important a case as this too! the hearts of the whole family engaged in it! *You did indeed*, says she, *want an interposing friend — but were I to have been in your situation, I would have torn his eyes out, and left it to his heart to furnish the reason for it.* See! See! What sayest thou to this, Jack?

Villain, fellow that he is! follow. And for what? Only for wishing that the next day were to be my happy one; and for being dutiful to my nearest relation.

It is the cruellest of fates, she says, *for a woman to be forced to have a man whom her heart despises.* — That is what I wanted to be sure of — I was afraid that my beloved was too conscious of her talents; of her superiority! I was afraid that she *indeed* despised me. — And I cannot bear to think she does. But, Belford, I do not intend that this lady shall be bound down by so cruel a fate. Let me perish, if I marry a woman who has given her most intimate friend reason to say, *she despises me!* — A Lovelace to be *despised*, Jack!

His clenched fist to his forehead on your leaving him in just displeasure — that is, when she was not satisfied with my ardours, if it please ye! — I remember the motion; but her back was towards me at the time*. Are these watchful ladies all eye? — But observe what follows: *I wish it had been a pole-ax, and in the hands of his worst enemy —*

I *will* have patience, Jack; I *will* have patience! *My* day is at hand. — Then will I steel my heart with these remembrances.

But here is a scheme to be thought of, in order to *get my fair prize out of my hands, in case I give her reason to suspect me.*

This indeed alarms me. Now the contention becomes arduous. Now wilt thou not wonder if I let loose my plotting genius against them both. I will not be *out-Noris'd*, Belford.

But once more, *she has no notion,*

* She tells Miss Howe, that she saw this motion in the pier-glass. See p. 297.

she says, *that I can or dare to mean her dishonour.* But then the man is a *fool — that's all* — I should indeed be a fool, to proceed as I do, and mean matrimony! *However, since you are thrown upon a fool,* says she, *marry the fool, at the first opportunity; and though I doubt that this man will be the most unmanageable of fools, as all witty and vain fools are, take him as a punishment, since you cannot as a reward.* — Is there any bearing this, Belford?

But *such men as myself. are the men that the women do not naturally hate.* — True as the gospel, Jack! The truth is out at last. Have I not always told thee so? Sweet creatures and true christians these young girls! They love their enemies. But rakes in their hearts all of them! Like turns to like; *that's* the thing. Were I not well assured of the truth of this observation of the vixen, I should have thought it worth while, if not to be a good man, to be more of a hypocrite than I found it needful to be.

But in the letter I came at to-day while she was at church, her scheme is further opened; and a cursed one it is.

*Mr. Lovelace then transcribes from his short-hand notes that part of Miss Howe's letter, which relates to the design of engaging Mrs. Townsend (in case of necessity) to give her protection till Colonel Morden come:** and repeats his vows of revenge; especially for these words*; that should he at-

* See Letter c. p. 327, 328.

tempt any thing that would make him obnoxious to the laws of society, she might have a fair riddance of him, either by flight or the gallows; no matter which.

He then adds: — 'Tis my pride, to subdue girls who know *too much* to *doubt* their knowledge, and to convince them, that they know *too little* to defend themselves from the inconveniencies of knowing *too much.*

How passion drives a man on! proceeds he. — I have written a prodigious quantity in a very few hours! Now my resentments are warm, I will see, and perhaps will punish, this proud, this *double-armed beauty.* I have sent to tell her, that I must be admitted to sup with her. We have neither of us dined. She refused to drink tea in the after-noon; and I believe neither of us will have much stomach to our supper.

LETTER CIV.
Miss Clarissa Harlowe to Miss Howe.
Sunday morning, seven o'clock.

I was at the play last night with Mr. Lovelace and Miss Horton. It is, you know, a deep and most affecting tragedy in the reading. You have my remarks upon it in the little book you made me write upon the principal acting plays. You will not wonder, that Miss Horton, as well as I, was greatly moved at the representation, when I tell you, and have some pleasure in telling you, that Mr. Lovelace himself was very sensibly touched with some of the most affecting scenes. I mention this in praise of the author's performance; for I take Mr. Lovelace to be one of the most hard-hearted men in the world: upon my word, my dear, I do.

His behaviour, however, on this occasion, and on our return, was unexceptionable; only that he would oblige me to stay to supper with the women below, when we came back, and to sit up with him and them till near one o'clock this morning. I am not very sorry to have the pretence; for I love to pass the Sundays by myself.

To have the better excuse to avoid his teasing, I am ready dressed to go to church this morning. I will go only to St. James's church, and in a *chair;* that I may be sure I can go out and come in when I please, without being intruded upon by him, as I was twice before.

Near nine o'clock.

I have your kind letter of yesterday. He knows I have. And I shall expect that he will be inquisitive next time I see him after your opinion of his proposals. I doubted not your approbation of them, and had written an answer on that presumption; which is ready for him. He must *study* for occasions of procrastination, and to disoblige me, if now any thing happens to set us at variance again.

He is very importunate to see me. He has desired to attend me to church. He is angry that I have declined to breakfast with him. I am sure that I should not have been at my own liberty if I had—I bid Dorcas tell him, that I desired to have this day to myself. I would see him in the morning as early as he pleased. She says, she knows not what ails him, but that he is out of humour with every body.

He has sent again in a peremptory manner. He warns me of Singleton. I sent him word that if *he* was not afraid of Singleton at the playhouse last night, I need not at church to-day: so many churches to *one* playhouse. I have accepted of his servant's proposed attendance. But he is quite displeased, it seems. I don't care. I will not be perpetually at his insolent beck.—Adieu, my dear, till I return. The chair waits. He won't stop me, sure, as I go down to it.

* * *

I DID not see him as I went down. He is, it seems, excessively out of humour. Dorcas says, not with me neither, she believes: but something has vexed him. This is put on perhaps, to make me dine with him. But I will not, if I can help it. I shan't get rid of him for the rest of the day, if I do.

* * *

HE was very earnest to dine with me. But I was resolved to carry this one small point; and so denied to dine myself. And indeed I was endeavouring to write to my cousin Morden; and had begun three different times, without being able to please myself.

He was very busy in writing, Dorcas says; and pursued it without dining, because I denied him my company.

He afterwards *demanded*, as I may say, to be admitted to afternoon tea with me: and appealed by Dorcas to his behaviour to me last night; as if, as I sent him word by her, he thought he had a merit in being unexceptionable. However, I repeated my promise to meet him as early as he pleased in the morning, or to breakfast with him.

Dorcas says, he raved; I heard him loud, and I heard his servant fly from him, as I thought. You, my dearest friend, say, in one of yours,* that you must have somebody to be angry at, when your mother sets you up. I should be very loth to draw comparisons: but the workings of passion, when indulged, are but too much alike, whether in man or woman.

* * *

HE has just sent me word, that he insists upon supping with me. As we had been in a good train for several days past, I thought it not prudent to break with him for little matters. Yet, to be, in a manner, threatened into his will, I know not how to bear that.

* * *

WHILE I was considering, he came up, and tapping at my door, told me, in a very angry tone, he must see me this night. He could not rest till he had been told what he had done to deserve the treatment I gave him.

* See Letter lxviii, Paragr. 2.

Treatment I gave him! A wretch! Yet perhaps he has nothing new to say to me. I shall be very angry with him.

As the lady could not know what Mr. Lovelace's designs were, nor the cause of his ill-humour, it will not be improper to pursue the subject from his letter.

Having described his angry manner of demanding, in person, her company at supper: he proceeds as follows:

'Tis hard, answered the fair perverse, that I am to be so little my own mistress. I will meet you in the dining-room half an hour hence.

I went down to wait that half hour. All the women set me hard to give her cause for this tyranny. They demonstrated, as well from the nature of the *sex* as of the *case*, that I had nothing to hope for from my tameness, and could meet with no worse treatment, were I to be guilty of the last offence. They urged me vehemently to *try* at least what effect some greater familiarities than I had ever taken with her would have: and their arguments being strengthened by my just resentments on the discoveries I had made, I was resolved to take *some liberties*, and as they were received, to take *still greater*, and lay all the fault upon her *tyranny*. In this humour I went up, and never had paralytic so little command of his joints, as I had, while I walked about the dining-room, attending her motions.

With an erect mien she entered, her face averted, her lovely bosom swelling, and the more charmingly protuberant for the erectness of her mien. O Jack! that sullenness and reserve should add to the charms of this haughty maid! But in every attitude, in every humour, in every gesture, is beauty beautiful. — By her averted face, and indignant aspect, I saw the dear insolent was disposed to be angry — but by the fierceness of mine, as my trembling hands seized hers, I soon made fear her predominant passion. And yet the moment I beheld her, my heart was dastardized; and my reverence for the virgin purity, so visible in her whole deportment, again took place. Surely, Belford, this is an angel. And yet, had she not been known to be a female, they would not from *babyhood* have dressed her as such, nor would she, but upon that conviction, have continued the dress.

Let me ask you, madam, I beseech you tell me, what I have done to deserve this distant treatment?

And let me ask *you*, Mr. Lovelace, why are my retirements to be thus invaded? — What can you have to say to me since last night, that I went with you so much against my will to the play? And after sitting up with you, equally against my will, till a very late hour?

This I have to say, madam, that I cannot bear to be kept at this distance from you under the same roof.

Under the same roof, sir!—How came you—

Hear me out, madam [letting go her trembling hands, and snatching them back again with an eagerness that made her start]—I have a thousand things to say, to talk of, relating to our present and future prospects; but when I want to open my whole soul to you, you are always contriving to keep me at a distance. You make me inconsistent with myself. Your heart is set upon delays. You must have views that you will not own. Tell me, madam, I conjure you to tell me, this moment without subterfuge or reserve, in what light am I to appear to you in future? I cannot bear this distance. The suspense you hold me in I cannot bear.

In what light, Mr. Lovelace! [visibly terrified] In no bad light I hope. — Pray, Mr. Lovelace, do not grasp my hands so hard [endeavouring to withdraw them]. — Pray let me go, —

You *hate* me, madam —

I hate nobody, sir —

You *hate* me, madam, repeated I.

Instigated and resolved, as I came up, I wanted some new provocation. The devil, indeed, as soon as my angel made her appearance, crept out of my heart: but he had left the door open, and was no further off than my elbow.

You come up in no good temper, I see, Mr. Lovelace — but pray be not violent — *I have done you no hurt* — pray be not violent —

Sweet creature! And I clasped one arm about her, holding one hand in my other.— *You have done me no hurt* — I could have devoured her — but restraining myself — You have done me the greatest hurt! — In what have I deserved the distance you keep me at? — I knew not what to say.

She struggled to disengage herself — Pray, Mr. Lovelace, let me withdraw. I know not why this is. I know not what I have done to offend you. I see you are come with *a design to quarrel with me*. If you would not terrify me by the ill humour you are in, permit me to withdraw. I will hear all you have to say another time — to-morrow morning, as I sent you word — but indeed you frighten me. I beseech you, if you have any value for me, permit me to withdraw.

Night, *mid-night*, *is* necessary, Belford. Surprise, terror, *must* be necessary to the ultimate trial of this charming creature, say the women below what they will. I could not hold my purposes. This was not the first time that I had *intended* to try if she could forgive.

I kissed her hand with a fervour, as if I would have left my lips upon it. — Withdraw, then, dearest and ever-dear creature. Indeed, I entered in a very ill humour. I cannot bear the distance at which you so causelessly keep me. Withdraw, madam, since it is your will to withdraw; and judge me generously; judge me but as I deserve to be judged; and let me hope to meet you to-morrow morning early in such a temper as becomes our present situation, and my future hopes.

And so saying, I conducted her to the door, and left her there. But, instead of going down to the women, I went into my own chamber, and locked myself in; ashamed of being awed by her majestic loveliness, and apprehensive virtue, into so great a change of purpose, notwithstanding I had such just provocations from the letters of her saucy friend, founded on her own representations of facts and situations between herself and me.

The lady (dating Sunday night) thus describes her terrors, and Mr. Lovelace's behaviour, on the occasion.

On my entering the dining-room, he took my hand in his in such a humour, as I saw plainly he was resolved to quarrel with me — and for what? — What had I done to him? — I never in my life beheld in any body such wild, such angry, such impatient airs. I was terrified; and instead of being as angry as I intended to be, I was forced to be all mildness. I can hardly remember what were his first words, I was so frighted. But, *You hate me, madam! You hate me, madam!* were some of them — with such a fierceness — I wished myself a thousand miles distant from him. I hate nobody, said I; I thank God, I hate nobody — you terrify me, Mr. Lovelace — let me leave you. — The man, my dear, looked quite ugly — I never saw a man so ugly as passion made him look — *and for what?* — And he so grasped my hands! — Fierce creature! — He so grasped my hands! In short, he seemed by his looks, and by his words, (once putting his arms about me) to wish me to provoke him. So that I had nothing to do but to beg of him (which I did repeatedly) to permit me to withdraw: and to promise to meet him at his own time in the morning.

It was with a very ill grace that he complied, on that condition: and at parting he kissed my hand with such a savageness, that a redness remains upon it still.

Do you not think, my dear, that I have reason to be incensed at him, my situation considered: am I not under a *necessity*, as it were, of quarrelling with him, at least every other time I see him? No prudery, no coquetry, no tyranny in my heart, or in my behaviour to him, that I know of. No affected procrastination. Aiming at nothing but decorum. He as much concerned, and so he ought to think, as I, to have that observed. Too much in his power: cast upon him by the cruelty of my relations. No other protection to fly to but his. One plain path before us; yet such embarrasses, such difficulties, such subjects for doubt, for cavil, for uneasiness; as fast as one is obviated, another to be introduced, and not by myself — I know not how introduced — What pleasure can I propose to myself in meeting such a wretch?

Perfect for me, my dearest Miss Howe, perfect for me, I beseech you, your kind scheme with Mrs. Townsend, and I will then leave this man.

My temper, I believe, is changed. No wonder if it be. I question whether ever it will be what it was. But I cannot make *him* half so uneasy by the change as I am *myself.* See you not how, from step to step, he grows upon me? — I tremble to look back upon his encroachments. And now to give me cause to apprehend *more evil from him than indignation will permit me to express!* — O my dear, perfect your scheme, and let me fly from so strange a wretch!

Yet, to be first an eloper from my friends to him, as the world supposes; and now to be so from him [to *whom* I know not!] how hard to one who ever endeavoured to shun intricate paths! — But he must certainly have views in quarrelling with me thus, which he dare not own! — Yet what can they be? — I am terrified but to think of what they may be!

Let me *but* get from him! — As to my reputation, if I leave him — that is already too much wounded for me, now, to be careful about any thing, but how to act so, as that my own heart shall not reproach me. As to the world's censure, I must be content to suffer that — an unhappy composition however. — What a wreck have my fortunes suffered, to be obliged to throw overboard so many valuables, to preserve, indeed, the *only* valuable! A composition that once it would have half broken my heart to think there would have been the least danger that I should be obliged to submit to.

You, my dear, could not be a stranger to my most secret failings, although you would not tell me of them. What a pride did I take in the applause of every one! — What a pride even in supposing I had *not* that pride! — Which concealed itself from my unexamining heart under the specious veil of *humility,* doubting the merit to myself by the *supposed,* and indeed *imputed,* gracefulness in the manner of conferring benefits, when I had not a single merit in what I did, vastly overpaid by the pleasure of doing some little good, and impelled, as I may say, by talents given me — for what? — Not to be proud of.

So desirous, in short, to be considered as an *example!* A vanity which my partial admirers put into my head! — And so secure in my own virtue!

I am punished enough, enough mortified, for this my vanity — I hope *enough,* if it so please the all-gracious Inflictor: since now, I verily think, I more despise myself for my presumptuous self-security, as well as vanity, than ever I secretly vaunted myself on my good inclinations: *secretly,* I say, however; for indeed I had not given myself leisure to reflect, till I was thus mortified, how very imperfect I was; nor how much truth there is in what divines tell us, that we sin in our best performances.

23*

But I was very young — but here let me watch over myself again: for in those four words, *I was very young*, is there not a palliation couched, that were enough to take all efficacy from the discovery and confession?

What strange imperfect beings! — But *self* here, which is at the bottom of all we do, and of all we wish, is the grand misleader.

I will not apologize to you, my dear, for these grave reflections. Is it not enough to make the unhappy creature look into herself, and endeavour to detect herself, who, from such an high reputation, left to proud and presumptuous self, should, by one thoughtless step, be brought to the dreadful situation I am in?

Let me, however, look forward: to despond would be to add sin to sin. And whom have I to raise me up, whom to comfort me, if I desert myself? — Thou, O Father, who, I hope, hast not yet deserted, hast not yet cursed me! — For I am thine! — It is fit that meditation should supply the rest. —

* * *

I was so disgusted with him, as well as frighted by him, that, on my return to my chamber, in a fit of passionate despair, I tore almost in two the answer I had written to his proposals.

I will see him in the morning, because I promised I would. But I will go out, and that without him, or any attendant. If he account not tolerably for his sudden change of behaviour, and a proper opportunity offer of a private lodging in some creditable house, I will not any more return to this: — at present I think so. — And there will I either attend the perfecting of your scheme; or, by your epistolary mediation, make my own terms with the wretch; since it is your opinion that I must be his, and cannot help myself: or, perhaps, take a resolution to throw myself at once into Lady Betty's protection; and this will hinder him from making his insolently-threatened visit to Harlowe Place.

The lady writes again on Monday evening: and gives her friend an account of all that passed between herself and Mr. Lovelace that day; and of her being terrified out of her purpose, of going out: but Mr. Lovelace's next letters giving a more ample account of all, hers are omitted. It is proper, however, to mention, that she re-urges Miss Howe (from the dissatisfaction she has reason for from what passed between Mr. Lovelace and herself) to perfect her scheme in relation to Mrs. Townsend. She concludes this letter in these words.

I should say something of your last favour, (but a few hours ago received) and of your dialogue with your mother — are you not very whimsical, my dear? I have but two things to wish for on this occasion — the one, that your charming pleasantry had a *better subject* than that you find for it in this dialogue — the other, that my situation were not such, as must too often damp that pleasantry in you, and will not permit me to enjoy it as I used to do. Be, however, happy in yourself, though you cannot in

Your
CLARISSA HARLOWE.

LETTER CV.

Mr. Lovelace to John Belford, Esq.

Monday morning, May 22.

No generosity in this lady. None at all. Wouldst thou not have thought, that after I had permitted her to withdraw, primed for mischief as I was, she would meet me next morning early; and that with a smile; making me one of her best courtesies?

I was in the dining-room before six, expecting her. She opened not her door. I went up stairs and down; and hemmed; and called Will; called Dorcas; threw the doors hard to; but still she opened not her door. Thus till half an hour after eight fooled I away my time; and then (breakfast ready) I sent Dorcas to request her company.

But I was astonished, when (following the wench, as she did at the first invitation) I saw her enter dressed, all but her gloves, and those and her fan in her hand: in the same moment bidding Dorcas direct Will to get a chair to the door.

Cruel creature, thought I, to expose me thus to the derision of the women below!

Going abroad, madam?
I am, sir.

I looked cursed silly, I am sure. You will breakfast first, I hope, madam; in a very humble strain; yet with a hundred tenter-hooks in my heart.

Had she given me more notice of her intention, I had perhaps wrought myself up to the frame I was in the day before, and begun my vengeance. And immediately came into my head all the virulence that had been transcribed for me from Miss Howe's letters, and in that letter which I had transcribed myself.

Yes, she would drink one dish; and then laid her gloves and fan in the window, just by.

I was perfectly disconcerted. I hemmed, and was going to speak several times; but I knew not in what key. Who's modest now! thought I. Who's insolent now! — How a tyrant of a woman confounds a bashful man! She was acting Miss Howe, I thought; and I the spiritless Hickman.

At last, I *will* begin, thought I. She a dish — I a dish.

Sip, her eyes her own, she; like an haughty and imperious sovereign, conscious of dignity, every look a favour.

Sip, like her vassal, I; lips and hands trembling, and not knowing that I sipped or tasted.

I was — I was — I sip'd — (drawing in my breath and the liquor together, though I scalded my mouth with it) I was in hopes, madam —

Dorcas came in just then. — Dorcas, said she, is a chair gone for?

D—n'd impertinence, thought I, thus to put me out in my speech; and I was forced to wait for the servant's answer to the insolent mistress's question.

William is gone for one, madam.

This cost me a minute's silence before I could begin again. And then it was with my hopes, and my hopes, and my hopes, that I should have been early admitted to —

What weather is it, Dorcas? said she, as regardless of me as if I had not been present.

A little lowering, madam — the sun is gone in — it was very fine half an hour ago.

I had no patience. Up I rose. Down went the tea-cup, saucer and all — Confound the weather, the sunshine, and the wench! — Begone for a devil, when I am speaking to your lady, and have so little opportunity given me.

Up rose the saucy-face, half-frighted; and snatched from the window her gloves and fan.

You must not go, madam; — Seizing her hand — By my soul you must not —

Must not, sir! — But I must — you can curse your maid in my absence as well as if I were present — except — except — you intend for *me* what you direct to *her*.

Dearest creature, you must not go — you must not leave me — such determined scorn! such contempts! — Questions asked your servant of no meaning but to break in upon me — I cannot bear it!

Detain me not, struggling. I will not be withheld. I like you not, nor your ways. You sought to quarrel with me yesterday, *for no reason in the world that I can think of but because I was too obliging*. You are an ingrateful man; and I hate you with my whole heart, Mr. Lovelace.

Do not make me desperate, madam. Permit me to say, that you shall not leave me in this humour. Wherever you go I will attend you. Had Miss Howe been my friend, I had not been thus treated. It is but too plain to whom my difficulties are owing. I have long observed, that every letter you received from *her* makes an alteration in your behaviour to *me*. She would have *you* treat *me* as *she* treats Mr. Hickman, I suppose; but neither does that treatment become your admirable temper to offer nor me to receive.

This startled her. She did not care to have me think hardly of Miss Howe.

But recollecting herself, Miss Howe, said she, is a friend to virtue and to good men. If she like not you, it is because you are not one of those.

Yes, madam; and therefore to speak of Mr. Hickman, and myself, as you both, I suppose, think of each, she treats *him* as she would not treat a *Lovelace*. — I challenge you, madam, to shew me but one of the many letters you have received from her, where I am mentioned.

Miss Howe is just; Miss Howe is good, replied she. She writes, she speaks, of every body as they deserve. If you point me out but any one occasion, upon which you have reason to build a merit to yourself, as either just or good, or even generous, I will look out for her letter on that occasion [if such an occasion there be, I have certainly acquainted her with it]; and will engage it shall be in your favour.

Devilish severe! And as indelicate as severe, to put a modest man upon hunting backward after his own merits.

She would have flung from me: I will *not* be detained, Mr. Lovelace. I *will* go out.

Indeed you must not, madam, in this humour. And I placed myself between her and the door. — And then, fanning, she threw herself into a chair, her sweet face all crimsoned over with passion.

I cast myself at her feet. Begone, Mr. Lovelace, said she, with a rejecting motion, her fan in her hand; for your own sake leave me! — My soul is above thee, man! with both her hands pushing me from her! — Urge me not to tell thee how sincerely I think my soul above thee! — Thou hast in mine, a proud, a too proud heart, to contend with! — Leave me, and leave me for ever! — Thou hast a proud heart to contend with! —

Her air, her manner, her voice, were bewitchingly noble, though her words were so severe.

Let me worship an angel, said I, no woman. Forgive me, dearest creature! — Creature if you be, forgive me! — Forgive my inadvertencies! Forgive my inequalities! — Pity my infirmities! — Who is equal to my Clarissa?

I trembled between admiration and love; and wrapt my arms about her knees as she sat. She tried to rise at the moment; but my clasping round her thus ardently, drew her down again; and never was woman more affrighted. But, free as my clasping emotion might appear to her apprehensive heart, I had not at that instant any thought but what reverence inspired. And till she had actually withdrawn [which I permitted under promise of a speedy return, and on her consent to dismiss the chair] all the motions of my heart were as pure as her own.

She kept not her word. An hour I waited before I sent to claim her promise. She could not possibly see me yet, was her answer. As soon as she could she would.

Dorcas says she still excessively trembled; and ordered her to give her hartshorn and water.

A strange apprehensive creature! Her terror is too great for the occasion. Evils are often greater in apprehension than in reality. Hast thou never observed, that the terrors of a bird caught, and actually in the hand, bear no comparison to what we might have supposed those terrors would be, were we to have formed a judgment of the same bird by its shyness before it was taken?

Dear creature! — Did she never romp? Did she never, from

girlhood to now, hoyden? The *innocent* kinds of freedom, taken and allowed on these occasions, would have familiarised her to greater. Sacrilege but to touch the hem of her garment!—Excess of delicacy! O the consecrated beauty! how can she think to be a wife!

But how do I know till I try, whether she may not, by a less alarming treatment, be prevailed upon, or whether [*day*, I have done with thee!] she may not *yield to nightly surprises?* This is still the burden of my song, I can marry her when I will. And if I do, after prevailing, (whether by *surprise* or by *reluctant consent*) whom but myself shall I have injured?

* * *

It is now eleven o'clock. She will see me as soon as she can, she tells Polly Horton, who made her a tender visit, and to whom she is less reserved than to any body else. Her emotion, she assures her, was not owing to perverseness, to nicety, to ill humour; but to *weakness of heart.* She has not *strength of mind* sufficient, she says, to enable her to support her condition.

Yet what a contradiction!—*Weakness of heart,* says she, with such *a strength of will!* — O Belford! she is a lion-hearted lady, in every case where her honour, punctilio rather, calls for spirit. But I have had reason more than once, in her case, to conclude, that the passions of the gentle, slower to be moved than those of the quick, are the most flaming, the most irresistible, when raised. — Yet her charming body is not equally organised. The unequal partners pull two ways; and the divinity within her tears her silken frame. But had the same soul informed a masculine body, never would there have been a truer hero.

Monday, two o'clock.

Not yet visible! — My beloved is not well. What *expectations* had she from my ardent admiration of her! — More rudeness than revenge apprehended. Yet how my soul thirsts for revenge upon both these ladies! I must have recourse to my *master-strokes.* This cursed project of Miss Howe and her Mrs. Townsend (if I cannot contrive to render it abortive) will be always a sword hanging over my head. Upon every little disobligation, my beloved will be for taking wing; and the pains I have taken to deprive her of every other refuge or protection, in order to make her absolutely dependent upon me, will be all thrown away. But, perhaps, I shall find out a smuggler to counterplot Miss Howe.

Thou rememberest the contention between the sun and the north-wind, in the fable, which should first make an honest traveller throw off his cloak.

Boreas began first. He puffed away most vehemently; and often made the poor fellow curve and stagger; but with no other effect than to cause him to wrap his surtout the closer about him.

But when it came to Phœbus's turn, he so played upon the traveller with his beams, that he made him first unbutton, and then throw it quite off: — nor left he, till he obliged him to take to the friendly shade of a spreading beech; where, prostrating himself on the thrown-off cloak, he took a comfortable nap.

The victor-god then laughed outright, both at Boreas and the traveller, and pursued his radiant course, shining upon, and warming and cherishing a thousand new objects, as he danced along: and at night, when he put up his fiery coursers, he diverted his Thetis with the relation of his pranks in the passed day.

I, in like manner, will discard all my boisterous inventions: and if I can oblige my sweet traveller to throw aside, *but for one moment*, the cloak of her rigid virtue, I shall have nothing to do, but, like the sun, to bless new objects with my rays. But my chosen hours of conversation and repose, after all my peregrinations, will be devoted to my goddess.

* * *

And now, Belford, according to my new system, I think this house of Mrs. Fretchville's an embarrass upon me. I will get rid of it, for some time at least. Mennel, when I am out, shall come to her, inquiring for me. What for? thou'lt ask. What for! — Hast thou not heard what has befallen poor Mrs. Fretchville? — Then I'll tell thee.

One of her maids about a week ago was taken with the small-pox. The rest kept their mistress ignorant of it till Friday; and *then* she came to know it by accident. The greater half of the plagues poor mortals of condition are tormented with proceed from the servants they take, partly for show, partly for use, and with a view to lessen their cares.

This has so terrified the widow, that she is taken with all the symptoms that threaten an attack from that dreadful enemy of fair faces. — So must not think of removing: yet cannot expect that we should be further delayed on her account.

She now wishes, with all her heart, that she had known her own mind, and gone into the country at first when I treated about the house: this evil then had not happened! A cursed cross accident for *us*, too! — Heigh-ho! Nothing else, I think, in this mortal life! People need not study to bring crosses upon themselves by their petulancies.

So this affair of the house will be over; at least, for one while. But then I can fall upon an expedient which will make amends for this disappointment. I must move *slow* in order to be *sure*. I have a charming contrivance or two in my head, even supposing my beloved should get away, to bring her back again.

But what is become of Lord M. I trow, that he writes not to me, in answer to my invitation? If he would send me such a letter as I could shew, it might go a great way towards a perfect reconciliation. I have written to Charlotte about it. He shall soon hear from me, and that in a way he won't like, if he writes not quickly. He has sometimes threatened to disinherit *me*, but if I should renounce *him*, it would be but justice, and would vex him ten times more than any thing he can do will vex me. Then, the settlements unavoidably delayed by his neglect! — How shall I bear such a life of procrastination! — I, who, as to my will, and impatience, and so forth, am of the true *lady make*, and can as little bear controul and disappointment as the best of them!

* * *

Another letter from Miss Howe. I suppose it is *that* which she promises in her last to send her relating to the courtship between old Tony the uncle and Annabella the mother. I should be extremely rejoiced to see it. No more of the smuggler-plot in it, surely! This letter, it seems, she has put in her pocket. But I hope I shall soon find it deposited with the rest.

Monday evening.

At my repeated request she condescended to meet me in the dining-room to afternoon-tea and not before.

She entered with bashfulness, as I thought; in a pretty confusion, for having carried her apprehensions too far. Sullen and slow moved she towards the tea-table. — Dorcas present, busy in tea-cup preparations. I took her reluctant hand, and pressed it to my lips — Dearest, loveliest of creatures, why this distance? Why this displeasure? How can you thus torture the faithfullest heart in the world?

She disengaged her hand. Again I would have snatched it.

Be quiet, peevishly withdrawing it. And down she sat; a gentle palpitation in the beauty of beauties indicating mingled sullenness and resentment; her snowy handkerchief rising and falling, and a sweet flush overspreading her charming cheeks.

For God's sake, madam; — and a third time I would have taken her repulsing hand.

And for the same sake, sir; no more teasing.

Dorcas retired; I drew my chair nearer hers, and with the most respectful tenderness took her hand; and told her, that I could not forbear to express my apprehensions (from the distance she was so desirous to keep me at) that if any man in the world was more *indifferent* to her, to use no harsher a word, than another, it was the unhappy wretch before her.

She looked steadily upon me for a moment, and with her other hand, not withdrawing that I held, pulled her handkerchief out of her pocket; and by a twinkling motion urged forward a tear or two, which having arisen in each sweet eye, it was plain by that motion she would rather have dissipated: but answered me only with a sigh, and an averted face.

I urged her to speak; to look

up at me; to bless me with an eye more favourable.

I had reason, she told me, for my complaint of her indifference. She saw nothing in my mind that was generous. I was not a man to be obliged or favoured. My strange behaviour to her since Saturday night, *for no cause at all that she knew of*, convinced her of this. Whatever hopes she had conceived of me were utterly dissipated: all my ways were disgustful to her.

This cut me to the heart. The guilty, I believe, in every case, less patiently bear the detecting truth, than the innocent do the degrading falsehood.

I bespoke her patience, while I took the liberty to account for this change on my part. — I re-acknowledged the pride of my heart, which could not bear the thought of that want of preference in the heart of a lady whom I hoped to call mine, which she had always manifested. Marriage, I said, was a state that was not to be entered upon with indifference on either side.

It is insolence, interrupted she; it is presumption, sir, to expect tokens of value, without resolving to *deserve* them. You have no whining creature before you, Mr. Lovelace, overcome by weak motives, to love where there is no merit. Miss Howe can tell you, sir, that I never loved the *faults* of my friend: nor ever wished her to love me for mine. It was a rule with us not to spare each other. And would a man who has nothing but faults (for pray, sir, what are your virtues?) expect that I should shew a value for him? Indeed, if I did, I should not deserve even *his* value; but ought to be despised by him.

Well have you, madam, kept up to this noble manner of thinking. You are in no danger of being despised for any marks of tenderness or favour shewn to the man before you. You have been perhaps, *you'll* think, *laudably* studious of making and taking occasions to declare, that it was far from being owing to your *choice*, that you had any thoughts of me. My whole soul, madam, in all its errors, in all its wishes, in all its views, had been laid open and naked before you, had I been encouraged by such a share in your confidence and esteem, as would have secured me against your apprehended worst constructions of what I should from time to time have revealed to you, and consulted you upon. For never was there a franker heart; nor a man so ready to accuse himself [*this*, Belford, *is true*]. But you know, madam, how much otherwise it has been between us. — Doubt, distance, reserve, on your part, begat doubt, fear, awe, on mine. — How little confidence! as if we apprehended each other to be a plotter rather than a lover. How have I dreaded every letter that has been brought you from Wilson's! — And with reason, since the last, from which I expected so much, on account of the proposals I had made to you in writing, has, if I may judge by the effects, and by your denial of seeing me yesterday, (though you could go abroad, and in a *chair* too, to avoid my attendance on you) set you against me more than ever.

I was guilty, it seems, of going to church, said the indignant charmer; and without the company of a man, whose choice it would not have been to go, had I not gone—I was guilty of desiring to have the whole Sunday to myself, after I had obliged you, against my will, at a play; and after you had detained me (equally to my dislike) to a very late hour over-night. — These were my faults: for these I was to be punished: I was to be compelled to see you, and to be terrified when I did see you, by the most shocking ill-humour that was ever shewn to a creature in my circumstances, and not bound to bear it. You have pretended to find free fault with my father's temper, Mr. Lovelace: but the worst that he ever shewed *after* marriage was not in the least to be compared to what you have shewn twenty times *beforehand*. — And what are my prospects with you, at the very best?—My indignation rises against you, Mr. Lovelace, while I speak to you, when I recollect the many instances, equally ungenerous and unpolite, of your behaviour to one whom you have brought into distress — and I can hardly bear you in my sight.

She turned from me, standing up; and lifting up her folded hands, and charming eyes swimming in tears, O my father, said the inimitable creature, you might have spared your heavy curse, had you known how I have been punished, ever since my swerving feet led me out of your garden door to meet this man! — Then, sinking into her chair, a burst of passionate tears forced their way down her glowing cheeks.

My dearest life, taking her still folded hands in mine, who can bear an invocation so affecting, though so passionate?

And, as I hope to live, my nose tingled, as I once, when a boy, remember it did (and indeed once more very lately) just before some tears came into my eyes; and I durst hardly trust my face in view of hers.

What have I done to deserve this impatient exclamation? — Have I, at any time, by word, by deeds, by looks, given you cause to doubt my honour, my reverence, my *adoration*, I may call it, of your virtues? All is owing to misapprehension, I hope, on both sides. Condescend to clear up but your part, as I will mine, and all must speedily be happy. — Would to heaven I loved that heaven as I love you! And yet, if I doubted a return in love, let me perish if I should know how to wish you mine! — Give me hope, dearest creature, give me but hope, that I am your preferable choice! — Give me but hope that you hate me not; that you do not *despise me.*

O Mr. Lovelace, we have been

long enough together to be tired of each other's humours and ways; ways and humours so different, that perhaps you ought to dislike *me* as much as I do *you*. — I think, I think, that I cannot make an answerable return to the value you profess for me. My temper is utterly ruined, you have given me an ill opinion of all mankind; of yourself in particular; and withal so bad a one of myself, that I shall never be able to look up, having utterly and for ever lost all that self-complacency, and conscious pride, which are so necessary to carry a woman through this life with tolerable satisfaction to herself.

She paused, I was silent. By my soul, thought I, this sweet creature will at last undo me!

She proceeded. — What now remains, but that you pronounce me free of all obligation to you? And that you hinder me not from pursuing the destiny that shall be allotted me?

Again she paused. I was still silent: meditating whether to renounce all further designs upon her; whether I had not received sufficient evidence of a virtue, and of a greatness of soul, that could not be questioned or impeached.

She went on: Propitious to me be your silence, Mr. Lovelace! — Tell me, that I am free of all obligation to you. You know I never made *you* promises. You know, that you are not under any to *me*. — My broken fortunes I matter not —

She was proceeding — My dearest life, said I, I have been all this time, though you fill me with doubts of your favour, busy in the nuptial preparations. I am actually in treaty for equipage.

Equipage, sir! — Trappings, tinsel! — What is equipage; what is life; what is any thing; to a creature sunk so low as I am in my own opinion! Labouring under a father's curse! — Unable to look backward without self-reproach, or forward without terror! — These reflections strengthened by every cross accident! — And what but cross accidents befal me! — All my darling schemes dashed in pieces, all my hopes at an end; deny me not the liberty to refuge myself in some obscure corner, where neither the enemies you have made me, nor the few friends you have left me, may ever hear of the supposed rash one, till those happy moments are at hand, which shall expiate for all!

I had not a word to say for myself. Such a war in my mind had I never known. Gratitude, and admiration of the excellent creature before me, combating with villainous habit, with resolutions so premeditately made, and with views so much gloried in! — An hundred new contrivances in my head, and in my heart, that to be honest, as it is called, must all be given up, by a heart delighting in intrigue and difficulty — Miss Howe's virulences endeavoured to be recollected — yet recollection refusing to bring them forward with the requisite efficacy — I had certainly been a lost man, had not Dorcas come seasonably in, with a letter. — On the superscription written. — *Be pleased, sir, to open it now.*

I retired to the window — opened it — it was from Dorcas herself. — These the contents — "Be pleased to detain my lady: a paper of importance to transcribe. I will cough when I have done."

I put the paper in my pocket, and turned to my charmer, less disconcerted, as she, by that time, had also a little recovered herself. — One favour, dearest creature — let me but know whether Miss Howe approves or disapproves of my proposals? — I know her to be my enemy. — I was intending to account to you for the change of behaviour you accused me of at the beginning of the conversation; but was diverted from it by your vehemence. Indeed, my beloved creature, you were *very* vehement. Do you think, it must not be matter of high regret to me, to find my wishes so often delayed and postponed in favour of your predominant view to a reconciliation with relations who will not be reconciled to you? — To this was owing your declining to celebrate our nuptials before we came to town, though you were atrociously treated by your sister, and your whole family; and though so ardently pressed to celebrate by me — to this was owing the ready offence you took at my four friends: and at the unavailing attempt I made to see a dropped letter; little imagining, from what two such ladies could write to each other, that there could be room for mortal displeasure. — To this was owing the week's distance you held me at, till you knew the issue of another application. — But when they had rejected that; when you had sent my coldly-received proposals to Miss Howe for her approbation or advice, as indeed I advised; and had honoured me with your company at the play on Saturday night) my whole behaviour unobjectible to the last hour); must not, madam, the sudden change in your conduct, the very next morning, astonish and distress me? — And this persisted in with still stronger declarations, after you had received the impatiently-expected letter from Miss Howe; must I not conclude, that all was owing to her influence; and that some other application or project was meditating, that made it necessary to keep me again at a distance, till the result were known, and which was to deprive me of you for ever? for was not that your constantly proposed preliminary? — Well, madam, might I be wrought up to a half-phrensy by this apprehension; and well might I charge you with hating me. — And now, dearest creature, let me know, I once more ask you; what is Miss Howe's opinion of my proposals?

Were I disposed to debate with you, Mr. Lovelace, I could very easily answer your fine harangue. But, at present, I shall only say, that your ways have been very unaccountable. You seem to me, if your meanings were always just, to have taken great pains to embarrass them. Whether owing in you to the want of a clear head, or a sound heart, I cannot determine; but it is to the want of one of them, I verily think, that I am to ascribe the greatest part of your strange conduct.

Curse upon the heart of the little devil, said I, who instigates you to think so hardly of the faithfullest heart in the world!

How dare you, sir! And there she stopped; having almost overshot herself; as I designed she should.

How dare I *what*, madam? And I looked with meaning. How dare I *what?*

Vile man! — And do you — and there again she stopt.

Do I *what*, madam?— And why *vile man?*

How dare you curse *any body* in my presence?

O the sweet receder! But that was not to go off so with a Lovelace.

Why then, dearest creature, is there *any body* that instigates you? — If there be, again I curse them, be they whom they will.

She was in a charming pretty passion. And this was the first time that I had the odds in my favour.

Well, madam, it is just as I thought. And now I know how to account for a temper that I hope not *natural* to you.

Artful wretch! And is it thus you would entrap me? But know, sir, that I receive letters from nobody but Miss Howe. Miss Howe likes some of your ways as little as I do; for I have set every thing before her. Yet she is thus far *your* enemy as she is mine: she thinks I should not refuse your offers; but endeavour to make the best of my lot. And now you have the truth. Would to heaven you were capable of dealing with equal sincerity!

I *am*, madam. And here on my knee, I renew my vows, and my supplication, that you will make me yours. Yours for ever. And let me have cause to bless you and Miss Howe in the same breath.

To say the truth, Belford, I had before begun to think, that the vixen of a girl, who certainly likes not Hickman, was in love with *me*.

Rise, sir, from your too-ready knees; and mock me not.

Too-ready knees, thought I! Though this humble posture so little affects this proud beauty, she knows not how much I have obtained of others of her sex, nor how often I have been forgiven for the last attempts, by kneeling.

Mock you, madam! And I arose, and re-urged her for the day. I blamed myself at the same time for the invitation I had given to Lord M. as it might subject me to delay from his infirmities: but told her, that I would write to him to excuse me, if she had no objection; or to give him the day she would give me, and not wait for him, if he could not come in time.

My day, sir, said she, is never. Be not surprised. A person of politeness, judging between us, would not be surprised that I say so. But, indeed, Mr. Lovelace [and wept through impatience] you either know not how to treat with a mind of the least degree of delicacy, notwithstanding your birth and education, or you are an ingrateful man; and [after a pause] a *worse* than an ingrateful one. But I will retire. I will see you again to-morrow. I cannot before. I think I hate you. You *may* look. Indeed I think I hate you. And if, upon a re-examination of my own heart, I find I do, I would not for the world that matters should go on further between us.

But I see, I see, she does not *hate* me! How it would mortify my vanity, if I thought there was a woman in the world, much more this, that could *hate* me! 'Tis evident, villain as she thinks me, that I should not be an *odious* villain, if I could but at last in *one* instance cease to be a villain! She could not hold it, determined as she had thought herself, I saw by her eyes, the moment I endeavoured to dissipate her apprehensions, on my *too-ready knees*, as she calls them. The moment the rough covering my teasing behaviour has thrown over her affections is quite removed, I doubt not to find all silk and silver at the bottom, all soft, bright, and charming.

I was, however, too much vexed, disconcerted, mortified, to hinder her from retiring. And yet she had not gone, if Dorcas had not coughed.

The wench came in, as soon as her lady had retired, and gave me the copy she had taken. And what should it be of but the answer the truly-admirable creature had intended to give to my written proposals in relation to settlements?

I have but just dipped into this affecting paper. Were I to read it attentively, not a wink should I sleep this night. To-morrow it shall obtain my serious consideration.

LETTER CVI.

Mr. Lovelace to John Belford, Esq.

Tuesday morning, May 23.

THE dear creature desires to be excused seeing me till the evening. She is not very well, as Dorcas tells me.

Read here, if thou wilt, the paper transcribed by Dorcas. It is impossible that I should proceed with my projects against this admirable woman, were it not that I am resolved, after a few trials more, if as nobly sustained as those she has already passed through, to make her (if she really hate me not) legally mine.

" TO MR. LOVELACE.

"WHEN a woman is married, that supreme earthly obligation requires that in all instances where her husband's real honour is concerned she should yield her own will to his. But, beforehand, I could be glad, conformably to what I have always signified, to have the most explicit assurances, that every possible way should be tried to avoid litigation with my father. Time and patience will subdue all things. My prospects of happiness are extremely contracted. A husband's right will be always the same. In my lifetime I could wish nothing to be done of this sort. Your circumstances, sir, will not oblige you to extort violently from him what is in his hands. All that depends upon *me*, either with regard to my person, to my diversions, or to the economy that no married woman, of whatever rank or quality, should be above inspecting, shall be done, to prevent a necessity for such measures being taken. And if there will be no *necessity* for them, it is to be hoped that motives *less* excusable will not have force — motives which must be founded in a littleness of mind, which a woman, who has *not* that littleness of mind, will be under such temptations as her duty will hardly be able at all times to check, to despise her husband for having; especially in cases where her own family, so much a part of herself, and which will have obligations upon her (though then but *secondary* ones) from which she can never be freed, is intimately concerned.

"This article, then, I urge to your most serious consideration, as what lies next my heart. I enter not here minutely into the fatal misunderstanding between them and you: the fault may be in both. But, sir, *yours* was the foundation-fault: at least, you gave a too plausible pretence for my brother's antipathy to work upon. Condescension was no part of your study. You chose to bear the imputations laid to your charge, rather than to make it your endeavour to obviate them.

"But this may lead into hateful recrimination — let it be remembered, I will only say, in this place, that in *their* eye, you have robbed them of a daughter they doated upon; and that their resentments on this occasion rise but in proportion to their love, and their disappointment. If they were faulty in some of the measures they took, while they themselves did not think so, who shall judge for *them?* You, sir, who will judge every body as you please, and will let nobody judge you in *your own* particular, must not be their judge. — It may therefore be expected, that they will stand out.

"As for *myself*, sir, I must leave it [so seems it to be destined] to your justice, to treat me as you shall think I deserve: but if your future behaviour to *them* is not governed by that harsh-sounding implacableness, which you charge upon some of *their* tempers, the splendour of your family, and the excellent character of *some* of them, (of *all* indeed, unless your own conscience furnishes you with one *only* exception) will, on better consideration, do every thing with them: for they *may* be overcome; perhaps, however, with the more difficulty, as the greatly prosperous less bear controul and disappointment than others: for I will own to you, that I have often in secret lamented, that their great acquirements have been a snare to them; perhaps as great a snare, as some *other* accidentals have been to you; which, being less immediately your own gifts, you have still less reason than they to value yourself upon them.

"Let me only, on this subject, further observe, that condescension is not meanness. There is a glory in yielding, that hardly any violent spirit can judge of. My brother perhaps is no more sensible of *this* than you. But as you have talents which he has not, (who, however, has, as I hope, that regard for morals, the want of which makes one of his objections to you) I could wish it may not be owing to *you* that your mutual dislikes to each other do not subside; for it is my earnest hope, that in time you may see each other without exciting the fears of a wife and a sister for the consequence. Not that I should wish you to yield in points that truly concerned your honour: no, sir, I would be as delicate in such, as you yourself: *more* delicate, I will venture to say, because more *uniformly* so. How vain, how contemptible, is that pride, which shews itself in standing upon diminutive observances; and gives up, and makes a jest of the most important duties!

"This article being considered as I wish, all the rest will be easy. Were I to accept of the handsome separate provision you seem to intend me; added to the considerable sums arising from my grandfather's estate since his death (more considerable than perhaps you may suppose from your offer); I should think it my duty to lay up for the family good, and for unforeseen events, out of it: for, as to my donations, I would generally confine myself in them to the tenth of my income, be it what it would. I aim at no glare in what I do of that sort. All I wish for, is the power of relieving the lame, the blind, the sick, and the industrious poor, and those whom accident has made so, or sudden distress reduced. The common or bred beggars I leave to others, and to the public provision. They cannot be lower: perhaps they wish not to be higher: and, not able to do for every one, I aim not at works of supererogation. Two hundred pounds a year would do all I wish to do of the separate sort: for all above, I would content myself to ask you: except, mistrusting your own economy, you would give up to my management and keeping, in order to provide for future contingencies, a larger portion; for which, as your steward, I would regularly account.

"As to clothes, I have particularly two suits, which, having been only in a manner tried on, would answer for any present occasion. Jewels I have of my grandmother's, which want only new setting: another set I have, which on particular days I used to wear. Although these are not sent me, I have no doubt being merely personals, but they will, when I send for them in *another name*; till when I should not choose to wear any.

"As to your complaints of my diffidences, and the like, I appeal to your own heart, if it be possible for you to make my case your own for one moment, and to retrospect some parts of your behaviour, words, and actions, whether I am not rather to be justified than censured: and whether, of all men in the world, *avowing what you avow*, you ought not to think so. If you do not, let me admonish you, sir, from the very *mismatch*, that then must appear to be in our minds, never to seek, nor so much as wish to bring about the *most intimate* union of interests between yourself and
May 20. "CLARISSA HARLOWE."

The original of this charming paper, as Dorcas tells me, was torn almost in two. In one of her pets, I suppose! What business have the sex, whose principal glory is meekness, and patience, and resignation, to be in a passion, I trow? — Will not she, who allows herself such liberties as a maiden, take greater when married?

And a *wife* to be in a passion! — Let me tell the ladies, it is an impudent thing, begging their pardon, and as *imprudent* as impudent, for a *wife* to be in a passion, if she mean not eternal separation, or wicked defiance, by it: for is it not rejecting at once all that expostulatory meekness, and gentle reasoning, mingled with sighs as gentle, and graced with bent knees, supplicating hands, and eyes lifted up to your imperial countenance, just running over, that should make a reconciliation speedy, and as lasting as speedy? Even suppose the husband is in the wrong, will not his being so give the greater force to her expostulation?

Now I think of it, a man *should* be in the wrong now-and-then, to make his wife shine. Miss Howe tells my charmer, that adversity is *her* shining time. 'Tis a generous thing in a man to make his wife shine at his own expense: to give her leave to triumph over him by patient reasoning: for were he to be *too imperial* to acknowledge his fault *on the spot*, she will find the benefit of her duty and submission *in future*, and in the high opinion he will conceive of her prudence and obligingness — and so, by degrees, she will become her master's master.

But for a wife to come up with a kimboed arm, the other hand thrown out, perhaps with a pointing finger — Look ye here, sir! — Take notice! — If *you* are wrong, *I'll* be wrong! — If *you* are in a passion, *I'll* be in a passion! — Rebuff, — for rebuff, sir! — If *you* fly, *I'll* tear! — If *you* swear, *I'll* curse! — And the same room, and the same bed, shall not hold us, sir!—For, remember, I am married, sir!—I am a wife, sir!—You can't help yourself, sir!—Your honour, as well as your peace, is in my keeping!—And, if you like not this treatment, you may have worse, sir!

Ah! Jack! Jack! what man who has observed these things, either *implied*, or *expressed*, in *other* families, would wish to be an husband?

Dorcas found this paper in one of the drawers of her lady's dressing table. She was reperusing it, as she supposes, when the honest wench carried my message to desire her to favour me at the tea-table: for she saw her pop a paper into the drawer as she came in; and there, on her mistress's going to meet me in the dining-room, she found it; and to be this.

But I had better not to have had a copy of it, as far as I know: for, determined as I was before upon my operations, it instantly turned all my resolutions in her favour. Yet I would give something to be convinced, that she did not pop it into her drawer before the wench, in order for me to see it; and perhaps (if I were to take notice of it) to discover whether Dorcas, according to Miss Howe's advice, were most *my* friend, or *hers*.

The very suspicion of this will do her no good: for I cannot bear to be *artfully dealt with*. People love to enjoy their own peculiar talents in *monopoly*, as I may say. I am aware that it will strengthen thy arguments against me in her behalf. But I know every tittle thou canst say upon it. Spare, therefore, thy wambling nonsense, I desire thee; and leave this sweet excellence and me to our fate; that will determine *for* us as it shall please itself: for as Cowley says,

An unseen hand makes all our moves:
And some are great, and some are small;
Some climb to good, some from good fortune fall:
Some wise men, and some fools we call:
Figures, alas! of speech! For destiny plays us all.

But, after all, I am sorry, *almost* sorry (for how shall I do to be *quite* sorry, when it is not *given* to me to be so?) that I cannot, until I have made further trials, resolve upon wedlock.

I have just read over again this intended answer to my proposals: and how I adore her for it!

But yet; another *yet!*—She has not given it or sent it to me.—It is not therefore *her* answer. It is not written *for* me, though to me. Nay, she has not *intended* to send it to me: she has even torn it, perhaps with indignation, as thinking it too *good* for me. By this action she absolutely retracts it. Why then does my foolish fondness seek to establish for her the same merit in my heart, as if she avowed it? Pr'ythee, dear Belford, once more leave us to our fate; and do not thou interpose with thy nonsense, to weaken a spirit already too squeamish, and strengthen a conscience that has declared itself of her party.

Then again, remember thy

recent discoveries, Lovelace! Remember her indifference, attended with all the appearance of contempt and hatred. View her, even *now*, wrapped up in reserve and mystery; meditating plots, as far as thou knowest, against the sovereignty thou hast, by right of conquest, obtained over her. Remember, in short, all thou hast *threatened* to remember against this insolent beauty, who is a rebel to the power she has listed under.

But yet, how dost thou propose to subdue thy sweet enemy! — Abhorred be *force*, be the *necessity* of force, if that can be avoided! There is no triumph in *force* — no conquest over the will — no prevailing by gentle degrees, over the gentle passions! *Force* is the devil!

My cursed character, as I have often said, was against me at setting-out — yet is she not a *woman?* Cannot I find one yielding or but half-yielding moment, if she do not absolutely hate me?

But with what can I tempt her? — RICHES she was born to, and despises, knowing what they are. JEWELS and ornaments, to a mind so much a jewel, and so richly set, her worthy consciousness will not let her value. LOVE — if she be susceptible of love, it seems to be so much under the direction of prudence, that one unguarded moment, I fear, cannot be reasonably hoped for: and so much VIGILANCE, so much apprehensiveness, that her fears are ever aforehand with her dangers. Then her LOVE of VIRTUE seems to be *principle*, native principle, or, if *not* native, so deeply rooted, that its fibres have struck into her heart, and, as she grew up, so blended and twisted themselves with the strings of life, that I doubt there is no separating of the one without cutting the others asunder.

What then can be done to make such a matchless creature get over the first tests, in order to put her to the grand proof, *whether once overcome, she will not be always overcome?*

Our mother and her nymphs say, I am a perfect Craven, and no Lovelace: and so I think. But this is no simpering, smiling charmer, as I have found others to be, when I have touched upon affecting subjects at a distance; as once or twice I have tried to her, the mother introducing them (to make sex palliate the freedom to sex) when only we three together. She is above the affectation of not seeming to understand you. She shews by her displeasure, and a fierceness not natural to her eye, that she judges of an impure heart by an impure mouth, and darts dead at once even the embryo hopes of an encroaching lover, however distantly insinuated, before the meaning hint can dawn into *double entendre.*

By my faith, Jack, as I sit gazing upon her, my whole soul in my eyes, contemplating her perfections, and thinking when I have seen her easy and serene, what would be her thoughts, did *she* know my heart as well as *I* know it; when I behold her disturbed and jealous, and think of the *justness* of her apprehensions, and that she cannot fear so much, as there is *room* for her to fear; my heart often misgives me.

And must, think I, O creature so divinely excellent, and so beloved of my soul, those arms, those incircling arms, that would make a monarch happy, be used to repel brutal force; all their strength unavailingly, perhaps, exerted to repel it, and to defend a person so delicately framed? Can violence enter into the heart of a wretch, who might entitle himself to all thy willing, yet virtuous love, and make the blessings he aspires after, thy *duty* to confer? — Begone, villain-purposes! Sink ye all to the hell that could only inspire ye! And I am then ready to throw myself at her feet, to confess my villainous designs, to avow my repentance, and put it out of my power to act unworthily by such an excellence.

How then comes it, that all these compassionate, and, as some would call them, *honest* sensibilities go off? — Why, Miss Howe will tell thee: she says, I am the *devil*. — By my conscience, I think he has at present a great share in me.

There's ingenuousness! — How I lay myself open to thee! — But seest thou not, that the more I say against myself, the less room there is for thee to take me to task? — O Belford, Belford! I cannot, cannot — (at least *at present*) I cannot marry.

Then her family, my bitter enemies — to supple to them, or if I do not, to make her *as* unhappy as she can be from my *attempts* —

Then does she not love them too much, me too little?

She now seems to despise me: Miss Howe declares that she really does despise me. To be *despised by a* WIFE — what a thought is that! — To be *excelled by a* WIFE too, in every part of praise-worthy knowledge! — To *take lessons*, to *take instructions*, from a WIFE! — *More* than despise me, she herself has taken time to consider whether she does not *hate* me: — *I hate you*, Lovelace, *with my whole heart*, said she to me but yesterday! *My soul is above thee, man!* — *Urge me not to tell thee, how sincerely I think my soul above thee!* How poor indeed was I then, even in my own heart! — So *visible* a superiority, to so proud a spirit as mine! — And *here* from below, from BELOW indeed! from these *women!* I am so goaded on —

Yet 'tis poor too, to think myself a machine in the hands of such wretches. — I am *no* machine. — Lovelace, thou art base to thyself, but to *suppose* thyself a machine.

But having gone thus far, I should be unhappy if after marriage, in the petulance of ill humour, I had it to reproach myself, that I did not try her to the utmost. And yet I don't know how it is, but this lady, the moment I come into her presence, half-assimilates me to her own virtue. — Once or twice (to say nothing of her triumph over me on Sunday night) I was prevailed upon to fluster myself, with an intention to make some advances, which, if obliged to recede, I might lay upon raised spirits: but the instant I beheld her, I was soberized into awe and reverence: and the majesty of her even *visible* purity first damped, and then extinguished, my *double* flame.

What a surprisingly powerful effect, so much and so long in my power *she!* so instigated by some of her own sex, and so stimulated by passion, *I!* — How can this be accounted for in a Lovelace!

But, what a heap of stuff have I written! — How have I been run away with! — By what? — Canst thou say, by what! — O thou lurking varletess CONSCIENCE! — Is it thou, that hast thus made me of party against myself? — How camest thou in? — In what disguise, thou egregious haunter of my more agreeable hours? — Stand *thou*, with *fate*, but neuter in this controversy; and, if I cannot do credit to human nature, and to the female sex, by bringing down such an angel as this to class with and adorn it (for adorn it she does in her foibles) then I am all yours, and never will resist you more.

Here I arose. I shook myself. The window was open. Away the troublesome bosom-visitor, the intruder, is flown. — I see it yet! — I see it yet! — And now it lessens to my aching eye! — And now the cleft air is closed after it, and it is out of sight! — And once more I am ROBERT LOVELACE.

LETTER CVII.

Mr. Lovelace to John Belford, Esq.

Tuesday, May 23.

WELL did I, but just in time, conclude to have done with Mrs. Fretchville and the house: for here Mennell has declared, that he cannot in conscience and honour go any further. — He would not for the world be accessary to the deceiving of such a lady! — I was a fool to let either you or him see her; for ever *since*, ye have both had scruples, which neither would have had were a *woman* to have been in the question.

Well, I can't help it!

Mennell has, however, though with some reluctance, consented to write me a letter, provided I will allow it to be the last step he shall take in this affair.

I presumed, I told him, that if I could cause Mrs. Fretchville's *woman* to supply *his* place, he would have no objection to that.

None, he says — *but is it not pity* —

A pitiful fellow! Such a ridiculous kind of pity *his*, as those silly souls have, who would not kill an innocent chicken for the world; but, when killed to their hands, are always the most greedy devourers of it.

Now this letter gives the servant the small-pox: and she has given it to her unhappy vapourish lady. Vapourish people are perpetual subjects for diseases to work upon. *Name* but the malady, and it is *their's* in a moment. Ever fitted for inoculation. The physical tribe's milch-cows. — A vapourish or splenetic patient is a fiddle for the doctors; and they are eternally playing upon it. Sweet music does it make them. All their difficulty, except a case extraordinary happens, (as poor Mrs. Fretchville's, who has *realized* her apprehensions) is but to hold their countenance, while their patient is drawing up a bill of indictment against himself; — and when they have heard it, proceed to *punish* — the right word for *prescribe*. Why should they not, when the criminal has confessed his guilt? — And *punish* they generally do with a vengeance.

Yet, silly toads too, now I think of it. For why, when they know they cannot do good, may they not as well endeavour to gratify, as to nauseate, the patient's palate?

Were I a physician, I'd get all the trade to myself: for Malmsey and Cyprus, and the generous product of the Cape, a little disguised, should be my principal doses: as these would create new spirits, how would the revived patient covet the physic, and adore the doctor!

Give all the paraders of the faculty whom thou knowest, this hint. — There could but one inconvenience arise from it. The APOTHECARIES would find their medicines cost them *something:* but the demand for quantities would answer that: since the honest NURSE would be the patient's taster; perpetually requiring repetitions of the last cordial julap.

Well, but to the letter — yet what need of further explanation after the hints in my former? The widow can't be removed; and that's enough: and Mennell's work is over; and his conscience left to plague him for his own sins, and not another man's: and, very possibly, plague enough will it give him for those.

This letter is directed, *To Robert Lovelace, Esq. or, in his absence, To his Lady.* She had refused dining with me, or seeing me: and I was out when it came. She opened it: so is my lady by her own consent, proud and saucy as she is.

I am glad at my heart that it came before we entirely make up. She would else perhaps have concluded it to be *contrived for a delay;* and, now moreover, we can accommodate our old and new quarrels together: and that's contrivance, you know. But how is her dear heart humbled to what it was when I knew her first, that she can apprehend any delays from me; and have nothing to do but to vex at them!

I came in to dinner. She sent me down the letter, desiring my excuse for opening it. — Did it before she was aware. Lady-pride, Belford! — Recollection, then retrogradation!

I requested to see her upon it

that moment. — But she desires to suspend our interview till morning. I will bring her to own, before I have done with her, that she can't see me too often.

My impatience was so great, on an occasion so *unexpected*, that I could not help writing to tell her, "How much vexed I was at the accident: but that it need not delay my happy day, as that did not depend upon the house. [*She knew that before, she'll think; and so did I:*] and as Mrs. Fretchville, by Mr. Mennell, so handsomely expressed her concern upon it, and her wishes, that it could suit us to bear with the unavoidable delay, I hoped, that going down to the Lawn for two or three of the summer months, when I was made the happiest of men, would be favourable to all round."

The dear creature takes this incident to heart, I believe: she has sent word to my repeated request to see her notwithstanding her denial, that she cannot till the morning: it shall be then at six o'clock, if I please!

To be sure I *do* please!

Can see her but once a day now, Jack!

Did I tell thee, that I wrote a letter to my cousin Montague, wondering that I heard not from Lord M. as the subject was so very interesting! In it I acquainted her with the house I was about taking; and with Mrs. Fretchville's vapourish delays.

I was very loth to engage my own family, either man or woman, in this affair; but I must take my measures securely: and already they all think as bad of me as they well can. You observe by my Lord M.'s letter to yourself, that the well-manner'd peer is afraid I should play this admirable creature one of my *usual dog's tricks*.

I have received just now an answer from Charlotte.

Charlotte is not well. A stomach disorder!

No wonder a girl's stomach should plague her. A single woman, that's it. When she has a man to plague, it will have something besides itself to prey upon. Knowest thou not moreover, that man is the woman's sun; woman is the man's earth? — How dreary, how desolate, the earth, that the sun shines not upon!

Poor Charlotte! But *I heard* she was not well: that encouraged me to write to her; and to express myself a little concerned, that she had not of her own accord thought of a visit in town to my charmer.

Here follows a copy of her letter. Thou wilt see by it, that every little monkey is to catechise *me*. They all depend upon my good-nature.

DEAR COUSIN, M. Hall, May 22.

We have been in daily hope for a long time, I must call it, of hearing that the happy knot was tied. My lord has been very much out of order: and yet nothing would serve him but he would himself write an answer to your letter. It was the only opportunity he should ever have, perhaps, to throw in a little good advice to you, with the hope of its being of any signification; and he has been several hours in a day, as his gout would let him, busied in it. It wants now only his last revisal. He hopes it will have the greater weight with you, if it appear all in his own hand-writing.

Indeed, Mr. Lovelace, his worthy heart is wrapped up in you. I wish you loved yourself but half as well. But I believe too, that, if all the family loved you less, you would love yourself more.

His lordship has been very busy, at the times he could not write, in consulting Pritchard about those estates, which he proposes to transfer to you on the happy occasion, that he may answer your letter in the most acceptable manner; and shew, by effects, how kindly he takes your invitation. I assure you, he is mighty proud of it.

As for myself, I am not at all well, and have not been for some weeks past, with my old stomach-disorder. I had certainly else before now have done myself the honour you wonder I have *not* done myself. Lady Betty, who would have accompanied me (for we had laid it all out) has been exceedingly busy in her law-affair; her antagonist, who is actually on the spot, having been making proposals for an accommodation. But you may assure yourself, that when our dear relation-elect shall be entered upon the new habitation you tell me of, we will do ourselves the honour of visiting her, and if any delay arises from the dear lady's want of courage, (which considering her man, let me tell you, may very well be) we will endeavour to inspire her with it, and be sponsors for you; — for, cousin, I believe you have need to be christened over again before you are entitled to so great a blessing. What think you?

Just now, my lord tells me, he will dispatch a man on purpose with his letter to-morrow: so I needed not to have written. But now I have, let it go; and by Empson, who sets out directly on his return to town.

My best compliments, and sister's, to the most deserving lady in the world [you will need no other direction to the person meant] conclude me,

Your affectionate cousin and servant,
CHARL. MONTAGUE.

Thou seest how seasonably this letter comes. I hope my lord will write nothing but what I may shew to my beloved. I have actually sent her up this letter of Charlotte's; and hope for happy effects from it.
R. L.

The lady, in her next letter, gives Miss Howe an account of what has passed between Mr. Lovelace and herself. She resents his be-

haviour with her usual dignity: but when she comes to mention Mr. Mennell's letter, she re-urges Miss Howe to perfect her scheme for her deliverance; being resolved to leave him. But, dating again, on his sending up to her Miss Montague's letter, she alters her mind, and desires her to suspend for the present her application to Mrs. Townsend.

I HAD begun, *says she*, to suspect all he had said of Mrs. Fretchville and her house; and even Mr. Mennell himself, though so well-appearing a man. But now that I find Mr. Lovelace had apprised his relations of his intention to take it, and had engaged some of the ladies to visit me there; I could hardly forbear blaming myself for censuring him as capable of so vile an imposture. But may he not thank himself for acting so very unaccountably, and taking such needlessly-awry steps, as he has done; embarrassing, as I told him, his own meanings, if they were good?

LETTER CVIII.
Mr. Lovelace to John Belford, Esq.
Wednesday, May 24.

He gives his friend an account of their interview that morning; and of the happy effects of his cousin Montague's letter in his favour. Her reserves, however, he tells him, are not absolutely banished. But this he imputes to form.

IT is *not* in the power of woman, says he, to be altogether sincere on these occasions. But why? — Do they think it so great a disgrace to be found out to be really what they are?

I regretted the illness of Mrs. Fretchville; as the intention I had to fix her dear self in the house before the happy knot was tied, would have set her in that independence in *appearance*, as well as *fact*, which was necessary to shew to all the world, that her choice was free; and as the ladies of my family would have been proud to make their court to her there; while the settlements and our equipages were preparing. But on any other account, there was no great matter in it; since when my happy day was over, we could, with so much convenience, go down to the Lawn, to my Lord M.'s, and to Lady Sarah's or Lady Betty's, in turn; which would give full time to provide ourselves with servants, and other accommodations.

How sweetly the charmer listened!

I asked her, if she had had the small-pox?

Ten thousand pounds the worse in my estimation, thought I, if she has not; for not one of her charming graces can I dispense with.

'Twas always a doubtful point with her mother and Mrs. Norton, she owned. But although she was not afraid of it, she chose not unnecessarily to rush into places where it was.

Right, thought *I* — else, I said, it would not have been amiss for her to see the house before she went into the country; for, if *she* liked it not, I was not obliged to have it.

She asked, if she might take a copy of Miss Montague's letter? I said she might keep the letter itself, and send it to Miss Howe, if she pleased; for *that*, I supposed, was her intention.

She bowed her head to me.

There, Jack! I shall have her courtesy to me by-and-bye, I question not. What a-devil had I to do, to terrify the sweet creature by my termagant projects!— Yet it was not amiss, I believe, to make her afraid of me. She *says*, I am an unpolite man — and every instance of politeness from such a one, is deemed a favour.

Talking of the settlements, I told her, I had rather that Pritchard (mentioned by my cousin Charlotte) had not been consulted on this occasion. Pritchard, indeed, was a very honest man; and had been for a generation in the family; and knew the estates, and the condition of them, better than either my lord or myself: but Pritchard, like other old men, was diffident and slow; and valued himself upon his skill as a draughtsman; and for the sake of that paltry reputation, must have all his forms preserved, were an imperial crown to depend upon his dispatch.

I kissed her unrepulsing hand no less than five times during this conversation. Lord, Jack, how my generous heart ran over!— She was quite obliging at parting. — She in a manner asked me *leave* to retire; to re-peruse Charlotte's letter.— I think she bent her knees to me; but I won't be sure.— How happy might we have both been long ago, had the dear creature been always as complaisant to me! For I do love respect, and, whether I deserve it or not, always had it, till I knew this proud beauty.

And now, Belford, are we in a train, or the deuce is in it. Every fortified town has its strong and its weak place. I had carried on my attacks against the impregnable parts. I have no doubt but I shall either *shine* or *smuggle* her out of her cloak, since she and Miss Howe have intended to employ a smuggler against *me*. — All we wait for now is my lord's letter.

But I had like to have *forgot* to tell thee, that we have been not a little alarmed, by some inquiries that have been made after me and my beloved, by a man of good appearance; who yesterday procured a tradesman in the neighbourhood to send for Dorcas: of whom he asked several questions relating to us; and particularly (as we boarded and lodged in one house) whether we were married?

This has given my beloved great uneasiness. And I could not help observing upon it, to her, *how right a thing it was, that we had given out below, that we were married.* The inquiry, most probably, I said, was from her brother's quarter; and now, perhaps, that our marriage was owned, we should hear no more of his machinations. The person, it seems, was curious to know the *day* that the ceremony was performed. But Dorcas refused to give him any other particulars, than that we *were* married; and she was the more reserved, as he declined to tell her the motives of his inquiry.

LETTER CIX.
Mr. Lovelace to John Belford, Esq.

May 24.

THE devil take this uncle of mine! He has at last sent me a letter, which I cannot shew, without exposing the head of our family for a fool. A confounded parcel of pop-guns has he let off upon me. I was in hopes he had exhausted his whole stock of this sort, in his letter to you. — To keep it back, to delay sending it, till he had recollected all this *farrago* of nonsense — confound his *wisdom of nations*, if so much of it is to be scraped together, in disgrace of itself, to make one egregious simpleton! — But I am glad I am fortified with this piece of flagrant folly, however; since, in all human affairs, the *convenient* and *inconvenient*, the *good* and the *bad*, are so mingled, that there is no having the one without the other.

I have already offered the bill inclosed in it to my beloved: and read to her part of the letter. But she refused the bill: and as I am in cash myself, I shall return it. She seemed very desirous to peruse the whole letter. And when I told her, that were it not for exposing the writer, I would oblige her; she said, it would not be exposing his lordship to shew it to her; and that she always preferred the heart to the head. I knew her meaning; but did not thank her for it.

All that makes for me in it, I will transcribe for her — yet hang it, she shall have the letter, and my soul with it, for one consenting kiss.

* * *

SHE has got the letter from me, without the reward. Deuce take me, if I had the courage to propose the condition. A new character this of bashfulness in thy friend. I see, *that a truly modest woman may make even a confident man keep his distance.* By my soul, Belford, I believe, that nine women in ten, who fall, fall either *from their own vanity*, or *levity*, or for want of *circumspection* and *proper reserves*.

* * *

I DID intend to take my reward on her returning a letter so favourable to us both. But she sent it to me, sealed up, by Dorcas. I might have thought that there were two or three hints in it, that she would be too nice immediately to appear to. I send it to thee; and here will stop, to give thee time to read it. Return it as soon as thou hast perused it.

LETTER CX.
Lord M. to Robert Lovelace, Esq.

Tuesday, May 23.

IT is a long lane that has no turning — do not despise me for my proverbs — you know I was always fond of them; and if you had been so too, it would have been the better for you, let me tell you. I dare swear the fine lady you are so likely to be soon happy with, will be far from despising them; for I am told that she writes well, and that all her letters are full of sentences. God convert you! for nobody but he and this lady can.

I have no manner of doubt now but that you will marry, as your father, and all your ancestors, did before you: else you would have had no title to be my heir; nor can your descendants have any title to be yours, unless they are legitimate; that's worth your remembrance, sir! — *No man is always a fool, every man is sometimes.* — But your follies, I hope, are now at an end.

I know, you have vowed revenge against this fine lady's family: but no more of that now. You must look upon them all as your relations; and forgive, and forget. And when they see you make a good husband and a good father, [which God send, for all our sakes!] they will wonder at their nonsensical antipathy, and beg your pardon: but while they think you a vile fellow, and a rake, how can they either love you, or excuse their daughter?

And methinks I could wish to give a word of comfort to the lady, who, doubtless, must be under great fears, how she shall be able to hold-in such a wild creature as you have hitherto been. I would hint to her, that by strong arguments, and gentle words, she may do any thing with you; for though you are too apt to be hot, gentle words will cool you, and bring you into the temper that is necessary for your cure.

Would to God, *my* poor lady, your aunt, who is dead and gone, had been a proper patient for the same remedy! God rest her soul! No reflections upon her memory! *Worth is best known by want!* I know *hers* now; and, if I had went first, she would by this time have known *mine.*

There is great wisdom in that saying, *God send me a friend, that may tell me of my faults: if not, an enemy, and he will.* Not that I am your enemy: and that you well know. *The more noble any one is, the more humble*: so bear with me, if you would be thought noble. — Am I not your uncle? And do I not design to be better to you than your father could be? Nay, I will be your father too, when the happy day comes; since you desire it; and pray make my compliments to my dear niece; and tell her, I wonder much that she has so long deferred your happiness.

Pray let her know as that I will present HER (not *you*) either my Lancashire seat, or *the Lawn* in Hertfordshire, and settle upon her a thousand pounds a year pennyrents, to shew her, that we are not a family to take base advantages; and you may have writings drawn, and settle as you will — honest Pritchard has the rent-roll of both these estates; and as he has been a good old servant, I recommend him to your lady's favour. I have already consulted him: he will tell you what is best for you, and most pleasing to me.

I am still very bad with my gout, but will come in a litter, as soon as the day is fixed: it would be the joy of my heart to join your hands. And, let me tell you, if you do not make the best of husbands to so good a young lady, and one who has had so much courage for your sake, I will renounce you; and settle all I can upon her and hers by you, and leave you out of the question.

If any thing be wanting for your further security, I am ready to give it; though you know, that my word has always been looked upon as my bond. And when the Harlowes know all this, let us see whether they are able to blush, and take shame to themselves.

Lady Sarah and Lady Betty want only to know the day, to make all the country round them blaze, and all their tenants mad. And, if any one of mine be sober upon the occasion, Pritchard shall eject him. And on the birth of the first child, if a son, I will do something more for you, and repeat all our rejoicings.

I ought indeed to have written sooner. But I knew, that if you thought me long, and were in haste as to your nuptials, you would write and tell me so. But my gout was very troublesome; and I am but a slow writer, you know, at best: for composing is a thing, that though formerly I was very ready at it (as my Lord Lexington used to say); yet having left it off a great while, I am not so now. And I chose, on this occasion, to write all out of my own head and memory; and to give you my best advice; for I may never have such an opportunity again. You have had [God mend you!] a strange way of turning your back upon all I have said: this once, I hope, you will be more attentive to the advice I give you for your own good.

I had still another end; nay, two other ends.

The one was, that now you are upon the borders of wedlock, as I may say, and *all your wild oats will be sown*, I would give you some instructions as to your public as well as private behaviour in life; which, intending you so much good as I do, you ought to hear; and perhaps would never have listened to, on any less extraordinary occasion.

The second is, that your dear lady-elect (who is it seems herself so fine and sententious a writer) will see by this, that it is not our faults, nor for want of the best advice, that you was not a better man than you have hitherto been.

And now, in few words, for the conduct I would wish you to follow in public, as well as in private, if you would think me worthy of advising. — It shall be short; so be not uneasy.

As to the *private* life: love your lady as she deserves. *Let your actions praise you.* Be a good husband; and so give the lie to all your enemies: and make them ashamed of their scandals. And let us have pride in saying, that Miss Harlowe has not done either herself or family any discredit by coming among us. Do this; and I, and Lady Sarah, and Lady Betty, will love you for ever.

As to your *public* conduct — this as follows is what I could wish: but I reckon your lady's wisdom will put us both right — no disparagement, sir; since, with all your wit, you have not hitherto shewn much wisdom, you know.

Get into parliament as soon as you can: for you have *talents* to make a great figure there. Who so proper to assist in making new holding laws, as those whom no law in being could hold?

Then, for so long as you will give attendance in St. Stephen's chapel — its being called a chapel, I hope, will not *disgust* you: I am sure I have known many a riot there: — a Speaker has a hard time of it! but we *peers* have more decorum — but what was I going to say? — I must go back.

For so long as you will give your attendance in parliament, for so long will you be out of mischief; out of *private* mischief, at least: and may St. Stephen's fate be yours, if you wilfully do *public* mischief!

When a new election comes, you will have two or three boroughs, you know, to choose out of: but, if you stay till then, I had rather you were for the Shire.

You will have interest enough, I am sure; and being so handsome a man, the women will *make* their husbands vote for you.

I shall long to read your speeches. I expect you will speak, if occasion offer, the very first day.

You want no courage; and think highly enough of yourself, and lowly enough of every body else, to speak on all occasions.

As to the methods of the house, you have spirit enough, I fear, to be too much above them: take care of that. I don't so much fear your want of good manners. To *men*, you want not decency, if they don't provoke you: as to that, I wish you would only learn to be as patient of contradiction from *others*, as you would have other people be to *you*.

Although I would not have you to be a courtier; neither would I have you to be a malecontent. I remember (*for I have it down*) what my old friend Archibald Hutcheson said; and it was a very good saying —(to Mr. Secretary Craggs, I think, it was) — "I look upon an administration as entitled to every vote I can with good conscience give it; for a House of Commons should not needlessly put drags upon the wheels of government: and, when I have *not* given it my vote, it was with regret: and, for my country's sake, I wished with all my heart, the measure had been such as I could have approved."

And another saying he had, which was this; "Neither can an opposition, neither can a ministry, be always wrong. To be a plumb man, therefore, with either is an infallible mark, that that man must mean more and worse than he will own he does mean."

Are these sayings bad, sir? Are

they to be despised?—Well then, why should I be despised for remembering them, and quoting them, as I love to do? Let me tell you, if you loved my company more than you do, you would not be the worse for it. I may say so without any vanity; since it is *other men's* wisdom and not *my own*, that I am so fond of.

But to add a word or two more on this occasion; and I may never have such another; for you *must* read this through — *love honest men, and herd with them, in the house and out of the house:* by whatever names they be dignified or distinguished: *keep good men company, and you shall be of their number.* But did I, or did I not, write this before?— Writing, at so many different times, and such a quantity, one may forget.

You may come in for the title when I am dead and gone — God help me!— So I would have you keep an equilibrium. If once you get the name of being a fine speaker, you may have any thing: and to be sure, you have naturally a good deal of elocution; a tongue that would delude an angel, as the women say — to their sorrow, some of them, poor creatures!— A leading man in the House of Commons is a very important character; because that House has the giving of money: and *money makes the mare to go;* aye, and queens and kings too, sometimes, to go in a manner very different from what they might otherwise choose to go, let me tell you.

However, methinks, I would not have you take a place neither — it will double your value, and your interest, if it be believed, that you will not: for, as you will then stand in no man's way, you will have no envy; but pure sterling respect; and both sides will court you.

For your part, you will not want a place as some others do, to piece up their broken fortunes. If you can now live reputably upon two thousand pounds a year, it will be hard if you cannot hereafter live upon ten or twelve — less you will not have, if you oblige me; as now by marrying so fine a lady, very much you will — and all this, over and above Lady Betty's and Lady Sarah's favours! What, in the name of wonder, could possibly possess the proud Harlowes! — That son, that son of theirs! — But for his dear sister's sake, I will say no more of him.

I never was offered a place myself: and the only one I would have taken, had I been offered it, was *Master of the Buckhounds;* for I loved hunting when I was young; and it carries a good sound with it for us who live in the country. Often have I thought of that excellent old adage; *he that eats the king's goose, shall be choked with his feathers.* I wish to the Lord, this was thoroughly considered by place-hunters! It would be better for them, and for their poor families.

I could say a great deal more, and all equally to the purpose. But really I am tired; and so I doubt are you. And, besides, I would reserve something for conversation.

My nieces Montague, and Lady Sarah and Lady Betty, join in compliments to my niece that is to be. If she would choose to have the knot tied among us, pray tell her that we shall see it *securely done:* and we will make all the country ring and blaze for a week together. But so I believe I said before.

If any thing further may be needful towards promoting your reciprocal felicity, let me know it: and how you order about the day; and all that. The inclosed bill is very much at your service. 'Tis payable at sight, as whatever else you may have occasion for, shall be.

So God bless you both; and make things as convenient to my gout as you can; though, be it whenever it will, I will hobble to you; for I long to see you; and still more to see my niece; and am (in expectation of that happy opportunity)

Your most affectionate uncle
M.

LETTER CXI.

Mr. Lovelace to John Belford, Esq.

Thursday, May 25.

Thou seest, Belford, how we now drive before the wind. — The dear creature now comes almost at the first word, whenever I desire the honour of her company. I told her last night, that apprehending delay from Pritchard's slowness, I was determined to leave it to my lord to make his compliments in his own way; and had actually that afternoon put my writings into the hands of a very eminent lawyer, Counsellor Williams, with directions for him to draw up settlements from my own estate, and conformable to those of my mother; which I put into his hands at the same time. It had been, I assured her, no small part of my concern, that her frequent displeasure, and our mutual misapprehensions, had hindered me from advising with her before on this subject. Indeed, indeed, my dearest life, said I, you have hitherto afforded me but a very thorny courtship.

She was silent. *Kindly* silent. For well know I that she could have recriminated upon me with a vengeance. But I was willing to see, if she were not loth to disoblige me now. I comforted myself, I said, with the hopes that all my difficulties were now over; and that every past disobligation would be buried in oblivion.

Now, Belford, I have actually deposited these writings with Counsellor Williams: and I expect the drafts in a week at furthest. So shall be doubly armed. For if I *attempt*, and *fail*, these will be ready to throw in, to make her have patience with me *till I can try again.*

I have more contrivances still in embryo. I could tell thee of an hundred, and yet hold another hundred in petto, to pop in as I go along, to excite thy surprise, and keep up thy attention. Nor rave thou at me; but, if thou art my friend, think of *Miss Howe's letters*, and of her *smuggling scheme*. All owing to my fair captive's informations and incitements. Am I not a *villain*, a *fool*, a *Beelzebub*, with them already? — Yet no harm done by me, nor so much as attempted!

Every thing of this nature the dear creature answered, (with a downcast eye, and a blushing cheek) she left to me.

I proposed my lord's chapel for the celebration, where we might have the presence of Lady Betty, Lady Sarah, and my two cousins Montague.

She seemed not to favour a public celebration; and waived this subject for the present. I doubted not but she would be as willing as I, to decline a public wedding; so I pressed not this matter further just then.

But patterns I *actually produced;* and a jeweller was to bring as this day several sets of jewels for her choice. But the patterns she would not open. She sighed at the mention of them: the second patterns, she said, that had been offered to her.* And very peremptorily forbid the jeweller's coming; as well as declined my offer of causing my mother's to be new set at least for the present.

I do assure thee, Belford, I was in earnest in all this. My whole estate is nothing to me, put in competition with her hoped-for favour.

* See Vol. I. pp. 190, 191.

She then told me, that she had put into writing her opinion of my general proposals; and there had expressed her mind, as to clothes and jewels: but on my strange behaviour to her *(for no cause that she knew of)* on Sunday night, she had torn the paper in two.

I earnestly pressed her to let me be favoured with a sight of this paper torn as it was. And after some hesitation, she withdrew, and sent it to me by Dorcas.

I perused it again. It was in a manner new to me, though I had read it so lately; and by my soul, I could hardly stand it. An hundred admirable creatures I called her to myself. But I charge thee, write not a word to me in her favour, if thou meanest her well; for, if I spare her, it must be all *ex mero motu.*

You may easily suppose, when I was re-admitted to her presence, that I ran over in her praises, and in vows of gratitude and everlasting love. But here's the devil; she still receives all I say with reserve; or, if it be not with reserve, she receives it so much *as her due*, that she is not at all raised by it. Some women are undone by praise, by flattery. I myself, a man, am proud of praise. Perhaps thou wilt say, that those are most proud of it, who least deserve it; as those are of riches and grandeur, who are not born to either. I own, that to be superior to these foibles it requires a soul. Have I not then a soul? — Surely I have. — Let me then be considered as an exception to the rule.

25*

Now have I foundation to go upon in my terms. My lord, in the exuberance of his generosity, mentioned a thousand pounds a year penny-rents. *This I* know, that were I to marry this lady, he would rather settle upon her all he has a mind to settle, than upon me. He has even threatened, that if I prove not a good husband to her, he will leave all he can at his death from me to her. Yet considers not that a woman so perfect can never be displeased with her husband but to *his* disgrace; for who will blame *her?* — Another reason why a LOVELACE should not wish to marry a CLARISSA.

But what a pretty fellow of an uncle is this foolish peer, to think of making a wife independent of her emperor, and a rebel of course: yet smarted himself for an error of this kind.

My beloved, in her torn paper, mentions but two hundred pounds a year, for her separate use. I insisted upon her naming a larger sum. She said it might then be three; and I, for fear she should suspect very large offers, named only five; but added the entire disposal of all arrears in her father's hands, for the benefit of Mrs. Norton, or whom she pleased.

She said that the good woman would be uneasy if any thing more than a competency were done for her. She was for suiting all her dispositions of this kind, she said, *to the usual way of life of the person.* To go beyond it, was but to put the benefitted upon projects, or to make them awkward in a new state; when they might shine in that to which they were accustomed. And to put it into so good a mother's power to give her son a beginning in his business at a proper time; yet to leave her something for herself, to set her above want, or above the necessity of taking back from her child what she had been enabled to bestow upon him; would be the height of such a worthy parent's ambition.

Here's prudence! Here's judgment in so young a creature! How do I hate the Harlowe's for producing such an angel! — O why, why, did she refuse my sincere address to tie the knot before we came to this house!

But yet, what mortifies my pride, is, that this exalted creature, if I *were* to marry her, would not be governed in her behaviour to me by love, but by generosity merely, or by blind duty; and had rather live single than be mine.

I cannot bear this. I would have the woman whom I honour with my name, if ever I confer this honour upon any, forego even her *superior duties* for me. I would have her look after me when I go out as far as she can see me, as my Rosebud after her Johnny; and meet me at my return with rapture. I would be the subject of her dreams, as well as of her waking thoughts; I would have her think every moment lost that is not passed with me: sing to me, read to me, play to me when I pleased: no joy so great as in obeying me. When I should be inclined to love, overwhelm me with it; when to be serious or solitary, if apprehensive of intrusion, retiring at a nod: approaching me only if I smiled encouragement: steal into my presence with silence; out of it, if not noticed, on tiptoe. Be a *Lady Easy* to all my pleasures, and valuing those most who most contributed to them: only sighing in private, that it was not *herself* at the time. Thus of old did the contending wives of the honest patriarchs; each recommending her handmaid to her lord, as she thought it would oblige him, and looking upon the genial product as her own.

The gentle Waller says, *women are born to be controlled.* Gentle as he was, he knew that. A tyrant husband makes a dutiful wife. And why do the sex love rakes, but because they know how to direct their uncertain wills, and manage them?

* * *

Another agreeable conversation. The day of days the subject. As to fixing a particular one, that need not be done, my charmer says, till the settlements are completed. As to marrying at my lord's chapel, the ladies of my family present, that would be making a public affair of it! and the dear creature observed with regret, that it seemed to be my lord's intention to make it so.

It could not be imagined, I said, but that his lordship's setting out in a litter, and coming to town, as well as his taste for glare, and the joy he would take to see me married at last, and to her dear self, would give it as much the air of a public marriage, as if the ceremony were performed at his own chapel, all the ladies present.

I cannot, said she, endure the thoughts of a public day. It will carry with it an air of insult upon my whole family. And for my part, if my lord will not take it amiss, [and perhaps he will not, as the motion came not from himself, but from you, Mr. Lovelace] I will very willingly dispense with his lordship's presence; the rather, as dress and appearance will then be unnecessary; for I cannot bear to think of decking my person while my parents are in tears.

How excellent this! Yet do not her parents richly deserve to be in tears?

See, Belford, with so charming a niceness, we might have been a long time ago upon the verge of the state, and yet found a great deal to do, before we entered into it.

All obedience, all resignation— no will but hers. I withdrew, and wrote directly to my lord; and she not disapproving of it, I sent it away. The purport as follows; for I took no copy.

"That I was much obliged to his lordship for his intended goodness to me, on an occasion the most solemn of my life. That the admirable lady, whom he so justly praised, thought his lordship's proposals in her favour too high. That she chose not to make a public appearance, if, without disobliging my friends, she could avoid it, till a reconciliation with her own could be effected. That although she expressed a grateful sense of his lordship's consent to give her to me with his own hand; yet presuming, that the motive to this kind intention was rather to do her honour, than it otherwise would have been his own choice (especially as travelling would be at this time so inconvenient to him) she thought it advisable to save his lordship trouble on this occasion; and hoped he would take as meant her declining the favour.

"That the Lawn will be the most acceptable to us both to retire to; and the rather, as it is so to his lordship.

"But, if he pleases, the jointure may be made from my own estate; leaving to his lordship's goodness the alternative."

I conclude with telling him, "That I had offered to present the lady his lordship's bill; but on her declining to accept of it, (having myself no present occasion for it) I return it inclosed, with my thanks, &c."

And is not this going a plaguy length? What a figure should I make in rakish annals, if at last I should be caught in my own gin?

The sex may say what they will, but a poor innocent fellow had need to take great care of himself, when he dances upon the edge of the matrimonial precipice. Many a faint-hearted man, when he began in jest, or only designed to ape gallantry, has been forced into earnest, by being over-prompt, and taken at his word, not knowing how to own that he meant less than the lady supposed he meant. I am the better enabled to judge that this must have been the case of many a sneaking varlet; because I, who know the female world as well as any man in it of my standing, am so frequently in doubt of myself, and know not what to make of the matter.

Then these little sly rogues, how they lie couchant, ready to spring upon us harmless fellows the moment we are in their reach! — When the ice is once broken for them, how swiftly can they make to port — meantime, the subject they can least *speak* to, they most *think* of. Nor can you talk of the ceremony before they have laid out in their minds how it is all to be. Little saucy-face designers! how first they draw themselves in, then us!

But be all these things as they will, Lord M. never in his life received so handsome a letter as this from his nephew

LOVELACE.

The lady, after having given to Miss Howe the particulars contained in Mr. Lovelace's last letter, thus expresses herself:

A principal consolation arising from these favourable appearances, is, that I, who have now but one only friend, shall most probably, and if it be not my own fault, have as many new ones as there are persons in Mr. Lovelace's family; and this whether Mr. Lovelace treat me kindly or not. And who knows, but that by degrees, those new friends, by their rank and merit, may have weight enough to get me restored to the favour of my relations? Till which can be effected, I shall not be tolerably easy. Happy I never expect to be. Mr. Lovelace's mind and mine are vastly different; different in *essentials*.

But as matters are at present circumstanced, I pray you, my dear friend, to keep to yourself every thing that might bring discredit to him, if revealed.—Better any body expose a man than a wife, if I *am* to be his; and what is said by you will be thought to come from me.

It shall be my constant prayer, that all the felicities which this world can afford, may be yours: and that the Almighty will never suffer you nor yours, to the remotest posterity, to want such a friend as my Anna Howe has been to her

CLARISSA HARLOWE.

LETTER CXII.
Mr. Lovelace to John Belford, Esq.

AND now, that my beloved seems secure in my net, for my project upon the vixen Miss Howe, and upon her mother; in which the officious prancer Hickman is to come in for a dash.

But why upon her mother? methinks thou askest; who, unknown to herself, has only acted, by thy impulse, through thy agent Joseph Leman, upon the folly of old Tony the uncle?

No matter for that: she believes she acts upon her own judgment; and deserves to be punished for pretending to judgment, when she has none.—Every living soul, but myself, I can tell thee, shall be punished, that treats either cruelly or disrespectfully so adored a lady. — What a plague! is it not enough that she is teased and tormented in person by me?

I have already broken the matter to our three confederates; as a *supposed*, not a *resolved on* case indeed. And yet they know, that with me, in a piece of mischief, execution with its swiftest feet, is seldom three paces behind projection, which hardly ever limps neither.

MOWBRAY is not against it. It is a scheme, he says, worthy of us: and we have not done any thing for a good while, that has made a noise.

BELTON indeed hesitates a little, because matters go wrong between him and his Thomasine; and the poor fellow has not the courage to have his sore place probed to the bottom.

TOURVILLE has started a fresh game, and shrugs his shoulders, and should not *choose* to go abroad at present, *if I please*. For I apprehend that (from the *nature* of the project) there will be a kind of necessity to travel, till all is blown over.

To ME, one country is as good as another; and I shall soon, I suppose, choose to quit this paltry island; except the mistress of my fate will consent to cohabit at home; and so lay me under no necessity of *surprising her into foreign parts.* TRAVELLING, thou knowest, gives the sexes charming opportunities of being familiar with one another. A very few days and nights must now decide all matters betwixt me and my fair inimitable.

DOLEMAN, who can act in these causes only as chamber-counsel, will inform us, by pen and ink, [his right hand and right side having not yet been struck, and the other side beginning to be sensible] of all that shall occur in our absence.

As for THEE, we had rather have thy company than not; for, although thou art a wretched fellow at contrivance, yet art thou intrepid at execution. But as thy present engagements make thy attendance uncertain, I am not for making thy part necessary to our scheme; but for leaving thee to come after us when abroad. I know thou canst not long live without us.

The project, in short, is this: Mrs. Howe has an elder sister in the Isle of Wight, who is lately a widow: and I am well informed, that the mother and daughter have engaged, before the latter is married, to pay a visit to this lady, who is rich, and intends Miss for her heiress; and in the interim will make her some valuable presents on her approaching nuptials; which, as Mrs. Howe, who loves money more than any thing but herself, told one of my acquaintance, would be *worth fetching.*

Now, Jack, nothing more need be done, than to hire a little trim vessel, which shall sail a pleasuring backward and forward to Portsmouth, Spithead, and the Isle of Wight, for a week or fortnight before we enter upon our parts of the plot. And as Mrs. Howe will be for making the best bargain she can for her passage, the master of the vessel may have orders (as a perquisite allowed him by his owners) to take what she will give him: and the master's name, be it what it will, shall be *Ganmore* on the occasion; for I know a rogue of that name, who is not obliged to be of any country, any more than we.

Well, then, we will imagine them on board. I will be there in disguise. They know not any of ye four — supposing (the scheme so inviting) that thou canst be one.

'Tis plaguy hard, if we cannot *find*, or *make*, a storm.

Perhaps they will be sea-sick: but whether they be or not, no doubt they will keep their cabin. Here will be Mrs. Howe, Miss Howe, Mr. Hickman, a maid, and a footman, I suppose; and thus we will order it:

I know it will be hard weather: I *know* it will: and before there can be the least suspicion of the matter, we shall be in sight of Guernsey, Jersey, Dieppe, Cherbourg, or any whither on the French coast that it shall please us to agree with the winds to blow us: and then, securing the footman, and the women being separated, one of us, according to lots that may be cast, shall overcome, either by persuasion or force, the maid servant: that will be no hard task; and she is a likely wench [I have seen her often:] one, Mrs. Howe; nor can there be much difficulty there; for she is full of health and life; and has been long a widow: another [*that*, says the princely lion, must be *I!*] the saucy daughter; who will be too much frightened to make great resistance [*violent* spirits, in that sex, are seldom *true* spirits — 'tis but where they *can* —] and after beating about the coast for three or four days for recreation's sake, and to make sure work, and till we see our sullen birds begin to eat and sip, we will set them all on shore where it will be most convenient; sell the vessel, [to Mrs. Townsend's agent, with all my heart, or to some other smugglers] or give it to Ganmore; and pursue our travels, and tarry abroad till all is hushed up.

Now I know thou wilt make difficulties, as it is thy way; while it is mine to conquer them. My other vassals made theirs; and I condescended to obviate them: as thus I will thine, first stating them for thee according to what I know of thy phlegm.

What, in the first place, wilt thou ask, shall be done with Hickman? who will be in full parade of dress and primness, in order to shew the old aunt what a devilish clever fellow of a nephew she is to have.

What! — I'll tell thee — Hickman, in good manners, will leave the women in the cabin — and, to shew his courage with his breeding, be upon deck. —

Well, and suppose he is?

Suppose he is! — Why then I hope it is easy for Ganmore, or any body else, myself suppose in my pea-jacket and great watchcoat, (if any other make a scruple to do it) while he stands in the way, gaping and staring like a novice, to stumble against him, and push him overboard! — A rich thought! — Is it not, Belford? — He is certainly plaguy officious in the ladies' correspondence; and, I am informed, plays double between mother and daughter, in fear of both. — Dost not see him, Jack? — I do — popping up and down, his wig and hat floating by him; and paddling, pawing, and dashing, like a frighted mongrel — I am afraid he never ventured to learn to swim.

But thou wilt not drown the poor fellow; wilt thou?

No, no! — That is not necessary to the project — I hate to do mischiefs supererogatory. The skiff shall be ready to save him, while the vessel keeps its course: he shall be set on shore with the loss of wig and hat only, and of half of his little wits, at the place where he embarked, or any where else.

Well, but shall we not be in danger of being hanged for three such enormous rapes, although

Hickman should escape with only a bellyful of sea-water?

Yes, to be sure, when caught — but is there any likelihood of that? — Besides, have we not been in danger before now for worse facts? — And what is there in being only in *danger?* — If we actually were to appear in open day in England before matters are made up, there will be greater likelihood that these women will not prosecute, than that they *will.* — For my own part I should wish they *may.* Would not a brave fellow choose to appear in court to such an arraignment, confronting women who would do credit to his attempt? The country is more merciful in *these* cases than in *any others:* I should therefore like to put myself upon my country.

Let me indulge a few reflections upon what thou mayest think the *worst* that *can* happen. I will suppose that thou art one of us, and that all five are actually brought to trial on this occasion: how bravely shall we enter a court, *I* at the head of you, dressed out each man, as if to his wedding-appearance! — You are sure of all the women, old and young, of your side — What brave fellows! — What fine gentlemen! — There goes a charming handsome man! — meaning me, to be sure! — Who could find in their hearts to hang such a gentleman as that? whispers one lady, sitting, perhaps, on the right hand of the Recorder [I suppose the scene to be in London:] while another disbelieves that any woman could *fairly* swear against me. All will crowd after *me:* it will be each man's happiness (if ye shall chance to be bashful) to be neglected: I shall be found to be the greatest criminal; and my safety, for which the general voice will be engaged, will be yours.

But then comes the triumph of triumphs, that will make the accused look up, while the accusers are covered with confusion.

Make room there! — stand by — give back! — One receiving a rap, another an elbow, half a score a push a piece! ——

Enter the slow-moving, hood-faced, down-looking plaintiffs. —

And first the widow, with a sorrowful countenance, though half veiled, pitying her daughter more than herself. The people, the women especially, who on this occasion will be five-sixths of the spectators, reproaching her — You'd have the conscience, would you, to have five such brave gentlemen as these hanged for you know not what?

Next comes the poor maid — who perhaps had been ravished twenty times before; and had not appeared now, but for company's sake; mincing, simpering, weeping, by turns: not knowing whether she should be sorry or glad.

But every eye dwells upon Miss! — See, see the handsome gentleman bows to her!

To the very ground, to be sure, I shall bow; and kiss my hand.

See her confusion! See! She turns from him! — Ay; that's because it is in open court! cries an arch one. While others admire her — Aye! that's a girl worth venturing one's neck for!

Then shall we be praised — even the judges, and the whole crowded bench will acquit us in their hearts; and every single man wish he had been me! — The women, all the time, disclaiming prosecution, were the case to be their own. To be sure, Belford, the sufferers cannot put half so good a face upon the matter as we. Then what a noise will this matter make! — Is it not enough, suppose us moving from the prison to the Sessions House*, to make a noble heart thump it away most gloriously, when such an one finds himself attended to his trial by a parade of guards and officers, of miens and aspects warlike and unwarlike; himself their whole care, and their business! — Weapons in their hands, some bright, some rusty, equally venerable for their antiquity and inoffensiveness! Others of more authoritative demeanour, strutting before with fine painted staves! Shoals of people following, with a — Which is he whom the *young* lady appears against? — Then, let us look down, look up, look round, which way we will, we shall see all the doors, the shops, the windows, the sign irons and balconies, (garrets, gutters, and chimney-tops included) all white-capt, black-hooded, and periwig'd, or crop-eared up by the *immobile vulgus:* while the floating *street swarmers*, who have seen us pass by at one place, run with stretched out necks, and strained eye-balls, a round-about way, and elbow and shoulder themselves into places by which we have not passed, in order to obtain another sight of us; every street continuing to pour out its swarms of late comers, to add to the gathering snowball; who are content to take descriptions of our persons, behaviour, and countenances, from those who had the good fortune to have been in time to see us.

Let me tell thee, Jack, I see not why (to judge according to our principles and practices) we should not be as much elated in our march, were this to happen to us, as others may be upon any other the most *mob-attracting* occasion — suppose a Lord Mayor on his *gaudy;* suppose a victorious general, or embassador, on his public entry — suppose (as I began with the *lowest*) the *grandest* parade that can be supposed, a coronation — for in all these, do not the royal guard, the heroic trained bands, the pendent, clinging throngs of spectators, with their waving heads rolling to-and-fro from house-tops to house-bottoms and street-ways, as I have above described, make the principal part of the raree-show?

And let me ask thee, if thou dost not think, that either the mayor,

---

* Within these few years past, a passage has been made from the prison to the sessions-house, whereby malefactors are carried into court without going through the street. Lovelace's triumph on their supposed march shews the wisdom of this alteration.

the embassador, or the general, would not make very pitiful figures on their galas, did not the trumpets and tabrets call together the canaille to gaze at them? — Nor perhaps should we be the most guilty heroes neither: for who knows how the magistrate may have obtained his gold chain? While the general probably returns from cutting of throats, and from murder, sanctified by custom only. — Cæsar, we are told*, had won, at the age of fifty-six, when he was assassinated, fifty pitched battles, had taken by assault above a thousand towns, and slain near 1,200,000 men; I suppose exclusive of those who fell on his own side in slaying them. Are not you and I, Jack, innocent men, and babes in swaddling-clothes, compared to Cæsar, and to his predecessor in heroism, Alexander, dubbed for murders and depredation *Magnus?*

The principal difference that strikes me in the comparison between us and the mayor, the embassador, the general, on *their* gaudies, is that the mob make a greater noise, a louder huzzaing, in the one case than the other, which is called *acclamation*, and ends frequently in *higher* taste, by throwing dead animals at one another, before they disperse; in which they have as much joy, as in the former part of the triumph: while they will attend us with all the marks of an awful or silent (at most only a whispering) respect;

* Pliny gives this account, putting the number of men slain at 1,100,092. See also Lipsius *de Constantia.*

their mouths distended, as if set open with gags, and their voices generally lost in goggle-eyed admiration.

Well, but suppose, after all, we are convicted; what have we to do, but in time to make over our estates, that the sheriffs may not revel in our spoils?

There is no fear of being hanged for such a crime as this, while we have *money* or *friends.* — And suppose even the worst, that two or three were to die, have we not a chance, each man of us, to escape? The devil's in them, if they'll hang five for ravishing three!

I know I shall get off for one — were it but for family sake: and being a handsome fellow, I shall have a dozen or two of young maidens, all dressed in white, go to court to beg my life — and what a pretty show they will make, with their white hoods, white gowns, white petticoats, white scarves, white gloves, kneeling for me, with their white handkerchiefs at their eyes, in two pretty rows, as Majesty walks through them and nods my pardon for their sakes! — And, if once pardoned, all is over: for, Jack, in a crime of this nature there lies no appeal, as in a murder.

So thou seest the worst that can happen, should we *not* make the grand tour upon this occasion, but stay and take our trials. But it is most likely, that they will not prosecute at all. If not, no risk on our side will be run: only taking our pleasure abroad, at the worst; leaving friends tired of us, in order, after a time, to return to the same friends endeared to us, as we to them, by absence.

This, Jack, is my scheme, at the first running. I know it is capable of improvement — for example: I can land these ladies in France; whip over before they can get a passage back, or before Hickman can have recovered his fright; and so find means to entrap my beloved on board — and then all will be right; and I need not care if I were never to return to England.

Memorandum, to be considered of — whether, in order to complete my vengeance, I cannot contrive to kidnap away either James Harlowe or Solmes? or both? A man, Jack, would not go into exile for nothing.

LETTER CXIII.

Mr. Lovelace to John Belford, Esq.

IF, Belford, thou likest not my plot upon Miss Howe, I have three or four more as good in my own opinion; better, perhaps, they will be in thine: and so 'tis but getting loose from thy present engagement, and thou shalt pick and choose. But as for thy three brethren, they must do as I would have them: and so, indeed, must thou — else why am I your general? But I will refer this subject to its proper season. Thou knowest that I never absolutely conclude upon a project, till 'tis time for execution; and then lightning strikes not quicker than I.

And now to the subject next my heart.

Wilt thou believe me, when I tell thee that I have so many contrivances rising up and crowding upon me for preference, with regard to my Gloriana, that I hardly know which to choose? — I could tell thee of no less than six princely ones, any of which *must* do. But, as the dear creature has not grudged giving me trouble, I think I ought not, in gratitude, to spare combustibles for her; but, on the contrary, to make her stare and stand aghast, by springing three or four mines at once.

Thou rememberest what Shakspeare, in his Troilus and Cressida, makes Hector, who, however, is not used to boast, say to Achilles in an interview between them; and which, applied to this watchful lady, and to the vexation she has given me, and to the certainty I now think I have of subduing her, will run thus; supposing the charmer before me; and I meditating her sweet person from head to foot.

Henceforth, O watchful fair-one! guard thee well:
For I'll not kill thee there! nor there! nor there!
But, by the zone that circles Venus' waist,
I'll kill thee every where; yea, o'er and o'er.
Thou wisest Belford, pardon me this brag.
Her watchfulness draws folly from my lips;
But I'll endeavour deeds to match the words,
Or may I never ——

Then I imagine thee interposing to qualify my impatience, as Ajax did to Achilles.

—— Do not chafe thee, cousin: —— And let these threats alone, Till accident or purpose bring thee to it.

All that vexes me, in the midst of my gloried-in devices, is, that there is a sorry fellow in the world, who has presumed to question, whether the prize, when obtained, is worthy of the pains it cost me; yet knows, with what patience and trouble a birdman will spread an acre of ground with gins and snares; set up his stalking-horse, his glasses: plant his decoy birds, and invite the feathered throng by his whistle; and all his prize at last (the reward of early hours, and of a whole morning's pains) only a simple linnet.

To be serious, Belford, I must acknowledge, that all our pursuits, from childhood to manhood, are only trifles of different sorts and sizes, proportioned to our years and views; but then is not a fine woman the noblest trifle, that ever was or could be obtained by man? —And to what purpose do we say *obtained*, if it be not in the way we wish for? — If a man is rather to be *her* prize than she *his*?

* * *

And now, Belford, what dost think?

That thou art a cursed fellow, if ——

If — No ifs — but I shall be very sick to-morrow. I shall, 'faith.

Sick — Why sick? What a devil shouldst thou be sick for?

For more good reasons than one, Jack.

I should be glad to hear but one.

—Sick, quotha! Of all thy roguish inventions I should not have thought of this.

Perhaps thou thinkest my view to be, to draw the lady to my bed-side. That's a trick of three or four thousand years old; and I should find it much more to my purpose, if I could get to hers. However, I'll condescend to make thee as wise as myself.

I am excessively disturbed about this smuggling scheme of Miss Howe. I have no doubt, that my fair one, were I to make an attempt, and miscarry, will fly from me, if she can. I once believed she loved me: but now I doubt whether she does or not: at least, that it is with such an *ardour*, as Miss Howe calls it, as will make her overlook a premeditated fault, should I be guilty of one.

And what will being sick do for thee?

Have patience. I don't intend to be so very bad as Dorcas shall represent me to be. But yet I know I shall retch confoundedly, and bring up some clotted blood. To be sure, I shall break a vessel: there's no doubt of that: and a bottle of Eaton's Styptic shall be sent for; but no doctor. If she has *humanity*, she will be concerned. But, if she has *love*, let it have been pushed ever so far back, it will, on this occasion, come forward and shew itself; not only in her eye, but in every line of her sweet face.

I will be very intrepid. I will not fear death, or any thing else. I will be sure of being well in an hour or two, having formerly found great benefit by this astringent medicine, on occasion of an inward bruise by a fall from my horse in hunting, of which, perhaps, this malady may be the remains. And this will shew her, that those about me may make the most of it, I do not; and so can have no design in it.

Well, methinks thou sayest, I begin to think tolerably of this device.

I knew thou would'st, when I explained myself. Another time prepare to wonder and banish doubt.

Now, Belford, if she be not much concerned at the broken vessel, which in one so fiery in his temper, as I had the *reputation* to be thought, may be very dangerous; a malady which I shall calmly attribute to the harasses and doubts under which I have laboured for some time past; and this would be a further proof of my love, and will demand a grateful return.

And what then, thou egregious contriver?

Why then I shall have the *less remorse*, if I am to use a little violence: for can *she* deserve compassion, who shews none?

And what if she shew a *great deal of concern?*

Then I shall be in hopes of building on a good foundation. Love hides a multitude of faults, and diminishes those it cannot hide. Love when acknowledged, authorizes freedom; and freedom begets freedom; and I shall then see how far I can go.

Well but, Lovelace, how the deuce wilt thou, with that full health and vigour of constitution, and with that bloom in thy face, make any body believe thou art sick?

How! — Why, take a few grains of ipecacuanha; enough to make me retch like a fury.

Good! — But how wilt thou manage to bring up blood, and not hurt thyself?

Foolish fellow! are there not pigeons and chickens in every poulterer's shop?

Cry thy mercy.

But then I will be persuaded by Mrs. Sinclair, that I have of late confined myself too much; and so will have a chair called, and be carried to the Park; where I will try to walk half the length of the Mall, or so; and in my return, amuse myself at White's or the Cocoa.

And what will this do?

Questioning again! — I am afraid thou'rt an infidel, Belford —why then shall I not know if my beloved offers to go out in my absence? — And shall I not see whether she receives me with tenderness at my return? But this is not all: *I have a foreboding that something affecting will happen while I am out.* But of this more in its place.

And now, Belford, wilt thou, or wilt thou not, allow, that it is a right thing to be sick? — Lord, Jack, so much delight do I take in my contrivances, that I shall be half sorry when the occasion for them is over; for never, never shall I again have such charming exercise for my invention.

Meantime these plaguy women are so impertinent, so full of reproaches, that I know not how to do any thing but curse them. And then, truly, they are for helping me out with some of *their* trite and vulgar artifices. Sally particularly, who pretends to be a mighty contriver, has just now in an insolent manner told me, on my rejecting her proffered aids, that I had no mind to conquer; and that I was so *wicked* as to intend to marry, though I would not own it to her.

Because this little devil made her first sacrifice at my altar, she thinks she may take any liberty with me: and what makes her outrageous at times, is, that I have, for a long time, *studiously*, as she says, slighted her too readily offered favours. But is it not very impudent in her to think, that I will be any man's *successor?* It is not come to that neither. This, thou knowest, was always my rule—*once any other man's* and *I* know it, and *never more mine.* It is for such as thou, and thy brethren, to take up with *harlots.* I have been always aiming at the merit of a first discoverer.

The more devil I, perhaps thou wilt say, to endeavour to corrupt the uncorrupted.

But I say, *not;* since, hence, I have but very few adulteries to answer for.

One affair, indeed, at Paris, with a married lady (I believe I never told thee of it] touched my conscience a little: yet brought on by the spirit of intrigue, more than by sheer wickedness. I'll give it thee in brief:

"A French marquis, somewhat in years, employed by his court in a public function at that of Madrid, had put his charming young new married wife under the control and *wardship*, as I may say, of his insolent sister, an old prude.

"I saw the lady at the opera. I liked her at first sight, and better at second, when I knew the situation she was in. So, pretending to make my addresses to the prude, got admittance to both.

"The first thing I had to do, was to compliment my prude into shyness by complaints of shyness: next to take advantage of the marquis's situation, between her husband's jealousy, and his sister's arrogance; and to inspire her with resentment, and, as I hoped, with a regard to my person. The French ladies have no dislike to intrigue.

"The sister began to suspect me: the lady had no mind to part with the company of the only man who had been permitted to visit there; and told me of her sister's suspicions. I put her upon concealing the prude, as if unknown to me, in a closet in one of her own apartments, locking her in, and putting the key in her own pocket: and she was to question me on the sincerity of my professions to her sister, in her sister's hearing.

"She complied. My mistress

was locked up. The lady and I took our seats. I owned fervent love, and made high professions: for the marquise put it home to me. The prude was delighted with what she heard.

"And how dost think it ended? — I took my advantage of the lady herself, who durst not for her life cry out; and drew her after me to the next apartment, on pretence of going to seek her sister, who all the time was locked up in the closet."

No woman ever gave me a private meeting for nothing; my dearest Miss Harlowe excepted.

"My ingenuity obtained my pardon: the lady being unable to forbear laughing through the whole affair, to find both so uncommonly tricked; her gaoleress her prisoner, safe locked up, and as much pleased as either of us."

The English, Jack, do not often out-wit the French.

"We had contrivances afterwards equally ingenious, in which the lady, the ice once broken [*once subdued, always subdued*] co-operated — but a more tender tell-tale revealed the secret — revealed it, before the marquis could come to cover the disgrace. The sister was inveterate; the husband, irreconcileable; in every respect unfit for a husband, even for a *French* one — made, perhaps, more delicate to these particulars by the customs of a people among whom he was then resident, so contrary to those of his own countrymen. She was obliged to throw herself into my protection — nor thought herself unhappy in it, till childbed pangs seized her: then penitence, and death, overtook her the same hour!"

Excuse a tear, Belford! — She deserved a better fate! What had such a vile inexorable husband to answer for! — The sister was punished effectually — that pleases me on reflection — the sister was effectually punished! — But perhaps I have told thee this story before.

LETTER CXIV.

Mr. Lovelace to John Belford, Esq.

Friday evening.

Just returned from an airing with my charmer, complied with after great importunity. She was attended by the two nymphs. They both stopped their parts; kept their eyes within bounds; made moral reflections now-and-then. O Jack, what devils are women, when all tests are got over, and we have completely ruined them!

The coach carried us to Hampstead, to Highgate, to Muswell Hill; back to Hampstead to the Upper Flask: there, in compliment to the nymphs, my beloved consented to alight, and take a little repast. Then home early by Kentish Town.

Delightfully easy she, and so respectful and obliging I, all the way, and as we walked out upon the Heath, to view the variegated prospects which that agreeable elevation affords, that she promised to take now-and-then a little excursion with me. I think,

Miss Howe, I *think*, said I to myself, every now-and-then as we walked, that thy wicked devices are superseded.

But let me give thee a few particulars of our conversation in the *circumrotation* we took, while in the coach — She had received a letter from Miss Howe I presumed?

She made no answer. How happy should I think myself to be admitted into their correspondence? I would joyfully make an exchange of communications.

So, though I hoped not to succeed by her consent, [and little did she think, I had so happily in part succeeded without it] I thought it not amiss to urge for it, for several reasons: among others, that I might account to her for my constant employment at my pen; in order to take off her jealousy, that *she* was the subject of thy correspondence and mine: and that I might justify *my* secrecy and *uncommunicativeness* by her *own*.

I proceeded therefore — That I loved familiar letter writing, as I had more than once told her, above all the species of writing: it was writing from the heart (without the fetters prescribed by method or study) as the very word *correspondence* implied. Not the heart only; the *soul* was in it. Nothing of body, when friend writes to friend: the mind impelling sovereignly the vassal fingers. It was, in short, friendship recorded; friendship given under hand and seal; demonstrating that the parties were under no apprehension of changing from time or accident, when they so liberally gave testimonies, which would always be ready, on a failure, or infidelity, to be turned against them. — For my own part, it was the principal diversion I had in her absence; but for this innocent amusement, the distance she so frequently kept me at would have been intolerable.

Sally knew my drift; and said, she had had the honour to see two or three of my letters, and of Mr. Belford's; and she thought them the most entertaining that she had ever read.

My friend Belford, I said, had a happy talent in the letter writing way; and upon all subjects.

I expected my beloved would have been inquisitive after our subject: but (lying perdue, as I saw) not a word said she. So I touched upon this article myself.

Our topics were various and diffuse; sometimes upon literary articles [she was very attentive upon this]; sometimes upon the public entertainments; sometimes amusing each other with the fruits of the different correspondences we held with persons abroad, with whom we had contracted friendships; sometimes upon the foibles and perfections of our particular friends; sometimes upon our own present and future hopes; sometimes aiming at humour and raillery upon each other. — It might indeed appear to savour of vanity, to suppose my letters would entertain a lady of her delicacy and judgment. But yet I could not but say, that perhaps she would be far from thinking so hardly of me as sometimes she had seemed to do, if she were to see the letters which generally passed between Mr. Belford and me [I hope, Jack, thou hast more manners, than to give me the lie, though but in thy heart.]

She then spoke: after declining my compliment in such a manner, as only a person could do, who deserved it, she said, for her part, she had always thought me a man of sense [a man of sense, Jack! what a niggardly praise!] — and should therefore hope, that, when I wrote, it exceeded even my speech: for that it was impossible, be the letters written in as easy and familiar a style as they would, but that they must have that advantage from sitting down to write them, which prompt speech could not always have. She should think it very strange, therefore, if my letters were barren of sentiment: and as strange, if I gave myself liberties upon *premeditation*, which could have no excuse at all, but from a thoughtlessness, which itself wanted excuse. — But, if Mr. Belford's letters and mine were upon subjects so general, and some of them equally (she presumed) instructive and entertaining, she could not but say, that she should be glad to see any of them; and particularly those which Miss Martin had seen and praised.

This was put close.

I looked at her, to see if I could discover any tincture of jealousy in this hint; that *Miss Martin* had seen what I had not shown to *her*. But she did not look it: so I only said, I should be very proud to show her not only those, but all that passed between Mr. Belford and me; but I must remind her, that she knew the condition.

No, indeed! with a sweet lip pouted out, as saucy as pretty; implying a lovely scorn, that yet can only be lovely in youth so blooming, and beauty so divinely distinguished.

How I long to see such a motion again! *Her* mouth only can give it.

But I am mad with love — yet eternal will be the distance, at the rate I go on: now fire, now ice, my soul is continually upon the *hiss*, as I may say. In vain, however, is the trial to quench — what, after all, is unquenchable.

Pr'ythee, Belford, forgive my nonsense, and my Vulcan-like metaphors — Did I not tell thee, not that I am *sick* of love, but that I am *mad* with it? Why brought I such an angel into such a house? into such company! — And why do I not stop my ears to the sirens, who, knowing my aversion to wedlock, are perpetually touching that string?

I was not willing to be answered so easily: I was sure, that what passed between two such young ladies (friends so dear) might be seen by every body: I had more reason than any body to wish to see the letters that passed between her and Miss Howe; because I was sure they must be full of admirable instruction, and one of the dear correspondents had deigned to wish my entire reformation.

She looked at me, as if she would look me through; I thought I *felt* eye-beam, after eye-beam, penetrate my shivering reins. — But she was silent. Nor needed her eyes the assistance of speech.

Nevertheless, a little recovering myself, I hoped that nothing unhappy had befallen either Miss Howe or her mother. The letter of Sunday sent by a particular hand; she opening it with great emotion — seeming to have expected it sooner — were the reasons for my apprehensions.

We were then at Muswell Hill: *A pretty country within the eye*, to Polly, was the remark, instead of replying to *me*.

But I was not so to be answered — I should expect some charming subjects and characters from two such pens: I hoped every thing went on well between Mr. Hickman and Miss Howe. Her mother's heart, I said, was set upon that match: Mr. Hickman was not without his merits: he was what the ladies called a SOBER man: but I must needs say, that I thought Miss Howe deserved a husband of a very different cast.

This, I supposed, would have engaged her into a subject from which I could have wiredrawn something: — for Hickman is one of her favourites — why, I can't divine, except for the sake of opposition of character to that of thy honest friend.

But she cut me short by a look of disapprobation, and another cool remark upon a distant view; and, *How far off, Miss Horton, do you think that clump of trees may be* pointing out of the coach. — So I had done.

Here endeth all I have to write concerning our conversation on this our agreeable airing.

We have both been writing ever since we came home. I am to be favoured with her company for an hour, before she retires to rest. All that obsequious love can suggest, in order to engage her tenderest sentiments for me against to-morrow's sickness, will I aim at when we meet. But at parting will complain of a disorder in my stomach.

* * *

We have met. All was love and unexceptionable respect on my part, ease and complaisance on hers. She was concerned for my disorder. So sudden! — Just as we parted! But it was nothing. I shall be quite well by morning.

Faith, Jack, I think I am sick already. Is it possible for such a giddy fellow as me to *persuade* myself to be ill! I am a better mimic at this rate than I wish to be. But every nerve and fibre of me is always ready to contribute its aid, whether by health or by ailment, to carry a resolved on roguery into execution.

Dorcas has transcribed for me the whole letter of Miss Howe, dated Sunday, May 14*, of which before I had only extracts. She found no other letter added to that parcel: but this, and that which I copied myself in character last Sunday while she was at church, relating to the smuggling scheme**, are enough for me.

* * *

Dorcas tells me, that her lady has been removing her papers from the mahogany chest into a wainscot box, which held her linen, and which she put into her dark closet. We have no key of that at present. No doubt but all her letters, previous to those I have come at, are in that box. Dorcas is uneasy upon it: yet hopes that her lady does not suspect her; for she is sure that she laid in every thing as she found it.

LETTER CXV.

Mr. Lovelace to John Belford, Esq.

Cocoa-tree Saturday, May 27.

THIS ipecacuanha is a most disagreeable medicine. That these cursed physical folks can find out nothing to do us good, but what would poison the devil! In the other world, were they only to take physic, it would be punishment enough of itself for a misspent life. A doctor at one elbow, and an apothecary at the other, and the poor soul labouring under their prescribed operations, he need no worse tormentors.

But now this was to take down my countenance. It has done it:

* See p. 278, & seq.
** See p. 327, & seq.

for, with violent retchings, having taken enough to make me sick, and not enough water to carry it off, I presently looked as if I had kept my bed a fortnight. *Ill jesting*, as I thought in the midst of the exercise, *with edge tools*, and worse with *physical ones.*

Two hours it held me. I had forbid Dorcas to let her lady know any thing of the matter, out of tenderness to her; being willing, when she knew my prohibition, to let her see that I *expected* her to be concerned for me. —

Well, but Dorcas was nevertheless a *woman*, and she can *whisper* to her lady the secret she is enjoined to keep!

Come hither, toad! [sick as a devil at the instant] Let me see what a mixture of grief and surprise may be beat up together in thy pudding-face.

That won't do. That dropped jaw, and mouth distended into the long oval, is more upon the horrible than the grievous.

Nor that pinking and winking with thy *odious eyes*, as my charmer once called them.

A little better *that;* yet not quite right: but keep your mouth closer. You have a muscle or two which you have no command of, between your cheek-bone and your lips, that should carry one corner of your mouth up towards your crow's-foot, and that down to meet it.

There! begone! Be in a plaguy hurry running up stairs and down to fetch from the dining-room what you carry up on purpose to fetch, till motion extraordinary put you out of breath, and give you the sigh natural.

What's the matter, Dorcas?

Nothing, madam.

My beloved wonders she has not seen me this morning, no doubt; but is too shy to say she wonders. Repeated, What's the matter, however, as Dorcas runs up and down stairs by her door, bring on, Oh! madam! my master! my poor master!

What! How! When! — And all the monosyllables of surprise.

[*Within parentheses* let me tell thee, that I have often thought that the little words in the republic of letters, like the little folks in a nation, are the most significant. The *trisyllables* and the *rumblers* of syllables more than *three*, are but the good-for-little *magnates*.]

I must not tell you, madam — my master ordered me not to tell you — but he is in a worse way than he thinks for! — But he would not have *you* frighted.

High concern took possession of every sweet feature. She pitied me! — By my soul, she pitied me!

Where is he?

Too much in a hurry for good manners [*another parenthesis, Jack!* Good-manners are so little natural, that we ought to be *composed* to observe them: politeness will not live in a storm.] I cannot stay to answer questions, cries the wench — though desirous to answer [*a third parenthesis* — like the people crying proclamations, running away from the customers they want to sell to.] This hurry puts the lady in a hurry to ask [*a fourth*, by way of embellishing the third!] as the other does the people in a hurry to buy. And I have in my eye now a whole street raised, and running after a proclamation or express crier, as if the first was a thief, the others his pursuers.

At last, O Lord! let Mrs. Lovelace know — there is danger to be sure! whisper'd from one nymph to another; but at the door and so loud, that my listening fair-one might hear.

Out she darts — As how! as how, Dorcas!

O madam — a vomiting of blood! A vessel broke, to be sure!

Down she hastens; finds every one as busy over my blood in the entry, as if it were that of the Neapolitan saint.

In steps my charmer, with a face of sweet concern.

How do you, Mr. Lovelace?

O my best love! — very well — very well! — Nothing at all! nothing of consequence! — I shall be well in an instant! — Straining again! for I was indeed plaguy sick, though no more blood came.

In short, Belford, I have gained my end! I see the dear soul loves me. I see she forgives me all that's past. I see I have credit for a new score.

Miss Howe, I defy thee, my dear. — Mrs. Townsend! — Who the devil are you? — Troop away with your contrabands. No smuggling! nor smuggler, but myself! Nor will the choicest of my fair-one's favours be long prohibited goods to me!

* * *

Every one now is sure that she loves me. Tears were in her eyes more than once for me. She suffered me to take her hand, and kiss it as often as I pleased. On Mrs. Sinclair's mentioning, that I too much confined myself, she pressed me to take an airing; but obligingly desired me to be careful of myself. Wished I would advise with a physician. *God made physicians*, she said.

I did not think that, Jack. God indeed made us all. But I fancy she meant *physic* instead of *physicians;* and then the phrase might mean what the vulgar phrase means — *God sends meat, the devil cooks.*

I was well already, on taking the styptic from *her* dear hands.

On her requiring me to take the air, I asked if I might have the honour of her company in a coach; and this, that I might observe if she had an intention of going out in my absence.

If she thought a chair were not a more proper vehicle for my case, she would with all her heart!

There's a precious!

I kissed her hand again! She was all goodness! Would to Heaven I better deserved it, I said! — But all were golden days before us! — Her presence and generous concern had done every thing. I was well! nothing ailed me. But since my beloved will have it so, I'll take a little airing!

— Let a chair be called! — O my charmer! — *were I to have owed this indisposition to my late harasses,* and *to the uneasiness I have had for disobliging you;* all is infinitely compensated by your goodness — All the art of healing is in your smiles! — Your late displeasure was the only malady!

While Mrs. Sinclair, and Dorcas, and Polly, and even poor silly Mabell [for Sally went out, as my angel came in] with uplifted hands and eyes, stood thanking Heaven that I was better, in audible whispers: See the power of love, cried one! — What a charming husband, another! Happy couple, all!

O how the dear creature's cheek mantled — how her eyes sparkled! — How sweetly acceptable is praise to conscious merit, while it but reproaches when applied to the undeserving! — What a new, what a gay creation it makes at once in a diffident or dispirited heart!

And now, Belford, was it not worth while to be sick! And yet I must tell thee, that too many pleasanter expedients offer themselves, to make trial any more of this confounded ipecacuanha.

LETTER CXVI.

Miss Clarissa Harlowe to Miss Howe.

Saturday, May 27.

Mr. Lovelace, my dear, has been very ill. Suddenly taken. With a vomiting of blood in great quantities. Some vessel broken. He complained of a disorder in his stomach over-night. I was the more affected with it, *as I am afraid it was occasioned by the violent contentions between us.* — But was I in fault?

How lately did I think I hated him! — But hatred and anger, I see, are but temporary passions with me. One cannot, my dear, hate people in danger of death, or who are in distress or affliction. My heart, I find, is not proof against kindness and acknowledgment of errors committed.

He took great care to have his illness concealed from me as long as he could. So tender in the violence of his disorder! so desirous to make the best of it! — I wish he had not been ill in my sight. I was too much affected — every body alarming me with his danger — the poor man, from such high health, so *suddenly* taken! — And so unprepared!

He is gone out in a chair. I advised him to do so. I fear that my advice was wrong; since quiet in such a disorder must needs be best. We are apt to be so ready, in cases of emergency, to give our advice, without judgment or waiting for it! — I proposed a physician indeed; but he would not hear of one. I have great honour for the faculty; and the greater, as I have always observed, that those who treat the professors of the art of healing contemptuously, too generally treat higher institutions in the same manner.

I am really very uneasy. For I have, no doubt, exposed myself to him, and to the women below. *They* indeed will excuse me, as they think us married. But if he be not generous, I shall have cause to regret this surprise; which (as I had reason to think myself unaccountably treated by him) has taught me more than I knew of myself.

'Tis true, I have owned more than once, that I could have liked Mr. Lovelace above all men. I remember the debates you and I used to have on this subject, when I was your happy guest. You used to say, and once you wrote*, that men of his cast are the men that our sex do not *naturally* dislike: while I held, that such were not (however *that* might be) the men we *ought* to like. But what with my relations precipitating of me, on one hand, and what with his unhappy character and embarrassing ways on the other, I had no more leisure than inclination to examine my own heart in this particular. And this reminds me of a passage in one of your former letters, which I will transcribe, though it was written in raillery, *May it not be,* say you**, *that you have had such persons to deal with, as have not allowed you to attend to the throbs; or, if you had them a little now-and-then, whether, having had two accounts to place them to, you have not by mistake put them to the wrong one?* A passage, which although it came into my mind when Mr. Lovelace was least exceptionable, yet that I have

* See p. 302.
** See Vol. I. p. 50.

denied any efficacy to, when he has teased and vexed me, and given me cause of suspicion. For, after all, my dear, Mr. Lovelace is not wise in all his ways. And should we not endeavour, as much as is possible, (where we are not attached by *natural* ties) to like and dislike as reason bids us, and according to the merit or demerit of the object? If love, as it is called, is allowed to be an excuse for our most unreasonable follies, and to lay level all the fences that a careful education has surrounded us by, what is meant by the doctrine of subduing our passions? — But, O my dearest friend, am I not guilty of a punishable fault, were I to love this man of errors? And has not my own heart deceived me, when I thought I did not? And what must be that love, that has not some degree of purity for its object? I am afraid of recollecting some passages in my cousin Morden's letter.* — And yet why fly I from subjects that, duly considered, might tend to correct and purify my heart? I have carried, I doubt, my notions on this head too high, not for practice, but for *my* practice. Yet think me not guilty of prudery neither; for had I found out as much of myself before; or, rather, had he given me heart's ease enough before to find it out, you should have had my confession sooner.

Nevertheless let me tell you (what I hope I may justly tell you) that if again he give me cause

* See p. 247, & seq. of this volume.

to resume distance and reserve, I hope my reason will gather strength enough from his imperfections, to enable me to keep my passions under. — What can we do more than govern ourselves by the temporary lights lent us?

You will not wonder that I am grave on this detection — *detection*, must I call it? What can I call it? —

Dissatisfied with myself, I am afraid to look back upon what I have written: and yet know not how to have done writing. I never was in such an odd frame of mind. — I know not how to describe it — Was *you* ever *so?* — Afraid of the censure of her you love — yet not conscious that you deserve it?

Of this, however, I am convinced, that I should *indeed* deserve censure, if I kept any secret of my heart from you.

But I will not add another word, after I have assured you, that I will look still more narrowly into myself: and that I am

Your equally sincere and
affectionate
Cl. Harlowe.

LETTER CXVII.

Mr. Lovelace to John Belford, Esq.

Sat. evening.

I HAD a charming airing. No return of my malady. My heart perfectly easy, how could my stomach be otherwise?

But when I came home, I found that my sweet soul had been alarmed by *a new incident* — the inquiry after us both, in a very suspicious manner, and that by description of our persons, and not by names, by a servant in a blue livery turned up and trimmed with yellow.

Dorcas was called to him, as the upper servant; and she refusing to answer any of the fellow's questions unless he told his business, and from whom he came, the fellow (as short as she) said, that if she would not answer *him*, perhaps she might answer somebody *else;* and went away out of humour.

Dorcas hurried up to her lady, and alarmed her not only with the fact, but with her own conjectures; adding, that he was an ill-looking fellow, and she was sure could come for no good.

The livery and the features of the servant were particularly inquired after, and as particularly described — *Lord bless her! no end of her alarms, she thought!* And then did her apprehensions anticipate every evil that could happen.

She wished Mr. Lovelace would come in.

Mr. Lovelace came in soon after; all lively, grateful, full of hopes, of duty, of love, to thank his charmer, and to congratulate with her upon the cure she had performed. And then she told the story, with all its circumstances; and Dorcas, to point her lady's fears, told us, that the servant was a sun-burnt fellow, and looked as if he had been at sea.

He was then, no doubt, Captain Singleton's servant, and the next news we should hear, was, that the house was surrounded by a whole ship's crew; the vessel lying no further off, as she understood, than Rotherhithe.

Impossible, I said. Such an *attempt* would not be ushered in by such a *manner of inquiry.* And why may it not rather be a servant of your cousin Morden, with notice of his arrival, and of his design to attend you?

This surmise delighted her. Her apprehensions went off, and she was at leisure to congratulate me upon my sudden recovery; which she did in the most obliging manner.

But we had not sat long together, when Dorcas again came fluttering up to tell us, that the footman, the *very* footman, was again at the door, and inquired, whether Mr. Lovelace and his lady, *by name*, had not lodgings in this house? He asked, he told Dorcas, for no harm: but his disavowing of harm was a demonstration with my apprehensive fair-one, that harm was intended. And as the fellow had not been answered by Dorcas, I proposed to go down to the street-parlour, and hear what he had to say.

I see your causeless terror, my dearest life, said I, and your impatience — will you be pleased to walk down — and without being observed (for he shall come no further than the parlour door) you may hear all that passes?

She consented. We went down. Dorcas bid the man come forward.

Well, friend, what is your business with Mr. or Mrs. Lovelace?

Bowing, scraping, I am sure *you* are the gentleman, sir. Why, sir, my business is only to know if your honour be here, and to be spoken with; or if you shall be here for any time?

Whom came you from?

From a gentleman who ordered me to say, if I was made to tell, but not else, it was from a friend of Mr. John Harlowe, Mrs. Lovelace's eldest uncle.

The dear creature was ready to sink upon this. *It was but of late that she had provided herself with salts.* She pulled them out.

Do you know any thing of Colonel Morden, friend? said I.

No; I never heard of his name.

Of Captain Singleton?

No, sir. But the gentleman, my master, is a captain too.

What is his name?

I don't know if I should tell.

There can be no harm in telling the gentleman's name, if you come upon a good account.

That I do; for my master told me so; and there is not an honester gentleman on the face of God's yearth — his name is Captain Tomlinson, sir.

I don't know such a one.

I believe not, sir. He was pleased to say, he don't know your honour, sir; but I heard him say as how he should not be an unwelcome visitor to you for all that.

Do you know such a man as Captain Tomlinson, my dearest life [*aside*], your uncle's friend?

No; but my uncle may have acquaintance, no doubt, that I don't know. — But I hope [trembling] this is not a trick.

Well, friend, if your master has any thing to say to Mr. Lovelace, you may tell him that Mr. Lovelace is here; and will see him whenever he pleases.

The dear creature looked as if afraid that my engagement was too prompt for my own safety; and away went the fellow — *I wondering, that she might not wonder*, that this Captain Tomlinson, whoever he were, came not himself, or sent not a letter the second time, when he had reason to suppose that I might be here.

Meantime, for fear that this should be a contrivance of James Harlowe, who, I said, loved plotting, though he had not a head turned for it, I gave some precautionary directions to the servants, and the women, whom, for the greater parade, I assembled before us. And my beloved was resolved *not to stir abroad till she saw the issue of this odd affair.*

And here must I close, *though in so great a puzzle.*

Only let me add, that poor Belton wants thee; for I dare not stir for my life.

Mowbray and Tourville skulk about like vagabonds, without heads, without hands, without souls; having neither you nor me to conduct them. They tell me, they shall rust beyond the power of oil or action to brighten them up, or give them motion.

How goes it with thy uncle?

LETTER CXVIII.
Mr. Lovelace to John Belford, Esq.

Sunday, May 28.

This story of Captain Tomlinson employed us, not only for the time we were together last night, but all the while we sat at breakfast this morning. She would still have it, that it was the prelude to some mischief from Singleton. I insisted (according to my former hint) that it might much more probably be a method taken by Colonel Morden to alarm her, previous to a personal visit. Travelled gentlemen affected to surprise in this manner. And why, dearest creature, said I, must every thing that happens, which we cannot immediately account for, be what we least wish?

She had had so many disagreeable things befal her of late, that her fears were too often stronger than her hopes.

And this, madam, makes me apprehensive, that you will get into so low-spirited a way, that you will not be able to enjoy the happiness that seems to await us.

Her duty and her gratitude, she gravely said, to the Dispenser of all good, would secure her, she hoped, against all unthankfulness. And a thankful spirit was the same as a joyful one.

So, Belford, for all her future joys she depends entirely upon the invisible good. She is certainly right; since those who fix least upon second causes are the least likely to be disappointed — and is not this gravity for her gravity?

She had hardly done speaking, when Dorcas came running up in a hurry — she set even *my* heart into a palpitation — thump, thump, thump, like a precipitated pendulum in a clock case — flutter, flutter, flutter, my charmer's, as by her sweet bosom rising to her chin I saw.

This lower class of people, my beloved herself observed, were for ever aiming at the *stupid wonderful*, and for making even common incidents matter of surprise.

Why the devil, said I to the wench, this alarming hurry? — And with your spread fingers, and your O madams, and O sirs! — And be cursed to you! Would there have been a second of time difference, had you come up slowly?

Captain Tomlinson, sir!

Captain Devilson, what care I? — Do you see how you have disordered your lady?

Good Mr. Lovelace, said my charmer, trembling, [see, Jack, when she has an end to serve, I am *good* Mr. Lovelace] if — if my brother, if Captain Singleton should appear — pray now — I beseech you — let me beg of you — to govern your temper — my brother is my brother — Captain Singleton is but an *agent*.

My dearest life, folding my arms about her [when she asks favours, thought I, the devil's in it, if she will not allow of such innocent freedom as this, from *good* Mr. Lovelace too] you shall be witness of all that passes between us. — Dorcas, desire the gentleman to walk up.

Let me retire to my chamber first! — Let me not be known to be in the house!

Charming dear! — Thou seest, Belford, she is afraid of leaving me! — O the little witchcrafts! Were it not for surprises now-and-then, how would an honest man know where to have them?

She withdrew to listen — and though this incident has not turned out to answer *all I wished from it*, yet is it necessary, if I would acquaint thee with my *whole circulation*, to be very particular in what passed between Captain Tomlinson and me.

Enter Captain Tomlinson in a riding-dress, whip in hand.

Your servant, sir — Mr. Lovelace, I presume?

My name is Lovelace, sir.

Excuse the day, sir. — Be pleased to excuse my garb. I am obliged to go out of town directly, that I may return at night.

The day is a good day. Your garb needs no apology.

When I sent my servant, I did *not know that I should find time to do myself this honour.* All that I thought I could do to oblige my friend this journey, was *only* to assure myself of your abode; and whether there were a probability of being admitted to the speech either of you, or your lady.

Sir, you best know your own motives. What your time will permit you to do, you also best know. And here I am attending your pleasure.

My charmer owned afterwards her concern on my being so short. Whatever I shall mingle of her emotions, thou wilt easily guess I had afterwards.

Sir, I hope no offence. I intend none.

None — none at all, sir.

Sir, I have no interest in the affair I come about. I may appear officious; and if I thought I should, I would decline any concern in it, after I have just hinted what it is.

And pray, sir, what is it?

May I ask you, sir, without offence, whether you wish to be reconciled, and to co-operate upon honourable terms, with *one* gentleman of the name of Harlowe; preparative, as it may be hoped, to a general reconciliation?

O how my heart fluttered! cried my charmer.

I can't tell, sir — [*and then it fluttered still more, no doubt:*] the whole family have used me extremely ill. They have taken greater liberties with my character than are justifiable; and with my family *too;* which I can less forgive.

Sir, sir, I have done. I beg pardon for this intrusion.

My beloved was then ready to sink, and thought very hardly of me.

But, pray, sir; to the immediate purpose of your present commission; since a commission it seems to be.

It is a commission, sir; and such a one, as I thought would be agreeable to all parties, or I should not have given myself concern about it.

Perhaps it *may*, sir, when known. But let me ask you one previous question; Do you know Colonel Morden, sir?

No, sir. If you mean *personally*, I do not. But I have heard my good friend Mr. John Harlowe talk of him with great respect; and as a co-trustee with him in a certain trust.

Lovel. I thought it probable, sir, that the colonel might be arrived; that you might be a gentleman of his acquaintance; and that something of an agreeable surprise might be intended.

Capt. Had Colonel Morden been in England, Mr. John Harlowe would have known it; and then I should not have been a stranger to it.

Lovel. Well but, sir, have you then any commission to me from Mr. John Harlowe?

Capt. Sir, I will tell you, as briefly as I can, the whole of what I have to say; but you'll excuse me also a previous question, for which curiosity is not my motive; but it is necessary to be answered before I can proceed; as you will judge when you hear it.

Lovel. What, pray, sir, is your question?

Capt. Briefly, whether you are actually, and *bona fide*, married to Miss Clarissa Harlowe?

I started, and in a haughty tone, Is this, sir, a question that *must* be answered before you can proceed in the business you have undertaken?

I mean no offence, Mr. Lovelace. Mr. Harlowe sought to me to undertake this office. I have daughters and nieces of my own. I thought it a good office, or I, who have many considerable affairs upon my hands, had not accepted of it. I know the world; and will take the liberty to say, that if that young lady —

Captain Tomlinson, I think you are called?

My name is Tomlinson.

Why then, Captain Tomlinson, no *liberty*, as you call it, will be taken well, that is not extremely delicate, when that lady is mentioned.

When you had heard me out, Mr. Lovelace, and had found, I had so behaved, as to make the caution necessary, it would have been just to have given it. — Allow me to say, I know what is due to the character of a woman of virtue, as well as any man alive.

Why, sir! Why, Captain Tomlinson, you seem warm. If you intend any thing by this [O how I *trembled!* said the lady, *when she took notice of this part of our conversation afterwards*] I will only say, that this is a privileged place. It is at present my home, and an asylum for any gentleman who thinks it worth his while to inquire after me, be the manner or end of his inquiry what it will.

I know not, sir, that I have

given occasion for this. I make no scruple to attend you *elsewhere*, if I am troublesome here. I was told, I had a warm young gentleman to deal with: but as I knew my intention, and that my commission was an amicable one, I was the less concerned about that. I am twice your age, Mr. Lovelace, I dare say: but I do assure you, that if either my message, or my manner, give you offence, I can suspend the one or the other for a day, or for ever, as you like. And so, sir, any time before eight to-morrow morning, you will let me know your further commands. —And was going to tell me where he might be found.

Captain Tomlinson, said I, you answer well. I love a man of spirit. Have you not been in the army?

I have, sir; but have *turned my sword into a ploughshare*, as the scripture has it [*there was a clever fellow, Jack!*— *He was a good man with somebody, I warrant!* O what a fine coat and cloak for an hypocrite will a text of scripture, properly applied, make at any time in the eye of the pious! — How easily are the good folks taken in!] — And all my delight, added he, for some years past, has been in cultivating my paternal estate. I love a brave man, Mr. Lovelace, as well as ever I did in my life. But let me tell you, sir, that when you come to my time of life, you will be of opinion that there is not so much true bravery in youthful choler, as you may now think there is.

A clever fellow again, Belford!— Ear and heart, both at once, he took in my charmer! — 'Tis well, she says, *there are some men who have wisdom in their anger.*

Well, captain, that is reproof for reproof. So we are upon a foot. And now give me the pleasure of hearing the import of your commission.

Sir, you must first allow me to repeat my question: are you really, and *bona fide*, married to Miss Clarissa Harlowe? Or are you not yet married?

Bluntly put, captain. But, if I answer that I *am*, what then?

Why then, sir, I shall say, that you are a man of honour.

That I hope I am, whether *you* say it or not, Captain Tomlinson.

Sir, I will be very frank in all I have to say on this subject — Mr. John Harlowe has lately found out, that you and his niece are both in the same lodgings; that you have been long so; and that the lady was at the play with you yesterday was se'nnight; and he hopes that you are actually married. He has indeed heard that you *are:* but as he knows your enterprising temper, and that you have declared, that you disdain a relation to their family, he is willing by me to have your marriage confirmed from your own mouth, before he takes the steps he is inclined to take in his niece's favour. You will allow me to say, Mr. Lovelace, that he will not be satisfied with an answer that admits of the least doubt.

Let me tell you, Captain Tomlinson, that it is a high degree of vileness for any man to suppose —

Sir — Mr. Lovelace — don't put yourself into a passion. The lady's relations are jealous of the honour of their family. They have prejudices to overcome as well as you — advantage may have been taken — and the lady, at the *time*, not to blame.

This lady, sir, could give no such advantages: and if she *had*, what must the *man* be, Captain Tomlinson, who could have taken them? — Do you know the lady, sir?

I never had the honour to see her but once; and that was at church! and should not know her again.

Not know her again, sir! — I thought there was not a man living who had once seen her, and would not know her among a thousand.

I remember, sir, that I thought I never saw a finer woman in my life. But, Mr. Lovelace, I believe you will allow, that it is better that her relations should have wronged *you*, than you the *lady;* I hope, sir, you will permit me to repeat my question.

Enter Dorcas, in a hurry.

A *gentleman*, this minute, sir, desires to speak with your honour — [*my lady, sir! — Aside.*]

Could the dear creature put *Dorcas* upon telling this fib, yet want to save *me* one? —

Desire the gentleman to walk into one of the parlours. I will wait on him presently. [*Exit Dorcas.*

The dear creature, I doubted not, wanted to instruct me how to answer the captain's home put. I knew how I intended to answer it — plump, thou mayst be sure — but Dorcas's message staggered me. And yet I was upon one of my master-strokes — which was, to take advantage of the captain's inquiries, and to make her *own her marriage before him*, as she had done to the people below; and if she had been brought to that, to induce her, for her uncle's satisfaction, to write him a letter of gratitude; which of course must have been signed *Clarissa Lovelace*. I was loth, therefore, thou may'st believe, to attend her sudden commands: and yet, afraid of pushing matters beyond recovery with her, I thought proper to lead him from the question, to account for himself, and for Mr. Harlowe's coming at the knowledge of where we are; and for other particulars which I knew would engage her attention; and which might possibly convince her of the necessity there was for her to acquiesce in the affirmative I was disposed to give. And this for her own sake; for what, as I asked her afterwards, is it to me, whether I am ever reconciled to her family? — A family, Jack, which I must for ever despise.

You think, captain, that I have answered doubtfully to the question you put. You *may* think so. And you must know, that I have a good deal of pride; and, only that you are a gentleman, and seem in this affair to be governed by generous motives, or I should ill brook being interrogated as to my honour to a lady so dear to me. — But before I answer more directly to the point, pray satisfy me in a question or two that I shall put to *you*.

With all my heart, sir. Ask me what questions you please: I will answer them with sincerity and candour.

You say, Mr. Harlowe has found out that we were at a play together; and that we were both in the same lodgings — how, pray, came he at this knowledge? — for, let me tell you, that I have, for certain considerations, (not respecting myself, I will assure you) condescended, that our abode should be kept secret. And this has been so strictly observed, that even Miss Howe, though she and my beloved correspond, knows not directly whither to send to us.

Why, sir, the person, who saw you at the play, was a tenant of Mr. John Harlowe. He watched all your motions. When the play was done, he followed your coach to your lodgings. And early the next day, Sunday, he took horse, and acquainted his landlord with what he had observed.

Lovel. How oddly things come about! — But does any other of the Harlowes know where we are?

Capt. It is an absolute secret to every other person of the family; and so it is intended to be kept: as also that Mr. John Harlowe is willing to enter into treaty with you, by me, if his niece *be actually married;* for perhaps he is aware, that he shall have difficulty enough with some people to bring about the desirable reconciliation, although he could give them this assurance.

I doubt it not, captain — to James Harlowe is all the family-folly owing. — Fine fools! [*heroically stalking about*] to be governed by one to whom malice, and not genius, gives the busy liveliness that distinguishes him from a natural! — But how long, pray, sir, has Mr. John Harlowe been in this pacific disposition?

I will tell you, Mr. Lovelace, and the occasion; and be very explicit upon it, and upon all that concerns you to know of me, and of the commission I have undertaken to execute; and this the rather, as when you have heard me out, you will be satisfied, that I am not an officious man in this my present address to you.

I am all attention, Captain Tomlinson.

And so I doubt not was my beloved.

Capt. "You must know, sir, that I have not been *many months* in Mr. John Harlowe's neighbourhood. I removed from Northamptonshire, partly for the sake of better managing one of two executorships, which I could not avoid engaging in (the affairs of which frequently call me to town, and are part of my present business); and partly for the sake of occupying a neglected farm, which has *lately* fallen into my hands. But though an acquaintance of no

Clarissa. II. 27

longer standing, and that commencing on the Bowling-green [*uncle John is a great bowler, Belford*] upon my decision of a point to every one's satisfaction, which was appealed to me by all the gentlemen; (and which might have been attended with bad consequences) no two brothers have a more cordial esteem for each other. You know, Mr. Lovelace, that there is a *consent*, as I may call it, in some minds, which will unite them stronger together in a few hours, than years can do with others, whom yet we see not with disgust."

Lovel. Very true, captain.

Capt. "It was on the foot of this avowed friendship on both sides, that on Monday the 15th, as I very well remember, Mr. Harlowe invited himself home with me. And when there, he acquainted me with the whole of the unhappy affair that had made them all so uneasy. Till then, I knew it only by report; for intimate, as we were, I forbore to speak of what was so near his heart, till he began first. And then he told me, that he had had an application made to him, two or three days before, by a gentleman whom he named,* to induce him not only to be reconciled himself to his niece, but to forward for her a general reconciliation.

"A like application, he told me, had been made to his sister Harlowe, by a good woman whom every body respected; who had intimated, that his niece, if encouraged, would again put herself into the protection of her friends, *and leave you;* but, if not, that *she must unavoidably be yours.*"

I hope, Mr. Lovelace, I make no mischief. — You look concerned — you sigh, sir.

Proceed, Captain Tomlinson. Pray proceed. — *And I sighed still more profoundly.*

Capt. "They all thought it extremely particular, that a lady should decline marriage with a man she had so lately gone away with."

Pray, captain — *Pray,* Mr. Tomlinson — no more of this subject. My beloved is an angel. In every thing unblameable. Whatever faults there have been, have been *theirs* and *mine*. What you would further say, is, that the *unforgiving* family rejected her application. They did. She and I had had a misunderstanding. *The falling out of lovers* — you know, captain. — We have been happier ever since.

Capt. "Well, sir; but Mr. John Harlowe could not but better consider the matter *afterwards*. And he desired my advice how to act in it. He told me that no father ever loved a daughter as he loved this niece of his; whom, indeed, he used to call his *daughter-niece*. He said, she had really been unkindly treated by her brother and sister: and as your alliance, sir, was far from being a discredit to their family, he would do his endeavour to reconcile all parties, if he could be sure that ye were actually man and wife."

* See Miss Howe's Letters, p. 266, 279.

Lovel. And what, pray, captain, was your advice?

Capt. "I gave it as my opinion, that if his niece were unworthily treated, and in distress (as he apprehended from the application to him) he would soon hear of her again: but that it was likely, that this application was made without *expecting* it would succeed; and as a salvo only, to herself, for marrying without their consent. And the rather thought I so, as he had told me, that it came from a young lady, her friend, and not in a direct way *from herself;* which young lady was no favourite of the family; and therefore would hardly have been employed, had success been expected."

Lovel. Very well, Captain Tomlinson, pray proceed.

Capt. "Here the matter rested till last Sunday evening, when Mr. John Harlowe came to me with the man who had seen you and your lady (as I presume she is) at the play: and who had assured him, that you both lodged in the same house. — And then the application having been so lately made, which implied, that you were not then married, he was so uneasy for his niece's honour, that I advised him to dispatch to town some one in whom he could confide to make proper enquiries."

Lovel. Very well, captain — and was such a person employed on such an errand by her uncle?

Capt. "A trusty and discreet person was accordingly sent; and last Tuesday, I think it was (for he returned to us on the Wednesday) he made the inquiries among the neighbours first." [*The very inquiry, Jack, that gave us all so much uneasiness**.] But finding that none of them could give any satisfactory account, the lady's woman was come at, who declared, that you were actually married. But the inquirist keeping himself on the reserve as to his employers, the girl refused to tell the day, or to give him other particulars."

Lovel. You give a very clear account of every thing, Captain Tomlinson. Pray proceed.

Capt. "The gentleman returned; and on his report to Mr. Harlowe, having still doubts, and being willing to proceed on some grounds in so important a point, besought me (as my affairs called me frequently to town) to undertake this matter. "You, Mr. Tomlinson, he was pleased to say, have children of your own: you know the world: you know what I drive at? You will proceed, I am sure, with understanding and spirit: and whatever you are satisfied with shall satisfy me."

Enter Dorcas again in a hurry.

Sir, the gentleman is impatient. I will attend him presently.

The captain then accounted for his not calling in person, when he had reason to think us here.

He said he had business of consequence a few miles out of town, whither he thought he must have gone yesterday, and having been obliged to put off his little journey till this day, and understanding

* See p. 380.

27*

that we were within, not knowing whether he should have such another opportunity, he was willing to try his good fortune before he set out; and this made him come booted and spurred as I saw him.

He dropped a hint in commendation of the people of the house; but it was in such a way, as to give no room to suspect that he thought it *necessary* to inquire after the character of persons who make so genteel an appearance, as he observed they do.

And here let me remark, that my beloved might collect another circumstance in favour of the people below, had she doubted their characters, from the silence of her uncle's inquirist on Tuesday among the neighbours.

Capt. "And now, sir, that I believe I have satisfied you in every thing relating to my commission, I hope you will permit me to repeat my question — which is" —

Enter Dorcas again, out of breath.

Sir, the gentleman will step up to you. [*My lady is impatient. She wonders at your honour's delay. Aside.*]

Excuse me, captain, for one moment.

I have staid my full time, Mr. Lovelace. What may result from my question and your answer, whatever it shall be, may take us up time. — And you are engaged. Will you permit me to attend you in the morning, before I set out on my return?

You will then breakfast with me, captain?

It must be early if I do. I must reach my own house to-morrow night, or I shall make the best of wives unhappy. And I have two or three places to call at in my way.

It shall be by seven o'clock, if you please, captain. We are early folks. And this I will tell you, that if ever I am reconciled to a family so implacable as I have always found the Harlowes to be, it must be by the mediation of so cool and so moderate a gentleman as yourself.

And so, with the highest civilities on both sides, we parted. But for the private satisfaction of so good a man, I left him out of doubt, that we were man and wife, though I did not directly aver it.

LETTER CXIX.

Mr. Lovelace to John Belford, Esq.

Sunday night.

This Captain Tomlinson is one of the happiest as well as one of the best men in the world. What would I give to stand as high in my beloved's opinion as he does! But yet I am as good a man as he, were I to tell my own story, and have equal credit given to it. But the devil should have had him before I had seen him on the account he came upon, had I thought I should not have answered my principal end in it. I hinted to thee in my last what that was.

But to the particulars of the conference between my fair-one and me, on her hasty messages; which I was loth to come to, because she has had an half triumph over me in it.

After I had attended the captain down to the very passage, I returned to the dining-room, and put on a joyful air, on my beloved's entrance into it — O my dearest creature, said I, let me congratulate you on a prospect so agreeable to your wishes! And I snatched her hand, and smothered it with kisses.

I was going on; when interrupting me, you see, Mr. Lovelace, said she, how you have embarrassed yourself, by your obliquities! You see, that you have not been able to return a direct answer to a plain and honest question, though upon it depends all the happiness on the prospect of which you congratulate me.

You know, my best love, what my prudent, and I will say, my *kind* motives were, for giving out that we were married. You see, that I have taken no advantage of it; and that no inconvenience has followed it. You see that your uncle wants only to be assured from ourselves, *that it is so* —

Not another word on this subject, Mr. Lovelace, I will not only risk, but I will forfeit the reconciliation so near my heart, rather than I will go on to countenance a story so untrue!

My dearest soul — would you have me appear —

I would have you appear, sir, as *you are!* I am resolved that I will appear to my uncle's friend and to my uncle as *I am.*

For one week, my dearest life! Cannot you for one week — only till the settlements —

Not for one hour, with my own consent. You don't know, sir, how much I have been afflicted, that I have appeared to the people below what I am not. But my uncle, sir, shall never have it to upbraid me, nor will I to upbraid myself, that I have wilfully passed upon him in false lights.

What, my dear, would you have me to say to the captain to-morrow morning? I have given him room to think —

Then put him right, Mr. Lovelace. Tell the truth. Tell him what you please of the favour of your relations to me: tell him what you will about the settlements: and if, when drawn, you will submit them to his perusal and approbation, it will show him how much you are in earnest.

My dearest life! — Do you think, that he would disapprove of the terms I have offered?

No.

Then may I be accursed, if I willingly submit to be trampled under foot by my enemies!

And may I, Mr. Lovelace, never be happy in this life, if I submit to the passing upon my uncle Harlowe a wilful and premeditated falsehood for truth! I have too long laboured under the affliction which the rejection of all my friends has given me, to purchase my reconciliation with them now at so dear a price as that of my veracity.

The women below, my dear —

What are the women below to me? I want not to establish myself with them. Need they know all that passes between my relations and you and me?

Neither are they any thing to me, madam. Only that when, for the sake of preventing the fatal mischiefs which might have attended your brother's projects, I have made them think us married, I would not appear to them in a light which you yourself think so shocking. By my soul, madam, I had rather die, than contradict myself so flagrantly, after I have related to them so many circumstances of our marriage.

Well, sir, the women may believe what they please. That I have given countenance to what you told them, is my error. The many circumstances which you own *one* untruth has drawn you in to relate, is a justification of my refusal in the present case.

Don't you see, madam, that your uncle wishes to find that we are married? May not the ceremony be privately over, before his mediation can take place?

Urge this point no farther, Mr. Lovelace. If you will not tell the truth, *I* will to-morrow morning (if I see Captain Tomlinson) tell it myself. Indeed I will.

Will you, madam, consent that things pass as before with the people below? This mediation of Tomlinson *may* come to nothing. Your brother's schemes *may* be pursued; the rather, that now he will know (perhaps from your uncle) that you are not under a legal protection. — You will, at least, consent that things pass *here* as before? —

To permit this, is to go on in an error, Mr. Lovelace. But as the occasion for so doing (if there *can* be in your opinion an occasion that will warrant an untruth) will, as I presume, soon be over, I shall the less dispute that point with you. But a new error I will not be guilty of, if I can avoid it.

Can I, do you think, madam, have any dishonourable view in the step I supposed you would not scruple to take towards a reconciliation with your own family? Not for *my own* sake, you know, did I wish you to take it; for what is it to me, if I am never reconciled to your family? I want no favours from them.

I hope, Mr. Lovelace, there is no occasion, in our present not disagreeable situation, to answer such a question. And let me say, that I shall think my prospects still more agreeable, if, to-morrow morning, you will not only own the very truth, but give my uncle's friend such an account of the steps you have taken, and are taking, as may keep up my uncle's favourable intentions towards me. This you may do under what restrictions of secrecy you please. Captain Tomlinson is a prudent man; a promoter of family peace, you find; and, I dare say, may be made a friend.

I saw there was no help. I saw that the inflexible Harlowe spirit was all up in her. — A little witch! — A little — forgive me, Love, for calling her names! And so I said, with an air, we have had too many misunderstandings, madam, for me to wish for new ones: I will obey you without reserve. Had I not thought I should have obliged you by the other method, (especially as the ceremony might have been over, before any thing could have operated from your uncle's intentions, and of consequence no untruth persisted in) I would not have proposed it. But think not, my beloved creature, that you shall enjoy, without condition, this triumph over my judgment.

And then, clasping my arms about her, I gave her averted cheek (her charming lip designed) a fervent kiss — And your forgiveness of this sweet freedom [bowing] is that condition.

She was not mortally offended. And now must I make out the rest as well as I can. But this I will tell thee, that although her triumph has not diminished my love for her; yet it has stimulated me more than ever to *revenge*, as thou wilt be apt to call it. But *victory* or *conquest* is the more proper word.

There is a pleasure, 'tis true, in subduing one of these watchful beauties. But, by my soul, Belford, men of our cast take twenty times the pains to be rogues, that it would cost them to be honest; and dearly, with the sweat of our brows, and to the puzzling of our brains (to say nothing of the hazards we run) do we earn our purchase; and ought not therefore to be grudged our success when we meet with it — especially as, when we have obtained our end, satiety soon follows; and leaves us little or nothing to show for it. But this,

indeed, may be said of all worldly delights. — And is not that a grave reflection for me?

I was willing to write up to the time. Although I have not carried my principal point, I shall make something turn out in my favour from Captain Tomlinson's errand. But let me give thee this caution; that thou do not pretend to judge of my devices by *parts;* but have patience till thou seest the *whole*. But once more I swear, that I will not be *out-Norris'd* by a pair of novices. And yet I am very apprehensive, at times, of the consequences of Miss Howe's smuggling scheme.

My conscience, I should think, ought not to reproach me for a contrivance, which is justified by the contrivances of two such girls as these: one of whom (the more excellent of the two) I have always, with her own approbation as I imagine, proposed for my imitation.

But here, Jack, is the thing that concludes me, and cases my heart with adamant: I find by Miss Howe's letters, that it is owing to *her*, that I have made no greater progress with my blooming fair-one. She loves me. The Ipecacuanha contrivance convinces me that she loves me. Where there is love, there must be confidence, or a desire of having *reason* to confide. Generosity, founded on my supposed generosity, has taken hold of her heart. Shall I not now see (since I must be for ever unhappy, if I marry her, and leave any trial unessayed) what I can make of her love, and her newly-raised confidence? — Will it not be to my glory to succeed? and to hers, and to the honour of her sex, if I cannot? — Where then will be the hurt to either, to make the trial? And cannot I, as I have often said, reward her when I will by marriage?

'Tis late, or rather early; for the day begins to dawn upon me. I am plaguy heavy. Perhaps I need not to have told thee that. But will only indulge a doze in my chair for an hour; then shake myself, wash and refresh. At my time of life, with such a constitution as I am blessed with, that's all that's wanted.

Good night to me! — It cannot be broad day till I am awake, — Aw-w-w-waugh — pox of this yawning!

Is not thy uncle dead yet? What's come to mine, that he writes not to my last? — Hunting after more *wisdom of nations*, I suppose? — Yaw-yaw-yawning again? — Pen, begone!

LETTER CXX.

Mr. Lovelace to John Belford, Esq.

Monday, May 29.

Now have I established myself for ever in my charmer's heart.

The captain came at seven, as promised, and ready equipped for his journey. My beloved chose not to give us her company till our first conversation was over — ashamed, I suppose, to be present at that part of it which was to restore her to her *virgin state* by my confession, after her *wifehood* had been reported to her uncle. But she took her cue nevertheless, and listened to all that passed.

The modestest women, Jack, must *think*, and think deeply sometimes. I wonder whether they ever blush at those things by themselves, at which they have so charming a knack of blushing in company. If not; and if blushing be a sign of grace or modesty; have not the sex as great a command over their blushes, as they are said to have over their tears? This reflection would lead me a great way into female minds were I disposed to pursue it.

I told the captain, that I would prevent his question; and accordingly (after I had enjoined the strictest secrecy, that no advantage might be given to James Harlowe; and which he answered for as well on Mr. Harlowe's part as his own) I acknowledged nakedly and fairly the whole truth — to wit, "that we were not yet married. I gave him hints of the causes of procrastination. Some of them owing to unhappy misunderstandings: but chiefly to the lady's desire of previous reconciliation with her friends; and to a delicacy that had no example."

Less nice ladies than this, Jack, love to have delays, wilful and *studied* delays *imputed to them* in these cases — yet are indelicate in their affected delicacy; for do they not thereby tacitly confess, that they expect to be the greatest gainers in wedlock; and that there is *self-denial* in the pride they take in delaying.

"I told him the reason of our passing to the people below as married — yet as under a vow of restriction, as to consummation, which had kept us both to the height, one of *forbearing*, the other of *vigilant* punctilio; even to the denial of those innocent freedoms, which betrothed lovers never scruple to allow or take.

"I then communicated to him a copy of my proposal of settlement; the substance of her written answer; the contents of my letter of invitation to Lord M. to be her nuptial-father; and of my lord's generous reply. But said, that having apprehensions of delay from his infirmities, and my beloved choosing by all means (and that from principles of *unrequited* duty) a private solemnization, I had written to excuse his lordship's presence, and expected an answer every hour.

"The settlements, I told him, were actually drawing by Counsellor Williams, of whose eminence he must have heard —"

He had.

"And of the truth of this he might satisfy himself before he went out of town.

"When these were drawn, approved, and engrossed, nothing, I said, but signing, and the nomination of my happy day, would be wanting. I had a pride, I declared, in doing the highest justice to so beloved a creature, of my own voluntary motion, and without the intervention of a family from whom I had received the greatest insults. And this being our present situation, I was contented that Mr. John Harlowe should suspend his reconciliatory purposes, till our marriage were actually solemnized."

The captain was highly delighted with all I said: yet owned, that as his dear friend Mr. Harlowe had expressed himself greatly pleased to hear that we were actually married, he could have wished it had been so. But, nevertheless, he doubted not that all would be well.

He saw my reasons, he said, and approved of them, for making the gentlewomen below [whom again he *understood to be good sort of people*] believe, that the ceremony had passed; which so well accounted for what the lady's maid had told Mr. Harlowe's friend. Mr. James Harlowe, he said, had certainly ends to answer in keeping open the breach; and *as* certainly *had formed a design to get his sister out of my hands*. Wherefore it as much imported his worthy friend to keep this treaty a secret, as it did me; at least till he had formed his party, and taken his measures. Ill-will and passion were dreadful misrepresenters. It was amazing to him, that animosity could be carried so high against a man capable of views so pacific and so honourable, and who had shewn such a command of his temper, in this whole transaction, as I had done. Generosity, indeed, in every case, where love of stratagem and intrigue (I would excuse him) were not concerned, was a part of my character.

He was proceeding, when breakfast being ready, in came the empress of my heart, irradiating all around her, as with a glory — a benignity and graciousness in her aspect, that, though natural to it, had been long banished from it.

Next to prostration lowly bowed the captain. O how the sweet creature smiled her approbation of him! Reverence from one begets reverence from another. Men are more of monkeys in imitation, than they think themselves — involuntarily, in a manner, I bent my knee — my dearest life — and made a very fine speech on presenting the captain to her. No title, myself, to her lip or cheek, 'tis well *he* attempted not either. He was indeed ready to worship her: — could only touch her charming hand.

I have told the captain, my dear creature — and then I briefly repeated (as if I had supposed she had not heard it) all I had told him.

He was astonished, that any body could be displeased one moment with such an angel. He undertook her cause as the highest degree of merit to himself.

Never, I must need say, did the angel so much *look* the angel. All placid, serene, smiling, self-assured: a more lovely flush than usual heightening her natural graces, and adding charms, even to radiance, to her charming complexion.

After we had seated ourselves, the agreeable subject was renewed, as we took our chocolate. How happy should she be in her uncle's restored favour!

The captain engaged for it — no more delays he hoped, on *her* part! Let the happy day be but *once* over, all would then be right. But was it improper to ask for copies of my proposals, and of her answer, in order to shew them to his dear friend her uncle?

As Mr. Lovelace pleased — O that the dear creature would always say so!

It must be in strict confidence then, I said. But would it not be better to shew her uncle the draught of the settlements, when drawn?

And will you *be so good* as to allow of this, Mr. Lovelace?

There, Belford! We were once *the quarrelsome*, but now we are *the polite lovers.*

Indeed, my dear creature, I will, *if you desire it*, and if Captain Tomlinson will engage, that Mr. Harlowe shall keep them absolutely a secret; that I may not be subjected to the cavil and control of any others of a family that have used me so very ill.

Now indeed, sir, you are very obliging.

Dost think, Jack, that my face did not now also shine.

I held out my hand (first consecrating it with a kiss for hers). *She condescended to give it me.* I pressed it to my lips: you know not, Captain Tomlinson (with an air) all storms overblown, what a happy man —

Charming couple! [His hands lifted up] how will my good friend rejoice! O that he were present! You know not, madam, how dear you still are to your uncle Harlowe! —

I am unhappy ever to have disobliged him!

Not too much of that, however, fairest, thought I!

The captain repeated his resolutions of service, and that in so acceptable a manner, that the dear creature wished, that neither he nor any of his, might ever want a friend of equal benevolence.

Nor any of his, she said; for the captain brought it in, that he had five children living, by one of the best of wives and mothers, whose excellent management made him as happy, as if his eight hundred pounds a year (which was all he had to boast of) were two thousand.

Without economy, the oraculous lady said, *no* estate was large enough. *With* it, the *least* was not too small.

Lie still, teasing villain! lie still — I was only speaking to my conscience, Jack.

And let me ask you, Mr. Lovelace, said the captain; yet not so much from doubt, as that I may proceed upon sure grounds — you are *willing* to cooperate with my dear friend in a general reconciliation?

Let me tell you, Mr. Tomlinson, that if it can be distinguished, that my readiness to make up with a family, of whose generosity I have not had reason to think highly, is entirely owing to the value I have for this angel of a woman, I will not only co-operate with Mr. John Harlowe, as you ask; but I will meet Mr. James Harlowe senior, and his lady, *all the way.* And furthermore, to make the son James and his sister Arabella quite easy, I will absolutely disclaim any further interest, whether living or dying, in any of the three brothers' estates; contenting myself with what my beloved's grandfather has bequeathed to her: for I have reason to be abundantly satisfied with my own circumstances and prospects — enough rewarded, were she not to bring a shilling in dowry, in a woman who has a merit superior to all the goods of fortune. True as the Gospel, Belford! — Why had not this scene a real foundation?

The dear creature, by her eyes, expressed her gratitude before her lips could utter it. O, Mr. Lovelace, said she — you have infinitely — and there she stopped.

The captain run over in my praise. He was really affected.

O that I had not such *a mixture of revenge and pride in my love,* thought I! — But (my old plea) cannot I make her amends at any time? And is not her virtue now in the height of its probation? — Would she lay aside, like the friends of my uncontending Rosebud, all thoughts of defiance — would she throw herself upon my mercy, and try me but one fortnight in the life of honour — what then? — *I cannot say, what then.* —

Do not despise me, Jack, for my inconsistency — In no two letters perhaps agreeing with myself — Who expects consistency in men of our character? — But I am mad with love — fired by revenge — puzzled with my own devices — my invention is my curse — my pride my punishment — drawn five or six ways at once, can *she* possibly be so unhappy as *I?* — O why, why, was this woman so divinely excellent? — Yet how know I that she is? What have been her trials? Have I had the courage to make a single one upon her *person*, though a thousand upon her *temper?* — Enow, I hope, to make her afraid of ever disobliging me more! —

* * *

I MUST banish reflection, or I am a lost man. For these two hours past I have hated myself for my own contrivances. And this not only from what I *have* related to thee; but from what I have *further* to relate. But I have now once more steeled my heart. My vengeance is uppermost; *for I have been re-perusing some of Miss Howe's virulence.* The contempt they have both held me in, I cannot bear —

The happiest breakfast time, my beloved owned, that she had ever known *since she had left her father's house* [*she might have let this alone*]. The captain renewed all his protestations of service. He would write me word how his dear friend received the account he should give him of the happy situation of our affairs, and what he thought of the settlements, as soon as I should send him the drafts so kindly promised. And we parted with great professions of mutual esteem; my beloved putting up vows for the success of his generous mediation.

When I returned from attending the captain down stairs, which I did to the outward door, my beloved met me as I entered the dining-room; complacency reigning in every lovely feature.

"You see me already, *said she,* another creature. You know not, Mr. Lovelace, how near my heart this hoped-for reconciliation is. I am now willing to banish every disagreeable remembrance. You know not, sir, how much you have obliged me. And Oh! Mr. Lovelace, how happy shall I be, when my heart is lightened from the all-sinking weight of a father's curse! When my dear mamma — you don't know, sir, half the excellencies of my dear mamma! and what a kind heart she has, when it is left to follow its own impulses — when this blessed mamma, shall once more fold me to her indulgent bosom! When I shall again have uncles and aunt, and a brother and sister, all striving who shall shew most kindness and favour to the poor outcast, then *no more* an outcast — and you, Mr. Lovelace, to behold all this, and to be received into a family so dear to me, with welcome — what though a little cold at first? When they come to know you better, and to see you oftener, no fresh cause of disgust occurring, and you, as I hope, having entered upon a new course, all will be warmer and warmer love on both sides, till every one will perhaps wonder, how they came to set themselves against you."

Then drying her tears with her handkerchief, after a few moments pausing, on a sudden, as if recollecting that she had been led by her joy to an expression of it which she had not intended I should see, she retired to her chamber with precipitation; leaving me almost as unable to stand it as herself.

In short, I was — I want words to say how I was — my nose had been made to tingle before; my eyes had before been made to glisten by this soul-moving beauty; but so *very* much affected I never was — for, trying to check my sensibility, it was too strong for me, and I even sobbed — yes, by my soul, I *audibly* sobbed, and was forced to turn from her before she had well finished her affecting speech.

I want, methinks, now I have owned the odd sensation, to describe it to thee — the thing was so strange to me — something choaking, as it were, in my throat — I know not how — yet I must needs say, though I am out of countenance upon the recollection, that there was something very pretty in it; and I wish I could know it again, that I might have a more perfect idea of it, and be better able to describe it to thee.

But this effect of her joy on such an occasion gives me a high notion of what that virtue must be [what other name can I call it?] which in a mind so capable of delicate transport, should be able to make so charming a creature in her very bloom, all frost and snow to every advance of love from the man she hates not. This must be all from education too — must it not, Belford? Can *education* have stronger force in a woman's heart than *nature?* — Sure it cannot. But if it can, how entirely right are parents to cultivate their daughters' minds, and to inspire them with notions of reserve and distance to our sex; and indeed to make them think highly of their own! For pride is an excellent substitute, let me tell thee, where virtue shines not out, as the sun, in its own unborrowed lustre.

LETTER CXXI.

Mr. Lovelace to John Belford, Esq.

AND now it is time to confess (and yet I know that thy conjectures are aforehand with my exposition) that this Captain Tomlinson, who is so great a favourite with my charmer, and who takes so much delight in healing breaches and reconciling differences, is neither a greater man nor a less than honest Patrick M'Donald, attended by a discarded footman of his own finding out.

Thou knowest what a various-lived rascal he is; and to what better hopes born and educated.

But that ingenious knack of forgery, for which he was expelled the Dublin university, and a detection since in evidenceship, have been his ruin. For these have thrown him from one country to another; and at last into the way of life which would make him a fit husband for Miss Howe's Townsend with her contrabands. He is, thou knowest, admirably qualified for any enterprise that requires adroitness and solemnity. And can there, after all, be a higher piece of justice, than to keep one smuggler in readiness to play against another?

"Well but, Lovelace, (methinks thou questionest) how camest thou to venture upon such a contrivance as this, when, as thou hast told me, the lady used to be a month at a time at this uncle's; and must therefore, in all probability, know, that there was not a Captain Tomlinson in all the neighbourhood; at least no one of the name so intimate with him as this man pretends to be?"

This objection, Jack, is so natural a one, that I could not help observing to my charmer, that she must surely have heard her uncle speak of this gentleman. No, she said, she never had. Besides she had not been at her uncle Harlowe's for near ten months [*this I had heard her say before*]: and there were several gentlemen who used the same green whom she knew not.

We are all very ready, thou knowest, to believe what we like.

And what was the reason, thinkest thou, that she had not been of so long a time at this uncle's? — Why, this old sinner, who imagines himself entitled to call me to account for my freedoms with the sex, has lately fallen into familiarities, as it is suspected, with his housekeeper, who assumes airs upon it. — A cursed deluding sex! — In youth, middle age, or dotage, they take us all in.

Dost thou not see, however, that this housekeeper knows nothing, nor is to know any thing, of the treaty of reconciliation designed to be set on foot; and therefore the uncle always comes to the captain, the captain goes not to the uncle? and this I surmised to the lady. And then it was a natural suggestion that the captain was the rather applied to, as he is a stranger to the rest of the family — need I tell thee the meaning of all this?

But this intrigue of the *ancient* is a piece of private history, the truth of which my beloved cares not to own, and indeed affects to disbelieve: as she does also some puisny gallantries of her foolish brother; which, by way of recrimination, I have hinted at, without naming my informant in the family.

"Well but, methinks, thou questionest again, is it not probable that Miss Howe will make inquiry after such a man as Tomlinson? — And when she cannot—

I know what thou wouldst say — but I have no doubt that Wilson will be so good, if I desire it, as to give into my own hands any letter that may be brought by Collins to his house, for a week to come. And now I hope thou art satisfied.

I will conclude with a short story.

"Two neighbouring sovereigns were at war together, about some pitiful chuck-farthing thing or other, no matter what; *for the least trifles will set princes and children at loggerheads.* Their armies had been drawn up in battalia some days, and the news of a decisive action was expected every hour to arrive at each court. At last issue was joined; a bloody battle was fought; and a fellow who had been a spectator of it, arriving, with the news of a complete victory, at the capital of one of the princes some time before the appointed couriers, the bells were set a ringing, bonfires and illuminations were made, and the people went to bed intoxicated with joy and good liquor. But the next day all was reversed: the victorious enemy, pursuing his advantage, was expected every hour at the gates of the almost defenceless capital. The first reporter was hereupon sought for, and found; and being questioned, pleaded a great deal of merit, in that he had in so dismal a situation taken such a space of time from the distress of his fellow citizens, and given it to festivity, as were the hours between the false good news and the real bad."

Do thou, Belford, make the application. This I know, that I have given greater joy to my beloved than she had thought would so soon fall to her share. And as human life is properly said to be chequer-work, no doubt but a person of her prudence will make the best of it, and set off so much good against so much bad, in order to strike as just a balance as possible.

The lady, in three several letters, acquaints her friend with the material passages and conversations contained in those of Mr. Lovelace preceding. These are her words, on relating what the commission of the pretended Tomlinson was, after the apprehensions that his distant inquiry had given her:

At last, my dear, all these doubts and fears were cleared up and banished; and in their place, a delightful prospect was opened to me. For it comes happily out (but at present it must be an absolute secret, for reasons which I shall mention in the sequel) that the gentleman was sent by my uncle Harlowe [I thought he could not be angry with me for ever]: all owing to the conversation that passed between your good Mr. Hickman and him. For although Mr. Hickman's application was too harshly rejected at the time, my uncle could not but think better of it afterwards, and of the arguments that worthy gentleman used in my favour.

Who, upon a passionate repulse, would despair of having a reasonable request granted? — Who would not, by gentleness and condescension, endeavour to leave favourable impressions upon an angry mind; which, when it comes coolly to reflect, may induce it to work itself into a condescending temper? to request a favour, as I have often said, is one thing; to challenge it as our due is another. And what right has a petitioner to be angry at a *repulse*, if he has not a right to *demand* what he sues for as a *debt?*

She describes Captain Tomlinson on his breakfast visit, to be a grave good sort of a man. And in another place, a genteel man of great gravity and a good aspect; she believes upwards of fifty years of age. "I liked him, *says she*, as soon as I saw him."

As her prospects are now, as she says, more favourable, than heretofore, she wishes, that her hopes of Mr. Lovelace's so-often-promised reformation were better grounded than she is afraid they can be.

We have both been extremely puzzled, my dear, *says she*, to reconcile some parts of Mr. Lovelace's character with other parts of it: his good with his bad; such of the former, in particular, as his generosity to his tenants; his bounty to the innkeeper's daughter; his readiness to put me upon doing kind things to my good Norton, and others.

A strange mixture in his mind, as I have told him! For he is certainly (as I have reason to say, looking back upon his past behaviour to me in twenty instances) *a hard-hearted man.* Indeed my dear, *I have thought more than once, that he had rather see me in tears than give me reason to be pleased with him.*

My cousin Morden says that free livers are remorseless.* And so they must be in the very nature of things.

Mr. Lovelace is a proud man. We have both long ago observed that he is. And I am truly afraid, that his very generosity is more owing to his *pride* and his *vanity* than to that *philanthropy* (shall I call it!) which distinguishes a beneficent mind.

Money he values not, but as a means to support his pride and his independence. And it is easy, as I have often thought, for a person to part with a *secondary* appetite, when by so doing he can promote or gratify a *first.*

I am afraid, my dear, that there must have been some fault in his education. His natural bias was not, I fancy, sufficiently attended to. He was instructed, perhaps, (as his power was likely to be large) to do good and beneficent actions; but not, I doubt, from *proper motives.*

If he *had*, his generosity would not have stopped at *pride*, but would have struck into *humanity;* and then would he not have contented himself with doing praise-

* See page 250. See also Mr. Lovelace's own confession of the delight he takes in a woman's tears, in different parts of his letters.

worthy things by fits and starts, or, as if relying on the doctrine of merits, he hoped by a good action to atone for a bad one;* but he would have been uniformly noble, and done the good for its *own* sake.

O my dear; what a lot have I drawn! *Pride* this poor man's *virtue;* and *revenge* his other predominating quality! — This one consolation, however, remains: he is not an infidel, an unbeliever: had he been an *infidel,* there would have been no room at all for hope of him; but (priding himself, as he does, in his fertile invention) he would have been utterly abandoned, irreclaimable, and a savage.

---

* That the lady judges rightly of him in this place, see Vol. I. p. 160, where, giving the motive for his generosity to his Rosebud, he says — "As I make it my rule, whenever I have committed a very capital enormity, to do some good by way of atonement; and as I believe I am a pretty deal indebted on that score: I intend to join an hundred pounds to Johnny's aunt's hundred pounds, to make one innocent couple happy." Besides which motive, he had a further view to answer in that instance of his generosity; as may be seen, Vol. I. Letters lxx. lxxi. lxxii. See also the note, Vol. I. p. 317.

To shew the consistency of his actions, as they now appear, with his views and principles, as he lays them down in his *first letters,* it may not be amiss to refer the reader to his Letters, Vol. I. Numb. xxxiv. xxxv.

See also Vol. I. p. 132—134, and p. 184—186, for Clarissa's early opinion of Mr. Lovelace. Whence the coldness and indifference to him, which he so repeatedly accuses her of, will be accounted for, more to *her* glory than to *his* honour.

When she comes to relate those occasions, which Mr. Lovelace in his narrative acknowledges himself to be affected by, she thus expresses herself:

He endeavoured, as once before, to conceal his emotion. But, why, my dear, should these men (for Mr. Lovelace is not singular in this) think themselves above giving these beautiful proofs of a feeling heart? Were it in my power again to choose, or to refuse, I would reject the man with contempt, who sought to suppress, or offered to deny, the power of being visibly affected upon *proper* occasions, as either a savage-hearted creature, or as one who was so ignorant of the principal glory of the human nature, as to place his pride in a barbarous insensibility.

These lines, translated from Juvenal by Mr. Tate, I have been often pleased with:

Compassion *proper* to *mankind* appears;
Which Nature witness'd, when she lent us tears.
Of tender sentiments *we* only give
These proofs; to weep is *our* prerogative:
To shew by pitying looks, and melting eyes,
How with a suffering friend we sympathize.
Who can all sense of others' ills escape,
Is but a brute at best, in human shape.

It cannot but yield me some pleasure, hardly as I have sometimes thought of the people of the house, that such a good man as Captain Tomlinson had spoken well of them upon inquiry.

And here I stop a minute, my

dear, to receive, in fancy, your kind congratulation.

My next I hope, will confirm my present, and open still more agreeable prospects. Meantime be assured, that there cannot possibly any good fortune befal me, which I shall look upon with equal delight to that I have in your friendship.

My thankful compliments to your good Mr. Hickman, to whose kind intervention I am so much obliged on this occasion; conclude me, my dearest Miss Howe,

Your ever affectionate and grateful
CL. HARLOWE.

LETTER CXXII.

Mr. Lovelace to John Belford, Esq.

Tuesday, May 30.

I HAVE a letter from Lord M. Such a one as I would wish for, if I intended matrimony. But as matters are circumstanced, I cannot think of shewing it to my beloved.

My lord regrets, "that he is not to be the lady's nuptial-father. He seems apprehensive that I have still, specious as my reasons are, some mischief in my head."

He graciously consents, "that I may marry when I please: and offers one or both of my cousins to assist my bride, and to support her spirits on the occasion; since, as he understands, she is so much afraid to venture with me.

"Pritchard, he tells me, has his final orders to draw up deeds for assigning over to me in perpetuity 1000 *l. per annum*; which he will execute the same hour that the lady in person owns her marriage."

He consents, "that the jointure be made from my own estate."

He wishes, "that the lady would have accepted of his draft; and commends me for tendering it to her. But reproaches me for pride in not keeping it myself. *What the right side gives up, the left*, he says, *may be the better for*."

The girls, the *left sided* girls, he means.

With all my heart. If I can have my Clarissa, the devil take every thing else.

A good deal of other stuff writes the stupid peer; scribbling in several places half a dozen lines, apparently for no other reason, but to bring in as many musty words in an old saw.

If thou askest, "How I can manage, since my beloved will wonder, that I have not an answer from my lord to such a letter as I wrote to him; and if I own I have one, will expect that I should shew it to her, as I did my letter?"— This I answer — that I can be informed by Pritchard, "that my lord has the gout in his right-hand; and has ordered him to attend me in form, for my particular orders about the transfer:" and I can see Pritchard, thou knowest at the King's Arms, or wherever I please, *at an hour's warning; though he be at M. Hall, I in town;* and he, by word of mouth, can acquaint me with every thing in my lord's letter *that is necessary for my charmer to know.*

Whenever it suits me, I can *restore the old peer to his right hand,* and then can make him write a much more sensible letter than this that he has now sent me.

Thou kuowest that an adroitness in the art of *manual imitation* was one of my earliest attainments. It has been said on this occasion, that had I been a *bad* man in *meum* and *tuum* matters, I should not have been fit to live. As to the girls, we hold it no sin to cheat them. And are we not told, that in being *well deceived* consists the whole of human happiness?

Wednesday, May 31.

ALL still happier and happier. A very high honour done me: a chariot instead of a coach, permitted, purposely to indulge me in the subject of subjects.

Our discourse in this sweet airing turned upon our future manner of life. The day is bashfully promised me. *Soon* was the answer to my repeated urgency. Our equipage, our servants, our liveries, were part of the delightful subject. A desire that the wretch who had given me intelligence out of the family (honest Joseph Leman) might not be one of our menials; and her resolution to have her faithful Hannah, whether recovered or not, were signified; and both as readily assented to.

Her wishes, from my attentive behaviour, when with her at St. Paul's,* that I would often accom-

* See p. 215.

pany her to the divine service, were gently intimated, and as readily engaged for. I assured her, that I ever had respected the clergy in a body; and some individuals of them (her Dr. Lewen for one) highly: and that, were not going to church an act of religion, I thought it [as I told thee once*] a most agreeable sight to see rich and poor, all of a *company*, as I might say, assembled once a week in one place, and each in his or her best attire, to worship the God that made them. Nor could it be a hardship upon a man liberally educated, to make *one* on so solemn an occasion, and to hear the harangue of a man of letters (though far from being the principal part of the service, as it is too generally looked upon to be) whose studies having taken a different turn from his own, he must always have something new to say.

She shook her head, and repeated the word *new:* but looked as if willing to be satisfied for the present with this answer. To be sure, Jack, she means to do great despite to his Satanic Majesty in her hopes of reforming me. No wonder therefore if he exerts himself to prevent her, and to be revenged — but how came this in? — I am ever of party against myself. — One day I fancy, I shall hate myself on recollecting what I am about at this instant. But I must stay till then. We must all of us do something to repent of. The reconciliation prospect was

* Ibid. p. 214.

28*

enlarged upon. If her uncle Harlowe will but pave the way to it, and if it can be brought about she shall be happy, — happy, with a sigh, *as it is now possible she can be.* She won't forbear, Jack!

I told her that I had heard from Pritchard, just before we set out on our airing, and expected him in town to-morrow from Lord M. to take my directions. I spoke with gratitude of my lord's kindness to me; and with pleasure of Lady Sarah's, Lady Betty's, and my two cousins Montague's veneration for her: as also of his lordship's concern that his gout hindered him from writing a reply *with his own hand* to my last.

She pitied my lord. She pitied poor Mrs. Fretchville too; for she had the goodness to inquire after her. The dear creature pitied every body that seemed to want pity. Happy in her own prospects, she had leisure to look abroad, and wishes every body equally happy.

It is likely to go very hard with Mrs. Fretchville. Her face, which she had valued herself upon, will be utterly ruined. "This good, however, as I could not but observe, she may reap from so great an evil — as the greater malady generally swallows up the less, she may have a grief on this occasion, that may diminish the other grief, and make it tolerable."

I had a gentle reprimand for this light turn on so heavy an evil — "for what is the loss of beauty to the loss of a good husband?" — Excellent creature!

Her hopes (and her pleasure upon those hopes) that Miss Howe's mother would be reconciled to her, were also mentioned. *Good* Mrs. Howe was her word, for a woman so covetous, and so remorseless in her covetousness, that no one else will call her *good.* But this dear creature has such an extension in her love, as to be capable of valuing the most insignificant animal related to those whom she respects. *Love me, and love my dog,* I have heard Lord M. say. — Who knows, but that I may in time, in compliment to myself, bring her to think well of *thee,* Jack?

But what am I about? Am I not all this time arraigning my own heart? — I know I am, by the remorse I feel in it, while my pen bears testimony to her excellence. But yet I must add (for no selfish consideration shall hinder me from doing justice to this admirable creature) that in this conversation she demonstrated so much prudent knowledge in every thing that relates to that part of the domestic management which falls under the care of a mistress of a family, that I believe she has no equal of her years in the world.

But, indeed, I know not the subject on which she does not talk with admirable distinction; insomuch that could I but get over my prejudices against matrimony, and resolve to walk in the dull beaten path of my ancestors, I should be the happiest of men — and, if I cannot, perhaps I may be ten times more to be pitied than she.

My heart, my heart, Belford, *is not to be trusted*—I break off, to reperuse some of Miss Howe's virulence.

* * *

Cursed letters, these of Miss Howe, Jack!—Do thou turn back to those of mine, where I take notice of them—I proceed—

Upon the whole, my charmer was all gentleness, all ease, all serenity, throughout this sweet excursion. Nor had she reason to be otherwise: for it being the first time that I had the honour of her company alone, I was resolved to encourage her, by my respectfulness, to *repeat the favour*.

On our return, I found the counsellor's clerk waiting for me, with a draft of the marriage-settlements.

They are drawn, with only the necessary variations, from those made for my mother. The original of which (now returned by the counsellor) as well as the new drafts, I have put into my beloved's hands.

These settlements of my mother made the lawyer's work easy: nor can she have a better precedent; the great Lord S. having settled them, at the request of my mother's relations; all the difference, my charmer's are 100*l.* per annum more than my mother's.

I offered to read to her the old deed, while she looked over the draft; for she had refused her presence at the examination with the clerk: but this she also declined.

I suppose she did not care to hear of so many children, first, second, third, fourth, fifth, sixth, and seventh sons, and as many daughters, *to be begotten upon the body of the said Clarissa Harlowe.*

Charming matrimonial recitativoes!—though it is always said *lawfully begotten* too—as if a man could beget children *unlawfully* upon the body of his own wife.— But thinkest thou not that these arch rogues the lawyers hereby intimate, that a man may have children by his wife *before marriage?*—This must be what they mean. Why will these sly fellows put an honest man in mind of such rogueries?—But hence, as in numberless other instances, we see, that *law* and *gospel* are two very different things.

Dorcas, in our absence, tried to get at the wainscot-box in the dark closet. But it cannot be done without violence. And to run a risk of consequence *now*, for mere curiosity-sake, would be inexcusable.

Mrs. Sinclair and the nymphs are all of opinion, that I am now so much a favourite, and have such a visible share in her confidence, and even in her affections, that I may do what I will, and plead for excuse, violence of *passion;* which, they will have it, makes violence of *action* pardonable with their sex; as well as an *allowed extenuation* with the unconcerned *of both sexes;* and they all offer their helping hands. Why not? they say: has she not passed for my wife before them all?—

And is she not in a fine way of being reconciled to her friends? And was not the want of that reconciliation the pretence for postponing the consummation?

They again urge me, since it is so difficult to make *night* my friend, to an attempt in the *day*. They remind me, that the situation of their house is such, that no noises can be heard out of it; and ridicule me for making it necessary for a lady to be undressed. *It was not always so with me*, poor old man! Sally told me; saucily flinging her handkerchief in my face.

LETTER CXXIII.
Mr. Lovelace to John Belford, Esq.

Friday, June 2.

NOTWITHSTANDING my studied-for politeness and complaisance for some days past; and though I have wanted courage to throw the mask quite aside; yet I have made the dear creature more than once look about her, by the warm though decent expression of my passion. I have brought her to own, that I am *more* than indifferent with her: but as to LOVE, which I pressed her to acknowledge, *what need of acknowledgments of that sort, when a woman consents to marry?* — And once repulsing me with displeasure. *The proof of true love I was vowing for her, was* RESPECT, *not* FREEDOM. And offering to defend myself, she told me that all the conception she had been able to form of a faulty passion, was, that it must demonstrate itself as mine sought to do.

I endeavoured to justify my passion, by laying over-delicacy at her door. Over-delicacy, she said, was not *my* fault, if it were hers. She must plainly tell me, that I appeared to her incapable of distinguishing what were the requisites of a pure mind. Perhaps, had the *libertine* presumption to imagine, that there was no difference in *heart*, nor any but what proceeded from difference of *education* and *custom*, between the pure and the impure — and yet custom *alone*, as she observed, if I *did* so think, would make a second nature, as well in *good* as in *bad* habits.

* * *

I HAVE just now been called to account for some innocent liberties which I thought myself entitled to take before the women; as they suppose us to be married, and now within view of consummation.

I took the lecture very hardly; and with impatience wished for the happy day and hour when I might call her all my own, and meet with no check from a niceness that had no example.

She looked at me with a bashful kind of contempt. I thought it *contempt*, and required the reason for it; not being conscious of offence, as I told her.

This is not the first time, Mr. Lovelace, said she, that I have had cause to be displeased with you, when *you*, perhaps, have not thought yourself exceptionable.

— But, sir, let me tell you, that the married state, in my eye, is a state of purity, and [I *think* she told me] not of *licentiousness;* so, at least, I understood her.

Marriage purity, Jack! — Very comical, faith — yet, sweet dears, half the female world ready to run away with a rake, *because* he is a rake; and for no *other* reason; nay, every other reason *against* their choice of such a one.

But have not you and I, Belford, seen young wives, who would be thought modest; and when maids were fantastically shy; permit freedoms in public from their uxorious husbands, which have shewn, that both of them have forgotten what belongs either to prudence or decency? While every modest eye has sunk under the shameless effrontery, and every modest face been covered with blushes, for those who could *not* blush.

I once, upon such an occasion, proposed to a circle of a dozen, thus scandalized, to withdraw; since they must needs see that as well the *lady*, as the gentleman, wanted to be in private. This motion had its effect upon the amorous pair; and I was applauded for the check given to their licentiousness.

But, upon another occasion of this sort, I acted a little more in character. For I ventured to make an attempt upon a bride, which I should not have had the courage to make, had not the unblushing passiveness with which she received her fond husband's public toyings (looking round her with triumph rather than with shame, upon every lady present) incited my curiosity to know if the same complacency might not be shewn to a private friend. 'Tis true, I was in honour obliged to keep the secret. But I never saw the turtles bill afterwards, but I thought of number two to the same female; and in my heart thanked the fond husband for the lesson he had taught his wife.

From what I have said, thou wilt see, that I approve of my beloved's exception to *public* loves. That, I hope, is all the charming icicle means by *marriage purity*. But to return.

From the whole of what I have mentioned to have passed between my beloved and me, thou wilt gather, that I have not been a mere dangler, a Hickman, in the passed days, though not absolutely active, and a Lovelace.

The dear creature now considers herself as my wife-elect. The *unsaddened* heart, no longer prudish, will not now, I hope, give the sable turn to every address of the man she dislikes not. And yet she must keep up so much reserve, as will justify past inflexibilities. "Many and many a pretty soul would yield, were she not afraid that the man she favoured would think the worse of her for it." This is also a part of the rake's creed. But should she resent ever so strongly, she cannot now break with me; since, if she does, there will be an end of the family reconciliation; and that in a way highly discreditable to herself.

Saturday, June 3.

JUST returned from Doctors' Commons. I have been endeavouring to get a licence. Very true, Jack. I have the mortification to find a difficulty, as the lady is of rank and fortune, and as there is no consent of father or *next friend*, in obtaining this *all-fettering* instrument.

I made report of this difficulty. "It is very right, she says, that such difficulties should be made." — But not to a man of my known fortune, surely, Jack, though the woman were the daughter of a duke.

I asked, if she approved of the settlements? She said, she had compared them with my mother's, and had no objection to them. She had written to Miss Howe upon the subject, she owned; and to inform her of our present situation.*

* * *

JUST now, in high good humour, my beloved returned me the drafts of the settlements: a copy of which I sent to Captain Tomlinson. She complimented me, "that she never had any doubt of my honour in cases of this nature."

In matters between man and man nobody ever had, thou knowest.

I had need, thou wilt say, to have some good qualities.

* As this letter of the lady to Miss Howe contains no new matter, but what may be collected from those of Mr. Lovelace, it is omitted.

Great faults and great virtues are often found in the same person. In nothing *very* bad, but as to women: and did not one of them begin with me?*

We have held, that women have no souls. I am a very Turk in this point, and willing to believe they have not. And if so, to whom shall I be accountable for what I do to them? Nay, if souls they have, as there is no sex in etherials, nor need of any, what plea can a lady hold of injuries done her in her lady-*state*, when there is an end of her lady-*ship*?

LETTER CXXIV.

Mr. Lovelace to John Belford, Esq.

Monday, June 5.

I AM now almost in despair of succeeding with this charming frost-piece by love or gentleness. — A copy of the drafts, as I told thee, has been sent to Captain Tomlinson; and that by a special messenger. Engrossments are proceeding with. I have been again at the Commons. — Should in all probability have procured a licence by Mallory's means, had not Mallory's friend the proctor been suddenly sent for to Cheshunt, to make an old lady's will. Pritchard has told me by word of mouth, *though my charmer saw him not*, all that was necessary for her to know in the letter my lord wrote, which I could not shew her: and taken my directions about the estates to be made over to me on my nuptials. — Yet, with

* See Vol. I. p. 135.

all these favourable appearances, no conceding moment to be found, no improveable tenderness to be raised.

But never, I believe, was there so true, so delicate a modesty in the human mind as in that of this lady. And this has been my security all along; and, in spite of Miss Howe's advice to her, will be so still; since, if her delicacy be a fault, she can no more overcome it than I can my aversion to matrimony. Habit, habit, Jack, seest thou not? may subject us both to weaknesses. And should she not have charity for me, as I have for her?

Twice, indeed with rapture, which once she called rude, did I salute her; and each time resenting the freedom, did she retire; though, to do her justice, she favoured me again with her presence at my first entreaty, and took no notice of the cause of her withdrawing.

Is it policy to shew so open a resentment for innocent liberties, which, in her situation, she must so soon forgive?

Yet the woman who resents not initiatory freedoms must be lost. For love is an encroacher. Love never goes backward. Love is always aspiring. Always must aspire. Nothing but the highest act of love can satisfy an indulged love. And what advantages has a lover who values not breaking the peace, over his mistress who is solicitous to keep it!

I have now at this instant wrought myself up, for the dozenth time, to a half-resolution. A thousand agreeable things I have to say to her. She is in the dining-room. Just gone up. She always expects me when there.

* * *

High displeasure! — followed by an abrupt departure.

I sat down by her. I took both her hands in mine, I would *have* it so. All gentle my voice. Her father mentioned with respect. Her mother with reverence. Even her brother amicably spoken of. I never thought I could have wished so ardently, as I told her I did wish, for a reconciliation with her family.

A sweet and grateful flush then overspread her fair face; a gentle sigh now-and-then heaved her handkerchief.

I perfectly longed to hear from Captain Tomlinson. It was impossible for her uncle to find fault with the draft of the settlements. I would not, however, be understood, by sending them down, that I intended to put it in her uncle's power to delay my happy day. When, when was it to be?

I would hasten again to the Commons; and would not return without the licence.

The Lawn I proposed to retire to, as soon as the happy ceremony was over. This day and that day I proposed.

It was time enough to name the day, when the settlements were completed, and the licence obtained. Happy should she be, could the kind Captain Tomlinson obtain her *uncle's presence privately.*

A good hint! — It may perhaps be improved upon — either for a delay or a *pacifier.*

No new delays for heaven's sake, I besought her; and reproached her gently for the past. Name but the day — (an *early* day, I hoped it would be, in the following week) — that I might hail its approach, and number the tardy hours.

My cheek reclined on her shoulder — kissing her hands by turns. Rather bashfully than angrily reluctant, her hands sought to be withdrawn; her shoulder avoiding my reclined cheek — apparently loth, and more loth to quarrel with me; her downcast eye confessing more than her lips could utter. Now, surely, thought I, is my time to try if she can forgive a still bolder freedom than I had ever yet taken.

I then gave her struggling hands liberty. I put one arm round her waist: I imprinted a kiss on her sweet lip, with a *be quiet only,* and an averted face, as if she feared another.

Encouraged by so gentle a repulse, the tenderest things I said; and then with my other hand, drew aside the handkerchief that concealed the beauty of beauties, and pressed with my burning lips the most charming breast that ever my ravished eyes beheld.

A very contrary passion to that, which gave her bosom so delightful a swell, immediately took place. She struggled out of my encircling arms with indignation. I retained her reluctant hand. Let me go, said she. *I see there is no keeping terms with you.* Base encroacher! Is this the design of your flattering speeches? Far as matters have gone, I will for ever renounce you. You have an odious heart. Let me go, I tell you.

I was forced to obey, and she flung from me, repeating *base,* and adding, *flattering* encroacher.

* * *

In vain have I urged by Dorcas for the promised favour of dining with her. She would not dine *at all.* She *could not.*

But why makes she every inch of her person thus sacred? — So near the time too, that she must suppose, that all will be my own by deed of purchase and settlement?

She has read no doubt of the part of the eastern monarchs, who sequestered themselves from the eyes of their subjects, in order to excite their adoration, when, upon some solemn occasions, they think fit to appear in public.

But let me ask thee, Belford, whether (on these solemn occasions) the preceding cavalcade; here a great officer, and there a great minister, with their satellites, and glaring equipages; do not prepare the eyes of the wondering beholders, by degrees, to bear the blaze of canopied majesty (what though but an ugly old man perhaps himself? yet) glittering in the collected riches of his vast empire?

And should not my beloved, for

her own sake, descend, by *degrees*, from *goddess-hood* into *humanity?* If it be *pride* that restrains her, ought not that pride to be punished? If, as in the eastern emperors, it be *art* as well as *pride*, *art* is what she of all women need not use. If *shame*, what a shame to be ashamed to communicate to her adorer's sight the most admirable of her personal graces?

Let me perish, Belford, if I would not forego the brightest diadem in the world, for the pleasure of seeing a twin Lovelace at each charming breast, drawing from it his first sustenance; the pious task, for physical reasons*, continued for one month and no more!

I now, methinks, behold this most charming of women in this sweet office: her conscious eye now dropt on one, now on the other, with a sigh of maternal tenderness, and then raised up to my delighted eye, full of wishes for the sake of the pretty varlets, and for her own sake, that I would deign to legitimate; that I would condescend to put on the nuptial fetters.

LETTER CXXV.
Mr. Lovelace to John Belford, Esq.

Monday afternoon.

A LETTER received from the worthy Captain Tomlinson has introduced me into the presence of my charmer sooner than perhaps I should otherwise have been admitted.

Sullen her brow, at her first entrance into the dining-room. But I took no notice of what had passed, and her anger of itself subsided.

"The captain, after letting me know, that he chose not to write, till he had the promised draft of the settlements, acquaints me, that his friend, Mr. John Harlowe, in their first conference (which was held as soon as he got down) was extremely surprised, and even grieved (*as he feared he would be*) to hear that we were not married. The world, he said, who knew my character, would be very censorious, were it owned, that we had lived so long together unmarried in the same lodgings; although our marriage were now to be ever so publicly celebrated.

"His nephew James, he was sure, would make a great handle of it against any motion that might be made towards a reconciliation; and with the greater success, as there was not a family in the kingdom more jealous of their honour than theirs."

This is true of the Harlowes, Jack: they have been called *the proud Harlowes:* and I have ever found, that all *young honour* is supercilious and touchy.

But seest thou not how right I was in my endeavour to persuade

---
* In Pamela, Vol. IV. Letter vi. these reasons are given, and are worthy of every parent's consideration, as is the whole letter, which contains the debate between Mr. B. and his Pamela, on the important subject of mothers being nurses to their own children.

my fair-one to allow her uncle's friend to think us married; especially as he came *prepared* to believe it; and as her uncle *hoped it* was so? — But nothing on earth is so perverse, as a woman when she is set upon carrying a point, and has a *meek* man, or one who loves his *peace*, to deal with.

My beloved was vexed. She pulled out her handkerchief: but was more inclined to blame me, than herself.

Had you kept your word, Mr. Lovelace, and left me when we came to town — and there she stopped, for she knew, that it was her own fault that we were not married before we left the country; and how could I leave her *afterwards*, *while her brother was plotting to carry her off by violence?*

Nor has this brother yet given over his machinations.

For as the captain proceeds, "Mr. John Harlowe owned to him (but in confidence) that his nephew is at this time busied in endeavouring to find out where we are; being assured, (as I am not to be heard of at any of my relations, or at my usual lodgings) that we are together. And that we are not married, is plain, as he will have it, *from Mr. Hickman's application so lately made to her uncle; and which was seconded by Mrs. Norton to her mother.* And her brother cannot bear that I should enjoy such a triumph unmolested."

A profound sigh, and the handkerchief again lifted to the eye. But did not the sweet soul deserve this turn upon her for feloniously resolving to rob me of herself, had the application made by Hickman succeeded?

I read on to the following effect:

"Why (asked Mr. Harlowe) was it said to his other inquiring friend, that we *were married;* and that by his niece's woman, who ought to know? Who could give convincing reasons, no doubt" —

Here again she wept; took a turn cross the room; then returned — Read on, says she —

Will you, my dearest life, read it yourself?

I will take the letter with me, by-and-bye — I cannot *see* to read it just now, wiping her eyes — read on — let me hear it all — that I may know *your* sentiments upon this letter, as well as give *my own.*

"The captain then told uncle John, the reasons that induced me to give out that we were married; and the conditions, on which my beloved was brought to countenance it; which had kept us at the most punctilious distance.

"But still, Mr. Harlowe objected my character. And went away dissatisfied. And the captain was also so much concerned, that he cared not to write what the result of his first conference was.

"But in the next, which was held on receipt of the drafts, at the captain's house, (as the former was, for the greater secrecy) when the old gentleman had read them, and had the captain's opinion, he was much better pleased. And yet he declared, that it would not be easy to persuade *any other person of his family to believe so favourably of the matter*, as he was *now* willing to believe, were they to know that we had lived so long together unmarried.

"And then the captain says, his dear friend made a proposal: — it was this — *That we should marry immediately, but as privately as possible, as indeed he found we intended* (for he could have no objection to the drafts) — *But, yet he expected to have present one trusty friend of his own, for his better satisfaction.*" —

Here I stopped, with a design to be angry — but she desiring me to read on, I obeyed.

"— *But that it should pass to every one living, except to that trusty person, to himself, and to the captain, that we were married from the time that we had lived together in one house; and that this time should be made to agree with that of Mr. Hickman's application to him from Miss Howe.*"

This, my dearest life, said I, is a very considerate proposal. We have nothing to do, but to caution the people below properly on this head. I did not think your uncle Harlowe capable of hitting upon such a charming expedient as this. But you see how much his heart is in the reconciliation.

This was the return I met with — You have always, as a mark of your politeness, let me know, how *meanly* you think of every one of my family.

Yet, thou wilt think, Belford, that *I could forgive her for the reproach*.

The captain does not know, he says, how this proposal will be relished by us. But, for his part, he thinks it an expedient that will obviate many difficulties, and may possibly put an end to Mr. James Harlowe's further designs; and on this account he has, *by the uncle's advice*, already declared to two several persons, by whose means it may come to that young gentleman's ears, that he [Captain Tomlinson] has very great reason to believe, that we were married soon after Mr. Hickman's application was rejected.

"And this, Mr. Lovelace, (says the captain) will enable you to pay a compliment to the family, that will not be unsuitable to the generosity of some of the declarations you were pleased to make to the lady before me (and which Mr. John Harlowe may make some advantage of in favour of a reconciliation); in that you have not demanded your lady's estate so soon as you were entitled to make the demand." An excellent contriver, surely, she must think this worthy Mr. Tomlinson to be!

But the captain adds, that if either the lady or I disapprove of his report of our marriage, he will retract it. Nevertheless, he must tell me, that Mr. John Harlowe is very much set upon this way of proceeding; as the only one, in his opinion, capable of being improved into a general reconciliation. But if we do acquiesce in it, he beseeches my fair one not to suspend my day, that he may be authorized in what he says, as to the truth of the main fact [*how conscientious this good man!*] Nor must it be expected, he says, that her uncle will take one step towards the wished-for reconciliation till the *solemnity is actually over.*"

He adds, "that he shall be very soon in town on other affairs; and then proposes to attend us, and give us a more particular account of all that has passed, or shall further pass, between Mr. Harlowe and him."

Well, my dearest life, what say you to your uncle's expedient? Shall I write to the captain, and acquaint him that we have no objection to it?

She was silent for a few minutes. At last, with a sigh, See, Mr. Lovelace, said she, what you have brought me to, by treading after you in such crooked paths! — See what disgrace I have incurred! — Indeed you have not acted like a wise man.

My beloved creature, do you not remember, how earnestly I besought the honour of your hand before we came to town? — Had I been *then favoured* —

Well, well, sir, — there has been much amiss somewhere; that's all I will say at present. And since what is passed cannot be recalled, my uncle must be obeyed, I think.

Charmingly dutiful! — I had nothing then to do, that I might not be behind-hand with the worthy captain and her uncle, but to press for the day. This I fervently did. But (as I might have expected) she repeated her former answer; to wit, that when the settlements were completed; when the licence was actually obtained; it would be time enough to name the day: and, O Mr. Lovelace, said she, turning from me with a grace inimitably tender, her handkerchief at her eyes, what a happiness, if my dear uncle could be prevailed upon to be personally a father, on this occasion, to *the poor fatherless girl!*

What's the matter with me! — Whence this dew-drop! — A tear! As I hope to be saved it is a tear, Jack! — Very ready methinks! — Only on reciting! — But her lovely image was before me, in the very attitude she spoke the words — and indeed at the time she spoke them, these lines of Shakspeare came into my head:

Thy heart is big. Get thee apart and weep!
Passion, I see, is catching: — For my eye,
Seeing those beads of sorrow stand in thine,
Begin to water —

I withdrew, and wrote to the captain to the following effect — "I desired that he would be so good as to acquaint his dear friend, that we entirely acquiesced with what he had proposed; and had already *properly* cautioned the gentlewomen of the house, and their servants, as well as our own: and to tell him, that if he would in person give me the blessing of his dear niece's hand, it would crown the wishes of both. In this case,

I consented, that his own day, as *I presumed it would be a short one*, should be ours: that by this means the secret would be with fewer persons: that I myself, as well as he, thought the ceremony could not be too privately performed; and this not only for the sake of the wise end he had proposed to answer by it, but because I would not have Lord M. think himself slighted; since that nobleman, as I had told him [the captain] had once intended to be our nuptial-father; and actually made the offer; but that we had declined to accept of it, and that for no other reason than to avoid a public wedding; which his beloved niece would not come into, while she was in disgrace with her friends — but that if he chose not to do us this honour, I wished that captain Tomlinson might be the trusty person whom he would have to be present on the happy occasion."

I shewed this letter to my fair-one. She was not displeased with it. So, Jack, we cannot now move too fast, as to settlements and licence: the day is her *uncle's day*, or *Captain Tomlinson's*, perhaps, as shall best suit the occasion. Miss Howe's smuggling-scheme is now surely provided against in all events.

But I will not by anticipation make thee a judge of all the benefits that may flow from this my elaborate contrivance. Why will these girls put me upon my *master-strokes?*

And now for a little mine which I am getting ready to spring. The *first* that I have sprung, and at the rate I go on (now a *resolution*, and now a *remorse*) perhaps the last that I shall attempt to spring.

A *little* mine, call it. But it may be attended with great effects. I shall not, however, absolutely depend upon the success of it, having much more effectual ones in reserve. And yet great engines are often moved by small springs. A little spark falling by accident into a powder-magazine, has done more execution in a siege than an hundred cannon.

Come the worst, the *hymeneal torch*, and a *white sheet*, must be my *amende honorable*, as the French have it.

LETTER CXXVI.

Mr. Belford to Robert Lovelace, Esq.

Tuesday, June 6.

UNSUCCESSFUL as hitherto my application to you has been, I cannot for the heart of me forbear writing once more in behalf of this admirable woman: and yet am unable to account for the zeal which impels me to take her part with an earnestness so sincere.

But all her merit thou acknowledgest; all thy own vileness thou confessest, and even gloriest in it: what hope then of moving so hardened a man? — Yet, as it is not too late, and thou art nevertheless upon the crisis, I am resolved to try what another letter will do. It is but my writing in vain, if it do no good; and if thou wilt let me prevail, I know thou wilt hereafter think me richly entitled to thy thanks.

To argue with thee would be folly. The case cannot require it. I will only *entreat* thee, therefore, that thou wilt not let such an excellence lose the reward of her vigilant virtue.

I believe there were never libertines so vile, but purposed, at some future period of their lives, to set about reforming; and let me beg of thee, that thou wilt, in this great article, make thy future repentance as easy, as some time hence thou wilt wish thou *hadst* made it.

If thou proceedest, I have no doubt, that this affair will end tragically, one way or other. It *must*. Such a woman must interest both gods and men in her cause. But what I most apprehend, is, that with her own hand, in resentment of the perpetrated outrage, she (like another Lucretia) will assert the purity of her heart: or, if her piety preserve her from this violence, that wasting grief will soon put a period to her days. And in either case, will not the remembrance of thy *ever-during* guilt, and *transitory* triumph, be a torment of torments to thee?

'Tis a seriously sad thing, after all, that so fine a creature should have fallen into such vile and remorseless hands: for, from thy cradle, as I have heard thee own, thou ever delightedst to sport with and torment the animal, whether bird or beast, that thou lovedst, and hadst a power over.

How different is the case of this fine woman from that of any other whom thou hast seduced! — I need not mention to thee, nor insist upon the striking difference: justice, gratitude, thy interest, thy vows, all engaging thee; and thou certainly loving her, as far as thou art capable of love, above all her sex. She not to be drawn aside by art, or to be made to suffer from credulity, nor for want of wit and discernment (that will be another cutting reflection to so fine a mind as hers): the contention between you only unequal, as it is between naked innocence and armed guilt. In every thing else, as thou ownest, her talents greatly superior to thine! — What a fate will hers be, if thou art not at last overcome by thy reiterated remorses!

At first, indeed, when I was admitted into her presence* (and till I observed her meaning air, and heard her speak) I supposed that she had no very uncommon *judgment* to boast of: for I made, as I thought, but *just* allowances for her blossoming youth, and for that loveliness of person, and for that ease and elegance in her dress, which I imagined must have taken up half her time and study to cultivate; and yet I had been prepared by thee to entertain a very high opinion of her sense and her reading. Her choice of this gay fellow, upon such hazardous terms, (thought I) is a confirmation that her *wit* wants that maturity which only *years*

* See p. 220.

and *experience* can give it. Her *knowledge* (argued I to myself) must be all *theory;* and the complaisance ever consorting with an age so green and so gay, will make so inexperienced a lady at least forbear to shew herself *disgusted* at freedoms of discourse in which those present of her own sex, and some of ours (so learned, so well read, and so travelled) allow themselves.

In this presumption, I ran on; and having the advantage, as I conceited, of all the company but you, and being desirous to appear in her eyes a mighty clever fellow, I thought I *showed away*, when I said any foolish things that had more sound than sense in them; and when I made silly jests, which attracted the smiles of thy Sinclair and thy specious Partington: and that Miss Harlowe did not smile too, I thought was owing to her youth or affectation, or to a mixture of both, perhaps to a greater command of her features. — Little dreamt I, that I was incurring her contempt all the time.

But when, as I said, I heard her speak, which she did not till she had fathomed us all: when I heard her sentiments on two or three subjects, and took notice of that searching eye, darting into the very inmost cells of our frothy brains; by my faith, it made me look about me, and I began to recollect and be ashamed of all I had said before; in short, was resolved to sit silent, till every one had talked round, to keep my folly in countenance. And then I raised the subjects that she *could* join in, and which she *did* join in, so much to the confusion and surprise of every one of us! — For even thou, Lovelace, so noted for smart wit, repartee, and a vein of raillery, that delighteth all who come near thee, sattest in palpable darkness, and lookedst about thee, as well as we.

One instance only of this, shall I remind thee of?

We talked of *wit*, and of *wit*, and aimed at it, bandying it like a ball from one to another, and resting it chiefly with thee, who wert always proud enough and vain enough of the attribute; and then more especially as thou hadst assembled us, as far as I know, principally to shew the lady thy superiority over us: and us thy triumph over her. And then Tourville (who is always satisfied with wit at *second-hand;* wit upon memory; other men's wit) repeated some verses as applicable to the subject; which two of us applauded, though full of *double entendre*. Thou, seeing the lady's serious air on one of those repetitions, appliedst thyself to her, desiring her notions of wit: a quality, thou saidst, which every one prized, whether flowing from himself or found in another.

Then it was that she took all our attention. It was a quality much talked of, she said, but, she believed, very little understood. At least, if she might be so free as to give her judgment of it from what had passed in the present conversation, she must say, that wit with men was one thing; with women another.

This startled us all: — how the women looked! — how they pursed in their mouths! A broad smile the moment before, upon each, from the verses they had heard repeated, so well understood, as we saw, by their looks! While I besought her to let us know, for our instruction, what wit was with *women*; for such I was sure it *ought* to be with *men*.

Cowley, she said, had defined it prettily by negatives. Thou desiredst her to repeat his definition.

She did; and with so much graceful ease and beauty, and propriety of accent, as would have made bad poetry delightful.

A thousand diff'rent shapes it bears;
Comely in thousand shapes appears.
'Tis not a *tale*, 'tis not a *jest*,
Admir'd with *laughter* at a *feast*,
Nor *florid talk*, which must this title gain:
The proofs of wit for ever must remain.
Much less can that have any place
At which a virgin hides her face.
Such dross the fire must purge away: —
'Tis just
The author blush there, where the reader must.

Here she stopped, looking round her upon us all with conscious superiority, as I thought. Lord, how we stared! Thou attemptedst to give us thy definition of wit, that thou mightest have something to say, and not seem to be surprised into silent modesty.

But, as if she cared not to trust thee with the subject, referring to the same author as for his more positive decision, she thus, with the same harmony of voice and accent, emphatically decided upon it.

Wit, like a luxuriant vine,
Unless to *virtue's* prop it join,
Firm and erect, tow'rd heaven bound,
Tho' it with beauteous leaves and pleasant fruit be crown'd,
It lies deform'd and rotting on the ground.

If thou recollectest this part of the conversation, and how like fools we looked at one another; how much it put us out of conceit with ourselves, and made us fear her, when we found our conversation thus excluded from the very character which our vanity had made us think unquestionably ours; and if thou profitest properly by the recollection, thou wilt be of my mind, that there is not so much wit in wickedness as we had flattered ourselves there was.

And after all, I have been of opinion ever since *that* conversation, that the wit of all the rakes and libertines I ever conversed with, from the brilliant Bob Lovelace, down to little Johnny Hartop the punster, consists mostly in saying bold and shocking things, with such courage as shall make the modest blush, the impudent laugh, and the ignorant stare.

And why dost thou think I mention these things, so mal-à-propos, as it may seem! — Only, let me tell thee, as an instance (among many that might be given from the same evening's conversation) of this fine woman's superiority in those talents which ennoble nature, and dignify her sex —

evidenced not only to each of us, as we offended, but to the flippant Partington, and the grosser but egregiously hypocritical Sinclair, in the correcting eye, the discouraging blush, in which was mixed as much displeasure as modesty, and sometimes, as the occasion called for it, (for we were some of us hardened above the sense of feeling *delicate* reproof) by the sovereign contempt, mingled with a disdainful kind of pity, that shewed at once her own conscious worth, and our despicable worthlessness.

O Lovelace! what then was the triumph, even in my eye, and what is it still upon reflection, of *true* modesty, of *true* wit, and *true* politeness, over frothy jest, laughing impertinence, and an obscenity so shameful, even to the guilty, that they cannot hint at it but under a double meaning!

Then, as thou hast somewhere observed,* all her correctives *avowed* by her eye. Not poorly, like the generality of her sex, affecting ignorance of meanings too obvious to be concealed; but so resenting, as to shew each impudent laugher the offence given to, and taken by, a purity, that had mistaken its way, when it fell into such company.

Such is the woman, such is the angel, whom thou hast betrayed into thy power, and wouldst deceive and ruin. — Sweet creature! did she but know how she is surrounded, (as I then thought, as well as now think) and what is

* See p. 373.

intended, how much sooner would death be her choice, than so dreadful a situation! — "And how effectually would her story, were it generally known, warn all the sex against throwing themselves into the power of ours, let our vows, oaths, and protestations be what they will!"

But let me beg of thee, once more, my dear Lovelace, if thou hast any regard for thine own honour, for the honour of thy family, for thy future peace, or for my opinion of thee, (who yet pretend not to be so much moved by principle, as by that dazzling merit which ought still more to attract *thee*) to be prevailed upon — to be — to be *humane*, that's all — only, that thou wouldest not disgrace our common humanity!

Hardened as thou art, I know that they are the abandoned people in the house who keep thee up to a resolution against her. O that the sagacious fair-one (with so much innocent charity in her own heart) had not so resolutely held those women at distance! — That, as she *boarded* there, she had oftener *tabled* with them! Specious as they are, in a week's time, she would have seen through them; they could not have been always so guarded, as they were when they saw her but seldom, and when they *prepared* themselves to see her; and she would have fled their house as a place infected. And yet, perhaps, with so determined an enterpriser, this discovery might have accelerated her ruin.

I know that thou art nice in thy loves. But are there not hundreds of women, who, though not utterly abandoned, would be taken with thee for mere *personal* regards! Make a toy, if thou wilt, of principle with respect to such of the sex as regard it as a toy; but rob not an angel of those purities, which, in her own opinion, constitute the difference between angelic and brutal qualities.

With regard to the passion itself, the less of soul in either man or woman, the more sensual are they. Thou, Lovelace, hast a soul, though a corrupted one; and art more intent (as thou even gloriest) upon the preparative stratagem, than upon the end of conquering.

See we not the natural bent of idiots and the crazed? the very appetite is *body;* and when we ourselves are most fools, and crazed, then are we most eager in these pursuits. See what fools this passion makes the wisest men! what snivellers, what dotards, when they suffer themselves to be run away with by it! — An *unpermanent passion!* Since, if (ashamed of its *more proper* name) we must call it *love*, *love gratified, is love satisfied — and love satisfied, is indifference begun.* And this is the case where *consent* on one side adds to the obligation on the other. What then but remorse can follow a forcible attempt?

Do not even chaste lovers chuse to be alone in their courtship preparations, ashamed to have even a child to witness to their foolish actions, and more foolish expressions? Is this deified passion, in its greatest altitudes, fitted to stand the day? Do not the lovers, when mutual consent awaits their wills, retire to coverts, and to darkness, to complete their wishes? and shall such a sneaking passion as this, which can be so easily gratified by viler objects, be permitted to debase the noblest?

Were not the delays of thy vile purposes owing more to the awe which her majestic virtue has inspired thee with, than to thy want of adroitness in villainy, [I *must* write my free sentiments in this case; for have I not *seen* the angel?] I should be ready to censure some of thy contrivances and pretences to suspend the expected day, as *trite*, *stale*, and (to me, who know thy intention) *poor;* and too often resorted to, as nothing comes of them, to be gloried in; particularly that of Mennel, the vapourish lady, and the ready-furnished house.

She must have thought so too, at times, and in her heart despised thee for them, or love thee (ungrateful as thou art!) to her misfortune: as well as entertain hope against probability. But this would afford another warning to the sex, were they to know her story; "as it would shew them what poor pretences they must seem to be satisfied with, if once they put themselves into the power of a designing man."

If *trial* only was thy end, as

once was thy pretence,* enough surely hast thou tried this paragon of virtue and vigilance. But I knew thee too well, to expect, at the *time*, that thou wouldest stop there. "Men of our cast put no other bound to their views upon any of the sex, than what want of power compels them to put." I knew that from one advantage gained, thou wouldest proceed to attempt another. Thy habitual aversion to wedlock, too well I knew; and indeed thou avowest thy hope to bring her to *cohabitation*, in that very letter in which thou pretendest *trial* to be thy principal view.**

But do not even thy own frequent and involuntary remorses, when thou hast time, place, company, and every other circumstance, to favour thee in thy wicked design, convince thee, that there can be no room for a hope so presumptuous? Why then, since thou wouldest chuse to marry her rather than lose her, wilt thou make her hate thee for ever?

But if thou darest to meditate *personal* trial, and art sincere in thy resolution to reward her, as she behaves in it, let me beseech thee to remove her from this vile house. That will be to give her and thy conscience fair play. So entirely now does the sweet deluded excellence depend upon her supposed happier prospects, that thou needest not to fear that she will fly from thee, or that she will wish to have recourse to that scheme of Miss Howe, which has put thee upon what thou callest thy *master-strokes*.

But whatever be thy determination on this head; and if I write not in time, but that thou hast actually pulled off the mask; let it not be one of thy devices, if thou wouldest avoid the curses of every heart, and hereafter of thy own, to give her, no not for one hour, (be her resentment ever so great) into the power of that villainous woman, who has, if possible, less remorse than thyself; and whose *trade* it is to break the resisting spirit, and utterly to ruin the heart unpractised in evil. O Lovelace, Lovelace, how many dreadful stories could this horrid woman tell the sex! And shall that of a Clarissa swell the guilty list?

But this I might have spared. Of this, devil as thou art, thou canst not be capable. Thou couldst not enjoy a triumph so disgraceful to thy wicked pride, as well as to humanity.

Shouldest thou think, that the melancholy spectacle hourly before me has made me more serious than usual, perhaps thou wilt not be mistaken. But nothing more is to be inferred from hence, (were I even to return to my former courses) but that whenever the time of cool reflection comes, whether brought on by our own disasters, or by those of others, we shall undoubtedly, if capable of thought, and if we have time for it, think in the same manner. We neither of us are such fools

---

* See Letter xlv.
** See p. 57. See also Letters xii. xiii.

as to disbelieve a futurity, or to think, whatever be our practice, that we came hither by chance, and for no end but to do all the mischief we have it in our power to do. Nor am I ashamed to own, that in the prayers which my poor uncle makes me read to him in the absence of a very good clergyman who regularly attends him, I do not forget to put in a word or two for myself.

If, Lovelace, thou laughest at me, thy ridicule will be more conformable to thy *actions* than to thy *belief*. — *Devils believe and tremble.* Canst thou be more abandoned than they?

And here let me add, with regard to my poor old man, that I often wish thee present but for one half hour in a day, to see the dregs of a gay life running off in the most excruciating tortures, that the colic, the stone, and the surgeon's knife can unitedly inflict, and to hear him bewail the dissoluteness of his past life, in the bitterest anguish of a spirit every hour expecting to be called to its last account. — Yet, by all his confessions, he has not to accuse himself, in sixty-seven years of life, of half the *very* vile enormities, which you and I have committed in the last seven only.

I conclude with recommending to your serious consideration all I have written, as proceeding from the heart and soul of

Your assured friend
J. BELFORD.

LETTER CXXVII.

Mr. Lovelace to John Belford, Esq.

Tuesday, afternoon, June 6.

DIFFICULTIES still to be got over in procuring this plaguy licence. I ever hated, and ever shall hate, these spiritual lawyers, and their court.

And now, Jack, if I have not secured *victory*, I have a *retreat*.

But hold — thy servant with a letter. —

* * *

A confounded *long* one, though not a *narrative* one. — Once more in behalf of this lady! Lie thee down, oddity! What canst thou write that can have force upon me at this crisis? — And have I not, as I went along, made thee to say all that was necessary for thee to say?

* * *

Yet once more, I will take thee up.

Trite, stale, poor (sayest thou) are some of my contrivances? that of the widow particularly. — I have no patience with thee. Had not that contrivance its effect at the time, for a procrastination? — And had I not then reason to fear, that the lady would find enough to make her dislike this house? And was it not right (intending what I intended) to lead her on from time to time, with a notion, that a house of her own would be ready for her soon, in order to induce her to continue here till it was?

Trite, stale, and *poor!* — Thou

art a silly fellow, and no judge, when thou sayest this. Had I not, like a blockhead, revealed to thee, as I *went along*, the secret purposes of my heart, but had kept all in, till the event had explained my mysteries, I would have defied thee to have been able, any more than the lady, to have guessed at what was to befal her, till it had actually come to pass. Nor doubt I, in this case, that instead of presuming to reflect upon her for credulity, *as loving me to her misfortune*, and for *hoping against probability*, thou wouldest have been readier by far, to censure her for nicety and over-scrupulousness. And, let me tell thee, that had she loved me as I wished her to love me, she could not possibly have been so very apprehensive of my designs, nor so ready to be influenced by Miss Howe's precautions, as she has always been, although my general character made not for me with her.

But in thy opinion, I suffer for that simplicity in my contrivances, which is their principal excellence. No machinery make I necessary. No unnatural flights aim I at. All pure nature, taking advantage of nature, as nature tends; and so simple my devices, that when they are known, thou, even *thou* imaginest, thou couldest have thought of the same. And indeed thou seemest to *own*, that the slight thou puttest upon them, is owing to my letting thee into them beforehand — undistinguishing, as well as ungrateful as thou art!

Yet, after all, I would not have thee think, that I do not know my weak places. I have formerly told thee, that it is difficult for the ablest general to say what he *will* do, or what he *can* do, when he is obliged to regulate his motions by those of a watchful enemy.* If thou givest due weight to this consideration, thou wilt not wonder that I should make many marches and countermarches, some of which may appear to a slight observer unnecessary.

But let me cursorily enter into debate with thee on this subject, now I am within sight of my journey's end.

Abundance of impertinent things thou tellest me in this letter; some of which thou hadst from myself; others that I knew before.

All that thou sayest in this charming creature's praise, is short of what I have said and written on the inexhaustible subject.

Her virtue, her resistance, which are her *merits*, are my *stimulatives*. Have I not told thee so twenty times over?

Devil, as these girls between them call me, what of devil am I, but in my *contrivances?* I am not more a devil, than others, in the *end* I aim at; for when I have carried my point, it is still but *one* seduction. And I have perhaps been spared the guilt of *many* seductions in the time.

What of uncommon would there be in this case, but for her watchfulness? — As well as I love in-

* See p. 121.

trigue and stratagem, dost think, that I had not rather have gained my end with less trouble and less guilt?

The man, let me tell thee, who is as wicked as he *can* be, is a worse man than I am. Let me ask any rake in England, if, resolving to carry his point, he would have been *so long about it*, or have had *so much compunction* as I have had?

Were every rake, nay, were every man, to sit down, as I do, and write all that enters into his head, or into his heart, and to accuse himself with equal freedom and truth, what an army of miscreants should I have to keep me in countenance!

It is a maxim with some, that if they are left alone with a woman, and make not an attempt upon her, she will think herself affronted —are not such men as these worse than I am? What an opinion must they have of the whole sex!

Let me defend the sex I so dearly love. If these elder brethren of ours think they have general reason for their assertion, they must have kept very bad company, or must judge of women's hearts by their own. She must be an abandoned woman, who will not shrink as a snail into its shell, at a *gross* and *sudden* attempt. A modest woman must be naturally *cold*, *reserved*, and *shy*. She cannot be *so much*, and *so soon* affected, as libertines are apt to imagine. She must, *at least*, have some confidence in the *honour* and *silence* of a man before desire can possibly put forth in her, to encourage and meet his flame. For my own part, I have been always decent in the company of women, till I was *sure* of them. Nor have I ever offered a *great* offence, till I have found *little* ones passed over; and that they shunned me not, when they knew my character.

My divine Clarissa has puzzled me, and beat me out of my play: at one time, I hoped to overcome by *intimidating* her: at another by *love*; by the amorous *see-saw*, as I have called it.* And I have only to join *surprise* to the other two, and see what can be done by all three.

And whose property, I pray thee, shall I invade, if I pursue my schemes of love and vengeance? Have not those who have a right to her, renounced that right? Have not they wilfully exposed her to dangers? Yet must know, that such a woman would be considered as lawful prize, by as many as could have the opportunity to attempt her? — And had they not thus cruelly exposed her, is she not a *single woman*? And need I tell thee, Jack, that men of our cast, the *best* of them, [the *worst* stick at nothing] think it a great grace and favour done to the married men, if they leave them their wives to themselves; and compound for their sisters, daughters, wards, and nieces! Shocking as these principles must be to a reflecting mind, yet such thou knowest are the principles of thousands (who would not act so generously, as I

* See p. 49.

have acted by almost all of the sex, over whom I have obtained a power); and as often carried into practice, as their opportunities or courage will permit. Such therefore have no right to blame *me*.

Thou repeatedly pleadest her sufferings from her family. But I have too often answered this plea, to need to say any more now, than that she has not suffered for *my sake*. For has she not been made the victim of the malice of her rapacious brother and envious sister, who only waited for an occasion to ruin her with her other relations; and took this *as the first* to drive her out of the house; and as it happened, into my arms? — Thou knowest how much *against her inclination*.

As for her *own* sins, how many has the dear creature to answer for to *love* and to *me!* — Twenty times, and twenty times twenty has she not told me, that she refused not the odious Solmes in favour to me? and as often has she not offered to renounce me for the single life, if the implacables would have received her on that condition? — Of what repetitions does thy weak pity make me guilty!

To look a little further back: Canst thou forget what my sufferings were from this haughty beauty in the whole time of my attendance upon her proud motions, in the purlieus of Harlowe Place, and at the Little White Hart at Neale, as we called it? — Did I not threaten vengeance upon her then (and had I not reason?) for disappointing me of a promised interview?

O Jack! what a night had I in the bleak coppice adjoining to her father's paddock! — my linen frozen; my limbs absolutely numbed; my fingers only sensible of so much warmth, as enabled me to hold a pen; and that obtained by rubbing the skin off, and by beating with my hands my shivering sides! Kneeling on the hoar moss on one knee, writing on the other, if the stiff scrawl could be called writing! My feet by the time I had done, seeming to have taken root, and actually unable to support me for some minutes! Love and rage then kept my heart in motion, (and only love and rage could do it) or how much more than I *did* suffer, must I have suffered!

I told thee, at my melancholy return, what were the contents of the letter I wrote*. And I shewed thee afterwards, her tyrannical answer to it**. Thou, then, Jack, lovedst thy friend; and pitiedst thy poor suffering Lovelace. Even the affronted god of love approved then of my threatened vengeance against the fair promiser; though now with thee, in the day of my power, forgetful of the night of my sufferings, he is become an advocate for her.

Nay, was it not he himself that brought to me my adorable *Nemesis;* and both together put me upon this very vow, "that I would never rest till I had drawn in this goddess-daughter of the Harlowes to cohabit with me; and that in the face of all their proud family!"

* See Vol. I. p. 294.
** Ibid. p. 295.

Nor canst thou forget this vow. — At this instant I have thee before me, as then thou sorrowfully lookedst. Thy strong features glowing with compassion for me; thy lips twisted; thy forehead furrowed; thy whole face drawn out from the stupid round into the ghastly oval; every muscle contributing its power to complete the aspect grievous; and not one word couldst thou utter but *amen* to my vow.

And what of distinguishing love, or favour, or confidence, have I had from her since, to make me forego this vow?

I *renewed it not*, indeed, afterwards; and actually, for a long season, was willing to forget it; till repetitions of the same faults revived the remembrance of the former. And now adding to those the contents of some of Miss Howe's virulent letters, so lately come at, what canst thou say for the rebel, consistent with thy loyalty to thy friend?

Every man to his genius and constitution. Hannibal was called *the father of warlike stratagems*. Had Hannibal been a private man, and turned his plotting head against the *other sex;* or I had been a general, and turned mine against such of my fellow-creatures of *my own*, as I thought myself entitled to consider as my enemies, because they were born and lived in a different climate; Hannibal would have done less mischief; Lovelace more. — That would have been the difference.

Not a sovereign on earth, if he be not a *good man*, and if he be of a warlike temper, but must do a thousand times more mischief than I. And why? Because he has it in his *power* to do more.

An honest man, perhaps thou'lt say, will not wish to have it in his power to do hurt. He *ought not*, let me tell him: for, if he have it, a thousand to one but it makes him both wanton and wicked.

In what, then, am I so *singularly vile?*

In my *contrivances*, thou wilt say, (for thou art my echo) if not in my proposed *end* of them.

How difficult does every man find it, as well as I, to forego a predominant passion! I have three passions that sway me by turns; all imperial ones. Love, revenge, ambition, or a desire of conquest.

As to this particular contrivance of Tomlinson and the uncle, which perhaps thou wilt think a black one; that had been spared, had not these *innocent* ladies put me upon finding a husband for their Mrs. Townsend: that device, therefore, is, but a *preventive* one. Thinkest thou, that I could bear to be outwitted? And may not this very contrivance save a world of mischief? for dost thou think, I would have tamely given up the lady to Townsend's tars?

What meanest thou, except to overthrow thy own plea, when thou sayest *that men of our cast know no other bound to their wickedness, but want of power;* yet knowest this lady to be in mine?

Enough, sayest thou, *have I tried this paragon of virtue.* Not so; for

I have not tried her at all — all I have been doing, is but *preparation to a trial.*

But thou art concerned for the *means* that I may have recourse to in the *trial,* and for my *veracity.*

Silly fellow! — Did ever any man, thinkest thou, deceive a woman, but at the expense of his veracity? how, otherwise, can he be said to *deceive?*

As to the *means,* thou dost not imagine that I expect a *direct* consent. My main hope is but in a yielding reluctance; without which I will be sworn, whatever rapes have been attempted, none ever were committed, one person to one person. And good Queen Bess of England, had she been living, and appealed to, would have declared herself of my mind.

It would not be amiss for the sex to know, what our opinions are upon this subject. I love to warn them. I wish no man to succeed with them but myself. I told thee once, that *though a rake, I am not a rake's friend.**

Thou sayest, that I ever hated wedlock. And true thou sayest. And yet *as* true, when thou tellest me, that I *would rather marry than lose this lady.* And *will she detest me for ever,* thinkest thou, if I try her, and succeed not? — Take care — take care, Jack! — Seest thou not, that thou warnest me, that I do not try without resolving to conquer?

I must add, that I have for some time been convinced, that I have done wrong, to scribble to thee so

* See p. 57.

freely as I have done (and the more so, if I make the lady legally mine); for has not every letter I have written to thee, been a bill of indictment against myself? I may partly curse my vanity for it; and I think I will refrain for the future; for thou art really very impertinent.

A *good* man, I own, might urge many of the things thou urgest: but, by my soul, they come very awkwardly from thee. And thou must be sensible, that I can answer every tittle of what thou writest, upon the foot of the *maxims we have long held and pursued.* — By the specimen above, thou wilt see that I can.

And pry'thee tell me, Jack, what but this that follows would have been the epitome of mine and my beloved's story, *after ten years' cohabitation,* had I never written to thee upon the subject, and had I not been my own accuser.

"Robert Lovelace, a notorious woman-eater, makes his addresses in an honourable way to Miss Clarissa Harlowe; a young lady of the highest merit — fortunes on both sides out of the question.

"After encouragement given, he is insulted by her violent brother; who thinks it his interest to discountenance the match; and who at last challenging him, is obliged to take his worthless life at his hands.

"The family as much enraged as if he had *taken* the life he *gave,* insult him personally, and find out an odious lover for the young lady.

"To avoid a forced marriage, she is prevailed upon to take a step, which throws her into Mr. Lovelace's protection.

"Yet, disclaiming any passion for him, she repeatedly offers to renounce him for ever, if, on that condition, her relations will receive her, and free her from the address of the man she hates.

"Mr. Lovelace, a man of strong passions, and, as some say, of great pride, thinks himself under very little obligation to her on this account; and not being naturally fond of marriage, and having so much reason to hate her relations, endeavours to prevail upon her to live with him, what he calls the *life of honour:* and at last, by stratagem, art, and contrivance, prevails.

"He resolves never to marry any other woman: takes a pride to have her called by his name: a church-rite all the difference between them: treats her with deserved tenderness. Nobody questions their marriage but those proud relations of hers, whom he wishes to question it. Every year a charming boy. Fortunes to support the increasing family with splendour. A tender father. Always a warm friend; a generous landlord; and a punctual paymaster. Now-and-then however, perhaps, indulging with a new object, in order to bring him back with greater delight to his charming Clarissa — his only fault love of the sex, — which, nevertheless, the women say, will cure itself — defensible *thus far*, that he breaks no contracts by his rovings." — And what is there so very greatly amiss, AS THE WORLD GOES, in all this?

Let me aver, that there are thousands and ten thousands, who have worse stories to tell than this would appear to be, had I not interested thee in the progress to my great end. And besides, thou knowest that the character I gave myself to Joseph Leman, as to my treatment of my mistresses, is pretty near the truth.*

Were I to be as much in earnest in my defence, as thou art warm in my arraignment, I could convince thee, by other arguments, observations, and comparisons, [*is not all human good and evil comparative?*] that though from my ingenuous temper (writing only to thee, who art master of every secret of my heart) I am so ready to accuse myself in my narrations; yet I have something to say *for* myself *to* myself, as I go along; though no one else perhaps, that was not a rake, would allow any weight to it. — And this caution might I give to thousands, who would stoop for a stone to throw at me: "See that your own *predominant passions*, whatever they be, hurry you not into as much wickedness, as *mine* do *me*. See if ye happen to be better than I in some things, that ye are not worse in others; and in points too, that may be of more extensive bad consequence, than that of seducing a girl, (and taking care of her after-

* See p. 150, 151.

wards) who *from her cradle is armed with cautions against the delusions of men.* And yet I am not so partial to my own follies as to think lightly of *this* fault, when I allow myself to think.

Another grave thing I will add, now my hand is in: "So dearly do I love the sex, that had I found that a character for virtue had been generally *necessary* to recommend me to them, I should have had a much greater regard to my morals than to the sex, than I have had."

To sum up all—I am sufficiently apprised, that men of worthy and honest hearts, who never allowed themselves in *premeditated* evil, and who take into the account the excellences of this fine creature, will and must not only condemn, but *abhor* me, were they to know as much of me as thou dost. But, methinks, I would be glad to escape the censure of those men, and of those women too, who have never known what capital trials and temptations are; of those who have no genius for enterprise; of those who want rather courage than will; and most particularly of those, who have only kept their secret better than I have kept, or wish to keep, mine. Were these exceptions to take place, perhaps, Jack, I should have ten to acquit, to one that would condemn me. Have I not often said, *that human nature is a rogue?*

* * *

I THREATENED above to refrain writing to thee. But take it not to heart, Jack—I must write on, and cannot help it.

LETTER CXXVIII.

Mr. Lovelace to John Belford, Esq.

Wednesday, night, 11 o'clock.

FAITH, Jack, thou hadst half undone me with thy nonsense, though I would not own it in my yesterday's letter: my conscience of thy party before.—But I think I am my own man again.

So near to execution my plot; so near springing my mine; all agreed upon between the women and me; or I believe thou hadst overthrown me.

I have time for a few lines preparative to what is to happen in an hour or two; and I love to write to the *moment*.

We have been extremely happy. How many agreeable days have we known together!—What may the next two hours produce!

When I parted with my charmer (which I did, with infinite reluctance, half an hour ago) it was upon her promise that she would not sit up to write or read. For so engaging was the conversation to me (and indeed my behaviour throughout the whole of it I was confessedly agreeable to her), that I insisted, if she did not directly retire to rest, that she should add another happy hour to the former.

To have sat up writing or reading half the night, as she sometimes does, would have frustrated my view, as thou wilt observe, when my little plot unravels.

* * *

WHAT — what — what now! — Bounding villain! wouldst thou choak me! —

I was speaking to my heart, Jack! — It was then at my throat. — And what is all this for? — These shy women, how, when a man thinks himself near the mark, do they *tempest* him!

* * *

Is all ready, Dorcas? Has my beloved kept her word with me? — Whether are these billowy heavings owing more to love or to fear? I cannot tell for the soul of me, of which I have most. If I can but take her before her apprehension, before her eloquence, is awake —

Limbs, why thus convulsed? — Knees, till now so firmly knit, why thus relaxed? Why beat you thus together? Will not these trembling fingers, which twice have refused to direct the pen, fail me in the arduous moment?

Once again, Why and for what all these convulsions? This project is not to end in *matrimony*, surely!

But the consequences must be greater than I had thought of till this moment — my beloved's destiny or my own may depend upon the issue of the two next hours!

I will recede, I think! —

* * *

SOFT, O virgin saint, and safe as soft, be thy slumbers!

I will now once more turn to my friend Belford's letter. Thou shalt have fair play, my charmer. I will re-peruse what thy advocate has to say for thee. Weak arguments will do, in the frame I am in! —

But, what, what's the matter! — What a *double* — but the uproar abates! — What a *double coward* am I? — Or is it that I am taken in a cowardly minute? for heroes have their fits of *fear;* cowards their *brave* moments; and virtuous women, all but my Clarissa, their moment *critical* —

But thus coolly enjoying thy reflections in a hurricane! — Again the confusion is renewed — What! Where! — How came it. Is my beloved safe —

O wake not too roughly, my beloved!

LETTER CXXIX.

Mr. Lovelace to John Belford, Esq.

Thursday morning, five o'clock,
(June 8.)

Now is my reformation secured; for I never shall love any other woman! O she is all variety! she must be ever new to me! *Imagination* cannot form; much less can the pencil paint; nor can the soul of painting, *poetry*, describe an angel so exquisitely, so elegantly lovely! — But I will not by anticipation pacify thy impatience. Although the subject is too hallowed for profane contemplation, yet shalt thou have the whole before thee as it passed: and this not from a spirit wantoning in description upon so rich a subject; but with a design to put a bound to thy roving thoughts. It will be iniquity *greater than a Lovelace was ever guilty of*, to carry them further than I shall acknowledge.

Thus then, connecting my last with the present, I lead to it.

Didst thou not, by the conclusion of my former, perceive the consternation I was in, just as I was about to re-peruse thy letter, in order to prevail upon myself to recede from my purpose of awaking in terrors my slumbering charmer? And what dost think was the matter?

I'll tell thee —

At a little after two, when the whole house was still, or seemed to be so, and as it proved, my Clarissa in bed, and fast asleep; I also in a manner undressed (as indeed I was for an hour before) and in my gown and slippers, though, to oblige thee, writing on! — I was alarmed by a trampling noise over head, and a confused buz of mixed voices, some louder than others, like scolding, and little short of screaming. While I was wondering what could be the matter, down stairs ran Dorcas, and at my door, in an accent rather frightedly and hoarsely inward, than shrilly clamorous, she cried out, Fire! Fire! And this the more alarmed me, as she seemed to endeavour to cry out louder, but could not.

My pen (its last scrawl a benediction on my beloved) dropped from my fingers; and up started I; and making but three steps to the door, opening it, cried out, Where! Where! almost as much terrified as the wench; while she, more than half undressed, her petticoats in her hand, unable to speak distinctly, pointed up stairs.

I was there in a moment, and found all owing to the carelessness of Mrs. Sinclair's cook-maid, who, having sat up to read the simple *History of Dorastus and Faunia*, when she should have been in bed, had set fire to an old pair of calico window-curtains.

She had had the presence of mind, in her fright, to tear down the half-burnt vallens, as well as curtains, and had got them, though blazing, into the chimney, by the time I came up; so that I had the satisfaction to find the danger happily over.

Meantime Dorcas, after she had directed me up stairs, not knowing the worst was over, and expecting every minute the house would be in a blaze, out of tender regard for her lady [*I shall for ever love the wench for it*] ran to her door, and rapping loudly at it, in a recovered voice, cried out, with a shrillness equal to her love, *Fire! Fire! The house is on fire! — Rise, madam! — This instant rise — if you would not be burnt in your bed!*

No sooner had she made this dreadful outcry, but I heard her lady's door with hasty violence unbar, unbolt, unlock, and open, and my charmer's voice sounding like that of one going into a fit.

Thou mayest believe that I was greatly affected.

I trembled with concern for her, and hastened down faster than the alarm of fire had made me run up, in order to satisfy her, that all the danger was over.

When I had *flown down* to her chamber door, there I beheld the most charming creature in the world, supporting herself on the arm of the gasping Dorcas, sighing, trembling, and ready to faint, with nothing on but an under petticoat, her lovely bosom half open, and her feet just slipped into her shoes. As soon as she saw me, she panted, and struggled to speak; but could only say, Oh, Mr. Lovelace! and down was ready to sink.

I clasped her in my arms with an ardour she never felt before: My dearest life! fear nothing: I have been up — the danger is over — the fire is got under — and how, foolish devil [to Dorcas] could you thus, by your hideous yell, alarm and frighten my angel?

O Jack! how her sweet bosom, as I clasped her to mine, heaved and panted! I could even distinguish her dear heart flutter, flutter, flutter against mine; and for a few minutes, I feared she would go into fits.

Lest the half-lifeless charmer should catch cold in this undress, I lifted her to her bed, and sat down by her upon the side of it, endeavouring with the utmost tenderness, as well of action as expression, to dissipate her terrors.

But what did I get by this my generous care of her, and my *successful* endeavour to bring her to herself? — Nothing (ungrateful as she was!) but the most passionate exclamations: for we had both already forgotten the occasion, dreadful as it was, which had thrown her into my arms; I, from the joy of encircling the almost disrobed body of the loveliest of her sex; she, from the greater terrors that arose from finding herself in my arms, and both seated on the bed, from which she had been so lately frighted.

And now, Belford, reflect upon the distance at which the watchful charmer had hitherto kept me: reflect upon my love, and upon my sufferings for her: reflect upon her vigilance, and how long I had laid in wait to elude it; the awe I had stood in, because of her frozen virtue and over-niceness; and that I never before was so happy with her; and then think how ungovernable must be my transports in those happy moments! — And yet in my own account, I was both decent and generous.

But, far from being affected, as I wished, by an address so fervent, (although from a man for whom she had so lately owned a regard, and with whom, but an hour or two before, she had parted with so much satisfaction) I never saw a bitterer, or more moving grief, when she came fully to herself.

She appealed to heaven against my *treachery*, as she called it, while I, by the most solemn vows, pleaded my own equal fright, and the reality of the danger that had alarmed us both.

She conjured me, in the most

solemn and affecting manner, by turns threatening and soothing, to quit her apartment, and permit her to hide herself from the light, and from every human eye.

I besought her pardon, yet could not avoid offending; and repeatedly vowed, that the next morning's sun should witness our espousals: but, taking, I suppose, all my protestations of this kind as an indication that I intended to proceed to the last extremity, she would hear nothing that I said; but redoubling her struggles to get from me, in broken accents, and exclamations the most vehement, she protested, that she would not survive what she called a treatment so disgraceful and villainous; and, looking all wildly round her, as if for some instrument of mischief, she espied a pair of sharp pointed scissars on a chair by the bed-side, and endeavoured to catch them up, with design to make her words good on the spot.

Seeing her desperation, I begged her to be pacified; that she would hear me speak but one word; declaring that I intended no dishonour to her: and having seized the scissars, I threw them into the chimney; and she still insisting vehemently upon my distance, I permitted her to take the chair.

But, O the sweet discomposure! — Her bared shoulders, and arms so inimitably fair and lovely: her spread hands crossed over her charming neck; yet not half concealing its glossy beauties: the scanty coat, as she rose from me, giving the whole of her admirable shape, and fine-turned limbs: her eyes running over, yet seeming to threaten future vengeance: and at last her lips uttering what every indignant look and glowing feature portended; exclaiming as if I had done the worst I could do, and vowing never to forgive me; wilt thou wonder if I resumed the incensed, the already too much provoked fair one?

I did; and clasped her once more to my bosom: but, considering the delicacy of her frame, her force was amazing, and shewed how much in earnest she was in her resentment; for it was with the utmost difficulty that I was able to hold her: nor could I prevent her sliding through my arms, to fall upon her knees: which she did at my feet: and there, in the anguish of her soul, her streaming eyes lifted up to my face with supplicating softness, hands folded, dishevelled hair; for her night head-dress having fallen off in her struggling, her charming tresses fell down in naturally shining ringlets, as if officious to conceal the dazzling beauties of her neck and shoulders; her lovely bosom too heaving with sighs, and broken sobs, as if to aid her quivering lips, in pleading for her — in this manner, but when her grief gave way to her speech, in words pronounced with that emphatical propriety, which distinguishes this admirable creature in her elocution from all the women I ever

Clarissa. II. 30

heard speak; did she implore my compassion, and my honour.

"Consider me, *dear* Lovelace," [*dear* was her charming word!] "on my knees I beg you to consider me, as a poor creature who has no protector but you; who has no defence but your honour. — By that honour! by your humanity! by all you have vowed; I conjure you not to make me abhor myself! — Not to make me vile in my own eyes!"

I mentioned to-morrow, as the happiest day of my life.

Tell me not of to-morrow. If indeed you mean me honourably, *Now*, this very instant NOW! you must shew it, and be gone! You can never in a whole long life repair the evils you may NOW make me suffer.

Wicked wretch! — Insolent villain! — Yes, she called me insolent villain, although so much in my power! And for what! — only for kissing (*with passion indeed*) her inimitable neck, her lips, her cheeks, her forehead, and her streaming eyes, as this assemblage of beauties offered itself at once to my ravished sight; she continuing kneeling at my feet as I sat.

If I *am* a villain, madam — and then my grasping, but trembling hand — I hope I did not hurt the tenderest and loveliest of all her beauties — If I *am* a villain, madam —

She tore my ruffle, shrunk from my happy hand, with amazing force and agility, as with my other arm I would have encircled her waist.

Indeed you are! — The worst of villains! — Help! dear blessed people! and screamed out — No help for a poor creature!

Am I then a villain, madam? — *Am* I then a villain, say you? — And clasped both my arms about her, offering to raise her to my bounding heart.

O no! — And yet you are! — And again I was her *dear* Lovelace! — Her hands again clasped over her charming bosom: Kill me! Kill me! — If I am odious enough in your eyes to deserve this treatment; and I will thank you! — Too long, much too long has my life been a burden to me! — Or, wildly looking all around her, give me but the means, and I will instantly convince you, that my honour is dearer to me than my life!

Then, with still folded hands, and fresh streaming eyes, I was her *blessed* Lovelace; and she would thank me with her latest breath, if I would permit her to make that preference, or free her from further indignities.

I sat suspended for a moment: by my soul, thought I, thou art, upon full proof, an angel and no woman! Still, however, close clasping her to my bosom, as I had raised her from her knees, she again slid through my arms, and dropped upon them. — "See, Mr. Lovelace! — Good God! that I should live to see this hour, and to bear this treatment! — See at your feet a poor creature, imploring your pity; who, for your sake, is abandoned of all the world!

Let not my father's curse thus dreadfully operate! Be not *you* the inflicter, who have been the *cause* of it: but spare me, I beseech you spare me! — For how have I deserved this treatment from you? For *your own sake*, if not for *my sake*, and as you would that God Almighty, in your last hour, should have mercy upon *you*, spare me."

What heart but must have been penetrated?

I would again have raised the dear suppliant from her knees; but she would not be raised, till my softened mind, she said, had yielded to her prayer, and bid her rise to be innocent.

Rise then, my angel! Rise, and be what you are, and all you wish to be! Only pronounce me pardoned for what has passed, and tell me you will continue to look upon me with that eye of favour and serenity which I have been blessed with for some days past, and I will submit to my beloved conqueress, whose power never was at so great an height with me, as now, and retire to my apartment.

God Almighty, said she, hear your prayers in your most arduous moments, as you have heard mine! And now leave me, this moment leave me, to my own recollection: in *that* you will leave me to misery enough, and more than you ought to wish to your bitterest enemy.

Impute not every thing, my best beloved, to design, for design it was not —

O Mr. Lovelace! —

Upon my soul, madam, the fire was real — [*and so it was, Jack!*] — The house, my dearest life, might have been consumed by it, as you will be convinced in the morning by ocular demonstration.

O Mr. Lovelace! —

Let my passion for you, madam, and the unexpected meeting of you at your chamber door, in an attitude so charming —

Leave me, leave me, this moment! — I beseech you leave me; looking wildly and in confusion about her, and upon herself.

Excuse me, dearest creature, for those liberties, which innocent as they were, your too great delicacy may make you take amiss —

No more! No more! — Leave me, I beseech you; Again looking upon herself, and round her, in a sweet confusion — Begone! Begone! —

Then weeping, she struggled vehemently to withdraw her hands, which all the while I held between mine. — Her struggles! — O what additional charms, as I now reflect, did her struggles give to every feature, every limb, of a person so sweetly elegant and lovely!

Impossible, my dearest life, till you pronounce my pardon! — Say but you forgive me! — Say but you forgive me!

I beseech you to begone! Leave me to myself, that I may think what I *can* do, and what I *ought* to do.

That my dearest creature, is not enough. You must tell me, that I am forgiven; that you will

30*

see me to-morrow, as if nothing had happened.

And then I clasped her again in my arms, hoping she would not forgive me —

I will — I do forgive you — wretch that you are!

Nay, my Clarissa! And is it such a reluctant pardon, mingled with a word so upbraiding, that I am to be put off with when you are thus (clasping her close to me) in my power?

I do, I *do* forgive you!

Heartily?

Yes, heartily!

And freely?

Freely!

And will you look upon me to-morrow as if nothing had passed?

Yes, yes!

I cannot take these peevish affirmatives, so much like intentional negatives! — Say, you will, upon your honour.

Upon my honour, then — O now, begone! begone! — And never, never —

What, never, my angel! — Is this forgiveness?

Never, said she, let what has passed be remembered more!

I insisted upon one kiss to seal my pardon — and retired like a fool, a woman's fool, as I was! — I sneakingly retired! — Couldst thou have believed it?

But I had no sooner entered my own apartment, than reflecting upon the opportunity I had lost, and that all I had gained was but an increase of my own difficulties; and upon the ridicule I should meet with below upon a weakness so much out of my usual character; I repented and hastened back, in hope, that through the distress of mind which I left her in, she had not so soon fastened the door; and I was fully resolved to execute all my purposes, be the consequence what it would; for thought I, I have already sinned beyond cordial forgiveness, I doubt; and if fits and desperation ensue, I can but marry at last, and then I shall make her amends.

But I was justly punished; for her door was fast: and hearing her sigh and sob, as if her heart would burst; my beloved creature, said I, rapping gently [her sobbings then ceasing] I want but to say three words to you, which must be the most acceptable you ever heard from me. Let me see you but for one moment.

I thought I heard her coming to open the door, and my heart leapt in that hope; but it was only to draw another bolt, to make it still the faster; and she either could not or would not answer me, but retired to the further end of her apartment, to her closet probably: and more like a fool than before, again I sneaked away.

This was my mine, my plot! And this was all I made of it.

I love her more than ever! — And well I may! — Never saw I polished ivory so beautiful as her arms and shoulders; never touched I velvet so soft as her skin: her virgin bosom — O Belford, she is all perfection! Then such an elegance! — In her struggling losing her shoe (but just slipt on, as I told thee) her pretty foot equally white and delicate as the hand of any other woman, or even as her own hand!

But seest thou not that I have a claim of merit for a grace that every body hitherto had denied me? And that is, for a capacity of being moved by prayers and tears — Where, where, on this occasion, was the *callus*, where the flint, by which my heart was said to be surrounded?

This, indeed, is the first instance, in the like case, that ever I was wrought upon. But why, *Because I never before encountered a resistance so much in earnest:* a resistance, in short, so irresistible.

What a triumph has her sex obtained in my thoughts by this trial, and this resistance?

But if she can *now* forgive me — *Can!* — She *must.* Has she not upon her honour already done it? — But how will the dear creature keep that part of her promise, which engages her to see me in the morning, as if nothing had happened?

She would give the world, I fancy, to have the first interview over! — She had not best reproach me — yet *not* to reproach me! — What a charming puzzle! — Let her break her word with me at her peril. Fly me she cannot — no appeals lie from my tribunal — What friend has she in the world, if my compassion exert not itself in her favour? — And then the worthy Captain Tomlinson, and her uncle Harlowe, will be able to make all up for me, be my *next* offence what it will.

As to thy apprehensions of her committing any rashness upon herself, whatever she might have done in her passion if she could have seized upon her scissars, or found any other weapon, I dare say, there is no fear of that from her *deliberate* mind. A man has trouble enough with these truly pious, and truly virtuous girls [*now I believe there are such*]; he had need to have some benefit *from,* some security *in,* the rectitude of their minds.

In short, I fear nothing in this lady but grief: yet that's a slow worker, you know; and gives time to pop in a little joy between its sullen fits.

END OF VOL. II.

www.ingramcontent.com/pod-product-compliance
Lightning Source LLC
Chambersburg PA
CBHW022059300426
44117CB00007B/512